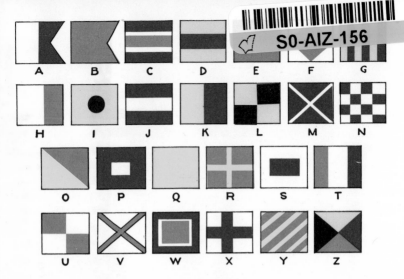

ALPHABET

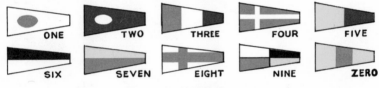

NUMBERS

INTERNATIONAL CODE FLAGS AND PENNANTS

NAMES AND DESIGNS OF INTERNATIONAL ALPHABET FLAGS

A	ALFA	J	JULIET	R	ROMEO
B	BRAVO	K	KILO	S	SIERRA
C	CHARLIE	L	LIMA	T	TANGO
D	DELTA	M	MIKE	U	UNIFORM
E	ECHO	N	NOVEMBER	V	VICTOR
F	FOXTROT	O	OSCAR	W	WHISKEY
G	GOLF	P	PAPA	X	X RAY
H	HOTEL	Q	QUEBEC	Y	YANKEE
I	INDIA			Z	ZULU

THE
BOATMAN'S
MANUAL

BOOKS BY CARL D. LANE

NONFICTION

The Boatman's Manual
The Cruiser's Manual
Boatowner's Sheet Anchor
How to Sail
Go South Inside
Navigation the Easy Way
American Paddle Steamboats
What You Should Know About the Merchant Marine

FICTION
The Fleet in the Forest
River Dragon
The Fire Raft
Black Tide
Mystery Trail
Treasure Cave
Steam vs. Steam

FOURTH REVISED
AND ENLARGED
EDITION

THE
BOATMAN'S
MANUAL

A Complete Manual of Boat Handling,
Operation, Maintenance, and Seamanship

by CARL D. LANE

Drawings by the Author

W · W · NORTON & COMPANY
New York · London

Copyright © 1979, 1962, 1951, 1942 by W. W. Norton & Company, Inc.

Published simultaneously in Canada by
Penguin Books Canada Ltd,
2801 John Street, Markham, Ontario L3R 1B4.

Library of Congress Cataloging in Publication Data

Lane, Carl Daniel, 1899–
   The boatman's manual.

   Editions for 1962 and 1967 published under title: The new boatman's
manual.
   Includes bibliographical references and index.
   1. Boats and boating.   I. Title.
VK541.L3 1979   623.88   78-32139

ISBN 0-393-03190-X

W. W. Norton & Company, Inc.
500 Fifth Avenue, New York, N.Y. 10110
W. W. Norton & Company Ltd.
37 Great Russell Street, London WC1B 3NU

3 4 5 6 7 8 9 0

NOTICE

The reader of this Manual is cautioned that no words and none of his time are wasted in it. Facts are stated once and not repeated.

In addition to a complete index, each chapter is divided into subheads and numbered paragraphs. Illustrations bear the same figure number as the number of the paragraph to which they refer. The first component of the number signifies the chapter number; the second, the paragraph or illustration number.

PREFACE TO THE FOURTH REVISED EDITION

THE NEED that prompted the original publication of this manual is even greater today, some thirty-seven years later. The small-craft fleet of our country—from outboards to spit-and-polish yachts—has multiplied in fantastic numbers, boating has moved from an obscure sport to one as common as bowling or skiing. Millions of men and women have discovered the pleasures of boating and demand an accurate, concise, and well-arranged handbook to help meet the myriad problems of sailing and navigating.

In this edition, its fourth major revision, *The Boatman's Manual* remains the most complete guide available for the small-craft skipper, owner, and crew member. It is still the book that thousands of seamen have come to rely upon and keep, above all others, on the chart table, but it has been thoroughly modernized, with much new material, new drawings, and diagrams added.

It was pointed out by the many organizations and individuals who reviewed this *Manual* in outline that two things above all were essential to its usefulness: (a) that it be concise yet give all information however basic, elemental, or obvious it may appear to the boatman of long experience, and (b) that its arrangement and illustration be truly in manual or handbook form, the contents quickly available, clear and bare of all narrative writing.

What is here presented is neither startlingly new nor in any way novel, but it is orderly, useful, and complete. It is the gleaning, the assiduous gathering, of all information vital and necessary to the small-boat operator, owner, or crew member. Over a hundred books, pamphlets, articles, and other publications were consulted in its preparation. This manual, together with the proper *Coast Pilot*, charts, and tables, should enable the small-boat mariner to take his boat, in safety, anywhere in American and Canadian waters, and should prepare him to meet any one of the scores of situations even the shortest of passages creates.

The author freely acknowledges the great help received from the publications of the United States Coast Guard, United States Navy, the Department of Commerce, the United States Hydrographic Office, the United States Army Engineer Office, the service pamphlets and the specially prepared material on the marine engine by the Gray Marine Motor Company; from many articles appearing in *Motorboating, Yachting, Boating, The Rudder*; from H. I. Chapelle's *Yacht Designing and Planning*, and his *Boatbuilding*; and, of course, those great source books, Kright's *Modern Seamanship*, Riesenberg's *Standard Seamanship for the Merchant Service*, and Dutton's *Navigation and Nautical Astronomy*.

For the reviews and critical readings, which assisted so much in the preparation of this revised edition, I thank many but especially:

Mr. Wolcott Gibbs of *Yachting*

Mr. Roland Birnn, of Washington, D. C.

Mr. T. P. Sanders, of Chestertown, New York

Mr. Robert Lane, my son, of the Penobscot Boat Works, Rockport, Maine

—and the many readers who have over the years been kind enough to write me with a helpful thought or suggestion.

CARL D. LANE

Cranberry Island, Maine

CONTENTS

Part Two BOAT OPERATION

Part Three PILOTING AND NAVIGATION.

PART I
BOAT HANDLING

CHAPTER I

HANDLING SMALL BOATS

A BOAT is defined by Webster as "a small open vessel, or watercraft, usually moved by oars or rowing."

A deepwater man used to consider a boat any small craft, usually auxiliary to his own larger ship, which could be bodily lifted from the water and stowed on a large vessel. However, with the coming of power and modern sail rigs, replacing oars, the "boat" has reached far beyond its meaning of only a few decades ago.

For the purposes of this manual, a boat shall be considered any hull, however moved that is not a ship. This, of course, raises the question: How small is a ship? Rather than try to answer that moot, and sometimes embarrassing, question, or to attempt to place a limit of size or tonnage on the vessels to which this *Manual* applies, let us merely state that the canoeist, the small-sailboat man, and the pleasure powerboat man should find this work advanced and complete. However, for all our avowed practicality, we have tried, at the same time, to preserve some of the language, lore, and romance of the "tall ships."

In most cases the boat is, or can be, operated singlehanded; the lone operator must be his own deck man, navigator, reefer, engineer, and cook; serve his vessel as owner, master, and crew. He must thoroughly understand the elements of a great many subjects—be his vessel a dinghy, a 40-ton schooner, or a dragger—and he must have a basic working knowledge of them all.

Before he ever sets foot on his boat, certainly before he will require a knowledge of detailed seamanship, navigation, or maintenance, he will need to understand the handling of the boat of his choice.

Logically, a manual purporting to be complete and useful should commence at the beginning—at boat handling.

Logically, the subject of boat handling should commence at the beginning also—with the handling of the basic elemental type of boat, that which is propelled by man power.

Handling Boats Under Oars

The ancient, straddling his logboat, without doubt first propelled his rude craft by a setting pole, a satisfactory device until he sailed into deep water. Once "off soundings," he was up against trouble, and his answer was to kick his feet violently and then discover that the broad bulk of his calves actually moved his boat independently of any contact with the solid land beneath him. It was a short step from this discovery to the conversion of his spare setting pole to a paddle by attaching a wide, flat section of bark to it. The need for an efficient means of propelling larger craft led to a further evolution of the paddle to an oar.

The types of rowing boats are myriad. Each region has developed its own peculiar type, best suited to local wind, weather, and beaching conditions as well as to basic purposes. In general the dory is considered the safest deepwater boat. It is high-sided and has marked *flare*, making it a good weight carrier and a fairly dry boat. Its construction is strong enough not to depend upon thwarts for strength, and so it can be nested or banked, four or more dories to a bank. It is generally rowed by pushing the oars rather than pulling them, the boatman facing forward in a standing position. Dories will sail only moderately well, and they require a small sail with low centers. Unusual among small craft, the classic dory is likely to be cranky and tender when lightly loaded, but will gain stability rapidly as her load is increased and she settles more deeply into the water.

In very small sizes, the flat-bottomed rowboat is satisfactory and is easily propelled except in very rough water. It is a good carrier and is strong, but it can seldom be towed satisfactorily. However, it has the advantages of cheapness, ease in building and repair, and of being able to take a lot of punishment on a beach or at a wharf; for these reasons, it is a common type. Properly designed and taken out of the "box" class, the flat-bottomed, or sharpie, rowboat makes the best all-round boat for most small-boat uses.

Round and V-bottomed small boats are treacherous, unstable craft until they reach a length of about 12′. In the smaller sizes they have most of the bad characteristics of the canoe and none of its good characteristics. They tow fairly well, they can be sailed, and they look well in conjunction with a smart yacht when davited or decked. Repairs are difficult, however, and unless very lightly built, they are heavier than the flat-bottomed boat and therefore offer more difficulty in beaching and stowing. In larger sizes, such as cutters and whaleboats, the advantages of round-bottomed con-

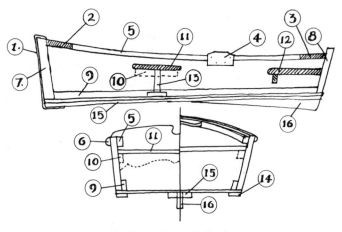

101 Parts of a small dinghy

1. Stem iron	9. Clintle or nailing strip
2. Breasthook	10. Seat risers
3. Quarter knee	11. Thwart
4. Oarlock block	12. Seat
5. Sheer clamp	13. Seat brace
6. Gunwale	14. Grounding strip
7. Stem	15. Keel
8. Transom	16. Skeg

struction and design become apparent, and they become able boats.

In selecting the small boat the prime consideration should be that it fit the uses to which it will be put.

101 The flat-bottomed rowboat up to 12′. For lake and river recreation and fishing, protected salt water fishing, dinghy use, work boats; can take outboard motor up to about four hp. Sails well except to windward in rough water.

102 The dory up to 21′. For exposed waters and offshore. Useful as tender for deepwater boats. Unless sections are modified (*See Figure 102*) will not sail well except off the wind.

103 The round-bottomed boat (and V-bottomed). Good, "fancy" dinghy in small sizes, but is tricky to handle until over 12′. Drives well under power and tows well. When so designed will sail very well. (Example: the "Frostbite" dinghy.) (Boats carried by ships are always round-bottomed and can reach the length of 40′.)

104 Modern inflatables, still called "rubber boats," by many, are usually made of rubber-coated synthetic fabric. They appear in three types—life rafts, dinghies, and so-called "sport boats," the last designed for high-speed outboard propulsion. Although the normal inflatable dinghy rows and powers sluggishly, and can be almost unmaneuverable in a high wind, it is very easy to strike and has a large carrying capacity compared to other craft its size.

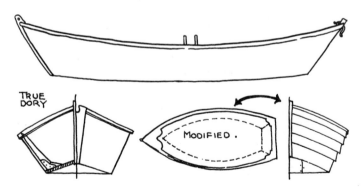

102 The dory The more deeply loaded (immersed), the steadier it becomes. *Right,* modified to about 10′ x 4′ the type makes an ideal, sturdy, yet fairly light tender.

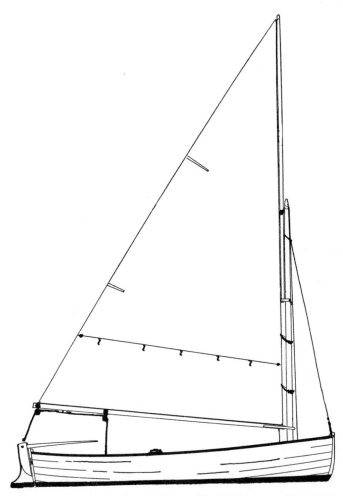

103 13′ utility round-bottom dinghy for sail, power, or rowing Center-board (drop keel) and gunter rig (spar that extends the mast) make it possible to stow all parts within the hull length for easy daviting, towing, or trailering. Usually lapstrake, if of wood, in order to maintain tight seams. Available in many forms in fiberglass.

THE OAR

105 Ash makes the best oar material. It may be kept white and clean by rubbing with sand and canvas. Always stow oars flat. For long life, the leather (which may be of leather, canvas, or fiber) is necessary as a rub shield. (*Figure 105*)

Rules for length of dinghy oars:

Boat length 7' OA   6' oar length
  "   "   9' OA   6½' oar "
  "   "   11' OA   7' oar   "
  "   "   13' OA   7½' oar "

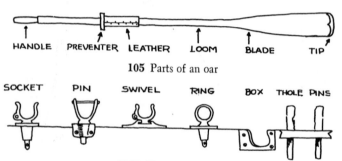

HANDLE   PREVENTER   LEATHER   LOOM   BLADE   TIP

105 Parts of an oar

SOCKET   PIN   SWIVEL   RING   BOX   THOLE PINS

105A Types of rowlocks

ROWING THE SMALL BOAT

106 Most good oarsmen prefer to row with the ends of the oar handles touching each other or even overlapping slightly. Either way, the result will produce considerably more power than when the handles are widely separated.

The complete stroke is made up of four distinct parts:

Catch—Place the blade in the water, ready to pull.

Pull—Sweep the blade aft to give headway.

Feather—Raise the blade out of the water and turn flat.

Recover—Swing oars to position of *Catch*.

To give the stroke power it is essential to:

1. Keep the upper edge of the blade at the surface of the water.
2. Keep hands about level; they move fore and aft as if in a fixed groove.

3. As the stroke is completed, give the wrists a smart flip so that the blade comes out of the water at about a 45° angle. The elbows are in close to the body.

4. Keep the back straight, chin up and in, and the feet against the stretcher. Keep your weight slightly abaft the center of buoyancy; never so that the boat trims down by the head.

Note: A good oarsman takes the stress of the pull with his back, never his arms; the arms' work is to guide the oars and complete the follow-through of the stroke

The pin-type lock (*Figure 105A*) will not permit proper rowing form. It is popular on lakes, for trolling where the oars must be dropped and trailed at times. Better for this same purpose is a ring rowlock that has a preventer inboard of the oar leather.

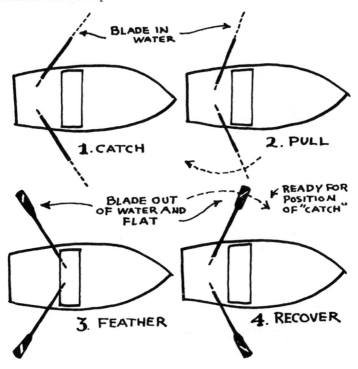

106 The rowing stroke

Learn to set a course and head the boat exactly for it (making due allowances for tide or wind if necessary). From then on steer by the wake or by lining up two objects on the shore you face as you row and keeping the proper relationship to them. It is lubberly and tiresome to peer forward after every few strokes.

Long pulls can be made less tedious by changing the position of the oars slightly or by facing forward and push-rowing for a while. More progress will be made against a head sea by quartering into it rather than meeting the seas head on. This is especially true with a flat-bottomed boat of generous beam.

The alternating "fisherman's stroke" is sometimes useful when not in a hurry and rowing a long-keeled boat. The rower dips one

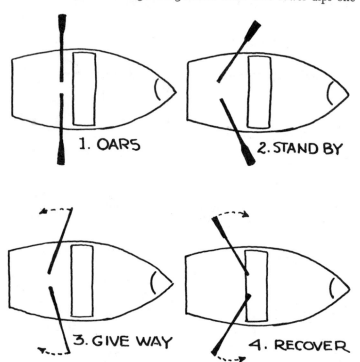

107 Rowing commands

oar-blade at a time in an alternating, unhurried rhythm. The stroke is a short one, the pull being taken entirely in the arms; the fisherman's stroke applied to a heavy, easy-running hull can be almost effortless once the boat is moving at speed.

107 Here are the basic rowing commands, which are sometimes required when directing the oarsmen of a small boat (as in a crowded harbor).

SCULLING

108 A single oar, properly handled, can move a boat almost as fast as a pair of oars used in the normal manner. This maneuver is called sculling; it is especially useful in congested waters, such as near a busy dock or in a narrow creek or channel.

The oar is shipped over the stern, or the quarter, in a rowlock or through a grommet that has been spliced into the transom, the sculler standing and facing aft. The oar is placed with the blade parallel to the stern. Grasp the handle in the right hand, turn the knuckles down, and move the handle to the right. At the end of the stroke, turn the knuckles up and move the handle to the left—knuckles up, push left; knuckles down, push right. Continue, and keep the oar blade pressing outboard—that's all there is to sculling. Steering is accomplished by easing the motion right or left, and so directing the boat.

108 Sculling *Right*, the successive blade positions

SPECIAL NOTES ON HANDLING BOATS
UNDER OARS

109 In going into a crowded or difficult landing, pull easily and keep the boat under control with the oars as long as possible, laying on oars if necessary, and boating oars only at the last moment.

In going through a narrow entrance, get good way on the boat, then trail or ship the oars.

A loaded boat holds her way much longer than a light one.

In pulling across a current, try to make good a straight line by steering upstream from the line you want to make good.

Having a long pull against the tide, run near shore where the tide is slacker than further out and where there is sometimes a counter current.

Remember that in certain waters, fog can roll in quickly and the wise rower is aware of his course and the vital bearings at all times.

The boat should, at all times, be equipped with at least the following:

> Bailer
> Small compass
> Flashlight
> Horn or whistle
> Spare oar (to double as a "setting pole")
> Bow line
> Anchor

> > *—and the federal law requires one life preserver for each person on board.*

TOWING, DECKING, DAVITING SMALL BOATS

110 Towing the small boat has always been a problem for people who cruise, especially in a sea or offshore. Dangers include the towed boat's swamping and filling and the consequent strain on and perhaps parting of the towline, and, under certain conditions, the towed boat's actually coming aboard the towing craft or ramming her stern.

Experienced deepwater men insist upon a deck design that allows the small boat to be carried there or in davits.

If the boat must be towed it is best secured to a cleat on the quarter. Towed off center thus, it exerts somewhat less pull and is less apt to "wander" in its course astern. Sometimes its inclination to veer can be cured quite easily by:

1. Dragging a length of line from the center of the towed boat.
2. Affixing a deeper or longer skeg.
3. Ballasting the towed boat a trifle out of trim, port, starboard, or by the stern, whichever proves, by experiment, to be a correction.
4. Lashing the tiller (if so equipped) to keep the towed boat edging slightly off the true course.
5. Towing the boat at "just the right point" aft, the point to be found by experimenting. The right point may vary depending upon speed, sea conditions, tide, and current. In a towing boat having a distinct wave drag, this spot is likely to be the forward side of the second following wave.

Most small boats tow best if provided with a towing ring on the stem near the waterline or even below it. This gives a lift to the forefoot which prevents the boat from "nosing" (burying the forefoot) and veering wildly.

Inflatables, both dinghies and sport boats, tow differently from other small craft. The best technique is to lash the inflatable's bow right up against the towing boat's transom at deck level, padding the gunwale with a rag to prevent chafe. Not only will this procedure reduce the inflatable's great drag, which can take a full knot off the speed of a sailing cruiser, but it will also keep the small boat from being swamped by the parent boat's wake.

111 Some method of actually taking the dinghy aboard a larger boat is necessary for any extended coastwise work. Davits are an abomination on the small cruiser unless there is beam enough to davit the dinghy thwartships across the stern in chocks on deck—in preference to its merely hanging over the water from the davits.

The dinghy, if it can be accommodated on deck, is best stowed about amidships and on the center line, overturned, if possible. Methods of decking the small boat are shown in Figure 111.

The most practical davits for the small cruiser are the ones of the round bar or radial type. A modification of the quadrant type, in which the davits hinge inboard and deliver the davited boat directly over its skids, is in use but cannot always be handled by one man.

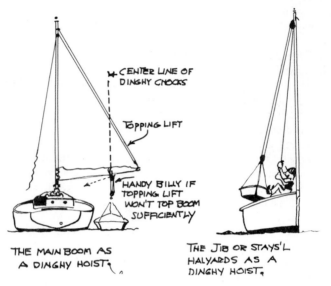

CENTER LINE OF
DINGHY CHOCKS

TOPPING LIFT

HANDY BILLY IF
TOPPING LIFT
WON'T TOP BOOM
SUFFICIENTLY

THE MAIN BOOM AS
A DINGHY HOIST.

THE JIB OR STAYS'L
HALYARDS AS A
DINGHY HOIST.

111 Two methods of decking a small boat

112 With the small boat actually on board, it should always
be provided with its own permanently secured skids and hold-down
arrangement.

If the boat is carried upright, the skids take the outside shape of
the sections at which they grip the boat and are padded to minimize chafing. These skids fold to the deck to facilitate handling the
boat. They should always be high enough to permit swabbing the
deck under the secured boat, usually at least 10".

A boat carried this way is held down by gripes which are easily
cast off by releasing the locking link (*See Figure 112*). A boat
cover must be provided, rigged over a ridgepole. It is usually fitted
with canvas straps passing under the boat for lashing down.

A boat carried upside down needs chocks as well as some method
of lashing it to the deck. Unless the boat is of fiberglass or plywood
construction, a cover is desirable to prevent undue drying of the
planking. On the dinghy rigged for sailing, a cover is necessary to
prevent soiling sails and running rigging.

Modern yacht designers have recognized the dinghy and its problems as a serious handicap to successful cruising and are gradually coming to include provisions for its stowage in the original design. This is accomplished by adjusting sail or deck plans to accommodate a small boat. Pram-type dinghies which fit over a part of the trunk, or become part of the cockpit or the deck, have been tried with some success.

Inflatables can be wholly or partially deflated (keeping one of the hull units blown up) but should always be lashed down. Fully inflated decked dinghies will generally tend to fly away.

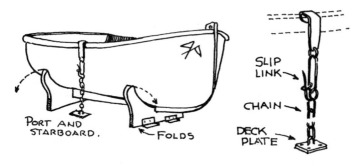

PORT AND STARBOARD.   FOLDS   SLIP LINK   CHAIN   DECK PLATE

112 Chocking a small boat on deck

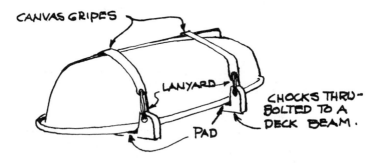

CANVAS GRIPES   LANYARD   CHOCKS THRU-BOLTED TO A DECK BEAM.   PAD

112A A light dinghy carried capsized on cabin trunk

LAUNCHING FROM A LARGE POWER YACHT OR SHIP

113 The launching of a heavy dinghy presents special problems. Launching mechanism may be quadrant davits, gravity davits or the common radial davits. The first two types operate by means of gears or levers that place the boat in position for lowering. The radial davits require careful maneuvering and drill in order to have them function to their designed purpose. Figure 113A gives the steps in diagrammatic form.

When the boat is swung out ready for lowering, it should be in such condition as to become waterborne without further effort. The cover should have been removed and it, with the spreaders, stowed within the boat, the boat plug in, the painter lead forward and outboard of all encumbrances, and rudder hung.

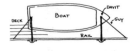

1. Clear Away. Falls are manned and the boat raised several inches above the chocks. Falls belayed. Chocks folded or knocked out. The after guy is cast off. (Boat plug checked.)

2. Launch Aft. The boat is swung forward, helped by a haul on the forward guy, and as it clears the after davit the forward guy is let go. Without loss of motion, the next step—

3. Bear out Aft. Haul away after guy—is completed. The stern is swung out.

4. Launch Forward. The boat is pushed aft, helped by a haul on the after guy.

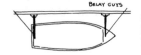

5. Bear out Forward. The boat is pushed outboard and both fore-and-aft guys securely belayed. The boat then can be lowered away.

113A Launching a davited boat

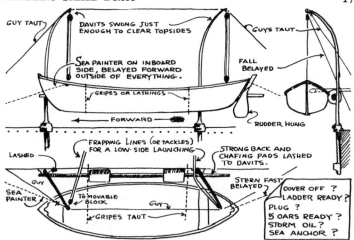

113B Life boat swung out ready for emergency lowering

Frapping lines leading from the lower (or movable) block of each fall will prevent the boat from swinging in a seaway or in the case of a severe outboard list. Such lines should lead from the swivel of the block or from a bight taken around the fall and should be handled from the boat deck.

Lowering is accomplished by paying out the boat falls from a sitting position and with the heels braced if possible. Gloves should be worn to avoid rope burns and the falls should be properly turned on a cleat to avoid a quick drop. The Jacob's ladder should be payed out as the boat is lowered from between the davits to the midships of the boat. If the ship has headway, the after end of the boat should be a trifle lower than the forward end and should reach the water first.

Releasing gear should be operated *before* the boat is completely waterborne and when the ship has reached the limit of a downward roll. If the ship has way on, the proper rigging of the sea painter from the boat to the ship will see the boat lying parallel to the ship, riding easy. Crashing may be avoided by use of the boat's rudder, putting the helm toward the ship slightly but not enough to cause a wild outward sheer and consequent danger of swamping or capsizing. The crew may board by the ladder.

Way is made by placing two oars ready for use and hauling ahead on the painter. When the painter is "up and down" it is cut smartly, the rudder put smartly away from the ship and the oars put into use. Get away from the ship at once on a right-angle course to avoid propeller suction.

Whenever possible launch from the lee side or from the lowest side.

Always release the stern falls first when the ship has headway on.

If launching from the low side of a listed ship no special instructions are required save to rig frapping lines to the falls.

If launching from the high side of a listed ship keep a strain on the falls while the boat gripes are cast off lest the boat slide to the low side. A "skate" of some design is necessary to launch from the high side so that the boat will clear extending members of the ship, porthole rims, bolts and plate edges and will not capsize as it is lowered. If the boat is not equipped with the usual iron midship skate, the strongback or another spar may be lashed along the inboard gunwale as a jury skate. It is almost hopeless to attempt to launch from the high side without a skate.

Most modern deep-water cruisers carry automatically-inflating life rafts in protective cases or drums, lashed down on deck. These rafts may be launched by the crew, who cast off the quick-release fittings on the case and roll it over the side—*being sure to retain the lanyard attached to it.* A sharp tug on the lanyard causes the raft to inflate and pop free from its container, at which point it is ready for boarding. Should the parent craft sink so fast that manual launching is impossible, the raft lashings will release automatically at a depth of about 15"; the raft will float to the surface, and the pull of the lanyard exerted by the sinking vessel will cause inflation. A weak link in the lanyard prevents the raft from being pulled under. Rafts should be carried where the crew can get to them in severe conditions without crossing stretches of wave-swept deck, and they should be positioned so they can easily be pushed over the side without cutting lifelines.

HANDLING ROWING BOATS AT SEA, BEACHING THEM, ETC.

114 In heavy sea conditions, the chief concern of the rowing craft is to meet the wave crests end on and so avoid a fatal "broaching to." The secret is to have way on when meeting crests, either by moderate forward motion or actual "holding" so that the crest passes ahead of the boat. Rudder or oar action can often "dodge" a crest of white tumbling water and this is recommended practice provided that, in so doing, the boat is not turned sufficiently to be endangered by receiving a sea on the beam and broaching to.

Running before a sea is always dangerous, the problem being to maintain course as the seas attack from astern. Rudder work and constant way are the best safeguards. If the bow seems to wish to "bury," get weight aft. Be sure the boat is dry, since water weight flowing fore and aft as the boat pitches adds to the bow weight when buoyancy there is most needed.

To make a landing in heavy surf, make a careful study of the situation and estimate of the power of the sea. One of the following methods, all designed to prevent the fateful broaching to which spells disaster in beach landings, should be used:

1. While still beyond the breakers, turn the boat stern to the shore, then back in, pulling a few strokes ahead to meet the heavier seas.
2. Come in bow first, but back up on the charge of each sea; then allow the "back" of the sea itself to carry the boat shoreward. This would be similar to the control of a surfboard.
3. Come in bow first dragging a drogue (basket, life-preserver, sea anchor, etc.), thus holding the stern into the wave crests.

115 Beaching the small boat, up to 100 pounds or so, presents no difficulties, except in surf or heavy seas. Within limitations the remarks in Paragraph 114 relating to the beaching of large pulling boats relate to small boats also. However, it is foolhardy to attempt beaching the small, light dinghy of 10′ or 12′ in length in heavy surf conditions unless it is of undisputed seaworthy design and build. The various dory types might possibly fall into this class; any boat with a broad-transom stern decidedly does not.

Sometimes a landing can be successfully made stern first, keeping the bows to the incoming seas and the weights slightly toward the bow. Headway and steerageway must be maintained under any conditions. Such a landing would probably only be made under emergency conditions, and the rower or passengers should be equipped with life preservers and resigned to a ducking and possible loss of the boat and/or its equipment.

116   The actual handling of the small boat on the beach is not difficult. Here are some hints:

1. Use rollers (logs, branches, tubular fenders, large tin cans, etc.) if at all possible. Oars, with the blade end boosted slightly by riding on a driftwood stringer or another oar, can sometimes be made to work.
2. A boat will slide easily on wet kelp or other seaweed, or on dry marsh grass.
3. Pull the boat, never push.
4. A fairly heavy boat can be "jogged"; i.e., lift one end and carry ahead, pivoting on the remaining end; then lift the pivot end and repeat.
5. Always secure the boat to a stake or a rock, no matter how high on the beach. If on a rocky shore, with danger of the tide rising, boost the boat up on its oars, using them as beams spanning a low spot between high, flanking rocks.
6. Unless the boat is resting on them, hide the oars. Leave a note or some other indication showing the Coast Guard patrol or police that the boat is not abandoned nor shipwrecked.

117   The boat which is regularly beached or taken ashore upon landing should be handled by gear designed especially for

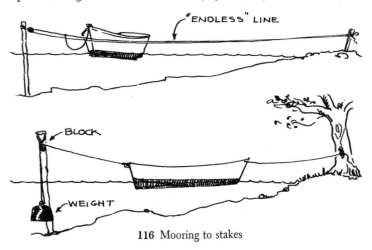

116 Mooring to stakes

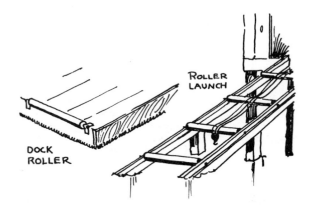

117A *Left,* a dock "roller" *Right,* a dinghy launch

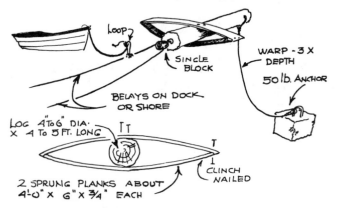

117B A small-boat offhaul The cross-section of the outboard float prevents capsizing and twisting of the line. Good in tidal waters and up to about 150' length. Apt to pick up seaweed and foul.

that purpose. A dock or a float should be provided with a wide, flush roller to facilitate the hauling to a safe position. Where there is a great rise and fall in the tide a "dinghy launch" serves well. The boat is usually handled by a tackle and possibly a small winch. (*Figure 117A*)

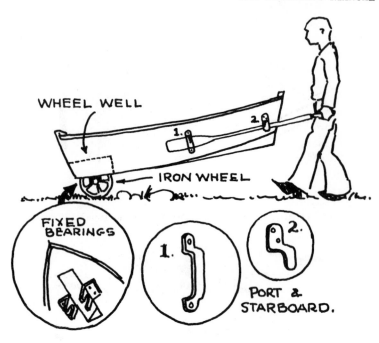

117C Trundle skiff

Small dinghies of wooden construction—especially if equipped with center-or daggerboards—frequently develop hull problems from the constant flexing of being beached. In general, it is a good idea to avoid grounding, if it is at all avoidable.

118 The carrying of boats on public highways presents problems. It is generally dangerous to carry even very small boats on the roof of a passenger car, especially at high speeds. In some states it is forbidden—and wisely.

The common carrying devices make use of gear which (a) grips a certain part of the car, usually the drip gutters, or (b) attaches by means of rubber suction caps. Both are weak in that they do not provide for the great strains of windage. The pocketing effect of an overturned boat being driven into the wind or against wind of the car's own making is tremendous and frequently has resulted in serious accidents.

The safest method of transporting boats over highways is by the use of a boat trailer. Such a trailer must be heavy enough to safely carry the boat and its gear.

Trailering a boat at highway speeds is demanding. Because trailering has become so popular in the last few years, techniques are still being developed, and in many states, laws pertaining to trailers are still in flux. There are some basics that apply nearly everywhere. The most obvious limiting factor is beam: For trailering without a special police permit, the maximum width of the boat or trailer (whichever is greater) is 8′, which in turn means that most boats designed for trailering are less than 25′ in length. Hull shape is also important—for launching, a flat or slightly rounded bottom is best. Most standard trailers are equipped with a number of rollers which can be adjusted fore and aft or vertically to provide the best support of the hull.

Your trailer will probably require license plates and lights, which can often be purchased as a demountable set; you can, and should, remove them before launching, as no electric lights can withstand repeated immersion. The electrical plug and socket connecting the car's electrical system to the trailer is especially vulnerable, and the wires should be under no strain, nor should they sag near the ground.

Brake requirements vary from state to state, but the American Boat & Yacht Council recommends brakes of some sort for all wheels of trailers designed for a gross weight of 1,500 pounds or more. There are three types of brakes in common use—*electrical, hydraulic,* and *surge.* The first two, integrated into the car's braking system, are preferable.

There are also three types of hitch—*bumper, frame,* and *weight-distributing.* The first is illegal in many states; the frame hitch, which bolts to at least two of the towing vehicle's structural members, is the most generally used. Very heavy loads require the weight-distributing hitch, a complicated device that uses leverage on car and trailer to distribute the load evenly. A frame hitch is generally considered suitable for gross weights—trailer *plus* load—up to 3,500 pounds.

Safety chains are required in most states. These consist of a pair of chains ending in S-hooks and running from the tongue of the trailer to the towing hitch, crossed under the hitch in such a way that, if the ball-and-socket joint fails, the trailer tongue won't drive into the ground and somersault the rig. The chains should be just long enough to permit free turning and should be welded steel, of a breaking strength equal to the trailer's recommended gross weight (marked on the trailer itself).

Boats are made to be supported at all points by water, so a trailer will always be an unnatural bed for your hull. In most cases, vital support points are the forefoot, the keel, the turn of the bilge (especially under built-in weight) and the transom.

On the road, at speeds to 55 mph., the boat will undergo rapid motion unlike anything on the water. All loose weights should be placed in the car trunk or firmly secured, and the boat itself must be lashed down. The primary point of attachment is forward, at the winch, whose drum should be mounted (if possible) directly in line with your boat's towing eye when the craft is fully cradled. Besides the winch line, an additional cable, preferably with a turnbuckle, should run from the towing eye to the winch pillar. There should be a non-stretching fabric strap (padded where it touches the hull) across the after part of the boat, as well as a pair of spring lines run aft from the bow cleat to the trailer frame alongside the wheels.

The key to successful towing is balancing the boat's weight so that the load on the trailer tongue is somewhere between 5% and 7% of the total gross weight—boat plus contents plus trailer. For the average small passenger car, the gross weight shouldn't be much more than 2,000 pounds, and the tongue weight about 100 pounds. You can easily measure tongue weight with a bathroom scale set on a couple of cinder blocks.

The mast and boom of a sailboat should be firmly secured to a padded rack, with the standing and running rigging bundled and lashed to the mast at intervals. If the mast protrudes over the stern, it should have a red flag tied to the end. Obviously, the rudder won't be attached when trailering, but an outboard may be left in place, as long as the transom is supported directly beneath the motor. A keel or weighted centerboard should be lowered to rest on a frame crosspiece.

CANOES

119 The handling of the American canoe, the design of which is based upon those of the North American Indians, is an art. Its handling calls for the nicest sense of balance. The man who can handle a canoe well, especially under sail, has learned a great deal of basic seamanship, which he will unconsciously apply to the handling of other and much larger boats.

PADDLING POSITIONS

120 The safest and fastest paddling position is the one in which the paddler kneels, usually on soft pads attached to the knees or on a cushion about 24" by 15". Kneeling positions keep the center of gravity lower than when sitting on the seats (sometimes provided) and permit the upper leg muscles to add their power to those of the arms and back. Cruising positions call for one or both knees on the pads, but the buttocks rest against a thwart. Racing positions call for the knee on the paddling side to be on the pad and the torso held more erect than in cruising.

Double paddles are used from a full kneeling position only, or from a seat. Such a seat is generally portable, is raised only 3" to 5" from the bottom, and sometimes has extensions to which a cross foot brace is attached.

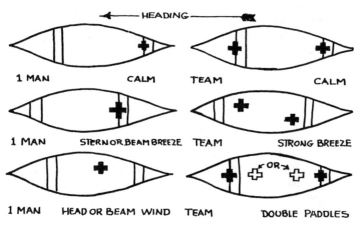

120 Paddling positions

When both paddlers of a team sit upon the caned seats found in many canoes, the boat becomes a very unstable and cranky craft. In general, unless there is cruising duffel low down to bring the center of gravity lower, it is best to have at least one paddler in a kneeling position. Expert canoeists, men with thousands of miles of water behind them without a spill, invariably use the kneeling positions as a matter of basic safety. The comfort of the sitting position, however, should not be denied, and many canoeists rehang the cane seats so that they are several inches below the gunwales. This is a simple operation, involving only longer carriage bolts from gunwale to seat frame and sometimes the removal or lowering of the thwart forward of the stern seat.

In white water and in rapids, the expert finds that a standing position will permit him to quickly counteract capsizing efforts by throwing his body weight from one leg to the other. A long, light pole rather than a paddle is then often used, the current being permitted to move the boat, the pole being used more or less as a fender or a setting pole.

CANOE STROKES

121   *The J Stroke.* Used for single paddling. Its curve is adjusted according to trim, windage, or current so that the boat is propelled forward on a straight course. After completion, a slight drag—using the paddle as a rudder, directs the bow in the opposite direction from that given it by the stroke.

The Bow Stroke. Used by the bowman of a team. It is perfectly parallel to the keel. The bow stroke sets the pace for the stern paddler. Regardless of the maneuver in the offing, the bow stroke is kept up in this manner and not changed until so ordered by the stern paddler, who is considered the helmsman.

The Sweep. Used for wide slow turns without loss of speed. Sometimes it is terminated in the draw stroke for quicker turning.

The Backwater. Simply the reverse of the bow stroke. The paddle is not removed for the back stroke but kept submerged and feathered.

The Draw. Used to move the canoe sideways as to a dock or float.

121 Canoe strokes

The Push-over. Used to move the canoe away from a dock or float. The gunwale is used as a fulcrum, the paddle as a lever. The stroke is feathered upon the return.

The Bow Rudder. Used by the bow paddler to swing the stern or to make quick turns. Also, for the same purpose, the paddle is extended forward of the stem and the blade projected into the water on the opposite side of the keel.

Sculling. To move the canoe sideways but at a 45° angle forward or backward.

CANOE ACCIDENTS

122   The canoe is its own life preserver in a sense. Even when it is filled, it will float and afford flotation to a man in the water. Overturnings are common, especially with the inexperienced. But they need not be dangerous—unless, of course, the canoeist is not a swimmer, in which case he has no business being in a canoe anyway.

Most canoe tragedies occur because the canoeist does not know how to right and reboard his boat. When understood, this is a simple trick. If the canoe has filled in upsetting (as is most likely) it must first be freed of water. The first step is to swim to either the bow or stern and take a vertical position facing the opposite end. Now, place one hand on the stemhead and the other beneath the curve of the stem under water. Slowly submerge the canoe, keeping it in even thwartship trim; as soon as possible bring your full weight on the end and with the free hand and legs start swimming forward. Most of the water will rush toward you and spill over the submerged end. Do not let go of the canoe or it will sheer wildly from you and make its recovery necessary. The gunwales will now be several inches above the water and the canoe out of an "awash" position.

Now swim to a point about amidships, on the leeward side, and using your full weight, rock the canoe from side to side, splashing the water out in small dollops. The trick is to time the application of your weight with the natural thwartship rush of the water, giving it a flip as the water bulk reaches its extreme surge at the near gunwale. Patience will soon reduce the water in the canoe to the amount where it can be dipped or scooped out.

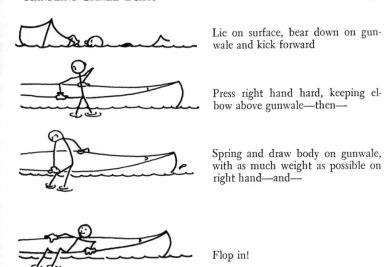

Lie on surface, bear down on gunwale and kick forward

Press right hand hard, keeping elbow above gunwale—then—

Spring and draw body on gunwale, with as much weight as possible on right hand—and—

Flop in!

122 Getting into a canoe in deep water

Once the canoe has been emptied, it is reboarded, as shown in Figure 122. Immediately upon a canoe's upsetting and swamping, at least one paddle should be retrieved and wedged into the bow or stern. Other gear can be picked up after the boat is again under way. If the canoe has not filled upon upsetting, under no circumstances let go of it. Even a gentle breeze will carry it away much more quickly than you can swim after it. With one hand always on the canoe and dragging it with you, go after the paddle.

CANOE SAILING

123   Canoe sailing has developed many forms of rigs, some of them of amazing and dangerous sail areas. For ordinary day sailing or cruising, a safe but efficient rig, such as the one shown in Figure 123 should suffice. Decked-in canoes, or canoes equipped with "hike boards" upon which the skipper may crawl to create windward ballast, of course, might have sail areas larger than shown.

The leeboards are detachable, and each is pivoted so that the leeward board alone is down when sailing. When running free, both boards are up or slightly trailing.

The sail center and leeboard center (center of lateral resistance) must have a certain definite relationship to each other and to the hull itself. (*See Chapter II.*) In a canoe these are easily adjusted by shifting the leeboards fore and aft until the perfect balance has been achieved. With your own weight approximately amidships and the leeboards vertical, the canoe, without rudder effort (the paddle is used for a rudder), should tend to round to into the wind or have a "weather helm."

Centers can be further shifted by pivoting the leeboard in use forward or aft of the pivot center until little or no rudder effort is required. A canoe sails best upright, not heeled. Do not hesitate to add to her stability by shifting your weight to windward, or by hooking a leg over the gunwale. Do not sit on the gunwale. The wind resistance will deaden the boat and a sudden slackening of the wind, or a pocket, might easily capsize you to windward. Windward courses are helped by shifting your weight slightly forward. Off the wind, a weight shift aft will help.

The expert sailor does not use his paddle for coming about. He stows his paddle, slides forward and, as the canoe heads into the wind, he sheets the sail in, keeping it full. With the boom amidships and the sail luffing, the leeboard is raised and secured, then, pushing the boom slightly to windward, he again slides aft. With the bow well around on the new tack, the boom is released, the paddle shipped, and, with the foot, the leeward leeboard is pushed down.

Traditionally, spars should be of Sitka spruce or of stock of equal weight, and running rigging should be very light, preferably of cotton line. Sails are of one-ounce canvas or so-called "balloon cloth," without bolt ropes; grommets should be of brass machine set. Leeboards are generally of one-inch stock, mahogany being the favorite, though spruce, white pine, or Spanish cedar are sometimes used. However, most canoes today are built of anodized aluminum; some of fiber-glass. Sailing rigs, too, are modern with metal spars and leeboards, while sails are of lightweight nylon or, rarely, of Dacron.

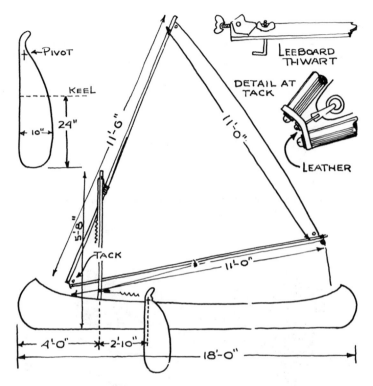

123 Details of a canoe sailing rig

OUTBOARD MOTORBOATS

124 Today's outboard motors are thoroughly reliable and sophisticated engines running to over 200 hp in size. They have brought forth a number of specialized hulls designed for this kind of detachable—rather than portable—propulsion. These range from the smallest yacht tenders to heavy, auxiliary sailboats and house-boats, and include the increasingly popular center-console utility craft, water ski runabouts and hydroplanes capable of speeds of 60 mph and more. In general, hulls suitable for outboard motors are of the planing type, and the best are characterized by a broad, flat

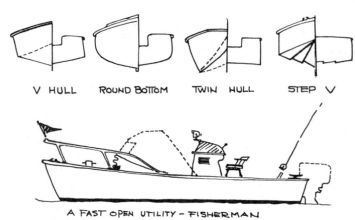

V HULL   ROUND BOTTOM   TWIN HULL   STEP V

A FAST OPEN UTILITY — FISHERMAN

124A An outboard runabout and typical lines

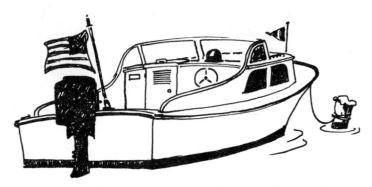

124B A typical trailerable outboard cruiser

stern section capable of supplying adequate buoyancy for one or two big engines. All but the smallest and simplest outboards are operated from consoles amidships or seats forward, with wheel steering and throttle-gearshift controls. (Only the smallest engines are without forward-neutral-reverse shifts.)

Hull shapes are varied. In the mid-size craft of 16′ to 20′ in length, some type of V-bottom is most common. Generally speaking, the sharper, deeper V-hulls, in which the V is carried aft all the way to the transom, provide a soft and seaworthy ride in steep seas, at the expense of stability and fuel economy (they drag a lot of hull through the water); shallower, flatter V-shapes tend to plane more easily and are more stable, but pound at higher speeds and in rough seas. Deep-V hulls have excellent directional stability —at planing speeds—while shallower hulls tend to yaw badly in seas, while being somewhat more maneuverable at slow speeds.

In an attempt to combine the seakindliness of the deep-V with the stability of the flat-bottom hull, designers came up with several multiple-hull configurations, carrying such commercial names as "tri-V," "cathedral" and "air slot." The basic idea behind all of them is similar: Taking one or two sharp-V hulls, builders stabilized them, either by separating them, as in the twin hull illustrated, or by adding a pair of sponsons, one on either side, as in the cathedral types. These elaborate hull shapes were only possible in fiberglass, where any shape is capable of being built if it can be molded.

Some designers have turned out successful outboard cruisers in the 17′-to-22′ class, weighing up to 2,000 pounds and performing well with single 200-hp or twin 140-hp engines. Most such designs suffer from poor weight distribution and have eccentric maneuvering habits at slow speeds, with little hull immersed forward. Because of the great strength of fiberglass, these boats will absorb far more punishment at high speeds than their passengers can stand—the pounding and vibration makes them especially prone to shedding bits and pieces of hardware. For the most part, however, the smaller cruiser is driven by a cross between outboard and inboard, the I/O, sterndrive or outdrive, to cite three of its more popular names.

As outboard power grew higher and higher with the demand for speed, fuel economy became a concern. Two-cycle outboard engines are not excessively greedy in smaller sizes—and "smaller" now seems to include engines to 75 hp—consuming 12 gallons an hour. There was, however, a limiting size beyond which the outboard configuration, with its tremendous load on the boat's transom, was simply impractical. By linking a standard inboard engine through the transom to a retractable outboard lower unit, it was possible to offer, at least in principle, the advantages of the inboard power unit plus those of the outboard—precise, responsive steering and the ability to raise the propeller. Even diesel power was available.

The sterndrive installation has survived its initial teething problems, associated with the engineering complexities of the engine-to-lower-unit hookup. It still requires a hull designed to carry inordinate weight aft, and the necessary engine box butted up against the transom results in some waste of cockpit space. Like almost everything else associated with boat design, it is a compromise.

Most outboard dealers also sell boats suitable for their engines, and of course inboard and sterndrive boat dealers supply engines as standard. It does not necessarily follow that a dealer is a good judge of the best engine for a given hull. In today's powerboats under 20', however, there is the limiting aspect of the Federal Boat Safety Act of 1971, which prescribes that all such craft built after October 31, 1972 (except sailboats, canoes, kayaks, inflatables, and multihulls) must carry a legible capacity plate attached by the manufacturer in a location clearly visible to the boat's operator.

Capacity plates for outboards list the boat's maximum horsepower, maximum passenger capacity in pounds, and maximum load capacity, including motor(s), equipment and crew, again in pounds. Inboard and sterndrive boats have a somewhat different style of wording, listing the maximum crew capacity in pounds, and the maximum capacity in pounds of crew and equipment—the engine in such craft being installed by the manufacturer, who must certify to the Coast Guard that it meets applicable safety standards, including those covered by the capacity plate.

Maximum allowable horsepower may be considerably more than

that necessary to accomplish what a particular owner desires of his boat. If in doubt, one may consult a naval architect or inquire along the waterfront as to the performance capabilities of similar boats: Almost any owner is only too willing to talk about his boat, although he may be less than forthright about his vessel's drawbacks.

CONSTRUCTION MATERIALS

125 A question that continues to arise is the one of the relative merits of construction and materials. Developments in materials in the last couple of decades have resulted in the possibility of building first-rate craft from any of the common materials. Unfortunately it is also possible to construct shoddy, badly-designed vessels from the same basic ingredients. The safety requirements of the Federal Boat Safety Act of 1971, which make the manufacturer responsible for the safety-related aspects of his products, is beginning to have a visible effect, mostly in the disappearance of some of the least reputable boatbuilders.

Here is a general guide to the salient characteristics of today's materials and their applications:

Sheet-construction aluminum. Generally satisfactory for all applications, in both fresh and salt water, if the material has been properly treated during construction. Lightweight pram types are especially prone to drumming noises and, if uninsulated, are cold in winter and hot in summer. Most aluminum boats are, however, both insulated and provided with positive flotation in case they are holed. Repair of gashes is still a professional job. A reputable firm whose products are well distributed in a given saltwater boating area is probably quite reliable. For freshwater use, the aluminum-hulled boat is probably the best.

Fiberglass construction. Actually plastic reinforced with strands or weaves of glass filaments, and the British name for it—fiberglass-reinforced plastic, or FRP—is more accurate. Some early fiberglass boats were horrors, disintegrating, fading, cracking and otherwise turning into perfect wrecks. Others, such as the first patrol craft commissioned by the Coast Guard, have shown no visible signs of deterioration after nearly 30 years' service.

With the passage of time, manufacturers' claims of "zero main-

tenance" have evaporated and the general level of fiberglass workmanship has improved. In general, the prospective buyer should
avoid boats with sharp corners, gunwales, or chines: Fiberglass
actually gains strength from easy curves, but abrupt bends are
sources of cracks and star-shaped crazing. Beware also of colored
hulls, which may fade—although this problem is not as severe as
it was. Check by sighting along the hull for "hard spots," where interior bulkheads or fittings have been pushed too hard against the
hull, creating a place for eventual failure of hull, fitting, or both.

Glass is today the most popular construction material, account-
ing for something over 80% of the boats under 26' in length. The
only close contender—and it is falling behind—is aluminum.
Whether this situation will continue with the increasing shortage
of petrochemicals (the source of the resin used in fiberglass boats)
is an open question.

The greatest asset of fiberglass as a designer's material is its
adaptability to endless hull forms of great complexity: It would
be financially impossible for a builder to market a cathedral-hull
boat of wood or aluminum. Unfortunately, while many manufacturers have used fiberglass creatively, in seaworthy new designs
or in glass versions of classic hulls, others have used the material's
versatility to produce untried, unsafe, and impractical hull forms.

Glass boats can be quite readily repaired by the owner who is
willing to take a little time to do a good job. Kits are available in
most marine supply stores for touch-up repairs or more serious
work. The resale value of glass boats—good ones, that is—has
been for some time far better than that of any other craft, and
this seems likely to continue.

Sheet-plywood construction. Reasonably satisfactory. Plywood
will eventually break down—much sooner than solid wood planking. Drums and is noisy. Repairs not difficult, except for holes.
Bottoms tend to "work" and hence fastenings *must* be large-headed
screws, or so-called annular construction nails. Plywood edges must
be protected at all times. Teredo worms adore the glue between the
laminates of some plywoods. The plywood grade should be
"marine"; i.e., with solid core and selected faces and backs. Mere
"exterior" grade is not good enough. Douglas fir is cheapest but
will not take a smooth paint job; for that use mahogany-faced

marine plywood, at least 5 ply. The glue must be waterproof.

Good for trailer boats. Begins to fail at high speeds; say 40 mph and up. The quality in a sheet plywood boat is found in the framing and ribbing more than the skin itself.

An inherent criticism of all sheet materials is that the sheet, unbendable into compound curves, dictates the hull form. Therefore such a hull must be a compromise between what a designer considers safe, fast, and weatherly and what form the sheet of material will permit. This is why some plywood and metal boats can truly be characterized as "boxes." Some of them are unsafe, indeed, man-killing. Lapstrake construction somewhat solves this very basic problem.

Lapstrake construction. A very strong hull form, yet not unduly heavy. Look for good glue bonds at laps and a sensible manner of clinching; namely, rivets and burrs, or clinch nails. Adjustable bolts and nuts seem to be a sales gimmick only. Some glues today stand without metal fastenings of any kind; lessons learned from the airframe industry. Plywood or solid plank will provide an equally good hull form. Solid plank will soak water and become much heavier than plywood in time; further, it will not take as much soaking and drying as plywood and is better for a boat which is to be left at a mooring rather than trailed home or beached.

There is no merit whatever in the claim that the laps of the boat actually are a planing surface or "lift" the boat and increase speed. These are claims for the unthinking.

A weak area is the fastening of the planks (a double plank, really) to the relatively light bent frames of a round-bottomed lapstrake boat. A rivet and burr is best here; the usual screw works out under stress of a speed-wracked hull. Keep sand and litter out of the bilges; once it is allowed to creep or sift between the laps (as when the boat is dry), the boat can be made tight again only by external gunks and compounds made to correct such leaks.

A lapstrake topside with a smooth bottom, on a chine-form hull (V-bottom), makes the fastest, lightest and most satisfactory boat for normal uses. Round bottom is usually good at sea but slower than the above form in smooth or lake waters. Because of its design flexibility, fiberglass is used to make most "lapstrake" hulls today. The laps give the fiberglass extra form strength.

Composite Construction. The limitations of sheet forms have led to a newer form of construction, the so-called sandwich hull. In one such process the hull is built up in wood strips, often of cedar, edge-glued and nailed and quite smoothly sanded and faired. It is then covered inside and out with laid-up fiberglass, plus a gel coat. Along with the hull work, the superstructure and decks are similarly treated, making a solid and durable assembly indeed. Another sandwich consists of a foam or balsa core, fiberglassed inside and out. Sandwich construction is practical only on larger boats, because of weight and cost, but it permits hull forms that are based on the operating conditions rather than on the limitations imposed by the material. It is especially applicable to sailing hull forms and to heavy workboats and cruisers of the displacement types. Its cost is higher than either wood or glass alone and is not often used in boats of the runabout type.

YACHT TENDERS

126   In combination with the small rowing-type dinghy, the smaller-size outboard engines serve the cruising yachtsmen well. Engines up to three hp are sufficiently powerful for a 10′ to 12′ displacement dinghy and do not offer a great problem in finding stowage space aboard the mother vessel. It is essential to keep such a motor in the true lightweight class (23 to 35 pounds, tank filled). A bracket in a vertical locker or a cradle in the lazarette should be provided. Be certain that such a space is ventilated and always wipe off oil and gas film before stowing. Store outboard-motor gas on deck and only in metal cans designed to carry inflammables.

OUTBOARD MOTORS AS AUXILIARY POWER

127   The detachable motor has come into wide use as auxiliary power for sailboats up to 30′. While hardly capable of driving a heavy hull into a head wind or tide, the outboard serves faithfully when the wind dies and calm waters prevail. The open sailboat has no problem in attaching the motor. However, the decked craft requires some type of well, extension bracket, or false transom on the stern. Ship chandlers stock various devices applicable to flat transom craft. Avoid the large "contraption" of the

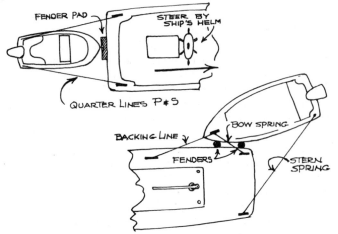

127A How to use an outboard-motor dinghy as auxiliary power

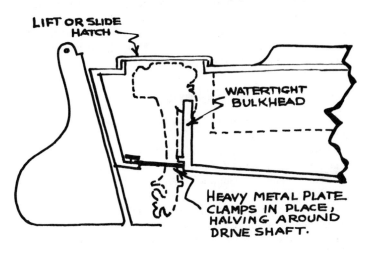

127B Typical motor well on a small sailing craft

Rube Goldberg variety too often seen; it requires more space for stowage than the motor itself. As neat and clean a device as there is consists of a small removable panel of deck in the way of the transom, just large enough to receive the motor clamp. It may be off-center to clear rudder and traveler. Steering is done by the ship's rudder, the engine being set in its "straight ahead" notch. Remember that an off-center outboard will give a boat a much smaller turning circle in one direction than in the other.

A few larger sailing cruisers use a dinghy–outboard-motor combination as a push boat. Pad the bow of the dinghy at the transom and rig lines from the dinghy quarters to the ship's quarters, lashing the dinghy bow amidships. These bridles may be used as steering lines, the dinghy itself becoming the rudder.

If the dinghy and motor are lashed 'longside, lay against fenders and rig a spring line from the dinghy bow to the ship's quarter on the same side; then a stern line from the dinghy stern to the opposite quarter—and don't forget a backing line rigged from the bow of the pushboat to a midship cleat on the moved vessel. Let the propeller extend somewhat aft of the ship's waterline (stern) and haul in the spring so the pushboat toes in to compensate for the extreme off-center power application.

Glossary

The recognized nomenclature of the principal parts of boats and their fittings is as follows:

Apron   A timber fitted abaft the stem to reinforce the stem and to give a sufficient surface on which to land the ends of the planks.

Beams   Transverse supports running from side to side to support the deck.

Bilge   The part of the bottom, on each side of the keel, on which the boat would rest if aground.

Binding strake   A strake of planking, usually thicker than other planks, fitted next to and under the sheer strake.

Blade, oar   The broad flattened part of an oar as distinguished from the loom.

Boat falls   Blocks and tackle with which the boats are hoisted aboard at davits.

Boat hook   A pole with a blunt hook on the end to aid in landing operations or hauling alongside.

Boat plug   A screwed metal plug fitted in the bottom planking of the boat at the lowest point to drain the bilges when boat is out of the water.

Bottom boards   The fore-and-aft planks secured to the frames, or to floor beams, forming the floor of the boat; frequently removable.

Breaker   A small cask for carrying potable water.

Breasthook   A wood or metal knee fitted behind the stem structure.

Capping   The fore-and-aft finishing piece on top of the clamp and sheer strake, at the frame heads, in an open boat.

Carling   A fore-and-aft beam at deck openings.

Chock   A metal casting used as a fair-lead for a mooring line or anchor chain.

Clamp   A main longitudinal strengthening member under the deck in decked-over boats and at the gunwale in open boats.

Cleat   A metal or wood fitting shaped like an anvil with two horns; for belaying lines.

Cockpit   A compartment, usually for passengers, in the stern of a cruising vessel.

Deadwood   Timber built on top of the keel or shaft log at either end of the boat to afford a firm fastening for the frames and to connect the keel to the end timbers.

Fenders   Portable bumpers hung over the side during landings to protect the hull. Never called bumpers.

Floors   The transverse timbers which reinforce the frames and carry the strength athwartships across the keel.

Frames   The ribs of the boat; curved timbers, frequently steambent, secured to the keel and extending upward to the gunwale or deck.

Garboard strake   The lowest board of outside planking, next to the keel.

Grapnel   A small multiple-fluked anchor used in dragging or grappling operations; a common small boat anchor.

Gripes   The fitting used to secure a boat in its stowage position on board ship.

Gudgeons   Small metal fittings, similar to eyebolts, secured to the sternpost of small boats on which the rudder hangs. Used in place of the rudder hanger of larger boats.

Gunwale   The upper edge of the side of a boat.

Hoisting pads   Metal fittings inside the boat often attached to the keel to take the hoisting slings or hoisting rods.

Horn timber   The after deadwood fastening the shaft log and transom knee together.

Keel   The principal timber of a boat, extending from stem to stern at the bottom of the hull and supporting the whole frame.

Keelsons   Fore-and-aft structural timbers either above or outboard of the keel.

Knee   A shaped timber for connecting construction members installed at an angle to each other. Some knees are sawn from straight-grained wood, while in other cases the grain follows the natural bend of the tree at a limb or root.

Leather   The portion of an oar which rests in the rowlock. This is usually covered with leather.

Loom   Rounded portion of an oar between the blade and handle.

Norman pin   A metal pin fitted in a towing post or bitt for belaying the line.

Painter   A rope used in the bow for towing or for securing the boat.

Pintles   Small straight pieces of metal secured to the rudder and fitting in the gudgeons on the sternpost of small boats, thus supporting the rudder. Pintles and gudgeons are used in place of the rudder braces of larger boats.

Plank sheer   The top plank at the side.

Risings   The fore-and-aft stringers inside a boat, secured to the frames, on which the thwarts rest.

Rowlocks.   Forked pieces of metal in which the leathers of oars rest while pulling. *Sunken rowlocks* are those which are set down in the gunwale of the boat. *Swivel rowlocks* rotate, the shank of the rowlock fitting in a socket in the gunwale.

Sheer   The line of form at the side, which the gunwale or deck edge follows in profile.

Sheet strake   The uppermost strake of planking at the side following the line of sheer.

Side fender   A longitudinal timber projecting beyond the outside line of the hull planking, often metal-faced, to protect the hull.

Slings   Gear made of wire rope and close-linked chain for handling boats at booms or cranes.

Spars   Masts, booms, and gaffs upon which, when stepped in the boat, the sails are spread.

Steering rowlock   A form of swivel rowlock, fitted near the stern of a boat, in which the steering oar is shipped; sometimes called a crutch.

Stem   The upright timber in the forward part of a boat, joined to the keel by a knee.

Stem band   A metal facing or cutwater fitted on the stempost.

Stem heel (The forward deadwood)   A timber, often called the sole piece, used to connect the stem knee to the keel.

Stern fast   A stern painter for use in securing the stern of a boat when moored or docked.

Stern hook   Same as breasthook, for stern on a double-ended boat.

Sternpost   The principal vertical piece of timber at the after end of a boat, its lower end fastened to the keel or shaft log by a stern knee.

Stern sheets   The space in the boat abaft the thwarts.

Strakes   Continuous lines of fore-and-aft planking. Each line of planking is known as a strake.

Stretchers   Athwartship, movable pieces against which the oarsmen brace their feet in pulling.

Stringers   Longitudinal strengthening timbers inside the hull.

Strongback   The spar between the davits to which a boat is griped.

Tarpaulin   A waterproof fabric cover.

Thole pin   A pin fitted in the gunwale plank for use in place of a rowlock. Used with manila ring about five inches in diameter, called a *thole-pin grommet*; also used when sculling.

Tiller   A bar or lever, fitted fore and aft in the rudder head, by which the rudder is moved.

Towing bitts (Often called towing posts). A vertical timber securely fastened for use in towing or mooring.

Trailing lines Small lines secured to the boat and around the oars to prevent the latter from getting adrift when trailed from swivel rowlocks.

Transom The planking across the stern in a transomed boat.

Yoke Athwartship piece fitting over the rudder head, by which the rudder is moved by yoke ropes when the tiller is not shipped.

⚓

CHAPTER II

HANDLING BOATS
UNDER SAIL

BOAT SAILING is done today almost entirely under fore-and-aft rigs. The square rig has always been the sail dress of ships capable of carrying the large crew necessary to handle the rig. It was essentially the rig of deep water where the ship had sea room enough to "go find a breeze"; and with one of the trades or other steady and predictable winds abeam or astern, long, fast passages were made with regularity and safety.

. Wind conditions near the land are never predictable except in so far as they generally provide breezes either from the land or toward the land in normal stormless periods. Any sailing vessel sails best with the wind abeam, or *reaching*. Small vessels, fishermen, and coasters that did not sail foreign seas nor engage in an overseas trade, soon learned that in their normal trade between coastal ports this beam wind, permitting fast reaching courses on either board, called for the fore-and-aft rig. Not only did this rig give them maximum day-in and day-out speed and safety, but it was also very handy for quick maneuvering in tight harbors and rivers, and required an absolute minimum of hands to sail.

Deepwater ships in island or short-run service, making many ports per voyage, learned the advantage of the fore-and-aft rig for inshore work and well knew the advantages of the square rig in the ocean trades. Hence, we find such combinations as the topsail schooner, the brigantine, the barkentine, and the jackass bark; rigs which were efficient for either deepwater or coasting.

The sail rig for the boat has always been the fore-and-aft rig for

45

obvious reasons. Occasionally, as in the case of a deepwater cruiser or an offshore banksman, a combination rig is carried, which makes use of one or more square sails, known on yachts as trade-wind sails and raffees. A sail often carried by fore-and-aft boats is the spinnaker in one of its several forms; a sail directly related to the square sail, though not rigged to a yard nor sheeted as an out-and-out square sail. Nevertheless, the working rig of all sailboats is the fore-and-aft rig.

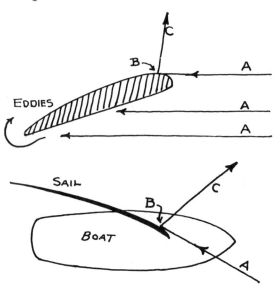

201 *Above*, the force of wind on an airplane wing. (Note change of direction of force AB.) *Below*, the same force on a sail

The principle and the basic handling of all fore-and-aft rigs are the same. If a sailor understands the handling of a catboat, the simplest form of the fore-and-aft rig, he can, with but little additional practice, also handle more complex forms, such as the sloop, the cutter, the yawl, the ketch, and the schooner.

201 Men have been sailing for centuries without understanding the force which drove them. Only in the last 50 years, with the subject much aired by the scientific approach of airplane and yacht designers, have we begun to understand the action of moving air or wind on our sails.

There is nothing strange in the phenomenon of a sailboat moving before the wind. The pressure of the wind on the spread sail is sufficient to overcome the retarding effect of the water on the hull, and the entire assembly, sail, spars, and hull, moves in the direction of the wind.

However, when the wind is on the beam or ahead and the assembly actually moves *against* the force which is moving it, entirely different, and until aerodynamics made them evident, unknown, principles come into play.

What happens when a boat moves against the wind is simply that the direction of the force of the wind has been changed. A certain proportion of this force or power is dispersed and wasted. A remaining proportion is conserved (through efficient design, setting, and handling of the sails) and becomes useful power.

In the language of the layman, this useful force is in the form of a vacuum, on the leeward side of the sail, which exerts a lift or pull. In Figure 201 is represented an airplane wing. The wind A exerts some force on the undersurface, "holding it up," but a far greater force is exerted at point B where a negative or lifting force comes into play because of the change in the direction of the force. This direction is approximately shown by the arrow C.

If we now stand the wing on end, so to speak, as if its leading edge were lashed to a boat's mast, this same force would exist but its changed direction would exert a suction not upward but forward—resulting in progress against the driving force. It should be stated that this theory has been accepted for many years as gospel but has recently come under attack as new methods of measurement and testing are developed.

Because our sail is of one thickness, without a "bottom" that is different in contour from the top surface (as in the airplane wing), it has certain advantages over the wing. Its inside or after shape is taken, as allowed by the suction on the opposite or forward side, as a result of the pressure of the wind against it. Being flexible, the sail becomes air-foiled, that is, perfectly balanced between the two components of the wind. This air-foiling is all-important, as it reduces to a minimum the eddies which tend to destroy the suction power on the forward side.

202 Some eddies cannot be entirely eliminated. These are chiefly those caused by the leach or after edge of the sail. These form the "dead areas" present to some degree in all sails, no matter how well designed or bent. (*Figure 202A*)

The leading edge of the sail does most of the work, for here, on its leeward side, occurs the pull or suction. The leading edge of a sail is called the *luff*. The efficiency of the luff is somewhat impaired by the eddies set up by the mast (in the "much-drive" area of the sails shown in Figure 202B).

In order to eliminate these hindering eddies, a foresail or a jib is used. The air spilling from the leach of the foresail or jib destroys the eddies and restores the drive of the sail aft of it. To some extent, the foresail, or the jib, helps the drive of the sail aft of it in another way. The wind velocity is increased in the narrow "funnel" between the two sails, and results in an increased pressure at the luff of the mainsail, exactly where it is needed most. If this funnel is made too narrow by excessive sheeting-in of the foresail or jib, or by the use of a jib that overlaps the mainsail too much, it backwinds the mainsail and invades the luff vacuum, destroying its suction power. Excessive narrowing of the funnel will so pocket the wind as to form a vacuum on the *after* side of the mainsail, drawing the boat *backwards*.

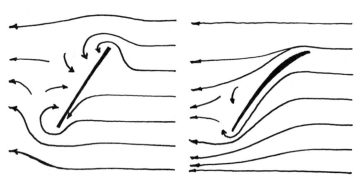

202A *Left*, excessive eddy-making of a flat surface *Right*, reduced eddy-making of an air-foiled surface

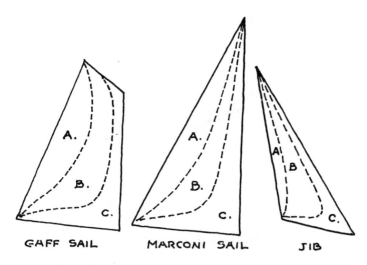

GAFF SAIL   MARCONI SAIL   JIB

202B a) Little or no drive b) Moderate drive c) Much drive

Many modern sailboats, however, set large jibs that overlap the mainsail. These foresails may provide considerably more drive, in some circumstances, than the "main" sail.

203 By applying the parallelogram of forces to the wind force (*Figure 203*) of a vessel sailing *into* the wind, the force is broken into its component parts. Its forward drive in a direction parallel to the keel is represented by lines AB and CD. Its side drive (called leeway) is represented by lines AC and BD. The resultant force, CB, is a compromise between the forward and sideways drives.

The object is to have the boat sail ahead as much as possible and sideways as little as possible. This is accomplished by designing the hull to offer the *greatest* resistance to the direct action of the wind's force, as represented by the lines AC and BD; to resist side motion; and simultaneously to design the hull so that it offers the *least* resistance to the forward suction produced by the wind's force, as represented by the lines AB and CD; the direction in which we wish the boat to go, or to windward.

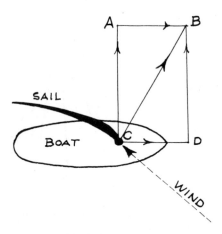

203 The parallelogram of forces

Resistance to side motion (lines AC and BD) is accomplished by fitting the boat with a keel or a centerboard so that a large surface or plane is presented to resist forces AC and BD. Inasmuch as this large surface is presented in water, a fluid of much greater density than air, it is obvious that the forces AC and BD cannot move the boat as quickly nor as much through the water as through the air.

In order to have the boat present the least resistance to being driven along the lines AB and CD (or ahead) its hull and upper parts are so designed as to offer the least forward resistance to the water and air through which it is to be driven.

Good hull design, sharp bows, easy runs and sterns, minimum *flat* planes and minimum areas of wetted surface are some of the elements combined to permit easy motion forward through the water.

Minimum above-the-water parts (such as deckhouses, spars, and rigging), and these of streamlined design, permit the easy motion forward through the air.

A happy combination of proper design will find the boat sailing approximately along lines AB and CD, the direction in which the boat is required to go. The forces AC and BD cannot be entirely overcome, and the boat will make a certain amount of leeway or side motion.

204 It is evident that the boat will not sail directly into the wind; or *against* its driving force. Consequently, tacking must be resorted to; that is, the boat is steered as closely into the wind as possible (about 45° from a true windward course), with the wind's force on one side and then the boat "put about" or veered about 90° into the wind, until the wind's force is exerted on the opposite side of the boat. Thus, in a series of steps or jogs, motion is made directly into the wind. Such a zig-zag course represents a greater distance sailed than a straight line to windward, of course. (*Figure 204*)

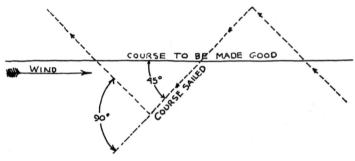

204 Tacking

205 The study of aerodynamics (which includes sailing) is a complicated and involved one and until recently was considered an exact science. However, worldwide investigations into aircraft design, plus international competition in the America's Cup matches, would appear to have given rise to further considerations, which amplify and modify the accepted theory. It is the "old" theory which we have presented in this discussion, partly because the "new" one is not even fully understood by the scientists, but mostly because to the layman it makes sense and is not impossible to apply to the art of sailing. It is the author's earnest suggestion that if the theory of sailing doesn't set well with you, forget it; very few sailors, even the good ones, understand it.

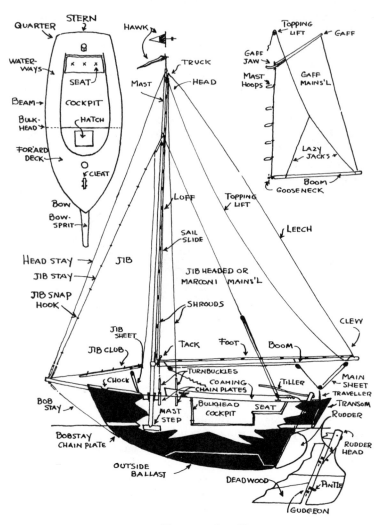

206A The parts of a sailboat

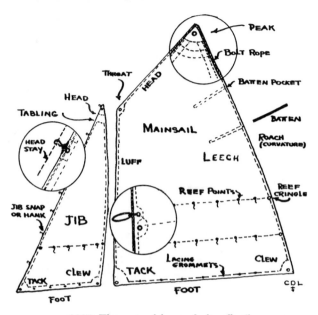

206B The parts of fore-and-aft gaff sails

It is entirely possible to sail, and sail well, without understanding any part of the theory of sailing. Anybody can sail—it becomes an art only when a person can sail well; that is, when sailing is done in the most efficient and safe manner, when there is nothing lubberly in the handling, and when the "boat and skipper become one." When that occurs the theory of sailing is utilized, though it may not be understood; the skipper has acquired a "feel" or a sixth sense, and the practical results are exactly the same as if the complicated phenomenon of sailing were thoroughly understood.

206 No book and no set of diagrams can teach anybody to sail. However there is precise terminology that you must know in order to give or take orders. There is but one school—the school of experience. Armed with the messages of the printed page, the student *must* sail to become a sailor. Text and diagrams, at best, can merely ease some of the knocks and bumps of the school of experience.

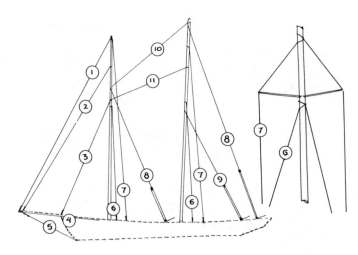

206C Principal standing rigging Each stay takes its name from the mast it supports, thus: No. 7 on a schooner—main upper shroud; No. 6 on a yawl—mizzen lower shroud.

1. Headstay
2. Jibstay
3. Forestay
4. Bowsprit shroud
5. Bobstay (sometimes ends in chain)
6. Lower shroud
7. Upper shroud
8. Backstay (partly running rigging)
9. Lowermast backstay
10. Springstay
11. Triatic stay

206D Principal running rigging of sailboats

HALYARDS

	1	2	3
Cat		Throat	Peak
Sloop Cutter	Jib Stays'l	Throat	Peak
Yawl	Jib	Main Throat or Mizzen Throat	Main Peak or Mizzen Peak
Ketch			
Schooner	Jib or Stays'l	Main Throat or Fore Throat	Main Peak or Fore Throat

SHEETS

	4	5	6	7	8	9
Cat			Main			
Sloop Cutter	Main	Jib or Stays'l	Main	Main		Down-haul
Yawl	Main or Mizzen	Jib	Main or Mizzen	Main or Mizzen		Down-haul
Ketch						
Schooner	Main or Fore	Jib or Stays'l	Main or Fore	Main or Fore	Vang	Down-haul

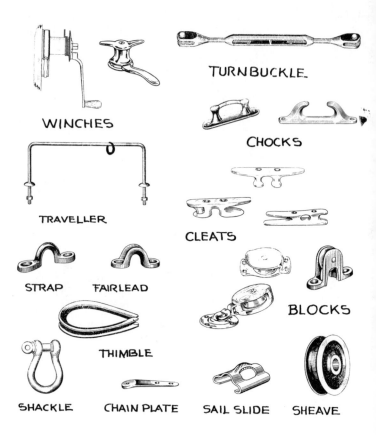

206E Sailboat gear

In giving the rudiments of sailing, the sloop will be used as an example in the following pages. Subsequent parts of this chapter will deal with only the special characteristics of other fore-and-aft types, as the basic handling is exactly the same as for the sloop.

The Sloop

207   Sails are sheeted to give maximum drive (adjusted in relation to the center line of the boat) in four general conditions: (*Figure* 207)

1. On the wind (or close-hauled).
2. Off the wind (or reaching).
3. Running before it (sailing free, sailing downwind scudding).
4. To give maximum drive.

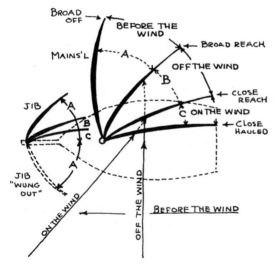

207 Sail position on different points of sailing

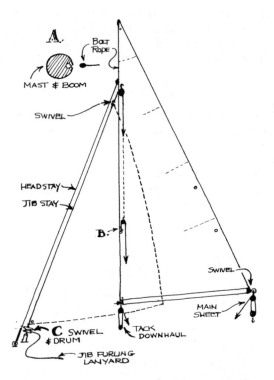

207A A modern jib-headed sloop rig The sails and lines will be of Dacron-type synthetics; the spars, hollow aluminum with slots into which the bolt roping of the luff and foot neatly fit and slide (A) The jib is hoisted on its own stay, which is usually a tackle (B) and fitted with swivels and a drum. (C) The jib is broken out with the sheets and furled on its own stay by furling lines which activate the drum. The mainsail may be stowed or shortened (reefed) simply by rolling it on the boom, just like a window shade.

ON THE WIND

208   A boat is sailing on the wind when the wind comes from a point forward of six points on the bow (*Figure 208*). The sails are sheeted in, almost parallel to the keel of the boat. The general rule for sailing on the wind is to keep the sails full, sheeted not too flat, but every sail drawing, and the boat definitely alive and moving. This trim is reached by having the boom somewhere between the rudder-head and the quarter, and the boat pointed, by steering, in a direction in which the luff of the mainsail is just about to flutter.

To actually permit it to flutter or collapse indicates that its power has been destroyed (by eddying). To permit the wind to strike the sail too broadly when close-hauled will cause excessive leeway, and thus loss of forward speed and forward distance.

A good helmsman steers by the luff. He keeps the boat headed so that there is neither flutter nor undue fullness on the after side of the sail. Helping to keep this course, in addition to constant watchfulness of the luff (using eyes and that sixth sense which all good sailors develop), is a wind pennant. This is a small flag of bunting or light metal mounted on the masthead and extending well beyond the eddies of the sail peak. It indicates the true direction of the wind, and the helmsman endeavors to maintain the angle that he finds by experimentation between it and the boat's course.

During the last decade or so, the demands of competition sailing have resulted in a number of sophisticated, electronic indicators to measure the force of the wind and its angle relative to the boat. None of these is as effective—at least in daytime—as the simple, inexpensive addition of *woollies* to one's headsails. Woollies are merely strips of wool yarn, each about 12″ to 18″ long, and of a color that contrasts with the sails.

About 6″ to 12″ aft of the luff, thread and woolly through the sail till it hangs evenly on either side, and knot it to keep it from pulling free. When sailing to windward, trim the foresail until it is just off the spreaders. Now watch the woollies: If they are streaming aft parallel to each other, your boat is at the optimum angle to the wind for efficient performance. If the woolly on the outer, or leeward, side of the sail is twirling or fluttering, you should

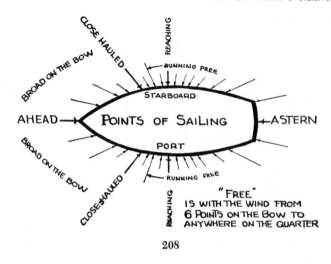

208

head up into the wind until it begins to stream again. If the windward woolly twirls, you're sailing too close to the wind and should
head off.

Keen sailors normally use three pairs of woollies per headsail,
spaced evenly up the luff. Some sailors also use woollies on the
mainsail, but because of the turbulence-creating effect of the mast,
these woollies must be farther aft of the sail's luff, at least 12″ and
perhaps more.

The wake also indicates the true course in relation to the wind.
Ranges of any fixed object ashore or afloat also serve as a bearing,
but when so used, allowance must be made for tide, current, and
leeway. Generally, a range is useful only for a short hitch. As current, tide, or leeway remove the boat from its first observed course
to the range, allowance must be made and another bearing taken,
even though to the same object.

209   While sailing close-hauled, the sail should be relatively
flat, topping lift slacked off, and luff stretched fully along the
mast, and foot stretched fully along the boom. The stronger the
wind, the flatter you should set your sail, and vice-versa. This point
of sailing is often the most dangerous of any, and in a small boat
the sheet is never belayed while close-hauled or "pointing." The

boat heels most on this point, and any sudden puff of wind, or any combination of normal wind and steep sea may find the boat heeled to dangerous angles.

This is parried by: (1) Immediately heading the boat up somewhat into the wind, so that the sails flutter, or luff. The boat will "stand up" at once, but will lose its headway if the course is held into the wind too long.

It is important to keep the boat moving, because a second gust can knock down a boat that is dead in the water. (2) Letting the sheet run out but keeping the basic course. The boat will at once stand up but not as straight as in maneuver (1), because the jib and part of the mainsail are still under wind pressure. However, not as much headway is lost; if the sail is promptly sheeted-in, there will be practically no time or speed lost. The sheet is never "let fly," merely slacked off a few feet. To "let fly" might permit the boom to strike the water and kill steerage-way entirely, creating a dangerous situation.

A boat is designed to sail in a heeled position. To have the seas lapping the rail is not a sign of danger nor an indication to shorten sail or luff up. Keelboats are in no danger until the seas actually begin spilling into the cockpit. However, nothing is actually gained by sailing with the rail buried for a long period, as the contours of the deck and deck fixtures decidedly slow the boat's speed. Centerboard boats generally become dangerous when the seas begin reaching inboard of the rail. They are then approaching a critical angle, beyond which it is unsafe to go. Most modern "board boats, such as the Sunfish, and light performance craft, such as the Laser, should be sailed nearly upright at all times. The factor of stability is relatively small in a centerboard or unballasted boat; it very quickly turns from a safe to a dangerous boat. Live ballast, of course, well to windward very much increases the safe heeling angle of the centerboarder.

The novice usually fails to recognize his sailing path, which is definitely not where he wants to go but rather to the point nearest his destination that is permitted by the best sailing course in terms of wind direction. To the experienced this invisible path in the sky is as definite as a path through a field—which also may not lead in a direct line to the destination. Learn to recognize this

"best way to get there" and stick with it, for there is *no other way.*
Pick a target to the left of the objective, as allowed by the course,
and steer for it; then pick a target to the right, and reach your
objective by tacking—eventually your objective will *automatically
have become the target* . . . and there you are. (*See Paragraph
213*)

210   In strong winds it may become apparent that the boat is
over-canvased, in which case reefing will have to be resorted to.
Figure 210 shows how to reef all common sails. If for some reason
reefing is not possible, it is still possible to continue sailing safely
and with reasonable speed by the following maneuver: Trim in the
jib flat amidships. Start (or slack off) the mainsheet until the sail is
about 50% luffing, or until the "much-drive" area has been destroyed. The boat will sail on providing it is not pinched too closely
into the wind. This is called lazy reefing. What it lacks in windward qualities it makes up for in speed, and it will see the same
point reached in about the same time as in usual reefing.

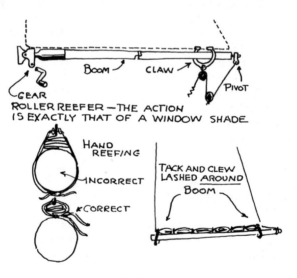

210 How to reef

211 A well-designed boat almost steers herself when close-hauled. Very little rudder effort is required to keep a straight course. However, this quality can be utterly destroyed by the improper sheeting of sails, as related to each other. Each boat has a different point at which the sails are set exactly right—this point is to be found by experimentation. Any unbalance in the proper set is reflected in undue rudder effort. If the rudder "pulls" hard (always providing that the boat is correctly hung and that the cause does not lie elsewhere, a matter to be discussed later), it usually can be eased by adjusting the set of the jib. This position is somewhat of a compromise between a position of the utmost drive and one of least rudder effort. Sharp rudder angles slow a boat enormously, and it is wise to sacrifice some jib drive to gain fair underwater lines.

212 If the wind is blowing on the starboard (right) side of the boat and the boom extends to the port (left), the boat is said to be sailing on the starboard tack.

If the wind is blowing on the port (left) side of the boat and the boom extends to the starboard (right), the boat is said to be sailing on the port tack.

TACKING

213 Tacking, or coming about, is the maneuver of putting a boat on the opposite tack from the one on which she has been sailing. On a crewed boat it is carried out as follows:

1. Sailing close-hauled on either tack, the boat may (if she is slow or reluctant to turn) be headed slightly off the wind to pick up speed, at the skipper's warning hail of *Ready about*.

2. When the skipper sees that the crew is prepared and the boat moving well, he calls out *Hard alee*, and puts the tiller over to leeward, or, if the boat has wheel steering, turns the wheel to windward.

3. As the boat swings up into the wind, the crew stands by to cast off the jib sheet as soon as (but not before) the foresail begins to luff. The boat's bow moves through the eye of the wind, and the crew trims in the opposite jib sheet as soon as the mainsail—which is self-sheeting—has begun to fill.

4. When the boat's heading is about 90° to the previous course, the skipper moves the tiller back to amidships, and the boat begins to pick up speed on the new tack.

Single-sailed catboats and sloops with self-trimming jib sheets will obviously require no sheet adjustment when tacking. The timing of sheet changes with large, overlapping Genoa jibs (*See Paragraph 232*) is tricky and requires considerable practice to achieve a smooth maneuver.

214   Failure of the boat to complete the tacking maneuver will find her without headway, possibly with sternway, and inclined to remain in a permanently luffing position. To get her sailing again it is necessary to:

1. (*a*) Trim the jib in as flat as possible.
   (*b*) Push the boom slightly away from the direction in which you wish the bow to swing. The boat will slowly swing on the tack desired. Appropriate rudder action must follow as soon as headway has been regained and the sails are drawing.
2. Go forward and *back the jib*—hold it away from the direction in which you wish the bow to swing—permitting the mainsail to luff the while.

A boat in the position just described is said to be in irons or in stays. Properly handled no boat should ever go into irons. Persistence in so doing may be cured by centerboard adjustments or by slacking off the jib sheets before going about. In strange waters boats go in irons because of unfamiliarity with local tides and currents, which sometimes upset the maneuver calculations of even the most careful helmsman. A small boat, willing to be branded as a lubber's ship, sometimes can work out of irons by using the rudder as a sculling oar, or by actually paddling the stern or bow around with an oar.

JIBING AND WEARING

215   Changing tacks when running before the wind is usually accomplished by *jibing*. With the mainsail fully extended on one side or the other, the steps for jibing are as follows:

1. The skipper calls *Stand by to jibe*. At his hail, the crew takes in the mainsheet until the boom is nearly amidships.
2. The skipper says *Jibe-ho*, and pushes the tiller to windward (or turns the wheel to leeward) just enough to move the boat's stern through the eye of the wind, which gets behind the mainsail and swings it across the boat.
3. The crew, standing by the mainsheet, feeds it out quickly and smoothly, braking the force of the wind in the sail, until the boom is fully extended on the opposite side, but not touching the shrouds. As noted in 217 below, the jib is usually blanketed by the main and can be ignored during the jibe.

In a modern sailboat, jibing is as safe a maneuver as tacking as long as the mainsheet is controlled during the actual jibe. Only an *uncontrolled jibe*, when the mainsail suddenly snaps from one side of the boat to the other, with no one trimming the sheet, can be dangerous—to the crew's heads, to the rigging, to the boom, and even to the boat.

Wearing is another method of tacking or coming about onto the opposite tack. In a light or moderate breeze, the boat is slowly rounded to a position with the wind aft. As the head is brought around and the wind begins to cross the stern, the sails are sheeted in smartly, being held amidships as the wind actually reaches and passes the center line of the boat. Now, as the head swings round to the new course, the sheets are slowly paid out and belayed when at the proper point of trim. The boat is kept sailing during the entire maneuver.

REACHING OR OFF THE WIND

216   Reaching is the fastest and sportiest point of sailing for most sailboats. The boat not only moves ahead faster but makes considerably less leeway than when sailing close-hauled. In consequence, a course can be sailed by bearings or by compass with more accuracy than when close-hauled.

No special sailing instructions are required to sail on a reach. Under certain conditions of sea, a boat on a reach will roll quite easily, and it is always good therefore to look to the topping lift and see that the boom is kept well out of the sea. Ordinarily, only about 60% of the centerboard area is required on a reach (the sheathing of the board alone contributes much to speed), but exposing its full area will often lessen the roll.

In entering other points of sailing from a reach, it is of the utmost importance that the skipper know his boat well before attempting to skip a step. While most boats can be brought from a port reach to a starboard reach without loss of motion or without going into stays, the tyro would do best to first close-haul the boat, then come about in the usual manner, and then slowly come from the new tack to the new reach.

BEFORE THE WIND

217 When running before the wind, or sailing downhill, as it is called, the mainsail should be at approximately right angles to the keel of the boat. While the boat will still continue to sail downhill if the sail is sheeted in, it will then begin to make leeway and not sail a straight downwind course. Very little leeway is made, however, by sheeting the sail aft just enough to clear the shrouds. Such leeway can be compensated for by setting the jib out on the opposite side from the mainsail by rigging a temporary boom (a boat hook or whisker pole). Speed will be increased as well.

If the jib is not boomed out it will often hang idle from its stay and have no driving value whatsoever. In reasonably flat water, a good crew can usually make the jib stand on the side opposite from the main, without a whisker pole.

When sailing before the wind, the topping lift should be set up to prevent the boom from dragging in the water and to give the sail more pocket or belly, a desirable feature on this point of sailing.

A danger always present when sailing before the wind is that of an accidental jibe. A sudden wind shift or a yaw of the boat may very easily bring the wind to bear on the forward side of the sail and whip it against its sheet on the opposite board.

If the jib is not "wung out" (boomed out, or sailing wing-and-wing) it becomes an ideal jibe warning. As long as it remains quietly asleep forward of the mainsail there is no danger of jibing. If, however, it suddenly fills on the opposite side from the mainsail, or lashes forward against the head or jibstay (called a scandalized jib), it is giving timely warning that the point of a jibe is being approached. In general, in sailing before the wind it is safest to keep the wind over the quarter that is opposite the side the mainsail is on. This may necessitate a slightly longer course, seldom more than a few yards per mile, however, and is called tacking downwind.

In light airs, the boom can be kept on the side where it belongs by heeling the boat (by live ballast) toward the boom. In heavy weather, a downwind course can be made under jib alone with more safety than under a reefed mainsail.

GIVING MAXIMUM DRIVE TO A SAIL

218   To get the greatest drive out of a sail it is essential that the area of "much drive" be in no way violated. The sail must be bent and hoisted so that this area is free from wrinkles. The luff should be fitted with ample track slides or mast hoops so that it does not present a scalloped effect.

When sheeting a sail, the important angle is that of the "much-drive" area to the keel rather than the angle of the boom. This angle must be correctly reached and maintained, even at the cost of a slight flopping of the leach.

On the wind and close-reaching, the mainsail drives best if it is reasonably flat, its halyard and outhaul pulled tight. Before the wind a belly or pocket effect is more efficient; generally this latter condition can be achieved by easing the outhaul and halyard.

The drive of small boats is very easily killed by the injudicious placing of passengers or crew. In general, sitting high on the rails, or hanging in the shrouds, or sprawling on the forward deck or cabin top, creates eddies which reduce the efficiency of the sail. Objects placed on the deck (like dinghies or bundled spare sails) have a similar effect. In racing boats, such as the Stars, this idea is carried out even to streamlining or eliminating most of the common small-deck fittings, guardrails, combings, etc.

The jib often kills the drive of the mainsail. As a rule the jib (or any foresail) is set at an angle of about 15° greater to the wind than the mainsail. There is, however, no hard-and-fast rule. Many modern boats get more drive from the jib than the main, and in some cases it is possible to trim only one of the two properly.

When a boat is on the wind, it is a decided advantage to so dispose the live ballast as to bring it as near to an even keel as possible. Eddies from the lifted windward topsides sometimes completely kill the drive along the foot of the sail.

CENTERBOARD AND KEELS

219   The keelboat has its underwater parts permanently fixed. Its skin friction cannot be changed. However, the boat that is equipped with a centerboard can greatly increase its sailing speed by the proper use of the centerboard. The correct positions for various points of sailing are shown in Figure 219. However, try different amounts of board until you find out what's best for your boat and the conditions.

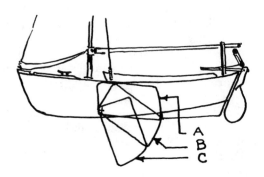

219 Correct centerboard positions for various points of sailing: A) Before the wind, B) Reaching, C) Close hauled.

If, *while reaching,* the boat rolls excessively, lower the board to position C. If, *while before the wind,* the boat rolls excessively, lower the board to position B.

TRIM

220   Proper trim is the position in which the boat will sail best after the distribution of the ballast, both live and otherwise, and after the correct setting of the sails.

Thwartship trim should find the fixed ballast low down and the boat standing with its mast plumb when viewed from bow or stern. Thwartship trim on small boats can be adjusted to suit sailing conditions by the disposal of the live weights to windward in breezes and winds, amidships in gentle breezes, and to leeward in calms or near calms.

Fixed ballast (inside ballast in the form of iron or lead pigs, bags of sand or stone) is never adjusted to meet sailing conditions requiring thwartship trim. Certain racing boats called sandbaggers, now obsolete, were an exception to this statement. Thwartship trim is seldom required in the well-designed and properly sailed boat except after a certain point of heeling has been reached, when the shifting to windward of passengers will extend the margin of the safe heeling angle.

221   Boats are considered in trim when the waterline is parallel to the water, always assuming that the hull then presents its best form for driving. However, in boats up to about 25′ waterline, the shifting of fore-and-aft ballast will have a marked effect upon sailing. Centerboard or shallow boats are more sensitive to this ballast adjustment than keelboats.

The ballast adjustment is usually made by shifting passengers or crew (and occasionally sandbags) fore or aft under the following conditions:

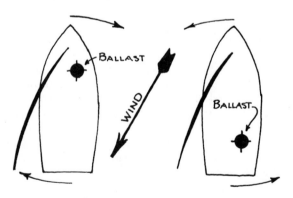

221 Effect of ballast shift on helm

1. Shifting the ballast forward will give the boat a tendency to head into the wind. It will relieve a lee helm.
2. Shifting the ballast aft will give the boat a tendency to fall away from the wind. It will relieve a weather helm. When running before the wind, the ballast moved aft will give the boat a beneficial drag by the stern and hold the rudder deeper in the water.

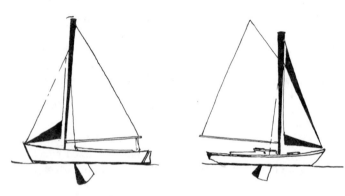

222 *Left,* to cure a mild lee helm: Reduce jib area, rake mast aft, drop centerboard (CE and CLR must be closer). *Right,* to cure a mild weather helm: Add to jib area, rake mast forward, partly hoist centerboard (CE and CLR must be separated)

LEE AND WEATHER HELM

222   A boat that, with rudder amidships, tends to head into the wind is said to carry a *weather helm.* Most boats are designed to carry a slight weather helm, so that if for any reason the tiller must be abandoned the boat will immediately cease sailing (by heading into the wind and luffing). A slight weather helm is desirable.

A boat that, without rudder effort, tends to swing her bow away from the wind is said to carry a *lee helm.* Boats are designed so as to avoid a lee helm because, if, for any reason, the helm must be abandoned, the boat will fall off away from *the wind,* wear, and possibly jibe. A Lee helm is undesirable and dangerous.

Lee or excessive weather helm can be cured by:

1. Adjusting fore-and-aft ballast (trimming).
2. Adjusting the set of the jib or other headsails.
3. Checking the balance of the sails to see that one end of the boat does not overpower the other. This balance is usually perfect under plain or working sails. It is often upset when carrying light-weather sails, or storm canvas, or when reefed. (For example, when tucking in a reef in the mainsail, its area is so reduced that the jib may upset the sail balance. If so, the jib must be reefed as well, or a storm jib of reduced area set.)
4. Checking the relationship of the center of effort of the sails to the center of lateral resistance of the hull.

223 This relationship (#4, *above*) is established according to well-known engineering rules. If an engineer or naval architect has designed the boat and the boat has been built according to design, this relationship is probably correct. However, changes in rig, in hull, in trim, in mast positions may have upset the balance, with resultant objectionable lee or weather helm, poor sailing, dangerous sailing, or failure to sail at all.

In calculating the factors entering into this relationship, both the sails and the hull profile are considered as flat planes; the sail plane subject to pressure by the wind, and the hull plane subject to resistance in making leeway through the water. Each is given a reference point, this point being the center of the pressure of the wind and the center of the resistance of the water pressure.

These centers are found by the methods shown in Figures 223 A, B, C, D, E and F.

If transferred to drawing paper, the relationship can readily be checked. The center of sail pressure is called the center of effort (CE) and is a common center of the effort of all working sails. The amount of bellying and the overlap of overlapping sails (such as a Genoa) are not considered in calculating the area of sails. The center of hull resistance is called the center of lateral resistance (CLR). The rudder is not considered in the calculations but the centerboard, fully dropped, is. Large rudders, such as those found on catboats, are sometimes partly considered, and the forward one third of the area is calculated as part of the lateral plane.

Upon being diagramed on paper, the center of effort should lead the center of lateral resistance. No fixed amount can be determined before hand as it varies with every design. The separation, or amount of lead, will, however, be somewhere around 6% of the waterline-length separation between the two points. The important point of such a check is to find out whether the center of effort actually does lead the center of lateral resistance. If a safe boat having a weather helm is required, the CE *must* lead the CLR.

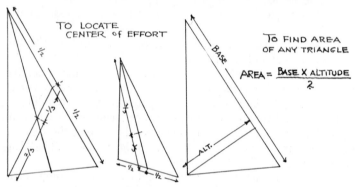

FIND CENTER OF ANY SIDE AND PROJECT LINE FROM IT TO OPPOSITE APEX. ONE THIRD THE LENGTH OF THIS LINE FROM THE SIDE DIVIDED IS THE C. of E.

223A Jib-headed sails

To locate the center of effort of a jib-headed sail: Find the center of any side and project a line from it to the opposite apex. One third the length of this line from the side divided is the CE.

To find the area of any triangle use formula:

$$\text{Area} = \frac{\text{base} \times \text{altitude}}{2}$$

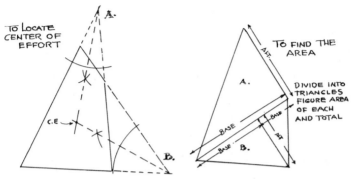

223B Gaff-headed sails

To locate center of effort: Extend the sides to form two triangles. Bisect each angle (A & B). The intersection of the extended bisecting lines is the CE.

To find the area: Divide into triangles and figure area of each (Figure 223A) and total.

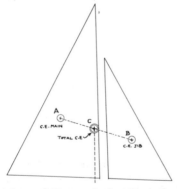

223C *Finding the total Center of effort* Draw the sails in their exact relationship and connect the two centers by the line A-B. Divide the product of multiplying the area of the jib by the scaled length of A-B by the sum of the areas of the jib and the mainsail. The result is the scaled distance from C to A.

$$\text{Rule: } AC = \frac{\text{area of jib} \times AB}{\text{area of jib} + \text{area of mainsail}}$$

223D *Finding C of E of two-masted vessels* In sail plans of more than two sails the following practice is used: The sail areas are treated in rotation for CE. The common center of any two is found; then this is taken as a single area and combined with the next, and so on.

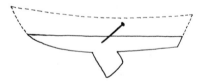

223E *Finding the center of lateral resistance* Cut out of cardboard, metal, or plywood the exact *underwater* shape of the hull drawn to scale. Balance at the outer edge with a pin or needle. The point from which the waterline hangs level is the CLR. The point is transferred to the master drawing. The CLR is anyplace along a vertical line drawn through the point.

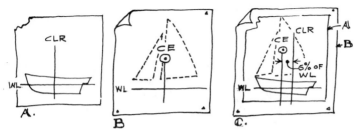

223F To determine the relationship of the CE and CLR. Draw, on tracing paper, a base line (waterline) and locate the CLR as per Figure 223E. In the same scale, draw the sail plan, on drawing paper, with the waterline and CE located as per Figure 223C. With waterlines matching, adjust so that CE *leads* CLR by not more than 6% of the *waterline* length. From this determine where the mast should be located in the hull.

This is a calculation that will hardly be necessary unless a check is being made for poor performance or, possibly, for the original design or alteration of a sail rig in its entirety.

224 A radical upset of the relationship must be corrected by redesigning the sail plan. But before assuming basic balance problems, sail the boat under a variety of weather conditions and sail combinations.

A slight upset of the relationship can be corrected by adjusting the present sail plan or by adjusting the rake of the masts, the position of the centerboard, etc.

HEAVY-WEATHER SAILING

225 Heavy-weather sailing on the wind is always made easier and more comfortable by quartering into the seas rather than by meeting them head on. To attempt to "buck" steep seas will only result in the boat's being stopped by each attacking sea and perhaps even being thrown backward, if headway has not been regained between attacks.

If the boat becomes too hard-pressed, assuming a dangerous angle of heel, sail must be shortened, or reefed. Careful and smart sailors reef before it is absolutely necessary. Not only does such a precaution give them a fairly large margin of safety, but it results in a better course and faster time. The boat carrying full sail in reefing weather must frequently luff or spill her wind. To avoid being stopped dead, the sails should be luffed by easing sheets, rather than turning up into the wind. It is important to keep the boat both on her feet and moving. However, the reefed boat will not need to luff, and she can maintain course and speed without loss of time.

It is time to reef an open boat when the seas begin to approach the lee rail, not after the water has actually come aboard.

It is time to reef a decked boat when the seas begin to regularly flood the deck, not after the cockpit has been flooded.

It is time to reef a cabin boat when any part of the deck or deck fixtures (trunks, cabins, etc.) are being regularly submerged.

226 Reefing is accomplished by reducing the areas of existing sails by mechanical means (*Figure 210*). Balance must always be maintained; the reefed sail plan must have its common center of effort at approximately the same place as the full sail plan.

Multisailed craft reduce areas by reefing and also by varying sail combinations. (*Figure 226*)

Small boats are best reefed by dropping all sails and tying in the reefs without way on. When reefed, the mainsail is hoisted first, acting somewhat like a weather vane and tending to swing the bow into the wind. The jib is then hoisted, the mainsail sheeted in, the jib sheeted in, and the boat put on its course.

A reef on a small boat is best shaken out (or untied) by reversing the above procedure.

When reefing underway, the boat must be sailing close-hauled in order to have the boom inboard. The helm should be manned constantly while reefing underway.

A hand reef is tied in by first lashing the tack and the clew, passing several turns of light line through the cringles and *around* the boom. The reef points are then tied in, starting forward and proceeding aft, the points passing between the boom and the foot boltrope, and being tied, all on the same side, with a square or reef knot. A loop (or half bow) will permit easy shaking out again.

A hand reef is shaken out by casting off the points first, then the clew lashing, then the tack lashing.

A slight modern variant on standard reefing is so-called *slab reefing.* In this system (most used on larger racing yachts), the mainsail is fitted with a vertical hook on the gooseneck and a cheek block toward the end of the boom, slightly abaft where the clew reef cringle will be when the sail is reefed. To shorten sail, the main is lowered until the gooseneck hook fits through the tack reef cringle. A line from the boom runs up through the clew reef cringle and back down to the boom cheek block, thence to a winch on the boom; by pulling on this line, the boom is literally

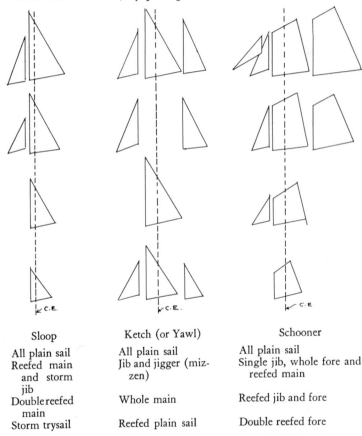

Sloop	Ketch (or Yawl)	Schooner
All plain sail	All plain sail	All plain sail
Reefed main and storm jib	Jib and jigger (mizzen)	Single jib, whole fore and reefed main
Double reefed main	Whole main	Reefed jib and fore
Storm trysail	Reefed plain sail	Double reefed fore

226 Preserving balance under shortened sail

winched up to the clew reef cringle. The halyard is then sweated up again, and the reef is complete; since the sail is reinforced, it is not necessary to have reef points between luff and leech, although some sails are fitted thus, for neatness.

Slab reefing, also known as *jiffy reefing*, is so fast when accomplished by a well-trained crew that *roller reefing* is now losing its previous popularity in many classes. It is still fitted, however, in many boats both large and small. A roller-reefing mainsail is rolled, like a window shade, around its own boom, which revolves around its long axis; the turning mechanism, worked by a crank, is normally located at the gooseneck. To reef, the boat is headed slightly off the wind and the sail allowed to luff a bit. While the skipper tends the helm, the crew eases the main halyard, taking up the slack with the roller crank until the desired sail reduction is made. Of course, battens must be removed before they are rolled into the reef. To avoid uneven rolling around the boom, it is often necessary to exert tension aft, by pulling the leech of the sail.

Although not, strictly speaking, a form of reefing, *roller-furling* jibs also allow for sail reduction in a hurry. In essence, a jib is rolled around its luff wire in much the same way a mainsail is rolled around its boom. Because of differences in cut and sheet location between the two sails, it is difficult to roller-reef a jib properly: the reduced sail will almost always exhibit a poor shape, which, if stressed by strong winds, may well result in permanently deforming the sail.

227   Running before a sea is always dangerous.

There is danger of rolling the boom into the sea, in which event it will act like a rudder, take charge of the boat, and result in a broach, accompanied by a jibe.

To prevent this danger:
1. Top the boom sharply by means of the topping lift.
2. Steer with a long oar instead of the rudder (which frequently "rolls" out of the water).
3. Lower the centerboard to prevent rolling.
4. Ballast the side opposite the one the boom is on.

There is danger of being "pooped." A boat sailing up the back of a wave submerges her stern and quarters, and the next sea (especially if it is breaking) is liable to come aboard and flood the cockpit by the stern. Tacking down wind so as to take the seas on the quarter, parting them, will help prevent *pooping;* so will ballast forward (but not too far forward lest the rudder be raised out of the water), or running under jib alone.

There is danger of broaching to. A hard sea striking the quarter opposite to the one on which the sail is set will drive the bow around and tend to push the boat beam to the seas. Broaching to often results in capsizing. If the jib is sheeted in flat it will help somewhat by making the bow hard to swing; as the boat flies against the rudder, the wind pressure on the jib helps to pay her off again and take the boat out of its yaw. A drag of some kind, trailed from astern, will help to prevent excessive yawing, the primary cause of broaching to.

228 If the sea makes up so that progress becomes impossible or too dangerous, boats may resort to *heaving to* or *laying to.*

Heaving to is a maneuver calculated to stop the boat from sailing and to maintain her approximate position without the use of an anchor. While hove to, the boat makes leeway and is also carried by tide or current. Sea room is needed to leeward, and heaving to is not recommended in confined sounds, bays, or estuaries.

To heave to, the boat is headed into the wind to the point where she begins making sternway. The tiller is then lashed down or to leeward, and the sheets are trimmed so that she does not sail.

The boat is then said to "go to sleep." What she is doing, in endless cycles, is this: She starts moving backwards. As the helm is lashed down, the bow will slowly fall off, whereupon the boat will slowly sail ahead and again round into the wind, and then repeat the process over and over.

The trick is to so adjust the helm and the sheets that both a minimum of sternway and a minimum of sailing ahead take place. This point can be found only by experimenting, but once the point is found, the boat will lie quietly and not sail. In practice, the sail will be fluttering, the sheets slightly slackened and the boom about over the quarter (about in the same position as in a close reach).

On small boats, even though *hove to* and "in the groove," the shifting of live ballast will upset the balance entirely. The helm and sheet adjustments are made from the hatch, the skipper remaining in the approximate position from which he made the adjustment while heaving to. Ketches and yawls will usually heave to very well under mizzen alone.

229   If the boat will stand no canvas at all, a safe and fairly comfortable lay can be made by laying to a sea anchor.

The effect of a sea anchor is to keep the bow of the boat heading into the seas rather than beam to. As in heaving to, leeway is made, and the tide and the current affect the boat's position as well (*Figure 229*).

A long warp is required so that the surge of the boat, as she pitches, does not snap too smartly and part the line or tear the canvas cone of the anchor. When rigged, the anchor should be invisible, from 5' to 12' beneath the surface. Chain should not be used for the warp of a sea anchor.

A jury sea anchor, having a similar effect, can be made by lashing together spare spars, timbers, hatch covers, etc., and launching the bundle over the bow; it should be rigged so that it presents the greatest resistance to the tugging of the boat. A swamped small boat, towed by a bridle from its stem to sternpost, can readily be used for a jury sea anchor.

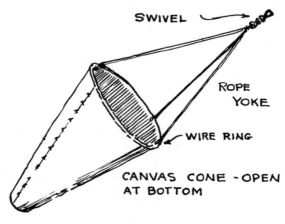

229 A sea anchor or drogue

230   The use of oil reduces seas and prevents their breaking, and oil bags are often called into service when either heaving to or laying to a drogue (sea anchor). Experimenting with oil is not a good idea, except in genuine need, as the release of oil over the side is prohibited by Federal law.

Large boats pump the oil overboard, using the bilge pump, or discharge it from watercloset or sink drains.

231   Thunderstorms seldom make permanent heavy weather. They rise and disappear quickly, and it is not necessary to heave to during one. Upon the approach of a thunderstorm, and during the calm that always precedes it, all sail should be taken in, stopped down, and extra lashings placed on the boom, and the boat anchored.

If at all possible use an anchor with plenty of warp. Thunderstorms seldom build up great seas, and the strain is from the wind alone. If no bottom is found, the approach of a storm should find the boat sailing away from the shore, which will be a lee one when the storm breaks. Prepare to scud before it if there is sea room, using a small jib to maintain steerageway.

If in really tight quarters, without either sea room or the possibility of anchoring to bottom, a sea anchor may be used. With a boat where it is possible to do so, removing the mast will greatly reduce the windage and slow up the boat's motion. Unless forced to, do not anchor on a lee shore. Lightning is an ever-present danger during thunderstorms, and it is wise to keep away from masts, halyards, and shrouds. Lightning will not usually harm you if your body is generally at or below the waterline. It is difficult to be sure about what lightning will do—its most reliable characteristic is unpredictability.

A thunderstorm expends most of its wind before the rain. If the rain comes first, then the wind, look out for dirty weather; the storm is more than merely a local thunderstorm. Beware of the split storm, one with two centers, or one at the turn of the tide, as there is liable to be a repetition almost at once. Sail had best not be made until the storm has definitely passed away—and then quickly —for thunderstorms often are followed by long periods of dead calm or confused light winds.

Fishermen use the verse below to diagnose the severity of and length of thunderstorms:

> *If the wind before the rain,*
>   *Soon you may make sail again.*
> *If the rain before the wind,*
>   *Shorten sail and halyards mind.*

LIGHT-WEATHER SAILING

232   The jib and mainsail of a sloop are referred to as the *plain sails* or *working sails*. In light airs they are of insufficient area to drive the boat efficiently. Working sails were designed to meet average weather conditions with safety and ease of handling. Today, however, the term is somewhat misleading, as most sailing craft are designed to carry mainsail and Genoa jib as the customary rig when going to windward. Genoas, or jennies, may be of several sizes and weights of sailcloth (*Figure 232A*). The larger ones, usually referred to as "Number Ones," often have a foot that reaches well aft of the mast to somewhere around mid-cockpit. Smaller Genoas may be either shorter on the foot, on the luff, or both. In boats of approximately 16′ and longer, trimming Genoa sheets is done with cockpit-mounted winches.

Next to the Genoa, the most popular light-weather sail, and usually the largest, is the spinnaker (*Figure 232B*). This is a triangular sail with two equal, convex sides and a smaller foot, set at or near the masthead, outside the highest forestay. The spinnaker is *set flying*—secured only at its three corners—one clew being secured to a line running through the outer end of a pole that is pivoted to the forward side of the mast, the other clew made fast to a sheet that normally leads to a turning block at the transom, thence forward to a cockpit winch.

Except in serious competition, the spinnaker is used when the wind is abaft the beam, and for beginners, it is best to set the sail with the wind on the quarter. The spinnaker sets on the opposite side of the boat from the main, boomed out into the wind by its pole. Most of the time, the spinnaker pole and the main boom will be opposite each other, each being at right angles to the wind. Although the two sides of a spinnaker are identical, the windward

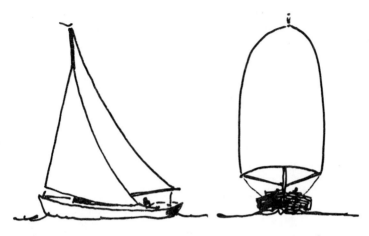

232A Genoa jib   Parachute spinnaker

side (when the sail is set) is called the luff, and the leeward is called the leech. The tack is at the foot of the luff, while the clew is at the corner of the leech and the foot. The two identical control lines are the guy, attached by a snap-hook to the tack, and the sheet, snapped to the clew.

Setting and recovering spinnakers can be critical moments for the crew. Although there are numerous gadgets to simplify both maneuvers, it is a good idea to first learn how to set and douse the sail without them. To prepare a spinnaker for hoisting, perhaps the easiest method is to stretch the sail out on a lawn, then fold it at the center, so one clew is on top of the other. Next roll it into a snakelike bundle from the center toward the leeches. Now the sail may be stuffed into a bag or box, with head and clews exposed; or, alternatively, it may be tied with heavy thread or very light twine at about 4' or 5' intervals.

Before hoisting sail, make sure the running rigging is in order: The sheet and guy are led forward, outside of all the rigging, lifeline stanchions, and pulpit. The guy is led through the fitting at the outer end of the pole, then sheet and guy are snapped to the clew and tack, respectively.

Next, the pole is attached to an eye (often running on a track) on the forward side of the mast, and is then raised with the pole topping lift until it is parallel to the water's surface, and (of course) on the side opposite the main boom. The pole should be about halfway between the shrouds and the forestay, to begin with; it is held from swinging by a foreguy, which runs from it to a block on the foredeck.

Under normal conditions, the spinnaker is hoisted either after the jib is dropped or behind (to leeward of) it, while it is still raised. If you adopt the latter course, be sure the spinnaker halyard is led down outside the jib, then under its foot, but above the lifeline. While two hands aft tend the sheet and guy, a crew member on the foredeck raises the sail until its head is slightly—6″ to 1′— from its halyard block.

The sail may well fill by itself, unless it has been stopped with thread as described above, in which case a slight pull by the sheet and guy tenders will snap the bottom threads, and air pressure will take care of the rest. With the sail up and open, trim the sheet and guy so that the spinnaker pole—which should remain horizontal— is at right angles to the wind.

There are several ways to cut a spinnaker, from very flat, for reaching and heavy weather, to extremely full, for running in light airs. The average sailor will require only one spinnaker, of a moderate cut designed to be carried with the wind well abaft the beam. Although it is possible to carry a spinnaker with the wind forward of the beam, in most cases it is both safer and more effective to use a Genoa under these conditions.

Recovering a spinnaker is not hard, if the maneuver hasn't been postponed too long. The simplest way is to release the guy, allowing it to run through the pole end fitting, then pull the sail into the cockpit as the halyard is eased. It is also possible to hoist the Genoa inside the spinnaker; the spinnaker will then be blanketed, and the chute can be pulled in under the foot of the jib.

To jibe a spinnaker, a maneuver that should be attempted only in moderate winds, head the boat nearly directly downwind. With the spinnaker pole at right angles to the centerline, or nearly, un-snap it from the mast and re-snap it to the spinnaker clew fitting. Then, as the cockpit crew jibe the mainsail, unsnap the other

end of the pole from the tack fitting, and secure it to the mast
eye. If done smoothly without losing control of the main, the
spinnaker will remain filled throughout the operation.

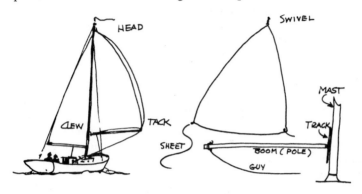

232B The spinnaker

233 Used mostly by dedicated racers, *reachers* and *drifters*
are light-air headsails that are cut high in the clew, so that they
sheet well aft, either through a block at the end of the main boom
or via a turning block on the transom. Reachers, as the name sug-
gests, are employed on headings from a close reach to a broad
reach. Drifters, made from the lightest Dacron or nylon, are sometimes cut with only half as many luff snaps as normal, or even none
at all. They are useful in winds of five knots or less, and will suffer
permanent damage if hoisted in breezes much above that figure.

234 "Staysail" is an all-purpose term that covers a number
of auxiliary sails. On a cutter, the staysail is a working sail, often
on a self-tacking boom, rigged aft of the jib and set to a stay
shorter than the jibstay. On racing sloops, staysails tend to be tall,
thin splinters of cloth used to amplify the effect of genoa or spinnaker off the wind. Mizzen staysails on ketches and yawls are
valuable reaching sails, often nearly as large as the main. They are
hoisted to the mizzen masthead, sheeted to a block at the outer
end of the mizzen boom, and tacked down on deck near the
weather side of the mainmast. Often, a mizzen staysail will only
function properly after the mizzen itself has been furled. A fisher-

man's staysail, on the other hand, is a reaching sail used aboard schooners, where it is set between the fore- and mainmast heads; it may occupy nearly the entire quadrilateral area between the masts and exerts tremendous drive.

235 Twin Genoas are often carried by cruising sailboats making extended downwind passages. Usually set on twin head-stays, about 6″ apart, with separate halyards, the sails are boomed out with whisker poles. If raised, the mainsail is usually sheeted flat amidships to help keep the boat on course.

HANDLING A SAILBOAT IN A TIDEWAY

236 Waters affected by tidal or other current are moving *en masse*. Sailing in such waters is no different from sailing in any other waters. Nothing is changed except the relative position of the boat to the land.

However, if a land objective is sought, certain problems arise which the sailor must solve in order to make the best course to such an objective.

In sailing across, that is, with the current on the beam, the course must be laid well above the objective. If the wind and tide are on the same beam, leeway must also be allowed for in setting the course, which is then set an even greater amount above the objec-tive. If wind and tide are on opposite beams, a nearly straight course can often be laid, as the drift and leeway tend to blank each other out. Drift is usually somewhat greater than leeway. If the wind is astern, drift only must be allowed for.

In sailing *into* a current the practice of lee-bowing will make for a faster passage. Set the course so as to take the tidal current on the lee bow, slack off the sheets slightly, and the tide will con-stantly be advancing the boat to windward—the desired direction. A straight course can be made to the objective. Oftentimes, re-membering that drift is generally more than leeway over a given distance, it will be necessary to set the course to *leeward* of the objective.

When sailing in a tideway with a centerboard boat, against the current, only enough board is exposed to prevent leeway. More will merely increase the wetted surface or skin friction and make the boat harder to push against water already affecting the boat adversely.

It is a fallacy to assume that the direction of the current always reverses itself changing from flood to ebb, or vice versa. This is not so. Knowledge of local conditions is required to predict the tides intelligently. Lacking this, the government's annual publications entitled *Tide Tables* and *Tidal Current Tables* should be consulted.

The current runs strongest in the middle of areas of water; weakest alongshore. In estuaries and sounds, the tide will sometimes flow one way in mid-channel, and the opposite way at the edges; it flows much stronger in deep channels than over shallows. Back eddies that occur around points and headlands and underwater obstructions can be used in making progress against the tide. (*See Chapter XI*). In a curving watercourse, such as a river, the strongest current is usually on the outside of the bends.

When obliged to sail against a strong tide and light wind, put over to the lee shore, close under, and beat against it. Sail over shallow areas in preference to deep ones. If ground is still lost, there is no recourse but to anchor the boat.

DOCKING AND MOORING A SAILBOAT

237 When a sailboat is in irons she will sail no more. In making a landing or in picking up a mooring, the object *is* to sail the boat exactly to the spot and then sail no more. This is done by sailing the boat to a position where it is estimated that her own momentum will carry her forward, putting her in irons, and steering her to the desired dock, mooring, or small boat.

It can be successfully done only after the sailor has become thoroughly familiar with his boat and has learned her habits and her approximate distance of "shooting" under various wind velocities.

Whenever possible, and it usually is, the objective should be approached from leeward. Thus, if the boat is sailing toward a mooring from windward, the course is held until it is *past* the mooring and well to one side of it. The boat is then put off the wind, swung quickly on the wind, and when it is at a point well to leeward of the mooring it is sharply put in irons (luffed), and the

headway is depended upon to carry it to the mooring and to reach
it without appreciable headway, leeway, or sternway. The jib is
immediately lowered and the mainsheet let run. The boat will lie
quietly, like a weather vane, and not sail thereafter. (*Figure 237A*)

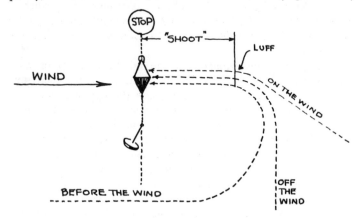

237A Approaching a mooring under sail

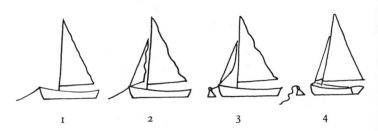

237B Steps in getting away from a mooring

1. Raise mainsail and ready all gear, lower centerboard, set *backstays*
   (if so equipped) for desired tack. Bend jib but do not raise. Do
   not belay mainsheet; let run.
2. Raise jib. Do not belay jib sheet. Draw boat to mooring or prepare
   to cast off mooring warp.
3. Hold jib aweather on tack desired to sail on. As head pays off, cast
   off mooring.
4. Sheet in main; sheet in jib. Trim both.

Casting off from a mooring and picking a mooring up are shown, step by step, in Figures 237B and 237C, with additional advice in Figure 237D.

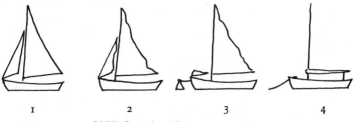

1   2   3   4

237C Steps in picking up a mooring

1. Sail at mooring from leeward.
2. Luff and shoot into the eye of the wind, at mooring.
3. Let all sheets run. Pick up mooring and drop jib or vice versa.
4. Drift back on mooring warp, douse main and snug down.

237D Long painter for the boat left at the mooring to give room for maneuvering

238 When a sailboat is anchored, the anchor is hove up short, then the sail set. As she is put on the wind, the cable is smartly handed in and the anchor lifted as the boat sails over it. If the anchor needs to be broken out, sail hard against it on one tack, drift to leeward, then get off on the other tack. The second jerk should break out the anchor. An anchor will break out easier with a short cable than with a long one.

239 When a sailboat wants to anchor, she is handled exactly as in picking up a mooring. As soon as she has stopped sailing and commenced making sternway, the anchor is put over and the cable payed out slowly as the leeward drift takes it. The mainsail is left up until the cable is taut; it will set the anchor better than the drift of the uncanvased boat alone.

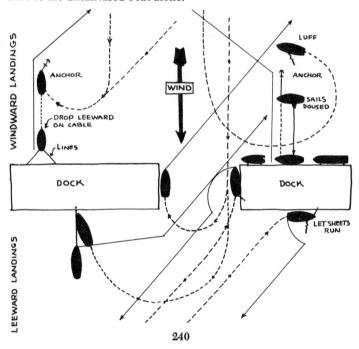

240

Dotted line—docking
Solid line—leaving the dock and returning to the original direction

If it is necessary to set an anchor especially deep or well, drop it over the stern, sail it in hard; then, as the boat rounds to, lead it forward.

240 In making a dock, approach it from leeward whenever possible. (*Figure 240*)

Immediately the dock is made, let all sheets run, get a line from the bow to the dock, raise the centerboard, and lower the jib. She will lie there quietly.

In the event that too much way is on as the dock is approached, fenders should be kept handy. A boat hook can be used as a fender or to grab the dock in case the "shoot" has been too short.

In holding off with a boat hook, hold it on the side of the body, like a long-handled shovel—not with the inboard end pointing at your midriff. In holding a boat off with the feet, sit on the deck, bracing against the mast or a trunk, and fend with both feet.

Windward approaches to a dock are dangerous and should be attempted only if absolutely necessary. It requires the nicest timing and expert seamanship and helmsmanship. (*Figure 240*)

The tide and current must often be reckoned with in approaching a dock. Be certain that their effects upon the boat are completely forecast and, if favorable, fully used to help in the maneuver of docking.

Both tide and wind can be of much use in getting a boat properly headed for leaving a dock. Stern lines from the boat to a turn around a dock bollard and thence back to the boat are very useful. One end of the line is cast off on deck and later hauled aboard.

In getting away from the windward side of a dock, sea room is gained by having someone ashore shove the boat to windward, using the main boom. As soon as it is clear, sheet the sail home and get on the wind.

In getting away from the leeward side of a dock the boat can be backed out in the following ways:

1. By "fanning the jib." Hold the jib out. The wind will drive the boat backwards and will drive the stern in the opposite direction. As this occurs, swing the jib to the other side. The course will be a series of "sashays" astern and can be kept up indefinitely, provided the stern is not permitted to swing too much.

2. By sailing the boat backwards. Jib and mainsail are trimmed
   absolutely flat amidships and the centerboard is raised entirely. The tiller is held (or lashed, if single-handed) about
   2" to port or starboard. The boat is shoved off from the dock
   exactly to leeward; it will sail backwards until the helm is put
   over and the sheets started. It is important that trim be maintained during the maneuver, especially in the small boat.

RULES OF THE ROAD FOR SAILBOATS

241   Like all American ships and boats, sailing craft are
governed, at any given moment, by one of four sets of Rules of
the Road: On the Mississippi River system, they are called Western
Rivers Rules; Great Lakes Rules cover those bodies of water;
coastal waters and such popular boating areas as the major bays
and sounds are in the Inland Rules' jurisdiction; offshore, although
not just in international waters, the International Rules hold sway.
The dividing line between Inland and International Rules runs
generally along the shore, jumping in straight lines from headland
to headland. The dividing line is marked on charts, but not, alas,
on the water.

Although the four Rules are much the same, there are significant
differences in detail. Because most small-boat sailors operate on
inland waters, those are the Rules reproduced here. Where there
are exceptions, they are noted.

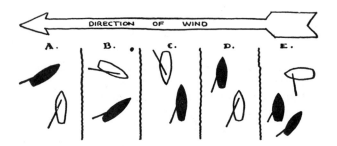

241 Rules of the road illustrated In each situation the white boat
keeps clear

242

(1) When two boats under sail are approaching one another so as to involve risk of collision, one of them shall keep out of the way of the other as follows:

    (*a*) A boat that is running free shall keep out of the way of a boat that is close-hauled.

    (*b*) A boat which is close-hauled on the port tack shall keep out of the way of a boat that is close-hauled on the starboard tack.

    (c) When both are running free, with the wind on different sides, the boat that has the wind on the port side shall keep out of the way of the other.

    (*d*) When both are running free, with the wind on the same side, the boat that is to windward shall keep out of the way of the boat that is to leeward.

    (*e*) A boat that has the wind aft shall keep out of the way of other boats.

It is important to note the sequence of privileged-burdened: *first*, running free gives way to close-hauled; if this is not applicable, *then* port tack gives way to starboard tack; if this does not apply, *then* windward gives way to leeward. Under International Rules, however, the first and overriding situation between sailing craft is port versus starboard, then (if both are on the same tack) leeward versus windward. Under the new International Rules, no distinction is made between running free and close-hauled.

(2) When a boat under power and a boat under sail are proceeding in such directions as to involve risk of collision, the boat under power shall keep out of the way of the boat under sail.

    (*a*) A sailboat under power *and* sail is, for legal purposes, a *boat under power*.

    (*b*) No boat, sail or power, may force a large vessel from a narrow channel within which she must remain or run aground.

    (*c*) Power and sail craft shall keep out of the way of commercial fishing craft while they are fishing.

    (*d*) In International Rule jurisdictions, power and sail craft shall also keep out of the way of one that is not under command and/or any vessel restricted in its ability to maneuver.

(3) Where, by any of these rules, one of the two boats is to keep out of the way, the other shall keep her course and speed.

(4) Every boat that is directed by these rules to keep out of the way of another boat shall, if the circumstances of the case permit, avoid passing ahead of the other.

(5) Every boat, whether under power, oars, or sail, when overtaking any other shall keep out of the way of the overtaken boat.

243   Closely related to the sloop are the other types of single-masted boats. Their handling is essentially the same as for the sloop, since all are fore-and-aft rigs. Two-masted ketches, yawls and schooners also derive from the original single-mast concept.

243 *Left,* Marconi or Bermuda rig, peak or jib-headed mainsail

Right,   gaff   rig,   gaff-headed mainsail

THE CATBOAT

244   The cat is a single-masted boat with but one large mainsail, the mast set far forward and the sail usually gaff-headed. Generally the mast is very heavy, the deck at the mast being too narrow to give adequate "spread" for usual shrouds. A single headstay (or jackstay) is often provided.

While the rig is simple and easily handled by a small crew, the single sail is of tremendous proportions, and the long boom required is sometimes a danger when running in a beam sea or before the wind with a roll. The topping lift must be used more often than with the sloop or other types.

Much more frequently seen in recent years are the single-sailed craft technically described as being "cat-rigged," but perhaps more meaningfully referred to as being "uni-rigged." The most numerous of these are the boardboats—oversize surfboards with, perhaps, a small footwell and a daggerboard. Most boardboats are lateen-rigged, an arrangement in which the gaff (here called the *yard*) extends down forward of the mast and meets a forward extension of the boom.

There are as well an increasing number of light racing boats with high masts, short booms, and a single Bermuda sail. Inexpensive to own, quick to rig and unrig on the beach, these craft offer planing performance in most breezes over 10 knots or so.

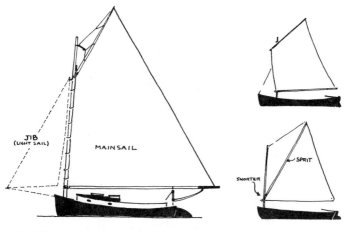

244 The cat

Above right, standing lug
rig *Below right,* sprit rig

THE CUTTER

245   The cutter is essentially a sloop rig having her sails so arranged that many combinations of areas may be obtained. Originally the rig carried a mainsail, two or three jibs, a topsail, and a square sail (or course) as well. It was a work-boat rig, much used on fishing or pilot boats, and was pretty well able to meet any ordinary sea conditions, especially when fitted with a reefing bowsprit (as was usual in the past).

A cutter with plain sail set carries a proportionately larger area of canvas than does a sloop with plain sail and is therefore faster than the sloop and will generally be slightly more weatherly. One advantage this rig has over the sloop is that under staysail it is easier to heave to.

There is actually little difference between the modern cutter and the sloop. The cutter generally carries two or more headsails in the

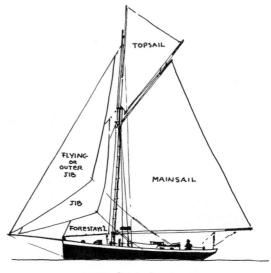

245A Original cutter rig

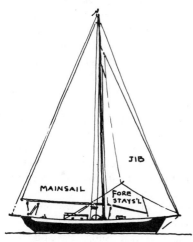

245B A modern cutter rig

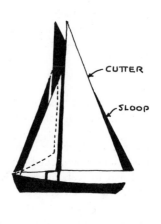

Right, location of rigs in relation to hull in the sloop and cutter

working rig and her mast is farther aft than that of a sloop. This location is about two fifths of the waterline length aft. Her mast usually rakes aft more than a sloop's. (*Figure 245B*)

Mainsail, staysail, and jib are the working sails; jib topsail and topsail are used in light airs. Under heavy weather conditions, sail may handily be reduced to reefed main and full jib or staysail, or reefed main and reefed staysail, or reefed staysail alone.

The type presents no new problems in handling save in the trimming of the headsails. The jib is not self-trimming and must be sheeted after each new tack. The staysail is set at a greater angle to the wind than the mainsail, and the jib at a greater angle than the staysail.

THE YAWL AND KETCH

246 The yawl and ketch (and schooner) make use of the divided rig, which has the advantage of spreading a large area of canvas with no single sail too big to handle comfortably. Briefly, that is the why and wherefore of all divided rigs in small craft. Some divided rigs have the additional advantage of quick adjustment of sail area to replace reefing. The yawl in particular lends itself well to sailing under shortened canvas either under just the mainsail or just the jib and jigger (mizzen).

All divided rigs on small boats have the disadvantage of requiring considerably more sparring, staying, and rigging than single-masted rigs. While they can carry more canvas than the undivided rig and work under shortened sail for some time after the single-sticker has had to reef, much of the additional sail drive merely goes to overcome the adverse effect of the additional rigging.

The divided rig has some marked advantages at sea and for cruising purposes, in that repairs can be made aloft, a matter sometimes impossible on tall, single masts. It is a "snug" rig, and, because it is relatively easily handled, greatly increases the limits of the "one-man boat." A smaller crew can handle a large yawl or ketch than they can a sloop. However, any sail rig is a compromise or a personal preference, and the owner has his own good reasons for selecting the rig he has.

The yawl or ketch is sailed exactly like all fore-and-afters; the rig involves no new principles.

The yawl is essentially a racing rig; in the last few years the racing handicap rule has ceased to favor yawls, and virtually none have been built. In principle, most yawls are sloops with a small balancing sail aft. The majority of yawls will balance fairly well with or without the mizzen, which is seldom effective when beating to windward in any case. Under extreme conditions, a yawl may sail a reach under jib and mizzen; it should also balance well under mainsail alone. Off the wind, the mizzen is usually replaced by a mizzen staysail—a light, Dacron sail hauled to the masthead, sheeted to the end of the mizzen boom and tacked to an eye on the weather-side deck about level with the mainmast. Other light-air sails include spinnakers, drifter, and reacher.

While the yawl is really a sloop with a small extra sail aft, the ketch is a true, two-masted sailing craft in which all of the sails are working elements of the rig. Going to windward, the mizzen seldom or never adds any useful drive, being in the dirty air of the mainsail; it is thus frequently dropped on this point of sailing. In addition, many ketches drop the mizzen as a sort of first reef, while many others reduce sail proportionately in fore triangle, main, and mizzen. Reaching in heavy weather, jib and mizzen usually form an effective and controllable combination.

The ketch carries the same light-air sails as the yawl, although a ketch's mizzen staysail is of course much larger, often nearly as large as the main. Some Bermuda ketches also carry a fisherman (or mule) which is set on the main backstay and sheeted to the mizzen masthead. This sail can offer a good deal of drive on close

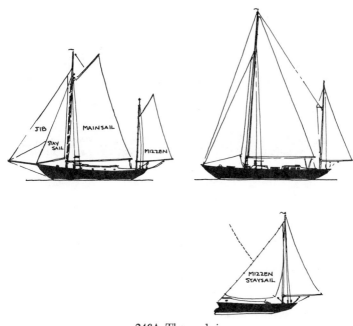

246A The yawl rig

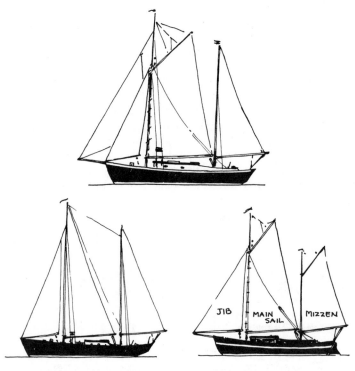

246B The ketch rig

reaches, when a mizzen staysail will not fill. When the wind is abaft the beam, the mizzen staysail takes over.

247 A ketch is visually distinguished from a yawl (and vice versa) in the following ways:

1. The mizzenmast of a yawl is aft of the rudderhead; the mizzenmast of a ketch is forward of the rudderhead.
2. The mizzen sail of a yawl is one fourth the area of the mainsail; the mizzen sail of a ketch is between one third and one half the area of the mainsail. The combined area of foretriangle and mizzen is about equal to the area of the main.

248 Going to windward, peak-headed rigs are more efficient in the yawl or ketch rig than gaff-headed rigs. This is due to the fact that there is a proportionately greater "much-drive" area (luff), and because there is no part of the sail which sags excessively to leeward as does the head of a gaff sail. This sagging can be overcome fairly well, however, by use of a vang on the mainsail gaff which is led to a block on the mizzen and then to a cleat on or near the deck.

THE SCHOONER

249 The schooner rig, while not having originated in America as is so often stated, reached its highest development here and remains a typically American rig. (*Figure 249A*)

The combinations of schooner sails are almost without end. The rig is basically three sails; a headsail, foresail, and mainsail. It can be handled by a small crew, is fast and weatherly, and permits combinations of sail shortening and reefing to meet any sea conditions.

No new principles of sailing are involved in its handling. When running before the wind, the large mainsail is quite apt to blanket the sail forward of it, and it is usual to set the main and foresail wing-and-wing and tack downwind. When on or off the wind, the foresail must be set at a greater angle to the wind than the main-

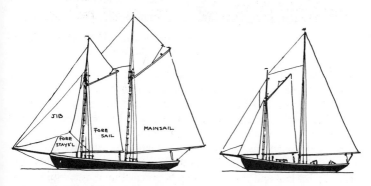

249A *Left,* fisherman schooner *Right,* schooner yacht

249B *Left,* Staysail schooner *Right,* Knockabout schooner

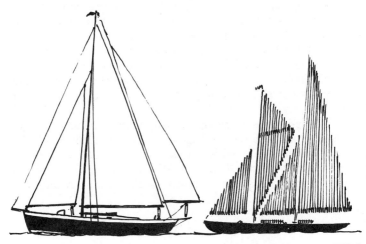

249C Rig oddments *Left,* the mizzen staysail yawl *Right,* the "Wish-bone" or Vamarie-rig schooner

sail. A loose-footed foresail or an overlapping foresail (boomless, of course) is a very effective and powerful schooner sail.

Under heavy weather conditions the schooner reduces to plain sail, then reefs, as required. She will heave to well under foresail or reefed foresail alone; or under storm trysail; or quite often under bare poles, particularly if the mainmast is taller and more heavily rigged than the foremast. Light sails include fisherman, staysail, or balloon staysail hung between the masts. Spinnakers and light headsails, while carried, are not as efficient as on other rigs because of the relatively short foremast.

A bald-headed schooner is one carrying gaff-headed sails on both fore and mainmasts.

A knockabout schooner is one with the rig entirely inboard; i.e., no bowsprit. (*Figure 249B*)

The staysail schooner is one on which the common foresail is absent, and in its place is a triangular sail hanked to a stay from the base of the foremast to the head of the mainmast. In the space above it, a huge staysail (or several smaller ones) is spread.

250 By far the greatest number of sailboats are engaged in the ancient sport of racing. Usually, fleets of one-design craft are organized, often sponsored by a yacht club, and strict rules are imposed and enforced so that the race, in fact, is between sailing brains and not sailing boats. This is as it should be, of course.

America has literally hundreds of racing classes, some numbering 4,000 fleet units. More are added each year as new gimmicks and designs are developed. The trend at present is toward planing hulls—sailing craft which attain such high speeds that they rise, or plane, and skim not through but over the water. Some of the lasting contributions to sailing have come from the racing fleets and the sport is definitely the richer for their experiments and innovations.

Rule-beating designs in the racing classes have resulted in the discovery of some sound new sailing principles; i.e., the trend toward increased area in the foretriangle (jibs) and consequent lessening of the mainsail area, a useful trend for cruising yachts. Jibs almost all overlap now and the Genoa has become a powerful working sail. Even hull form has been affected as designers try for advantageous handicap ratings by juggling normal relations among waterline length, overall length, deck length and overhangs. This fluctuation has been most evident in small ocean racers of the Quarter Ton and Half Ton classes.

An excellent combination, especially for cruising, is the keel-centerboard craft, wherein the hull carries a slotted fixed outside keel of lead or iron, ample for off-the-wind sailing and a boon to the shallow water sailor, plus a centerboard for the heavy windward, on-the-wind work. This almost obviates the straight centerboarder, which depends so much upon beam for stability with consequent loss of windward seakindliness because of pounding.

Racing, too, has been responsible for many of the newer materials—nylon, Dacron, and other synthetics that make canvas obso-

A PAGE OF CHARACTER WIND BOATS

JUNK

BRIG

24 FOOT GLOUCESTERMAN

A "JACHT"

A "COWHORN"

THE "SPRAY"

A.   B.

250B Vessel A has almost no fore-and-aft bearing and requires beam to stand up, with consequent loss of speed. Vessel B has long overhangs which, when heeled under press of wind, immerse and provide considerable bearing. Beam would then be at a minimum making for a stable vessel in hard going but with very little immersed hull in light airs. She would be a fast boat.

lete today; plastics which are rapidly replacing metal for fittings in rigging and on deck; and reefing and winching gear that makes boating safer and easier.

MULTIHULLS

251 The search for speed under sail has resulted in the borrowing and modernization of an ancient Maori art, the application of the outrigger canoe principle to modern vessels and materials. Thus we now have both catamarans and trimarans, even up to cruising, seagoing sizes. Both attain fantastic speeds, with simple working sails (cats have been clocked at 28 knots!) and do so standing up, for multihull vessels heel only less than one third as much as most single-hulled boats.

They provide the full thrill of sailing and seldom carry any light-air sails—save the spinnaker—because they are sailed on all tacks with sails seldom started more than for a close reach. The angle of heel, especially in the catamaran, is usually only 5° to 10°, contributing to both comfort and safety. The outfit, in general, must be kept very light in weight and thus these craft usually become Rube-Goldberg-type combinations of fiberglass flotation, extruded aluminum shapes, aircraft rigging, hollow tubular spars and ultra-light sail cloth; they horrify traditional skippers as much as they please the modern sailors. Yet they sail—and well—and make a great many people happy.

In normal cruising sizes, there are considerable differences between mono- and multihulls, and between cats and tris. Up to about 35' overall, catamarans offer more interior space than monohulls, counting both of the hulls and the bridge- or wingdeck. Often, however, this extra cubic footage is an illusion, since if it is used, the weight of the load cripples the cat's performance. Cats from about 35′ and up will have standing headroom in the hulls, but not until a cat is about 45′–50′ long does she have standing headroom in the bridge-deck accommodation.

Trimarans, at least those with any pretense to performance, have the smallest accommodation of all three types of boat in sizes under about 40′ overall. The reason is simple: At these sizes, only the tri's main hull is available for cabin use, although the cabin can be extended out over the wings to provide berths. The floats are just that—they provide buoyancy and stability, and must remain empty or very lightly stowed, otherwise the effect on performance will be dramatic. Above about 40′–45′, the floats can contain sleeping cabins, at which point the tri's possibilities begin to be realized.

However, the multihull is a recognized part of the yachting scene and is available from many manufacturers. Especially popular are the small ones, those readily trailerable and collapsible, and so easily beached.

There are no special problems to the handling or sailing, save that of high speed, which makes even small mistakes doubly hazardous. At these high speeds, losses from current, leeway, and hull friction are negligible and need not be considered in making good short courses. Keep the multihull's sails inboard (about over the quarter) on all points of sailing, especially when before the wind, to avoid running one of the pontoons under. Sail as you would sail a sloop but do not make the mistake of believing that capsizing is impossible. You *can* capsize—and when you do, the cat goes all

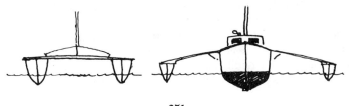

251

Hull of a small   Hull of a cruising
   "cat"   "tri"

the way over, bottoms up, with the mast hanging straight down. It requires a boat with a high tackle to right it. On small cats, it is usual to carry a balloon or tank on the masthead to prevent complete capsizing.

Both cats and tris frequently have trouble tacking, being prone to getting into irons. They must be put about at reasonably high speeds. Jibing, on the other hand, is simplicity itself, as neither cats nor tris stagger or lurch even under an abrupt jibe.

It would seem that multihulled boats are taking their place in the boating scene as racing and thrill craft . . . just pure fun. And what's wrong with that?

Glossary of Sailboat Terms

Abaft   Toward the stern

Abeam   On the side of the vessel, amidships, or at right angles

Aboard   Within, on board the vessel

About   To go on the opposite tack

Abreast   Alongside of, side by side

Adrift   Broken from moorings or dock

Afloat   Resting on the surface of the water

Aft   Near or toward the stern

Aground   Touching the bottom

Ahead   In the direction of the vessel's bow; *Wind ahead* is from the direction toward which the vessel's head points

Alee   When the helm is in the opposite direction from that in which the wind blows

All Hands   The entire crew

All in the wind   When all the sails are shaking

Aloft   Above the deck

Amidships   In the center of the vessel, either with reference to her length or to her breadth

Apeak   When the vessel is hove taut so as to bring the vessel over her anchor

Arm, Yardarm   The extremity of a yard

Astern   In the direction of the stern, the opposite of ahead

Athwart   Across

Athwartships   Across the length of a vessel, the opposite to fore and aft

Avast   To stop. "Avast heaving!"

Awning   A covering of canvas over a vessel's deck, or over a boat, to keep off sun and rain

Backstays   Rigging running from the masthead to the vessel's side, slanting a little aft

Ballast   Heavy material, as iron, lead, or stone, placed in the bottom of the hold to keep a vessel steady

Bare poles   The condition of a vessel when she has no sail set

Bark, or Barque   A three-masted vessel having her fore and main-masts rigged like a ship's, and her mizzenmast like the mainmast of a schooner, with a spanker and gaff topsail

Battens   Lightweight strips inserted in pockets along the leech of a sail to make it set flat

Beams   *On the weather* or *lee beam*—a direction to windward or leeward, at right angles with the keel; *on beam ends*—the situation of a vessel when listing so that her beams are in almost the vertical

Bear   *To bear down upon a vessel* is to approach her from the windward

Bearing   The direction of an object from the person looking

Beating   Going toward the direction of the wind, by tacks

Becalm   To intercept the wind; a vessel to windward is said to becalm another. One sail becalms another to leeward of it

Becket   A piece of rope, with an eye or knot at either end, placed so as to confine a spar or another rope; a handle made of rope, in the form of a half circle

Belay   To make a rope fast, but not to hitch or tie it

Belaying pins   Movable pins placed in pinrails, on which to belay running gear

Bend   To make fast; *bend a sail* is to put it on a yard, gaff, or boom; *bend a cable*, make it fast to anchor; *bend*, the knot with which one rope is made fast to another

Bight   The double part, bend, or loop of a rope

Bilge   That part of a ship on which she would rest, besides the keel, if aground; also the part of the ship's interior over the bilge; *bilgewater* is the drainage within the bilge; *bilged*, a ship resting on its bilges

Bitts   Upright timbers running through the deck of a large boat on which hawsers and other lines are secured

Block   Wooden or metal frame containing a wheel through which ropes run. (Land term is pulley)

Board   Course of a vessel on one tack. *Sternboard,* when a vessel is going astern. *By the board,* when a ship's masts fall over side

Boat hook   Staff with iron hook at one end, for holding small boats to wharves or ships' sides; also useful for picking up various floating objects, and mooring lines

Bobstays   Standing rigging running from bowsprit to cutwater or stem

Bollard   Upright post, sometimes a cannon, half sunk in ground used for mooring lines. Sometimes called *dolphin* (Navy)

Boltrope   Outer edge of sail to which canvas proper is sewed

Booby hatch   Small, raised hatchway

Boom   Spar used to extend foot of a fore-and-aft sail

Bow   Rounded part of a vessel forward

Bowsprit   Heavy spar rigged from bow of vessel carrying the headsails

Brace   Rope used to swing a yard about

Breaker   Keg for drinking water used in small boats

Brig   Square-rigged vessel with two masts

Brigantine or *Hermaphrodite Brig* is square-rigged on foremast; fore-and-aft rigged on main; this is rarely seen

Bring to   Throwing a vessel up into the wind

Broach   To open a cask or box

Broach to   To swing a vessel running before the wind broadside to wind or at right angles to course; very dangerous if the sea is heavy

Broadside   Side of a vessel

Bull's-eye   A small piece of stout wood with a hole in the center for a stay or rope to reeve through, without a sheave, and with a groove round it for the strap, which is usually of iron. Also a piece of thick glass inserted in the deck to let in light

Bulwarks   Woodwork around a vessel above decks

Bunting   Thin woolen stuff of which flags are made

Bush   The centerpiece of a wooden sheave in a block

Butt   The end of a plank where it unites with the end of another. *Scuttle butt,* a cask with a hole cut in its bilge and kept on deck to hold drinking water

By the head   When the head of a vessel is lower in the water than her stern. If her stern is lower, she is *by the stern*

Cable   A large, strong fiber or wire rope or chain, made fast to the anchor, by which the vessel is secured

Canvas   Sail cloth; strength indicated by numbers 0 to 9. That numbered 0 is the heaviest. Also is used to mean sails ship may be carrying

Capsize   Upset, overturn

Careen   Heave a vessel on her side

Carry away   Break a spar or rope

Carry on   To crack on all sail possible

Catamaran   A vessel, power or sail, with two equal-sized hulls

Catboat   A sailing vessel with one mast and one sail (the mainsail). To differentiate the classic gaff-rigged cat boat from modern, Bermudan-rigged craft, the latter are sometimes referred to as *una rigs*

Cat-ketch   A sailboat with the largest mast in the bows plus a smaller mizzen aft. It carries no jib(s)

Cat's-paw   Light air or the circular riffles made on the water by this small breeze

Chains   Metal plates bolted to ships' sides, on which standing rigging is set up. *Rudder chains* lead from rudder head to tiller ropes

Channels   Broad planks bolted to outside of vessel to spread lower rigging

Chockablock   When the lower block of a tackle is run close to the upper one, so that you can hoist no higher

Clawing Off   To beat off close-hauled from a lee shore

Cleat   A horned fitting used to belay ropes

Clew   The after corner of fore-and-aft sails

Close-hauled   When a vessel is sailing as close to the wind as she will go

Close-reefed   When all the reefs have been taken in

Coamings   Raised borders around the hatches, to prevent water from running below

Coat   *Mast coat* is a piece of canvas, tarred or painted, placed around a mast or bowsprit where it enters the deck, to keep out water

Coil   To lay a rope up in a circle, with one turn, or fake, over another. A coil is a quantity of rope laid up in this manner

Collar   An eye or bight in the end of a shroud or stay, to go over the masthead

Companion   A wooden covering over the staircase to a cabin. *Companionway*, the staircase to the cabin. *Companion ladder*, leading from the poop to the main deck

Conning   Directing the helmsman in steering a vessel

Counter   That part of a vessel between the bottom of the stern and the wing transom and buttock; the overhang of the stern

Courses   Common term for the sails that hang from a square-rigged ship's lower yards. The foresail is called the *forecourse* and the mainsail the *maincourse*

Cranky   Vessel that rolls a great deal and cannot carry much sail; of any boat, touchy, unstable

Cringle   Rope spliced into the boltrope of a sail to enclose iron ring or thimble producing a circular eye

Cutter   By definition, a single-masted sailing boat in which the mast is stepped at least 40 percent of the waterline length aft of the bow. Usually refers to a single-masted yacht designed to carry a double-head-rig as working sail. The outer headsail is the jib; the inner is the staysail

Deadeyes   Bits of hardwood through which lanyards are rove to set up and connect rigging

Dog vane   A small vane, usually made of bunting, to show the direction of the wind

Douse   To lower suddenly

Downhaul   A rope used to haul down jibs, staysails, and studding sails

Draw   A sail *draws* when it is filled by the wind

Drive   To scud before a gale, or to drift in a current

Driver   A spanker

Drogue   A sea anchor to keep the head of the vessel to the wind

Drop   The depth of a sail, from head to foot, amidships

Earing   A rope attached to a cringle, used in bending on or reefing sails

Even keel   The position of a vessel when she is so trimmed that she rests evenly upon the water

Eye   Shroud or stay where it goes over mast

Eyebolt   Bar with circular hole at end

Eye splice   Bit of rope spliced to form loop at end

Eyes of ships   Extreme forepart of bows

Fake   One of the layers of a coil of rope

Fall   Ropes running through blocks, by which a boat is hoisted

Fast   Secured. *All fast, make fast* are common sea terms

Fenders, Fender spars   Rope rolls or wood hung from side of ship or boat to prevent chafing

Fid   Wooden block at heel of mast holding it in place. Wooden marlin-spike

Fife rail   Rail around mast for belaying running rigging

Flat   A sheet is said to be hauled flat when it is hauled down close

Flaw   A gust of wind

Foot   The lower end of a mast or sail

Foot rope   A rope upon which to stand when reefing or furling sail on squareriggers

Fore   Used to distinguish the forward part of a vessel, or things forward of amidships; as, *foremast, forehatch.* The opposite to aft or after

Fore and aft   Lengthwise with the vessel. The opposite to athwartships

Forecastle   That part of the upper deck forward of the foremast; or, forward of the afterpart of the forechannels. Also, the forward part of the vessel, under the deck, where the sailors live. (Often spelled fo'c'sle)

Forefoot   A piece of timber at the forward extremity of the keel, upon which the lower end of the stem rests

Formast   The forward mast of a vessel

Forward   In front of; in the direction of the bow

Foul   The opposite of clear

Founder   When a vessel fills with water and sinks

Free   Running before the wind. *Free of water,* clear of water

Freeboard   Part of vessel out of water

Full and by   Sailing order meaning to keep the sails full yet to steer a course as close to the wind as possible

Furl   To roll a sail snugly on boom or yard

Gadget   Any little handy contraption, such as a scraper, or special sailmaker's palm, etc.

Gaff   Spar to which head of fore-and-aft sail is bent

Gaff topsail Light fore-and-aft sail rigged to a gaff

Gooseneck An iron ring fitted to the end of a yard or boom

Grating Open latticework of wood. Used principally to cover hatches in good weather; also, to let in light and air

Gripes Bars of iron, with lanyards, rings, and clews, by which a boat is lashed to the ringbolt of the deck. Those for a quarter boat are made of long strips of canvas, going around her and set taut by a lanyard

Grommet A ring formed of rope, by laying around a single strand

Gun-tackle purchase A purchase made by two single blocks

Gunwale The upper rail of a boat or vessel

Guy A rope attached to anything to steady it, and bear it one way or another in hoisting

Hail To speak or call to another vessel or to men in a different part of the ship

Halyards or Halliards Ropes or tackle used for hoisting and lowering yards, gaffs, and sails

Hand *To hand a sail* is to furl it. *Bear a hand*, make haste; *lend a hand*, assist; *hand-over-hand*, hauling rapidly on a rope, by putting one hand before the other, alternately

Handspike A long wooden bar, used for heaving at the windlass

Hatch, or Hatchway An opening in the deck to afford a passage up and down. The coverings over these openings are called *hatch covers*

Hatch Bar An iron bar going across the hatches, to keep them down

Haul *Haul her wind*, when a vessel comes up close upon the wind

Hawse block A block of wood fitted into a hawsehole when at sea

Hawsehole The hole in the bows through which the anchor cable runs

Hawser A large rope used for various purposes, as warping, for a spring, etc.; usually of large diameter

Head Prow of a vessel. Also the upper end of a mast, called the *masthead.*

Headsails All sails that set forward of the foremast

Heave in stays   To go about, tacking

Heave to   (*See Lie to*)

Heel   The after part of the keel. The lower end of the mast or boom. Also, the lower end of the sternpost. *To heel* is to careen to one side

Heeling   The square part of the lower end of a mast, through which the fid hole is made

Helm   The machinery by which a vessel is steered, including the rudder, tiller, wheel, etc.

Home   The sheets of a sail are said to be home when the clews are hauled chock out to the sheave holes. An anchor *comes home* when it is loosened from the ground and hove in

Horns   The pieces that form the jaws on booms and gaffs

Hounds   Projections on the mast serving as shoulders for the stays to rest upon

House   Lowering a mast and securing it to the spar below

Irons   When a ship misses stays in tacking and hangs in the wind she is *in irons*

Jacob's Ladder   Flexible ladder, made of rope with wooden rungs used far aloft. Smaller ones are used over ship's side for entering boats

Jaws   Inner ends of gaffs and booms partly encircling the mast

Jib   Chief headsail running on a stay to bowsprit. Flying jib and outer jib run on other stays

Jib Boom   Boom rigged to bowsprit to which tack of jib is secured

Jibe   To change the position of the sails of a fore-and-aft vessel from one side to the other when before the wind but without tacking

Jigger   Fourth mast in a square-rigged vessel; small tackle used for tautening sheets, halliards, etc.; small after mast of a yawl

Jury Mast   Temporary mast rigged to replace one lost

Keel   Lowest and chief timber in a vessel, running its entire length

Ketch   A sailing boat with two masts. The larger mainmast is forward; the mizzen is stepped forward of the rudder post. The classic formula for a ketch rig is that the area of the mainsail equals the combined area of mizzen and foretriangle

Knightheads   Timbers next to the stem and running up to support the bowsprit

Labor   A vessel is said to labor when she rolls or pitches heavily

Lacing   Rope used to lash a sail to a spar, or a bonnet to a sail

Landfall   Making land

Lanyards   Ropes rove through deadeyes for setting up rigging. Also a rope made fast to anything to secure it

Leading wind   A fair wind. Applied to a wind abeam or quartering

Lee   The side opposite to that from which the wind blows; if a vessel has the wind on her starboard, that will be the *weather* side, and the port will be the *lee* side. A *lee shore* is the shore upon which the wind is blowing. *Under the lee* of anything is when you have that between you and the wind

Leeboard   A board fitted to the side of small craft to prevent its drifting to leeward.

Leech, or *Leach*   The border or edge of a sail, at the sides; the after edge of a fore-and-aft sail

Leech line   A rope used for hauling up the leech of a sail on squareriggers; a line to tighten the leech of a fore-and-aft sail

Leeward   The lee side. In a direction opposite to that from which the wind blows, which is called *windward*. The opposite of *lee* is *weather*; but of *leeward*, *windward*

Leeway   What a vessel loses by drifting to leeward

Lie to, or *Lay to*   To stop progress of a vessel at sea either by counterbracing the yards or by reducing sail so that she will make little or no headway, but will merely come to and fall off by the counteraction of the sails and helm

Life lines   Ropes carried along yards, booms, etc., or at any part of the vessel to hold on by

Lift   A rope or tackle, going from the yardarms to the masthead, to support and move the yard. Also a term applied to the sails when the wind strikes them on the leeches and raises them slightly

List   Inclination of a vessel to one side; *heavy list to starboard* means much tilted over to the right

Locker   Chest or box for stowing things. *Chain locker*, place for anchor chain; *bosun's locker*, storage place for small stuff used in ship's work

Luff   To bring the ship closer to the wind

Luff tackle   Purchase composed of a double and a single block

Lugsail   Used in small boats; is bent to a yard or *lug* suspended obliquely from the mast

Lurch   Sudden rolling of a vessel

Main   Principal mast or sail

Mainropes   Safety lines used in going over the ship's side

Marlin   Fine two-stranded small cord, usually tarred

Marlinspike   Pointed instrument used in splicing rope

Martingale   A short, perpendicular spar, under the bowsprit end, used for guying the headstays. Sometimes called a *dolphin striker*

Mast   A spar set upright from the deck, to support rigging, yards, booms and sails

Master   The commander of a vessel

Midships   The timbers at the broadest part of the vessel; a position midway between the stem and stern

Miss stays   To fail of going about from one tack to another

Mizzenmast   The aftermost mast of a ship. The spanker is sometimes called the *mizzen*; the after mast in a ketch or yawl

Mouse   To put a turn of rope yarn or spun yarn around the end of a hook and its standing part when it is hooked to anything, so as to prevent it from slipping out

Nip   A short turn or twist in a rope

Off and On   To stand on different tacks toward and from the land

Offing   Distance from the shore

Outhaul   A rope used for hauling out the clew of a sail

Overhaul   Applied to rigging it means to examine and repair. Applied to rope it means to keep it clear for running through the blocks. To overhaul a ship is to catch up with or overtake it

Painter   Rope at bows of a small boat to make her fast

Part   To break. Also a section of rope when rove through a block, as the *standing part* and the *running part*

Pay   To *pay off* is to let vessel go away from the wind. To *pay out* a line is to let it run

Peak   *Forepeak* is extreme forward part of the ship; *afterpeak*, extreme after part of ship; both below deck. *Peak of a sail* is the top, outer corner of a gaff sail

Pennant, or *Pendant*   Narrow flag of bunting triangular in shape. Also, a short rope on which is hooked a purchase

Pillow   Block supporting inboard end of bowsprit

Pin   Center axle of a block. *Belaying pin,* iron or wooden bar used for making lines fast. Belaying pins are set in *pinrails*

Poop   Raised deck at extreme stern of vessel

Port   Left side of vessel looking forward. A habor. Also holes in vessel's side through which cargo is worked; *bunkerport,* holes leading to the coal bunkers.

Preventer   Additional stay or spar used to support one already in place

Purchase   Extra power applied, usually by means of a block and tackle

Quarter   Side of vessel toward the stern; opposite of bow

Quarter-deck   That part of the deck aft of the mainmast, in squareriggers

Rack   To seize parallel ropes together, but not to "marry" them.

Rake   Angle at which masts or funnels are set

Ratlines   Light lines running across the shrouds, thus forming a rope ladder

Ready about   Order to stand by for tacking

Reef   To shorten sail

Reef band   Extra width of canvas sewed in sail to support strain of *reef points*

Reef points   Small lines sewn in a sail with which to secure shortened sail when reefing

Reef tackle   Small tackle used to stretch the leech of a reef tightly to yard or boom

Reeve   To pass the end of a rope through a block

Rigging   The general term for all the ropes of a vessel. Also, the common term for the shrouds with their ratlines

Right   To right the helm is to put it amidships

Ringbolt   An eyebolt with a ring through the eye.

Rope yarn   A twisted thread of hemp, or other fiber, of which a rope is made

Round in   To haul in on a rope

Round up   To haul up on a tackle

Rowlocks   The receptacles for the oars in rowing; also called oar-locks

Rudder   A device by which a vessel or boat is steered

Run   The after part of a vessel's bottom

Runner   A rope to increase the power of a tackle. It is rove through a single block, and a tackle is hooked to each end, or to one end, the other being fast

Running Rigging   The ropes that reeve through blocks and are pulled and hauled, such as braces, halyards, etc.; in contrast to the standing rigging, the ends of which are securely seized, such as stays, shrouds, etc.

Sag   To sag to leeward is to drift off bodily to leeward

Sails   Pieces of fabric spread so as to catch wind, in either of two ways: *square sails*, which hang from yards, their foot lying across the line of the keel, as the course, topsail, etc.; and *fore-and-aft sails*, which set upon gaffs, booms, etc., their foot running with the line of the keel.

Schooner   A vessel with two or more masts. A *fore-and-aft schooner* has only fore-and-aft sails. A *topsail schooner* carries a square topsail, and frequently topgallant sail

Score   A groove in a block or deadeye

Scud   To drive before a gale with no sail or only enough to steady the vessel. Also, low, thin clouds that fly swiftly before the wind

Scuppers   Holes cut in the waterways for the water to run from the decks

Scuttle   A hole cut in a vessel's deck, as a hatchway. Also, a hole cut in any part of a vessel. To *scuttle* is to cut or bore holes in a vessel to make her sink

Scuttle butt   Cask on deck containing drinking water; slang for rumors

Seize   To fasten ropes together by turns of small stuff, to secure hooks, etc.

Seizings   The fastenings or bindings that seize ropes together

Sennit, or *Sinnit*   A braid, formed by plaiting rope yarns or spun yarns together

Serve   To wind small stuff, marlines, spun yarns, etc., around a rope to keep it from chafing. It is wound and hove around taut by a serving mallet

Set   To *set up rigging* is to tighten it. The *set of a current* is the direction in which the water is moving

Shackles   Links in a chain cable fitted with a movable bolt so that the chain can be separated. U-shaped fittings with a movable pin across the opening for attaching rigging

Shank   The main piece of an anchor; the stock is made fast at one end, and the arms at the other

Shear legs   Two or more spars, raised at angles or lashed together near their upper ends, used for lowering or hoisting heavy objects

Sheave   Wheel within a block. (Pronounced "shiv")

Sheepshank   Hitch used to shorten a rope without cutting it

Sheer   Longitudinal curvature from bow to stern when viewed from the side. *Sheer strake*, top line of planking running fore and aft along a vessel's gunwale

Sheet   In fore-and-afters, a line to hold booms from swinging too far and to control the sails

Sheet Anchor   The ship's largest anchor; now usually called *best bower*

Shell   Outside casing of a block

Shore   Prop

Shrouds   Standing rigging running from masthead to channel plates, to support masts laterally

Slack   Anything loose. To *slack away* means to loosen gradually

Slings   Rope support of a yard

Sloop   Small vessel with one mast, carrying at least jib and main-sail

Small Stuff   Spun yarn, marline, and other light rope

Snatch Block   Single block made so that the sheave can be opened and the bight of a rope led through

Snub   To check a rope suddenly by taking a turn around a fitting

Spars   General term for masts, yards, gaffs, booms

Spill   To shake wind out of sail by luffing

Spindrift   Seaspray swept from crests of waves

Spring   To crack, as to "*spring*" a mast

Sprit   A pole set diagonally across a rectangular fore-and-aft sail from the mast to the peak. Also temporary bowsprit. *Spritsail*—Sail used in small boats rigged on a sprit

Spun yarn   A rope formed by laying together two or three rope yarns

Square sail   A sail set at the foremast of a schooner or the mainmast of a sloop when going before the wind; the working sails, hung from yards, on squareriggers

Staff   A pole or mast used to hoist flags upon

Stanchions   Upright posts of wood or iron placed so as to support the beams of a vessel. Also, upright pieces of timber placed along the sides of a vessel to support the bulwarks and rail. Also, any fixed, upright support.

Standing rigging   That part of a vessel's rigging that is made fast to the sides; its chief use is to support the masts

Starboard   The right side of a vessel looking forward

Stay   To tack a vessel, or to put her about, so that the wind, from being on one side, is brought upon the other, around the vessel's head. To *stay a mast* is to incline it forward or aft or to one side or the other, by the stays and backstays. A mast is said to be *stayed* too much forward or aft, or too much to port, etc.

Stays   Large wire cables used to support masts, and leading from the head of one mast down to another, or to some part of the vessel. Those that lead forward are called *fore-and-aft stays*, and those that lead down to the vessel's sides *backstays*. *In stays*, a vessel when she is *staying* or going from one tack to another

Steady   To keep the helm as it is

Stem   Extreme forward timber in a vessel

Step   Block of wood at base of mast that holds its heel

Stern   After end of vessel. (Never say rear, back, or behind)

Sternpost   Aftermost timber in a vessel

Sternway   Motion of vessel backward

Stiff   Vessel able to carry plenty of sail safely. Opposite of cranky

Strand   A component part of a rope; a strand is composed of yarns

Strap   Rope or metal binding around a block

Strip   Dismantle, remove rigging from

Surge   To *surge* a rope or cable is to slack it up suddenly where it renders around a pin, or around the windlass or capstan

Sway   To hoist up, usually referring to mast or spars

Sweep   To drag the bottom. Also, a large oar used in small vessels for steering or sculling

Swift   To bring two shrouds or stays close together by ropes

Swifter   The forward shroud to a lower mast

Swivel   A long link of iron, used in chain cables, made so as to turn upon an axis intended to keep the kinks out of a chain

Tack   To put a ship about, so that from having the wind on one side it is brought around on the other by way of her head. The opposite of wearing. A vessel is on the *starboard tack,* or has her *starboard tack* on board, when she has the wind on her starboard side. The *tack* of a fore-and-aft sail is the lower forward corner

Tackle   A purchase; formed by a rope rove through one or more blocks

Taffrail   The rail around a ship's stern

Tail   A rope spliced into the end of a block and used for making it fast to rigging or spars is called a *tail block.* A ship is said to *tail up* or *down stream* when at anchor, according as her stern swings up or down with the tide; the opposite to *heading* one way or another. *To tail* is to assist another of the crew by taking up the slack of a line as he is hauling or winching it in

Taut   Tight, snug

Thimble   An iron ring, having its rim concave on the outside for a rope or strap to fit snugly

Throat   The inner end of a gaff, where it widens and hollows in to fit the mast. Also, the hollow part of a knee. The *throat brails,* halyards, etc., are those that hoist or haul up the gaff or sail near the throat. Also, the angle where the arm of an anchor is joined to the shank

Thrum   To stick short strands of yarn through a mat or canvas to make a rough surface

Tiller   A bar of wood or iron put into the head of the rudder, by which it is moved

Timberheads   The ends of the timbers that come above the deck. Used on large boats for belaying hawsers and heavy ropes

Toggle   A pin placed through the bight or eye of a rope, block strap, or bolt to keep it in its place, or to put the bight or eye of another rope upon, securing them together

Top   A platform placed over the head of a lower mast, resting on the trestletrees, to spread the rigging and for the convenience of men aloft, on squareriggers

Topgallant mast   The third mast above the deck. *Topgallant*

sail—The third sail above the deck

Topmast   The second mast above the deck. Next above the lower mast

Topping lift   A wire line used for topping up the end of a boom

Topsail   The second sail above the deck

Traveler   Terminal for lower end of a sheet that moves on a deck fitting in self-trimming sails, or similar arrangement

Triatic stay   Heavy rope or wire secured to heads of the fore-and-aft mainmasts

Trice   To haul up by a rope

Trim   The way a vessel floats. *Trimmed by the head* means with bows lower than they should be. *To trim*, arrange the sails in the most efficient manner for using the wind

Trimaran   A three-hulled vessel. Normally, the center hull carries the accommodation, while the wing hulls, or floats, are for balance

Truck   Uppermost end of the uppermost mast

Trysail   Triangular fore-and-aft sail on a square-rigger; used in heavy weather

Turn   *Half turn, round turn* applied to rope means passing it about a pin. *Turn in*, stop work or go to bed; *turn out*, get up or get on the job

Vane   Light bunting at masthead used as weather vane

Vang   Rope leading from a gaff to ship's side to steady the gaff

Veer   To pay out chain; also the action of the wind when it changes against the compass (from westward to eastward, or clockwise); it *shifts* when it changes from eastward to westward or counterclockwise

Warp   To move a vessel from one place to another by means of a rope made fast to some fixed object, or to a kedge. A *warp* is a rope used for warping. If the warp is bent to a kedge which is let go, and the vessel is hove ahead by the capstan or windlass, it is called *kedging*

Washboard   Board placed above the gunwale of the boat to keep out spray

Watch tackle   A small luff purchase with a short fall, the double block having a tail to it, and the single one a hook. Used about deck

Waterways   Long pieces of timber running fore and aft on both sides, connecting the deck with the vessel's side. The scuppers run through them

Wear   To turn a vessel around so that from having the wind on one side, the wind will be on the other side, carrying her stern around by the wind. In *tacking* the same result is produced by carrying a vessel's head around by the wind

Weather   In the direction from which the wind blows. A ship carries a *weather helm* when she tends to come up into the wind. A *weatherly ship* is one that works well to windward, making but little leeway

Weather roll   The roll which a ship makes to windward

Whip   A purchase formed by a rope rove through a single block. To *whip* is to hoist by a whip; also, to secure the end of a rope from fraying by a seizing of twine

Wing-and-wing   The situation of a fore-and-aft vessel when she is going dead before the wind, with her foresail on one side and her mainsail on the other

Worm   To fill up between the lays of a rope with small stuff wound around spirally, between the strands

Yard   A long piece of timber, tapering slightly toward the ends, and hung by the center to a mast, to spread the square sails upon

Yardarm   The extremities of a yard

Yaw   The motion of a vessel when she goes off her course

Yawl   A two-masted sailing boat (but not a schooner). Basically, the yawl is a sloop with a small balancing sail (the mizzen) set on a mast stepped abaft the rudder post (see Ketch)

⚓

CHAPTER III

HANDLING BOATS UNDER POWER

AT SEA

301 The powerboat at sea, with plenty of space in which to navigate, constitutes no special problem in handling, save to steer and keep the course desired. A minimum of seamanship is required, and handling becomes even simpler than the handling of an automobile. This is because under ordinary conditions all the components of the problem remain relatively fixed (the surface of the sea, the power, the trim, for example) and are not constantly varying as they are when handling a boat under sail.

The navigator has but to know the characteristics of his particular boat, her responsiveness to rudder and to power, and the boat may be handled in a carefree and effortless manner. In addition to the problems raised by navigation, which are thoroughly discussed in Chapter XI, only three situations might arise calling for special handling. One is the presence of traffic; another, the coming of a storm; the third, an on-board emergency.

MOTORBOAT RULES OF THE ROAD

302 Inland and International Rules are similar in prescribing the conduct of each boat when meeting, to prevent the possibility of collision. It should be noted that the former terms applied to two vessels in a right-of-way situation—"privileged" and "burdened"—have now been changed, respectively, to "stand-on" and "give-way." The traditional term suggested, incorrectly, that one of two craft approaching a potential collision had a superior position; in fact, both such vessels have complementary obligations.

General points of the Rules—and there are four sets applicable to boats in various territorial waters of the United States—are as follows:

1. *Overtaking situation.* Any vessel overtaking any other shall keep out of the way of the vessel being overtaken. The method of propulsion does not apply here: A fast sailboat overtaking a slow powerboat must keep clear.

2. *Head-on situation.* When two vessels are approaching on reciprocal or nearly reciprocal courses, so that the threat of collision exists, each shall alter her course to starboard.

3. *Crossing situation.* When two power-driven vessels are crossing so as to involve risk of collision, the vessel which has the other on her own starboard side shall give way and, if necessary, avoid crossing ahead of the other vessel, which shall maintain her course and speed.

4. Powerboats should, with the exceptions noted in Chapter V, keep clear of sailing craft.

5. A boat is underway when she is not moored or anchored, and should be considered as underway even if she is not apparently moving.

6. All craft underway under power—inboards, outboards, auxiliary sailboats propelled by power or by sail and power—are powerboats for the purpose of the Rules of the Road.

7. Whether or not there is a posted speed limit, a boat is responsible for any damage her wake may create.

STORM AND ROUGH WATER

303 Waves are of two forms; trochoidal and cycloidal. (*Figure 303*) Trochoidal waves are the waves of deep water, and while they may be of tremendous dimensions, they are never dangerous until they begin to break at the crests. It takes a mighty storm to make them break, and the ordinary cruise will seldom find the motorboat so far offshore as not to have been able to run to shelter.

Cycloidal waves are the waves of shallow and confined waters. They are whipped up in shallow bodies (such as at inland lakes or

303 Wave forms

in shallow coastal bays) by a comparatively moderate breeze, one that would have little effect upon deepwater waves. There is but a small span between crests, and consequently they "drop" from beneath a boat quickly and cause a short, jerky, and unpleasant motion, which makes steering difficult. They are dangerous to small open boats, and most uncomfortable to even the decked-in large boat, particularly when they are attacking on the beam. The cycloidal wave will break under wind velocities that would scarcely ruffle the trochoidal wave.

A sea may be composed of a combination of both types, as in shoal areas, or over a bar, or when a strong tidal current opposes the direction of the waves.

304 Some hints for handling boats under power in seas follow:

RUNNING BEFORE A SEA

This is probably the most potentially dangerous of any position at sea. The boat is lifted by the stern, both steerageway and power are lost because the rudder and propeller are clear, or almost clear, of the water, and the boat goes into a wide and perhaps wild yaw. She may yaw to such an extent, as she is carried forward upon the breast of the wave, that she will broach to, or slither into the trough and wind up broadside to the seas. In this position she is almost helpless for a time, and is liable to be boarded by the beam by the next sea, or rolled over.

Both yawing and broaching to can be avoided by a combination of careful, "compensating" steering and throttle control. At all costs the rudder must be used to keep the boat's stern to the seas. Abruptly checking speed will permit the sea to pass. Reduced speed is indicated always. Dragging a long, heavy rope astern will help to slow the forward swing of the stern; in extreme cases, a rope into which many figure-eight knots have been tied may be towed.

A combination of excessive speed imparted by the motor and the waves and a sharp lift of the stern may result in pitchpoling. The bow is completely submerged, and as it staggers the stern is lifted and the vessel turned over end for end. Heavy, 50′ keelboats have been pitchpoled during violent storms. Open boats which are pitchpoled fill instantly. Careful helmsmanship, slow speed, and, if necessary, shifting of weights and ballast to the stern will reduce the likelihood of pitchpoling.

RUNNING INTO A SEA

Running into a sea is wet and sloppy going, but is seldom dangerous if speed has been reduced to avoid strain on the boat, the engine, her gear, and her company. The speed must be regulated so that the bow lifts to the oncoming seas and is not driven into them. It helps, in unusually heavy or breaking head seas, to take them slightly on one bow. Some of the sea's energy will then be expended in a slight, rolling motion, and pitching will be lessened.

The great dangers in "slamming" into head seas are that (a) the hull will be strained to the point of springing a plank, or breaking some frames; (b) something might be torn adrift (ballast, engine, tanks, and particularly such fixtures on the ends) and will need to be captured and tamed before they pound through the planking; and (c) the engine, or the gear, or the shaft may break down under the alternate heavy load of a submerged and then wildly racing propeller as the boat pitches.

RUNNING IN THE TROUGH

If this becomes necessary, and the wind and seas attack on the beam, there is no course but to "take it" at reduced speed and with careful steering. The helmsman should be ready to meet the largest of the seas by quartering into it momentarily; that is, by receiving the force of the crest on the weather (windward) bow, then straightening to true course to take advantage of the calm that follows a particularly heavy wave.

If the seas are too heavy, a series of open legs must be made to the objective, first taking the seas on the weather bow and then

steering the same distance on the opposite side of the true course
and taking them on the weather quarter. It is often possible to set
a course so that, instead of running in the trough, a slightly windward direction can be taken to a lee, and then the boat swung so
that the lee-flattened seas will attack only the quarter.

The advantage and comfort of running under a lee shore, if a
beam sea course lies ahead, should always be carefully considered.
It is just as good (and far more comfortable and safe) to run to a lee,
skirt it, and then run away from it at normal speed as it is to run
in the trough half the distance at half the speed.

HEAVING TO

When headway becomes nil or the punishment too severe, there
is nothing to do but heave the boat to (providing, of course, there
is sufficient sea room). Small boats will not heave to without aid as
steamers will, and a sea anchor, or drogue, becomes a necessity.
Lacking a sea anchor, the motor may be operated just enough to give
bare steerageway, and to keep the boat facing the seas at an angle
on either bow. The use of oil will sometimes help and is recommended. See Chapter II for sea anchors and the use of oil.

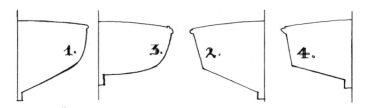

304 1 and 2 are better sea boats than 3 and 4

305 Cycloidal waves in a sea of generally trochoidal waves indicate a shallowing of the water under them, or the preesnce of an
opposing or cross current of some strength, which, in effect, "shallows" the water, so far as wave-making is concerned.

Run through such areas only if the cause is thoroughly understood
and the bottom beneath known from experience, or from the chart.
Cycloidal waves over coastal bars are common. Such breakers do not
necessarily denote shallow or dangerous water, but it may be taken

for granted that the smoothest of these areas are the deepest. In running into an area of breakers over a bar it behooves the helmsman to carefully study the wave groups and to count the light waves between the heavy ones. They will "make" in groups of at least three. The best time to cross the bar is directly after a large wave has passed and broken; then "gun" over in the relatively less violent other waves of the group.

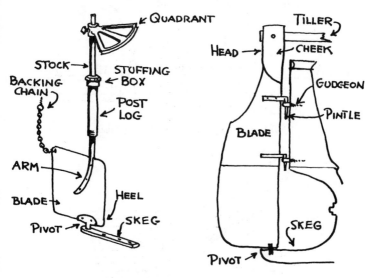

306 *Left,* balanced metal powerboat rudder with stop (backing) chains 35° each side of amidships

Right, unbalanced wooden sailboat rudder

HANDLING INBOARD BOATS IN CLOSE QUARTERS

306 Considerably more knowledge and experience are required to maneuver a motorboat in congested waters or to dock or moor it than is required to handle it at sea. Here the action of the rudder and propeller, particularly in turning and backing, must be thoroughly understood. (*Figure 306*)

THE RUDDER

307 A boat without rudder will, except as will be noted in Paragraph 310, proceed in a straight line in still water and air because the water pressure is equal on both sides of the hull. In order to change the course, or to divert the boat from going in a straight line, the rudder is moved by means of a wheel or a tiller, either right or left, as desired. The effect is to throw the water pressures out of balance, and the boat will turn toward the side with the most pressure retarding it. (*Figures 307A and 307B*)

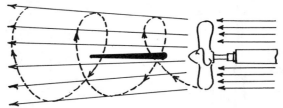

307A The propeller stream driving ahead

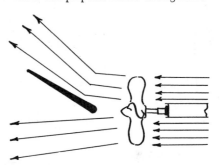

307B The propeller stream broken by the rudder and part of it converted into "side motion"

What is actually happening is that water is "bunched" between the deadwood and the rudder and the *stern is being pushed away from a straight course.* As the stern swings, forcing the boat from a straight course, the bow moves slightly in the opposite direction, and, as the boat is still moving approximately along her original course but not now with her keel parallel to that course, an additional pressure comes into play against the bow, helping in the turning effect desired.

The bow never swings to as great a radius as the stern but both have a common center of arc, always forward of amidships, called the *pivoting point*. This is shown in Figure 307C. While the swing is shown as if the boat were stationary, swinging about the pivoting point, it must be remembered that the vessel is all the while moving along an arc of the turning radius.

Every boat has a different pivoting point, but it is *always forward of amidships*. Any turn made will therefore always move the stern a greater distance toward the outside of the turning circle than it will move the bow toward the inside of the turning circle. This is a cardinal rule to remember and must always be considered when maneuvering in limited spaces or in docking or getting away from the dock.

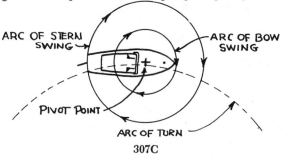

ARC OF STERN SWING →

← ARC OF BOW SWING

PIVOT POINT →

ARC OF TURN

307C

308 The location of the pivoting is of minor importance. However, after handling a boat in various situations, the point is very soon "sensed," and thereafter any turn is visualized as revolving around this point, and the point itself following around the arc of the turn. Its exact location depends upon the design of the boat and the rudder. A boat with a deep forefoot will be slow on the bow swing, or a boat with little or no deadwood will be fast on the stern swing. It is a matter of side-resistance of the hull to the water. The shape and balance of the rudder will determine the "swing" of the boat as well. A boat that will "spin on a dime" is usually one with little deadwood or forefoot. Such a boat is hard to steer and needs constant watch, except at very high speeds, when other course-maintaining forces come into play.

While astern speeds are usually slow and therefore under full control, it is wise to remember that when reversing, the pivot point moves *aft* and is located about the same distance from the true hull pivot (balance point) as when moving forward.

A boat that turns slowly, "takes a long time to make up her mind," is usually one with a deep forefoot and a full deadwood. Such a boat is easy to steer and requires a minimum of wheel watch.

Both types have their uses. Both types will require some special rudder handling when in wind or current.

309 A head wind or current will retard the progress of a boat but will not affect her course.

A wind or current on either bow will retard speed not only because of direct pressure but also because the helm must be carried to keep the boat headed on her true course; the boat will be slowed by the additional water pressure thus built up.

A wind or current on either beam will not directly retard speed, but the considerable amount of helm carried will.

PROPELLERS

310 Practically all gasoline-powered single-screw motorboats are equipped with a right-handed propeller. A right-handed propeller tends to throw the boat, with rudder amidships, slightly to the port, or left. This is due to the fact that upper and lower blades work in waters of different density, the lower blades exerting a thrust to port—which the upper blades cannot quite neutralize, even though turning in the same direction—and tending to throw the boat slightly to port, or left. If the propeller is left-handed, as is the case with most small diesels, the effect will be just opposite to the above.

The hand of a propeller is gauged by watching the propeller from aft, looking forward. A right-handed wheel, to move the boat forward, turns clockwise, or to the right at the top. A left-handed wheel does the reverse.

In smooth water, therefore, the rudder will have to be moved slightly to compensate for this tendency to fall off. Sometimes this propeller force is enough to compensate for a beam wind without the aid of the helm.

Twin propellers balance each other (the screws turn in opposite directions, the tops turning outboard), and if revolutions are equal, the boat does not have this falling-off tendency. The propellers may be used for steering, or maneuvering, or turning without the helm; or to breast a wind or current by slightly adjusting the speed of one.

MANEUVERING

311 The most powerful steering effect is produced by the thrust of the propeller stream against the rudder. A quick "shot" of the engine against the rudder of a boat without headway will swing the boat without giving it substantial headway. This principle is used extensively in maneuvering in tight spaces. Full left or right rudder is required, and the *stern* will swing—not the bow. With a balanced or semibalanced rudder, which when hard over kills most of the propeller thrust except on itself, this maneuver becomes fairly simple.

Forward speeds constitute no problem in tight places. However, the seamanlike (but undramatic) manner of handling the boat is to send it ahead *slowly*, "ticking" the clutch or throttle rather than dashing forward and then snapping into high speed reverse. Such maneuvers are hard on the engine and are liable to stall it, with consequent disaster and damage to self and property.

Backing presents a peculiar situation for single-screw boats. Depending upon the propeller and design of the hull, a boat with a right-handed wheel will have a marked inclination to depart from a straight backward course, even with the helm amidships, and yaw off to the port. Sometimes no amount of opposite helm will straighten the boat out. She will always reverse with a swing to port (or to the right, if one is facing aft).

To back in a straight line, experimentation will produce a rudder position somewhere to port where rudder and propeller action become neutralized. The boat will always back, in turning, better to port than to starboard.

This principle, too, is used in maneuvering. A complete turn in confined areas is not attempted except clockwise, or from left to right, the easiest turning direction of the boat with a right-handed wheel. The extreme left-hand limit of the maneuver is approached first, the rudder put hard to starboard, stopped, and backed; then reversed, with the rudder hard to port. The inclination of the boat to back to port is here distinctly an advantage and will reduce the turning to three fifths of the moves necessary if it were made from right to left. (*Figure 311B*)

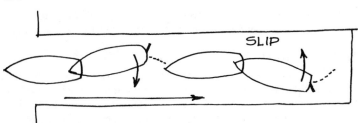

311A Correcting a backing course Few single-crew inboard boats will back under complete control, exceptions being some long-ended sailing craft with rudders of large area. Most power boats will require correction as the backing proceeds. *As the boat is moving,* turn the rudder *opposite* to the swing desired and gently "gun" the motor *forward,* just enough to get the stern into the backing course but not enough to kill way. This may have to be repeated several times, and wind or current may complicate the maneuver.

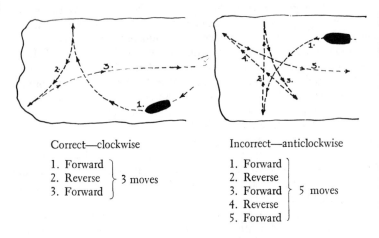

Correct—clockwise

1. Forward ⎫
2. Reverse   ⎬ 3 moves
3. Forward ⎭

Incorrect—anticlockwise

1. Forward ⎫
2. Reverse   ⎪
3. Forward   ⎬ 5 moves
4. Reverse   ⎪
5. Forward ⎭

311B Complete turn for boats with right-handed wheels

DOCKING

312 Under ordinary conditions, docking is a simple enough matter if it is remembered always that the boat turns on a pivot; that sea room is required not only ahead or astern but on either side as well. Wind or tide or both are usually present, however, and must be taken into consideration and even utilized. In the maneuvers diagramed in the following figures it is assumed that the water and the air are still.

Both wind and tide can be *used* in docking maneuvers. The complete evolutions of the maneuver must be fully visualized, step by step, before attempting the first step. If the tide or wind will help or hinder any step, an estimate of that help or hindrance must be made and allowances made for it in the various steps.

Tide will move a boat over the bottom but will not alter its relative bearing to the compass points or the objective. Currents within the tide (or this moving body of water), such as around pierheads, will alter the relative bearing.

Wind will move a boat over the bottom *after* first swinging the boat broadside to the wind. The broadside angle will vary with the topside areas of the boat. Thus a raised-deck cruiser will move broadside but with the bow farther to leeward than the stern.

The judicious use of fenders is recommended for all docking maneuvers. Fenders are imperative when docking on the windward side of a dock. The use of the spring line and the proper mooring lines is explained in detail in Chapter XIV.

It is always preferable to approach a dock or lie to it on the leeward side. Wind and tide shifts should be forecast and the berth chosen that will afford the best "lay" for the duration of the stay. If the boat must be shifted while at the dock, the diagrams following will give some helpful hints.

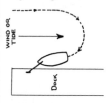

313 Approaching with the wind. Turn to face the wind, get a bow line out first, let the stern drift alongside.

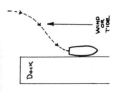

314 Approaching against the wind. Maneuver alongside, get a bow line out first, let the stern drift alongside.

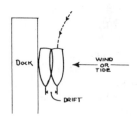

315 Approach the windward side. Stop alongside and parallel, drift into the dock. The bow will probably touch first.

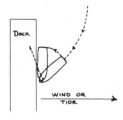

316 Approaching the leeward side. Touch with the bow, put a bow spring line out. Go forward under power with the rudder *away* from the dock to swing stern in.

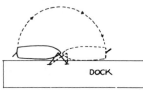

317 To reverse the heading while at a dock. Put out double bow lines, swing rudder *toward* the dock, go forward under engine. When half way around, stop engine, reverse, then, as bow strains against the *opposite* bow line, proceed as before.

318 To warp from a pierhead to alongside. Put out stern spring line, rudder toward dock and reverse on engine *tending the bow line*. As the boat swings alongside, slack and tend spring line.

319 To warp from alongside to a pierhead. Put out bow spring line. Go forward with rudder amidships, until pivoting point is beyond pierhead; then put rudder toward the dock and as the boat comes round put rudder away from the dock.

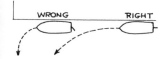

320 Right and wrong way to leave a dock. Go forward with rudder amidships and, as speed is picked up, move it *slightly* away from dock, increasing the angle as the boat slowly bears away and clear. To set the rudder sharply and then go forward will swing the stern into the dock with considerable force, and be dangerous.

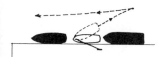

321 Clearing when dockbound. Put out a bow spring line and with rudder toward the dock, go forward on engine. When clear, cast off and reverse; then go forward.

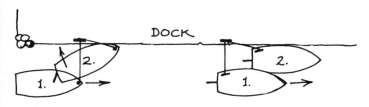

322 After bow spring. Slow ahead with right rudder.

323 After quarter spring. Slow ahead with zero rudder.

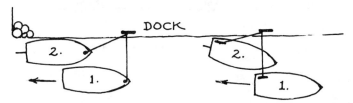

324 Forward bow spring. Slow astern, zero rudder.

325 Forward quarter spring. Slow astern, zero rudder, pass bow line at once.

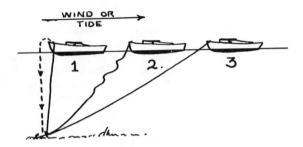

326 To anchor: Run into the wind or tide until directly over the spot in which the anchor is to be set. Put over the anchor when *stopped*. Then sag back or move back under reversed engine, paying out the cable as needed (about five times the depth of the water); take a turn around the bitts or Samson post, and *set* the anchor under the momentum of reversed engine.

327 To pick up a mooring: Approach against the tide or wind, drifting toward the buoy or float without power but with enough way on to steer. Do not sag back under power.

328 To moor between two stakes (or a stake and a dock): Approach as in position number one. Put the rudder hard over and "kick" the stern over by a forward "shot" on the engine. Reverse (if necessary) and put a stern line on the stern stake that is at least as long as the distance between both stakes (position number two). Now run ahead, paying out the stern line to position number three. Put a bow line over the forward stake. Middle to position number four by hauling or power.

FOULING THE PROPELLER

329 An ever-present danger when handling lines is that one will be sucked into the propeller. When reversing or running ahead over a line, the line should be hauled taut and clear of the water. Dinghy painters must be watched very carefully when maneuvering, and good seamanship requires that the painter should be taken up short when planning to dock or moor. A series of net floats of wood or cork are often strung on the dinghy painter to keep it afloat. They should be spaced so that no bight deep enough to reach the propeller may form between floats. Polypropylene line (synthetic, usually yellow) which floats, will serve well as a dinghy painter, although it remains an abomination to the sailor. A line which has become fouled in a wheel generally must be cut away. Reversing will sometimes help, but any power, forward or reverse, is liable to snub the line around the shaft or wheel blades, enough to throw them out of line or spring them. A line is cut away best with a hacksaw or a serrated knife blade.

If a lobster or net buoy is picked up, the mishap may be suspected of being more than merely a fouled propeller. Sometimes the wooden buoys jam between wheel and deadwood or hull, and cause split planks or other broken or strained underwater parts, and nearly always a bent propeller blade or blades.

Always be careful to pass to leeward, or around the "stern" of any pot buoy sighted. Watch also for a "trawl" of buoys or several buoys or warp floats secured together by underwater bridles, and do not pass between them.

Sometimes it is possible to retrieve both ends of a fouled line, in which case it can often be "sawed" off by pulling and slacking. A boat hook might be helpful to throw loops off the wheel blades. *In extremis*, cut off both ends as close to the wheel as possible and proceed with this tail hanging out behind . . . *at slow speed*. Be sure, if it is not your line, to secure both ends to each other. Lobstermen and crabbers expect severed lines as a hazard of the trade. But they reasonably expect not to lose their gear or trawls because a thoughtless yachtsman has failed to attach a buoy (his own buoy) to the trawl line. A lobster trap these days, rigged and baited, costs over $35; the more you destroy, the more your lobsters will cost. Custom-made stainless steel cages around the propeller are much in use in "pot buoy" infested waters as in Maine and Nova Scotia. They cost about $150 per wheel.

Eelgrass and seaweed can generally be "reversed" off without damage. Specially designed antifouling wheels are required in weed- or grass-infested waters.

TOWING

SOME GENERAL NOTES ON TOWING
330

1. A light dinghy will tow best on the forward breast of the second following wave.
2. A heavy tow, close up, should be towed with its center just slightly forward of the crest of one of the stern waves; never on the after breast of a wave.
3. In a broken or rolling sea, a long towing rope will provide the spring necessary between boats.
4. For maneuvering, always tow from the center line, rigging a bridle for the purpose if there is no center chock or bitt.
5. It is always better to tow a heavy boat from a point forward of the towing boat's transom than from its transom, and thus permit the stern some side motion when steering.

6. In towing a boat from a position alongside, get to the leeward of her, and with the towing boat's rudder and propeller somewhat astern of the towed boat's stern.

7. Pushboats (as an outboard dinghy used for power of a sailboat in a calm) are rigged on either quarter, well fended off, with a bow spring line and a stern line, and headed slightly outboard of the course of the pushed boat. Stern pushboats are lashed bow to center line at the transom, well fended, and lines are rigged from each quarter of the pushboat to the same quarter on the pushed boat.

8. Tow inflatables with their bows lashed upon the towboat's transom.

ATTRACTION (SUCTION)

331   Large vessels passing close abreast of each other often experience a mutual attraction caused by the water's being "dragged" along with the boat's movement.

It is seldom dangerous when passing, as the situation changes too rapidly for either vessel to be swung enough to collide, though collision is possible, of course. However, when one vessel is overtaking another and the situation exists for several minutes, there is often a marked suction, described as follows: (*Figure 331A*)

As the overlap commences, the overhauling vessel may expect the bow to be slightly attracted toward the vessel overtaken. There will be a simultaneous repulsion of the stern. As the vessels haul abreast, the attraction forward increases, and repulsion astern changes gradually to attraction.

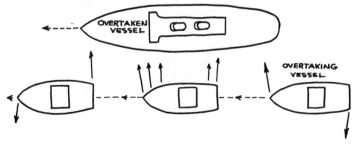

331A Attraction of vessels

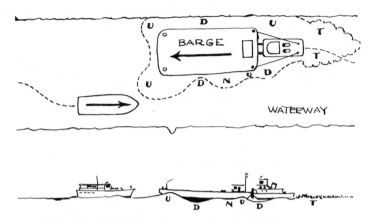

331B What you are up against when mixing with a fast "tow" in a narrow waterway, exaggerated for emphasis. U = up D = down N = neutral T = turbulence. The "downs" are most dangerous since they tend to draw you *into* the tow, especially if exposed to the attraction for a considerable time as when overtaking.

As the overtaking vessel hauls ahead, the bow attraction changes rapidly to repulsion, and the attraction of the stern becomes greater, diminishing only after a brief repulsion when entirely clear of the overtaken vessel.

The attraction of a large vessel for a small one may be so great as to cause the small one to yaw wildly and dangerously. The suction lessens in force at slow speeds and in deep water. Generally, there is little danger, at normal speeds, from small boats, except in very shallow water or in a narrow channel.

Attraction and repulsion in conjunction with still another phenomenon is especially noticeable in confined waters such as the Intracoastal Waterway and some Western rivers. This third effect occurs when passing or overtaking in narrow waters, or in running a dug channel of moderate width. In this situation, a huge bow wave *leads* the larger vessel, often a barge, oil tanker, or dry cargo "flattie," moved, as is necessary for such loads, at fairly high speeds (about 6 knots minimum). The smaller (yacht) passing vessel must actually steam *uphill* to overcome the bow wave, then, at the stern, fight a steep *downhill* wave plus heavy propeller turbulence. The defenses are chancy:

1. Bull through at high speed, which won't bother the barge, but since you may be practically on the shore or bank, is foolhardy seamanship.
2. Pass slowly, at half speed, with moderate rudder *away* from the threat and *reserve* power at your fingertips.
3. Stop and lay-to in any convenient cove or widening *before* engaging this adversary in sticky surroundings.
4. If you have a right-hand wheel, pass to starboard; if left-handed, pass to port (though the barge, after all a pretty decent fellow, may have already played it by the book and crowded to his starboard). If twin screw, either side.

We are conservative, and favor Number 3,—having once been set deep into Georgia mud by the vanishing stern wave.

RUNNING COASTAL INLETS

332 The soundest seamanship plus local knowledge is required to run inlets in surf conditions. Inlet waves are as fast as 47 knots and as high as 52'! Figure 332A shows an average wave pattern in cross section. It may take other or reverse forms due to shoaling, channels and the state of the tide. The ideal manner in which to "ride in" is on the back of a wave. Avoid over-running by the use of the drogue and lagging by "gunning" the boat out of the reverse-current area under the following crests. (*Figure 332B*)

Auxiliaries, in general, should avoid inlets in heavy weather. Twelve knots or better are required from a lively engine for safety.

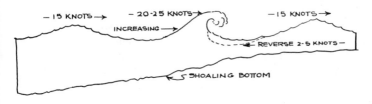

332A Average wave section and relative wave speeds over bars and shoaling inlets The reverse current is present in all troughs but strongest under crests.

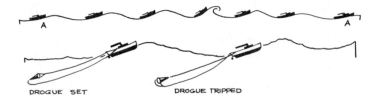

DROGUE SET   DROGUE TRIPPED

332B *Top*, select position on back of wave A as it forms well ahead of the breaker area and ride it beyond the breaker. *Bottom*, use of the drogue to control speed and prevent "runs" when passing through breaker areas or inlets.

Do not attempt to tow small boats; collision will result. Under no circumstances attempt an inlet under sail alone. And do not hesitate to anchor or run off to await a favorable tide as the experienced surfmen do.

HANDLING TWIN-SCREW BOATS

333   While there is no greater problem in handling twin-screw boats, operation thereof will be greatly improved and become more efficient after a thorough knowledge of single-screw handling. There is very little in the horizontal plane that cannot be achieved by the knowledgeable use of twin screws and rudders. It is essential to understand what happens when power and rudder combinations are applied.

A proper twin-screw application should see both propellers fitted with rudders operating in unison, under one helm, and the screws turning in *opposite directions* and *both outboard*; i.e., RH prop to starboard and LH prop to port. The tendency for the vessel to swing in the direction of the prop rotation (as in a single-screw plant) is now nullified and, with both engines at the same rpm and the rudders dead ahead, the boat will move dead ahead.

Now, since there is a choice of using either the right- or a left-side propeller (and the advantage of each in steering) maneuvering can be refined to precise dimensions, using the propeller characteristic required by the circumstances. Example: a port turn may be made (at maneuvering speeds of, say, up to six knots) by left rudder, power on the port propeller, and a dead starboard propeller. Or by increased left rudder, power on the starboard propeller, and a dead port propeller. Or by no rudder, with reverse power on the port propeller and forward power on the starboard propeller. In endless combinations, best suited to solve the problems of current, wind, and target, the choices are at the discretion of the skipper. (*See Figure 333A*)

Steering may be done with the throttles alone, adjusting the engine speeds of the appropriate side to overcome the force which causes deviation from a straight course. Thus, in a strong beam current, increased engine speed on the side opposite to the attack would tend to veer the bow into the current and achieve, by rpm adjustment, a straight course. Rudder might not be required at all.

It should be noted that twin screws fail to perform fully in maneuvering unless each screw has a rudder. Twin screws with a single rudder, which are sometimes seen, especially on sailing craft, simply provide more power and only limited twin-screw maneuverability. Such an installation cannot provide all the advantages of a proper twin-screw propulsion plant.

After some trial and error, it is perfectly possible, in still water and air, to turn a vessel around in a circle little greater in diameter than her own length. This is accomplished without rudders. Engines only are used; one forward and one reverse at individually selected rpms determined by experiment. (*Figure 333B*) With both engines at the same speed and rudders set amidships, a twin-screw boat has none of the difficulties of the single-screw boat in backing. She can back in a straight line, drift and windage possibly corrected by more or less engine speed on the appropriate side. The rudder is not required in backing. Even sharp turns may be made by controlled engine speeds, port or starboard.

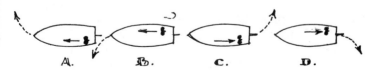

333A All are twin-screw boats. A and B have *one propeller only* moving forward. C and D have *one propeller only* moving in reverse. The rudder is amidships, or zero.

In backing to a necessary course (as, perhaps, in entering a slip stern first) a straight course may be held against tide or wind, by reversing at *slow* speed, avoiding the deplorable "cowboy" handling of far too many skippers and "aiming" and correcting the course by judicious use, *in slow ahead with appropriate rudder action*, of the proper engine. Thus, while backing, a course correction is required to starboard. With the starboard engine still in reverse, put the rudder to port and give the port engine a slight "gun" *ahead*. The stern will swing to starboard and regain the proper course; the engine is now put astern with rudders amidships.

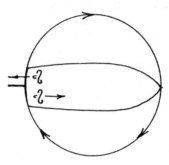

333B Turning a twin-screw vessel in its own length *To starboard:* zero rudder, port prop forward, starboard prop reverse. Since reverse wheel is less powerful than forward, more rpms will be required on the starboard wheel. Marked rpm increase on either wheel will move the vessel forward or backward. *To turn to port:* reverse the above order.

In the event of the breakdown of one of the motors, the remaining one, while having ample power to move the vessel briskly, may not respond to the rudder (usually very small). Most twin-screw boats have adequate balance to operate under either engine—that being the main rationale for the twin-screw design. There will, however, be some handling differences and the owner of a twin-engine boat is well advised to practice maneuvers under one engine alone before he finds that he must handle her this way in earnest.

Obviously, a boat with a single propeller skewed off the centerline will require a certain amount of corrective rudder to hold a straight course. She will tend to turn toward the dead engine, which-ever one it may be. This tendency is amplified by the fact that, in most twin-screw installations, the starboard engine is right-handed and the port engine is left-handed. (Only in outboard or inboard-outboard twins do both propellers usually turn the same way.) Thus, in close-quarters maneuvering, a boat with only her starboard engine running will turn much more easily to port, and will need to have the helm held slightly to starboard to maintain a straight course. This problem can be minimized in outboards and outdrives by re-tracting the dead lower unit—which will, in many cases, make it possible to get back up on plane.

One damaged rudder, or both of them, may be the problem. In this event, steer by the engines, even though they may be very much out of synchronization. There will be no engine or drive train dam-age; merely some annoying engine beat, mostly audible to other boats.

Twin screws at sea are often difficult, especially in a beam sea, because one or the other propeller rises to the surface or above it. There is no practical cure save to stand by the throttles and ease off on the prop that occasionally races. A steadying sail or a motor-sailer can set a rag to give the vessel some leeward heel and thus keep at least the leeward wheel well submerged, while the wind-ward wheel can be cut down to a lesser speed and so avoid violent "racing" as the vessel rolls. In some hull forms, notably double-enders, there is danger of cavitation in even a slight seaway and a throttle watch must be maintained. Almost any twin-screw boat must be most carefully handled when running an inlet for it is en-tirely possible that *both* wheels might be whizzing in thin air. Few propulsion plants can take such punishment for long.

The main reasons for a twin- as opposed to single-screw installa-tion are two: maneuverability and safety. While some power racers and larger commercial vessels use twin engines geared to the same shaft, this practice is almost unheard of in pleasure boats—except in some trawler or displacement yachts, where the main generator (itself a sizeable engine) may be belted to the single propeller shaft to provide emergency propulsion. And in some powered catamarans, a single engine is connected, by hydraulic drive, to two propellers, one in each hull.

HANDLING OF OUTBOARD AND
INBOARD-OUTBOARD BOATS

334 Handling the rudderless I/O or outboard boats is radically different from the handling of single- or twin-screw, rudder-equipped craft. An outboard or sterndrive's propeller both drives and steers the vessel—it ejects a slipstream of water, almost a solid, and it in effect becomes a solid rudder, as the slipstream is changed in direction to achieve a change in course.

On very small outboards, four hp or less, the engine is always in forward, and to reverse, the whole unit is turned in its bracket through 180°. Larger outboards and all inboard-outboards have forward-neutral-reverse gearing. In reverse, the propeller provides the same propulsive and directional thrust as in forward, and the boat will steer just as well—a major advance in handling over single-screw inboards.

Because the drive shaft and wheel are on a horizontal plane, these installations do not have the tendency to veer the boat in the direction of the motor rotation (usually right-handed with a veer to starboard). There is, however, a torque effect due to the high rpms of the more powerful of the outboard engines and most engines have a compensating exhaust nozzle tab which corrects torque. It must be adjusted by trial and error to suit the boat-motor combination.

Most outboards have wheel steering that works just like inboard steering. Some small outboards, however, steer by means of a lever-like handle, exactly like the tiller steering (on most sailing craft). The tiller is moved to the side *opposite* the desired course change.

Actual handling at docks and piers is similar to that of inboard-powered craft except that, once power is cut, the outboard boat tends to slog down rapidly; because of the relatively light boat weight and the dampening effects of carrying forward the bulk of the outdrive underwater casing and wheel(s), it does not carry way.

It is almost impossible to steer the boat once power is cut off. Turning, too, is apt to be a savage, sheering turn in close quarters because the turn must be made with power applied. In general, it is wise to plan landings and departures with wind and current effects clearly in mind. Plan to land *near* the dock, and let the wind or current move you in. Plan to shove off by hand, letting the wind or current move you *away* from the dock before applying the power.

Obviously, it will sometimes be necessary to make landings into an offshore breeze. In such situations, a rather fast final approach is necessary to maintain maneuverability, and the skipper should know from experience just how much power he requires to retain the outboard's traditional ability to pivot sharply. At the same time, cutting the boat's power sharply will kill her way much more effectively than pulling back the throttle of an inboard.

Twin outboard or sterndrive motors are linked to each other at the steering points, so some of the flexibility of twin-screw inboards is lost. Much, however, remains, as the two engines' throttles and shift levers remain individually operated; it is easy to turn a twin-screw outboard or outdrive in her own length or drop her into a slip without using the steering wheel.

Twin-screw outboard and inboard-outboard installations normally turn right-hand wheels only. This will create torque and veering problems that are counteracted by tab adjustments or slightly toeing the motors to throw them very slightly off power application that is exactly parallel to the keel. Both are matters of careful adjustment in the field.

335 Practically all planing OB and I/O craft are high-powered and extremely fast, and they become almost projectiles under certain conditions. This is especially noticeable in a seaway, even a moderate seaway of, say, 3′ waves, for there is a tendency for boats at full throttle, or full plane, to jump from wave to wave with consequent hull, engine, and crew strain and the danger of capsizing. A great deal depends upon the hull form and the total weight and distribution of weight. Deep-V's seem to be able enough sea boats. The flats and so-called cathedral hulls can become dangerous at high sea speeds.

There is one sane cure: cut down speed to near displacement speeds and proceed, with an eye on the larger or cresting waves. Not many OB boats have self-bailing cockpits but those under 20′ in length are required by law to have built-in flotation in the form

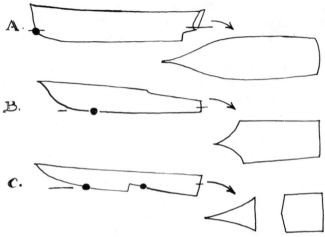

335A How hull form (type) affects the underwater form and gives rise to problems of steering and control. A is a common displacement hull, very limited in speed but easy to steer. B is a planing hull, quite fast since there is relatively small wetted surface to cause skin friction. Steers fairly well at high speed, sometimes almost uncontrollable at low speeds. C is a deep V, with a minimum of skin friction yet with kindly steering characteristics. The black dot in each case indicates the point of waterline impact. The plan drawings on the right suggest the underwater hull shapes underway.

335B A) Overload aft causes squatting. B) Overload forward causes the boat to plow. C) Proper trim results in maximum performance and safety.

of plastic foam baulks or sealed air chambers. Such flotation should be high in the boat; under the gunwales if possible, to encourage the craft to float upright if swamped. All outboard boats require the protection of an inner bulkhead, forward of the transom and motor(s), to prevent flooding of the main hull, plus quick-drain scuppers in the resultant "motor well." Usually boats requiring over 15- or 20-hp motors are built for long-shaft engines and require a transom cutout of 20″ above the waterline.

336 The U.S. Coast Guard regulations call for manufacturers, after October 31, 1972, to attach a capacity plate to any boat under 20′ indicating the allowable weight of motor, gear, and passengers. If I-O, inboard, or unpowered boat, the plate shows the limits of weight for gear and persons only.

Following are the formulas for determining approximate capacities. (It is important to remember that these formulas are rules-of-thumb for boats of average shape. Boats of unusual form—including some classics like the Grand Banks dory—won't fit into these figures.)

1. $\dfrac{\text{Length} \times \text{Beam}}{15}$ = number of persons that can be carried.

$$\left(\text{Example: } \frac{\text{Boat } 18' \times 6'}{15} = 7 \text{ persons}\right)$$

2. Formula to determine approximate carrying capacity:

$7.5 \times \text{Length} \times \text{Beam} \times \text{Minimum freeboard}$ * = Pounds for persons, engine, fuel, and all other gear.

   * (Usually from the waterline to the transom cut-out in feet and tenths.)

(Example: Boat 18′ x 6′, with 20″ transom cut-out)
7.5 x 18 x 6′ x 1.66′ = 1,344.6 pounds.

3. To determine weight of legal "live load" or weight of (not number of) persons permitted:

LIVE LOAD CAPACITY IN POUNDS

Weight carrying capacity of boat (from Table 2)			1,344 pounds
Motor weight	Assume	120 lbs.	
Battery "	"	30 "	
Tank and fuel weight*	"	72 "	
Gear and all other equipment	"	65 "	
Total deadweight	"	287 "	287 pounds
Remaining weight available for persons			1,057 pounds.

* Tank *and* gasoline fuel is taken at eight pounds per gallon, including tank.

Thus, the limit of passengers, including the skipper, is seven persons, averaging about 150 pounds each. If their combined weight is more than 1,057 pounds, their number must be reduced and the skipper (owner) is required to abide by the result of Formulas 1 or 3, whichever is the least.

337   Coast Guard regulations also require that all *outboard* boats over 20′ in length (but not sailboats and some special purpose boats) built after October 31, 1972, show a plate indicating the maximum allowable motor horsepower. The following formulas (either, not both) must be applied.

TABLE 1

Multiply overall length _____ x stern width _____ = factor _____ (nearest whole number)					
If this factor is	thru 35	36–39	40–42	43–45	46–52
hp capacity is	3	5	7–1/2	10	15

Dimensions are in feet and tenths. If the factor is greater than 52.5, use Table 2.

TABLE 2

	Remote Steering and 20" Transom or Equivalent	**No Remote Steering or Transom Less Than 20" or Equivalent**	
		Flat Bottom Hard Chine Boats	**Other Boats**
If this factor is	over 52.5	over 52.5	over 52.5
hp capacity is	$(2 \times factor) - 90$	$(\frac{1}{2} factor) - 15$	$(0.8 factor) - 25$
hp capacity = _____ (raise to next higher multiple of 5)			

HANDLING BOATS ON LAND

338 This rather startling heading does not refer to the stranded or beached boat, it refers to the ever-increasing numbers of OB, I/O and sailing craft that are trailered from a land base, usually one side of a two-car garage or an adjacent plot of land. Trailering is one way to help beat the high cost of boating, for the trailer and private storage area do not begin to match the costs of year-round dockage, several hauls for bottom work, and winter storage.

The combination of trailer and boat should be specified by an expert of some experience. While the limit of overall length for a trailable boat is not fixed, some states do specify a maximum length of 50' for trailer and towing vehicle. For trailering without a special highway permit, a maximum beam of 8' is prescribed in most states. In terms of launching and recovery, a flat- or round-bottomed boat is best, but the supports of trailers (called "rollers" and "bunks") can usually be adjusted to accommodate most normal hull shapes.

Most boat trailers require both license plates and lights. The best combination of these is a demountable set; although it is vastly preferable not to immerse a trailer when launching or recovering your boat, sooner or later it will be unavoidable, and lighting systems are least able to resist water damage.

The related questions of weight and balance are very important. Not only must your trailer be able to support the weight of the boat and her gear, but the gross weight of trailer and boat should be within your car's pulling abilities. The trailer's capacity is noted on a plate or decal affixed to its frame; check your car dealer for the load it can be expected to haul (most ordinary sedans can handle about a ton of towed load).

To determine the load on the trailer, take your boat's hull weight (add a bit extra for watersoaking if she is wood), and add to it the weights of whatever she will be carrying while on the trailer—engine, fuel and tank, battery, tools, safety and other gear. If the gross weight—boat and equipment—comes to 2,500 pounds or less, a two-wheel trailer is adequate; over that and four- or even six-wheel trailers are required.

Make sure the load is properly balanced on the trailer: With the boat strapped down in her over-the-road position, place all the gear aboard in its proper location. Now put an ordinary bathroom scale on the ground or on a couple of cinder blocks and rest the trailer tongue on it. The weight on the tongue should not be much more than 100 pounds if yours is a small passenger car. More important, the weight on tongue should be between 5% and 7% of the gross weight of boat plus gear plus the trailer itself.

Brake requirements for trailers vary from state to state, but the American Boat & Yacht Council recommends that trailer manufacturers offer brakes of some type for all wheels of trailers designed to carry a gross weight over 1,500 pounds. There are three types of brakes in common use: electrical and hydraulic brakes are integrated with the tow vehicle's own system, and are preferred. Surge brakes are activated by the trailer's own momentum and are not under the driver's control. They are illegal in an increasing number of states.

Like brakes, towing hitches come in three sorts. For very light loads, a bumper hitch, which fastens directly to the tow vehicle's rear bumper, may be adequate. It may, however, also be illegal: check with your police department. Far better is the frame hitch, for trailer-and-load gross weights up to 3,500 pounds. This attachment bolts to at least two of the towing vehicle's structural members. For very heavy loads, there is the weight-distributing hitch, which applies leverage on both car and trailer to even the load and keep the towing vehicle level with the ground.

Insurance coverage should be checked with your agent. Policies do not always automatically include trailer coverage and in no case will they cover insurance on the boat being hauled. That requires a separate policy or an endorsement to a marine policy.

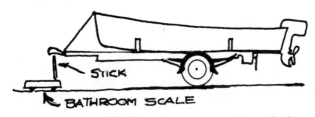

338 How to find your "tongue weight" Acceptable weight is up to 10% of the gross (load) weight.

339   Some Checks Before Open-Road Trailering:

1. Check total weight against trailer and car capacity. Make certain all gear in your boat is lashed down.
2. Check wheel bearings, brakes.
3. Check lights, stop light(s), electric brakes.
4. Carry trailer license, car license, all insurance policies or proof of coverage.
5. Check tire pressures; equalize them. If four tires, deflate forward tires about 7% to improve trailering.
6. Cover the boat against rain, dust, thrown cigarettes (from other cars) and for property protection.
7. Carry simple tools, spare trailer wheel, jack, and dolly wheel. Also useful are extra brake-light bulbs, extra set of wheel bearings, extra padding.
8. Check—and check again as you move on the road—holddowns, gripes, ties, or whatever device holds the boat in the cradle.
9. Be doubly sure that the transom weight is *directly* over the stern bearer, and that all intermediate bearers are wedged *up*

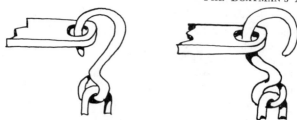

339 *Left,* [wrong] Hook can easily jump out. *Right,* correct If in
doubt, mouse the hook.

and secure; and that the bow hold-down is winched hard into
the bow yoke and the bow tied down to the cradle as well.
Check all adjustment bolts with a wrench.

10. Check safety chains and rig them correctly. (*Figure 339*)
11. Check your car for overheating, excessive oil consumption,
    tire pressures, and excessive hitch weight (should be 5 to
    7% of the gross weight (or load weight).
12. Remember: no riders in the boat, no passenger car speeds.
    (Trucks and trailers usually about 15% slower).
13. Stop once an hour—check wheels, tie-downs, loose gear,
    adjustment bolts.

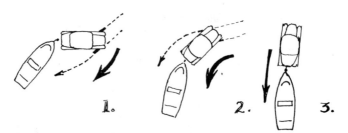

340 The trailer will back in the direction *opposite* to that of the
car or truck. 1) Car wheels to left. 2) Car wheels to right. 3) Car
wheels straight.

TO HANDLE THE TRAILER

340 It takes practice at *slow speeds* and application of the
basic rule at all times and under all conditions, namely: The trailer
always backs in the direction opposite to that of the car.

Figure 340 will help. Understand it . . . and practice. If failure (jackknife) is evident, stop *immediately*, move ahead slowly to get the car and trailer in a straight in-line position, and try again. Turn wide at corners and apply brakes slowly and easily.

LAUNCHING AT A RAMP

341 Assuming a proper ramp (not too steep, well surfaced, and of anti-skid material or construction), with no dangerous drop-off, and with maneuvering room, "aim" the rig at the water and prepare the boat:

1. Plug in (or drain closed).
2. Fuel connected, battery connected (but motor *up*).
3. Equipment load in the boat adjusted (for trim).
4. Bow *and* stern handling lines rigged.
5. Trailer wheel bearings cool; comfortable to the touch.
6. Hull blocking and bow hold-down removed (or lowered). Winch kept set and line snug and snubbed.

Now let the rig drift down the ramp—slowly—and straight, and stop it just before the trailer *axle* goes under. Set the brakes and put blocks under the rear car wheels. Keep the car engine running, with automatic transmission in Park. Man the trailer winch, with somebody standing by the bow and stern painters.

1. Trip the tilt latch and let the winch run, conrolling it with the hand brake, shoving the boat slightly if it needs a start on the rollers.
2. When the boat is afloat, disengage the winch line and temporarily snap it onto a rear frame member; tighten and lock.
3. Haul the boat over to a dock, or convenient boarding point, using fenders if necessary.
4. Prepare the boat for service. Lower motor, break out cushions, up the Navy top, take on fuel, etc., *while*
5. The tilted cradle is hauled down.
6. Blocks are removed from car wheels.
7. The rig is slowly moved to a parking place.
8. Car is locked and trailer chained and locked to car bumper.

Now you are in business.

RELOADING (OR RETRIEVING)

342 Again (as before) back the rig to the ramp edge and, with the motor(s) up, hand-haul the boat with the bow nuzzling the trailer's after rollers, pulling it up as far as it will go. Attach the winch hook to the bow eye, drop the winch into lowest gear, and start cranking; or, if you are lucky, trip the switch and let electricity from the car battery do the job for you. Be sure the boat comes ashore with its keel on center and in line with the fore-and-aft center of the trailer.

As the boat comes in, the tilt bed will flatten and assume a horizontal position at which it may be latched. When the bow of the boat is in the yoke, snub the winch and move the blocking into position, taking the load. Now slowly move the rig up the ramp and to an area where you can complete the road preparation; tie-downs, more blocking, restow the boat, cut off fuel and battery lines, cover the boat, go through the road check list . . . and you are off.

TRAILERING SAILBOATS

343 Centerboard boats in small sizes (say to 24′) pose no special problem save that of transporting the spars. These usually require specially designed and built jacks or crutches to hold the spars above the boat and as far ahead as possible. Any extension over the stern must be fitted with a red flag and at night, possibly, a red light, as dictated by your state law. The jacks should be fitted with cleats or other belaying gear so that spars can be *very securely* lashed down, and in such a foolproof manner that they can move neither vertically nor horizontally. Remember, a loose load in a vehicle tends to move ahead and to dash astern with some violence when starting.

And a last caution: When launching or recovering make certain that there are no overhead electrical wires in the area; several trailer-sailors have been electrocuted when their rigged masts hit such wires.

PART II

BOAT OPERATION

CHAPTER IV

GOVERNMENT REGULATIONS

THE LAWS, both federal and state, that govern pleasure boating have been changing in recent years, reflecting both the increase in the number of ill-trained boating people on the nation's waters and the trend toward consumer-oriented protection under law. From the boatman's point of view, there are two quite different effects.

First, the list of government-required safety equipment grows longer and more detailed. The responsibility for having and maintaining this gear is on the skipper. On the other hand, Federal regulations, notably the Federal Boat Safety Act of 1971, impose on boat and equipment manufacturers a growing responsibility for the safety of their products, impose penalties on them for violations, and give the owner some legal recourse in certain cases.

401 To include in this *Manual* a digest of the text of the three Acts of Congress now applying would serve no useful purpose and might very well confuse and obfuscate. However, for those who might require such information, full texts may be obtained from the Library of Congress, Washington, D. C., as follows:

Motor Boat Act of 1940   Public Law 484, 76th Congress
Bonner Act   9/2/1958   Public Law 85–911
Federal Boat Safety Act 8/8/1971 Public Law 92–75
The Coast Guard has also issued three helpful booklets:
CG-258   Regulations issued to implement the MBA/1940 and will be in effect, in part, until superseded by newer regulations under authority of FBSA/1971

CG-267   Relating to the numbering of pleasure vessels
CG-290   General summation of the present regulations applying to pleasure boating.

All are free of charge from USCG Headquarters, Washington, D. C., 20590. The larger Coast Guard bases have these booklets in stock for the asking.

It should here be noted that the job of the U. S. Coast Guard is far from complete; changes, additions, and new regulations, in new areas as well as old, occur almost daily. There is no way that any manual can keep current. However, the latest regulations controlling pollution by yachts were made public only months before this work went to press and, happily, became possible to include.

The best and easiest way to make sure one's boat exceeds the equipment and seaworthiness standards of the government is to obtain a free Courtesy Motorboat Examination from a member of the United States Coast Guard Auxiliary. These men and women are civilian volunteers, and the examination itself may only be performed if you request it. The standards applied are somewhat in advance of minimum legal requirements but are not unrealistic in any way, and the Vessel Examiners are specially trained for the job. If your craft passes the examination, she will receive a windshield decal that will normally exempt her for the calendar year, from being boarded by Coast Guard or other enforcement personnel, except in cases of visible violation.

If your boat does not pass, you will be told why and what's necessary to correct the situation. But no one else will know. You will not be reported to any agency, even if your boat is in legal violation, and the Examiner will not pressure you in any way. If your Coast Guard Auxiliary flotilla isn't listed in the telephone book, the nearest Coast Guard unit can tell you how to reach one.

At this time the Coast Guard has issued regulations in two new areas:

REGULATION OF MARINE ELECTRICAL SYSTEMS

This concerns itself with providing safe standards for all electrical systems on pleasure boats equipped with permanent inboard gasoline engines and/or generators, including inboard-outboard installations (but not outboard motors). It specifies wire sizes, and types of approved insulations based on ampere capacity, requires every circuit to be protected by fuses or circuit breakers, requires conduit systems or, in some situations, secure fastening by approved methods. It pays special attention to high-tension (ignition) systems and their insulation.

Especially important is the requirement for engine-room non-arcing equipment such as starter motors, generators, alternators, and fuel pumps. All engine-room switching devices are required to be enclosed and sparkproof. Diesel-powered boats are exempt. So is wiring for communications, electronics, and portable appliances.

REGULATION OF FUELING PRACTICES AND FUEL STORAGE

Studies indicate that inboard gasoline-powered boats that "blow" do so, in the great majority of cases, immediately after being fueled. New rules control fuel pumps, carburetors, flame arresters, vents, and fuel fills. Tankages are a prime target and in the future will be subject to flame exposure tests as well as shock impact and pressure tests. Diesel-powered craft and outboards will be exempt.

REGULATIONS FOR SEWERAGE DISCHARGE MARINE HEADS

After several years of indecision, the Coast Guard and the Environmental Protection Agency seem finally to have come up with permanent regulations affecting marine heads. These regulations, which have the force of law, are applicable to two classifications of waterways: The first and most common consists generally of federal and other officially navigable waters—the coastal waters and Great Lakes, major river systems, and the like. Into these waters (with some exceptions) properly treated effluent may be discharged. The other category consists of freshwater lakes that are largely closed systems, outside of interstate commerce, where *no* effluent may be discharged. The exceptions to the first type of waters consist of certain specified areas that require a no-discharge regulation—near bathing beaches, for instance, or over shellfish beds—despite their being part of a larger body of water suitable for treated effluent discharge.

As for treatment systems, which are what marine heads have become, there are three approved types: Type I is a flow-through device that treats sewage until it has a coliform count of not more than 1,000 per 100 milliliters and no visible floating solids. Type II is a refined version of the first, treating sewage to produce an effluent of no more than 200 coliform per 100 milliliters. Type III devices are all no-discharge holding tank systems, designed to be pumped out into shore-station tanks.

As of the time of publication of this book, all new boats are required to have either Type 1, II, or III units attached to their toilets. On January 30, 1980, Type I units will no longer be acceptable in new boats, though existing vessels may retain their Type I units as long as they are in working order.

Obviously, boatmen are hardly equipped to count coliform bacteria themselves, but they can, and should, insist that anyone selling them a marine head system provide a document or label certifying that the device in question is a Coast Guard-approved Type I, II, or III unit, as the case may be.

The smallest cruisers will almost certainly wind up with the self-contained portable heads of the Porta-Potti, Tota-Toilet kind. These contrivances have a detachable tank which can be taken ashore and emptied into a standard toilet. Because they are not permanently installed in the boat, they are exempt from federal regulation. They will generally function without the need for emptying during a weekend cruise. Type 1 devices, such as the Raritan Lectra-san, do not take up too much room, but they do draw a considerable amount of electricity and are thus practical only in power cruisers or aboard larger auxiliaries. Type II devices draw even more power.

Unsettled at the moment is the question of flushing waste water (as from a galley sink or a lavatory). The applicable rule at this writing is simply that the effluent from a marine unit shall not exceed a fecal coliform bacterial count of 1,000 per 100 milliliters nor contain visible solids. Normally, wash water would not contain illegal matter but, as environmentalists point out, they could. Look for a ruling on this soon.

402 Here then, without reference to their source, are the federal regulations and laws, applying to yachts and—a basic change in concept—to vessels that carry no more than six passengers for hire. As additional Coast Guard regulations appear and become

SUMMARY OF EQUIPMENT REQUIRED BY FEDERAL REGULATIONS

Note: for exceptions and explanations, see text following this table.

Item	Boat Length			
	0–16'	16–26'	26–40'	40'–65'
Fire Extinguishers	1 B-I	1 B-I	2 B-I or 1 B-II	3 B-I or 1 B-I and 1 B-II
Whistle or Horn	Not required	1 hand, mouth, or power. Capable of producing 2-sec. blast audible ½ mi.	1 hand or power. 2-sec. blast audible 1 mi.	1 power-operated 2-sec. blast audible 1 mi.
Hull Identification Number	All boats built after October 31, 1972			
Capacity Information Plate	All monohull boats under 20', built after October 31, 1972			
Personal Flotation Devices	At least one Type II, III, or IV (wearable) device for each person aboard, plus at least one Type I (throwable) device Boats under 16' may carry all Type I devices, if desired.			
Ventilation System	At least two ventilators, one intake/one exhaust, for each engine or fuel compartment of boats constructed or decked after April 25, 1940, using gasoline or other fuel with a flashpoint of 110° F. or less			
Flame Arrester	1 on each carburetor of each gasoline engine installed after November 19, 1952			
Lights	Required after dark only, according to several possible patterns (*See text*)			

law under the 1971 act, provisions under former acts disappear;
indeed the act of 1958 will become entirely obsolete in time. It is
well to remember that individual states (excepting, at present,
New Hampshire, Alaska, and Washington), while having no lesser
laws, may have further or different or tougher state laws. (*See
Appendix I and II.*) This is entirely legal under the FBSA/1971
and is, in truth, federal law. It is also well to remember that
certain other state and federal agencies may have additional or dif-
fering regulations. These would be (on the state level) regulation
of boating on small lakes, on water supply sources or their tributaries, in fish-rearing areas, near harbor facilities such as docks,
wharves, bridges, fireboat stations, seaplane operating areas; and
they may, and frequently do, regulate speed on the water. Other
federal agencies may regulate locally. These might be the National
Park Service, the U.S. Army Corps of Engineers, dam and port
authorities, naval shipyards and bases, and those concerned with
submarine-operating areas, trial courses, and target practice areas.

GENERAL NOTES ON AND DESCRIPTIONS
OF REQUIRED EQUIPMENT

403   "Coast Guard-Approved Equipment" is equipment that
has been approved by the Commandant of the U. S. Coast Guard
and has been determined to be in compliance with the U. S. Coast
Guard specifications and regulations relating to the materials, construction, and performance of such equipment. Manufacturers label-
ing their products "U. S. Coast Guard Approved," or a similar designation, are legally bound to truth and will be under severe penalties
for mislabeling. There is a strong Coast Guard influence at work
to require approval of the design and construction, as well as material, quality, and workmanship, of *all recreational boats.*

These paragraphs will refer to the physical *specifications* of the
required equipment, in part to determine acceptable types. The
use of this equipment is presented in the appropriate following
chapters and sections. Example: Lights. Under Rules of the Road,
Chapter V.

LIGHTS

404 The regulations do not specify the type or shape of light required, merely its power, and this in the most inexact terms; namely, "visible X number of miles on a clear, dark night." In order to convert this to a workable specification the Coast Guard has prepared the following tables:

Distance of visibility, in nautical miles	Candlepower
1	1.0
2	5.5
3	17.6
5	100.0

Table 404A To determine the candlepower (outside the lens) and the distance it can be seen.

Distance of visibility, in nautical miles	Color / Voltage	Lamp number for certain voltage systems—					
		With fresnel lens			Without fresnel lens		
		6	12	32	6	12	32
1.......... Red		82	90	1 266	1 130	1 142	1 230
1.......... Green		88	94	1 228	....	....	....
2.......... White		64	68	1 224	82	90	1 226
3.......... White		82	90	1 226	1 130	1 142	1 230

Table 404B To determine a Coast Guard recommended lamp power (by number) for use in either plain or Frésnel lenses. For plain green use the most powerful bulb that it is possible to insert in the lamp; green "kills" candlepower rapidly.

Thus, if you need to be seen, using a white light, for 3 miles, Table 404A indicates that you need a bulb of 17.5 candlepower *outside* the lens. This is probably true with white lens but for red add 50% candlepower; for green double it or more. Table 404B tells us (assuming a 12-volt system) that bulb #90 will provide the required candlepower. Bulb numbers are also suggested for red and green lights, but note that, while they may be visible the required one mile, bad weather, mist or fog, dirty lenses, or low battery power could reduce this substantially. In general, colored lights, especially green and blue, need the most powerful bulb the lamp will accept.

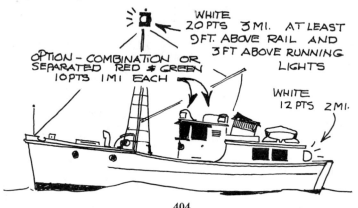

404

Vessels of less than 65' using International Waters
(May be used on Inland waters)

International: (1) Vessels 40 to less than 65' in length must carry 20 point white light 9' above gunwale as well as 3' higher than colored sidelights. (2) All vessels may display either separate colored sidelights or combined lanterns except vessels under sail alone 40 to less than 65' in length must display separate colored sidelights.

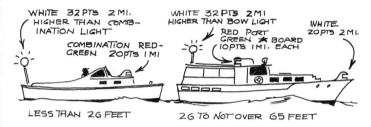

404A Vessels using only inland waters (including Great Lakes and Western rivers)

404B Vessels under sail alone, up to 40', may carry combination or separate running lights plus white stern light. If between 40 and 65', *must* carry separated running lights.

Exceptions: 1) Western River Rules. Sidelights for vessels under sail must be visible for three miles. 2) Great Lakes. On the Great Lakes sailing vessels show a white light (in lieu of a stern light) upon that portion of the vessel which is being approached by another vessel.

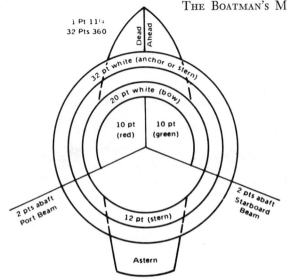

404C Arcs required for the various legal lights. Blacking out parts of the arc is done with screens, light boards, or the construction of the lamp shell.

The placement of navigation lights on the vessel is specified also. Except in the case of an outboard motorboat or other craft where such placement is necessary, white lights are to be placed *on the center line*, and colored lights equidistant from the center line and on the bows, at least forward of amidships and preferably about one third the length from the stem. No superstructure may interfere with the light visibility, and the required points of arc (*See Figure 404A*) must be "clear." All lights must be placed at such a height that persons moving about do not, at any time, blank them out.

A boat carrying side lights and range light (two colored and one white) must show the white or range light at least 3′ above the colored lights. This is usually done via a short mast or flagstaff and presents little problem if the side lights are let into the hull below the sheer line. Vessels requiring the display of two white lights (no matter what the arc of light shown) must have the stern light higher than the bow light. The exception to this is the vessel carrying (under her proper rules) only a 20-point white light. She

Table of Required Lights under International Rules for Vessels 0–65' LOA

	Option 1 (or) Option 2	
POWER (same as sail and power)		
Bow light	×	×
Running lights (pair)		×
Running lights (comb.)	×	
Stern light	×	×
SAIL AND POWER (same as power)		
Bow light (on mast)	×	×
Running lights (pair)		×
Running lights (comb.)	×	
Stern light	×	×
SAIL ALONE		
Running lights (pair)	×	
Running lights (combination on masthead)		×
Stern light	×	×

Table 404C International Rules for lights on vessels 0–65' LOA—also legal under Inland, Western River, and Great Lakes Rules. Note: On Great Lakes, vessels over 40 gross tons *must* use option 2.

Table of required lights under Inland Rules, Great Lakes, and Western Rivers for vessels 0–26' LOA and 26–65' LOA

	0–26' LOA	26–65' LOA
POWER (same as sail and power)		
Bow light		×
Running lights	×	×
Range light	×	×
SAIL AND POWER (same as power)		
Bow light		×
Running lights	×	×
Range light	×	×
SAIL ONLY		
Running lights	×	×
Stern light*	×	×
* Not required on Great Lakes		

Table 404D Inland and Great Lakes and Western River Rules for vessels 0–65' LOA

may show a low stern light, usually on the transom, at the same level as the colored lights; or she may flash or illuminate her after hull or superstructure when being overtaken. See the special Inland and Western River rules, Chapter V.

Lights may be powered by any source desired, the sole requirement is that of visibility. Boats under oars, or small sailboats that are capable of being rowed, show no permanent lights but must have on board a lantern (oil- or electric-powered), which is shown to an approaching or overtaking boat in order to avoid collision. The light is usually shown against a sail. It must *never* be flashed directly at the approaching boat.

Outboard boats have no special light regulations; they are under the same rules regarding equipment as heavier vessels up to 65′.

WHISTLE OR HORN

405   All pleasure boats over 16′ must be equipped with a whistle or horn. No sizes are specified but—obviously—the whistle (or horn) suitable for an outboard cruiser would not serve a 50-footer or a high-speed racing boat. The requirements are somewhat vague and might be interpreted to mean: "suitable for the boat on which used." It may be operated by any pressure means: mouth, manual, cylinder gas, electric, or compressor—or any other means devised by an owner. It must be capable of producing a blast of not less than two seconds duration and must be audible at least one-half mile for boats up to 26′ and at least one mile when carried by larger craft.

Boat Length:	Type:
0–16′	Not required (*See note following*)
16–26′	Mouth, hand, or power
26–40′	Hand or power
40–65′	Power

Table 405 Suggested types of whistles for boats.

Special Note: While motorboat regulations do not require boats under 16′ to carry a whistle (or bell), the Rules of the Road require such vessels to sound both under certain circumstances. International Rules (offshore passages) definitely require *all* boats to be equipped with whistle and bell.

Mouth whistles are usually of the chime variety, of non-ferrous metal or plastic. A foghorn will "pass" if it meets the audibility requirements. Hand-operated whistles are usually cannisters of compressed gas, which activates a powerful high-pressure bell horn, or a pump-compressor type, operated by a husky shove of the piston. "Power" horns, often twin trumpets, are usually driven by an electro-vibrator (diaphragm) system, or by compressed air, stored in a tank under high pressure and automatically kept at full pressure by compression motors or the engine cylinder pressure.

Horns (trumpets, bugles, etc.) are legal, though rare, and have some uses (such as echo navigation) that may make their shipping aboard desirable.

Portable aerosol-powered horns are legally acceptable for all classes of pleasure craft.

BELL

406 Motorboats and sailboats over 26' must carry a fog bell. It need not be rigged for use at all times. This is usually a brass stamped or cast bell, with a cast clapper attached to a lanyard. It is best located on a part of the superstructure, or a standing spar, so that it can be heard all around the board (360°) since it is used mostly for signifying a vessel anchored in a fairway. The only legal requirement is that the bell emit a "rounded, bell-like tone."

If boats of under 26' wish to be legal, they, too, should carry a bell even though not required by direction. The Rules of the Road specify that *all* boats must sound the bell under some conditions.

LIFE-SAVING DEVICES

407 Entirely new and updated regulations relating to life-saving devices (now called Personal Flotation Devices or PFDs) went into effect under the FBSA/1971 on October 1, 1973. There are no other regulations, no exceptions (save for racing craft and certain decked kayaks). *All* boats—canoes, sail-boats, kayaks, rafts, inflatable boats, yacht dinghies—*must* carry the appropriate PFD.

These devices are available in a great variety of sizes, colors, and styles and are offered by many manufacturers. To meet the requirements, each unit must be manufactured to Coast Guard specifications and standards and, after personal inspection, be stamped as Coast Guard-approved. Styles include the life preserver (practical for most craft), the bib style, the buoyant vest (like a sleeveless sweater), and many special-purpose styles for sport, hunting, waterskiing, and arctic wear.

Ring buoys (approved as a "throwable device") are available in diameters of 20″ to 36″. These must be kept "ready for use"; i.e., hung or secured near the steering station, possibly on a hook on the superstructure or after lifelines. Approved ring buoys are stamped with the Coast Guard approval and date. Horse-collar style buoys are in the same category as ring buoys.

These are the classes or types, by purpose:

Type I PFD   Designed to turn an unconscious person from a face downward position in the water to a vertical or beyond position, and to have more than 20 pounds of buoyancy.

Type II PFD   Designed for the same purpose as Type I PFD but to have at least 15½ pounds of buoyancy.

Type III PFD   Designed to keep a conscious person in a vertical or beyond position and to have at least 15½ pounds buoyancy.

Type IV PFD   Designed to be thrown to a person in the water and grasped rather than worn and have at least 16½ pounds buoyancy.

Type V PFD   Designed for a restricted or special purpose (as a work vest) and approved by the Coast Guard. No type V is currently legally acceptable for recreational boats.

All boats, not only motorboats, must have, at their option, one of Type I, II, or III on board and in good usable condition. All boats over 16′ must *also* have on board, ready for use, one Type IV PFD. This can be a ring buoy or a buoyant cushion of at least 16½ pounds buoyancy. Thus, it will be seen, the popular buoyant cushion is illegal as a *primary* PFD on any boat over 16′.

From the practical viewpoint, the life preserver type (Type I PFD) is the least comfortable because of its extreme bulk (20 pounds buoyancy). It is, however, the type most likely to give extended service and provide a long flotation period. For sport and deck wear, one of the Type II or III is preferable, providing comfort, light weight, and reasonable security. These are the types recommended for water skiing, white-water canoeing, canoe sailing, and deck wear on a sailing craft.

Most styles can be obtained in general sizes—medium and large —and children's sizes.

Older type life preservers (before October 1, 1973) may still be "passed" if in good condition and if they are included in the Coast Guard's list of acceptable "equivalent devices." The numbers of these devices, *stamped on the device by the Coast Guard,* is listed in Paragraph 402, Section 175.23 or as follows:

Type I PFD	Equivalent	160.002
		160.003
		160.004
		160.005
		160.055
Type II PFD	Equivalent	160.047
		160.052
		160.060
Type III PFD	Equivalent	160.009
		160.048
		160.049

At all times, life preserving devices must be kept in good, clean, and repaired order. They must be instantly available, preferably in marked, unlocked boxes or overhead racks. Most states require a PFD to be worn when waterskiing, racing, and sometimes canoeing and sailing.

Attaching whistles, flare kits, balloons (for locating), and automatic lights to PFDs is legal and under certain deepwater conditions is prudent seamanship. An ongoing Coast Guard program seeks to discover or invent a design which would make all types of life preservers more comfortable and less restrictive. If and when such new types appear, they will be announced by the manufacturers as well as by the Coast Guard.

FLAME ARRESTERS

408 Flame arresters are usually engine equipment and are included in the power package. Those approved by the Coast Guard are sometimes so marked on a part of the arrester frame, or so listed in the bill of materials or parts of the engine. The arrester's connection to the carburetor must be flameproof as well as the grid itself; this is often a point the Coast Guard will inspect. Outboard motors do not require flame arresters.

Engines installed prior to April 25, 1940, are exempt from current standards. Engines installed prior to November 19, 1952, if they meet the standards previous to that time, are also exempt. Special designs of engines, free from backfire, may be exempt as well as engines that exhaust into the air (as an air boat).

In general, marine engines are equipped with acceptable backfire devices. Converted auto engines, especially those home-engineered, are apt to fall short of regulations.

Diesel engines, of course, do not have carburetion systems and are not subject to inspection.

VENTILATION

409 It is almost impossible to be specific and objective in presenting the matter of vessel ventilation. The system will vary with almost every craft; indeed, the Coast Guard itself makes a minimum requirement and bases its final judgment upon the adequacy of the system *after it is built*. About all that is positive is that at least two cowls are required (inlet and outlet), that ducts are a must, and that certain area relationships must be maintained between duct area and cubic footage of the area to be ventilated. The simplest method, and the one most used—because the ventilating system involves mainly labor, with a minimum of material —is to overbuild; it costs little or nothing extra. Nevertheless, no matter what the capacity of the system, it must work. This section is designed to provide some guides as to how to make it work.

First, note that each engine must have a complete two-cowl system and that each fuel compartment, as well as any cooking gas storage locker or box (legal *only* on pleasure boats), must also be separately ventilated. Ventilation is a system that exchanges the air in a remote, usually low, area. Ducts must be used to reach the area. A "vent," which is merely a hole in a box, hull, or bulkhead, is by no stretch of the imagination a ventilator—in spite of what the former law(s) said. Coast Guard regulations in 1967 and in 1972 replaced the old, lenient law with some tough measures, and a Coast Guard inspecting party is under orders to give particular attention to ventilating systems. *They must work!*

An open boat is exempted; so are some outboard motorboats. To be classed as an open boat, or one of "open construction," the boat should be almost primitive, having neither engine box, cabin, nor bulkheaded fuel tank compartment(s). Here are the Coast Guard rules:

. . . To qualify for exemption from the bilge ventilation regulations, the boat must meet *all* of the following conditions.

(1) As a minimum, engine and fuel tank compartments must have 15 square inches of open area directly exposed to the atmosphere for each cubic foot of *net* compartment volume. (Net volume is found by determining total volume and then subtracting the volume occupied by the engine, tanks, fixtures, etc.

(2) Fuel and engine compartments must have at least one square inch of open area per cubic foot within one inch of the compartment bilge level, or floor, so that vapors can drain out into the atmosphere.

(3) There must be no long or narrow unventilated spaces accessible from the engine or fuel tank compartments into which a fire could spread, unless the space meets requirements of item 4 below.

(4) Long, narrow compartments, such as side panels, if joining engine or fuel tank compartments and not serving as ducts, must have at least 15 square inches of open area per cubic foot through frequent openings along the compartment's full length.

In *all* cases, *all* ducts must be positioned so as to efficiently empty the area of fumes. This means an entrance duct, from an outside cowl, scoop, or turbine head to the upper area of the space to be exhausted, and an exhaust duct from the bottom of the space (but not so low as to be in danger of normal bilge water blocking the opening). The exhaust duct must pull, downward, from the entrance duct. Exhaust blowers (electric, with spark-proof motors) do not replace naturally ventilated systems; they only complement them. The duct of power blowers must be separate from the required system(s) and pull from the average low spot in the compartment being exhausted.

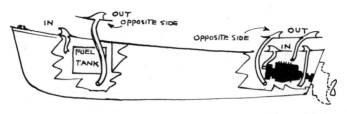

FUEL COMPARTMENT   ENGINE/BATTERY COMPARTMENT

409A Standards of ventilation. Tank, engine, and battery compartments *must* be "properly" ventilated. It is always wise to place intakes and exhaust cowls on opposite sides of the boat, well separated, to avoid recirculating exhaust fumes. Intakes should feed to the middle and upper areas: exhausts should pull from the bottom or bilges. Power exhausts should exit in the stern if possible, to avoid an intake picking up fumes.

A complete system is required for each compartment (engine and fuel) no matter how many there are, and good sense will dictate a double system for any installation which is side-ventilated (as opposed to a system with cowls forward, aft, or overhead). Great care, including tests with a smoke-producing device, must be exercised that no cowl is defeated in its purpose by being installed too close to a deck fixture, superstructure, spars, or other wind baffles. Intake cowls cannot be near fuel vents or fill caps, or close to smoke heads that might throw sparks. Exhausts from power blowers should be led to the stern area, or transom, in such a location that their discharge is not picked up by a system entrance cowl, or by other through-hull fittings.

While devices for the detection of escaping gases are not required by regulations, they are obviously a great protection and should be part of the installation of a prudent boatowner. A separate pick-up head should be in every area containing engine, generator, fuel tanks, cooking gas tanks, gas refrigerators or stoves, outboard motor storage or fuel, and the paint locker.

The regulations refer to gasoline-powered machinery only; diesel-powered boats are exempt. However, if the vessel with diesel propulsion engine(s) has other equipment using gasoline, cooking gas, etc., a ventilating system *is* required. In any case, diesel engines require healthy supplies of fresh air for proper aspiration. A blower exhaust system is also useful to cool down a diesel engine compartment.

Small craft, with a more or less definite engine box (as on an inboard-outboard boat) or tank compartment (as under a forward deck or after thwartship seat) may be guided by the following table for recommended duct sizes:

TABLE 409A FOR 1 INTAKE AND 1 EXHAUST

Net Compartment Volume in cubic feet	Minimum inside diameter, each duct, in inches	Area of cowl face in square inches
8	2	3
12	2½	5
17	3	7
23	3½	10
30	4	13
39	4½	16
48	5	20

Note: Systems with 2 intakes and 2 exhausts use 3″ diameter ducts throughout with cowl faces of from 12–16 square inches.

TABLE 409B FOR LARGER VESSELS, CRUISERS, AND AUXILIARY SAILING CRAFT REQUIRING 2 INTAKE AND 2 EXHAUST SYSTEMS

Beam in feet	Minimum inside diameter, each duct, in inches	Area of cowl face in square inches
7	3	7
8	3¼	8
9–10	3½	10
11–13	4	13
14–15	4½	15

Note: Cats and tris use beam of hull(s) in which the engine(s) are carried. Auxiliaries carrying outboard power or fuel tank *in a separate enclosed well or compartment* use Table 409A.

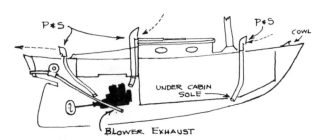

409B An auxiliary requires special engineering for airflow to reach into the deepest areas of the hull. Standing cowls are best since flush deck air scoops are apt to bring in water when heeled down in hard going. Ventilators should be placed so that off-draft from the sails do not negate or reverse the desired action. Sailboat exhaust cowls should be capable of being removed, and the openings securely capped, when sailing in heavy weather. In addition, sailboat cowls ought to be able to swivel, so they can be faced for most efficient operation, no matter what the boat's heading may be.

FIRE EXTINGUISHERS

410 The four essential elements of any fire are fuel, heat, oxygen (air), and chemical reaction. If any single element is interrupted or removed, the fire will cease to burn. In this principle lies the reason for the various types of fire-extinguishing materials. They are (plus water, of course):

Foam Sprayers	Effective, legal, not often used except as auxiliary fire fighters in passenger and cargo compartments. Will freeze. Leaves a damaging residue and can effect engine parts. Not pressurized.
Dry Chemical	Chemical under pressure. Can readily be recharged. Convenient. Modest cost. Suitable for fighting most boat fires (inflammable liquids and gases). Leaves a fine powder residue. This is the popular B type required by regulations.

Carbon Dioxide   Effective as an auxiliary to the dry chemical type. Often used in automatic installations. Clean; leaves no mess or engine damage. Frost-proof.

Note: Carbon tetrachloride and other vaporizing-liquid types which produce toxic gases, while effective for fire suppression, are not recommended and do not fill legal requirements. Dangerous to personnel in some types of fire.

Dry chemical types are the most commonly used. They must be from an approved manufacturer, along with other legal types, and the approved manufacturers are listed in Coast Guard publication CG-190 (Equipment Lists). An approved fire extinguisher wil have a brass nameplate attached denoting manufacturer, type, and capacity. If manufactured since 1965 it will also carry the legend: Approval No. 162.068/_____.

These are the approved types that are now legal equipment:

APPROVED FIRE EXTINGUISHERS

Class	Foam (Min. gallons)	Carbon Dioxide (Min. pounds)	Dry Chemical (Min. pounds)
B-I	1¼	4	2
B-II	2½	15	10

Refer to Table of Required Equipment for number of units on various sized boats.

If the boat has a permanent manual or automatic fire-suppressing system and is over 26', deduct one B-1 extinguisher from the required number. Boats driven by outboard motor need carry no extinguisher *if* the motor or its tankage is not enclosed in a box, covered well or compartment and is truly of "open construction." Further, it must have a tight cockpit floor; i.e., moulded to the hull or filled *completely* with flotation material, and it must not have a built-in tankage system (moulded-in-hull tanks). It has been determined that open slatted floors, bait wells, fish boxes, ice chests, and small glove-compartment type lockers, alone, do not call for fire extinguishers.

Fire extinguishers, to be approved, must be found in clean, non-rusted or corroded condition, ready for use, accessible, and filled to within 90% of capacity by volume or weight (depending upon type). They must have the approval plate attached.

"Accessible" means accessible upon the threat of a fire. In general, extinguishers should be near the helmsman, near the galley, near (never in) the engine room, and never in such a position as to be *beyond* the most likely fire areas and the most likely location of the crew. Determine where a fire might drive you; then put the extinguisher there.

A frequent check of contents should be part of routine boat maintenance. Foam is not pressurized and cannot be checked for content. Annually, upon commissioning, recharge such types. Dry chemical types can be recharged (but not always by the purchaser) by inserting a replacement cylinder when the gauge (required on Coast Guard-approved types) needle is in the red sector of the dial. The charge is under gas pressure. The CO_2 type is a gas-under-pressure type, sealed by lead tabs, and can be checked for content only by weighing by a servicing station. (Local fire departments often offer this service, and a recharge, free or at nominal cost). It must contain at least 90% of the full charge, by weight.

REGULATIONS OF THE NON-EQUIPMENT TYPE

411   Many of the following regulations are administered by the Coast Guard, on the water, by means of inspecting officers especially trained for the service. An official inspection must be made when the vessel is in operation, or has been observed in operation in the immediate past. Dockside inspections called "courtesy inspections" are carried out by members of the Coast Guard Auxiliary who have no law-enforcement powers. It is a kindly, cooperative effort by trained civilians to asisst the Coast Guard and the state boating departments to educate and to maintain boating as a safe and sane recreational sport.

An official inspection will take place, at sea, from a Coast Guard small craft, plainly marked on both bows by the distinctive Coast Guard red, white, and blue stripes running diagonally aft from the sheer to the boot top. The boat will fly the United States Coast Guard ensign, and the flag of the United States and her crew will be in uniform. She may flash a blue strobe light similar to that of police cars ashore. Upon her hail, the skipper is obliged to stop and lay to, and maneuver in such a manner that the boarding officer may safely

411 A typical Coast Guard patrol unit. It will *always* fly the Coast Guard ensign, possibly also the U.S. flag; will have uniformed crew; carry a blue "police" light; and display on both bows the Coast Guard identifying hash mark (large red, small blue & white bands with a Coast Guard device). The hull will be either white or black.

board. If you feel that the stop order is made in an unsafe place (in heavy water traffic, in dangerous currents, confused wakes, etc., or while you are experiencing engine trouble, leaking, etc.) so advice the officer and ask for another location or, if necessary, another time. Don't use the privilege capriciously; for example, just because you are in a hurry, for you will have to show why you requested the delay. Failure to comply without reasonable cause can bring penalties of up to $100.

Be prepared to show and demonstrate all required equipment, plus registration or documentation. Requests to test navigational lights are valid, but you cannot be faulted if they are inoperable if the inspection is made in daylight hours. Contrary to past requirements, the Coast Guard *has* inspection rights for documented pleasure boats up to 65′. The Steamboat Inspection Service takes care of documented boats above that length at the moment but look for a transfer of this authority to the Coast Guard.

Under the general heading of "Termination of Unsafe Use," Coast Guard officers have the authority to halt or turn back a boat when it is observed in use without a sufficient number of PFDs or fire extinguishers; if it is manifestly overloaded; or if, in the boarding officer's opinion, any other especially hazardous conditon exists. A similar, but far more limited, authority is vested in Coast Guard District Commanders—Rear or Vice Admirals—with respect to calling off announced voyages that seem to the Commander to pose inordinate danger to the participants because of the unsuitability or lack of seaworthiness of the boat. This authority, unlike that wielded by boarding officers, reposes only in the District Commander and cannot be delegated.

412 The United States Coast Guard Auxiliary, which is an organization of civilian volunteers, operating under Coast Guard auspices and trained by the Coast Guard, sets boat safety standards that go even further. Failure to meet these standards is not illegal and carries no penalty or stigma; they are merely desirable standards beyond the lawful regulations. The Auxiliary will gladly inspect to these standards after inspecting for the legally required standards and, if the vessel passes, will award a handsome decal, which may be displayed with honor on the vessel.

The following equipment standards are those used by the U.S. Coast Guard Auxiliary in its Courtesy Motorboat Examination program. Many of them derive directly from those of the federal government, but are in excess of legal requirements; others are "good judgment" standards applied voluntarily in areas where the Coast Guard has yet to create legally binding regulations. In all cases, they show the Coast Guard's considered thinking as to safety equipment and construction standards.

While not cause for withholding the CME decal, these standards of condition and equipment are recommended by the Auxiliary.

- Through-hull fittings should have shut-off valves or wooden plugs accessible for use in case of failure (*see Chapter* XV *for a universal plug*).
- Fuel lines should lead from the top of the tank and be equipped with shut-off valves at both the tank and the engine.
- Auxiliary generators should have tanks separate from the engine fuel tanks.
- All switches located in the bilges should be designed for submerged use.
- Distress-signaling equipment should be carried on every boat. (Flares, mirror, light, water dye etc.)

- A manual bilge pump should be carried on every boat irrespective of any mechanical pumping devices.
- Handrails should be secured with through-bolts.
- Spare canisters should be carried for horns or whistles which operate from compressed gas.
- Spare batteries and spare bulbs should be carried for battery-operated lights.
- A fully-equipped first-aid kit and manual should be carried in every boat.
- Tools and spare parts on board should be in usable condition.
- The safe-loading plate affixed at the time of manufacture should be legible and the load capacities indicated thereon should not be exceeded.

In addition, there should be:

- Marine-type galley stove, if any, properly installed.
- Paddles or oars and a bailer for boats under 16'.
- Fire extinguishers in powerboats under 16' even if not required.
- A drip pan under carburetors.
- Electrical wiring in good condition.
- An anchor and line suitable for the local waters.
- Portable fuel tanks, of sturdy construction and never of glass or other breakable material.
- A hull identification number (the responsibility of the boat builder to supply and affix).

In general, the vessel should be in good condition; sound, fuel lines and wiring intact and properly installed; equipment in shipshape and seaworthy condition in all departments.

NUMBERING OF BOATS

413 Since all states but Alaska, New Hampshire, and Washington have now qualified to register, number, and tax boats under the FBSA/1971, numbering has ceased to be a Coast Guard function, or almost so. Where it does license (the above three states mentioned, the District of Columbia, American Samoa, and Guam, the charges are: original numbering, $6; renewal of number, $6; replacement of lost or destroyed certificate, $1; replacement of lost validation sticker, 25¢.

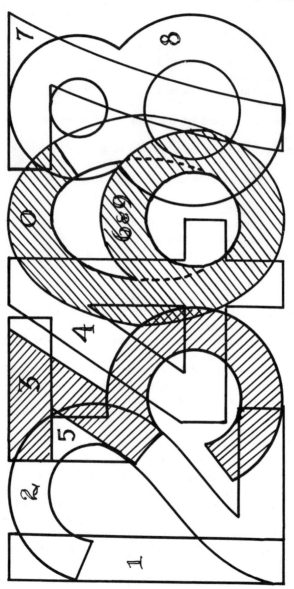

413A These numerals are exactly three inches high as required by the motorboat numbering regulations. They may be transferred to the boat by tracing or cutting out, and painted with a lettering or artist's brush.

B7   143—   0   □

correct and legal

B7143—0   □

incorrect and illegal

413B Correct manner in which to compose a boat number The square represents an annual validation sticker. Plain block letters of the typeface shown are the only legal and permitted kind. Script, ornamental, or archaic lettering is illegal.

Some states issue a validation sticker, usually a logo of distinctive color or shape, which must be shown within 6″ of the number. It shows current status of the license, tax, etc.

At its option, a state may require property, sales, and other state tax receipts to be exhibited before issuing a number.

Air boats (wingless) are boats and so licensed.

Temporary engines (such as outboards on a sailing craft or a fishing skiff) even though not in use at all times (when sailing or rowing) qualify as "power" and the boat must be numbered.

Boats of all sizes and types *if fitted with propulsion engine(s)* are required to be registered and numbered. The sole exceptions are: vessels of the U. S. government, documented vessels, ship's lifeboats and, in waters where the Coast Guard, not a state, issues registrations, yacht dinghies attached to a parent vessel and used solely for transportation to and from the parent vessel.

States may, and do, set their own fees and award their own numbers and validation stickers. The numbering system *must* adhere to the federal system in number size, shape, and color. Numbers are available from varying sources, depending upon state law, such as sporting goods stores, sheriff's departments, police departments, Fish and Game Commissions, and from central agencies.

The system of numbering (standard) is described in the extract from the regulations in the Appendix.

Certificates of Number award must be kept on board at all times (sealed in plastic or in a glass jar on small, open boats; framed on a cruiser or cabin boat). They can be renewed for a small fee if lost or destroyed. They cannot be used for or appiled to any other boat save the one for which it was issued. Renewals (in some states automatic notification is mailed to the licensee) must be made *before* expiration of the old certificate to obtain the low renewal rate.

In the event that the boat was obtained by lien or inheritance, and a bill of sale cannot be shown, most states require that a clarifying statement, duly authenticated, accompany the application. In general, the numbering record is public record and is freely revealed to law enforcement agencies, the U. S. Government, police, etc. In general, remember:

- Documentary proof of title and ownership is *not* required by the federal regulations; it may be required by a state.
- If there is a change of address, or if a vessel is destroyed, transferred, or abandoned, the certificate must be surrendered within 15 days.
- A change of motor does not need to be reported.
- If the state in which the boat is principally used is changed, the old certificate must be surrendered, and application for a new number in the new state made within 90 days.
- Upon sale within the same state, the original number will be assigned to the new owner.
- False certification on the application can be followed by a voiding of the certificate and number.
- Each state will recognize the validity of a number from another state for a period of 90 days.

DOCUMENTATION

414 Documentation is another form of registering or licensing available to pleasure boats of five net tons or over. It gives certain advantages to the yachtsman, especially if sailing foreign:

1. The privilege of recording legal documents relating to the boat or her business, with federal officials at her home port, making for simplified and recorded relationships between owner, mortgagers, purchasers, and others.
2. Freedom from numbering requirements; although some states require documented yachts to be registered as well, but omit the requirement to *display* numbers.

3. Status, not necessarily legal, when sailing foreign and in foreign ports.

To be eligible for documenting, the owner and his captain (if he has one) must be American citizens and the boat must be of at least five net tons. (*See Paragraph* 736.) If owned by a corporation, the corporation must be 51% owned by American citizens. Since 1966, documentation has been the duty of the Coast Guard, which has issued a helpful booklet (free of charge from Coast Guard offices) called *"Yacht Admeasurement and Documentation,"* that gives all and detailed information, including application forms.

An original documentation starts with admeasurement, or measuring the vessel to determine its net tonnage. Note that net tonnage has nothing to do with actual weight (displacement) but is a measurement of the cargo-carrying capacity of the vessel—roughly the cubic tonnage less the cubic tonnage of machinery and tank spaces, crew quarters, wheel house, galley, etc. For the purposes of yacht measurement a simplified formula is used: length × beam × depth (L × B × D). Note that depth is *not* draft but an interior measurement akin to depth of hold. From these figures gross tonnage is obtained as follows:

For powerboats ⅔ of L × B × D/ 100 = Gross tons

For sailboats ½ of L × B × D/ 100 = Gross tons

To obtain net tonnage:

For powerboats ⅘th of gross tons = net tons

For sailboats ⁹⁄₁₀ths of gross tons = net tons

If there is no engine, the net tons will be the same as gross tons.

This certification is made by the owner, builder, or dealer and submitted with a "Master Carpenter's Certificate." This is simply a document (Form 1261) prepared and signed by the builder (called, quaintly, the "Master Carpenter" even if the boat is glass or steel) giving the boat a recorded start in life. This too can be handled by mail. It is usual for the builder or dealer to take care of the matter as part of the transaction.

Upon the award of the official document and its number, that boat forever after, until destroyed, lost, or abandoned, carries that and no other number. It must immediately be attached permanently to a structural part of the vessel. On a wooden boat, it must be carved ⅜″ deep into the main beam (forward of the hatch, on the main deck or other permanent, heavy beam, carling, lodging knee, etc.) in block letters as near 3″ high as the member will allow. It must read: NO. ———, NET ———, with no changes of any kind allowed; *exactly as above.*

Steel and aluminum boats are marked, on a main structural member, near deck level, by punch marks, drill holes, or a welding torch; then painted a contrasting color and wiped clean so that the legend stands out. Glass boats may carve the legend into a sheet of stock and epoxy it to the hull near the bow—inside, of course.

Further, all documented boats *must* carry, on the transom (or both sides of the stern if a double ender) the name of the boat and the *port*, either of hail or of registration. The letters *must* be plain block letters, at least 4″ high, and of a contrasting color. They can be painted, plastic, metal, or carved. They cannot be of fancy script or with ornamental flourishes and cannot be on a board and the board attached to the transom. The port of hail is where the owner lives, or where the boat is kept, or where she has business, or where she is registered. Note that the port of registry need not be the port of hail, but the port of hail and the port of registry must be within the same Coast Guard district.

Numbers may also be required (state registration) but need not be shown. If there is a power dinghy, used solely for ship-to-shore service, it carries the same document number as the parent vessel with the number 1 (one) preceding it, on both bows, and it need not be state licensed. Documented boats are given the same 90-day reciprocal courtesy period as other boats when visiting other ports and states.

Each year, about a month previous to the anniversary of the award date, the Coast Guard notifies the owner, by mail, that the document must be taken or sent into the district office for endorsement for another year. No charge. The document must be aboard at all times and shown upon demand to Coast Guard officers, officers of the Marine Inspection Services, and state inspectors or police. It is illegal for anyone to take, hold, or possess your document; it belongs to the boat. Under no circumstances surrender it to over-zealous police or sheriff's officers.

The transfer of ownership of a previously documented boat is simple: provide the Coast Guard documentation office with the original document and two copies of an official bill of sale (on forms provided by the office, free)—and the transfer is made.

A name change involves further official forms, publication in a local newspaper's "Personal" columns of the intention to change the name (giving the old and new names), and a brief waiting period for interested persons, or creditors, to note and react. There is a nominal charge as well as the cost of the newspaper insertion. Allow about two weeks. It can be done by mail.

There are other forms of documentation for vessels in various commercial enterprises and fisheries, but only two concern the pleasure boatman: the "yacht license" for vessels of five to 20 net tons and the "yacht enrollment and license" for vessels over 20 net tons. The foregoing procedures will obtain documentation in either class.

The streamlined procedure for documenting is not obligatory. At the option of the owner, a boat may be "formally measured" (in the former manner), in which case application in writing is made to the Office of Marine Inspection within your local district and an appointment made to meet and physically measure the vessel. There is no advantage save to have the record completely official, possibly for some future use or reason. A slight traveling charge is made if the officer must travel beyond a fixed mileage.

SAILING FOREIGN

415   Since many boats are documented because they sail to foreign ports, or mean to, the following notes are included:

Regulations for a pleasure yacht sailing foreign have been made relatively simple and consist merely of entering and clearing.

Permissions for entering and clearing are obtained from local customs officials. To clear, the ship's registry papers or documentation must be exhibited. Upon entering, the master or owner must report to the customs officials, meanwhile holding passengers and crew on board until the boat has been inspected. *All* boats must report to the immigration officials upon return to a United States port and no person landed until permission has been granted. If a paid crew is carried they must be reported on a Crew Manifest Form.

Note that:

A documented yacht need not clear an American port.

All yachts over 16 gross tons must enter customs when returning to an American port.

All yachts under 16 gross tons need enter only when they carry dutiable merchandise.

All yachts must clear an American port if there is dutiable merchandise aboard.

Any vessel of 5 gross tons or over not used for pleasure (i.e., not a yacht) must both enter and clear, whether documented or not.

A Bill of Health is not required when clearing an American port. However, to comply with vague and changing regulations of foreign ports, especially those of the West Indies, it is wisest to request a Bill of Health. It is furnished free by the U. S. Department of Health.

When a yacht of 16 gross tons or more enters, she is required to file a manifest at the customhouse and pay a fee of $1.50. Yachts over 100 tons must pay $2.50. Additional charges are made if entry is on a holiday or if between the hours of 5 p. m. and 8 a. m. The matter must be taken care of within 48 hours of arrival.

Yachts clearing for Canada must secure a cruising permit which provides free entry and clearing from May 1 to October 1. The permit is obtained free at the first Canadian port entered and must be surrendered upon clearing for home. A similar exchange arrangement prevails for Canadian yachts entering the United States. No entry fees are assessed unless the yacht enters by sea. Thus the Great Lake ports of both Canada and the United States are "free ports" for pleasure vessels.

Upon request the Secretary of Commerce will issue a sea letter to a yacht engaged in ocean racing or a special single voyage. Such a letter is good only for the voyage specified and must be surrendered upon entering.

Customs regulations for other neighboring foreign countries (such as those of the Caribbean, Central America, etc.) change from time to time and seem to be interpreted more or less by individual port authorities and it is therefore wise to make a careful check. If there seem to be no regulations at a foreign port, assume that there are and take every document possible with you. Talk with yachtsmen, fishermen, or shipping people at the last U. S. port; they have the "latest." Always carry in the flag locker the national ensign of the countries to be visited. Not only is this a courtesy—in some lands failure to fly the flag of that nation is punishable by fine and imprisonment.

Nearly all foreign countries require a complete crew list—often in several copies—when clearing. It is a good idea to have several such lists available in advance. It is also a good idea to list everyone aboard as "crew" rather than as "passengers," as some foreign officials then take the yacht to be a passenger-carrying vessel, and charge heavy fees accordingly. Passports should always be carried by all hands, and a number of foreign-going yachtsmen have found it convenient to carry a full-size photostat of the yacht document, which can be temporarily surrendered to especially insistent officials.

LICENSED OPERATORS AND CREW ON YACHTS

416 No motorboat under 300 tons, documented as a yacht and not carrying passengers or freight for hire, is required to carry any licensed officers or personnel.

Motorboats of 15 tons or more, which carry passengers or freight for hire, or yachts of 300 tons and over (seagoing), must carry the licensed personnel required by the certificate of inspection. Fishing vessels are exempt from this requirement.

Motorboats of 15 tons or over but less than 65′ in length that carry passengers or freight for hire may be operated by personnel licensed under the Motorboat Law. On boats of such dimensions engaged in trade (commercial vessels, such as tugs, cargo carriers, etc.), as well as on vessels of 300 tons or over, and which are subject to hull and machinery inspection, a licensed pilot, or engineer, or other officers may be required, and will be so noted on the certificate of inspection by the local Officer in Charge, Marine Inspection, United States Coast Guard. (Thus, a steam-propelled boat of 40′, though documented as a yacht, is subject to inspection and might possibly require licensed operators, depending upon its use.)

LICENSE TO OPERATE MOTORBOATS CARRYING PASSENGERS FOR HIRE

417 In general, a motorboat is carrying passengers for hire when, by *prearrangement*, some form of payment is made for the voyage or for use of the vessel. Payment may be in cash, gifts, services, or some other form.

Here are some opinions on typical situations:

These passengers are *not* being carried for hire:

1. Business associates, invited by the owner.
2. Passengers who take the owner ashore for entertainment, or food, or lodging, or who bring, as gifts, food, boat's gear, books, etc.
3. Passengers who have chartered the boat before it has been placed in commission and without a crew, and who intend to use the vessel for pleasure, with or without a crew.

These passengers *are* being carried for hire:

1. Passengers who, in accepting an invitation to cruise or voyage, agree *in advance* to pay all or a proportionate share of the running expenses or other expenses (such as gasoline, canal tolls, stores, etc.).
2. Passengers who have chartered a boat for their exclusive use, the charter having included a crew.

SERIAL NUMBER   ISSUE NUMBER

United States Coast Guard
License to
Operate or Navigate Motorboats Carrying Passengers for Hire

This is to certify that _____
has given satisfactory evidence to the undersigned Officer in Charge, Marine Inspection for the district of _____,
that he can safely be intrusted with the duties and responsibilities of operator of motorboats as defined in the Act of April 25, 1940, when carrying passengers for hire, on the navigable waters of the United States, and is hereby licensed to act as such operator for the term of five years from this date.

Given under my hand this _____ *day of* _____, 19__

OFFICER IN CHARGE, MARINE INSPECTION.

417 Motorboat Operator's License (Required only when carrying passengers for hire.)

For a license to carry passengers for hire, application is made to the Officer in Charge, Marine Inspection, United States Coast Guard. See next page for list of local depots.

The applicant (male or female) must be 18 years of age, must stand a physical examination by the United States Department of Health or a reputable private physician, and must pass an oral examination on boat handling and operating.

Physical examination consists of tests for color perception, blindness, impaired hearing, insanity, and certain degenerative diseases likely to affect the senses in the future.

Oral examination consists of questions relating to navigation laws, Rules of the Road, signals, elementary seamanship, safety on shipboard and at sea, and questions based on elementary first-aid knowledge. The examination is not difficult for the applicant familiar with boats and does not require a knowledge of extensive navigation, engineering, or maritime law.

Letters of character and ability are required.

Application is made on Form 866A. A license is issued, at no cost to the applicant, and is good for five years. It may be renewed during the 59th month, or within one year after expiration, upon showing proof of no major change in physical condition.

The license may be revoked upon the holder's being found guilty of endangering life, willfully violating laws or safety provisions, incompetency, unskillfulness, misbehavior, or negligence. When revoked, the license automatically expires.

Application offices of the United States Coast Guard are located as listed below:

District No.	Name	Depots or Offices at
1	Boston	Boston; Portland, Me.; and Providence, R. I.
2	St. Louis	St. Louis, Cairo, Dubuque, Cincinnati, Louisville, Memphis, Nashville, Pittsburgh, and Huntington, W. Va.
3	New York	New York, Albany, Philadelphia, and New London, Conn.
5	Norfolk	Norfolk, Baltimore, and Wilmington, N. C.
7	Miami	Miami, Charleston, Savannah, Tampa, Jacksonville, and San Juan, P. R.

8	New Orleans	New Orleans, Mobile, Port Arthur, Galveston, Corpus Christi, and Houston.
9	Cleveland	Cleveland, Buffalo, Oswego, Detroit, Duluth, Toledo, St. Ignace, Chicago, Milwaukee, and Ludington.
11	Long Beach	Long Beach, Calif.
12	San Francisco	San Francisco
13	Seattle	Seattle, Ketchikan Alaska and Portland
14	Hawaii	Honolulu
17	Alaska	Juneau

RECKLESS HANDLING OF BOATS

418   Reckless operation of boats—*all* boats, including boats of the United States Government, of states and cities, foreign vessels, fishermen, commercial vessels, tugs, liners—is controlled by both federal and local law. *Damage does not have to be shown.* If, in the opinion of an enforcement officer, a boat is being operated in a dangerous, reckless, or negligent manner, is proceeding at high or dangerous speeds, is overloaded, or her safety equipment is absent or in unusable condition, the owner may be stopped, arrested, hailed into court, or forbidden further operation of the boat.

Grossly negligent operation of a boat which endangers life, limb, or property is a *criminal* offense and can carry heavy fines as well as imprisonment. Coast Guard officers as well as local police and sheriff departments, all in marked boats and in uniform, do the policing. Both hail an offender into a local court, usually of the county in which the transgression occurs.

These are offenses coming under negligent or grossly negligent operation of a boat:

Overloading (persons or freight)

Reckless operation and speeding in a swimming area

Operating under the influence of alcohol or drugs

Speeding in dangerous waters or when passing other boats

Unsafe water skiing practices

Operating without proper lights at night

Riding bow, seatbacks, gunwale, or transom at dangerous speeds

Excessive wake

Continued use or refusal to terminate use of a boat after being ordered to correct an especially hazardous condition by an officer. These conditions might include: insufficient life-saving devices, insufficient fire-fighting devices, fuel leakages, fuel in bilges, improper ventilation system, improper backfire control. An officer may order the boat into her mooring or wharf and impound it until the offense is corrected. He may, if he deems it the proper course, tow the boat in; or order her anchored and take off her passengers.

Complaints against offending boats may be made, in writing, to the Coast Guard. Local police take care of offenders also if there is a formal complaint, especially if there are witnesses and/or damage (as to docks by excessive wakes). Operators of commercial vessels who offend are subject to revocation or suspension of their licenses.

REPORTING MARINE ACCIDENTS

419 In the case of collision, accident, or other casualty involving a motorboat or other vessel, the operator thereof, if the collision, accident, or other casualty results in death or injury to any person, or damage to property in excess of $100, shall file with the Secretary of the Department within which the Coast Guard is operating, unless such operator is required to file an accident report with the State a full description of the collision, accident, or other casualty, including such information as the Secretary may by regulation require.

A vessel is considered to be involved in a "boating accident" whenever the occurrence results in damage by or to the vessel or its equipment; in injury or loss of life to any person, or in the disappearance of any person from on board under circumstances which indicate the possibility of death or injury. A "boating accident" includes, but is not limited to, capsizing, collision, foundering, flooding, fire, explosion and the disappearance of a vessel other than by theft.

A report is required whenever a vessel is involved in a "boating accident" that results in any one or more of the following:

(1) Loss of life.
(2) Injury causing any person to remain incapacitated for a period in excess of 72 hours.
(3) Actual physical damage to property (including vessels) in excess of $100.

Whenever death results from a boating accident, a written report shall be submitted within 48 hours. For every other reportable boating accident, a written report shall be submitted within five (5) days after such accident.

The operator(s) of the boat(s) shall prepare and submit the written report(s) to the Coast Guard Officer in Charge, Marine Inspection, nearest to the place where such accident occurred or nearest to the port of first arrival after such accident, unless such operator is required to file an accident report with a state.

Every written report shall contain the following information:

(1) The numbers and/or names of vessels involved.
(2) The locality where the accident occurred.
(3) The time and date when the accident occurred.
(4) Weather and sea conditions at time of accident.
(5) The name, address, age, and boat-operating experience of the operator of the reporting vessel.
(6) The names and addresses of operators of other vessels involved.
(7) The names and addresses of the owners of vessels or property involved.
(8) The names and addresses of any person or persons injured or killed.
(9) The nature and extent of injury to any person or persons.
(10) A description of damage to property (including vessels) and estimated cost of repairs.
(11) A description of the accident (including opinions as to the causes).
(12) The length, propulsion, horsepower, fuel, and construction of the reporting vessel.
(13) Names and addresses of known witnesses.

The Coast Guard Form CG-3865 (Boating Accident Report) may be used for the written report. Some states have their own reporting form, available at police stations and sheriff's offices.

REGULATION OF MOTORBOATS DURING WARTIME

420 Under war conditions, a captain of the port may prescribe and enforce any special regulations as well as general wartime regulations of pleasure and other small boats.

In general, such regulations consist of registering the boat and every member of the crew with the port authorities and, under certain conditions, every passenger as well. Proof of citizenship must be shown, address, age, occupation, and purpose of being on the sea. Photographs and fingerprints are required.

Such regulations apply to any person or any boat on the water, including rowboats, sailboats, and motorboats.

Coastal waters are under the jurisdiction of the United States Coast Guard, and application for permits, etc., is made to that service.

Certain sea areas, rivers, or waters adjacent to maritime bases, factories, or wharves may be restricted or closed to boats. It may be required to report to guard vessels before entering or leaving such areas, or in passing through mine nets, booms, or mined areas, or between and past forts, etc.

Boats may be restricted to use during daylight hours, or to certain days, or weeks, or seasons.

SALE OF YACHTS TO FOREIGN COUNTRIES

421 A series of complex laws relate to the sale of pleasure craft to foreigners. Normally, the provisions are lenient but at this writing the United States is under a National Emergency (and has been since late 1950) and there are special restrictions, especially on documented boats, in force. In the case of large yachts, or fleets of recreational boats (such as might be sold by a manufacturer or dealer), the services of an admiralty lawyer are almost certainly required to steer the matter through the bureaus and services. A helpful pamphlet, "Transfer and Sale of U. S. Ships to Aliens," in available from the Maritime Administration, Department of Commerce, Washington, D. C. It is free.

⚓

CHAPTER V

LIGHTS, WHISTLE SIGNALS, RULES OF THE ROAD AND NAVIGATION LAWS

501 In laws going back to the early 19th Century, the term "federal waters" has been defined over and over. Federal waters (or waterways) are under federal jurisdiction and not that of any state bordering them or it. Coast Guard regulations specifically delineate them, control and patrol them, even though current regulations delegate some or all of the control and patrol powers back to the states under certain conditions.

Federal waters are: (1) those of the high seas along the coast, including all bodies of water (rivers, bays, sounds, etc.) that are connected to the coastal waters; (2) waters (rivers, lakes, ponds) that separate states or overlap state boundaries, even though not connected to coastal waters; (3) waters that can be navigated to or from a foreign country.

Note that the construction of dams or locks does not limit the federal authority—indeed might extend the authority. The federal jurisdiction need not be restrictive. It relates mostly to commerce under Interstate Commerce Regulations, navigational aids and rules by the Coast Guard, charting, channel improvement, and aid to safe navigating. A state may impose its own rules on such waters if not in conflict with federal rules. An example would be state speed limits in certain areas.

502 The jurisdiction of the United States extends into the coastal waters generally about 12 miles (200 in some matters concerned with fishing grounds), beyond which are international waters. Within the coastal waters controlled by the United States are certain boundaries, inshore of which are the Inland Waters. They are defined in the various *Coast Pilots* and other publications and are shown on coastal charts by a broken magenta line drawn from some natural or permanent mark to another. These marks are usually sea buoys, islands, lighthouses and lightships, or reefs. Inside these lines (that is, toward the land) are Inland Waters. In addition there are continental waters, known for jurisdiction's sake as the Great Lakes and the Western Rivers.

Because each of these four areas bears incomplete relationships to the other in terms of geography, physical descriptions, and navigation, as well as in terms of the types of vessels usually found there and their special uses, they cannot be regulated under a uniform set of pilot or navigation rules. Each has its own problems and its own rules, though all have their basis in a common set of regulations known as the International Rules of the Road. And so we have, also, specialized rules known as the Inland Rules, the Great Lakes Rules, and the Western Rivers Rules. The last two are so similar that efforts are being made to combine them into a single set of rules. These may become effective even before publication of this edition and, if so, will be noted in the daily *Federal Register*, to be found in most major public libraries.

At the time of writing, the Coast Guard has hopes of standardizing the various Rules of the Road so that they will correspond in nearly all cases with the newly-effective International Rules. It is only fair to say, however, that such a hope has been expressed in the past without any great result.

In one area of the Rules, the owner of a pleasure boat under 65′ can avail himself of an overriding system that supersedes all the others: In the case of running lights, the International Rule pattern is acceptable on *any* waters. It is also a pattern that is, in the opinion of many, best suited to the shapes of most pleasure craft, and is thus the type of light system normally installed by manufacturers. On the other hand, a pleasure boat skipper ought to be able at least to recognize the more common types of running lights he is likely to see at night in his boating area, whether aboard yachts or commercial craft.

Remember: the Motor Boat Act of 1940 and the Federal Boat Safety Act of 1971 supersede all other rules wherever they conflict in cases involving motorboats. It is pleasant, but not necessary, to understand and know the complex rules and regulations of the other systems, especially since two of them are about to be combined and somewhat changed. It would seem far more practical for the yachtsman to thoroughly understand his own regulations, to use and be guided by them, than to half-know all the others. It is highly unlikely that he will be called upon to apply the Rules of the Road to any vessel but another yacht and, should he be, his basic rules are the same as the basic rules of the other systems, so he has nothing to worry about. It is improbable that a pleasure boatman will ever be called upon to lash up six barges in tow and properly light them; or that he will be moored alongside of a submerged wreck and have to sound proper fog signals; or that he will be mackerel fishing, with holds empty, and, drifting without power, have to decide which he is: a steam vessel or a sailing craft over 40 gross tons out of control?

For those who wish to investigate the matter further, the Coast Guard has for distribution three free booklets covering Inland and International Water Rules of the Road (CG-169), the Great Lakes Rules of the Road (CG-172), and the Western Rivers Rules of the Road (CG-184). These are available from the U. S. Coast Guard Marine Inspection offices in principal ports and cities or from The Commandant (CHS), U. S. Coast Guard, Washington, D. C. 20226.

The rules here given are those authorized by the MBA/1940 or by the International Rules, with appropriate additions or exceptions as they may apply to the pleasure yacht.

LIGHT REQUIREMENTS

503   The light requirements for vessels under 65′ have been changed recently and the old bugaboo of identifying a sailing vessel has been partially obviated. Lights are no longer specified by lens area but, rather, by visibility. (*See also Chapter IV*)

Lights are required, operating and visible as specified, between sunrise and sunset when *underway*. Stopped vessels or vessels at anchor (if not fishing) must display anchor lights except those under 65′ anchored or moored in a "special anchor area." Such areas are indicated on local charts and, in general, whether or not marked,

Option #1   OR   Option #2

Power

RED

GREEN

OPTIONAL IN
INTERNATIONAL
WATERS ONLY

GREEN
8 PTS.

RED
8 PTS.

WHITE
4 PTS.

ON WORKING FISHING
VESSELS ONLY (TRAWLERS)
AT MASTHEAD.

Sail and power

503A International Rules These lights are required on International waters and the high seas and are legal as well on the Great Lakes, Inland waters and Western rivers. Powerboats between 40' and 65' in length *must* take the second option and the stern (12 point) light must be visible for five miles. Under sail alone on the Great Lakes, a stern light is not required, but a white light must be shown when being overtaken.

| 32 Pts. White
Vis. 2 mi. | 20 Pts. White
Vis. 2 mi. | 12 Pts. White
Vis. 2 mi. | 20 Pts. R&G
Vis. 1 mi.
(Combination) | 10 Pts. R&G
Vis. 1 mi.
(Separate) |

0'–26' LOA   26'–65' LOA

Power alone

Sail and power

Sail alone

503B Inland rules These lights are legal only on inland waters, the
Great Lakes and Western rivers. They must be shown by inboards,
outboards, auxiliaries and straight sailboats. They apply to powerboats under 40 gross tons and sailing vessels under 20 gross tons. An
auxiliary sailboat here is classed as a powerboat.

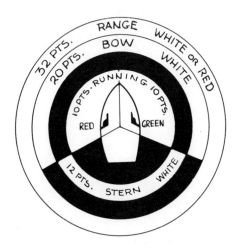

503C Characteristics, color, and range of navigation lights (except steam trawlers which carry combination masthead lights, red 8 pts. on port, white 4 pts. ahead and green 8 pts on starboard.

are areas in which numerous other vessels are anchored or, especially, moored. Such areas are likely to be off yacht clubs and marinas, near canal or waterway entrances, and in "inner" local natural harbors normally associated with small craft.

Outboard powered craft are required to conform to these laws.

A manually propelled craft, such as a canoe, rowboat, or a small sailing craft under oars in a calm, must have a white light ready to show an approaching boat in time to prevent collision. This light need be of no specified visibility and can be a lantern, flashlight or, in emergency, a white flare. Such a light need be displayed only "temporarily"; i.e., in time to avoid collision.

While it is unusual for an inspecting officer to test for himself the actual visibility of a light, this may be required in special cases. However, if your lights have a lens, either a Fresnel type (originally developed for oil flames) or a modern "wing tip" single or bull's-eye-type lens and an electric lamp of not less than 15 candle-power behind it, the light will "pass" as legal. Anchor lights, from a practical viewpoint, need not meet the visibility requirements when in areas exempt from display of an anchor light. Usually, cruising men show, in an anchoring area, a lantern hung from a forestay, an electric portable device designed for another light service, or the range light only of standard navigation lights.

A handy reference for quickly identifying the lights of a vessel at night at sea is found in the following light identification tables.

Color of light is indicated by letter within light: R—red; G—green; W—white

 32 point range light

 20 point bow light

 12 point stern light

 10 point red or green running light (this is not a combination light but signifies that either color may be seen)

 10 point red (port) running light

 10 point green (starboard) running light

 heading of vessel when observed

NOTE: *A sailboat, under power alone, or under power and sail, displays the lights of a power boat.*

ONE LIGHT

 Boat under 150' at anchor

 Row or paddle boat (lantern or flash light)

 Sailboat or powerboat when overtaking

 Sailboat, port side, forward of your beam

 Sailboat, starboard side, forward of your beam

TWO LIGHTS

 Sailboat, head on

 Powerboat under 26 feet, or boat under sail

 Ocean-going vessel or yacht over 150 feet at anchor

 Pilot vessel anchored on station

Vessel not under control

THREE LIGHTS

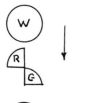

Powerboat, under 26 feet, head on

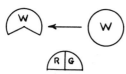

Powerboat, over 26 feet to 65 feet

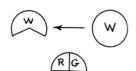

Sound or river steamer under Inland Rules

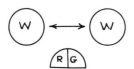

Ferry boat (may have line identification light amidships)

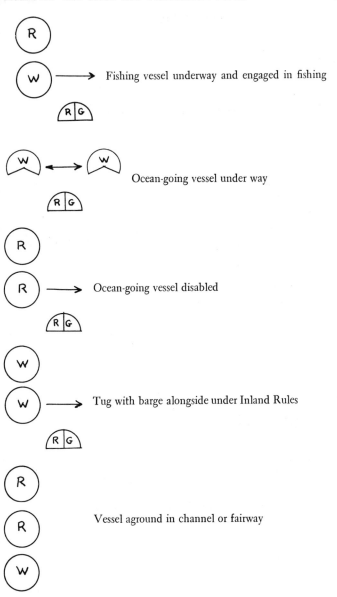

Fishing vessel underway and engaged in fishing

Ocean-going vessel under way

Ocean-going vessel disabled

Tug with barge alongside under Inland Rules

Vessel aground in channel or fairway

FOUR LIGHTS

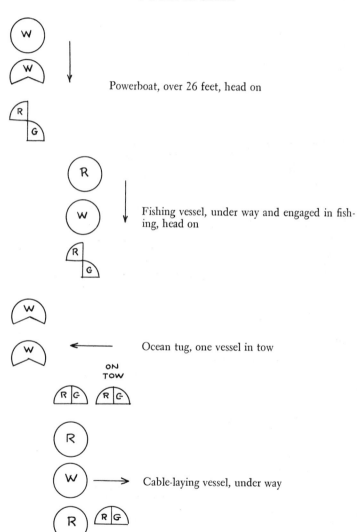

Powerboat, over 26 feet, head on

Fishing vessel, under way and engaged in fishing, head on

Ocean tug, one vessel in tow

ON TOW

Cable-laying vessel, under way

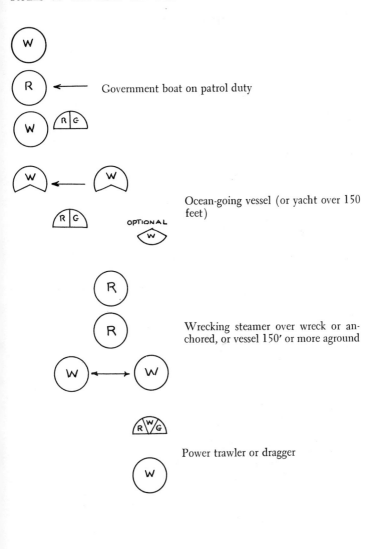

Government boat on patrol duty

Ocean-going vessel (or yacht over 150 feet)

OPTIONAL

Wrecking steamer over wreck or anchored, or vessel 150' or more aground

Power trawler or dragger

FIVE LIGHTS

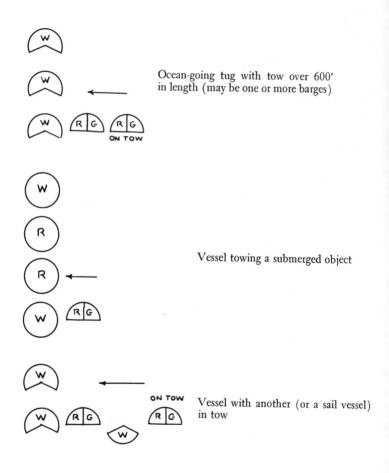

Ocean-going tug with tow over 600'
in length (may be one or more barges)

Vessel towing a submerged object

Vessel with another (or a sail vessel)
in tow

SIX LIGHTS

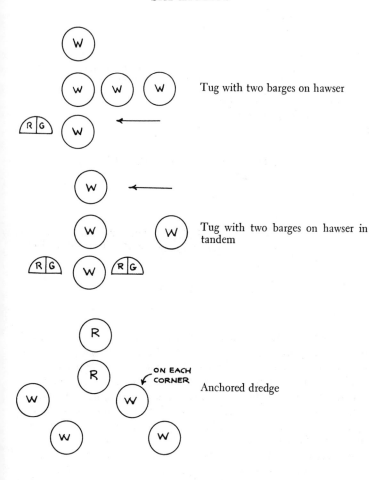

Tug with two barges on hawser

Tug with two barges on hawser in tandem

Anchored dredge

SEVEN LIGHTS

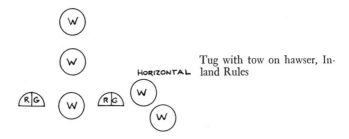

Tug with tow on hawser, Inland Rules

MORE THAN SEVEN LIGHTS

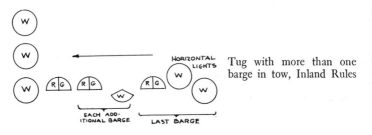

Tug with more than one barge in tow, Inland Rules

Count the number of lights sighted and deduct one if both colored running lights are seen. Then refer to the table showing all the possible vessels and conditions under which that number of lights might be seen. If but one colored running light is seen, count the actual number of lights, and (making no deductions) refer to the correct table. Example: Sighted one white light and port running light = two lights. The possibilities will be found in the table entitled *Two Lights*.

As nearly as possible, the lights have been shown in their proper relation to each other and to their height above deck. The arrow indicates the bow (or direction headed). It must be remembered that either a red or green running light may be seen, in which case the heading will be reversed. Lights of vessels being overtaken have not been shown, as few such combination can be identified until further lights are sighted from a position abeam.

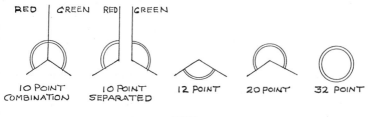

503D

RIGHT OF WAY AND WHISTLE SIGNALS

504 The vessel required to hold her course and speed is known as the "Stand-on Vessel" under International Rules, the "Privileged vessel" under other systems. The vessel required to take action to avoid collision is the "Give-way" (International) or "Burdened" (other) vessel.

A short blast (on the whistle) is from one to three seconds duration.

A long blast is from eight to ten seconds duration, but not less than eight.

A prolonged blast is a blast between short and long, or about five to six seconds in duration.

The danger signal is four or more rapid short blasts; used only when signals of another vessel are misunderstood or illegal or considered dangerous to either or both vessels.

The indication that the signaling vessel is in full reverse is three blasts of about two seconds each.

To clear up indecision and prevent accidents, these (and other) signals are in use to signify the intentions of vessels meeting on a possible collision course. When the possibility of a collision arises and common sense indicates that each of the vessels involved would be in a safer position if he knew what the other intended to make as a course, signals (or communications) are indicated. The Rules of the Road, to be sure, predetermine—by granting "right-of-way" to certain boats in certain situations that are likely to result in collision—the action that *must* be taken by the burdened vessel. The other vessel *must* maintain course and speed—legally, both have obligations.

It is prudent seamanship to take relative bearings when approaching another vessel and to alter course, or make signals, if there exists even a slight chance of collision. Make course changes in a firm, even exaggerated manner, so that your intentions are clearly recognized. Assume that the other boat (if a yacht or small outboard or sailing craft) does *not* know or understand the Rules of the Road; you will be right more often than wrong, we fear!

These are the whistle signals:

INTERNATIONAL RULES

One short blast—I am directing my course to starboard.

Two short blasts—I am directing my course to port.

Three short blasts—My engines are going full astern.

(*Note:* These are the only whistle signals permitted under International Rules.)

PILOT OR INLAND RULES

One short blast:

1. When changing course to starboard
2. When maintaining a course to starboard of a passing vessel
3. When on a crossing course, privileged vessel so signifies she will hold her course and speed
4. When on a crossing course, burdened vessel so signifies she will give way to the privileged vessel
5. When overtaking vessel desires to pass another on the overtaken vessel's starboard side
6. When overtaken vessel grants request to 5

Two short blasts:

1. When changing course to port
2. When maintaining course to port of a passing vessel
3. When overtaking vessel desires to pass another on the overtaken vessel's port side.
4. When overtaken vessels grants request to 3

Three short blasts:

My engines are going full astern.

Danger signal (four or more short blasts):

1. When the course or intention of another vessel is not understood
2. When answering the request of an overtaking vessel to pass in the negative (As soon as the situation preventing passing has cleared, the usual overtaking signals are made, one or two short blasts, depending upon the passing side of the original request.)
3. When immediate compliance with a whistle-signal request is impossible for any reason

Warning signal (one long blast):

1. When leaving a dock or berth
2. When visibility, because of bends, high banks, or other obstructions, has been reduced to one-half mile or less (The signal must be answered before passing signals are exchanged.)

GREAT LAKES RULES

Rules for the Great Lakes are exactly the same as Inland Rules. Unofficially, three short blasts, by usage, is recognized as a request for a passing vessel to slow down; also to indicate sternway. The danger signal is sometimes used to indicate that the course which another vessel has signified is not considered safe.

When situations develop that contain the elements of collision, the Rules of the Road usually prescribe the solution to the situation by recognizing a privileged vessel, or stand-on which must maintain course and speed, and a burdened or give-way vessel, requiring that she stay clear. They may or may not exchange whistle signals, but whether they do or not, such signals cannot change the resolution of the situation; indeed, if not confirming that maneuvers are being taken to solve the situation, such signals are illegal. Note that sailboats need not acknowledge a signal for the simple reason that they have the right-of-way over a powerboat under most conditions. (This can be carried too far, of course, and a privileged vessel—sailboat—should not demand her right in a situation involving a vessel of great tonnage, which cannot stop or maneuver as can a small yacht; or from an unwieldy tow, or a dredge.) A sailing vessel has no rights when overtaking a power boat, nor can she exercise any rights over a power boat if she drives the power boat into danger (such as into shallow water beyond a narrow channel).

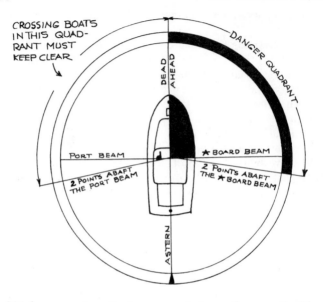

504 In a crossing situation a vessel in another vessel's "danger quadrant" has the right of way over that craft. She will show a red light at night and the burdened vessel's green light will be visible to her, signifying her right to cross. Similarly, the quadrant opposite the danger quadrant will warn off crossing boats since, then, this boat has the right of way and her red light at night will so signify to a crossing boat.

Here are the three "meeting" situations which the rules solve by proscribed action of the vessels concerned (*See Figures 504A–E*).

Head-on. This exists when two power-driven boats are meeting head-on or nearly so. Neither is a privileged vessel and neither therefore has any rights. Both must alter course to starboard and pass with a safe distance between. The legal definition of meeting is that approaching vessels shall be within one point (11¼°) of either bow; i.e., bearing one point on either bow (*See Figure 1418*). At night, a head-on situation exists if you can see both side lights of the other vessel.

504A First situation Here the two colored lights visible to each will indicate their direct approach "head and head" toward each other. In this situation it is a standing rule that both shall direct their courses to starboard and pass on the port side of each other, each having previously given one blast of the whistle.

Crossing. When two vessels are crossing so as to involve danger of collision, the vessel with the other on her starboard side must keep out of way and the "other" must maintain her course and speed until the situation ceases to exist.

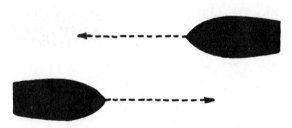

504B Second situation In this situation the red light only will be visible to each, the screens preventing the green lights from being seen. Both vessels are evidently passing to port of each other, which is rulable in this situation, each pilot having previously signified his intention by one blast of the whistle.

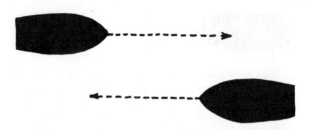

504C Third situation In this situation the green light only will be visible to each, the screens preventing the red light from being seen. They are, therefore, passing to starboard of each other, which is rulable in this situation, each pilot having previously signified his intention by two blasts of the whistle.

504D Fourth situation In this situation one powerboat is overtaking another powerboat from some point within the angle of two points abaft the beam of the overtaken powerboat. The overtaking powerboat may pass on the starboard or port side of the powerboat ahead after the necessary signals for passing have been given with the assent of the overtaken powerboat.

Overtaking. When any vessel comes up from behind a slower vessel and begins to catch up with her, she is the *overtaking* vessel and, as such, is the burdened vessel. She must keep clear of the overtaken (slower) vessel. Moreover, this relationship remains static for the duration of the encounter and does not change as (for example) when the overtaking vessel comes into the danger zone of the overtaken vessel and might be construed to now be a privileged crossing vessel.

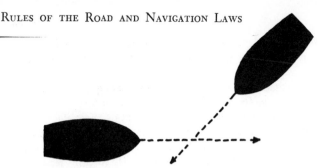

504E Fifth situation In this situation two powerboats are approaching each other at right angles or obliquely *in such manner as to involve risk of collision*, other than where one powerboat is overtaking another. The powerboat which has the other on her own *port* side shall hold course and speed, and the other shall keep clear by crossing astern of the powerboat that is holding course and speed, or, if necessary to do so, shall slacken her speed, stop, or reverse.

Under the new International Rules, there are several written clarifications of common-sense situations that have long been recognized by responsible seamen.

A vessel proceeding along the course of a narrow channel or fairway shall keep as near to the outer limit of the channel that lies on her starboard side as is safe and practicable.

A vessel of less than 20 meters in length (approximately 65′) or a sailing vessel shall not impede the passage of a vessel that can safely navigate only within a narrow channel.

A vessel shall not cross a narrow channel or fairway if such crossing impedes the passage of a vessel that can safely navigate only within such channel.

A power-driven vessel underway shall keep out of the way of:

1. a vessel not under command,
2. a vessel restricted in her ability to maneuver,
3. a vessel engaged in commercial fishing,
4. a sailing vessel.

A sailing vessel underway shall keep out of the way of the first three types of vessels listed above.

A vessel engaged in fishing when underway shall, as far as possible, keep out of the way of the first two types of vessels listed above.

Whistle signals here are vital. The overtaking vessel must propose a passing side (by signals; one blast to starboard or two blasts to port) and the overtaken vessel must accept or reject the proposal. If the proposal is acceptable, the overtaken vessel must immediately approve and consent by giving the same signal in return, whereupon the overtaking vessel may pass with care. If, for any reason, the proposal is considered dangerous by the overtaken vessel, she must give the danger signal (four blasts on the whistle) whereupon the overtaking vessel must surrender all attempts to pass until both are clear of the danger. She may again, when it appears clear, request passage through.

If an overtaking vessel fails to give a passing signal, she is obliged to stop and fall back if she receives the danger signal from the privileged vessel.

PASSING IN NARROW WATERWAYS

505 It is this passing situation that has become such a danger on narrow waterways, particularly on the Intracoastal Waterway from the Chesapeake Bay area to southern Florida. Much of the danger derives from pure stupidity, recklessness, and lack of common courtesy. Both vessels are often at fault. Here is the way for a fast vessel to pass a slower one, particularly a sailboat or small auxiliary:

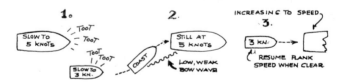

505 How to pass and be passed with safety and courtesy in a narrow waterway or canal. The key is to pass slowly, without excessive bow waves and the to-be-passed vessel slowed or stopped to permit this. It takes *two* courteous, prudent skippers and is a *joint maneuver.*

The usual passing signals should be given and approved. With the passing side determined, the overtaken (slow) boat drops down to about three knots and inches to the side away from the passing side, being careful not to get out of the deep water (for she will soon have to meet a fairly heavy bow wave and might be set on the mud). The overtaking vessel must also slow down, get off her plane if she is on one, and pass the slower boat at a speed not more than three knots faster than the slow boat (or about five knots or less). There *will be a bow wave*; it *can't* be avoided; it can only be reduced. Immediately the slow boat comes hard over to a crossing course, timed to pass into the faster boat's wake, and when she is over the slight pitch of the bow wave, she again turns hard over and into the wake. The overtaking boat then slowly comes up to speed, being careful not to create a dangerous wake, and when well clear (say 100 yards ahead) puts the throttle in the corner and continues. The slow boat resumes speed as soon as practicable.

This maneuver is gradually becoming standard, though covered by no Rules of the Road in specifics. If all hands understand the maneuver and play their proper, considerate role in it, there will be many more happy slow boat owners and possibly many fewer damage suits against the thoughtless and stupid.

Delivery captains complain about the loss of time (for they are paid by the trip) and don't have to pay for damage, but they are not the worst offenders by any means. These chaps, many of them superb seamen, are apt to come on a slow boat at a lively and alarming rate . . . but most of them cut back only 50 or so feet from the boat to be passed, after proper signals, and pass slowly. *But they cannot do the job alone.* They must be given the *opportunity* to pass slowly, without a dangerous bow wave, and they can do this only if the slow boat does its part—namely, slows down also so that the relative speed of the two boats does not produce the dangerous bow wave that everybody wants to avoid.

506 General Prudential Rule. It is recognized that situations might arise (as, for example, several boats proceeding on collision courses in a busy harbor) in which no involved vessel can sort out the rights and duties of each. In such a case there is almost certain to be the element of "immediate danger," and if that is present, it is legal—and applauded—to depart from the rules. This might take the form of the privileged vessel *not* maintaining speed and course or the burdened vessel stopping or backing. The key is the interpretation of "immediate danger." The courts have held that the rules cannot be abandoned when *perceptible* danger exists (for that is what the rules are designed to protect against); but only when *imminent or immediate danger exists* that can be avoided only by *imperative* action. It is a fine point and one seldom raised in yachting situations.

507   Right of Way of Vessels Engaged in Fishing. Other vessels must keep clear of vessels engaged in commercial fishing, including lobstermen, crabbers, and seiners. This is construed to mean keeping clear of nets (as towed by shrimpers, for example) or of toggles on a warp (as a lobsterman resetting his trap or trawl). In a moot status is the sport fisherman of the "for hire" type, who trolls baits; is he commercial or pleasure? Give him sea room and don't cross his lines is the practical and courteous answer, just as you would keep clear of a towed water skier or a towed dinghy.

508   When leaving a berth, especially a blind one, or when rounding a sharp river bend or pierhead, give one long blast of the whistle (10–12 seconds). The signal is precautionary only and gives no one any rights. Rights derive only after both vessels in a situation are *fully in sight.* The normal rules apply.

509   The signal to open a drawbridge (though not part of the Rules of the Road) is usually three short blasts. If possible, check the *Coast Pilot,* which lists all bridge signals. The bridge tender usually replies with a three-blast signal, if conditions permit him to open at once, or a four-blast signal, if he must delay (as might occur at a railroad bridge with a train in the block and expected shortly). Bridge tenders usually make a signal when closing the draw as well.

The signal to open a lock, again, is specified only in the Inland Rules. Commonly, the three-blast signal is given. However, the only legal signal, and the one used exclusively by commercial craft, is two longs and two shorts (— — · ·). It is acknowledged by light signal rather than sound: red—stop; amber—caution; green—proceed.

510   Whistle salutes between yachts are frowned upon, though illegal only in the sense that the rules forbid unnecessary sounding of the whistle. (The only correct salute is to dip the yacht ensign.)

511   Rules for the Great Lakes and Western rivers differ only slightly from the foregoing. Here are the main points of difference:

1. Vessels moving *with* the current (downstream) have the right-of-way (as through a bridge or cut or in a narrow channel).
2. There is no three-blast signal for backing; only the five-or-more danger signal is legal.
3. While some commercial vessels must have a range light co-ordinated with the whistle, this is not required under the MBA/1940, and yachts up to 65′ require a whistle only.

There are, of course, many other differences of no concern to yachtsmen. The departure from International and Inland rules is not great and the slight differences between Great Lakes and Western Rivers rules are gradually being reduced.

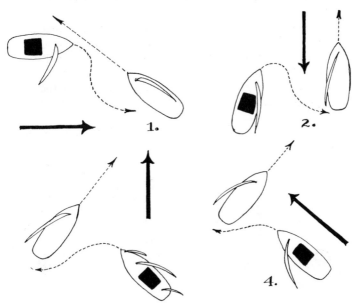

512 The right-of-way situations under the Inland Rules for two sailing vessels. The boat with the cabin (black square) is the burdened boat and must keep clear, while the other boat maintains course. The wind direction is noted by the heavy black arrow.

512 Inland Rules (the ones most in use in sailing circles) describe the five situations between two sailing vessels as follows:

When subject vessels are approaching one another so as to involve risk of collision, one must keep out of the way of the other in accordance with the following conditions:

1. A vessel that is running free must keep out of the way of a a vessel that is running close-hauled. (The one running free is the burdened vessel.)

2. A vessel that is close-hauled on the port tack must keep out of the way of a vessel that is close-hauled on the starboard tack. (The vessel on the port tack is the burdened vessel.)

3. When both vessels are running free with the wind on different sides, the vessel with the wind on her port side must keep out of the way of the other. (The vessel with the wind on the port side is the burdened vessel.)

4. When both vessels are running free with the wind on the same side, the vessel that is to windward must keep out of the way of the vessel that is to leeward. (The windward vessel is the burdened vessel.)

5. A vessel that has the wind aft must keep out of the way of the other vessel. (The vessel before the wind is the burdened vessel.)

Note that both vessels must be *under sail alone,* even though one or both may have auxiliary power.

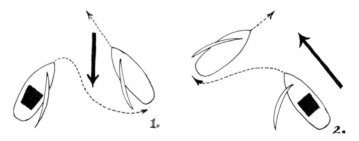

513 The right-of-way situations under the International Rules for two sailing vessels. The boat with the cabin (black square) is the give-way boat and must keep clear. The wind direction is shown by the heavy black arrow.

513   International Rules differ somewhat; they are brief and to the point, again remembering that in International Rules, give-way equals burdened; stand-on equals privileged:

1. When each has the wind on a different side, the vessel which has the wind on the port side must keep out of the way of the other. (The vessel with the wind on the port side is the give-way vessel.)

2. When both have the wind on the same side, the vessel which is to windward must keep out of the way of the vessel to leeward. (The vessel to windward is the give-way vessel.)

Note that the International Rule does not have a running free/close-hauled situation.

514   Racing rules are many and complex, their basis in these Rules of the Road, and must be studied as they pertain to each class. Boats racing under sail are, by courtesy, or by temporary ruling by the Coast Guard, exempt from normal sailboat rules and operate only under their own class rules—vis-à-vis other racers. Boats not racing should keep clear of a racing fleet and try to avoid courses within their racing buoys. Racing yachts occasionally carry, as identification, a numbered flag or device, most commonly the checkerboard "N" flag of the International Code of Signals.

FOG SIGNALS

515   Fog signals are given by day or night in thick weather of any kind (snow, heavy mist, fog, or heavy rain, or smoke). Signals are made on the whistle, foghorn, or bell as provided in the following regulations.

INTERNATIONAL RULES

Equipment—Power vessels are required to have a steam whistle (operated by steam or air) or a mechanical foghorn and bell. Sailing vessels must have a foghorn and bell. Boats under 20 tons require only equipment to make an efficient sound signal.

Signals underway:

Power vessels—One prolonged blast at intervals of not more than two minutes. (If underway but stopped—two prolonged blasts at intervals of not more than two minutes.)

A vessel not under command, one restricted in her ability to maneuver, a vessel engaged in fishing, and a vessel engaged in towing
or pushing another shall sound, at two-minute intervals, three blasts
in succession—one prolonged followed by two short.

Sailing vessels—One prolonged, followed by two short blasts, at
two-minute intervals.

Signals at anchor:

All vessels—Bell rung rapidly for five seconds at intervals of not
more than one minute.

Signals for towed or towing vessels:

One prolonged blast followed by three short blasts at intervals of
not more than two minutes.

Boats under 12 meters (40′)

Exempt from above rules but must make an efficient sound signal
at intervals of not more than one minute.

INLAND RULES

Equipment—Power vessels must have a whistle (operated by
steam or air) or mechanical foghorn and bell. Sailing vessels of 20
tons or over must have a bell and foghorn. Rafts, current boats, etc.,
must have a foghorn or the equivalent.

Signals underway:

Power vessels—One prolonged blast at intervals of not more than
one minute (on whistle).

Sailing vessels—Starboard tack—one blast. Port tack—two blasts.
Wind abaft the beam—three blasts. Intervals in each case of not
more than one minute (on foghorn).

Signals at anchor (or Not Underway):

All vessels—Bell rung rapidly for five seconds at intervals of not
more than one minute.

Signals for towed or towing vessels:

One prolonged whistle blast followed by two short blasts at intervals of not more than one minute. (Towed vessels make the same
signal but on a foghorn.)

Rafts, current boats, rowboats, etc.:
One blast of the foghorn, or equivalent, at intervals of not more than one minute.

GREAT LAKES RULES

Equipment—Power vessels must have a whistle, audible two miles, and a bell. Sailing vessels must have a foghorn and bell. Boats under 10 tons may have a foghorn or the equivalent. Tugs towing rafts must have a screeching or Modoc whistle.

Signals underway:
Power vessels—Three blasts at intervals of not more than one minute (except when towing)
Sailing vessels—Starboard tack—one blast. Port tack—two blasts. Wind abaft the beam—three blasts. Interval in each case of not more than one minute.

Signals at anchor:
All vessels—Bell rung rapidly for from three to five seconds at intervals of not more than two minutes. Grounded or stranded vessels near a channel or fairway make the same signal.

Signals for towed or towing vessels:
A vessel towed makes four bells on the fog bell—two short blasts, then two more short blasts, at intervals of one minute.
A steamer towing a raft must sound the screeching or Modoc whistle for from three to five seconds at intervals of not more than one minute.

Boats under 10 tons—fishing boats, current and rowboats, etc.:
One signal at intervals of not more than one minute on the foghorn or other sound apparatus.

Equipment—Power vessels must have a whistle; sailing vessels must have a foghorn; both have fog bells.

Signals underway:
Power vessel—One blast at intervals of not more than one minute.
Sailing vessel—One blast at intervals of not more than one minute.

Signals at anchor:

All vessels—Bell rung at intervals of not more than two minutes.

Signals for towing vessel:

Towboat sounds three blasts at intervals of not more than one minute.

Fishing boats, barges, current and rowboats, etc.:

When anchored or underway (but not anchored in port) they must sound the foghorn or equivalent (equal to steam whistle), at intervals of not more than two minutes.

⚓

CHAPTER VI

GROUND TACKLE

THE SAILOR throughout the ages has ever considered the anchor his staunch shipmate, ready to lower away and protect him when ill luck has driven his ship into a position of danger. In the symbolism of many civilizations, the anchor has appeared as the emblem of hope. No matter how bad conditions may appear, if the anchor can be firmly imbedded in something that will prevent matters from getting worse, there always is hope, and all is not lost.

Anchors were known to all maritime nations even in ancient times, and many of them were exactly like present-day anchors in principle. Seemingly, the old-fashioned anchor is the ultimate in a mechanism used to attach a ship to the ground beneath her.

601 The traditional old-fashioned, or Herreshoff, anchor has disappeared from the American yachting scene; indeed the demand has been so small that American foundries have discontinued the model.* The type had its faults but lack of holding power was not one of them. It has been largely replaced in yachting circles by anchors that stow more easily, are less prone to fouling (as the current reverses or the tide turns), and offer less problems in on-board handling.

While a new "old fashioned" anchor is difficult to buy today, some older vessels may be equipped with the type and so these comments are included for such owners. The type has two great faults:

---

* This kind of anchor is now available only from some Canadian yacht chandlers or from Nova Scotia foundries.

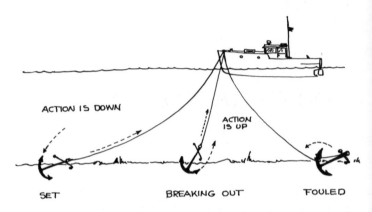

601A The action of an anchor with a stock under various conditions, old-fashioned type shown.

(1) It is subject to fouling, that is, picking up the anchor cable as the boat "walks" during anchored periods. There is no way to prevent this, short of heaving the cable up short after every 180° shift in the boat's heading, and being sure the cable leads directly to the ring (or shackle), and to pay the cable out as the boat sags against it. (2) It does not lend itself readily to stowing, although later design has removed the big objection of the original fixed stock, or cross arm; by removing a metal key it can be folded parallel to the shank. It is stowed on deck on three chocks or pads of wood or metal, folded, and lashed down. It is sometimes carried slung from the bowsprit, hanging from the roller chock by the cable and secured to the bobstay by a lashing. It would never be so carried at sea.

The stockless anchor (or patent anchor) is a type of anchor that has no stock and is therefore free of the danger of fouling the cable. Its action, however, is quite different from the old-fashioned anchor, and it has but 60% of the holding power.

Both flukes are buried when properly set. To keep them so, a longer cable (more scope) is required than for anchors of the old-fashioned type. A dragging stockless anchor will capsize if one fluke hits a stone or boulder in the mud. If it is on too short a cable, and

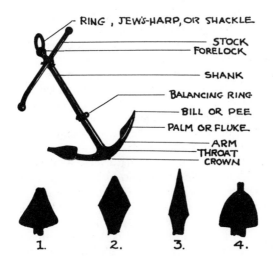

RING, JEW'S-HARP, OR SHACKLE
STOCK
FORELOCK
SHANK
BALANCING RING
BILL OR PEE
PALM OR FLUKE
ARM
THROAT
CROWN

1. Spade palm—good general holding type except in rock
2. Herreshoff palm—good general holding
3. Sand palm—for sand and some types of weed (usually a light anchor)
4. Ship palm—general holding including rock (note the prominent bill)

601B Parts of the old-fashioned anchor

a sea is running, it will step itself out as the yawing ship brings stress on first one fluke and then the other.

The grapnel is another stockless anchor of limited usefulness. This type of anchor makes an excellent rock and coral anchor, its only recommendation as a service anchor. A trip (*Figure 604*) is usually required to free it.

However, the grapnel makes a good dinghy or tender anchor and will hold reasonably well in weed, sand, and gravel. Another virtue of the grapnel is its effectiveness as a retrieving hook. Dragged on a short warp it can be used to pick up lost cables or to trip a fouled or bound anchor.

Never leave a grapnel unattended. There is no type which fouls its cable more readily or completely.

603 Other types. The demands of seaplanes for ultra-light ground tackle brought forth several types of lightweight anchors which have found their way to use on small boats. They are often referred to as "patent" anchors because they are—or were at some time—protected by patent. In general, these make use of the principle of the old-fashioned anchor in that they all have stocks in one form or another. Improved flukes give extra "bite" and digging-in powers, and weight can therefore be sacrificed.

In the best of these types, the makers claim holding power at the rate of 30 to 1 over other types.

Most of these "patent" types have the advantage of very light weight (a 12-pound anchor is alleged to do the work of a 100-pound common anchor), and they fold down for easy stowing. It is this light weight that appears to be a great disadvantage, for these "hooks" rather readily slide over oyster banks, hardpan, or shallow silt on clay. In kelp or heavy weed bottoms they sometimes fail to reach the bottom. However, once bedded they have adequate fluke area to hold well. Efficiency is much increased by bending a fathom

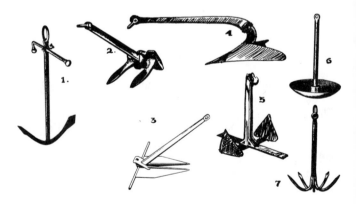

1. Yachtsman's anchor 2. "Navy" Type 3. Danforth anchor 4. CQR plow anchor 5. Light folding anchor 6. Mushroom anchor (for mooring) 7. Grapnel

603 Modern anchors

or two of chain between anchor and rope warp, but in so doing the advantages of the light weight are obviously lost.

The two most common types of "patent" anchors are the Danforth (and its imitators) and the Plow. Although both of these were for many years protected by patent, they are now available to any manufacturer who cares to imitate them, and many have. While some of the copies have had considerable success, others—especially versions of the original Plow, the CQR—have been disastrous.

The Danforth derives from a World War II design and is characterized by its oversized, sharp-edged flukes. It is generally considered to have its most effective use in reasonably hard sand or firm mud, where the flukes can penetrate fully. It is least effective in rock or kelp. The Plow has a single, plowshare-shaped fluke. It will not penetrate hard bottom as easily as the Danforth, and should be set by reversing the engine. On the other hand, it is not at all prone to fouling and holds very well once its fluke is buried.

Most experienced cruising people whose voyages take them to areas with varied types of holding ground carry two or three anchors —often one each of the three types described here. Skippers whose travels (and pocketbooks) are more restricted are probably best advised to use the type of hook that has most favor among the more experienced boatmen in their area.

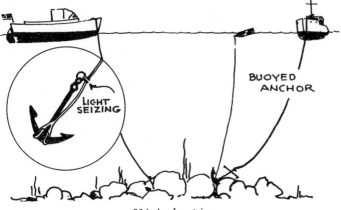

604 Anchor trips

604   Anchor trips are needed whenever the presence of rock is suspected. These are of two forms (*Figure 604*):

1. The cable is made fast at the crown, led along the shank, and secured to the ring by a few turns of light line. The cable should not lead through the ring. In the event that the anchor becomes wedged between rocks or in wreckage, an extra tug will break the ring lashing, and the lead will then be from the crown, and the anchor will break out easily.

2. A rope about half the diameter of the cable is bent to the anchor crown and led to the surface, where it is secured to a buoy. A fouled anchor can thus be freed by getting over it with a small boat or by picking up the tripping line from the bows with a boat hook. This method is to be recommended over number 1.

605   The anchor is always washed free of mud before decking and the cable cast off if its immediate re-use is not planned. It must be lashed down securely, otherwise pitching will surely send it adrift. An anchor adrift can do untold damage forward.

606 An example of a self-tripping anchor, this one called the "slip ring"

606   There are self-tripping anchors on the market today, but the wise owner of a large or cruising boat does not support the type. While it will indeed trip or free itself, no one knows just when this might occur: The manufacturers make the unwarranted assumptions that you will be awake, in a calm and protected anchorage, and have the manpower to retrieve the anchor if it is a heavy one. The type is essentially for fishermen or the afternoon sailor on a beach picnic; no skipper of a cruising vessel would normally trust the fate of himself, his crew, and his boat to a self-tripping anchor. The danger, of course, is that a current or wind change might very well "trip the hook" and see the boat drifting all by herself off toward possible danger.

607   To determine the anchor's holding power required for various types of craft, the following formula is used:

For sailing cruisers—8% of the gross weight
For power cruisers—7%   "
For launches, light cruisers—6% "
For centerboard sailers—5%   "

Thus a cruiser displacing (weighing) 8,000 pounds requires an anchor with a holding power of 560 pounds. The weight of the anchor will depend upon its style, and the makers usually have a table of holding powers for reference on various models of anchors.

608   There is no exact way to calculate the proper weight of anchors for any given boat. The recommended anchors, indicated by the table in Paragraph 607, while of sufficient size would be too large for easy and ordinary handling; i.e., while cruising or fishing. Small boats can be guided somewhat by the following rules:

1. Regular (light) anchor—one pound per foot of overall length.
2. Kedge anchor—three quarters of a pound per foot of overall length.
3. Heavy anchor—two pounds per foot of overall length. This rule applies to old-fashioned anchors only. Stockless "Navy" anchors should be from 25 to 40% heavier. Fisherman or dory anchors should be 15% heavier.

ANCHOR CABLES AND HAWSERS

609   Anchor cables are of chain (sometimes called chain cables or ship's cables).

Anchor hawsers are of synthetic rope (sometimes the outboard end will have a few fathoms of chain cable shackled to it to prevent undue chafing on the bottom). Hawsers are locally known also by the names of warps, rodes, or anchor fasts.

Wire cable is sometimes used for anchor hawsers. It must be handled by a drum winch, not by hand, and is seldom seen on small boats.

Boat cables are generally of BBB chain, galvanized, and composed of but two to four shots. A shot is one of the lengths of chain making up the cable, and in the merchant service is 15

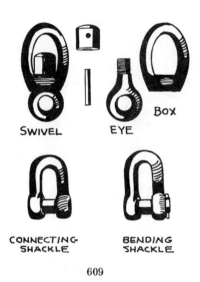

SWIVEL   EYE   BOX

CONNECTING
SHACKLE

BENDING
SHACKLE

609

BRAKE →   DEVIL'S-CLAW

SPILL
PIPE →

CHAIN
BIN

609A Chain cable—handling and stowing gear

fathoms long. Connections between shots are made by special links which permit the chain passing over the wildcat of the winch or windlass.

The outboard end is shackled to the anchor ring with the bow or rounded end of the shackle, called the bending shackle, facing the anchor. A stud link follows, then a swivel, then another stud link, then a shackle connecting to the first shot. Other combinations may be used, of course, providing the swivel is present. An old length of manila woven through the links of the first half fathom will do much to reduce wear of the chain here.

The inboard end, called the bitter end, after dropping through the spillpipe to the chain locker is securely shackled to an eye or ring let into part of the boat's framing. Sometimes a pelican hook or release hook is placed between shackle and chain so that the cable may be slipped quickly should the need arise.

It is important to match the strengths of all the components in a ground-tackle system. There is no point to a heavy rode and chain betrayed by a too-small shackle. The following table is based on average advertised safe working loads (not break strengths) of

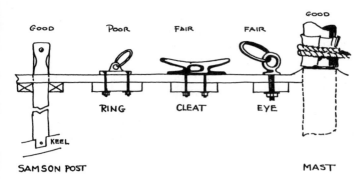

609B Small-boat mooring "bitts"

several rope, chain, and hardware manufacturers for items of given size:

Nylon Rode Diam/Load*	Galv. Chain Diam/Load*	Galv. Shackle Size/Load*
5⁄16″/570 lb.	3⁄16″/1,400 lb.	3⁄16″/670 lb.
3⁄8″/800 lb.	same	1⁄4″/1,000 lb.
7⁄16″/1,100 lb.	same	5⁄16″/1,500 lb.
1⁄2″/1,670 lb.	1⁄4″/4,350 lb.	3⁄8″/2,000 lb.
5⁄8″/2,400 lb.	same	7⁄16″/3,000 lb.

* Working load of nylon line is ⅕ breaking strength; Working load of chain is ½ breaking strength; Working load of shackle is ⅙ minimum strength; Shackle size is 1⁄16″ less than pin diameter.

610 Anchor windlasses are not usually found on small boats. However, when the anchor to be handled weighs 75 pounds or over, a windlass is necessary. Combination windlasses which handle chain cable or rope, or combination capstans having a chain wild-cat can be purchased to operate by hand or by electricity. (Figure 609)

Riding chocks are rarely found on small boats. These are steel chocks which guide the chain into the hawsepipe, and they have a locking device which is clamped to secure the chain and to take the strain from the windlass, leaving it free to be used for other purposes. A devil's-claw does the same thing. Sometimes the riding chocks are equipped with coil springs or rubber cushions, which take the shock of sudden jerks on the chain.

611 Chain is marked as follows (remembering a fathom equals 6′, or about 1.8 meters) to permit the exact scope to be known as cable is payed out. Paint is used for the markings:

20	fathoms	shackle	painted	red
35	"	"	"	white
50	"	"	"	blue
65	"	"	"	red
80	"	"	"	white
95	"	"	"	blue
110	"	"	"	red
125	"	"	"	white

For the small boat, which seldom requires great scope, some other system of marking is more practical. While many privately developed systems are in use, the following is one often found:

1 fathom	1 red band (painted on a link)	10 fathoms	1 red link
		15 "	2 red links
2 fathoms	2 red bands	20 "	3 "
3 "	3 "	25 "	1 white link
4 "	1 white band	30 "	2 white links
5 fathoms	2 white bands	35 fathoms	3 white links
6 "	3 "	40 "	1 blue link
7 "	1 blue band	45 "	2 blue links
8 "	2 blue bands	50 "	3 "
9 "	3 "		

(Approximately three fathoms from the bitter end, about a half fathom of chain is painted yellow, indicating approach of the bitter end.)

612

TABLE OF CHAIN SIZES FOR MEDIUM-HEAVY BOATS

Waterline Length	Diameter of Chain in Inches
For Motorboats	
25'	⅜"
35'	⁷⁄₁₆"
45'	½"
55'	⁹⁄₁₆"
For Sailboats (*Racing Type*)	
25'	⁵⁄₁₆"
35'	⅜"
45'	⁷⁄₁₆"
55'	⁹⁄₁₆"
For Sailboats (*Cruising Type*)	
25'	⁵⁄₁₆"
35'	⅜"
45'	⁷⁄₁₆"
55'	⁹⁄₁₆"

613 Chain cable is not subject to the rapid deterioration of rope. Its catenary curve (the curve of the chain between chocks and anchor) is greater than that of rope, and the chain, being of considerable weight, tends to act as a spring, and cushions the surge of the boat against the anchor. Even violent plunging of the boat against sufficient chain scope will not lift the chain very much from the bottom, thus keeping the strain in the position in which the anchor's holding power is best; i.e., pulling horizontally.

A chain anchor cable should be used on any boat large enough to carry the chain and its handling gear. A boat which regularly must anchor in rocky ground or in coral must always use chain cable or at least a chain cable pennant between anchor and warp.

613 *Left,* close link *Right,* stud link

ANCHOR RODE

614 Rope hawser should be of nylon in accordance with the following table of recommended sizes:

Waterline Length of Boat	Diameter of Nylon
20	⅜
25	½
30	9⁄16
35–40	¾
45–50	⅞
55–60	⅞
65–70	1

615 A knot in the rope weakens it at least 25%. An eye splice in the rope does not weaken it at all. Chafing gear must be provided wherever the cable rests against any fixed object. Chafing can weaken a rope by 50% in a few minutes; it can part a rope in an hour.

Natural-fiber rope is subject to marine borers but may be some-

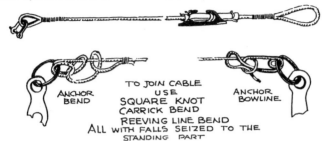

SHACKLE, EYE OVER THIMBLE   CHAFING GEAR   EYE SPLICE

ANCHOR BEND

TO JOIN CABLE
USE
SQUARE KNOT
CARRICK BEND
REEVING LINE BEND
ALL WITH FALLS SEIZED TO THE
STANDING PART

ANCHOR BOWLINE

615

what protected from attack by painting it with a poisonous paint (such as copper paint). A rope cable will weaken first at the ends, between wind and water (between chocks and the water), and near the anchor, where it chafes the bottom at the anchor ring. Weakening action here is much speeded by the presence of particles of sand, grit, and barnacles in the lay.

Polluted water containing acid (especially uric acid) will attack rope, as will oil or gasoline scum. One of its greatest enemies is dampness. A rope cable should never be stowed below until thoroughly dry—*and then it should be kept dry.* Prolonged exposure to sunlight damages nylon rope.

616 Anchor sprits, an ancient idea taken from Chinese junks, Persian sarowaks, and Down East schooners, have finally come to the yachting scene. These are simply small extensions that permit an average heavy anchor to be handled from deck without the necessity of lifting the anchor as dead weight. They have many forms.

The sailing vessel with a bowsprit is a natural, for not only can the anchor be handled from deck but it need never be taken on deck; it readily lends itself to lying "catted"—secured to bobstays or bowsprit shrouds and is thus ever ready for instant use. Not a small advantage is that a retrieved anchor does not deposit mud and silt over the forward deck area.

The CQR, or Plow anchor, lends itself most readily to the spirit

if the roller or sheave is sufficiently wide to accept the "knuckle" as well as the shank of the anchor. A catted anchor will lie with its shank parallel to the sprit, protrude out slightly, and be in an ideal launching position. A manufactured sprit, of metal, is available that lies over the stemhead, extending the anchor well outboard. As the anchor is retrieved and the knuckle meets the sprit head, the sprit neatly rises and folds aft, placing the whole combination squarely on the deck.

Sprits work particularly well with electric winches and capstans but the line must be fed, via fairleads or side blocks, to be directly in line with the sprit itself. With a foot-operated switch, leaving both hands free to handle the line and feed it to the bitt, much of the pain of anchoring or retrieving has been abolished.

ANCHORING

617 The anchor is let over crown first (not thrown) and held in an upright position on the bottom until the boat begins sagging to leeward. Cable is payed out when it is apparent that the shank and anchor ring will fall toward the boat, and is thereafter payed out only as needed, until the fully desired scope has been laid; then it is snubbed and the boat permitted to fully sag against the cable. (*Caution:* Never throw the anchor and follow it by a coil of rope. Fouling is certain to result.)

The stock of a traditional anchor will prevent the anchor from rolling and will assure the crown's being presented to the bottom in such a manner that the flukes can dig in and hold. Stockless anchors are held horizontal by their flukes.

A bearing is taken on a fixed object ashore and noted. Frequent checking immediately after anchoring will indicate whether the boat is holding or not. If not, more scope, or better holding ground, or a heavier anchor is required.

If two anchors are required, the second one is set somewhat to port or starboard of the first and the same distance to leeward of it. It is set by carrying it out in a small boat, or, if possible, by hauling ahead on the cable of the first with the rudder hard over (or a small headsail set), and planting it from deck.

The general rule for scope (chain or rope) is: Anchor cable scope at least five times the depth of the water anchored in.

Anchoring with chain cable requires the same basic rules as the handling of anchor and cable. However, the chain is controlled by the winch brake instead of by hand, the pawl of the wildcat being off and the chain free to pass outboard. When sufficient scope has been veered out, a stopper is clapped on the cable, either by rigging the devil's claw (a simple turnbuckle) or by tripping the pawl of the riding chock and then slacking off slightly on the windlass. The spillpipe is plugged, a conical stuffed canvas plug usually being used.

618 In crowded anchorages, the practice of mooring will provide holding scope and yet keep the boat confined to a relatively small area of swing. This procedure, of course, is distinct from lying to a permanent mooring.

Two anchors are used. The first is let go and its cable veered as the boat proceeds to the point where the second anchor is to be set, which point is distant from the first anchor by *twice* the scope of cable to be used on each anchor. The second anchor is let go; then the cable of the first is heaved in and the cable of the second veered out until the boat has the same amount of cable to each anchor (called *middling the cable*). Both cables are now shackled (or made fast) to a swivel piece, and a short cable is led from the swivel piece to the usual anchor bits. (*See Figure 618*)

The anchors are layed out in line with the tide or with the heaviest winds to be expected. The scope from the swivel piece to each anchor is five times the depth of the water; the lead from the swivel piece to the boat is the depth of the water. A boat moored will swing to but one fifth of the scope of an anchored boat and still have the same security.

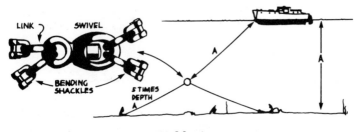

618 Mooring

In some very congested anchorages, boats are anchored and moored bow-and-stern: Each anchor is planted separately, its weight and scope calculated to hold the boat without assistance from the other anchor. The boat ties up with one rode to a hefty stern cleat, the other to the bitts or bow cleat. The boat's bow is oriented toward the direction of the prevailing wind or strongest current. Normally, the spliced loops of a permanent bow-and-stern mooring are connected by a pickup line rigged with floats every few feet: When picking up the line with a boathook, one has both rodes at a single swoop.

619 The use of a kellet is one of the traditional methods of giving spring to an anchor line and dampening the "snap" that often transmits to the vessel with damage to gear and spars. About halfway down the anchor line, a weight (anything heavy; preferably in a sack) of 20 to 30 pounds is lashed to the anchor line. It should be on a short scope so as not to thrash about and snarl up in the cable.

The use of chain will also provide spring. The cable should be either all chain or a much longer chain lead than is usually rigged.

Plastic or balsa buoys, also are used to dampen the "snap" by lifting the line rather than depressing it—but the result is the same. In emergency, any material that floats might serve; a plank, a capped oil drum or fuel tank, an old life-preserver. Finally, there is

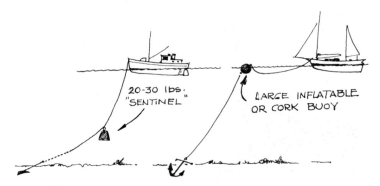

619A Two forms of the kellet, a device to introduce added spring to an anchor cable; it is highly efficient in a jumping sea or heavy current, or when the wind "comes from all over."

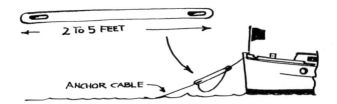

619B A rugged, stretchable link introduced into the anchor line will act as a kellet, these are for sale at chandleries. The cable need not be cut.

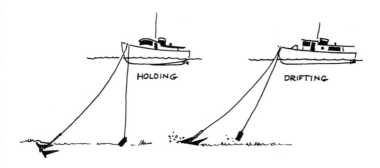

620 A light line and five-pound weight can be used as a drift warning: if the light line parallels the anchor line, a drift situation is developing.

on the market an extremely tough rubber link that is introduced between wind and water. (*See Figure 619B*) This effectively introduces spring to the anchor line yet does not weaken the cable. (It is manufactured by Rubbermaid Co.; available at most chandleries.)

620 A handy way to check for possible drift when anchored is this: drop a lead line (or any line with a weight that reaches the bottom) off the bow, securing it in approximately a straight up-and-down position, then giving it a few feet of slack. Any time this line extends beyond the bow, more or less in line with the anchor cable, and seems taut, the anchor may be slipping and the vessel drifting.

KEDGING

621 To kedge an anchor means to carry it out by small boat some distance from the boat, where it can be used to help pull off a grounded boat, or to careen a boat to lessen draft (as required when grounded), or for any number of purposes.

In the anchor weights liable to be found on boats, the elaborate methods of kedging a ship's anchor need not be explained. Figure 621 shows several methods of kedging anchors up to 300 pounds.

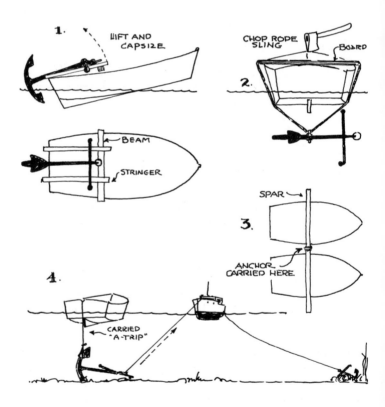

621 Kedging light anchors

The anchor should be set in such a place or in such depths as to be taken aboard directly to the mother ship. If this cannot be done, a tackle, which can be handled by man power, should be rigged to it and buoyed. A tripping line can be rigged. The anchor is tripped and held in a tripped position by making the tripping line fast to a small boat and heaving in on the anchor cable from the boat, an anchor first having been set off the stern.

PERMANENT MOORINGS

622 When a boat lies largely at a home port, it is usual to set a permanent mooring, which is more secure than an anchor. The requisites of a permanent mooring are:

1. That it be of sufficient weight to hold in any likely blow or current.
2. That it be positively antifouling.
3. That it can be left set, without need of servicing or inspection, for at least one boating season.
4. That the warp (or its bitter end) can be picked up under any conditions, night or day, with ease.

623 The commonest permanent mooring anchor is the mushroom anchor. (*Figure 623*) The action is exactly the same as a fluked anchor; the pull must be horizontal so that the edge of the mushroom (or disk) bites into the bottom and buries itself. Some mushroom anchors are made with a bulb on the shank to assure the anchor's remaining capsized and not sitting upright.

In mud or sand, a standard mushroom anchor is quite effective once it has dug in—but it may require a week or more to do so.

TABLE OF MUSHROOM ANCHOR WEIGHTS

Waterline Length of Boat	Light Boat	Cruising Boat
25'	50 pounds	100 pounds
30'	75 "	125
35'	100 "	150
40'	125 "	175–200
50'	200 "	300
60'	250 "	4–450

623 Mushroom mooring anchor

624   The mooring cable, because it cannot be taken up often, is always of chain and generally ends in a short rope warp.

Its parts consist of a shackle between mooring anchor ring, then a swivel, then one-third the total length of the chain cable of heavy chain, then a swivel, then lighter chain, then a long link, then a bending shackle to the rope warp. The rope warp is of sufficient length to keep the boat clear of the mooring buoy, if one is used, or one and one quarter times the depth of the water at high tide if a float buoy (carried on deck when moored) is used.

The scope of mooring cables is seven times the depth of the water; it should be greater under exposed-anchorage conditions or in swift tideways.

In crowded anchorages, such as most yacht anchorages are, there is seldom room to moor to the recommended scopes. Under such conditions the weight of the mooring must be increased as the scope is decreased. If a lay can be found which permits mooring bow and stern to the prevailing winds or tides, the problem is easily solved. In such a case the stern mooring should be 10% or more heavier than the bow mooring. The bow should face the storm quarter. The boat should be middled between the buoys so as not to override either.

625   Various types of mooring buoys are shown in Figure 625. If a rope pennant is used, it should be served for several feet fore and aft of where it leads through the regularly used chock, remembering that rope changes its length as it becomes wet and dry.

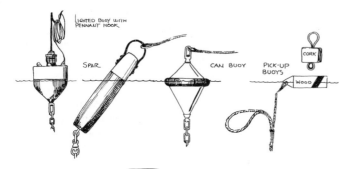

625 Types of mooring buoys

If the mooring buoy can be taken on deck and lashed, it makes a more satisfactory rig and prevents paint-chafing and scarring as buoy and boat collide between tides, or during calms, or when tides and winds come from opposite directions.

626 A very satisfactory permanent mooring, one that is particularly well suited to rocky anchorages, is a mooring anchor. This is simply an old-fashioned anchor, somewhat heavier in the shank and crown but having only one arm. It cannot foul the cable, and readily finds holding crevices in rocky bottoms. Cutting off the arm of an old-fashioned anchor with a hacksaw makes an entirely satisfactory mooring anchor, provided it is about twice as heavy as the ordinary heavy-service anchor.

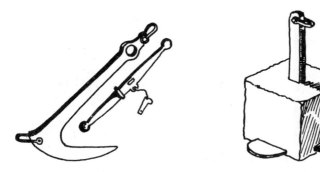

626 Mooring anchor   **627** The cement block mooring improved

627   Many other types of moorings, ranging from old auto engines and furnace castings, to cast cement, are in use. These types depend entirely upon dead weight for their holding power and should be used only for anchoring in places known to be free of tides or heavy seas. Possibly lakes, some rivers, and some salt ponds might fall into this class. Few salt-water anchorages could be considered safe for lying to one of this type of mooring. However, any one of this kind of mooring will be greatly improved in effectiveness if it is provided with some sort of a lever from which the cable lead can be taken. Anything that will tend to capsize the mooring object and make it difficult to drag through or over the bottom will help. An arrangement designed to dig in, as a fluke does, will also help greatly.

628   In deep mud bottoms, it is possible to drive a stake or stakes and lie to it with security and with a very short scope. The bottom must permit the stake to be driven into the mud to a depth equalling the depth of the water. One heavy stake will hold a small boat. Large boats require a "bundle," three or more stakes driven in somewhat like the frame of a wigwam and bound together at the common point of contact by several turns of rigging wire, well cleated. (*Figure* 628)

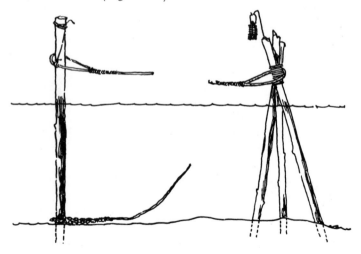

628 Mooring stakes

The mooring cable is secured to the stakes by a large eye splice passed over them and well served. A hold-up line is attached to prevent the eye from dropping to the base of the stake. Fishermen in Peconic Bay, Long Island, use a similar arrangement but pass a chain loop over the stake and attach the mooring cable to this, thus putting the strain on the stake at about the bottom. The chain can be lifted at any time for inspection or renewal.

The scope of a cable when moored to a stake should be about three times the depth of the water. The cable should be twice the size ordinarily used, as it comes in for hard use as it dips between wind and water; and the strain, as the boat surges, is severe.

Red cedar makes the longest-lived stakes, with black birch, juniper, and yellow pine following.

629 Moorings are generally moved by a scow equipped with a windlass, its tackle working through a large well amidships, over which is a sheerlegs.

Lacking such a scow a mooring can be moved by lashing a spar or beam across two small boats. The rig is placed over the mooring at low tide, the cable snubbed short and seized to the spar and let wait until high tide. Large moorings, even when deeply imbedded in the bottom, can thus be broken out and moved. To take such a mooring ashore, several tides are needed.

A boat lever can also be used. This rig is shown in Figure 629. A long boat of small beam is best. When securing or casting off the lever, beware of its swing and do not stand anywhere in its arc. When dropping a mooring from a boat lever, the lever will be shot a long distance astern. Be sure the water is clear of boats.

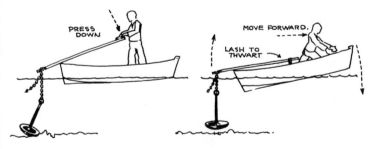

PRESS DOWN

MOVE FORWARD.

LASH TO THWART

629 *Left*, breaking out, and *right*, raising small moorings

Moorings can also be raised by swamping a boat over them and rigging a bridle to the snubbed cable. As the boat is pumped free of water, it will break out and raise the mooring.

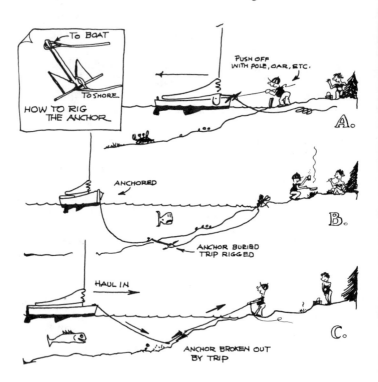

630 How to anchor a small boat off the beach or ledges. Rig the anchor as in the insert sketch and secure the anchor warp to the boat bitts, with its length two times as deep as the water to be anchored in. Rig a long line from the anchor crown (as for an anchor trip) to the shore. Lay the anchor on the edge of the forward deck. Shove the boat off with a hearty push as in A and yank the shore line sharply when you reach the anchoring spot. Belay the shore line. Then go fishing or whatever you came ashore for. The boat will ride safely as in B. To bring her in just haul away on the shore line, tripping the anchor as in C.

630 It is often handy to anchor a small boat offshore (as off a beach) and this may be done as shown in Figure 630.

This is an especially neat trick for outboarders and small sailboaters who do not carry a dinghy, yet wish to go ashore for swimming and picnicking.

MOORING AND ANCHORING REGULATIONS

631 While at anchor, all boats must show at least a white light visible all around the horizon. If under 150′ in length the light must be not more than 20′ above the water.

Exceptions are made in certain "anchorage areas" designated by the Coast Guard.

Vessels over 150′ in length must show two white lights, one forward and one aft.

Vessels 65′ in length or over must show anchor lights (or an anchor light) in any anchorage, including those designated as anchorage areas.

A boat lying to a permanent mooring is considered as being anchored.

No boat may lie at anchor in such a way as to obstruct a channel or to close any area beyond to the free passage of other boats. Most areas bordering on federal waters are under the direction of a port master, appointed by the government, who will assign permanent mooring locations upon application. He also hears complaints about offenders, may open or close an anchorage or mooring area, and investigate the types of moorings used, and forbid or permit their use.

In many local cruising harbors, moorings are maintained for the free use of visitors by civic organizations, Chamber of Commerce and yacht clubs. These are generally white and marked "Guest." Always check to see what the mooring will hold. Leave it as found —including the warp (sometimes attached).

632 With the passage of some control of federal waters to the states, there is, in crowded areas, a tendency to appoint a local "harbor master" who is placed in charge of moorings and the problems of permanent vessel moorage. Usually the harbor area is laid out in grids and certain areas designated as channels, mooring areas, turning basins, etc. In some cases double (bow and stern) moorings are required. Sometimes stakes are required, between which boats may lie on an endless bridle.

Unfortunately, some communities demand "rent" for mooring spaces (which is mumbo-jumbo, because the community does not own the land under the water). If seriously challenged, a local ordinance is sometimes passed forbidding all moorings save those owned by the community . . . and these are promptly "leased" to applicants. It's another case of "you can't win."

The harbor master is a properly authorized and empowered official of local government and should always be consulted before setting a permanent mooring, driving stakes, etc.

⚓

CHAPTER VII

BRIDGE AND QUARTERDECK

SINCE THE EARLY DAYS of the British sailing navy, the quarterdeck has been the traditional sanctuary of the "brains" of the ship. That these brains might function unhampered and uninterrupted, custom has decreed that no footstep, save in the rounds of duty, shall tread upon the quarterdeck to distract the master or his officers from their duty and their jobs. On modern vessels the bridge has the same sanctity.

Here, on bridge and quarterdeck, goes on the "extra" thought and planning so necessary to the success of any cruise, long or short. Those who do the brainwork of a cruise must know (and do know), first of all, the practical side of seamanship—every knot, and splice, and trick of sail handling, even the lowly swabbing of the deck. Every duty from that of the apprentice to the able-bodied seaman is thoroughly understood. In addition, such leaders must have a vast store of knowledge, much of it but distantly related to the sea. It is this knowledge, plus the ability to use it and to lead others, that constitutes the difference between officer and crew.

Roughly, this knowledge is divided into two major parts: one part, the knowledge required to solve the problems of the vessel while underway; the other, the knowledge required to meet the problems of a vessel while idle, or in port. And both parts overlap, of course.

Part one includes navigation (which is the subject of the three following chapters), weather lore, tide and currents, and many related subjects. Part two includes a knowledge of maritime law, insurance and insurance terms, stowage, port and clearance procedure, customs and immigration regulations, and like administrative matters.

Even the small-boat operator needs to know *some* of these things, and what follow, unrelated as they may appear, are the fundamentals of subjects which every merchant-marine officer knows intimately.

WEATHER LORE (METEOROLOGY)

701 Meteorology and weather forecasting are today almost exact sciences. They have nothing whatsoever to do with the position of heavenly bodies, or the "color of Mars," or the behavior of sea birds, and similar superstitions of not so long ago.

Unfortunately, weather data of a scientific nature is not available to the small-boat man at sea and, even if he had it, the highs and lows of pressure areas, wind directions, temperatures, etc., of thousands of square miles would have to be accurately known and the weather laws well understood in order to predict or forecast weather for the particular geographical area he is in. However, while it is an interesting study, meteorology need not be studied or understood in order to safely plan a cruise, for the United States government has made weather predictions available to anybody who is interested. Daily predictions and forecasting for weekly periods are made by experts and the information broadcast, by radio, to mariners, flyers, farmers, and others dependent upon the weather for their plans.

This information is available from at least the following sources:
1. By telephone from any National Weather Service office or Coast Guard station or base (at no charge).
2. From the daily press (in some cities).
3. From flag signals at Coast Guard stations, in the form of storm warnings (*See Chapter VIII*).
4. By radio from one of the network of VHF-FM radio stations operated by the National Weather Service (NWS).

This chain of VHF-FM stations, which will number 200 when the system is complete in 1980, will offer local, continuously updated weather forecasts to 90% of the population of the United States. To date, the coastal and Great Lakes areas have been fully covered by stations 40 to 80 miles apart. Since the average range of each station is between 25 and 40 miles (depending on the height of the receiving antenna), this spacing provides complete coverage with some overlap. Stations broadcast on either 162.40 or 162.55 MHz, just off the upper end of most commercial FM sets. Where there is danger of overlap on the same frequency, a third frequency, 162.45 MHz, is also available, though seldom used.

The broadcasts can be received on nearly all VHF-FM radiotelephones, which can be equipped with receive-only crystals for the appropriate channels; by nearly all radio direction finders; by some commercial FM receivers; and by special weather radios of various makes; these last are battery-powered, crystal-controlled, one- or two-frequency sets, with a price well within the means of even the least wealthy boatman. Slightly more expensive weather radios have a built-in alarm, triggered by a special signal broadcast over the (NWS) frequency.

702 With the ever-increasing popularity of boating, commercial and TV stations are more and more often offering genuine marine weather forecasts at least seasonally and during weekends.

Such marine information broadcasts originate from official weather sources and are distributed by local broadcast stations. They are quite "official" and not to be confused with local forecasts which, at times, tend to favor the advertiser who wants a sunny weekend to move his vacation merchandise. Many stations carry these broadcasts and practically any small craft is within range of one or more at all times, except if far out at sea. Local newspapers carry the schedules, or you may phone any broadcasting station or any Coast Guard station or depot for local schedules.

Information is broadcast at stated times during the day, on regular commercial frequencies, usually as part of a newscast. It is much appreciated by the hard-worked Coast Guard when yachtsmen listen to these broadcasts rather than call in at odd times and in odd circumstances. The ship-to-shore telephone earns its ugly reputation as a mere "yak-yak" instrument when it is used this way, as well as when it is used by bored yachtsmen or fishermen for the more obvious senseless chatter of "social" calls.

The Coast Guard also broadcasts occasional marine information broadcasts on its own frequencies following an announcement on 156.8 MHz or 2182 kHz. These broadcasts include other information of interest to the mariner (such as changes in navigational aids, obstructions to navigation, target practice near military bases, etc.).

703 Local "signs" may be used to give a clue to upcoming weather conditions, but it should be remembered that (a) such signs are not always reliable, and (b) such signs seldom will indicate the weather for more than the immediate succeeding 12 hours or less, which limits their value if planning an extended cruise. Local signs may include the appearance of the sky, the clouds, direction and velocity of the wind, and barometric pressure.

704 The barometer is a reliable and trustworthy instrument that indicates the changes in atmospheric pressure as they occur. Changes in weather or future weather are always accompanied by (or because of) changes in barometric pressure. Note that in the following table, readings are "at sea level." While most small boats will make readings at approximately sea level, barometers above or below sea level should be read with the following correction:

For every 10′ above or below sea level, add (or subtract) .01″. Adjustment can be made on the barometer itself so that the pointer reading is correct at all times. Correct readings at the time of setting may be obtained by calling the Coast Guard or the Weather Service.

Corrections for the Great Lakes follow:

Lake Superior	Add	0.64″
Lakes Michigan & Huron	"	0.62″
Lake Erie	"	0.61″
Lake Ontario	"	0.26″

Weather Signs

CLOUDS
705

1. Light scud clouds driving low under heavier cloud masses above indicate wind and rain.
2. Light scud clouds alone indicate wind.
3. Small black clouds indicate rain.
4. Light delicate clouds in soft fluffy masses foretell fine weather.

5. Hard clouds, sharply outlined and of bright hues promise rain and probably wind as well.

6. Misty "wet" clouds that form about heights, and either remain or descend, foretell wind and rain; if they disperse, improved weather may be expected.

7. High clouds that move against the direction of the lower clouds indicate the true future wind direction.

In general, the softer the cloud form, the less wind; the harder, more tufted, and sharper outlined, the more wind. The higher and more distant the clouds appear, the more gradual the weather change will come. Periods of bad weather are foretold by distant clouds breaking up into wisps, curls, and patches; the breaking up gradually increases and finally settles down over the sky as a murk, growing steadily in density.

Figures 705A and 705B show cross sections of cold- and warmfront approaches. The appearance and sequence of the several types and locations of clouds may, for the prudent mariner, foretell future weather. The practice of noting in the log the cloud disposition at the time of entry can lead to fairly accurate forecasting and serve as an alert in times of approaching foul weather.

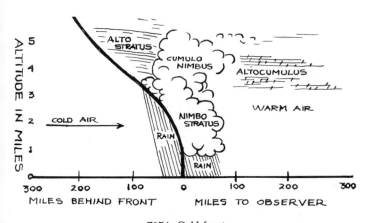

705A Cold front

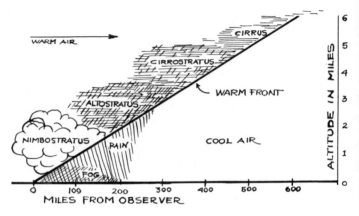

705B Warm front

The local thunderstorm is really local, though many different areas may experience "local" storms, locally born, at approximately the same time. Usually such a storm gives an advance "feel," confirmed by the appearance of tumbling, high white cumulous clouds some hours before it strikes. When a thunderstorm is predicted, the problems of the sailor become many. He must, by the predicted time of striking, be off a windward shore, either anchored or snugged down to ride out the savage gusts usual to thunderstorms. (Seas will not mount to dangerous heights, because of the short duration of the storm, but winds may well be of almost hurricane intensity.) He must also be in a position to reach port rapidly after the storm—for there will be little or no wind until the following day.

Figure 719 shows the general winds within a storm area as it moves along at average wind speed, usually toward the coast of a large body of water. The wind comes first; then the rain, knocking down the seas; then a cold or chilly front with diminishing wind and rain; and finally an uneasy calm. Such a storm often awaits the arrival of high tide before descending. Sometimes it splits, sparing a small local area; sometimes it "hits" twice. If first observed inland at or over the head of two or more bays or rivers, it will often divide and your best position is to leeward and between the mouths of these rivers or sounds. Mountains will often channel storms within storms through ravines or gaps, and these may hit the adjacent waters with wild fury. Stay *behind* high land if possible, not *between* two areas of high land.

A sure sign of the approach of a local thunderstorm is the presence of "static" on the ship's AM radio. This will commence quite early in the morning, be definitely noticeable by noon and stop comfortable reception several hours before the storm strikes. After the storm, the static will become weak or distant or cease, but if it does not, suspect a return engagement, possibly at night or at the next turn of the tide.

WEATHER PREDICTING BY THE BAROMETER
706

Wind Direction	Barometer Reduced to Sea Level	Character of Weather Indicated
SW to NW	30.10 to 30.20 and steady	Fair, with slight temperature changes, for one to two days.
SW to NW	30.10 to 30.20 and rising rapidly	Fair, followed within two days by rain.
SW to NW	30.20 and above and stationary	Continued fair, with no decided temperature change.
SW to NW	30.20 and above and falling slowly	Slowly rising temperature and fair for two days.
S to SE	30.10 to 30.20 and falling slowly	Rain within 24 hours.
S to SE	30.10 to 30.20 and falling rapidly	Wind increasing in force, with rain within 12 to 24 hours.
SE to NE	30.10 to 30.20 and falling slowly	Rain within 12 to 18 hours.
SE to NE	30.10 to 30.20 and falling rapidly	Increasing wind, and rain within 12 hours.
E to NE	30.10 and above and falling slowly	In summer, with light winds, rain may not fall for several days. In winter, rain within 24 hours.

E to NE	30.10 and above and falling rapidly	In summer, rain probable within 12 to 24 hours. In winter, rain or snow, with increasing winds, will often set in when the barometer begins to fall and the wind sets in from the NE.
SE to NE	30.00 or below and falling slowly	Rain will continue one to two days.
SE to NE	30.00 or below and falling rapidly	Rain with high wind, followed, within 36 hours, by clearing, and in winter by colder.
S to SW	30.00 or below and rising slowly	Clearing within a few hours, and fair for several days.
S to E	29.80 or below and falling rapidly	Severe storm imminent, followed, within 24 hours, by clearing, and in winter by colder.
E to N	29.80 or below and falling rapidly	Severe northeast gale and heavy precipitation; in winter, heavy snow, followed by a cold wave.
Going to W	29.80 or below and rising rapidly	Clearing and colder.

CLOUD DEFINITIONS
707

Cloud definitions follow. (*Figure* 707) The symbol in parentheses is used in recording the cloud state when making out the ship's log, or reporting.

1. *Cirrus* (Ci)—Detached clouds of delicate and fibrous appearance; silky, white, without shading.

2. *Cirrocumulus* (Cc)—In layers and patches, white, flaky or small globular shapes, usually without shadows. In groups, lines, or ripples.

3. *Cirrostratus* (Cs)—Thin, whitish veil, sometimes quite diffuse, giving sky a milky look. Sun or moon shows through, often forming a halo.

4. *Altocumulus* (Ac)—In layers or patches arranged in roughly horizontal groups, lines, or waves, following one or two directions with edges sometimes joining. *Altocumulus Castellatus* (Acc)—Same, but vertical developments from common horizontal base.

5. *Altostratus* (As)—Fibrous veil, gray or bluish in color, similar to a thick cirrostratus but without halo phenomena. Sun or moon seen only vaguely. Sometimes very thick and dark with light patches. Surface never shows real relief and fibrous structure is always seen in the body of the cloud.

6. *Stratocumulus* Sc)—In layers, or patches, in masses and rolls that seem to twist; soft and gray, with darker shading. In groups, lines and waves in one or two directions. Often closely formed, edges joined, giving entire sky a wavy appearance.

7. *Stratus* (St)— Low uniform layers of clouds resembling fog but not resting on ground. When the lowest layer is broken into shreds and wisps it is called *Fractostratus* (Fs).

8. *Nimbostratus* (Ns)—Low, dark gray, uniform colored, rainy, feebly illuminated. Precipitation can be either rain or snow, though it may not reach the earth. If this is so, the cloud base appears diffuse and "wet."

9. *Cumulus* (Cu)—Dense clouds with vertical development; upper surface dome-shaped, with rounded edges, base nearly horizontal. With the sun against them they appear bright and fleecy in centers; with sun on side, strong light and shade is seen; with sun behind, the edges become luminous. If the formation is not hard and well defined, but ragged and changing, it is called *Fractocumulus* (Fc).

10. *Cumulonimbus* (Cn)—Heavy masses of clouds, with great towering vertical development; upper parts often fibrous and spreading out in the shape of an anvil. The base often has a layer of ragged low clouds below it. The thundercloud.

707 Cloud forms: Their abbreviations and *common names.*

1. Cirrus   Ci *Feather*

2. Cirrocumulus Cc *Mackerel*

3. Cirrostratus   Cs *Web*

4. Altocumulus   Ac *Sheep*

5. Cumulus   Cu *Wool Pack*

6. Stratocumulus   Sc *Twist*

7. Stratus   St *Sheet*
8. Nimbostratus   Ns *Umbrella*

9. Altostratus   As *Curtain*

10. Cumulonimbus Ca *Thunder*

SKY

708 A red sunset sky foretells tomorrow's fair weather. When, after a fine-weather day, the sun sets behind cloud banks, rain may be expected within 12 hours; if the barometer is dropping at the same time, rain is certain. After sunset, if the western sky is whitish and yellow far up, rain may be expected on the following day. If the western sky blends from a horizon of purple or lavender into a blue high up, expect fair weather tomorrow.

A yellow sunset means wind is coming; a faint yellow or reddish hue indicates that rain is coming. Greenish tints foretell both rain and wind. If the sun itself sets pale and white, bad weather is in the offing.

A "high dawn," or the sunrise's first light seen above a cloud bank, mean wind is coming. A scorching morning sun, breaking from behind clouds, foretells thundershowers in the evening. A morning gray sky means good weather. A morning red sky brings wind and rain. Bright, clear blues in the sky indicate fair weather.

SUN AND MOON

709 A sun halo heralds bad weather. A moon halo indicates changing weather, usually bad before becoming good. A clear moon, seen in the daytime, means fair and cooler weather following shortly.

FOG AND DEW

710 Fog and dew both foretell that fine weather is coming. Heavy dew in hot weather promises a continuation of fair weather. Absence of dew after a hot day means rain soon.

SOUND AND SIGHT

711 Rain is foretold when distant objects stand "above the horizon" and are unusually clear. This phenomenon is sometimes called (erroneously) a "water mirage."

An unusual brightness and twinkling of the stars means wind. Lunar rainbows, or winddogs, or fragmentary rainbows signify increasing wind and possibly rain as well.

A "good hearing day," especially unusually good hearing from the wet quarter, means that rain will follow. A "poor hearing day" indicates a low humidity or moisture content of the air, and consequently fair weather may be expected.

SOME SAILOR'S SAWS TO REMEMBER
712

> *When sound travels far and wide,*
> *A stormy day will like betide.*

> *The farther the sight,*
> *The nearer the rain.*

> *Evening red and morning gray*
> *Are certain signs of a fine day.*

> *A red sky in the morning*
> *Is the sailor's warning.*
> *A red sky at night*
> *Is the sailor's delight.*

> *When the rain's before the wind,*
> *Halyards, sheets and braces mind.*
> *When the wind's before the rain,*
> *Soon you may make sail again.*

> Pertaining to the Barometer
> *First rise after low*
> *Indicates a stronger blow.*

> *Long foretold, long last;*
> *Short warning, soon past.*

> *When the glass falls low,*
> *Prepare for a blow;*
> *When it rises high,*
> *Let all your kites fly.*

Beaufort Scale with Corresponding Sea State Codes

Beaufort number	Wind speed — knots	mph	meters per second	km per hour	Seaman's term	World Meteorological Organisation (1964)	Effects observed at sea	Effects observed on land	Hydrographic Office — Term and height of waves, in feet	Code	World Meteorological Organization — Term and height of waves, in feet	Code
0	under 1	under 1	0.0-0.2	under 1	Calm	Calm	Sea like mirror.	Calm; smoke rises vertically.	Calm, 0	0	Calm, glassy, 0	0
1	1-3	1-3	0.3-1.5	1-5	Light air	Light air	Ripples with appearance of scales; no foam crests.	Smoke drift indicates wind direction; vanes do not move.	Smooth, less than 1	1	Calm, rippled, 0-⅓	1
2	4-6	4-7	1.6-3.3	6-11	Light breeze	Light breeze	Small wavelets; crests of glassy appearance, not breaking.	Wind felt on face; leaves rustle; vanes begin to move.	Slight, 1-3	2	Smooth, wavelets, ⅓-1⅔	2
3	7-10	8-12	3.4-5.4	12-19	Gentle breeze	Gentle breeze	Large wavelets; crests begin to break; scattered whitecaps.	Leaves, small twigs in constant motion; light flags extended.	Moderate, 3-5	3	Slight, 2-4	3
4	11-16	13-18	5.5-7.9	20-28	Moderate breeze	Moderate breeze	Small waves, becoming longer; numerous whitecaps.	Dust, leaves, and loose paper raised up; small branches move.			Moderate, 4-8	4
5	17-21	19-24	8.0-10.7	29-38	Fresh breeze	Fresh breeze	Moderate waves, taking longer form; many whitecaps; some spray.	Small trees in leaf begin to sway.	Rough, 5-8	4	Rough, 8-13	5
6	22-27	25-31	10.8-13.8	39-49	Strong breeze	Strong breeze	Larger waves forming; whitecaps everywhere; more spray.	Larger branches of trees in motion; whistling heard in wires.	Very rough, 8-12	5	Very rough, 13-20	6
7	28-33	32-38	13.9-17.1	50-61	Moderate gale	Near gale	Sea heaps up; white foam from breaking waves begins to be blown in streaks.	Whole trees in motion; resistance felt in walking against wind.				
8	34-40	39-46	17.2-20.7	62-74	Fresh gale	Gale	Moderately high waves of greater length; edges of crests begin to break into spindrift; foam is blown in well-marked streaks.	Twigs and small branches broken off trees; progress generally impeded.	High, 12-20	6	High, 20-30	7
9	41-47	47-54	20.8-24.4	75-88	Strong gale	Strong gale	High waves; sea begins to roll; dense streaks of foam; spray may reduce visibility.	Slight structural damage occurs; slate blown from roofs.	Very high, 20-40	7	Very high, 30-45	8
10	48-55	55-63	24.5-28.4	89-102	Whole gale	Storm	Very high waves with overhanging crests; sea takes white appearance as foam is blown in very dense streaks; rolling is heavy and visibility reduced.	Seldom experienced on land; trees broken or uprooted; considerable structural damage occurs.			Phenomenal, over 45	9
11	56-63	64-72	28.5-32.6	103-117	Storm	Violent storm	Exceptionally high waves; sea covered with white foam patches; visibility still more reduced.		Mountainous, 40 and higher	8		
12	64-71	73-82	32.7-36.9	118-133	Hurricane	Hurricane	Air filled with foam; sea completely white with driving spray; visibility greatly reduced.	Very rarely experienced on land; usually accompanied by widespread damage.	Confused	9		
13	72-80	83-92	37.0-41.4	134-149								
14	81-89	93-103	41.5-46.1	150-166								
15	90-99	104-114	46.2-50.9	167-183								
16	100-108	115-125	51.0-56.0	184-201								
17	109-118	126-136	56.1-61.2	202-220								

Note: Since January 1, 1955, weather map symbols have been based upon wind speed in knots, at five-knot intervals, rather than upon Beaufort number.

Courtesy of Bowditch/American Practical Navigator

713 Scales of Wind Force, Visibility, State of Weather and Sea, and Symbols for Recording in Log

VISIBILITY
714

0—Prominent objects not visible at 50 yards.

1—Prominent objects not visible at 200 yards.

2—Prominent objects not visible at 500 yards.

3—Prominent objects not visible at ½ mile.

4—Prominent objects not visible at 1 mile.

5—Prominent objects not visible at 2 miles.

6—Prominent objects not visible at 4 miles.

7—Prominent objects not visible at 7 miles.

8—Prominent objects not visible at 20 miles.

9—Prominent objects visible above 20 miles.

STATE OF WEATHER
715

b—Blue sky, cloudless.

bc—Blue sky with detached clouds.

c—Sky mainly cloudy.

d—Drizzling, or light rain.

e—Wet air, without rain.

f—Fog, or foggy weather.

g—Gloomy, or dark, stormy-looking.

h—Hail.

l—Lightning.

m—Misty weather.

o—Overcast.

p—Passing showers of rain.

q—Squally weather.

r—Rainy weather, or continuous rain.

s—Snow, snowy weather, or snow falling.

t—Thunder.

u—Ugly appearance, or threatening weather.

v—Variable weather.

w—Wet, or heavy dew.

z—Hazy weather.

To indicate great intensity of any feature, its symbol may be underlined; thus: $\underline{r}$, heavy rain.

STATE OF THE SEA

716

B—Broken or irregular sea.

C—Chopping, short, or cross sea.

G—Ground swell.

H—Heavy sea.

L—Long rolling sea.

M—Moderate sea or swell.

R—Rough sea.

S—Smooth sea.

T—Tide rips.

STORMS

717 Wind is caused by the movement of air as it "spills" from an area of high pressure into an area of low pressure. If this difference in pressure is great, the wind moves with speed and violence and the result is a storm. The small boat, in storm periods, is endangered not only by the high wind, but also by the sea that such winds make up. Storms are not to be confused with local thunderstorms or with the normal sea and land breezes caused by the air flowing upward from the heated earth during the daytime and per-

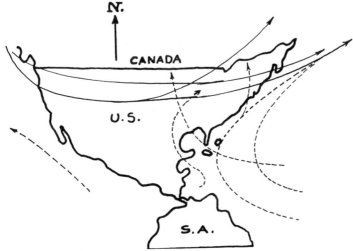

717 Principal storm tracks of the Western Hemisphere

———— Extratropical

- - - - - - Tropical (hurricanes)

mitting the cooler sea air to move inward toward the land—and the reversal of this process during the night when the earth is cool.

Storms make their advance according to well-known laws and follow well-known paths. Any small boat contemplating an ocean voyage of any extent should carefully prepare against storm danger, and the navigator should thoroughly understand the laws of the storms he is likely to encounter.

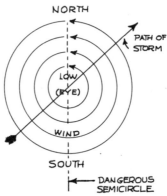

718 The cyclone (hurricane) in the Northern Hemisphere. It follows one of the storm tracks shown in Figure 717, rising from the south and generally dispersing at sea after recurving to the northeastward. Barometric pressures at the center range from 29.00 to 29.40 and at the outside edge 29.80 to 30.00. In low latitudes its diameter will be about 300 miles. After recurving, and at about latitude 40 North, it may be 1,000 miles in diameter. The center or "eye" is 10 to 15 miles in diameter, and the very "dead center" is always calm.

Such a storm moves along its track about 12 miles an hour at commencement, slows up around latitude 30 North and then, as it sweeps northward and eastward, increases to speeds as high as 35 miles an hour. The storm is most intense just before recurving.

The right half of the storm is known as the dangerous semicircle, and greater wind velocities prevail here than in the opposite half. Mariners always run for the left-hand semicircle when near the center if possible. Such a storm may find a pressure pocket inland or to the westward and northward and leave its usual course as did the great hurricanes of 1815 and 1938.

Detailed information may be had from any of the following publications of the United States Department of Agriculture, Washington, D. C. They are sent upon payment with the order (money orders or checks) and are sent post free to any address within the United States or any of its possessions.

The Hurricane—United States Department of Agriculture, National Weather Service (NWS). Illustrated. 14 pages. A paper dealing solely with the hurricane.

Florida Hurricanes—United States Department of Agriculture, NWS. Illustrated. Discusses frequency, time, and starting point of Florida hurricanes. The great hurricanes that reached the Florida coast in the last 50 years are described.

The Daily Weather Map—with Explanation—United States Department of Agriculture, NWS. Illustrated.

719 If caught at sea with a storm brewing, the mariner has but to locate the storm center and make all possible speed away from it, and thus avoid its full intensity. Familiarity with the law of storms and with the habits of hurricanes and cyclonic storms enables the informed boatman to do this.

You can make a rough estimate of where the storm center will be, after its approach has been indicated by a rapidly falling barometer, by noting cirrus clouds radiating from a point of great cloud density. A long swell is apt to come from the direction of the storm. Another detection method is to face directly into the wind. The center will be approximately (in the Northern Hemisphere only) 10 points to the observer's right. A ship heading directly into the wind will therefore find the storm center two points abaft the starboard beam.

If such an observation is taken every hour or so, the course of the storm may be plotted and the speed at which the center is moving estimated. If the storm is definitely cyclonic (such as the West Indian hurricane), the following maneuvers will take the ship away from the danger of the storm center. This, as will be noted, takes advantage of the fact that such storms *always* (in the Northern Hemisphere) revolve around the center anticlockwise, or from right to left. The sailing directions will see the ship heading away from the center and to higher barometric readings.

Right or Dangerous Semicircle. Powerboats: Bring the wind on the starboard bow, make as much way as possible, and if obliged to heave to, do so head to sea. Sailboats: Keep close-hauled on the starboard tack, make as much way as possible, and if obliged to heave to, do so on the starboard tack.

Left or Navigable Semicircle. Powerboats and sailboats: Bring the wind on the starboard quarter, note the course and hold it. If obliged to heave to, powerboats may do so stern to sea; sailboats on the port tack.

On the Storm Track in Front of Center. Powerboats and sailboats: Bring the wind two points on the starboard quarter, note the course and hold it, and run for the left semicircle, and when in that semicircle, maneuver as above.

On the Storm Track in Rear of Center. Avoid the center by the best practicable route, having due regard for the tendency of cyclones to recurve to the northward and eastward.

The common summer afternoon thunderstorm (*Figure 719*) needs warm weather and the approach or passage of a cooler front. Cumulus clouds will build up, darkening the sky, and reach great heights in the area of 30,000 feet. The storm is composed of three levels: ice on top, snow below it, and rain under the snow. When the build-up reaches a high altitude wind (40,000 feet or more) and the "anvil top" appears, cutting off the updraft, heavy rain, spiced by lightning activity, is sure to occur. It often delays (on the coasts) striking until the turn of the tide. It sometimes "splits" when each part follows a separate waterway (such as two parallel rivers) and the boatman may be spared both if he is between storms; or he may get both, one right after the other.

Because of the short duration of thunderstorms, there is seldom time for heavy seas to build up, it is mostly wind. With sea room it is hardly worth shifting to storm sail or reefing, for the whole display doesn't last very long. Bare poles are indicated. If in a confined body of water, furl down the canvas and drop a heavy anchor with more than average scope. There is nothing at all wrong with keeping the engine turning over, in gear at idle speed or a little better.

At the mature stage of the storm there is apt to be a sudden reversal of wind direction, a sharp increase in velocity, and a drop in temperature. Heavy rain (or hailstones) and lightning will occur for a short period; then, suddenly, it will be over and the wind will slowly come around to what it was before the storm, but at a much lower velocity, and it will gradually die.

Be on the alert for tornado formations; on the sea these can become dangerous waterspouts. The radio will advise if there is danger of one and where it might appear.

An alert for a *tornado watch* means that the possibility of one exists.

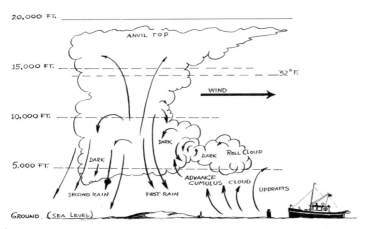

719 A "cross section" of a typical summer thunderstorm It usually makes up in the west and the oncoming anvil top and roll clouds are in evidence many hours before the storm strikes. The advance lower clouds "kill" the wind, then reverse it. Violent cyclone winds (really powerful updrafts) may be expected before the blackest clouds of all are overhead and release the rain—in two distinct falls. This diagram shows what to expect from a storm and in what order, as well as assisting in forecasting it. Obviously, sailing craft should prepare for the dangerous onslaught of the low cumulus clouds and the updrafts, which at sea level become heavy, varying winds that threaten knock-downs and jibes.

An alert for a *tornado warning* means that one has been sighted, visually or by radar.

You can do little about it save run from the danger area. It is highly unlikely that the traditional gunshot into a waterspout will cause it to collapse. Flash floods, inland, may dangerously affect the waters of a river mouth, creek, or bight in which you may have sought a lee; watch for signs (muddy waters, trash, tree limbs).

FOG

720 Fog is simply the bottom of a cloud lying over the sea, and consists of miniscule droplets of water through which it is difficult to see and hear. Fog forms from the sea upward in moisture-saturated air that is cooler than the sea water. If there are successive layers of cooler air above the one immediately above the water, the fog will be thick and densest at the bottom layer of cool air. There are four types of fog:

1. Radiation fog. This is the fog which forms at night over lakes and wide streams, sometimes called ground fog. It forms on still, almost airless nights, when it will reach a height of only a fathom or less; if there is a gentle wind (three knots or so) and a slight turbulence, it can become several hundred feet in height. It will disappear with the sunrise, as the sea warms slightly, sometimes the lower layers dispersing first and leaving an upper fog bank. Tides will carry the fog in or out to sea as it moves water of varying temperatures.

2. Advection fog. (*Figure* 720A) This fog, likely all year round, is caused by winds carrying warm, moist air over cooler waters. A condition that must exist for continued advection fog is that the water temperature must be progressively cooler in the direction toward which the fog is blowing. This is why, at times, fog seems to go and come with the tide; it is really the tidal movement of the favorable water temperature to form and maintain fog.

3. Coastal fog. (*Figure* 720B) This is the summertime fog which coastal yachtsmen (and those on the Great Lakes as well, under certain conditions) so often encounter. It is caused by warm oceanic air (as from the Gulf Stream) being blown across cold

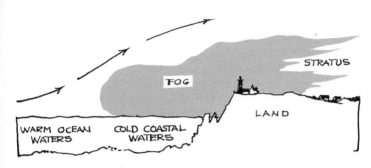

720A Advection fog

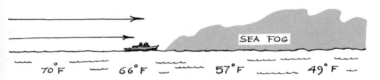

720B Coastal fog

720C Precipitation fog

coastal waters. It is a stubborn fog and may persist for several days and nights. Full sunlight above it in no way discourages it.

4. Precipitation fog occurs when rain falls through or from warm air and into cool air lying above the sea (*Figure 719C*). It is a heavy, wet fog; almost a rain—indeed can alternate between rain and fog. The lower air is always colder than the sea temperature below it. On the Great Lakes, Mississippi, Ohio, and other Western rivers, this is known as "steam fog" and is a hazard in the morning and evening, especially in the cooling days of autumn.

Unclassified is the fog known as "Arctic smoke," which occurs in bitter cold winter weather when arctic air of less than 10° blows over the sea (which may be in the low 30s). It is a stringy, light fog, wispy, and occurs in patches of varying densities.

Fog is measured—or, rather, the likelihood of fog is determined—by use of an instrument called the psychrometer. This is simply a dual thermometer instrument, its dry bulb measuring the air temperature and its wet bulb measuring the temperature of air when it is saturated. The difference between the temperatures on the two thermometers is applied to a scale, which assists in estimating the fact, density, and ETA of fog. The less the spread in readings, the closer is the fog; when they match there *is* fog.

TIDES

721   The tide is the diurnal, or twice daily, vertical rising and falling of the sea. It is caused by the attraction of the moon and sometimes by the sun and moon in combination.

While the moon affects tide the most, the sun has some influence, which is felt most when the attraction of sun and moon is combined. This occurs when both bodies are in the same or opposite quarters of the heavens, or at times of new and full moon; at these times they jointly produce the highest and lowest tides, called *spring tides*. At the first and third quarters of the moon the position of the sun and moon are such that high water produced by one body coincides with the low water of the other. The result is that the tides then have the least range (difference in level between high and low tide), and they are called *neap tides*.

Horizontal movements of the tide are called *tidal currents*. They flow inward to high-water levels (called the *flood tide*) and outward to low-water levels (called *ebb tides*). When vertical movement has ceased, the tide is said to be at the *stand*. When horizontal movement has ceased (usually at or before the stand), the tide is said to be at the *slack*.

The rise of the tide is the amount in feet and inches that the tide rises above a normal point, or datum plane of mean low water. This datum plane is used in marking the depths on charts, and all soundings are based on it—average (Mean) Low Water, MLW on the East and Gulf coasts of the United States. On the Pacific coast, where one of the two low tides in each 24-hour cycle is markedly lower, the chart datum is Mean Lower Low Water (MLLW).

The range of the tide is the extreme difference between high and low water (i.e., highest high water and lowest low water) expressed in feet and inches. This varies from zero (at the equator) to 40 or more feet (Bay of Fundy).

The set of a tidal current is the direction in which it flows.

The drift of the tidal current is the speed in which it sets, generally expressed in knots.

Tidal currents must be reckoned with when plotting courses for navigation and both set and drift considered. Tidal information and tables of data are published by the United States Department of Commerce for every part of the United States coast line, and must be referred to when plotting courses. (*See Chapter XI*)

UNITS OF MEASURE AT SEA

722 *Yard*—3 feet. Distance off is expressed in yards (or cables).

Fathom—6 feet. Depth is expressed in fathoms on some small-scale charts.

Cable—(units of 720 feet in U. S. Navy—largely obsolete). Distance from or to near-by objects, the shore, etc., can be expressed in cables.

Nautical mile—approximately 6,080 feet. The distance between two minutes of latitude, or between two minutes of longitude at the equator. Distance made good, lost, or away from, or toward is expressed in nautical miles.

Note: The knot is not a unit of measurement but of speed and is equal to a speed of one nautical mile per hour.

THE SHIP'S LOG

723 A log is a continuous, minute-by-minute record of the progress and life aboard the boat and upon the sea about her. In it is noted *anything* of interest to the boat, though nothing trivial or in the nature of a diary entry.

A harbor log will merely record the goings and comings of the crew and officers, stores and fuel taken aboard or used, visitors and officials on board, inspections made and the findings of such inspections, orders received, accidents or *unusual* happenings, the depth of water in the bilge (leak rate), and general weather recording.

A sea or cruise log records, in addition to some of the items listed above, course, speed, engine revolutions, change of course and speed, ships sighted, etc.

The following items may be noted in keeping a useful log.

Name of vessel, port of hail, where bound, date

In command; names of crew and/or guests

Amount of fuel in tanks, start and finish. Fuel consumed

Amount of water in tanks, start and finish

Running lights. Time of lighting and extinguishing

State of weather
State of sea
Wind force and direction   Recorded at fixed intervals, or at the
Visibility   change of course, or change of watch
Temperature
Barometric pressure

Where and when anchored (or moored) or docked

Orders to the watch

Orders for the morning

Supplies or stores needed

The actual recording of courses and distances run becomes valuable by comparing it with other similar runs and, of course, becomes necessary for running in fog or thick weather or away from the visible aids to navigation. Stock printed log forms for this purpose are many and may be procured from marine chandlers in bound blank form.

One of the most useful and complete has the following headings (running horizontally across the top of the page):

Actual Time Abeam
Place Abeam
Distance Off
Log Reading

Course to Next Objective { True Course
Magnetic Course
Compass Course

Current, Set, and Drift

Engine Speed (in rpm)
Speed, Actual
Predicted Time to Be Abeam
    Next Objective
Elapsed Time on Course
Distance by Log (Log Reading)
Depths

On the left-hand edge of the page, vertically, and in the boxes provided, the navigator fills in the time; then opposite it, under the proper heading, he makes the entry of the above items.

Thus a complete record of progress can be kept and used for comparison or for establishing position by dead reckoning if thick weather or night sets in.

A ship's log is legal and admissible evidence in any court of law and, when signed by the master at the time of its making, needs but certification as to its genuineness to help the court in rendering decisions upon legal action resultant from collision, property damage, etc. To give a log added weight, as evidence, it should be permanently bound and the pages consecutively numbered.

SHIP'S BELLS AND WATCHES

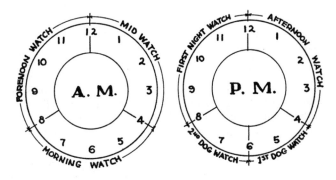

725 Order of watches

724   Time is denoted on shipboard by striking the ship's bell as follows, each dot representing one stroke of the clapper. Time is taken from the flagship or senior officer present:

A. M.		P. M.	
12:30—1 bell	.	12:30—1 bell	.
1:00—2 bells	..	1:00—2 bells	..
1:30—3 bells	...	1:30—3 bells	...
2:00—4 bells	.. ..	2:00—4 bells	.. ..
2:30—5 bells	.. .. .	2:30—5 bells	.. .. .
3:00—6 bells	.. .. ..	3:00—6 bells	.. .. ..
3:30—7 bells	.. ..	3:30—7 bells	.. ..
4:00—8 bells	.. ..	4:00—8 bells	.. ..
4:30—1 bell	.	4:30—1 bell	.
5:00—2 bells	..	5:00—2 bells	..
5:30—3 bells	...	5:30—3 bells	...
6:00—4 bells	.. ..	6:00—4 bells	.. ..
6:30—5 bells	.. .. .	6:30—5 bells	.. .. .
7:00—6 bells	.. .. ..	7:00—6 bells	.. .. ..
7:30—7 bells	.. ..	7:30—7 bells	.. ..
8:00—8 bells	.. ..	8:00—8 bells	.. ..
8:30—1 bell	.	8:30—1 bell	.
9:00—2 bells	..	9:00—2 bells	..
9:30—3 bells	...	9:30—3 bells	...
10:00—4 bells	.. ..	10:00—4 bells	.. ..
10:30—5 bells	.. .. .	10:30—5 bells	.. .. .
11:00—6 bells	.. .. ..	11:00—6 bells	.. .. ..
11:30—7 bells	.. ..	11:30—7 bells	.. ..
12 Noon—8 bells	.. ..	12 Mid.N.—8 bells	.. ..

725   At sea, the day is divided into watches of four hours each, the period representing the time that various members of the crew are on duty. The crew usually is divided into two watches, the starboard (or captain's watch) stood by the second mate and the port (or mate's watch) stood by the first mate. (*Figure 725*)

In order to rotate the watches from day to day, dogwatches of two hours each were instituted and are called first and second dogwatch (or dodge).

BILLET SYSTEM AND STATION BILLS

726 Some manner of organization is required on every boat engaged in extended cruising. Division of duties and responsibilities is absolutely necessary to achieve the purposes of the cruise, which for the small-boat man are fun, and pleasure, and relaxation.

By agreement in advance, each member of the ship's company should be made head of one of the boat's departments and take over the duties of that department (such as engine department, deck, bridge, or galley). If at sea, watches are stood in regular rotation, the agreement should indicate the relieving member and the time he is to relieve. Once a routine has been established, it should proceed without undue interruption of the ship's operation and without more than physical aid from other departments. The great advantage of such a system, even with a small crew of three or five men, is not that one man has to *do* everything in his department but that he is charged with *thinking and planning* for his department.

A routine cannot be laid down arbitrarily; it varies with ship and crew and cruising waters. In general it will be along the lines of the routine of a paid hand (*Chapter XIV*) and the ordinary procedure of the navigator, engineer, and cook.

Men detailed to such positions should be selected with extreme care. Not only should they thoroughly understand the details of their department but must, if they are to work congenially with other crew members, be leaders and cheerful, fair-minded companions. It is usual to have a round-table bull session before an important race or cruise, to thoroughly "hash over" all problems and duties and thus eliminate the jurisdictional "kicks" from both sides at the beginning. Of all department heads, the navigator's is perhaps the most important to the ship, but by all the experiences of habitual cruisers, the cook's department is the most important to the ship's company, and the appointment of a cook and the fixing of his allowances for "grub," mealtimes, and rules should be with the consent of the entire party.

725 The small boat seldom needs an elaborate station-bill system. However, some organization is needed, and quickly, to meet common emergencies, and station bills, carefully planned, before such emergencies will avoid the confusion of orders given at cross purposes that too often attend marine mishaps or disasters.

Crew members are each given a post and a duty for the several emergencies liable to occur on any boat, and instructions that, when the alarm is given, they must proceed to the assigned station at once and there do their assigned job or stand by for orders. The spirit of the station bill is simply that the various types of apparatus be manned and ready for use at the word of the leader. The leader has every right to consider the men under him as *part of the equipment* and to expect them at their posts, ready to perform and carry out orders without question, and without other, or different, or "better" ideas. A poorly co-ordinated plan is far better than no plan, or a plan ruined because one man is not to be relied upon.

Some simple station bills are suggested below:

FIRE

727 *Upon the alarm:*

1. Man fire extinguishers.
2. Head boat so that fire is to leeward.
3. Stand by signaling apparatus. Man the radio.
4. Break out and rig emergency tiller.
5. Launch and prepare small boat; distribute life preservers.
6. Stand by engineer for instructions to shut fuel lines or plug fuel vents.
7. Secure and be responsible for ship's papers, valuables, etc.

COLLISION

728 *Upon alarm:*

1. Stand by (and be prepared to man) all pumps.
2. Stand by for inspection and repair duty.
3. Stand by signaling apparatus. Man the radio.
4. Put out all fires.
5. Launch and prepare small boat; distribute life preservers.
6. Stand by to assist other boat involved.

ABANDON SHIP

729 *Upon orders:*

1. Launch and prepare small boat or raft; distribute life preservers.
2. Secure ship's papers, valuables, pets, etc.

3. Launch marker buoy for future locating of the wreck.
4. Stand by distress signals and radio.

MAN OVERBOARD

730   *Upon cry or alarm:*
1. Launch life rings (with water lights, night or day).
2. Locate man overboard and keep pointing directly at him and in sight of the navigator.
3. Prepare to launch small boat or raft.
4. At night, man the searchlight.
5. In daylight, send a man aloft to keep the man overboard in sight.
6. Take tacking stations (on a sailing vessel).

"JACKASS" NAVIGATION

731   This inelegant name applies to the art of taking a boat from here to there without the use of formal navigation as such. It is akin to the term "flying by the seat of your pants." All small craft, operating inshore or in confined waters, use jackass navigation in some degree, quite often in combination with standard compass, log, and lead practice. It refers to making good courses with the aid of local signs and knowledge, echo navigation, and just plain sea sense. It is not offered as a substitute for scientific navigation but as a complement to it. After all, many inshore courses are so short or varying that running a compass course and applying usual dead reckoning would result in error. Visible and audible "fixes" along such a course are of great safety value to the skipper who understands "signs."

Off the Connecticut shore, for example, the local lobstermen make some astoundingly accurate runs in thick fog. Few of them ship compasses. Yet their secret is simple once understood. They run inshore, the general direction of which is indicated by tide or wind or both, stop their engines and listen. Always in this busy area, laced by highways, bridges, railroads and industry, they obtain not only audible lines of position but actual identification of the locale as well. The hoot of a train at a certain crossing, or bridge, the bleat of a factory whistle, the roar of traffic on a hill or its honking at a blind intersection, the rumble of a long freight over a trestle—all these sounds become lines of position to the alert skipper and give him a fix as accurate as one obtained from standard aids to navigation such as lighthouses, buoys, and range marks.

To be sure, it requires an observant nature, of the type that, in fair weather, lays away many minute details, often quite unrelated, against a period of foul weather or stormy night. It is not impossible for the small-craft skipper to have this kind of intimate knowledge on tap for many areas around his home port and usual cruising grounds. Notes on charts are not uncommon; notes such as "You can see street light, corner Oak and Main, from here." or "Train blows three longs for Mystic Bridge."

In Maine, local navigation is much dependent upon lobster buoys. These string along deep ledges, often quite close to shore, and indicate a depth of water that at least a lobster boat can negotiate—usually about 15′ at the ebb stage. Large buoys or buoys with stick handles indicate deep waters such as are found a half mile or more offshore. Warps with toggles (bottles, wooden floats, or glass balls in nets) indicate swift currents, so possibly identify an entering gut or river. Buoys in a circle define a ledge; stay outside the circle for deep water. If you know the colors of the buoys used by various local lobstermen, or their license number, which is burned into the buoy, you can, if you know the fishing grounds of these men, obtain a remarkably accurate fix.

Oyster stakes in other areas, notably the Chesapeake and eastern Long Island Sound, indicate depths of about three fathoms and clear sand bottom. Fish weirs indicate a two-fathom depth and sufficient water for the net boats and carriers to operate in.

The color of the sea is also a clue to water depth and location. Sand shows up in a lighter sea color. Mud and clay give a dark cast to the waters. Ledge and rocky bottom is revealed almost always by streamers of kelp and ribbon weed floating a fathom or more *above* the sunken danger. Study the bottom from aloft. In the West Indies it is relatively simple to con a ship through vicious coral heads from the cross-trees, because of the clarity of the water.

In waters in which you catch flounder, you have mud or sand and probably level bottom. Mackerel sport in deep waters as a rule. Crabs come from deep but rocky bottoms. Cormorants fish in about two fathoms. When you see one pop to the surface nearby, you are in deep water. Porpoises play in mackerel waters—deep and moving—and this might indicate a main channel. Eel grass indicates shallowing waters; kelp deeper waters.

Tide rips, races, or small wavelets imposed upon the general wave pattern might mean shallowing waters, bars, or a submerged ledge. Do not confuse these with wind galls which move over the surface.

The local wind and tide patterns also give broad fixes. In fog the wind almost always comes from the easterly quarter. Along the coast, the morning wind usually comes from the land, changes to southwest along the Atlantic and southeast along the Pacific Coast during a normal day and backs off the land again in the evening. If the breeze smells of spruce woods or coke smoke or a fish plant or hay, you have a pretty good idea of direction if you know the local terrain and community. Inshore winds are apt to be "wet"; offshore dry.

The presence of garbage or wreckage floating in the tide may give a clue as to the boat's relative whereabouts. Brown waters, in Maine, identify one of the larger rivers that supports logging or textile mills. Spruce logs 4′ long indicate a pulp mill; random trunks or slab edges indicate a lumber mill nearby. If you know where these mills are you know roughly where you are. Oily waters, unfortunately, used to indicate a large city or town; now they can be pretty much anywhere.

732 The use of echoes in close inshore navigation is well understood in some areas, notably the rivers and sounds of the Northwest. It is based on the speed of sound waves, and measures, in time, the period required for a sound to be projected and bounce back to the point of origin; then convert the time into distance by the formula:

$$\frac{.18}{2} \times time = distance\ off\ in\ nautical\ miles$$

Sound travels at the approximate rate of 1,100 feet per second or .18 miles per second. Since the echo must be bounced by a solid object, the distance off must be the distance from that object to the receiving point or one-half of the total distance travelled by the sound wave. For quick calculation merely multiply the total time in seconds between sending and receiving the signal by .09. A rough estimate may be made by counting ten seconds one mile.

In general a sharp, high-pitched signal works best. Use the electric horn, especially if it may be swiveled to direct the sound abeam. Fog-horns and deep tones are not always reliable. A mouth whistle is quite satisfactory, especially if blown through a speaking megaphone. A megaphone to the ear also assists in picking up the echo when the engines are running. Be careful to keep flat areas (such as sails, deck houses, etc.) in back of you as you signal. A gun shot returns a clear and distinct echo. However, unless blanks are shot this is a dangerous practice. *In extremis* beat a pail or dish pan lustily.

The type of echo will be a clue as to the type of reflector returning it. A long, muttering echo indicates low shore, trees, marsh or flats. Clear-cut echoes indicate cliffs, high ledges, steep shores, or buildings. A weak echo, seemingly returned from a particular spot, may indicate another ship or an isolated object like a small islet, anchored craft, or bridge footing. Test such an echo carefully and get a bearing on the object; it may be a vessel underway and in danger of collision from or with you. Sails return such an echo. When nearby, cans and nuns return a soft whispering echo.

Dense fog dampens the echo and often distorts it. Wind, especially wind on the beam of the echo course, may whisk away all sound. By and large, echo navigation is a check, not a complete system of navigating unless you have extensive local experience under all weather conditions. It provides only *approximate* fixes. For accuracy combine echo navigation with sounding, compass courses, and other conventional methods. (*See Chapters IX, X, and XI.*)

The most common use to which echo navigation is put is to maintain a course in the mid-channel of a river or sound. In Figure 732A a boat is shown fogbound in mid-channel. A signal given on either side should result in the same distance off, signifying that the boat is in the center of the river. Figure 732B shows the boat off its course. It will hear a quick echo on one side and a slow echo on the other. To be sure, it may be desirable to follow a veering channel by using this very method. If so, lay out, on the chart, at regular time intervals, the time count of the echo return you expect to receive at these points; in this case converting distance to time. (*See Figure 732C.*)

It is possible to make a change in course by keeping an echo abeam during the turn. Plot the limit of the turn and convert it to a compass course. When the boat steadies on the corrected course, the echo should be directly abeam, thereafter fall to the quarter, and eventually be left astern.

Know the shoreline and coast contours. There is always danger that the echo signal may pass over a low beach or marsh and be returned by some higher elevation far inland. You may readily obtain a fix in this manner, however, provided you *know the coast.* (*Figure 732D*)

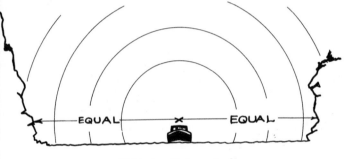

732A A mid-channel echo

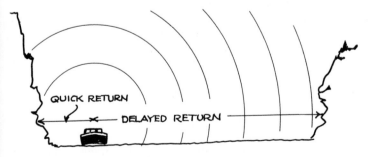

732B A side-channel echo

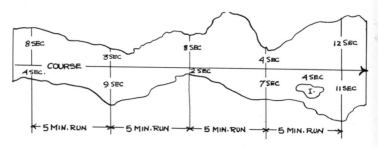

732C Plotting an echo course with distance laid off in time

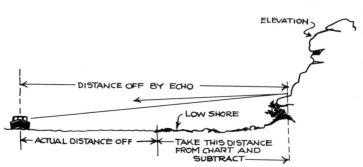

732D Why it is important to identify the shore returning the echo

Here on the coast of Maine, we have what is probably the strangest echo known. Coming in from Pemequid toward Friendship in a thick o' fog, we run out our time to Cranberry Island, and to confirm the dead-reckoned fix, a man goes forward and howls like a dog. Almost immediately a dog howls or barks back. We're on course—for no matter when you howl at Mord Libby's dog on Cranberry Island he howls right back.

Yacht Insurance

733 The wisdom of carrying the proper insurance to protect your investment and cover your liability in owning a boat needs no forwarding here. The considerations involved are exactly those involved in automobile or real-estate ownership.

Following is a purposely brief explanation of yacht insurance, intended to give those who may be unfamiliar with the subject an outline as to the general principles of this form of coverage.

HULL INSURANCE

Marine insurance is the oldest form of indemnity of which there is any record. Yacht insurance has naturally followed the time-honored principles applied to the insurance of ocean-going commercial vessels, with necessary adaptations to meet the requirements peculiar to the insurance of pleasure craft.

The coverage afforded under the standard yacht policy is extremely broad. It covers the hull, machinery, tackle, and equipment of the yacht against fire, theft, and what are commonly known as "the perils of the sea"—such as stranding, sinking, and collision damage sustained by the insured yacht—and liability for damage done to another vessel if the insured yacht be at fault; also, against heavy weather (storm damage) and similar perils.

Like most other forms of insurance, yacht policies normally cover the value of the insured item, less a deductible amount, which is normally 1% of the total value. As most claims are for amounts under 10% of the total value, the yachtsman who wants to be covered for total loss, but who is willing to take his chances with small damage, may secure a substantially lower premium by accepting a high deductible.

Better policies have relatively few exclusions—situations not covered under the policy—aside from such uncontrollable events as wars, revolutions, and nuclear explosions. Although damage caused to sails (especially spinnakers) when racing and hull or propulsion unit damage to powerboats engaged in formal races may be excluded in some policies, it is part of standard coverage in others.

Policies are customarily issued for a period of one year and provide continuous coverage whether the vessel be in port or at sea, at dock, on the ways, or in dry dock.

Certain cruising limits are always mentioned in the policy. Vessels on the eastern coast of the United States are usually written with navigating limits confined to coastwise and inland waters between Eastport, Maine and Cedar Key, Florida. Other navigating limits are allowed, such as Great Lakes and tributaries including the St. Lawrence River and tributaries not below Quebec or United States Gulf coast waters or other inland rivers and lakes. The policy usually is written allowing for specific layup periods according to the requirements of the assured, with rates adjusted accordingly. The usual lay-up period for vessels navigating northern waters is six months, from November 1 to May 1.

Provision is also made to cover equipment and gear that may be separately stored on shore. The value of such equipment is usually limited to a figure of 20% of the amount of the policy, subject to revision if necessary, and during such storage period, yacht equipment and gear is insured in accordance with full policy conditions.

The basic policy form provides that the vessel shall be used for private pleasure purposes only. Consequently, the policy will be invalidated if the yacht is used for the carrying of passengers for hire or for other commercial purposes. However, underwriters are generally willing to permit a time charter to responsible individuals for private pleasure purposes only.

Rates are based on a variety of factors peculiar to each risk. The principal determining factors are the value of the vessel, her age, motor equipment (if any) and whether gasoline or oil engines, cruising limits, and in-commission periods required (whether more or less than six months of the policy year). Rates on the higher-valued yachts are lower than rates on yachts of low values. The reason for this is that the cost of repairs on lower valued yachts is generally much higher in proportion to the value of the yacht than would be the case on those of higher values.

LIABILITY INSURANCE

The owner of a yacht, large or small, should give careful consideration to his legal obligation, not only with respect to the crew, if any, but also with respect to property damage and loss of life or personal injuries to any individual in connection with his ownership and operation of the vessel.

He may, like any other vessel owner, limit his liability at the discretion of the court. However, in order to do so, he has the burden of proving that the loss or damage occurred without his "privity or knowledge," which means, of course, knowledge of, or notice of, defects or errors causing the loss or damage.

In order that the yacht owner may insure his liability for property damage and loss of life or personal injury, what is known as the "Protection and Indemnity clause" may be added to the yacht policy.

This endorsement provides for property damage and also for loss of life and personal injuries for any reasonable limits, the exact amounts being specified in the endorsement. The premium is based on the value of the yacht and the limits of liability as may be required.

There is an important exception in the Protection and Indemnity endorsement to the effect that the policy is free from any claim arising directly or indirectly under the federal Longshoremen's and Harbor Worker's Compensation Act.

COMPENSATION INSURANCE

The Longshoremen's and Harbor Worker's Compensation Act is an act of Congress "To provide compensation for disability or death resulting from injury to employees in certain maritime employments and for other purposes." The act, however, does not provide for compensation in respect of disability or death of "a master or member of a crew of any vessel"; therefore these would be covered under Protection Indemnity insurance.

Under the provisions of the act, the employer is liable for and must secure the payment to his employees (other than a master or member of a crew) of the compensation payable, as specified in the act, for death, injuries, or disability, irrespective of fault on the part of the employer as a cause.

The yacht policy may be endorsed to cover the liability of the owner in accordance with the provisions of the federal act without additional premium wherever the Protection and Indemnity insurance is included.

MEDICAL PAYMENTS

For a small additional premium, wherever Protection and Indemnity insurance is endorsed under the policy, the contract may be extended to include Medical Payments insurance. Under this form, reasonable expenses for medical and surgical care, including hospitalization, etc., will be paid to or for the assured guests or others, excluding the assured or registered owner of the vessel, where injury results from an accident occurring aboard the insured vessel. Various limits of liability are available.

Yacht insurance is available through most insurance brokers and yacht brokers in three types of companies:

KINDS OF POLICIES

- *The stock company* charges a flat insurance rate depending upon the risk.
- *The "modified" stock company* charges a flat rate as above but returns from 10 to 20% of the premium if no claim is made thereunder.
- *The mutual company* charges a flat rate as above but pays an annual dividend, depending upon experience, of 15 to 20% to all policy holders. Dividends are not guaranteed.

Small sailboats, outboard boats, canoes, and rowing boats are often automatically covered under standard homeowners' policies. If in doubt, check with your agent before buying a separate marine policy.

The boating explosion of the last decades has made the yacht policy a paying deal for the insurers and they are now in competition for the yachtsman's dollars like other service and supply firms. Hence, it is today possible to get a better shake for your insurance dollar, and the local agent on his toes can often make up a very economical package for you, even to the point of combining several companies into a "pool."

Ask him about the advantages in rate for various deductible amounts—which means simply that you will insure yourself for the first $500 of loss (or other agreed-upon amount). Most of us insure against total loss and can afford a small loss as against a smaller rate accrued sometimes for many years. There is a lovely policy that counts your "lay days" and returns a part of your premium at policy end. The basis is your log; anytime, in season or out, that you "lay over"; i.e., do not move the boat for a specified period of days (usually 10), you enjoy a lesser rate. You may live aboard but not move. This is a boon to the Florida and California live-aboard people, who sometimes move their boats just twice a year—from yard to club or marina and back.

There are attractive "fleet" rates also. Boat and yacht clubs, or neighborhood groups can enjoy better rates under such a blanket policy, especially if all the boats are of the same design and value (as an outboard club, or sailing fleet). Local agents who really know their business can turn up the details. Ask them.

SALVAGE

734

"The right of salvage depends on no contract. A salvor who rescues valuable ships or cargoes from the grasp of wind and wave, the embrace of rocky ledges, or the devouring flame, need prove no bargain with its owner as the basis of recovering a reward.

"He is paid by the courts from motives of public policy—paid not merely for the value of his time and labor in the special case, but a bounty in addition, so that he may be encouraged to do the like again."

(From *Hughes on Admiralty*.)

In any case, the matter of determining salvage fees, rights, and other questions is for the court to decide. The spirit of the law is that all parties involved were functioning during an emergency but were unable because of the urgency of the situation to have come to an agreement on terms. Salvage questions seldom crop up in the small-boat fleet.

However, it is wise never to request a tow or ask for aid when disabled without being certain that a salvage situation is not being created. If wrecked and in dire danger, a salvage or potential salvage situation exists the moment that, without agreement, witnessed or in writing, the wrecked mariner accepts a line from the rescuing boat. Yachts performing such aid seldom consider it a salvaging job but commercial vessels or towboats might.

In any event, should the rescuer claim salvage, the courts will decide the amount of the award. This award is arrived at by a careful consideration of the actual danger that the wrecked vessel was in, the likelihood of her having got off without aid, etc. No salvage award is ever made for saving life, or for removing passengers or crew from a wrecked ship.

A towboat, or other boat which has been called to the scene by telephone or signal, is substantially "under a contract" even though the amount of payment for the service has not been specified, and her charges must be made accordingly and not as a salvage fee. Salvage generally can be claimed only when the wrecked ship has been "given up," or obviously should be given up, or when, without salvaging, she would shortly become a total loss.

Tows accepted from the Coast Guard or other government craft never constitute a salvage situation. Police or state boats may charge for services but not on a salvage basis. Under no interpretation of the law can it be called salvage when: (1) A sailboat is becalmed and in no danger and requests a tow; (2) a powerboat, suffering an engine breakdown and in no danger, requests a tow; (3) any boat, without crew or passengers on board, becomes "adrift" and is either towed to another mooring or her own anchors are let go, her engine started or sail raised and she is taken to a place of security.

CRUISING "FOREIGN" PAPERS

735   While the yachtsman cruising "foreign" need not be quite the sea lawyer the commercial seaman, on occasion, must be, it behooves him to understand some of the basic terms he is likely to require in processing the various "papers" involved.

The Crew Manifest. A separate paper, simply giving the names and ratings of the crew for purposes of health and Customhouse examination.

Clearance Papers. The official permission to sail from the boat's port of departure. Shows that all port dues and charges have been paid. Gives ports of destination.

Bill of Health. Shows condition of the health of the country (and the particular section of it) from whence the vessel sails.

Passenger List. If the boat is a passenger vessel, list must contain the names and destination of all passengers. It is really a part of the manifest.

Stores List. Contains list of the ship's stores. Must be complete when entering port, showing all unbroken and broken stores. Such stores not subject to duty.

Charter Party. A form of contract, or lease. It is a specified contract by which the owners of the vessel lease the entire vessel to another person, to be used by him either under their charge or his. The Yacht Charter Party takes various forms.

   a. Time Charter. The owner rents his ship out for a definite time and usually supplies crew, fuel, and stores.

   b. Voyage Charter. The owner hires the vessel out for a definite voyage as, for example, a run between two ports, or a round-trip voyage between two ports. Owner furnishes crew, fuel, and stores.

   c. Bareboat, or Barepole Charter. Charterer furnishes crew, fuel, and stores. With a partial bareboat charter, the charterer agrees to the owner's furnishing the crew, in which case he is responsible for their welfare. This is the most common form of Yacht charter.

Pratique. A certificate given after compliance with the quarantine regulations permitting a newly arrived ship to land her passengers and crew.

Port Charges. Pilotage, port, harbor, and possibly hospital dues. All based on tonnage except pilotage, which is based on draft.

TONNAGE

736 Gross tonnage is the internal capacity of the vessel expressed in units of 100 cubic feet and is strictly a measurement of volume, not weight.

Net tonnage is the measurement of volume, not weight, of the useful, cargo-carrying spaces left after deducting from the gross tonnage all the spaces required for machinery, tankage, crew quarters, galley etc.

Displacement tonnage (or simply displacement) is the actual weight in long tons (2,240 pounds) of the vessel and all that is in her. (Tons = volume of the vessel under water ÷ by 36 (or 35 if fresh water).

Deadweight tonnage is the carrying capacity of the vessel in long tons. It is the difference between the vessel "light" but with fuel and stores on board and the vessel loaded to her normal waterline.

Small boats are arbitrarily measured for tonnage by applying the Thames Tonnage Rule:

$$\frac{\text{Length} - \text{beam} \times \text{beam} \times \frac{1}{2} \text{beam}}{94}$$

Example: A vessel 30' overall with a beam of 9'.

$$\text{tonnage} = \frac{30 - 9 \ (\text{or } 21) \times 9 \times 4\frac{1}{2}}{94} = 9 + \text{tons}$$

CHAPTER VIII

SIGNALS AND SIGNALING

Distress Signals

INTERNATIONAL RULES
801

By day:

1. A gun or other explosive signal fired at intervals of about a minute
2. The International Code signal of distress indicated by NC
3. The distance signal, consisting of a square flag, having either above it or below it a ball or anything resembling a ball
4. Continuous sounding with any fog-signal apparatus
5. The signal SOS made by radiotelegraphy, or by any other distance signaling method or "MAYDAY" by radiotelephone
6. Orange Distress flag

By night:

1. A gun or other explosive signal, fired at intervals of about a minute (for vessels only)
2. Flames on the vessel, as from a burning tar barrel, oil barrel, etc. (for vessels only)
3. Rockets or shells throwing stars of any color or description, fired one at a time, at short intervals (for vessels only)
4. A continuous sounding with any fog-signal apparatus; in the case of aircraft, sound apparatus

5. The signal SOS made by radiotelegraphy, or by any other distance signaling method or "MAYDAY" by radiotelephone

INLAND RULES
802

By day:
1. A continuous sounding with any fog-signal apparatus, or firing a gun
2. Hand-held orange smoke signal
3. International Orange distress flag
4. Waving the American flag upside down
5. Repeatedly raising the arms over the head, then lowering them level with the shoulders

By night:
1. Flames on the vessel, as from a burning tar or oil barrel, etc
2. Continuous sounding with any fog-signal apparatus, or firing a gun
3. Red flares, hand or propelled

For Aircraft Only:
1. A succession of white lights projected into the sky at short intervals
2. The international distress call "MAYDAY" by radiotelephone

SUBMARINE DISTRESS SIGNALS

803 A submarine of the United States Navy that is attempting emergency surfacing releases a red smoke bomb. Keep clear.

A submarine that may be compelled to surface in the vicinity of surface craft releases two white or two yellow smoke bombs three seconds apart. Surface vessels should keep clear of the smoke bombs.

Any person sighting a red smoke bomb rising from the surface of the water should keep clear. If a submarine does not surface within a few minutes, report the time and location immediately to the nearest naval authority or Coast Guard unit, by radiotelephone if possible.

SIGNALS TO SUMMON A PILOT

804 A pilot may be obtained by displaying any of the following:

By day:

The International Code Flag Signal G, meaning "I require a pilot"

By night:

The International Code Signal G, by flashing light or horn

RADIO TIME SIGNALS

805 Official radio time signals are sent continuously from one Canadian and two United States government stations (as of February 1977). WWV, Fort Collins, Colorado, transmits GMT (Greenwich Mean Time) every minute on 5.0, 10.0, and 15.0 MHz. WWVH, Maui, Hawaii, transmits GMT every minute on 2.5, 5.0, 10.0, and 15.0 MHz. CHU, Ottawa, Ontario, transmits EST every minute on 3.33, 7.335 and 14.670 MHz.

Some U.S. radio and television stations also transmit hourly time beeps, which are quite accurate. Voice announcements are not so accurate.

DAY MARKS

806 Day marks are shown by boats operating under special conditions, such as towing or being towed, fishing, and dredging. The signal is made by a ball or cone shape. (*Figure 806*) Small boats are not required by law to show day marks, but every operator should understand and be able to read them when displayed on other vessels.

A vessel not under control shows a day mark consisting of two black balls, vertically arranged, and placed in a position where they can be best seen. The same day signal is displayed by self-propelled suction dredges underway with their suctions on bottom.

Vessels that are moored or anchored and engaged in laying pipe or operating on submarine construction display in daytime two balls in a vertical line, the upper ball being painted with alternate black and white vertical stripes and the lower ball in bright red.

A steam vessel under sail alone shows a day mark consisting of one black ball.
This same signal is used on vessels of over 300 gross tons when anchored.

A cable vessel in the daytime shows a day mark consisting of three shapes, the upper and lower of which are red balls and the center shape is in the form of a double cone base to base, painted bright white.

Dredges held in a stationary position show two balls in the daytime, vertically arranged, and placed in a position where they can best be seen.

A vessel towing a submerged boat in daytime shows two shapes, one above the other, in the form of two double cones base to base, the upper cone being painted with alternate horizontal stripes of black and white and the lower shape being painted bright red.

Steamers, lighters, and other vessels made fast alongside a wreck or moored over a wreck display two double cones base to base, both of which are painted bright red.

A fishing vessel in the daytime may display a basket in the rigging.

806 Day marks
307

STORM AND WEATHER SIGNALS

807   The storm flags are a triangular red pennant or a red square with a black center flown in various combinations. At night certain lantern combinations, hoisted vertically, give the same information. These are shown, together with their meanings, in Figure 807.

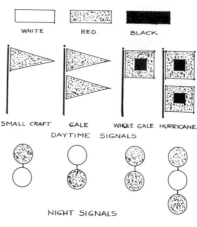

807

808   Explanation of small craft, storm, and hurricane advisories

Small craft advisory: One red pennant displayed by day and a red light above a white light at night to indicate that winds up to 38 mph (33 knots) and/or sea conditions dangerous to small craft operations are forecast for the area.

Gale warning: Two red pennants displayed by day and a white light above a red light at night to indicate that winds ranging from 39 to 54 mph (34 to 48 knots) are forecast for the area.

Whole gale warning: A single square red flag with a black center displayed during daytime and two red lights at night to indicate that winds ranging from 55 to 73 mph (48 to 63 knots) are forecast for the area.

Hurricane warning: Two square red flags with black centers displayed by day and a white light between two red lights at night to indicate that winds 74 mph (64 knots) and above are forecast for the area.

Both night and day storm signals are displayed at all Coast Guard stations, from the larger of the Coast Guard vessels (such as tugs, buoy tenders, cutters, etc.), from lightships on station—but *day signals only*—and from many private shore points. It is common for a yacht club, marina, shipyard or other boating facility to keep in touch with the local Coast Guard unit and, as a local service, display storm warnings. For full lists of display points as well as weather broadcasts, use "Storm-Warning Facilities Charts." These are charts covering coastal waters and the Great Lakes. Source is the Superintendent of Documents, Washington, D. C. 20402.

Storm-warning signals are displayed by the National Weather Service in maritime communities and ports, by the United States Coast Guard on some of their vessels, and by Coast Guard shore or surf stations. The various *Coast Pilots* contain local lists of points at which signals are displayed.

INTERNATIONAL CODE SIGNALING

809   Flag signaling is the oldest of the existing methods of visual signaling between vessels or between vessels and shore. The code used is international and standard in all civilized maritime nations.

The International Code consists of 26 letter flags, 10 numeral pennants, 3 repeater flags, and a code or answering pennant. The message, called a *hoist*, is read from top to bottom, and is sent aloft, if possible, in one string using a tack line (a length of halyard about one fathom long) to separate words, numbers, or meanings.

Messages often require more than one hoist. They are read in the following order:

First	Masthead
Second	Triatic stay
Third	Starboard yardarm
Fourth	Port yardarm

If all hoists are flown from the yardarm, the outboard hoist is the first read. If all hoists are flown from the triatic stay, the forward one is read first.

Signals remain flying until answered.

A signal is said to be *superior* to another if hoisted before the latter; it is *inferior* if hoisted after. It is also superior if hoisted in a preferred position (such as at the masthead), and inferior if hoisted in a secondary position (such as at the port yardarm).

HOW TO CALL

Unless the signal letters of a particular vessel are hoisted superior to the message, the message is understood to be addressed to all vessels. In the event that it is impossible to determine the signal letters of the ship desired to be addressed, letter "K" is displayed ("I wish to communicate with you") over numeral pennant as required: radio-telephone 2182 kHz—"8," radiotelephone VHF Channel 16—"9," International code flags—"6."

HOW TO ANSWER SIGNALS

The ship (or ships) addressed hoists the answering pennant *at the dip* (halfway up the halyard) as soon as it has seen each hoist made; and *close up* (fully up the halyard) as soon as read and understood. As soon as the hoist is hauled down on the transmitting ship, the answering pennant is lowered to *at the dip* on the receiving ship. Each hoist is so acknowledged until the message is completed.

Inasmuch as it is often difficult to distinguish between *at the dip* and *close up*, the answering pennant is not hoisted on the triatic stay signal halyards but rather to the masthead or a yardarm.

HOW TO COMPLETE A SIGNAL

The transmitting ship hoists the answering pennant alone after the last message hoisted to indicate that the message has been completed. The receiving ship answers this in a similar manner to answering all other hoists; then makes the reply.

IF THE SIGNAL IS NOT UNDERSTOOD

If the receiving ship cannot distinguish or understand the signal made, the answering pennant is kept at the dip and an appropriate signal made, informing the transmitting ship of the reason.

If the hoist can be distinguished but not understood the pennant is kept at the dip and the signal ZL made. (Meaning: Signal is not understood though flags are distinguished.)

810 The signal and practices have been revised and made more useful, especially on an international basis, effective April 1, 1969, and are fully described and detailed in HO 102 published by the Naval Oceanographic Office, Washington, D. C. 20390. While spelled-out messages are not barred, much further flexibility and speed is achieved by also giving the other and further meanings of the letters. The signals consist of:

1. Single-letter signals denote meanings which are common or urgent.
2. Two-letter signals denote general messages; not urgent.
3. Three-letter signals, the first letter of each being "M," are for medical messages.

A "complement," in the form of a numeral, may be added to a one- or two-letter signal denoting variations in the meaning of the signal; supplementary, specific, or more detailed meaning, or questions and answers relating to the signal.

The alphabetical signals in use before 1965 are no longer used. The single and two-letter signals, plus an extensive library of special-meaning signals (courses, time, bearings, geographical co-ordinates also found in HO 102) appear to meet 90% of the needs for ordinary, peace-time signaling. Spelled-out messages are used, of course, whenever there is no code and for proper names, places, etc. Such a hoist is preceded by the signal YZ to indicate that a plain-language message follows.

The three-letter medical signals or code is designed to exchange information (as between a ship carrying a doctor and one not carrying one) on the treatment, condition, diagnosis of a sick or injured person. It, like the single- and two-letter signals, is keyed to nine languages, so the entire new system is truly an international language. For any vessel in a foreign port the system can save life and suffering, and American offshore cruisers are urged to carry a copy of HO 102 and the appropriate flag bag.

The Medical Signal Code always begins with the letter M. The letter C (affirmative or yes) and the letter N (for negative or no) may follow the code group. Common diseases and medical situations are coded to a number and usual medical queries as to sex, age, pulse and temperature, breathing, duration and frequency of symptoms also have a code group. Standard medicines likely to be found in a ship's medicine chest are also coded. A chart of the human body is coded as well, so that an injury (for example) can be located exactly. Thus, by flag hoists (or blinker or semaphore) complete medical care can be given a patient from report and diagnosis to treatment and medication, in nine languages.

811   The following basic signals relate to medical situations which might arise (they are *not* preceded by flag "M"):

All made by International Code signal flags.

1.	"I need a doctor"	AN
2.	"I require medical assistance"	W
3.	"I have a doctor on board"	AL

812   In order to avoid confusion as the letters of a flag hoist are called out. (or letters are used in radiotelephone messages), the United States Navy has evolved a more or less foolproof system. Each letter is given a word sound rather than a letter sound, so that B, for example, cannot be confused with E, C, D or T. The word sound for B is *Bravo*, a word unlike any other word in the code. (*See end paper*)

813   These are the meanings of single-letter hoists:

A Diver, down, keep clear
B Dangerous cargo
C Yes, affirmative, ok
D Keep clear
E Altering course to starboard
F Disabled
G Want a pilot
H Pilot on board
I Altering course to port
J On fire, keep clear
K Wish to communicate
L Stop instantly
M I am stopped
N No
O Man overboard
P About to sail

Q Request pratique
R (No meaning)
S Engines going astern
T Keep clear of me
U Standing into danger
V Require assistance
W Require medical assistance
X Stop your intention
Y Am dragging anchor
Z Require a tug
Answering pennant is used for decimal. That is, number flag 9 + answering pennant plus number flag 5 equals 9.5 —

Two-letter hoists are listed in H.O. 102 and cover a great many situations of a general nature relating to business between ships and ship and shore. The single-letter hoists, time being of the essence with none of it to be spared to find the signals and make up a multiple flag hoist, are reserved for urgent or emergency communication (Example: O = Man overboard).

The general message can afford the time to make up a hoist. It would be on this order:

QX Request permission to anchor. (to harbor master)
PD Your navigation lights are not visible.
UT Where are you bound for?
CJ Do you require assistance?
KN I cannot take you in tow.

814 The yachting scene has developed many special signals, entirely unofficial in terms of the International Code; many stem from yacht clubs and some from flag manufacturers . . . and some, like those horrible ball-and-chain devices signifying that the wife is aboard, should be abolished under pain of the husband losing his silly pointed head.

These are common and valuable to know:

T Call for club launch (or transportation to shore)
W Doctor on board
Q Request pratique
B Explosives on board, or fueling, or oil cargo. (Also used as the racing protest flag by sailors)
H Pilot on board
G Request a pilot
P About to sail
Z Require a tug (or tow)
F Disabled

There are also special-purpose flags, not International Code flags, used by yachts. These are shown in the end paper and discussed in Chapter XVIII.

A very special flag, to be honored with concern whenever seen, is the diver's flag. It means that scuba divers are submerged, working or playing, and *all* boats are to keep well clear. (*Figure 814*)

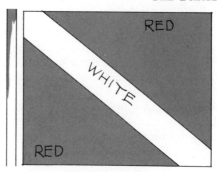

814 Diver's flag

THE INTERNATIONAL MORSE CODE
(DOT AND DASH SIGNALS)

815   The international Morse code is truly international, and may be used to communicate with a ship or the shore in any civilized land with a reasonable chance of the message's being understood and answered. It is used in radio, blinker light, sound, and visual signaling.

The code is shown in Figures 815A, B, C, and D.

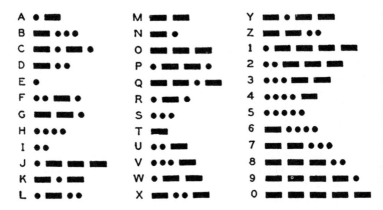

815A The international Morse code

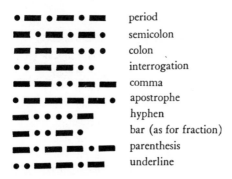

● ▬ ● ▬ ● ▬	period
▬ ● ▬ ● ▬ ●	semicolon
▬ ▬ ● ● ●	colon
● ● ▬ ▬ ● ●	interrogation
▬ ▬ ● ● ▬ ▬	comma
● ▬ ▬ ▬ ▬ ●	apostrophe
▬ ● ● ● ▬	hyphen
▬ ● ● ▬ ●	bar (as for fraction)
▬ ● ▬ ▬ ● ▬	parenthesis
● ● ▬ ▬ ● ▬	underline

815B International Morse code punctuation

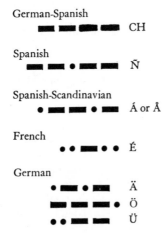

German-Spanish
▬ ▬ ▬ ▬ CH

Spanish
▬ ▬ ● ▬ ▬ Ñ

Spanish-Scandinavian
● ▬ ▬ ● ▬ Á or Å

French
● ● ▬ ● ● É

German
● ▬ ● ▬ Ä
▬ ▬ ▬ ● Ö
● ● ▬ ▬ Ü

815C International Morse code special language letters

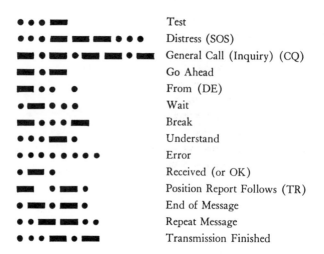

815D International Morse code calls

816 Blinker code is sent, using the Morse code, by various types of lights. Emergency blinker messages may be sent with a flashlight, a lantern and screen, or by using the main or navigating light switches as keys.

For long-distance visual signals, special equipment is required, usually a searchlight of some power, fitted with a key-operated shutter that breaks the beam of light. Such a light cannot be operated by turning the light on and off (as with an electrical switch) because the filament of the extinguised light continues to glow and, over a distance, there is no appreciable break in the light beam. If, in an emergency, the searchlight must be used, transmit at a *very* slow rate; not more than 10 or 12 letters a minute. A yardarm light has the same fault and its range is very short. A powerful flashlight that can be aimed is an excellent emergency blinker provided the signal is made, not with the switch, but by sliding the hand or a paper over the lens with the light on continually.

Blinker messages are divided into five component parts as follows:

Component	Transmitting Vessel Makes	Receiving Vessel Makes
1. Call	AA AA AA (general call)	TT TT TT (answer)
2. Identity	DE—signal letters or name	Repeats
3. Break sign	BT (text follows)	BT
4. Text	Message	Acknowledges each group of words or codes by TT TT
5. Ending	AR (message finished)	R (message received)

After a vessel has established her identity (if requested) future messages are carried on by the parts 1, 3, 4, and 5 only.

H.O. 10Z should be referred to for complete details of blinker signaling, especially if communication with naval vessels or bases is contemplated.

817   Sound signals by Morse code may be made on the whistle, foghorn, or other sounding device. It is to be considered purely as an emergency form of signaling, as such signals would create confusion in fog or in waters having heavy traffic.

The signals are made as follows:

Component	Transmitting Vessel Makes	Receiving Vessel Makes
1. Call	AA AA AA	TT TT TT
2. Break sign	BT (text follows)	(No acknowledgment)
3. Text	Message	"
4. Ending	AR	R

NOTE: If the message is not understood by the receiving ship she makes UD (repeat); otherwise the message is considered as having been understood and so acknowledged by making R.

WIGWAG MORSE CODE SIGNALING

818   The Morse code may be used in a system of flag manipulations which are basically very simple. The flag may be of any color easily seen against the background and should be bent to a staff about five feet long. (Figure 818)

Attention is called by waving, and is answered by TT TT.

The start is made by holding the staff vertical, flag up. Dots are made by a right dip and dashes by a left dip.

818 Wigwag signaling, using international Morse code

PRIVATE SIGNAL CODES

819 Private codes are used by some nautical organizations, particularly yacht clubs when racing or moving in squadron formation. A private signal-code book must be used, and a signal made from it is preceded by the International Code hoist NMM, indicating that the message is not to be interpreted from the International Code book.

In general, signals in the club code consist of:

Special, racing, and emergency signals (one or two flags, from A
to Z, and A to AZ).

General signals (two flags, BA to GZ).

Designation (two flags, HA to HZ).

Days of the week (two flags, IQ to IZ).

Hours of the day (two flags, JA to KY).

Names of places (two flags, NA to WZ).

Compass signals (three flags, AQD to AST).

RADIOTELEPHONY

820 Although, for practical purposes, no pleasure boat is required to be equipped with a radiotelephone, many are. So many, in
fact, that there are now four possible types of radio communication
open to the pleasure boat skipper; in addition, equipment may
range from the simplest portable or plug-in gear to elaborate, tun-
able ham systems. (Ham radio is an activity in itself, and beyond
the scope of this book.) The three kinds of radio remaining are the
AM transceivers operating in the 2–3 MHz band, the VHF-FM
sets occupying the 156–162 MHz band, and Citizens Band sets in
the 27 MHz band.

Of these, the VHF-FM is generally considered the most suitable
for short-range (25–40 miles) marine communications. VHF (for
Very High Frequency) FM works by line-of-sight, so the taller the
antenna, the greater the range. As there is no skip phenomenon,
VHF-FM transmissions stay more or less in the area where they are
broadcast, instead of turning up hundreds or thousands of miles
away. Many VHF-FM sets today come as transceiver-antenna packages, capable of being installed by anyone who can distinguish a positive terminal from a negative; unlike other forms of equipment,
these pretuned, matched sets do not require technician installation.

In the VHF-FM system, different channels are set aside for ship-
to-ship, ship-to-shore, safety, distress-and-calling, and other specialized uses. On most sets, one or two "receive-only" channels are
available for picking up the National Weather Service continuous
forecasts (*See Paragraph 701*). If you can afford it, experts recom-
mend a set with a minimum of six channels, offering Channels 6
(Safety), 16 (Distress and Calling), 22A (Coast Guard working),

two ship-to-ship and one ship-to-shore having the frequency of your local telephone company marine operator (through which you may call any telephone in the world). Twelve channels are even better—with the basic three, plus two or three for ship-to-ship, two or three for ship-to-coast, one for bridge or lock tenders if necessary, and two weather-receive. The latest official information on this and other kinds of marine radios is contained in a book entitled *How to Use Your Marine Radio Telephone*, published by the volunteer Radio Technical Commission for Marine Services, in cooperation with the Federal Communications Commission. Copies are available at most marine electronics dealers.

The marine radio system preceding the VHF-FM system was known technically as 2-3 MHz Double Sideband AM. Because of technical shortcomings of the system, and because of overcrowding, the Double Sideband (DSB) AM system has now been ruled illegal. What remains in this airspace is the Single Sideband AM system, a long-range radiotelephone service used largely by offshore cruising vessels. This system is extremely costly, technically demanding to install and operate, and only available (by FCC regulation) to boats whose skippers can (a) demonstrate a need for it and (b) already possess properly licensed VHF-FM equipment.

The Citizens Band Radio Service, created as an adjunct to small businesses ashore, has become a national fad, both on land and on the water. Although CB equipment is technically controlled under the same kind of FCC licensing as VHF-FM, SSB AM, or ham gear, in fact the CB operators are in many parts of the country out of all control, jamming the air with untraceable broadcasts from trucks, cars, boats, and homes. The Coast Guard and the FCC are both set against CB as a marine radio system for several reasons, some good and some merely bureaucratic: Limited by law to four watts DSB power or 12 watts for SSB sets, CB has a relatively short controllable range, which may be shortened still further by intervening structures and land masses. It is prone to atmospheric disturbance (as VHF-FM is not), and it is not monitored by any government safety organization, although CB Channel 9 has been designated as a distress and emergency frequency. Despite official disapproval, the low cost of CB equipment, its simplicity of installation, and the large number of operators both afloat and ashore do give it a convenience and safety aspect that is very important to hundreds of thousands of people.

RADIO LICENSES

821 For VHF-FM or SSB equipment, two licenses are required under Federal Communication Commission rules: one for the station and one for the operator, as follows:

Station License. Applicant must be a U. S. citizen or a U. S. corporation (requiring special procedures noted in Section 83.23 of the FCC rules). Use form 502. Mail to Federal Communication Commission, Gettysburg, Pennsylvania 17325 or carry to one of the 30 or more FCC offices in major cities. The fee is $4 with the application, and the license is good, under this single fee, for five years. It may be renewed for another five-year term upon payment of another $4 fee. The quickest manner in which to obtain a license is to visit a field office and conclude the business there, requesting immediate use of the equipment. This special permit, saving up to two or three months of waiting, costs $10.

The license is issued to the owner *and* the boat. It cannot be transferred to a new owner or to a different vessel. However, a change of boat name or registration number requires a letter to the FCC, explaining the matter, together with the posting of a copy with the station license. This license *must* be posted near the equipment and available to inspectors at all times.

To renew within the license period (as at the end of it) complete Form 405-B and send it into the FCC with $4, good for another five years. If the license has expired, you must start all over again. Discontinuance of the station must be advised to the FCC.

Operator's License (or Permit). The most popular of the two forms of license available is the Restricted Radiotelephone Operator Permit. It is for any U. S. citizen over 14 years of age and costs $4 for life. No test or examination is required but the applicant must certify that he can speak English, can keep a radio log in English or a common foreign language, and understands the general rules and regulations and his responsibility to keep current on these regulations. It is easily handled by mail to any FCC office.

While there is no significant advantage as a mere station operator to have a Third Class Radiotelephone Operator's License, it is available to those who pass the examination and wish the status of the Third Class Permit. However, any vessel carrying more than six passengers for hire must ship at least one crew member having a Third Class Permit. It is issued after passing a simple examination in operating procedures (nontechnical) and costs $3 for a five-year period. Preparation may be made with the help of a "Study Guide" issued by FCC offices.

A lost permit or license, or one mutilated (as by water or fire), may be replaced by reapplying and enclosing a letter of explanation and the original fee. Any person, licensed or not, may freely use the radiotelephone. The law requires only that someone on board must be licensed (master, owner, etc.).

The operator's permit does not give authority for the holder to make any frequency or other changes to the set. The experimenter or radio "ham" requires a second- or first-class license, obtainable only after technical examination. Any adjustments to the set must be made by or in the presence of a holder of a more advanced license. The restricted license is a license to *use* the radiotelephone only. CB operators require a station license, same cost and source as a ship station license, but no operator permit or license is necessary.

RADIO LOG

822   A radio log must be kept, showing the fact, time, etc. of all distress or emergency calls in and out of the boat, plus all calls heard of a distress or maritime safety nature. It should also show the start and end of a listening watch stood, as well as any adjustments made by an authorized technician. Each entry must be signed. There are penalties for failure to meet the regulations. It should be noted that a radio watch is not required on a small yacht. If, however, one is maintained, it must be on 2182 kHz on equipment in the 2–3 MHz band and Channel 16 on VHF equipment, and it must be posted in the log. The log itself is open upon demand to any FCC inspector at any reasonable time.

USE OF THE RADIOTELEPHONE

823   Using the radiotelephone is based on the premise that radiotelephone communication between vessels is important and has substance as compared to chit-chat. The sole exception is the call to a shore station (ship to shore), which is recognized to be of a more social or personal nature. Messages are graded as follows:

1st priority	Distress messages and further messages relating to the situation. Identified by the word "MAYDAY." (3 times)
2nd priority	Urgent messages relating to safety of the transmitting ship or any others of concern, including aircraft. Identified by the word "PAN." (3 times)
3rd priority	Safety messages relating to navigation, warnings, weather and hurricane warnings, identified by the word "SECURITY." (3 times)

Only then, after *carefully listening* to be certain that no priority message is on the air, may the ordinary ship's business be aired. It is this situation that most concerns the FCC and that it monitors at *all times*.

If a distress signal is on the air, or developing, listen but do not transmit. *Repeat: Do not transmit.*

If you hear the International signal (by voice) "Seelonce MAYDAY," cease transmitting at once. The only stations authorized to use this are the vessel needing assistance and the station controlling the distress traffic. "Seelonce Distress" means the same thing but is transmitted by any station, not the two above, who has reason to silence traffic. When the emergency is over and the air free to again use, the phrase is "Seelonce Feenee." These odd-looking words are phonetic for the French *silence* and *silence fini*, or silence finished. "Mayday" is the phonetic version of *m'aidez*—"help me"—in French.

If you hear a "Mayday" (repeated three times) listen first and try to determine (by listening to other traffic or the endangered vessel) if yours is the vessel that is nearest and can assist, or if another vessel is better equipped or located. Should you be the vessel tagged, reply to the MAYDAY, identify yourself by name and radio call number, give your position, your course and your estimated time of arrival (ETA).

If you hear the words "MAYDAY Relay," three times repeated, it is from another vessel relaying the distress call, and you should talk to her.

MAYDAY is to be used *only* in cases of genuine distress; not for minor mishaps such as stranding in protected waters, engine failure, or lack of a breeze. Hazard to life and/or property must be present to classify a message as a distress message. Should you, by any ill fortune, need to call for help, this is the form the message should take:

The *Distress Call* consists of:

—the Distress Signal MAYDAY, spoken three times;

—the identification (name and call sign) of the craft in distress, spoken three times;

—the call sign, spoken once.

The *Distress Message* follows and consists of:

—the Distress Signal MAYDAY, spoken three times;

—the identification of the craft;

—particulars of its position (latitude and longitude, or bearing and distance in miles from a known geographical position);

—the nature of the distress and the kind of assistance desired.

Be prepared to give a "long count" (a steady transmission signal) so that DF apparatus can locate you. Identify the source of the count both before and after your transmission by giving your call letters. Fight down the urge to hurry or to panic. Speak slowly, according to the prescribed message form, use phonetic words to assist in spelling. Ask for any advice, such as for a wounded person, after the distress message has been processed and help is on the way. It is quite likely that the Coast Guard will use aircraft (helicopter) to assist in a rescue operation, especially if there are wounded to be cared for, and in such case you will also have to talk to the aircraft, probably when he is overhead. The Coast Guard's directions to the rescued vessel are contained in Chapter XVI.

824 A call to a shore station telephone operator is made as follows:

The owner will first have duly registered with the telephone company, given the boat's call signal, set up an account, and requested the type of service desired (for yachts and noncommercial boats this is the General Service).

A call *from* the boat to a shore number is made by merely listening to hear if the channel is clear and if so, giving the answering operator the name of the boat calling and the number desired. If another boat is being called, give its call letters and probable location. Upon completion of the call the operator is given the calling boat's letters and the information that it is signing off.

A call from land *to* a boat is made by requesting Long Distance and then the Marine Operator. Give the called boat's name (or call letters and name), its probable location; then follow the operator's instructions.

Here is an example of a ship-to-ship call.

Begin on Channel 16 VHF-FM, wait for a break; then be brief.

Calling Vessel "Dog Star"	*Vessel Called "Windigo"*
"Windigo, this is WYP 7746, the yacht Dog Star. Over."	x
	"Dog Star, this is WAX 5678, the ketch Windigo. Shift to Channel 68. Over."
"Roger, switching." (Shifts to ship-to-shore channel 68) "Windigo. Dog Star."	"Go ahead."
(Sends message. Terminates communication within three minutes)	
"This is Dog Star WYP 7746. Out."	"Windigo, WAX 5678. Out."
x	x

HINTS

825 A call to the Coast Guard is made only in emergencies or for information that the Coast Guard usually gives. Request for weather information would hardly be fair (considering that it is sent out at frequent intervals anyway). Requests for medical advice, assistance, conditions over bars or in storm areas, or reporting vessels in distress are all legitimate reasons for using the Coast Guard frequency.

Any shore station will relay a call to the Coast Guard free of charge.

Telegrams may be sent via radiotelephone.

Do not break in on conversations. When you get on the air, be brief and concise, identify yourself by call number and yacht name at the start and finish of each message. If possible, sometime in the message work in your approximate position. This may help if you strike trouble or break down, for the Coast Guard is listening and picks just this kind of information out of the babble that pervades the radio air. Watch your language. No one will blame you for getting mad at the inane conversations that fill the small-craft channels, but don't—repeat *don't*—damn them. It is a criminal offense to use profanity or obscene language on the air.

If you carry, even temporarily, paying passengers and they number more than six, your vessel *must* be equipped with a radiophone. You will need at least a Third Class license and a set which puts out not less than 25 watts. Vessel operator's licenses are also required as indicated in Chapter IV. If your boat is chartered, it is not carrying passengers for hire if you go with the boat as a *guest* of the charterer. The charterer may use your radiophone under your license, but you are responsible for him and what he does or says.

⚓

PART III

PILOTING AND NAVIGATION

CHAPTER IX

THE INSTRUMENTS OF PILOTING

IN BROACHING the subject of navigation, let it be understood that the approach in this *Manual* is entirely from the viewpoint of the small-boat man. His navigating is done almost entirely by visible aids to navigation or by soundings (called *piloting*); when overtaken by thick weather or when making the occasional hundred-mile leg offshore he relies upon his compass, and log, and lead—and perhaps more than any of these, upon his lookout. And this is as it should be.

To introduce into this *Manual* a complete treatise on navigation (the average technical volume dealing with the subject reaches a thousand pages of this size) would be but to obfuscate the simple elements of the subject, which are all that the small-boat man needs to get from "here to there" in safety. Gyrocompasses and electronic logs are interesting and necessary to the deepwater navigator, but aren't necessary for the 'long-shore navigator; nor is his vessel likely to be equipped with such apparatus. Celestial navigation, too, while interesting to the student and necessary to the yachtsman who regularly make long ocean passages, is of no use to the coastwise navigator. *In extremis*, celestial navigation for the small-boat man is, as Alfred Loomis so soundly defined it: "the ability to distinguish sunrise from sunset, then to steer toward the sunset until a large continent looms in sight!" It may be pointed out that on the Pacific Coast it would be best to steer toward the sunrise. In either case, the navigator will come upon some aid to navigation, or a familiar coast line, or shipping lane and it behooves him then to thoroughly understand piloting.

901   The following instruments are required for piloting.

Compass:	Magnetic, at least 4″ card
Lead and line:	5 to 14 pounds and line marked to about 20 fathoms (or electronic depth sounder)
Log:	Patent, taffrail, or chip (or speedometer)
Course protractor:	Single arm
Dividers:	About 5″ legs
Binoculars:	7 x 35 (or 50), prismatic best
Time piece:	Accurate watch or chronometer
Deviation card:	For the compass and boat used
Charts:	Local
Publications:	Light List, Tide Tables, Current Tables, Coast Pilot for the locale
Logbook:	Or paper or notebook for calculations and record

Other tools, desirable but not absolutely necessary, are: parallel rules, drawing compass, straightedge, *Notices to Mariners*, pelorus (preferably to fit on standard compass), thermometer, stop watch, etc. Radio navigation requires at least a direction finder and a radio-beacon chart, and a standard-broadcast receiver is helpful at times.

THE MAGNETIC COMPASS

902   The magnetic compass is a mechanical contrivance making use of the electrical attraction of the magnetic poles. Basically it is a freely suspended magnet that tends always to point toward the magnetic North Pole. To this magnet is attached a graduated circular card, to be read at the lubber line, which is marked near the card on the inside of a stationary rim or bowl; the reading at the lubber line will be the vessel's heading. Thus a fixed pointer (the only such pointer on a vessel) is obtained. *It is always fixed and the boat always moves around it.* It is of the utmost importance that the novice fix this truth in his mind—in relation to the earth, *the compass card never moves*; the boat *moves around it to the extent shown by the lubber line.*

Various methods of suspending this magnet are in use; liquids are introduced to slow or steady the pointer and the entire device is suspended in gimbals, permitting it to remain level and accurate regardless of angle of heel or pitch. It is often enclosed in a binnacle, or stand, for protection and may be fitted with various hoods, magnifiers, and lighting devices for easy reading and for night use.

The compass is always installed with the lubber line, and the center of the pivot on which the magnet and its attached card rotates, on a fore-and-aft line of the boat. This line may be any distance from the center fore-and-aft line but must be parallel to it. It must never be assumed that a thwartships bulkhead is at perfect right angles to the center line and that the compass, affixed to such a bulkhead, will be accurate. A line must be stretched from the exact center of the stem to the exact center of the transom, and the lubber line and the center of the pivot be equidistant from such a line.

If the compass is thus accurately placed, a reading at the lubber line will be the compass course of the boat.

A magnifier is available, which clamps to the compass rim at approximately the lubber line, and enlarges the card *and* the lubber line so that the image is increased in size about five times. It is valuable when an exact course—one involving half or quarter points—must be steered and, on any compass, saves much eyestrain and fatigue.

903 The compass card is marked in several ways, only one of which is in common use. Figure 903A shows it. For most small craft, the 360° card is marked in 5° increments, with the cardinal (N, S, E, W) and sometimes intercardinal (NE, SW, SE, NW) points lettered.

On older compasses (*Figure 903*), the circumference of the card is divided into 32 points of 11¼° each. North, south, east, and west are the cardinal points, and midway between each cardinal point is an intercardinal point, northeast, southeast, southwest, and northwest. Between each cardinal and intercardinal point is an intermediate point. There are 16 intermediate points always recognized by the sign "x" or "by." An easy way to remember the intermediate points is to regard the "x" as saying "but." Thus NW x W is northwest (the intercardinal or cardinal point first) *but* west of it. S x W is south *but* west of it. The distance away from the cardinal or intercardinal point indicated by the second component of the intermediate point is always one point, or ¹⁄₃₂ of the circle.

Boxing the compass includes the ability to name the opposite

903 The traditional mariner's compass card, largely obsolete today except on large ships The outer card is the 360° or Navy card; the inner the quarter-point card used by sailors in the last century. It is available today only in compasses of at least 8″ diameter.

(across the card) point from any other point. First the cardinal and intercardinal points are thoroughly memorized, then the intermediate points, then the quarter points. The navigator should know how to box the compass, always visualizing the card as fixed and the lubber's line revolving about it.

The 360° or Navy card is divided into 360 degrees starting with zero (north) and proceeding clockwise. It is the most accurate of all the cards and makes fine steering possible. In small craft, however, the diameter of the card and the incessant movement of the boat makes 360 individual degrees difficult to deal with. The larger and steadier yachts normally use compasses marked in two-degree increments. On the more sophisticated—and expensive—compasses, some manufacturers offer a choice of cards. (*See also Figure* 903A)

The 5° card, probably the most used on yachts to-day. Easy to read and as accurate as a small-boat can be steered. In sizes from the smallest to 5", well within the needs of small yachts.

The 5°-point card, used by truly large sailing yachts on ocean passages. Available from to 5 to 8" diameter.

The popular 2° card used by the larger coastal and ocean cruisers. Available to 8" diameter.

903A Compass cards used by yachts today

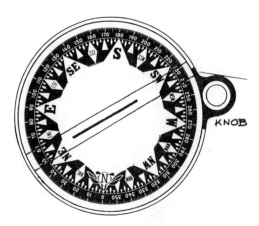

903B "Dead Beat" Steering Compass. From a practical viewpoint, the average yacht-sized compass has a card so small that continuous reading—"chasing a tiny number around"—becomes a tiresome and wearying chore and one that soon reduces the helmsman to anything but a reliable hand. This difficulty is increased at night, in fog, or in rain. Since no one can steer a small boat on an *exact* course for any length of time, the helmsman must develop a sense of averaging. Usually this can be confined to about a 5° variation, steering to left and right of the' exact course and compensating by meeting the understeering with oversteering or vice-versa. With a sense of timing applied (30 seconds right met with 30 seconds left) the course will average out remarkably true. To meet this situation and avoid the strain of following small numbers on a small card, set the desired course against the lubber line, and thereafter keep the two wire bars and the magnetic needle parallel. Usually the two bars and the needle are treated with a luminous material so they may be readily seen at night. This is an ideal sea compass, well suited for sail, and completely obviates the necessity to read numbers at any time save when setting the course. It is used extensively on aircraft.

RELATIVE BEARINGS

904   It will be noted that the system of relative bearings also makes use of 32 points that divide the imaginary circle around the vessel. They are definitely related to the compass bearings.

Thus a vessel heading north, having a stern wind, would refer to the wind as a 180° or a south wind. If the vessel were heading west with a stern wind, the wind would be a 90° or an east wind. If heading west with the wind broad on the port quarter, the wind would be a 135° or southeast wind.

Example of relative bearings compared to compass bearings of a vessel headed north (north to south, on the starboard side).

Wind

N	Ahead
NxE	One point on starboard bow
NNE	Two points on starboard bow
NExN	Three points on starboard bow
NE	Broad on starboard bow
NExE	Three points forward on starboard beam
ENE	Two points forward on starboard beam
ExN	One point forward on starboard beam
E	Abeam, or, broad on starboard beam
ExS	One point abaft starboard beam
ESE	Two points abaft starboard beam
SExE	Three points abaft starboard beam
SE	Broad on starboard quarter
SExS	Three points on starboard quarter
SSE	Two points on starboard quarter
SxE	One point on starboard quarter
S	Astern

It is necessary to know the boxing of the compass to convert such bearings to wind directions.

EMERGENCY DIRECTION FINDING

905   If the compass fails or becomes lost or broken, the navigator has two simple methods to give him general direction.

By day: north by watch—Hold a watch or clock, known to be reasonably accurate, level and in such a position that the hour hand points to the sun. Exactly halfway between the hour hand and twelve o'clock will be south, and directly opposite, of course, north. In summer months reset the watch to standard time. (South of the equator, the halfway mark will be north.)

By night: north by the Pole Star—The Dipper (7 stars in the shape of a common water dipper that are always visible on clear nights in most of the Northern Hemisphere) is found in the constellation of the Great Bear. A line drawn upward through the two front stars of the dipper's bowl will lead to a conspicuously bright star, which is Polaris, the North Star. (*Figure 905*)

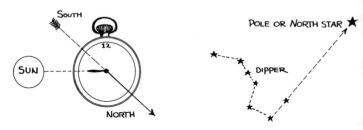

905 Emergency direction finders

Compass Error

VARIATION

906   Magnetic north and geographic or true north (to which all navigational charts are oriented) do not coincide. True north and south (the poles) are used as the chart poles because both are fixed and unvarying. Magnetic north is some 400 miles south of geographic north (73° N. Lat.; 100° W. Long.) and is constantly, though predictably, changing its exact location.

Therefore, when the compass needle points north it is not pointing to the north of the chart but to a different (magnetic) north. The amount of angular separation between these two points is called variation, and is expressed in degrees. (*Figure 906A*)

The amount of this variation may differ with the locality, as it follows certain magnetic channels between the poles; it may vary east or west of the true meridian, or there may be no variation at all.

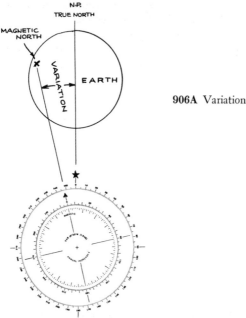

906A Variation

On coastwise charts the amount of variation for the locality shown on that chart is shown by a combination compass rose. This is a triple graduated circle (*Figure 906B*), the two outer roses marked in degrees and the inner marked in compass points. The outer circle is oriented to true or geographical north; its zero degrees is *true* north. The inner circle is oriented to magnetic north of the year noted in the center; its "north point" is *magnetic* north. The difference between the two points is the variation in the year noted at the center of the rose, top half. The innermost (point) circle is also oriented toward magnetic north.

The variation in the year as *read* is obtained by multiplying the annual increase or decrease noted in the lower half of the center by the number of years elapsed between printing and reading. Thus, on the chart rose shown in Figure 906B, the variation in 1975 was 0°15′ W (west). (Note information in the upper half of rose) The variation increases 8′ each year (Note information in lower half of rose.) The variation in 1978 therefore equaled 3 × 8′ (years elapsed × annual increase) or 0°15′ plus 24′, making the total variation since printing 0°39′ in the year 1978. Had the annual variation been decreased the amount would, of course, have been subtracted.

906B Combination compass rose

When a magnetic course is changed to a true course, *east variation* is always *added* and *west variation* is always *subtracted*. East variation is always shown to the right of the true north, and west variation to the left.

Unless the chart used is very old and the total annual increase or decrease amounts to a substantial part of a degree, the coastwise cruiser may safely disregard annual changes in variation on short courses. In practice, normal errors in steering and in estimating drift and windage will greatly outweigh the annual error in variation. Long sea courses should, however, take the annual variation into consideration.

DEVIATION

907 Deviation is another form of compass error. It is caused by magnetism within the vessel that may affect the accuracy of the compass; this must be corrected by placing compensating magnets about the compass—to cancel out the "errors"—or by calculating a table showing the deviation error on various headings (as the magnetism moves about the fixed compass needle). It is usual to eliminate as much of the deviation as possible by placing surrounding magnets, then to calculate a deviation chart for the remaining error. This error is applied to what would have been, without deviation, the correct course; the result is the compass course, which is the course steered, though neither a magnetic nor a true course.

All boats have varying magnetic characteristics peculiar to themselves and caused by a combination of factors, such as induced magnetism in iron ballast, in the iron masses of the machinery, in electrical apparatus, and in the hull, even though itself of wood.

Strong magnetic influences sometimes affect the compass sufficiently to make it worthless, but most of these can be eliminated by the careful location of the compass itself. It should be as far away as possible from the engine, and, especially, from such influences as a coil, generator, or other apparatus having a magnetic field. No part of the compass or binnacle should be electrically grounded. Wires passing nearby should be twisted around themselves to neutralize their fields, and iron or steel objects (such as knives, marlinspikes, etc.) should be kept away from the vicinity of the compass and out of the pockets of the helmsman. Magnetic energy will pass through anything and therefore shielding is of no avail.

Commercial vessels and some yachts engage a professional compass adjuster (cost $100 or thereabouts) who places the compensating magnets about the compass where needed and who furnishes the ship with a card showing the residual compass errors. These must be taken into consideration when laying out courses in the manner to be later detailed.

Modern pleasure-boat owners, with craft constructed of fiberglass, aluminum, or wood seldom require a compass adjuster. Virtually all good compasses, from the least expensive to the 5″ and up models, are provided with built-in compensating magnets and instructions for correcting deviation. Medium-priced and up instruments come with a non-magnetic screwdriver to assist in making accurate adjustments. The owner of a steel-hulled boat, or one with a navigating department very close to power plant, generator, or extensive electronic equipment may find that ordinary built-in compensators are not strong enough to correct the error. He will have to seek out an adjuster or himself affix basic corrective magnets around the compass and make final refinements with the built-in magnets.

908 While there are several do-it-yourself methods of compensating compasses the simplest for the small-boat man is the following ("Hoke" method). If you have a compass without built-in compensators, provide the boat with two bar compensating magnets (permanently magnetized small bars, usually enclosed in a copper sheath pierced for nailing). With the compass in its usual position and free of magnetic influences (including the two bars) take the boat out to a buoy (during slack water and preferably on a still day), around which there is a mile or more of sea room. Prepare, meantime, several large wads of balled newsprint, or a child's balloon weighted with about six to eight ounces on a 3′ line.

From the buoy, put the boat on a due north compass course and run, without change, for about 600 yards (zero course). Toss the balloon into the wake, make a quick complete turn, run over the balloon, and head directly back to the buoy. (*Figure* 908)

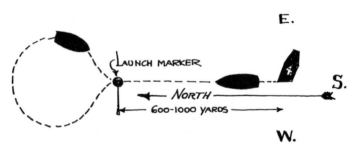

908 "Hoke" method of compensating the compass

The compass should read 180°, or south. If it does not (and it probably will not) it will require compensating.

This is done at once by placing one of the bar magnets ahead or astern of the compass with its long axis on an exact thwartship line and with its center exactly on the fore-and-aft (or lubber) line of the compass. It is turned end for end until the *error* is decreased; then moved toward or away from the compass until the compass course reads exactly halfway between south and the reading without the bar, and here lightly secured by tacks. The boat, meantime, must have been kept on a course exactly on the buoy.

Repeat the entire maneuver. The compass course of zero, reversed, should now be the compass course 180°. If it is not, do the whole maneuver again, making readjustments until you have eliminated the last remaining error by careful and minute positioning of the bar magnet. Permanently fasten the bar only after you have a perfect reading.

A similar procedure is followed for an east-west or west-east course (whichever is most convenient), but the compensating magnet is placed with its long axis on a fore-and-aft line, on either side of the compass, with its center on a thwartship line passing through the center of the compass.

To be sure, the same procedure may be followed in adjusting a compass with built-in compensating magnets. Be sure to use a non-magnetic adjusting tool (usually a screwdriver). After adjusting, try several courses with various auxiliaries operating—radio, windshield wipers, radar, generator, nearby lights, electric heaters, etc.—and with or without engine(s) operating. If any of these affect the compass, you must either (a) adjust the compass for the normal running effect—such as engine(s) operating on a power vessel—or (b) draw up deviation tables to apply at appropriate times.

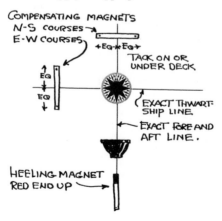

909 Finding heeling error

909 Heeling error is the compass error caused by the change of the relative position of large ballast castings. It is compensated for by placing a magnet *under* the compass, locating it with the north (red) end up—in the Northern Hemisphere.

As the greatest heeling error is found on north and south courses, the ship is so headed, and the compensating magnet moved toward or away from the compass until the compass does not deviate as the boat heels. Heeling error adjustment should be made before other adjustments. The heeling magnet has no effect on the compass when the boat is on level keel.

910 Compensating the compass may not cure all the problems of deviation; it merely reduces them to an irreducible (and often imperceptible) minimum. As the amount and direction of deviation vary with every course or bearing, a further correction may be required to arrive at accurate true courses.

Finding the deviation on various headings requires the comparing of compass bearings with magnetic bearings as the ship is headed on various courses. This is done by taking magnetic bearings on the sun; or by running over known ranges, maintained for the purpose by the government; or by running between any objects, such as buoys that have a known magnetic bearing; or by swinging ship and noting the bearings of some fixed object.

In any case, the difference between the magnetic bearing and the observed compass bearing on that heading is the deviation on that heading. The deviation is noted for each heading on some convenient form. Deviation is east if the magnetic bearing is greater than the compass bearing. Deviation is west if the magnetic bearing is less than the compass bearing.

Swinging ship is the simplest for the small-boat man. (*Figure 910*) The boat is anchored, bow and stern, off some prominent object (such as a lighthouse, steeple, etc.) about five miles away. By cross bearings, or soundings, or other methods, the exact location of the boat is established, and the magnetic bearing of the shore object to the boat noted. The difference between this magnetic bearing and the compass bearing as the ship is headed and steadied at various positions over the same spot will show the deviation on the respective heading.

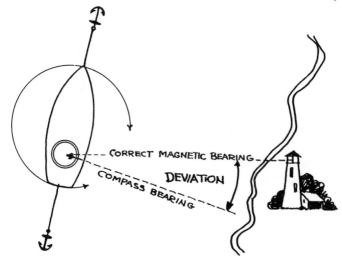

910 Swinging ship to determine deviation

The ship may be swung using a nearby object as well. In this case the boat's compass is taken ashore and the bearing noted from object to boat. This bearing is then reversed, the compass taken back on board and the ship swung as described. A chart is not required, as the compass ashore has indicated the correct magnetic bearing in reverse (it being free of the causes of the deviation on board).

While a complex pelorus form is used by professionals for taking bearings of distant objects, the average small-boat man will be well served by a simple azimuth attachment on the steering compass. It is merely a device for sighting and naming a bearing by reference to the compass.

911   A deviation card or table is made for handy reference so that the navigator can quickly apply deviation error for any course. For the coastwise sailor, a card in one of the forms shown in Figure 911 will suffice.

The card type is the one provided by professional compass adjusters. The double rose type is used generally by yachtsmen. Note that the outer rose shows the magnetic course from the chart and

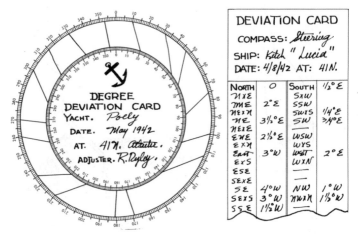

911 Deviation cards

that the inner shows the course to steer. Thus any course taken from the chart as the correct one is correct only if not connected to the inner one by a line. If such a line is present (and it is likely to be on all save the cardinal points), steer the course indicated on the inner rose to which it points.

When swinging ship as described, the powerboat should have its motor in operation (but not in gear, of course). Every iron or steel object belonging to the boat should be in its normal position exactly as it would be at sea.

The auxiliary vessel will often require two deviation cards, one made from errors noted with the engine in operation and one made without the engine.

As the ship is swung, nearby lights, searchlights, binnacle light, and the radio should be snapped on to be certain that their electrical fields do not disturb the compass. Low-tension disturbances (lights, windshield wipers, horns, etc.) can be neutralized by twisting the feed wires or running them parallel to each other. High-tension coils, magnetos, etc. might seriously offend. Separation from the compass is the only cure; if this is impossible a deviation card will be necessary. (*See Paragraph* 908)

Any shift of iron ballast, re-engining, rewiring, installation of an iron mass, such as a stove, relocation of the battery system, etc., should make the navigator view the deviation card with suspicion and cause him to check its accuracy on several headings.

TOTAL ERROR

912   By combining the errors of variation and deviation the navigator obtains the total compass error which must be applied to correct a compass course or bearing to true.

The rules for combining are:

When the names are alike, *add* and give the total error the same name. (Example: Dev. W 10° and Var. W 5° = Error W 15°.)

When the names are unlike *subtract* the lesser from the greater and give the total error the name of the greater. (Example: Dev. W 10° and Var. E 5° = Error W 5°.)

Error east is marked + (plus).

Error west is marked − (minus).

Examples:

RULE: When correcting *add* east, subtract west.

When uncorrecting *subtract* east, add west.

For practical purposes, it is easy to eliminate the arithmetic calculation involved in allowing for variation. When laying off a course, simply read the direction off the *inner* (magnetic) charted rose. To make any instant conversion from magnetic to true, or vice-versa, just lay a straightedge across the appropriate number on the rose, and through the rose's center, then read the corresponding true or magnetic number where the straightedge cuts the complementary circle of degrees. Be sure to use the compass rose nearest to the area of the chart where you're working.

Correcting: Compass to True

Compass Course		135°	Compass Course		212°
Dev. W	− 8		Dev. E	+ 4	
Var. E	+ 17		Var. E	+ 11	
Error		+ 9°	Error	+	15°
True		144°	True		227°

Uncorrecting: True to Compass

True		144°	True		227°
Dev. W	+ 8		Dev. E	− 4	
Var. E	− 17		Var. E	− 11	
		− 9°			− 15°
Compass		135°	Compass		212°

(*Note all signs reversed*)

Course Conversion Examples

True	142°	Magnetic	277°
Variation	13° E	Deviation	3° E
Magnetic	129°	Compass	274°

Compass	88°	Magnetic	199°
Deviation	9° W	Variation	12° E
Magnetic	79°	True	211°

THE DEPTH SOUNDER AND LEAD

913   While most boats, even small craft, are fitted with depth sounders these days, the prices thereof having, through competition, come down to reasonable levels, a knowledge of the old-fashioned sounding lead and its use is still good seamanship, and quite necessary for vessels without electrical power. An essential part of piloting is a knowledge of water depth, as will be seen later.

The hand lead is essentially a lead sinker that carries a marked line to the bottom, and that, in a tallow-filled pocket, picks up a sample of the bottom. Both the depth markings and the bottom sample help the navigator to fix position or estimate progress by referring to the chart.

The hand lead, its markings and handling, is thoroughly described in paragraph 1421, Chapter XIV.

Weights of five to seven pounds are adequate for soundings up to 40'. The standard 14-pound casting lead is ample for ordinary coastal uses.

The leadsman will report the actual depth from the bottom to the surface of the water. The navigator must make his own calculations to correlate the readings with the chart depths, which are for mean low water. The stage of the tide at the moment of sounding must be subtracted (or occasionally added) from the reported depth to coincide with the chart depths.

While hand sounding, speed should be somewhat reduced, depending upon the depth of the water, to, usually, around five mph.

The depth sounder is a simple electrical device which, from a transmitter-receiver unit attached to the hull, sends and receives a signal to and from the bottom. The time required for the round trip is translated into a visual signal in the form of a flash or a digital image, so that the navigator knows at all times the exact depth of water (in feet, fathoms, or meters, see Figure 913) in which he is navigating. An adjustment (manually achieved by a signal adjustment on some models) must be made for the depth of the hull unit (transducer) to obtain the accurate depth either to the water surface or to the bottom of the keel, whichever the navigator prefers. Some elaborate models record the depths as a continuing, varying line, made with an electrically activated stylus on a rolling paper tape. Such sophistication is hardly required by pleasure boatmen.

FATHOMS	1	2	3	4	5	6	7	8	9	10	11	12	13	14	15	16	17
FEET	6	12	18	24	30	36	42	48	54	60	66	72	78	84	90	96	102
METERS	1 2 3	4 5 6	7 8	9 10 11	12 13 14	15 16 17	18 19	20 21 22	23 24 25	26 27	28 29 30 31						

913 A useful conversion table for chart reading and for the navigator. Some depth sounders read in both feet and fathoms and soundings in meters are beginning to appear on newer charts.

The great advantage of the depth sounder over the hand line is that depth information can be obtained instantaneously and far more often per minute. It is quite possible to determine the character of the bottom by the character of the flash. Sharp, crisp flashes indicate a hard bottom. Fuzzy, shapeless flashes mean mud or heavy seaweed. Multiple flashes can mean rocks in singles or boulders on the soft bottom. An unusual, persistent pattern or erratic behavior could indicate a fouled transducer, such as a barnacle or seed oyster forming on the face.

The depth sounder usually contains one or more powerful magnets and therefore should be kept away from the compass.

LOGS

914   To navigate accurately, the mariner requires some means of knowing his speed over the bottom. The most practical devices for small boats all indicate speed through the water, and therefore allowances must be made for tide, current, and leeway (which will be detailed later).

Many boats today carry one or another type of mechanical or electronic log—or distance register—often coupled with a speedometer. The least expensive equipment consists of a miniature propeller mounted on the underside of the hull, transmitting speed and distance run through the water to a single dial that may be mounted virtually anywhere in the boat (except that some mechanical units are limited by the length of sending cable).

More advanced and expensive units are wholly electronic, and the sending head is a tiny paddlewheel whose rate of turning at different boat speeds is translated into speed through the water and distance run. In crowded waters, the best units are those which offer the least amount of projection for snagging garbage (especially plastic bags) and weed.

The patent or taffrail log is a traditional device suitable for high-seas use. It consists of a propeller-shaped rotator towed at the end of a long line attached to a mechanism, which, by means of a pointer, indicates on a dial the distance sailed. (*Figure 914A*)

The common type is calibrated for nautical miles of 6,080′ each. The large dial shows the miles run and the small dial the tenths of miles. The distance run is the difference between readings, of course.

914A Patent or taffrail log

The patent log is seldom completely accurate, and its error should be ascertained and recorded upon various runs in still water. It will underread in drifting calms and is quite likely to be very far "off" in heavy weather. Any erratic reading should make the navigator suspicious of a fouled rotator (seaweed, rubbish, or an attack by a fish), of bent rotator blades, or of mechanical failure of the recorder. Any inclination for the rotator to skip along the surface can be cured by either introducing a balanced tubular sinker some feet ahead of it or by giving the towing line more scope. The line should always be long enough to drop the rotator entirely clear of the wake and its eddies (about 100′ at 10 knots), and at sea it can well be twice that length.

The log is streamed by paying the rotator quickly over the stern; not by casting it as a sounding lead.

When the log is taken in, the line is unhooked from the wheel and, as the rotator is handed *in*, the line is let to pay *out*; the line will thus untwist and may be properly coiled down as it is hauled aboard. The recorder requires oiling frequently, and if salt-water soaked, it should be plunged into fresh hot water, then dried and oiled, before stowing.

Various other types of speed- and distance-measuring devices are in use, some applicable to the small boat. One is a delicate sub-surface pressure device, indicating speed. It is manufactured for sailboats zero to seven mph and for powerboats up to 40 mph. These gauges, called pitot-tube meters or pitometers, are at best only approximately accurate.

Any powerboat equipped with a tachometer may have its speed accurately charted on a conversion card. The calibration is made at various engine speeds over a measured course, or between buoys, etc., of known distances apart. Such measurements are preferably made in still water. However, if a current is suspected, the course may be run; then reversed, and the mean taken as the still-water time and distance.

CONVERSION CARD

rpm	mph
600	5.25
650	6.50
700	8.10
750	9.25
800	9.87

(etc.)

A log entirely suited for small-boat use, especially at speeds for two to five mph, is the chip log. (*Figure 914B*)

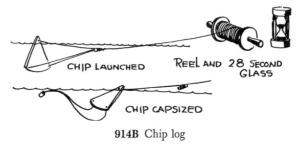

914B Chip log

It consists of a quadrant of wood, weighted on the arced side to hold it just awash when afloat. A bridle leads from this chip to the log line, the upper part being the bridle proper and the lower parts being pendants. These pendants are attached to a pine plug that fits into a wooden socket seized to the log line. With the three parts rigged, the chip, when launched, will assume a vertical position and rest there approximately stationary. Upon hauling in, the log line is jerked sharply, disengaging the plug and capsizing the chip so that it may be easily hauled aboard.

The log line is loosely laid, untarred hemp, similar to a lead line, and is marked (after being wetted and put on a stretch) as follows:

90′ from the chip (marking the end of the "stray line")	One piece red bunting
At every 47′3″ thereafter	Fish line seized to the log line

Each piece of fish line is knotted; one knot for the first piece, two knots for the second piece, three knots for the third piece, etc. The log line is stored on a free-running spool with a handled axle and is permitted to run freely out over the stern. Time is taken (or the sand glass capsized) when the red bunting leaves the reel. The line is checked when 28 seconds have elapsed (or the glass run out). The number of knots that have unreeled during the 28-second period is the *speed* of the boat in knots.

(It is almost impossible to purchase a chip log today. However, it is easily made by the boatman. The chip is of varnished ⅜″ soft wood, a quadrant section of a circle about 12″–16″ in diameter. The lead weight is usually a strip, sewn in leather, weighing about two ounces.)

Dutchman's Log

A speed formula for emergency use is as follows:

Between known distances abreast the length of the boat, take the amount of time it takes for a stick, paper, or other floating object to reach from the bow mark to the stern mark; then calculate—

Distance in feet is to feet per hour as the elapsed time in seconds is to the seconds in an hour (3,600).

> Example: Distance between marks 30 feet
> Time between marks 4 seconds
> 30 : ? :: 4 : 3,600 = 27,000 feet per hour
> To convert to nautical miles per hour divide by 6,080 (answer: 4.4 knots)
> To convert to statute miles per hour divide by 5,280 (answer: 5½ statute mph)

Dutch seamen were too poor to throw anything away—they just spit over the side; hence the name, Dutchman's Log.

ACCESSORIES

915 The vast number of transparent plastic course protractors available today have largely replaced the relatively clumsy parallel rules, except on large craft with extensive work surfaces. There is such a variety of course protractors on the market that no general text can accurately describe them all. They do, however, have some things in common. All are designed primarily to incorporate a compass rose and an angle-measuring device. By lining the protractor up with the desired course or bearing, and then orienting it on the nearest meridian of longitude, the vessel's true course or bearing is read off the instrument's compass rose. Some course protractors also allow for orientation on parallels of latitude, and some have overlay dials that can be adjusted so the device yields magnetic courses and bearings.

Any accurate timepiece is suitable for coastwise work. A chronometer is unnecessary, and unless carefully rated, is probably not as accurate on a small boat as a good wristwatch. Such a wristwatch should have a sweep second hand, and might be luminous and waterproof for sea use. A stop watch is very useful, especially for racing navigators and for timing light flashes.

Dividers should be of adequate span and of brass, not steel.

Binoculars are of two types: Galilean field and prismatic. Both are used extensively for navigating. Coastwise work requires better binoculars than offshore work.

Galilean field glasses of the better grade will magnify about five times, but they have small fields and uneven illumination. A field of 200 at 1,000 yards, bright in the center and ragged at the edges, is the best to be hoped for. They do not serve well as night glasses.

Prismatic glasses with the same magnification power as the Galilean glasses will provide a much larger field, and one of approximately the same relative brightness. Powers of 7×35 or 7×50 are perfect for marine use and make excellent night glasses.

All binoculars require extreme care in handling. They should be cleaned regularly, kept out of the direct sun and wet, and in general treated as precision instruments.

The telescope or "spy glass" has fallen into disfavor in modern times. However, while it is a clumsy instrument to use, there is no reason why a good one should not be used if desired.

The binocular is a navigating instrument, as vital as the compass, and should be treated as such. It should be "set" to the navigator's eyes and left so, ready for immediate use without adjustment, for it may well be needed in an instant. The average boatman fails to so regard the glasses, and anybody who wants to see a seagull closer or just "have a look" lifts the binocs and carries them to any vantage point on the ship. By all means ship two or more pairs of glasses—the "good" ones for the navigator, stowed in a padded box

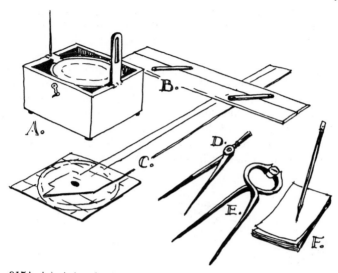

915A A.) Azimuth circle or sighting vane or hand-held pelorus. B.) Parallel rules, now largely obsolete in favor of the course prot actor. C.) and D.) Common draftsman's dividers. E.) British dividers that can be adjusted with one hand. F.) Scratch pad and medium hard pencil, with eraser, not round so it will not roll.

within reach of the helm and clearly marked "For Captain Only" or "Do Not Remove." Then at other locations there can be one or more pairs of glasses, in boxes marked "For Guests" or some such; these can be cheap or retired glasses. Let it be clearly understood by all that the "helm" glasses are as inviolate as the compass.

An accessory that more boats should have is a time ruler. It can't be purchased, but must be devised for your boat only. It is used on a chart to measure a known distance in terms of the time of *your boat* at various speeds (or engine rpms). When running in thick weather, especially short distances (such as winding up a river or into a tricky harbor where course changes are required every few moments and there is no time for formal calculations) the device becomes invaluable.

First, in the same scale as the chart to be used, lay out on a light stick (like a common ruler) or on stiff cardboard the distance your boat would go in one hour at various engine speeds—say, 1,500, 1,750, 2,000, and 2,250 rpms. This information is obtained from the conversion card for your boat. (*See Paragraph 914*) Lay each rpm conversion on one of the four edges of a stick or cardboard panel, using the same scale as the chart. Then divide each unit into six parts, marking the dividing lines 0, 10, 20, 30, etc., to 60. Then subdivide each part into halves and the halves again so that each of the 24 parts represents 1½ minutes in time. (*See Figure 915B*) To use, lay it on the course with zero at your then location, and the

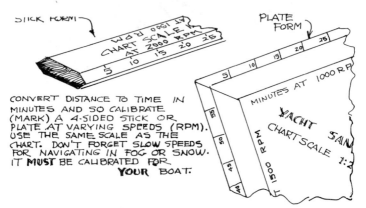

915B The time ruler—example of how to calibrate: Run at a known speed (five knots, eight knots, ten knots, etc.) over a measured course and record the rpm. Run the course both ways to strike an *average*; i.e., to cancel out effects of current and wind. Lay out on one of the above forms exactly an hour's run to the same scale as the chart that you will use. Now divide this run into 60 equal parts (or 12 or 30, etc.). Each division will represent the distance run in one minute (or five or two, etc.). Thus, with the zero mark on where you are, you may readily predict the running time *at that* rpm (speed) to where you want to go, or to a reference point, navigation aid, etc. Current must be added or substracted if present. For fog navigation the 60-point division is most practical and will give a fix *every* minute.

reading (on the scale representing your then rpms) at any point along the course will give you, in minutes, the time required to reach that point. Allowance must be made for current, plus or minus, usually almost negligible on short, changing courses, and drift or windage, if on the beam.

This device is most useful in confined waters and should be constructed to the scale of your local harbor charts. It may be wise to include a scale with your speed cut down to a crawl, such as 1,000 rpms or five knots, so that, in a real pea-souper or in traffic, you can cut down to a safe speed.

916   Figure 916A shows a popular device for solving navigational problems of speed, distance and time. If any two are known, it is possible to determine the third by simply twirling the rotary calculator. Not quite as rapid as the time stick, it nevertheless has great uses if there is time to make the calculation, as when you are offshore or coasting. It behooves the navigator to become thoroughly familiar with the operation of the device so that using it in times of stress is natural and rapid.

916A A speed-time-distance calculator

Still another device for solving the problems of speed-time-distance is the logarithmic scale found on ocean charts of the scale of 1 : 40,000 and over. (*See Figure 916B*) It is printed on the chart edge and requires only a dividers to solve the problem(s). To obtain speed you must know time and distance, thus:

Place one point of your dividers on the mark on the scale indicating the distance in nautical miles, and the other point on the number corresponding to the time in minutes. Without changing the spread between the divider arms, place the right point on the "60" at the right end of the scale; the left point will then indicate on the scale the speed in knots.

Distance can be determined as well. Set the right point of the dividers on "60" and the left point at the mark on the scale corresponding to the speed in knots. Without changing the spread, move the right point to the mark on the scale representing the time in minutes; the left point will now indicate the distance in nautical miles.

To determine the time required to cover a known distance at a specified speed, set the two divider points on the scale marks representing speed in knots and distance in miles. Move the dividers, without changing the spread, until the right point is at "60" on the scale; the other point will indicate the time in minutes.

Here again a thorough familiarity with the various methods of solution will pay off under stress; it should be almost automatic if the logarithmic scale is regularly used.

CHARTS AND CHART READING

917   A chart is a detailed picture or representation, on durable paper, of the navigable waters of the world. All charts are projected, in one way or another, to overcome the curvature of the earth's surface and show it on a two-dimensional plane. Three methods are used: the Mercator, the polyconic, and the gnomonic, or "great circle."

The Mercator is generally used, and it is *always* used for coast-wise charts. For the navigator, because its parallels of latitude and meridians of longitude are square to each other (which in reality they are not), the chart is simplicity itself, and as a projection, offers no problems. (*Figure* 917A)

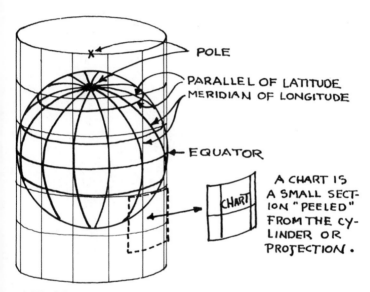

The Mercator projection (to which all large-scale and coastal charts are made) simply expands the spherical surface of the earth into a cylinder. The chart is a detailed representation of the expansion, made from the cylinder.

The advantage to the navigator is that the meridians of longitude are parallel to each other and at right angles to the parallels of latitude, thus permitting the course or track of a ship to be represented by a straight line. North is anywhere along the top perimeter of the cylinder.

917A Mercator projection

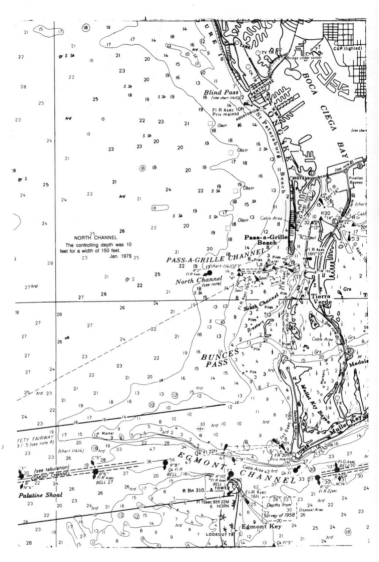

917B Section of a coastal chart

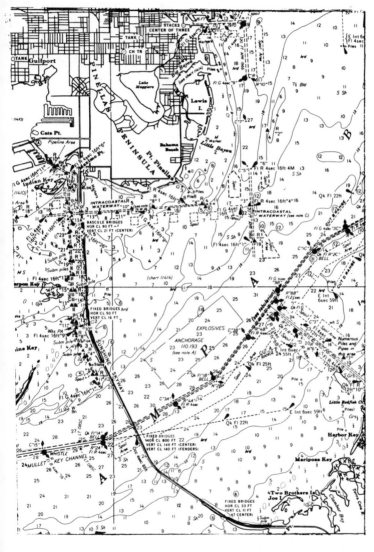

917B continued

The chart is always oriented to true or geographic north. Coastwise charts, however, are oriented to magnetic north as well and the year of the orientation noted on the chart rose, upper half. Measurements of distances are taken, with the dividers, from the scale of miles (nautical) and yards printed on all coastwise and harbor charts. It may also be taken from the latitude scale of minutes on the east and west perimeters of the chart. On Mercator charts of large areas, the minutes of latitude will be unequal, and there will be no scale on the chart. Distance is then measured from the latitude scale at a point opposite the area being worked.

The chart shows in detail *everything* of possible interest and aid to the mariner, including the depth and character of the bottom over which he sails, the nearby shore line, land contours, and objects to be used for bearings; aids and dangers to navigation, tidal and other currents, anchorages, radio stations, towns, Coast Guard stations, tidal interval and height, and many other things. (*Figure 917B*)

A careful study of the standard chart symbols and abbreviations will reveal the extent of the information to be gleaned from a chart.

SPECIAL NOTES ON CHART READING

1. Elevations given on land are from mean high water.
2. Depths given on water are to mean low water (feet or fathoms). Sailing and general charts give fathoms; coastal and harbor charts give feet. If combinations are used, the depths given in feet will be confined to a shaded inshore area. (Some recent charts are using meters.)
3. Floating lighted navigational aids are shown with a magenta disk. Fixed lighted aids are shown with a magenta disk; also, except on editions of charts published after 1975, fixed lights are indicated by a magenta exclamation point with a blade dot at the bottom for position. The color is for night navigation under special chart lighting.
4. The center of the base line of any symbol presenting a horizontal line is the exact location (such as a lightship, etc.).
5. The dot under the buoy symbol shows the *exact* location.
6. The bearings of ranges are given as true, in degrees, from north.

7. Bluffs are shown by a hatched band, the width denoting the height of the bluff, not the plan view. Thus a high bluff would be indicated by a wide band, a low bluff by a line or narrow band.

8. Any feature which is above high water at all times (such as a rock or reef) is named with VERTICAL lettering.

9. Any feature which is definitely part of the hydrography (such as character of the bottom, a channel, floating aids to navigation, etc.) is named with *leaning* lettering.

918 Coastal charts are on the scale of 1:80,000. Harbor charts are still larger to show all necessary information as sailing waters become restricted and therefore more dangerous. (*Figure 918A*)

Charts are dated in the lower, left-hand corner under the border. Both the consecutive number of edition and the date up to which the chart is correct are noted: "14th Ed., Jan. 4/75."

Charts show all necessary corrections as to lights, beacons, buoys, and dangers that have been received to the date of issue. All small but important corrections occurring subsequent to the date of issue of the chart are published in *Notice to Mariners* and should be applied by hand to the chart immediately after the receipt of the notices. The date of the edition of the chart remains unchanged until an extensive correction is made on the plate from which the chart is printed. The date is then changed and the issue is known as a new edition. All the notes on a chart should be read carefully, as in some cases they relate to the aids to navigation or to dangers that cannot be clearly charted. For a sampling of the types of information presented on a coastal chart, see Figure 918C.

Every chart table should have, as a starter, U. S. Chart No. 1 which is not a chart at all but a small booklet giving, in full detail, *all* the nautical chart symbols and abbreviations used on U. S. Charts. The latest edition of Chart No. 1 at the date of publication of this *Manual* is the Sixth Edition, July 1975. It gives the key to chart reading and is a *must* even for experienced skippers outside local waters. Chart No. 1 has illustrated tables (A to U) that show the symbols used; further sections cover *all* the abbreviations used in cartography (*See Figure 918B*) and diagramed charts of the navigational aids used in U. S. waters. It is available at all chart agencies and costs (in 1979) $2.25.

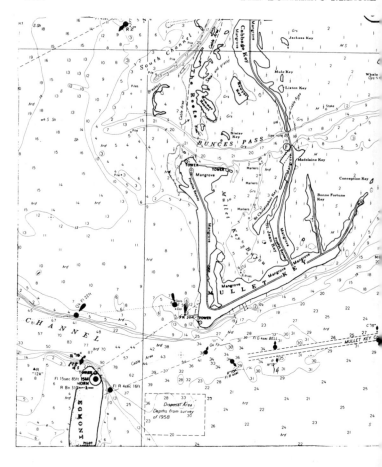

918A This shows the enlargement of a section of the coastal chart into the scale of the "harbor" charts. Note the additional information and detail it carries over the smaller scale of the chart in Figure 917B

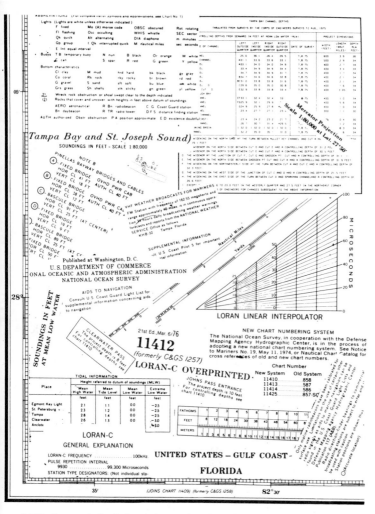

918B Some of the information to be gleaned from a coastal chart is shown above. The overlayed numbered grid lines are for Loran A and C navigation

Index of Abbreviations

A			Chan	Channel	B 10
aband	Abandoned	F 37	Chec	Checkered (buoy)	L 33
ABAND LT HO	Abandoned lighthouse	If	CHY	Chimney	I 44
abt	About	F 17	Cir	Cirripedia	S 38
AERO	Aeronautical	F 22; K 4	Ck	Chalk	S 12
AERO R Bn	Aeronautical radiobeacon	M 16	Cl	Clay	S 6
AERO R Rge	Aeronautical radio range	Md	CL	Clearance	Fd
alt	Altitude	E 18	cm	Centimeter	E 4b
Alt	Alternating (light)	K 26	Cn	Cinders	S 21
Am	Amber	K 67a; L 48a	Co	Company	II
anc	Ancient	F 9	Co	Coral	S 14
Anch	Anchorage	B 15; G 1, 2	Co Hd	Coral head	Sa
Anch prohib	Anchorage prohibited	G 12	concr	Concrete	Ff
Ant	Antenna	Ma	conspic	Conspicuous	F 12
approx	Approximate	F 34	C of E	Corps of Engineers	Df
Apprs	Approaches	Bg	cor	Corner	Fe
Apt	Apartment	Ij	Corp	Corporation	Im
Arch	Archipelago	B 20	Cov	Covers	O 33
Astro	Astronomical	D 9	corr	Correction	E 17
AUTH	Authorized	Fc	cps, c/s	Cycles per second	Ef
Aux	Auxiliary (' t)	K 51	Cr	Creek	B 5
Ave	Avenu⌐	I 26a	crs	Coarse	S 40
B				Causeway	H 3f
B				Courth⌐	SA

918C A portion of the Index of Abbreviations, U. S. Chart No. 1 (the notations to the right refer to tables of symbols and illustrate the use of an abbreviation on a chart)

The following special and general notes are contained in the fore-word of Chart No. 1.:

"All changes since the July 1972 edition of this publication are indicated by the dagger symbol in the margin immediately adjacent to the item identification of the symbol or abbreviation affected."

BUILDINGS. A conspicuous feature on a building may be shown by a landmark symbol with a descriptive label. Prominent buildings that are of assistance to the mariner may be shown by actual shape as viewed from above, and may be marked "CONSPICUOUS".

BUOYS and BEACONS. On entering a channel from seaward, buoys on starboard side are red with even numbers, on port side black with odd numbers. Lights on buoys on starboard side of channel are red or white, on port side white or green. Mid-channel buoys have black-and-white vertical stripes. Junction or obstruction buoys, which may be passed on either side, have red-and-black horizontal bands.

The position of a fixed beacon is represented by the center of the beacon symbol or the circle at the base of the symbol. The approximate position of a buoy is represented by the dot or circle associated with the buoy symbol. The approximate position is used because of practical limitations in positioning and maintaining buoys and their sinkers in precise geographical locations. These limitations include, but are not limited to, inherent imprecisions in position fixing methods, prevailing atmospheric and sea conditions, the slope of and the material making up the seabed, the fact that buoys are moored to sinkers by varying lengths of chain, and the fact that buoy body and/or sinker positions are not under continuous surveillance, but are normally checked only during periodic maintenance visits which often occur more than a year apart. The position of the buoy body can be expected to shift inside and outside the charting symbol due to the forces of nature. The mariner is also cautioned that buoys are liable to be carried away, shifted, capsized, sunk, etc. Lighted buoys may be extinguished or sound signals may not function as a result of ice, collisions, or other accidents. For the foregoing reasons, a prudent mariner must not rely completely upon the charted position or operation of floating aids to navigation, but will also utilize bearings from fixed objects and aids to navigation on shore. Further, a vessel attempting to pass close aboard always risks collision with a yawing buoy or with the obstruction the buoy marks.

COLORS are optional for characterizing various features and areas in the charts.

DEPTH contours and soundings are shown in meters on an increasing number of new charts and new editions; the depth unit is stated on all charts.

HEIGHTS of land and conspicuous objects are given in feet above Mean High Water, unless otherwise stated in the title of the chart.

IMPROVED CHANNELS are shown by limiting dashed lines with the depth and date of the latest examination placed adjacent to the channel except when the channel data is tabulated.

LETTERING styles and capitalization as indicated in Chart No. 1 are not always rigidly adhered to on the charts.

LONGITUDES are referred to the Meridian of Greenwich.

OBSOLESCENT SYMBOLIZATION on charts will be revised to agree with the current preferred usage as soon as opportunity affords.

SHORELINE shown on charts represents the line of contact between the land and a selected water elevation. In areas affected by tidal fluctuation, this line of contact is usually the mean high-water line. In confined coastal waters of diminished tidal influence, a mean water level line may be used. The shoreline of interior waters (rivers, lakes) is usually a line representing a specified elevation above a selected datum. Shoreline is symbolized by a heavy line.

APPARENT SHORELINE is used on charts to show the outer edge of marine vegetation where that limit would reasonably appear as the shoreline to the mariner or where it prevents the shoreline from being clearly defined. Apparent shoreline is symbolized by a light line.

919   Charts and related informational material are published by the following U. S. Government agencies:

National Ocean Survey, Department of Commerce, Rockville, Maryland 20852. Publishes NOS charts of coastal waters, rivers to head of tide, sounds, harbors, etc.

Defense Mapping Agency Hydrographic Office, Washington, D. C. 30290. Publishes H.O. charts of the high seas and foreign waters (except Canada), replacing former H.O. charts.

Lake Survey Center, National Ocean Survey, 630 Federal Building, Detroit, Mich. 48226. Publishes charts of the Great Lakes, Border Lakes, Lake Champlain, and N. Y. State Barge Canals.

U. S. Army Corps of Engineers (through district offices in many cities). Publishes charts of major rivers (Mississippi, Ohio, etc.) and many inland lakes and canal systems.

Hydrographic Chart Distribution Office, Department of the Environment, Ottawa, Ontario, Canada KTA 0E6. Distributes charts of the Seaway and Great Lakes.

All publish catalogs, mostly for the asking, and use private sales agencies extensively for distribution (marinas, boatyards, sporting goods outlets, boat clubs) at fixed prices. The average needs of the average boatman will be met by these outlets. Ocean and more special charts should be obtained from the agency concerned. Local custom houses list and will advise as to local outlets.

Charts average $3.25 and are the only accurate representation of the coast available to the navigator. No trust should be placed in charts which are presented free to the public on a "road-map" basis, nor do the publishers expect that such charts will serve the navigator in lieu of government-published and reliable charts.

PUBLICATIONS

920   The navigator will find the following publications supplement information given on the chart.

United States Coast Pilot Tide Tables Local Notice to Mariners	United States Coast and Geodetic Survey
Light Lists Tidal Current Tables	United States Coast Guard

Notice to Mariners is sent free, weekly, to any applicant if application is made to the nearest Coast Guard District Commander. It is a bulletin, noting both permanent and temporary changes to all charts issued. Permanent changes (such as relocating buoys, or a collapse of dredged channel walls, etc.) should be marked on the chart at once in India ink. Temporary changes (such as the placing of temporary buoys, notice of a dredge working, etc.) should be merely noted in the proper location on the chart in pencil and the notation erased upon the situation's again becoming normal.

Of special interest to small boat skippers is the *Local Notice to Mariners* which deals only with his own local area (Coast Guard District) and especially notes matters of interest that are inland and distant from the waters used by commercial craft. It may be subscribed to (free) at your District Coast Guard offices, % the Commander.

Copies of both types of notice are on file at all Customhouses, chart agencies, consulates, Coast Guard district offices, etc., and may be examined by navigators without cost.

921   *Tide Tables* are published annually, in advance, in four volumes, two of which cover the United States East and West coasts. They may be bought at any chart agency that handles the NOS charts, or direct from the NOS. (*See Paragraph 919*)

56

NEW YORK (THE BATTERY), N.Y., 1978

TIMES AND HEIGHTS OF HIGH AND LOW WATERS

JANUARY

DAY	TIME h.m.	HT. ft.	DAY	TIME h.m.	HT. ft.
1 SU	0029	3.8	16 M	0203	4.2
	0605	0.5		0825	0.3
	1229	3.9		1421	3.7
	1842	0.1		2047	0.0
2 M	0119	3.9	17 TU	0257	4.1
	0729	0.5		0927	0.3
	1323	3.8		1516	3.5
	2001	0.1		2143	0.0
3 TU	0213	4.1	18 W	0353	4.0
	0901	0.4		1021	0.2
	1424	3.7		1616	3.4
	2112	0.0		2233	0.0
4 W	0317	4.3	19 TH	0449	4.1
	1007	0.1		1112	0.1
	1538	3.7		1715	3.4
	2215	-0.3		2321	0.0
5 TH	0425	4.6	20 F	0542	4.3
	1105	-0.3		1201	-0.1
	1652	3.9		1806	3.5
	2311	-0.5			

FEBRUARY

DAY	TIME h.m.	HT. ft.	DAY	TIME h.m.	HT. ft.
1 W	0145	4.3	16 TH	0311	3.9
	0831	0.3		0946	0.5
	1403	3.7		1537	3.3
	2040	0.0		2200	0.4
2 TH	0250	4.4	17 F	0409	3.9
	0943	0.1		1041	0.3
	1517	3.7		1641	3.3
	2153	-0.1		2252	0.3
3 F	0403	4.5	18 SA	0505	4.0
	1046	-0.2		1131	0.2
	1636	3.8		1734	3.5
	2255	-0.4		2340	0.2
4 SA	0511	4.8	19 SU	0556	4.2
	1142	-0.6		1216	-0.1
	1743	4.1		1824	3.7
	2355	-0.7			
5 SU	0612	5.1	20 M	0027	0.0
	1238	-0.9		0641	4.4
	1843	4.4		1301	-0.3
				1905	4.0

MARCH

DAY	TIME h.m.	HT. ft.	DAY	TIME h.m.
1 W	0029	4.5	16 TH	0133
	0647	0.1		0806
	1254	3.9		1401
	1849	0.1		2021
2 TH	0129	4.5	17 F	0225
	0812	0.2		0907
	1359	3.8		1458
	2024	0.2		2124
3 F	0234	4.5	18 SA	0322
	0925	0.1		1004
	1511	3.8		1601
	2141	0.1		2220
4 SA	0348	4.5	19 SU	0423
	1030	-0.2		1054
	1626	3.9		1658
	2244	-0.2		2311
5 SU	0458	4.7	20 M	0518
	1126	-0.5		1142
	1732	4.3		1750
	2342	-0.5		2358

8

PICTOU, NOVA SCOTIA, 1978

TIMES AND HEIGHTS OF HIGH AND LOW WATERS

JANUARY

DAY	TIME h.m.	HT. ft.	DAY	TIME h.m.	HT. ft.
1 SU	0145	5.0	16 M	0300	4.9
	0750	2.1		0855	2.6
	1435	5.2		1520	5.3
	2020	2.8		2200	2.3
2 M	0230	4.8	17 TU	0425	4.5
	0820	2.4		0935	3.0
	1515	5.3		1610	5.2
	2115	2.6		2310	2.2
3 TU	0335	4.6	18 W	0540	4.3
	0910	2.7		1035	3.2
	1555	5.4		1705	5.2
	2225	2.4			
4 W	0450	4.5	19 TH	0020	2.1
	1000	2.9		0655	4.3
	1650	5.6		1135	3.4
	2345	2.0		1750	5.2
5 TH	0620	4.6	20 F	0115	1.9
	1105	3.2		0820	4.3
	1740	5.8		1240	3.4
				1855	5.3

FEBRUARY

DAY	TIME h.m.	HT. ft.	DAY	TIME h.m.	HT. ft.
1 W	0315	4.5	16 TH	0450	4.1
	0845	2.6		0940	3.1
	1515	5.5		1600	5.0
	2200	1.9		2340	2.0
2 TH	0440	4.3	17 F	0620	4.0
	0935	3.0		1050	3.3
	1610	5.6		1710	5.0
	2320	1.7			
3 F	0600	4.4	18 SA	0035	1.9
	1050	3.2		0720	4.1
	1710	5.7		1155	3.4
				1800	5.0
4 SA	0015	1.4	19 SU	0130	1.8
	0715	4.7		0825	4.2
	1205	3.4		1305	3.3
	1810	5.8		1910	5.1
5 SU	0115	1.0	20 M	0215	1.6
	0820	5.0		0900	4.4
	1315	3.3		1355	3.1
	1915	5.9		2000	5.3

MARCH

DAY	TIME h.m.	HT. ft.	DAY	TIME h.m.
1 W	0210	4.8	16 TH	0300
	0730	2.5		0810
	1355	5.4		1425
	2030	1.5		2115
2 TH	0315	4.5	17 F	0405
	0825	2.7		0900
	1450	5.4		1520
	2135	1.5		2235
3 F	0425	4.4	18 SA	0520
	0920	3.0		1000
	1540	5.4		1625
	2255	1.5		2350
4 SA	0550	4.5	19 SU	0635
	1030	3.2		1120
	1655	5.4		1730
5 SU	0005	1.4	20 M	0045
	0700	4.7		0725
	1145	3.2		1230
	1810	5.5		1835

921A Example of tables from *Tide Tables 1978 East Coast of North America*

They contain tables showing the times of high and low water at scores of reference stations, and tables showing the differences and constants at several thousand subordinate stations. It is thus possible to predict the exact time of high water and low water, and the stage of each on any given date in any waters of navigational importance.

In reading the table of reference stations, the bold-faced type always denotes p.m. time; the light-faced type a.m. time and all time is standard time. The heights (marked Ht.) indicate the difference in height of that tide from the depths given on the chart. Unless preceded by the sign — (minus) the height is always *added*.

In reading the table of subordinate stations (Table 2), the reference is to the reference station shown at the head of the table. The difference in time and height is shown; this is to be added or subtracted from the same tide at the reference point to obtain the time and height of the tide at the subordinate point.

The publication fully explains the workings of the tables.

While the tide information is normally accurate for all practical purposes the navigator should realize that the weather (which is not predictable) may greatly affect the tides. Offshore winds may very materially lower the high-water stage; onshore winds may raise the stage. Such considerations become important when crossing a bar, or navigating shallow water.

Coastal charts give limited tidal information in a legend, usually appearing in a lower corner.

Example: Chart #215, Connecticut River

Tide (referred to mean low water)

	Saybrook Light	Essex	Deep River
Mean high water	3.6′	2.7′	2.5′
Mean sea level	1.8′	1.4′	1.2′
Lowest tide to be expected	− 2.5′	− 2.5′	− 2.5′

This gives the information that, at Essex, the high-water depths will probably be 3.6′ above those shown on the chart, that the average level will be 1.8′ above those shown on the chart, and that lowest depths to be expected may reach 2.5′ below those shown on the chart.

TABLE 2.—TIDAL DIFFERENCES AND OTHER CONSTANTS

No.	PLACE	POSITION		DIFFERENCES				RANGES		Mean Tide Level
		Lat.	Long.	Time		Height		Mean	Spring	
				High water	Low water	High water	Low water			
		° ′ N.	° ′ W.	h. m.	h. m.	feet	feet	feet	feet	feet
	GREENLAND, West Coast—Continued *Time meridian, local*			on HARRINGTON HARBOUR, p.12						
87	North Star Bay, Wolstenholme Fjord--	76 32	68 50	+0 30	+0 32	*1.33	*1.12	5.4	7.0	4.5
89	Port Foulke------------------------	78 18	72 45	+0 28	+0 26	(*2.08-0.8)		7.9	10.7	6.5
91	Rensselaer Bugt--------------------	78 37	70 53	+1 05	+0 58	(*2.08-1.1)		7.9	10.8	6.2
93	Thank God Harbor, Polaris Bugt-----	81 36	61 40	+1 34	+1 31	-0.3	-0.4	3.9	5.4	3.2
	BAFFIN BAY, etc., West Side			on HALIFAX, p.20						
94	Fort Conger, Discovery Harbor------	81 44	64 44	+3 48	+3 25	-1.2	-1.1	4.3	5.9	3.0
95	Cape Lawrence----------------------	80 21	69 15	+3 46	+3 40	0.0	-1.1	5.5	7.2	3.6
96	Payer Harbour, Cape Sabine---------	78 43	74 23	+3 36	+3 30	+1.9	-0.7	7.0	9.4	4.7
97	Cape Adair-------------------------	71 33	71 30	+3 06	+3 06	+0.6	-1.0	6.0	7.8	3.9
98	Cape Hewett------------------------	70 16	67 47	+2 56	+2 56	+0.8	-0.3	5.5	7.2	4.4
	NEW YORK and NEW JERSEY **New York Harbor**									
1493	Coney Island-----------------------	40 34	73 59	-0 03	-0 19	+0.1	0.0	4.7	5.7	2.
1495	Norton Point, Gravesend Bay--------	40 35	74 00	-0 03	+0 01	+0.1	0.0	4.7	5.7	2.
1497	Fort Wadsworth, The Narrows--------	40 36	74 03	+0 02	+0 12	-0.3	0.0	4.3	5.2	2.
1499	Fort Hamilton, The Narrows---------	40 37	74 02	+0 03	+0 05	+0.1	0.0	4.7	5.7	2.3
				on NEW YORK, p.56						
1501	Bay Ridge--------------------------	40 38	74 02	-0 24	-0 24	+0.1	0.0	4.6	5.5	2.
1503	St. George, Staten Island----------	40 39	74 04	-0 21	-0 18	0.0	0.0	4.5	5.4	2.4
1505	Bayonne, New Jersey----------------	40 41	74 06	-0 19	-0 08	0.0	0.0	4.5	5.4	2.
1507	Gowanus Bay------------------------	40 40	74 01	-0 19	-0 15	-0.1	0.0	4.4	5.3	2.4
1509	Governors Island-------------------	40 42	74 01	-0 11	-0 06	-0.1	0.0	4.4	5.3	2.4
1511	NEW YORK (The Battery)-------------	40 42	74 01	Daily predictions				4.5	5.4	2.4

921B Tidal difference and other constants from *Tidal Current Tables 1978 Atlantic Coast of North America*

TABLE FOR FINDING HEIGHT OF TIDE ABOVE LOW WATER AT ANY HOUR OF THE EBB OR FLOOD

1. Find rise of tide for given day in *Tide Tables* (difference between heights of nearest high and low tides).
2. Enter column 1 or 3 on line corresponding to time for which height of tide is to be calculated.
3. In column 2 find constant given for that time.
4. Multiply constant obtained in (2) by total rise of tide.

1 Rising Tide Hours After Low Water	2 Constant Ebb or Flood	3 Falling Tide Hours After High Water
6	1.0	0
5½	0.98	½
5	0.92	1
4½	0.84	1½
4	0.75	2
3½	0.63	2½
3	0.50	3
2½	0.38	3½
2	0.26	4
1½	0.16	4½
1	0.08	5
½	0.025	5½

922 *Tidal Current Tables* are also published annually in advance for both the Atlantic and Pacific Oceans. They are similar to the *Tide Tables* in that two tables (reference and subordinate) are used. The time of maximum flood and maximum ebb, and slack ebb and flood ebb are given, as well as the velocity and direction of the current.

It should be remembered that the direction of a current is the one toward which the current moves, or sets. Most coastwise currents are caused by the rise and fall of the tides, rather than atmospheric phenomena, and therefore flood directions are toward the land, and contributaries and ebb directions away. Offshore, tidal currents are unconfined by channels and never reach a slack, flowing in any and all directions, and are known as rotary currents.

Tidal current charts are available for active boating areas (New

PORTSMOUTH HARBOR ENTRANCE (OFF WOOD I.), N.H., 1978

F-FLOOD, DIR. 355° TRUE   E-EBB, DIR. 195° TRUE

JANUARY

DAY	SLACK WATER TIME H.M.	MAX CURRENT TIME H.M.	VEL. KNOTS	DAY	SLACK WATER TIME H.M.	MAX CURRENT TIME H.M.	VEL. KNOTS
1 SU		0132	1.2F	16 M	0024	0221	1.2F
	0457	0801	1.6E		0624	0902	1.7E
	1153	1352	1.1F		1300	1442	0.9F
	1626	2023	1.8E		1838	2119	1.7E
2 M	0016	0223	1.3F	17 TU	0119	0312	1.0F
	0550	0856	1.7E		0720	1000	1.6E
	1250	1445	1.1F		1401	1536	0.7F
	1724	2116	1.8E		1937	2213	1.5E
3 TU	0107	0315	1.3F	18 W	0213	0403	0.9F
	0650	0950	1.7E		0814	1107	1.6E
	1348	1540	1.1F		1500	1630	0.6F
	1841	2209	1.8E		2034	2309	1.4E
4 W	0200	0410	1.4F	19 TH	0307	0454	0.9F
	0751	1045	1.9E		0906	1237	1.6E
	1447	1637	1.1F		1555	1956	0.7F
	2001	2306	1.9E		2130		

FEBRUARY

DAY	SLACK WATER TIME H.M.	MAX CURRENT TIME H.M.	VEL. KNOTS	DAY	SLACK WATER TIME H.M.	MAX CURRENT TIME H.M.	VEL. KNOTS
1 W	0033	0246	1.4F	16 TH	0138	0322	0.9F
	0612	0921	1.9E		0733	1012	1.5E
	1318	1512	1.1F		1424	1552	0.6F
	1817	2142	1.8E		1959	2229	1.4E
2 TH	0131	0341	1.4F	17 F	0233	0416	0.8F
	0719	1018	1.9E		0828	1108	1.5E
	1420	1611	1.1F		1520	1647	0.6F
	1941	2240	1.8E		2057	2326	1.3E
3 F	0231	0438	1.4F	18 SA	0327	0509	0.8F
	0826	1117	2.0E		0921	1207	1.5E
	1520	1712	1.2F		1612	1745	0.6F
	2054	2341	1.9E		2151		
4 SA	0330	0538	1.5F	19 SU		0022	1.4E
	0928	1217	2.1E		0417	0602	0.9F
	1618	1811	1.2F		1010	1259	1.6E
	2200				1700	1836	0.7F
					2240		

THE NARROWS, NEW YORK HARBOR, N.Y., 1978

F-FLOOD, DIR. 340° TRUE   E-EBB, DIR. 160° TRUE

JANUARY

DAY	SLACK WATER TIME H.M.	MAX CURRENT TIME H.M.	VEL. KNOTS	DAY	SLACK WATER TIME H.M.	MAX CURRENT TIME H.M.	VEL. KNOTS
1 SU	0221	0531	1.6E	16 M		0023	1.7F
	0913	1137	1.5F		0325	0642	1.8E
	1434	1756	1.8E		1021	1241	1.4F
	2140				1534	1900	1.8E
					2238		
2 M		0005	1.6F	17 TU		0119	1.6F
	0315	0632	1.7E		0424	0742	1.7E
	1013	1226	1.4F		1120	1348	1.2F
	1526	1855	1.8E		1631	1957	1.8E
	2229				2331		
3 TU		0056	1.7F	18 W		0228	1.6F
	0413	0733	1.8E		0523	0837	1.8E
	1110	1320	1.4F		1216	1504	1.2F
	1623	1951	1.9E		1728	2048	1.7E
	2319						
4 W		0151	-1.8F	19 TH	0022	0333	1.6F
	0513	0832	2.0E		0617	0928	1.8E
	1210	1417	1.4F		1311	1605	1.2F
	1723	2044	2.0E		1822	2137	1.7E

FEBRUARY

DAY	SLACK WATER TIME H.M.	MAX CURRENT TIME H.M.	VEL. KNOTS	DAY	SLACK WATER TIME H.M.	MAX CURRENT TIME H.M.	VEL. KNOTS
1 W		0028	1.8F	16 TH		0126	1.5F
	0343	0702	1.8E		0442	0802	1.7E
	1045	1253	1.4F		1144	1410	1.1F
	1553	1920	1.9E		1651	2016	1.6E
	2249				2350		
2 TH		0123	1.6F	17 F		0239	1.5F
	0445	0804	1.9E		0539	0855	1.7E
	1145	1352	1.4F		1239	1530	1.1F
	1656	2021	2.0E		1750	2107	1.6E
	2347						
3 F		0224	1.6F	18 SA	0042	0350	1.5F
	0547	0901	2.1E		0631	0943	1.8E
	1245	1458	1.4F		1331	1626	1.2F
	1759	2117	2.1E		1843	2154	1.7E
4 SA	0046	0328	2.1F	19 SU	0133	0439	1.6F
	0645	0957	2.3E		0718	1028	1.9E
	1342	1607	1.6F		1419	1711	1.4F
	1858	2212	2.2E		1931	2242	1.8E

922A Example from *Tidal Current Tables 1978 Atlantic Coast of North America*

York, Long Island Sound, San Francisco, etc.) which, together with the *Tidal Current Tables*, give direction and velocity of the current for any year and for various stages of ebb and flood.

In various parts of the country, private publishers issue annual directories giving tide, tidal current, and facilities information for the calendar year, in soft cover form.

TABLE 2: - ROTARY TIDAL CURRENTS

Station No.	Depth (ft.)		0.0	0.5	1.0	1.5	2.0	2.5	3.0	3.5	4.0	4.5	5.0	5.5	6.0	6.5	7.0	7.5	8.0	8.5	9.0	9.5	10.0	10.5	11.0	11.5	12.0
			(Time: Hours after Minimum before Flood at Boston Harbor)																							
393	10	knots	0.03	0.22	0.23	0.24	0.26	0.25	0.27	0.32	0.33	0.33	0.32	0.31	0.28	0.28	0.27	0.27	0.28	0.27	0.26	0.27	0.23	0.21	0.21		
		degrees	265	266	265	268	270	268	282	303	319	327	333	340	357	025	067	068	070	074	073	080	076	079	073	073	051
395	10	knots	0.30	0.40	0.45	0.43	0.46	0.48	0.50	0.53	0.51	0.52	0.50	0.51	0.51	0.52	0.49	0.50	0.48	0.52	0.49	0.46	0.46	0.43	0.40	0.40	0.36
		degrees	210	261	258	247	248	247	262	280	280	304	340	345	009	044	049	061	068	070	074	079	082	081	090	081	123
397	10	knots	0.29	0.50	0.50	0.31	0.32	0.34	0.34	0.35	0.37	0.36	0.35	0.35	0.34	0.34	0.35	0.34	0.36	0.35	0.34	0.36	0.35	0.34	0.32	0.18	
		degrees	200	209	212	222	229	243	247	259	265	268	284	331	002	018	042	056	058	064	065	075	080	085	086	095	132
399	10	knots	0.50	0.49	0.52	0.55	0.56	0.57	0.54	0.53	0.55	0.54	0.55	0.55	0.52	0.50	0.52	0.50	0.49	0.51	0.51	0.51	0.50	0.51	0.49	0.50	0.49
		degrees	138	140	220	243	284	260	252	241	250	244	240	228	211	160	078	062	081	093	085	093	091	087	095	116	130
401	10	knots	0.20	0.20	0.21	0.22	0.24	0.23	0.25	0.25	0.25	0.26	0.24	0.26	0.25	0.24	0.24	0.23	0.24	0.23	0.22	0.21	0.21	0.21	0.20	0.20	0.20
		degrees	306	342	340	244	228	232	223	232	200	210	216	271	290	351	357	051	059	048	045	028	037	052	028	035	011
403	10	knots	0.42	0.44	0.43	0.45	0.46	0.46	0.46	0.47	0.48	0.48	0.49	0.46	0.48	0.30	0.50	0.50	0.49	0.48	0.47	0.47	0.47	0.47	0.45	0.42	0.41
		degrees	221	223	216	221	213	211	215	219	227	235	230	221	254	019	015	009	357	052	053	055	070	135	193	206	
405	10	knots	0.42	0.44	0.45	0.45	0.47	0.50	0.46	0.47	0.45	0.44	0.44	0.40	0.45	0.47	0.44	0.44	0.47	0.44	0.42	0.43	0.47	0.40	0.43	0.45	
		degrees	213	199	193	182	175	135	178	183	222	247	267	306	330	346	328	344	335	327	334	341	337	338	306	276	240
417	15	knots	0.11	0.26	0.51	0.53	0.55	0.52	0.50	0.54	0.47	0.50	0.46	0.45	0.46	0.45	0.48	0.51	0.57	0.62	0.66	0.67	0.64	0.62	0.51	0.40	0.25
		degrees	191	292	295	304	303	312	308	319	313	331	354	358	010	030	046	059	089	108	109	122	121	119	132	129	134
419	10	knots	0.30	0.30	0.38	0.39	0.38	0.36	0.37	0.37	0.36	0.36	0.35	0.34	0.30	0.20	0.19	0.25	0.30	0.33	0.35	0.36	0.38	0.38	0.36	0.36	0.32
		degrees	251	307	331	342	332	336	343	341	343	350	347	006	029	081	114	138	146	160	165	172	173	190	203	233	
461	10	knots	0.34	0.39	0.41	0.42	0.35	0.35	0.34	0.37	0.39	0.38	0.40	0.39	0.41	0.36	0.40	0.41	0.35	0.31	0.32	0.31	0.27	0.29	0.20	0.25	
		degrees	267	264	261	261	259	251	235	230	220	209	199	197	146	087	069	070	071	046	030	018	024	046	024	269	272
489	10	knots	0.33	0.35	0.36	0.35	0.36	0.34	0.40	0.39	0.40	0.42	0.45	0.37	0.35	0.32	0.35	0.37	0.34	0.33	0.35	0.35	0.34	0.03	0.29	0.31	0.34
		degrees	007	010	024	034	060	343	348	007	063	025	095	064	081	103	102	103	104	117	135	139	158	215	339	353	355
*513	10	knots	0.17	0.16	0.18	0.16	0.13	0.17	0.19	0.21	0.22	0.18	0.19	0.21	0.18	0.22	0.25	0.26	0.26	0.27	0.28	0.28	0.29	0.29	0.28	0.25	0.18
		degrees	086	095	090	088	090	095	090	093	083	083	081	077	082	072	072	070	069	067	070	070	073	077	085	082	085
565	10	knots	0.22	0.27	0.29	0.09	0.37	0.40	0.44	0.45	0.44	0.44	0.44	0.50	0.51	0.47	0.42	0.39	0.37	0.37	0.34	0.30	0.23	0.10			
		degrees	217	199	209	199	052	061	074	077	066	047	032	025	029	041	061	077	082	076	071	070	070	064	069	070	085
565	20	knots	0.15	0.22	0.24	0.06	0.28	0.30	0.31	0.36	0.34	0.33	0.35	0.36	0.40	0.43	0.39	0.30	0.28	0.34	0.35	0.34	0.32	0.29	0.23	0.16	
		degrees	271	238	231	251	019	025	076	073	064	060	029	021	021	030	049	067	067	058	056	050	050	047	044	052	005
617	10	knots	0.20	0.23	0.27	0.45	0.41	0.40	0.35	0.30	0.28	0.32	0.34	0.35	0.33	0.29	0.29	0.32	0.33	0.32	0.33	0.32	0.30	0.26	0.24	0.24	
		degrees	246	232	282	351	019	025	024	009	355	343	338	339	345	007	013	008	002	356	345	336	333	331	331	320	305
617	20	knots	0.15	0.19	0.20	0.33	0.34	0.30	0.24	0.21	0.22	0.28	0.31	0.33	0.32	0.29	0.28	0.27	0.28	0.29	0.31	0.29	0.26	0.21	0.17	0.11	0.10
		degrees	220	214	232	001	020	027	024	003	345	340	333	332	331	351	009	008	003	350	339	334	329	322	322	315	254

* In Reserved Channel, the tidal current is weak, averaging less than 0.1 knot. During a 7-day observation period, the total current set was consistently eastward.

922B Example of a table for Rotary Tidal Currents

923 *United States Coast Pilot* is a publication, in series, giving extremely minute and detailed information of value and use to the navigator. It is published about every two years, and is corrected between publications by free supplements and by notes contained in the weekly *Notice to Mariners*. It provides exactly the type of information which enables the navigator to sail with safety in home or strange waters. The *Coast Pilot*, however, is primarily oriented toward the needs of commercial vessels. A cruising guide, of which many are available, provides supplementary information for small boats.

Example of information given for a harbor is shown in Figure 923.

Charts 13281, 13274.–Gloucester Harbor is one of the most important fishing ports in the United States and an important harbor of refuge. It is 5 miles southwestward of Emerson Point, the easternmost point of Cape Ann, 26 miles from Boston and 234 miles from New York. The entrance is marked on its eastern side by Eastern Point Light. There is an outer and inner harbor, the former having depths generally of 18 to 52 feet and the latter, depths of 15 to 24 feet.

Gloucester Inner Harbor limits begin at a line between Black Rock Daybeacon and **Fort Point.**

Gloucester is a city of great historical interest, the first permanent settlement having been established in 1623. The city limits cover the greater part of Cape Ann and part of the mainland as far west as Magnolia Harbor. Its principal industries are directly or indirectly connected with the fishing or related industries in the processing, freezing, canning, or shipment of fish and lobsters.

The principal imports are seafood and petroleum products. Limited amounts of canned meats, produce, and consumer goods are the principal exports.

Prominent   features.–Eastern   Point   Light (42°34.8′N., 70°39.9′W.), 57 feet above the water, is shown from a 36-foot white conical tower with a vay to a dwelling; a for signal is at the direction calibrat   at the 'iobeacon is 6̶ꞓ   of

The volumes of the *Coast Pilot* cover areas as follows:

> *Atlantic Coast*
> No. 1   Eastport to Cape Cod
> No. 2   Cape Cod to Sandy Hook
> No. 3   Sandy Hook to Cape Henry
> No. 4   Cape Henry to Key West
> No. 5   Gulf of Mexico, Puerto Rico, and
> Virgin Islands
> (Note: There is no Volume No. 6.)
> *Pacific Coast*
> No. 7   California, Oregon, Washington,
> and Hawaii
> *Alaska*
> No. 8   Dixon Entrance to Cape Spencer
> No. 9   Cape Spencer to Beaufort Sea

They are published by the National Ocean Survey and available from that agency directly (*see Paragraph 935*), or where NOS charts are sold. An upcoming program involving a new printing technique will soon make all volumes available on an annual basis.

For the Great Lakes and waters covered by the Lake Survey Charts, the applicable volume is *The Great Lakes Pilot*. It is published annually and kept current by issuing monthly advisories (to be posted in the *Pilot*) from May to November, the open navigating season for the Great Lakes.

924   Small Craft Charts. Lying somewhere between conventional charts and the *Coast Pilots* are the small-craft strip charts, or the "SC" series. These are accordion-folded charts, in a heavy-paper envelope, and are most convenient on small boats which have no chart tables or wheelhouses to accommodate standard charts. They are published by the National Ocean Survey for the most popular small boat areas and depict local areas such as rivers and inland bays and sounds, often with insets showing connecting waters or areas. The series are:

> 100SC to 199SC   Folios of several sheets,
> printed both sides

70 SC to 9500SC	Area charts from conventional plates but printed on lighter paper and with added small-craft information
600SC to 699SC	Routes on narrow waterways and rivers
800SC to 899SC	Intracoastal Waterway routes

All SC charts show features of particular interest to the small-boat man and day sailor. On some SC charts, long courses (as in crossing a sound or bay) are indicated and the course and reverse course noted with true compass course. On some, a magenta line threads the entire route and indicates the best depths, the route is divided, from a starting point, every five miles by a mileage notation.

Coast Pilot information on an SC chart is usually on the reverse side of the jacket or slip. This is information that usually would require checking in several publications, none of which would likely be found on a small boat. Thus, the information contains local annual tide tables, marine weather information sources, Rules of the Road, warning notes and signals in brief, and a list of repair and marina facilities located in the area covered, together with brief tabulation of available services, types of fuel (gas, diesel, etc.), depth alongside docks, and the like. Facilities are not, however, listed by name—only by location. Each chart is corrected and reissued annually.

The SC charts are real money savers, supplying information that would require many conventional charts of various scales, a *Coast Pilot, Tidal Current Tables,* and weather maps, plus private sources for marina and boatyard listings. The cost of conventional charts from Norfolk to Miami via the inland waterway would, with the supporting books, be upwards of $100. The SC charts for the same run cost about $20 (in 1979). The average folio size is 9″ by 15″ making for easy stowage on the small craft. At this writing there are about 100 charts in print, with more arriving years, and a small-boat skipper should check at local chart agencies regarding his own area. SC charts are listed in the NOS chart catalog and are available from chart agencies or from the NOS.

925 There are many other navigational tools, some quite sophisticated, many "gadgety" items that just get in the way of simple, here-to-there navigation. On the average cruiser, it behooves the master to reduce his navigational tools to a simple working set, with the use of each component so well understood as to be almost automatic. It is a far cry from the professional navigator—who daily uses the tools of his trade—to the recreational yachtsman who, with however complex and sophisticated navigational gear available, navigates his vessel 60 hours a year! There just isn't time or opportunity to become familiar with all the tools of the trade; far better to understand a few tools thoroughly and use only them. Except for the speedometer-log, depth sounder, and radio direction finder, the electronics—loran, radar, consolan, etc.—are often simply expensive gadgets (and possibly status symbols) that are useless unless one has a reasonably complete understanding of offshore navigation and how the operation and the application of the world of electronics fits into the problems. In addition to being navigator, the recreational yachtsman is likely also to be helmsman, engineer, officer of the watch, owner, lookout, and possibly bartender—all at the same time. He just cannot, besides all his other duties, handle complex electronic gadgetry.

On an ocean voyage, the navigator is sometimes considered to be such an essential crew member, and such a busy person with continuing responsibility and duties, that he is excused from all watch standing, wheel watches, and galley slavery. It looks like a soft berth but it definitely is not! It is recognized that he must be given the time to devote his full energies to the task of navigating, to become familiar with his tools, and by constant use and practice, to develop a reliable and accurate department of the ship. He simply has no time or energy for anything but navigation, and if he did take the time for other duties and responsibilities, his navigation would suffer in quality and accuracy. This all points up the fact that the average skipper, already burdened with many responsibilities, must keep his navigational procedures simple and clean-cut so that what he does need to know, he knows well—from familiarity born of experience.

Nevertheless, we shall discuss electronic navigational aids briefly, for conceivably some readers might have legitimate use for them.

ELECTRONIC NAVIGATIONAL AIDS

926   *The Radio Direction Finder (Figure 926A)* for the small boat is a self-contained device which utilizes the directional characteristics of the ferrite rod antenna. A movable antenna is manipulated by hand so that it rests at a null or silent point on the beam of a known radio wave. Its shaft is connected to a pointer from which a bearing may be taken from a dumb compass card, so mounted that readings can be taken from the ship's head in degrees or compass points. By applying the compass course, either a magnetic or true bearing of the radio beacon may be figured.

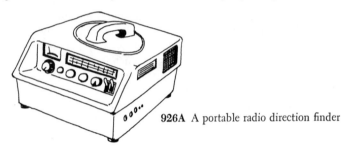

926A A portable radio direction finder

Direction finders are supplied by several manufacturers, and come with operating instructions relating to the particular type and model. The instrument is subject to error caused by deviation and must be calibrated upon installation and a deviation card calculated. This is usually done by observing radio bearings of a visible beacon and making the proper corrections on various headings on a direction-finder deviation card or circle.

It is affected by high land and by night reception. If the boat is over 100 miles from the beacon, corrections must be made to convert the great circle bearings to Mercator bearings. Any other radio antenna must be open while radio bearings are being taken.

The radio direction finder serves to give the navigator bearings and cross bearings from invisible marks, and thus to obtain a "fix." In some cases the beam may be followed for a distance by log, or by time, until usual methods of obtaining a "fix" are available (soundings, fog signals, lights, etc.). This is called *homing*. The danger, of course, is of over-running and crashing on the shore or into the radio-beacon ship.

An *ADF* (*Automatic Direction Finder*) does what the RDF does, but the antenna is mechanically or electronically rotated, saving manual rotating once it has been tuned. Power is from self-contained batteries and the ship's electrical supply. Most DF sets contain LW beacon bands, both marine and aero, MF ship-to-shore band, commercial radio bands (AM and FM), VHF ship band and continuous weather frequencies. The operation of an RDF is covered in the next chapter.

Loran is one of a family of hyperbolic navigational aids that includes Loran A, Loran C, Decca, Omega, Consol, and others. The system projects microwaves over large sea areas from two or more stations keyed to each other. On-board equipment (receiving only) measures the time difference and converts it into distance by obtaining a rough fix from electronic lines of position. It requires a trained operator for fast and accurate work, and certain tables must be part of the solution.

Loran is for genuine offshore navigation, especially under circumstances that forbid celestial sights. Loran A, when 1,000 miles distant from the transmitter, can obtain a fix within a quarter mile. Loran C will reach, on a direct wave, much farther. Another system using the same basics is Omega, which is worldwide. An international commission has set the date 1980 as the target for completion of worldwide coverage, requiring only eight transmitters. Five are presently in operation.

The equipment is expensive and requires abundant power and trained operators. It is hardly necessary for the small yacht, but is increasingly used by racing sailboats and small fishing craft down to 30′ or so.

Radar is a visual system that provides highly accurate bearings up to the optical horizon or slightly more. It times a radio-frequency wave to the target and back to the radar screen. Many ranges are available and most sets have multiple ranges, which may be selected at the screen. In order to "cover" the entire 360° electronic horizon, the transmitter-receiver unit is mechanically revolved to literally "sweep" the complete circle and report, on a screen, of which the

RADAR

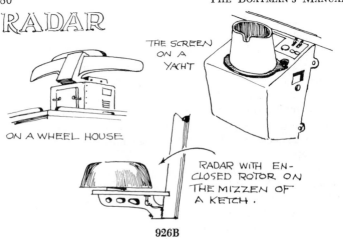

THE SCREEN ON A YACHT

ON A WHEEL HOUSE

RADAR WITH EN-CLOSED ROTOR ON THE MIZZEN OF A KETCH.

926B

ship is the center, *everything* within the circle. A trained operator can readily distinguish between land, buildings, other traffic, buoys, aircraft, etc. and can determine the nature of the object (trees, marsh, clouds, snow, fog, etc.) by density. While of particular value at night or in thick weather (for radar penetrates fog, rain, sleet, snow, smoke, and smog) it is often used in daytime to provide part of the component of a fix, particularly of a sighted object (on the screen) since the screen gives a distance reading—and thus two lines of position—and therefore a fix (a bearing and distance off).

Radar is expensive and the power demand hearty. Rather heavy equipment must be secured aloft—above fixtures and rigging and sparring—and considerable space must be allotted to the wheelhouse units (*see Figure 926B*). Nevertheless, many quite small craft are equipped with radar since it is not a complex device to interpret and is very useful in coasting in thick weather or at night. The screen does *not* give all the information in usable form. Generally, it merely alerts, and the factors of a navigational situation must still be plotted on the chart. Ordinary navigational practices then take over.

FURTHER TOOLS AND TRICKS OF NAVIGATION

927   Handy for chart work and part of the chart table equipment might also be:

A timer. Perfectly satisfactory is an oven timer (about $3.50) with an alarm which may be set for any time desired (as for running a known course between buoys, etc.).

2. In the absence of parallel rules or course protractor, just roll a round pencil from course to compass rose (to read a course).

3. A large magnifying glass is handy. Some are made with illumination from a bulb set into the edge.

4. If you need glasses to read chart or compass, hang them on loops that go around the neck and keep the glasses on your chest ready for use.

5. If you need glasses only for close reading, try "Ben Franklin" glasses—half glasses which magnify only when the gaze is lowered (as for reading) permitting distance sight over the nonmagnifying top half. (About $4 in five-and-dime stores.)

6. Provide weights (lead, a heavy ash tray, large nuts, etc.) to hold down the chart corners. Another idea is to use "drapery" weighted tape (tape with lead disks sewn in).

7. A pointer (any non-rolling object with a point) is handy to place on the chart in such a manner as to indicate your position from time to time. Saves much searching each time you wish to check. Useful to "tick off" passed buoys or markers as you steam (as on the Intracoastal, which has dozens of buoys per mile in places).

8. A chart-table light is a must. It should be a movable-arm type with a red bulb (since red does not induce night blindness).

9. Charts need to be stowed flat, not rolled. A large chart drawer should be provided, possibly (in a small-boat) of a size to permit one fold only. Overhead racks are OK.

10. A handy-by bookshelf is needed, big enough to hold the *Coast Pilots, Tide Tables,* this *Manual,* etc.

928   Following is a list of sources for charts, guides, tables, cruising information, and service publications.

U. S. COAST GUARD PUBLICATIONS

Recreational Boating Guide—CG-340. 77 pages. Information on boat numbering; equipment requirements; responsibilities when operating; aids to navigation; safety afloat; emergency procedures; and U. S. Coast Guard Auxiliary services. Federal Boating Act of 1958, and Motorboat Act of April 25, 1940; FSBA/71 Application for Number form; Boating Accident Report; and Radio Distress Information Sheet. Superintendent of Documents, Government Printing Office, Washington, D. C. 20402.

Federal Requirements for Recreational Boats—CG-290. Boating laws and regulations. Numbering. Boating accidents. Sales to aliens. Law enforcement. Documentation. C. G. approved equipment. Equipment requirements. Safety. U. S. Coast Guard offices.

Marine aids to Navigation of the United States—U. S. Coast Guard Publication CG-193. Illustrated. 32 pages. U. S. Coast Guard, Washington, D. C. 20590. Basic principles underlying the marking of coasts and waterways with lighthouses, lightships, fog signals, radiobeacons, loran, and buoys.

Emergency Repairs Afloat—U. S. Coast Guard publication CG-151. The Boatman's guide to engine troubleshooting, emergency repairs, how to stay afloat, and recommended basic tools and spare parts. Available from Boating Safety Offices at Coast Guard District Headquarters, or by mail from U.S.C.G. Headquarters, Washington, D. C. 20590.

Rules and Regulations for Uninspected Vessels—U. S. Coast Guard Publication C.G.-258. 16 pages. Copies may be obtained from District Coast Guard Offices. Requirements for all vessels not subject to inspection.

Rules and Regulations for Numbering Undocumented Vessels—U. S. Coast Guard Publication CG-267. Available from the Commandant (CHS), U. S. Coast Guard, Washington, D. C. 20590.

First Aid for the Boatman—U. S. Coast Guard/Coast Guard Auxiliary—AUX-206. Material on artificial respiration, wounds, bleeding, burns, shock. 20 pages. U.S.C.G., Washington, D. C. 20590.

CHARTS OF VARIOUS WATERWAYS

Charts, U. S. Coastal Waters—Charts of coastal waters, and the Atlantic and Gulf Intracoastal Waterways, are published by the National Ocean Survey, Rockville, Md., 20852, and are available from them, their distribution offices, or their sales agents.

Charts, Great Lakes—Charts of the Great Lakes and connecting rivers, Lake Champlain, New York State Canals, Lake of the Woods, and Rainy Lake are available from the Lake Survey Center, 630 Federal Bldg., Detroit, Mich. 48226. A catalog of charts is issued.

Charts, New York State Canals—A booklet of charts of the New York State canals is available from the Lake Survey Center, 630 Federal Bldg., Detroit, Mich. 48226.

Charts, Mississippi River and Tributaries—(*Middle & Upper Mississippi River; Cairo, Ill. to Minneapolis, Minn.*)

(*Middle Mississippi River; Cairo, Ill. to Grafton, Ill.*)

(*Mississippi River from Cairo, Ill. to Gulf of Mexico*)

(*Small Boat Navigation Chart; Alton, Ill. to Clarksville on the Mississippi River and Grafton, Ill., to LaGrange, Ill. on the Illinois River*)

(*Illinois Waterways; from Grafton, Ill. to Lake Michigan at Chicago and Calumet Harbors*)

U. S. Army Engineer District, 210 N. 12th Street, St. Louis, Missouri, 63101.

The offices listed below will supply lists of charts, detailing sources, prices, scales, and exact sections covered.

Mississippi River and connecting waterways, north of Ohio River—U. S. Army Engineer Division, North Central, 536 South Clark St., Chicago, Ill. 60605.

Mississippi River and tributaries, below Ohio River—Mississippi River Commission, P.O. Box 80, Vicksburg, Miss. 39181. This office also has a free booklet, "Mississippi River Navigation," relating to the history, development and navigation of the river.

Ohio River and tributaries; Pittsburgh, Pa., to the Mississippi River—U. S. Army Engineer Division, P.O. Box 1159, Cincinnati, Ohio 45201.

Tennessee and Cumberland Rivers—U. S. Army Engineer District, P. O. Box 1070, Nashville, Tenn. 37202. Tennessee Valley Authority, Maps and Engineering Records Section, 102A Union Bldg., Knoxville, Tenn.

Missouri River and tributaries—U. S. Army Engineer District, 6012 U. S. Post Office and Court House, Omaha, Neb. 68102.

Charts, Canadian Waters—Charts of Canadian waters are available from Hydrographic Chart Distribution, Canadian Hydrographic Service, Department of Mines and Technical Surveys, 615 Booth St., Ottawa, Ontario, Canada. These include charts of coastal waters; sections of the Great Lakes such as Georgian Bay; the St. Lawrence River; Richelieu River; Ottawa River; The Rideau Waterway; and other lakes, canals, etc.

A catalog, with prices of charts for any area in Canada are available free from the same address.

Charts, Foreign Waters—These are published by the Defense Mapping Agency Hydrographic Center, Washington, D. C. 20390, and are available through any of the sales agents listed semi annually in Notice to Mariners. A general catalog plus ten regional catalogs are available.

NOTICE TO MARINERS

Notice to Mariners—This is a weekly pamphlet published by the Defense Mapping Agency Hydrographic Center, Washington, D. C. 20390. It is issued so mariners may keep nautical charts and Coast Pilots up to date.

Local Notices, of interest to each of the Coast Guard Districts, are issued by Commanders of the districts, and are available from their district offices.

NEW YORK STATE CANALS

Rules and Regulations Covering Navigation and Use of the New York State Canal System—published by New York State Dept. of Transportation, Division of Operation and Maintenance,

Albany, N. Y. 12232. A description of the New York Canal System, and regulations pertaining to use of the canal.

Canal Guide Book for the New York State Barge Canal System and Connecting Navigable Waterways—Lists sources of supplies such as fuel, oil, engine repairs, fresh water, provisions, anchorage and dockage. Available from Cruising Guide Book, 146 Sheridan Avenue, Albany, N. Y. 12210.

The Northwest Passage—Guide book, with charts, for Hudson River, Champlain Canal, and Lake Champlain. Division of Motor Boats, New York Conservation Dept., Albany, N. Y. 12226.

The Grand Canal—Guide book, with charts, for Erie Canal, Oswego Canal, and the Cayuga Seneca Canals. Division of Motor Boats (See above).

INTRACOASTAL WATERWAYS

Intracoastal Waterway Booklets—Descriptions of the Intracoastal Waterway, with data on navigation, charts, distances, etc., by Corps of Engineers, U. S. Army, and available from Superintendent of Documents, Washington, D. C. 20402. In two sections: (1) Atlantic Section, Boston to Key West, (2) Gulf Section, Key West to Brownsville, Tex.

Intracoastal Waterway Bulletins—Timely bulletins giving latest information on the Intracoastal Waterway are published by the Corps of Engineers. Available from the following District Offices of the Army Engineers: 803 Front St., Norfolk, Va. 23510; P. O. Box 1890, Wilmington, N. C. 28401; P. O. Box 919, Charleston, S. C. 29402; P. O. Box 889, Savannah, Ga. 31402; P. O. Box 4970, Jacksonville, Fla. 32201; P. O. Box 2288, Mobile, Ala. 36601; P. O. Box 1229, Galveston, Tex. 77551.

Waterway Guide—A private annual guide detailing for the yachtsman all information concerning the inland waterways. The Northern Edition covers the coast from Maine to New York; the

Middle Atlantic Edition from New York to Sea Island, Ga.; the Southern Edition from Sea Island, Ga., to Florida and Gulf Coast to New Orleans; the Great Lakes Edition from New York to the Great Lakes with connecting Canadian canals and rivers. From Waterway Guide, Inc., 238 West St., Annapolis, Md. 21401, and many marinas and chandleries along the Intracoastal.

COAST PILOTS

Coast Pilots—For coastal waters, and the Atlantic and Gulf Intracoastal Waterways, published by the National Ocean Survey, Rockville, Md. 20852, and are available from them, their distribution offices, or sales agents. These volumes supplement the information given on charts, with detailed descriptions of routes, courses, distances, depths, harbors, sources of supplies, tides, currents, weather, list of yacht clubs, facilities for repairs, etc.

For the Great Lakes and other waters covered by Lake Survey charts, use the Great Lakes Pilot. This is an annual publication, kept up-to-date during the navigation season by monthly supplements issued from May to November. From the Lakes Survey Center, 630 Federal Bldg., Detroit, Mich. 48226.

For Canadian waters—Available from Hydrographic Chart Distribution, Canadian Hydrographic Office, Dept. of Mines and Technical Surveys, 615 Booth St., Ottawa, Ontario, Canada.

TIDE AND CURRENT TABLES

Tide Tables, Tidal Current Tables and Tidal Current Charts— Publications of the National Ocean Survey, Rockville, Md. 20852, and may be obtained from them, their distribution offices, or from any of their sales agents.

LIGHT LISTS

Light Lists—Published by the U. S. Coast Guard and for sale by the Superintendent of Documents, Washington, D. C. 20402, or any Coast Guard sales agent. They describe lighted aids, radio beacons, fog signals, unlighted buoys, and daymarks. Vol. I covers Atlantic Coast from St. Croix River, Me., to Little River, S. C. Vol. II, Atlantic and Gulf Coasts from Little River, S. C., to the

Rio Grande, Tex., and the Antilles. Vol. III, Pacific Coast and Islands. Vol. IV, Great Lakes. Vol. V, Mississippi River.

RULES OF THE ROAD

Rules of the Road—Rules of the Road are published for three areas, C.G. No. 169—Inland waters of the Atlantic and Pacific coasts and of the coast of the Gulf of Mexico; C.G. No. 172—The Great Lakes and their connecting and tributary waters and the St. Mary's River; and C.G. No. 184—The Western Rivers and the Red River of the North. Published by the U. S. Coast Guard—Copies may be obtained from Coast Guard Marine Inspection Offices in principal ports, or the Commandant (CHS), U. S. Coast Guard, Washington, D. C. 20226.

Handbook of Boating Laws—Four editions for Southern, Northeastern, North Central and Western states. Lists state requirements for registering, numbering, equipment and small-boat operation; fuel tax laws; boat trailer laws; and applicable federal regulations. From Outboard Boating Club, 333 N. Michigan Ave., Chicago, Ill. 60601.

WEATHER

Weather Forecasting—U. S. Department of Commerce, National Weather Service. Illustrated. 40 pages. Facts and theories of meteorology and some of the principles of weather forecasting. Superintendent of Documents, Washington, D. C. 20402.

The Hurricane—United States Department of Commerce, Weather Bureau. Illustrated. 22 pages. Dealing solely with the hurricane. Superintendent of Documents, Washington, D. C. 20402.

Circular R. W. B. 1151 Preparation and Use of Weather Maps at Sea—U. S. Department of Commerce, National Weather Service. Illustrated. 100 pages. The Ship's weather observation, Radio weather bulletins, Preparation of weather maps.

Florida Hurricanes—United States Department of Commerce, National Weather Service. Illustrated. 3 pages. Discusses frequency, time, and initial starting point of Florida hurricanes.

Circular F. Barometers and the Measurement of Atmospheric Pressure—U. S. Department of Commerce, National Weather Service. Illustrated. 3 pages. A treatise on barometers.

The Daily Weather Map—United States Department of Commerce, National Weather Service. Five weather maps of the United States, data for which are prepared from observations taken at hundreds of stations. A complete explanation of the maps, including all symbols and tables. Superintendent of Documents, Washington, D. C. 20402.

Manual of Cloud Forms and Codes for States of Sky—United States Department of Commerce, National Weather Service Circular S. Illustrated. 43 pages. Definitions and descriptions of cloud forms.

GENERAL CRUISING PUBLICATIONS

Cruising Guide to the New England Coast—Descriptions of harbors, anchorages, and waterways by Fessenden Blanchard. Includes Hudson River, Long Island Sound, and the New Brunswick coast. Available from Sailing Book Service, 34 Oak Ave., Tuckahoe, N. Y. 10707.

Cruising Guide to the Southern Coast—Blanchard's guide to the Intracoastal Waterway—Norfolk to New Orleans, including other Florida waterways. Sailing Book Service (address above).

Cruising Guide to the Chesapeake—Another Blanchard guide, with a wealth of information on Chesapeake Bay. Sailing Book Service (address above).

Yachtsman's Guide to Northern Harbors—Harbors, marinas and services on Long Island, and seacoast of New England. Seaport Publishing Co., 843 Delray Ave., S.E., Grand Rapids 6, Mich.

Guide for Cruising Maryland Waters—Maryland Dept. of Tidewater Fisheries. Full-color charts, with many courses and distances plotted. Maryland Board of Natural Resources, State Office Bldg., Annapolis, Md. 21404.

Boating Atlas of Tidewater Virginia—Charts in full color covering the ocean, lower Chesapeake Bay, the James, York, Rappahannock and Potomac rivers. Buoyage system, Rules of the Road, location of marine facilities, state and Coast Guard regulations, notes from the Coast Pilot, Tide Tables, safety suggestions, and a course protractor. Distributed by Paxton Co., 1019 Main St., Norfolk, Va.

Florida Boating—Pamphlet giving information on waterways, charts, Florida boat registration, and water safety regulations, area maps and information, plus a directory of marine facilities. Florida Development Commission, Carlton Bldg., Tallahassee, Fla., 32302.

Go South Inside by Carl D. Lane—A guide to the Atlantic Intracoastal Waterway with a listing of the favorite anchorages. Available from International Marine Publishing Company, Camden, Maine 04843 or from marinas and bookshops along the Waterway.

Yachtsman's Guide to the Great Lakes—For the Great Lakes, St. Lawrence, Richelieu and Hudson Rivers, Lake Champlain, and New York State Barge Canal. Seaport Publishing Co., 843 Delray Ave., S. E., Grand Rapids, Mich. 49506.

Cruising the Georgian Bay—Cruising information, with aerial survey maps and lists of services and facilities at ports. Bellhaven House, 12 Dyas Road, Don Mills, Ontario, Canada.

Cruising the North Channel—The waterway between Manitoulin Island and the north shore of Lake Huron. Bellhaven House, see address above.

Cruising the Trent-Severn Waterway—A cruising guide, with rules and regulations, services, mileages, etc. Bellhaven House, see address above.

Yachtsman's Guide to the Bahamas—A guide for the Bahamas with area charts, much like those of Coast Pilots. The customs and immigration information will be found especially valuable. Available from Tropic Isle Publishers, Inc., P. O. Box 613, Coral Gables, Fla. 33134.

Yachtsman's Guide to the Caribbean—Island, port, and anchorage charts from Florida through the Bahamas to the Greater Antilles and the Leeward and Windward Islands; facilities, refueling places, customs and port formalities. Seaport Publishing Co., 843 Delray Ave. S. E., Grand Rapids, Mich. 49506.

The Alluring Antilles—Provides accurate, and ample information about every island in the West Indies. D. Van Nostrand Co., Inc., 120 Alexander St., Princeton, N. J. 08540.

Virgin Islands—Descriptions of islands, harbors, passages, and facilities. Sailing Book Service, 34 Oak Avenue, Tuckahoe, N. Y. 10707.

CRUISING CHARTS AND GUIDES FROM THE OIL COMPANIES:

The larger oil companies offer detailed information about all areas of the United States, both coastal and inland, in the form of charts with courses noted, lists of facilities (with their own brand of fuel and oil featured, of course), much timely information, and even cruise outlines. They are free—along with a "cruise" service, which will plan a cruise for you just as it will an automobile tour. The service is free also. At least the following major companies offer this service:

Esso Touring Service, 15 West 51st Street, New York, N. Y. 10019.

Gulf Tourguide Bureau, Box 8056, Philadelphia, Pa. 19101.

Mobil Touring Service, 150 East 42nd Street, New York, N. Y. 10017.

Texaco Waterways Service, 135 East 42nd Street, New York, N. Y. 10019.

Most marine dealers have for distribution detailed local charts and other material from their parent company. Some dealers maintain spot weather reporting and can give information about the waters ahead.

MISCELLANEOUS PUBLICATIONS

The American Nautical Almanac—United States Naval Observatory. Copies available from the Superintendent of Documents,

Washington, D. C. 20402. A publication containing all the material essential for navigational position. Contains a Star Chart of the stars used in navigation and instructions for its use. The Star Chart may be purchased separately.

Tide and Current Investigations of the Coast and Geodetic Survey—U. S. Coast and Geodetic Survey, Washington, D. C. 20230. Illustrated. 50 pages. Types and forms of tides, earthquake waves, tidal currents, and wind currents.

First Aid—Supt. of Documents, Washington, D. C. 20402. Illustrated. 160 pages. Should be on every cruising boat.

The Ship's Medicine Chest and First Aid at Sea—United States Public Health Service. Illustrated. 498 pages. Prepared for sailors. An excellent treatise. Gives special instruction for emergency treatment, and First Aid by Radio. Superintendent of Documents, Washington, D. C. 20402.

Various government agencies as well as the U. S. Navy publish helps to the world-girdler, including charts for all the waters of the globe. Catalogs pertaining to foreign navigation are available from the National Ocean Survey, Rockville, Md., 20852. The list is too extensive to include here. Its distribution center (the place from which to order) is: Distribution Center (C44), National Ocean Survey, Washington, D. C. 20235.

Material may be ordered by mail. A check or money order in full should be enclosed. Material will be sent postage free.

Note: the Washington scene changes so rapidly these years as streamlining of government and the bureaucracy takes place that it is difficult to keep up with the changes of address and responsibility. If you cannot find the wanted information elsewhere, phone the office of your state representative or senator and ask their help; they are furnished the very latest information. Usually, his office will gladly send the free material available.

Further publications required in the navigating department are those furnished by the manufacturers of the navigating equipment —RDF, compass, auto-pilot, calculators, etc. Many modern aids require special information and rehearsed use in order to be truly valuable to the boatman. It all starts with reading the instructions, understanding the device, its use, maintenance, and repair so that it becomes as familiar—and comforting—as the king spoke of the wheel. Keep such booklets on the chart room bookshelf, available for instant use.

⚓

CHAPTER X

AIDS TO NAVIGATION

BUOYAGE SYSTEMS

1001 All waters of the United States, both federal and state, of importance to navigation are marked as to dangers, obstructions, best channels, etc., by an intricate buoyage system. The system is maintained by the United States Coast Guard (since 1940). All buoys of a permanent nature are shown on local charts and in the *Light Lists*. However, buoys tell their own story by shape, color, and number, and so, in a sense, chart the waters within sight of the navigator.

The federal system is known as the Lateral Buoyage System. Buoys and other markers and aids indicate a danger in relation to the course that should be followed or, approximately, in relation to the channel. Until recently the states used several varied systems, quite unrelated to each other or to the federal system. By an act of Congress establishing the Uniform State Waterway Marking System (USWMS) states are gradually adopting a uniform system, an essential part of which is the Lateral Buoyage System used by the federal government. Thus it is possible to steam to or from each area of jurisdiction (state or federal) and find identical buoyage systems. A second part of the state system consists of regulatory markers or advice relating to speed limits and traffic control, or indicating directions or general information.

The federal system is a one-part system and contains a minimum of control information, the message of the system being read entirely from the buoyage system itself, plus the chart and the *Coast*

Pilot. The system has two exceptions: a separate system of buoyage for the Intracoastal Waterway (Atlantic and Gulf Coasts) and another for the Western rivers (roughly the entire Mississippi system including all tributaries).

The basic federal system assumes passage from seaward to and toward the head of navigation. (It is read in reverse, of course, when heading toward the sea.) Coastal buoys and aids, including lighthouses and lightships or platforms) assume passage around the entire coast of the United States, including the Gulf of Mexico, the Pacific and Alaskan coasts, as *coming from seaward.* This simply indicates that the system is applied as if all shipping movement proceeded around the entire U. S. coastline in a clockwise direction. Further assumptions must be made for any area where the particular waters do not lead, directly, from the sea, but all such cases are marked and noted with special marks such as day marks, pointers, and ranges. U. S. lakes, entirely within the state boundaries and not part of an interstate waterway, may be found at variance with the federal system at the moment. It is the purpose of the legislature to eventually make the system uniform.

The Canadian system conforms to the federal system (though their buoys, etc., may be of different shape or construction) and American yachtsmen should be quite at home. Other foreign nations generally use the Cardinal System of Buoyage, sometimes in combination with the Lateral System, which indicates the direction of the danger *from the buoy.* The direction indicated is one of the cardinal points of the compass.

THE LATERAL BUOYAGE SYSTEM

1002 The system calls for the coloring, numbering, and shaping of the various buoys in reference to the channels that they define, when such channels are *entered from seaward* and followed to the head of navigation. Thus, the right-hand side of a channel is marked by buoys that are colored red, having conical (or nun) shapes and even numbers; the left-hand side is indicated by buoys that are colored black, having flat (or can) shapes, and odd numbers—This, of course, is as they are seen when entering from seaward. When leaving, proceeding to seaward, *exactly the reverse is true.*

Buoys having vertical black and white stripes are mid-channel or fairway buoys, and indicate that the center of the channel is directly beneath. They are to be passed close aboard. Buoys having horizontal black and red stripes indicate junctions, or middle grounds, or obstructions beneath, and are to be passed on either side with a *wide berth*.

The front and back endpaper illustrations give the shape, color, and numbering of all types of buoys.

SPECIAL NOTES ON DAYTIME AIDS AND BUOYS

1003 Can and nun buoys are divided into three types—tall, regular, and special—and each type is divided into six classes, the first class being the largest of the type. This division is merely to standardize buoys for all possible uses and locations (such as at sea, or in shallow waters, etc.), and neither type nor class changes the information that the buoy is giving in any way.

A yellow buoy of any type indicates quarantine areas.

A white buoy of any type indicates limits of anchorage grounds, or may mark out a torpedo range off a naval base.

A white buoy with a green-banded top indicates a dredging area.

A white buoy with black horizontal bands marks the limits (or ends) of fish nets, traps, or weirs.

A white buoy with two orange horizontal bands indicates a special purpose (and quite possibly temporary) buoy.

1004 Buoys are numbered, starting from *seaward*, in sequence. Sometimes, a buoy will carry a letter, such as 16 A, indicating that buoys have been added to the series, and the series has not been renumbered. Isolated sea buoys are sometimes given a number and letter, such as I CS, the letter indicating its station name (Cerberus Shoal).

Sometimes only letters are given to fairway or obstruction buoys.

Warning is here made that the chart symbol for a buoy of *any shape* is a diamond over, or, on new charts, connected to a dot (indicating the anchor ring or *exact* location). The symbol shows only the color, the legend nearby indicates the type and number. (C = can, N = nun, C "7," N "4," etc.)

Bush stakes, with white or colored bunting flags, indicate private oyster beds and are purely private marks. They are numerous in such oyster areas as Gardiners Bay, Long Island, and the Chesapeake. They are generally in water of at least 16′ depth and with flat sandy bottoms. At night, they constitute a real hazard to propellers and sails with sheets started.

Unlighted buoys are frequently fitted with reflectors, which are very useful in picking up a buoy at night with a searchlight. The reflector color is always white, red, or green, and has the same meaning as lights of these colors (*see Paragraph 1015*).

1005   In Maine waters when entering a thoroughfare (a river or channel connecting two bodies of water) from the eastward, the black buoys are taken to port (passed on the port side of the ship). This is also true in the Northwest when entering a thoroughfare (usually called passages there) from the west.

1006   Beacons are placed on shore or on sunken or awash obstructions where a floating buoy cannot be stationed. They may be of any shape and are often cairns, wooden shapes, baskets, kegs, dolphins, or stakes, on which are perched a cage, fish trap, flag, etc. If possible, the color will indicate the passing side. In spite of the word "beacon," such devices are usually unlit.

1007   Local marks (which are supposedly erected with the approval and under the direction of the harbor master) are often placed by fishermen and others using obscure local channels, creeks, and salt coves. They may be dolphins, bush stakes, anchored oil tins, or kegs, or merely wooden floats. If colored at all, they will be colored as the government buoys are. If not, they are generally (*not always*) to be left to starboard on coming from seaward. Lanterns, or pointers, or both sometimes indicate turning points and the direction of the turn.

Mistrust local marks until they have been clearly explained by some local boatman, or until a boat of equal draft has entered or cleared within sight of you.

1008   At night or in thick weather, when color is indistinguishable, proceed by shape, and (if a searchlight is available) by shape and number. If uncertain of the color or number (as between a channel can buoy and an obstruction or fairway buoy) pass it to starboard on entering for safety. Obstruction buoys are sometimes given a white-painted top. This is merely to facilitate picking it up by searchlight and in no way changes its meaning. Warning is given that gull guano often discolors a black buoy enough to be confusing at night. Running strange buoys at night always calls for slow speed and dependence upon log, lead, and lookout.

Right-angle metal silhouettes, sometimes observed atop buoys, are radar reflectors and, on the older type metal buoys, help in picking up a buoy in thick weather by ship's radar. The newer type buoys, both cans and nuns, are made in such a way that they appear to be solid cans or conical-shaped nun tops but special metal plates at the top are shaped to serve as radar pickups.

Buoys are liable to shift, to capsize from ice or collision, or to sink. They may also have been shifted from the chart location because of shoaling or channel changes, so the navigator should proceed with caution and the help of the pertinent *Notice to Mariners* whenever buoyage conditions vary from the chart.

LIGHT AND SOUND BUOYS

1009 The more important of the buoys are lighted, or are provided with a sound-making device, or both.

The painted color and number of any buoy is according to the standard buoyage system, whether lighted or unlighted. The addition of light or sound merely increases its usefulness in thick weather or at night, and in no way changes the meaning of the buoy. The shape alone may vary, but does not change the message given by the color and number.

The light, however, will definitely give the buoy a characteristic as indicated in the following table:

Red or black buoys: When marking the sides of channels—slow-flashing or occulting lights, at regular intervals. When marking turns, or dangerous spots—quick-flashing lights.

Horizontally banded red and black buoys: When marking junctions, obstructions, or middle grounds that may be passed on either side—interrupted, quick-flashing lights.

Vertically striped black and white buoys: When marking a fairway, mid-channel, or inlet entrance—short-long flashing light. (Fixed lights on buoys are not the rule but may be occasionally found, particularly on red or black buoys.)

Red buoys show red or white flashes.

Obstruction buoys show green or white if the preferred channel is to starboard, and red or white if the preferred channel is to port.

Fairway buoys show white only.

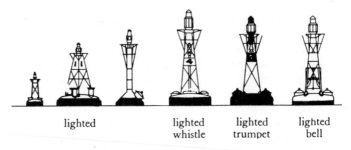

| lighted | lighted whistle | lighted trumpet | lighted bell |

1009A Lighted and sound buoys

The following table presents the meaning of various light patterns. Note that buoys never flash two colors, as that is a characteristic reserved for lighthouses.

Characteristic of Flashing	Purpose Indicated
1. Flashing: Less than 30 light periods per minute.	Channel sides and coasts.
2. Quick flashing: Not less than 60 flashes per minute.	Sudden constriction or sharp turns in channel. A distinctly cautionary significance is indicated.
3. Interrupted quick flashing (group): Quick flashing as above but interrupted by eclipse periods of four seconds at regular intervals about eight times per minute.	Obstructions, middle grounds, junctions, or wrecks. A distinctly cautionary significance is indicated.
4. Short-long flashes: Groups of a short and a long flash. Groups are repeated about eight times per minute. Called Morse code "A"	Mid-channels and fairways.
5. Isophase (also known as equal interval): the periods of light and darkness are of equal duration.	Channel sides
6. Occulting: light intervals longer than intervals of darkness.	Channel sides

LATERAL SYSTEM IN U. S. WATERS

Returning From Sea*	Color	Number	Unlighted Buoy Shape	Lights or Lighted Buoys			Daymark Shape
				Light Color	Light Phase Characteristic		
Right side of channel	red	even	nun	red or white	fixed, occulting, flashing or quick flashing isophase		triangular
Left side of channel	black	odd	can	green or white	fixed, occulting, flashing or quick flashing isophase		square
Channel junction or obstruction	red-and-black horizontally banded**	not numbered; may be lettered	nun or can**	red, green or white**	interrupted quick flashing		triangular or square**
Midchannel or fairway	black-and-white vertically striped	may be lettered	nun or can	white	Morse code "A" (· —)		octagonal

* Or entering a harbor from a larger body of water, such as a lake.
** Preferred channel is indicated by color of uppermost band (shape of unlighted buoy), color of light, if any.

1010   Any lighted or unlighted buoy may be equipped with a sound-producing device. This serves as further identification and is especially useful in fog, or in the case of the unlighted buoy.

Devices include the trumpet or "groaner," the bell, gong, and whistle. Most of them are operated by the motion of the sea, although mechanical clappers are being introduced, which operate by compressed air or electricity. Bells are usually located in harbors or tidal currents where a slight sea motion will actuate them. Gong buoys consist of four gongs of different tone and are used to avoid confusion in an area where there are several bell buoys. The whistle types are generally placed offshore where the normal seas provide sufficient motion to operate the self-contained air-compressing device.

No sound has special significance. It merely serves to locate and identify the buoy.

INTRACOASTAL WATERWAY BUOYAGE SYSTEM

1011   Intracoastal Waterway buoys, while having the color appropriate to the location, have a distinguishing yellow band or, in the case of daymarks, have a yellow border (*see back end-paper*)

They are numbered from north to south along the Atlantic, and from east to west along the coast of the Gulf of Mexico.

When the Intracoastal and regular coastal waters join or overlap, special markings are used as follows:

> *On black can buoys*—a yellow-painted triangle to indicate that the buoy is to be regarded as a red nun buoy.
>
> *On red nun buoys*—a yellow-painted square to indicate that the buoy is to be regarded as a black can buoy.

Thus, vessels sailing the Intracoastal Waterways use the conversion markings above when navigating in an overlap, while vessels sailing regular harbor or river routes use the buoys in their original meanings. (*See end papers*)

1012   The Western River Buoyage System is essentially the same as coastal and lake systems. However, the orientation is quite different. To match the coastal system of red to the right from seaward (red right returning) the Western river rule is red right *against* the current (flow). This must not be confused with tidal flow or a temporary condition. It means the normal flow of the river downstream from its source. Thus, the flow of the Mississippi River is from the north to the south (from the source to the mouth) no matter what the tide may be doing in the delta or a back current might be doing at the junction of the Ohio River.

Note that the western river system provides mileage markers at appropriate locations to help in identification. Many aids are in the form of daymarks; these, though placed on driven piles near the channel wherever possible, may be found on the land or on a jetty. Buoys and markers are often lighted and mean as follows:

Port side:	green or white	flashing
Starboard side:	red or white	group flash of two
Junction or obstruction:	red, green, or white	quick flashing

The buoyage system on the Western rivers does not quite tell the whole story as do coastal and Great Lakes buoys, and supplemental information is almost certainly required. (*See Chapter IX for charts, pilots, etc.*)

1013   The Great Lakes Buoyage System matches the coastal system and it is only necessary to remember that the outlet of the lake is the "sea" end—the direction *from* the outlet is the same as "*from* seaward." Thus on entering a lake through its outlet (the eastern end for Ontario, Erie, and Superior; the southern for Huron; and the northern end for Michigan, red is to starboard and black to port. Entering a harbor from the lake, you will find the buoyage exactly the same as entering a harbor from a larger bay, sound, etc. in the coastal system. If you cross into Canadian waters, the system does not change, although the constructional details of the buoys might; be guided by color, number, and shape as in U. S. systems.

1014   The uniform state system (USWMS) that eventually *all* states will have (*Figure 1001D*) is merely an extension of the federal system except that in some cases, where there is no well-defined channel or where an obstruction might be approached from several directions, it breaks away and goes into the Cardinal System. The buoys of the Cardinal System are shown in the figure and are basically white buoys, with colored divisions added. They have the indicated geographical direction meaning listed. Black, pass north or east; red, pass south or west. Note that the reflector, if present, is white and a light, if the buoy is lighted, is white and quick flashing. A mooring buoy, in a mooring area, is also white but has a blue band around it about midway between water and top. At night it shows a slow flashing white light unless it is in a fairway, in which event the light is quick flashing.

The system's second component relates to highway-sign practice. The "sign" may be shown on a board, or a board on a piling, or painted on a white buoy. Shapes have the following meanings:

Rectangle—Gives information, place names, distances.

Open Diamond—Warns of danger such as snags, dredges, dams, cable ferry, rock, or ledge.

Diamond with cross inside—Boats keep out! Rapids, swim area, waterfall, reservoir, etc.

Note: If the sign is painted on a regular waterway buoy, the buoy will have two stripes of international orange, one at the top of the shape and one just above the waterline.

1015   Any and all buoys, on any and all systems, may be fitted with *reflectors*. These are glass or plastic reflecting devices, or bands of luminous tape, 3″ to 6″ in width, which reflect the rays of a searchlight, often used in local "sweeps" to locate buoys at night. The reflector in all cases will be the same color as the light would be if the buoy were lighted. The reflector has the same meaning as the light color.

On unlighted buoys, the number or letter is sometimes also outlined with reflecting tape, making identification at night under searchlight quite easy. Any searchlight discovery, if too distant to read, can be brought in by binoculars if the user stands a few feet right or left of the beam. If in doubt, reduce speed and "creep" up on the aid until positive identification is made.

LIGHTHOUSES

1016   Lighthouses, unlike buoys, are in definitely fixed and known locations on land or just offshore, and they therefore become the mariner's prime nighttime aid in determining his position.

The chart gives all essential information about the particular light, its light characteristics, visibility, height above high water, and soundsignal character. The *Light List* gives further information, including the phase characteristic. Lights are divided into primary and secondary lights, the primary class being on the seacoast with the purpose of alerting high-seas traffic to the proximity of land. They are usually placed on high ground or elevated by means of a tall tower to achieve maximum range. While frequently white, they may be painted in various colors or designs so that they will stand out against a background and can be readily identified. While many are no longer manned by a keeper and crew (automatic equipment having been introduced) the old keepers' homes and service buildings are often to be seen. When located offshore, as on an island or ledge, they may serve a double purpose—to indicate land and to identify and warn of the offshore danger. Fog signaling equipment is usually present, sometimes augmented by radio signals.

1016 A lighthouse on the northeast coast

Secondary lights, usually of less intensity, serve the same purposes in bays, sounds, passages, and harbors. They are seldom as tall, and their physical structure varies greatly—from neat compact units, stone or wooden houses, to steel skeleton frames to a group of piles with an automatic light on it, to even a single pile or a simple steel box with a light, on shore.

Day identification of a lighthouse is made by the painted color (always one or a combination that stands out from the background seen from sea), the type of structure and its location—on land, bluff, shoal, sandspit, etc. The lantern itself is on the exact geo-

	Symbols and meaning		
Illustrations	Lights which do not change color	Lights which show color variations	Phase description
	F. = Fixed-------	Alt. = Alternating.	A continuous steady light.
	F. Fl. = Fixed and flashing.	Alt. F. Fl. = Alternating fixed and flashing.	A fixed light varied at regular intervals by a single flash of greater brilliance.
	F. Gp. Fl. = Fixed and group flashing.	Alt. F. Gp. Fl. = Alternating fixed and group flashing.	A fixed light varied at regular intervals by groups of 2 or more flashes of greater brilliance. The group may, or may not, be preceded and followed by an eclipse.
	Fl. = Flashing----	Alt. Fl. = Alternating flashing.	Showing a single flash at regular intervals, the duration of light always being less than the duration of darkness.
	Gp. Fl. = Group flashing.	Alt. Gp. Fl. = Alternating group flashing.	Showing at regular intervals groups of 2 or more flashes.
	Gp. Fl.(3 + 2) = Composite group flashing.	---------------	Group flashing in which the flashes are combined in alternate groups of different numbers.
	Mo. (K) = Morse Code.	---------------	Light in which flashes of different durations are grouped to produce a Morse *character* or *characters*.
	Qk. Fl. = Quick flashing.	---------------	Shows not less than 60 flashes per minute.
	Int.(L.)Qk. Fl. = Interrupted quick flashing.	---------------	Shows quick flashes for about 4 seconds, followed by a dark period of about 4 seconds.
	Iso.(E. Int.) Isophase.	---------------	Duration of light equal to that of darkness.
	Occ. = Occulting.	Alt. Occ. = Alternating occulting.	A light totally eclipsed at regular intervals, the duration of light always greater than the duration of darkness.
	Gp. Occ. = Group occulting.	Alt. Gp. Occ. = Alternating group occulting.	A light with a group of 2 or more eclipses at regular intervals.
	Gp. Occ.(3 + 4) = Composite group occulting.	---------------	Group occulting in which the occultations are combined in alternate groups of different numbers.

Light colors used and abbreviations: W=white, R=red, G=green.

1017 Characteristics of lights from *List of Lights and Fog Signals,*
1977 U. S. Government publication

CHESAPEAKE BAY   MARYLAND

(1) No.	(2) Name Characteristic	(3) Location Lat. N. Long. W.	(4) Nominal Range	(5) Ht. above water	Ht. above ground	(6) Structure	Daymark
	Chesapeake Channel						
	(For Annapolis Harbor, see No. 3500)						
2753	Hackett Point Shoal Buoy 1	In 18 feet				Black can	
	— Lighted Bell Buoy 78	In 57 feet		5		Red	
	Fl. W., 4ˢ	38 57.6 76 23.6					
2754	—Approach Lighted Buoy 79	In 51 feet		3		Black	
	Fl. G., 4ˢ						
2755	—Lighted Gong Buoy 80	In 50 feet		3		Red	
	Fl. R., 4ˢ						
2755.10	PIER 1 MARINA RANGE FRONT LIGHT.	On shore			18	KRB on pile	
	F. G.	38 58.7 76 20.1					
2755.11	PIER 1 MARINA RANGE REAR LIGHT.	On shore			33	KRB on pile	
	F. G.	38 58.7 76 19.9					
	Pier 1 Marina Daybeacon 1	In 9 feet				SB on pile	
	Pier 1 Marina Daybeacon 2	In 12 feet				TR on pile	
2756	Chesapeake Bay Bridge West Channel Fog Signal.	Suspended from center of main channel span.					
		38 59.6 76 22.9					

graphic spot stated in the *Light List*, and the height stated is from high water to the center of the lantern.

Night identification is made by the phase, period, and color of the light.

The period of a light (flashing or occulting, not fixed) is the time required for it to proceed through a full set of changes.

The phase of a light is the exact duration of the interval of light and darkness (or eclipse) which makes up the period.

The color of the light is the color, or colors, actually observed. Red, green, and white, or red or green in combination with white, are used, but never green and red.

1017 For the abbreviations, meanings, and phases used on charts and *Light Lists* for the description of lights, see pages 404–405.

1018 Upon first sighting a navigation light, extreme caution should be used in making identification. The visibility given on the chart and *Light List* is figured in miles from an observer's eye *15' above high water*. The vessel must be definitely known to be within the area of visibility of the light when its direct rays are seen; if definitely outside such an area, the light is to be but *tentatively* identified.

Correction for eye height above water is made with the aid of the Table of Distances of Visibility found in the *Light List*. The formula for obtaining distance of visibility follows:

$$\sqrt[2]{\text{height of light (ft.)}} \times 1.15 + \sqrt[2]{\text{height of observer's eye (ft.)}} \times 1.15$$
$$= \text{distance of visibility in miles}$$

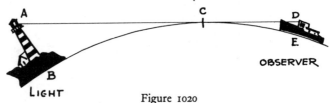

Figure 1020

$\frac{8}{7}\sqrt[2]{AB}$ in feet = AC in miles

$\frac{8}{7}\sqrt[2]{DE}$ in feet = CD in miles. Therefore: AC + CD = visibility (in nautical miles)

1018

Or:

1019

TABLE OF VISIBILITY AT SEA

Height	Visibility		Height	Visibility		Height	Visibility	
Feet	Stat. Miles	Naut. Miles	Feet	Stat. Miles	Naut. Miles	Feet	Stat. Miles	Naut. Miles
5	2.96	2.55	60	10.25	8.85	130	15.08	13.03
10	4.18	3.61	65	10.67	9.21	140	15.65	13.52
15	5.12	4.43	70	11.07	9.56	150	16.20	14.00
20	5.92	5.11	75	11.46	9.90	200	18.71	16.16
25	6.61	5.71	80	11.83	10.22	250	20.92	18.07
30	7.25	6.26	85	12.20	10.54	300	22.91	19.80
35	7.83	6.76	90	12.55	10.84	350	24.75	21.38
40	8.37	7.23	95	12.89	11.14	400	26.46	22.86
45	8.87	7.67	100	13.23	11.43	450	28.06	24.24
50	9.35	8.08	110	13.87	11.99	500	29.58	25.56
55	9.81	8.48	120	14.49	12.52			

1020 The glare of a light will usually be seen before the light itself, being reflected downward by the atmosphere, and it may take on an orange or reddish color.

Fixed lights, when first observed in a seaway, may appear to be flashing, or the phase or period of a flashing light made irregular or destroyed. An observation from a more lofty point will usually bring a distant light into clearer focus at once.

Two colored lights (as red and white flashing) are often obscured by atmospheric conditions, causing but one color to be seen at first. Fixed *and* flashing lights usually show the flash alone when it is first picked up, the lower-powered fixed light only appearing later.

When in doubt as to whether the light first sighted is a light-house or a vessel, observe it from a point below that from which it was first observed. The lighthouse light will disappear, or become erratic, or off-color. The vessel's light will remain as before.

It should always be remembered that the weather and atmospheric conditions at a distant lighthouse might be quite different from those prevailing at the point of observation and due allowance made.

1021 Lights may have a light sector of color different from the light itself. This sector is usually red and covers an area of danger. Such sectors are shown on the chart by dotted lines and a legend, and their bearings read from the chart rose. When passing into the sector, note that the color will not change at once; the change will be gradual. Example: From white to red, the white will pass through stages of pink, orange, red orange, etc.

When a light having a sector is located on an island or a headland, it may be first seen from such an angle that its sector alone is seen and is to be identified by the sector rather than its major characteristics. An example is North Dumpling light in Fisher's Island Sound. When approaching from the east, this light, which is fixed white, is first observed as red because of the red sector which covers Fisher's Island and its dangerous clumps and hummocks to northward. (*See Figure 1021*)

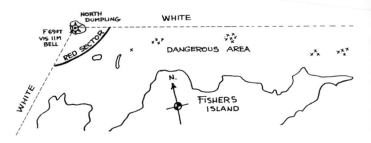

1021 Danger sector (or red sector)

LIGHTSHIPS

1022 Lightships serve the same purpose as lighthouses and are different only in that they are floating lights. They are fully described in the *Light List*; also on the chart. There is only one left in service.

As the lightship swings to an anchor, the light is not fixed but is some feet off the station shown on the chart, usually about seven times the depth of the water shown at the chart location or the *Light List* and in the direction of the tide, or wind, or both at the time of observation. In addition to the navigation light, the lightship carries a riding light forward (characteristics described in the

Light List), and from this may be ascertained the heading and the approximate distance off station.

A lightship is identified in daytime by a huge white-lettered station name on each topside, as well as by its *Light List* description as to shape, superstructure, color, number of masts, etc.

Except for the Nantucket light vessels, the coastal lightships of the Atlantic coast have been replaced by huge Class 6 offshore buoys, and light towers are set on the bottom. The light characteristics remain the same, although it is usually possible to achieve greater range. Most light towers are manned and have living quarters, a pad for the landing of supply helicopters, a radio beacon, facilities for communication, and oceanographic recording gear. Each is fully described in the *Light List*. Tower platforms are 50' to 60' above the water surface and have a high light tower on one corner; they are readily seen from long sea distances, usually up to 20 miles.

In some areas, notably deeper waters, unmanned navigational buoys are anchored as were the lightships before them. These have a single light tower, fog-signaling apparatus, and possibly a radio beacon and submarine bell. They are also listed and described in the *Light List*. Nearby is a *station buoy*, which is a simple lesser-class buoy to be used as a reference mark in the event the larger buoy is driven off course, hit by traffic, etc. Its message (in shape, color, and number or letter) is the same as that of the larger buoy.

Left, regular station ships, of which only one remains in service (1979), have red hull, white station name, port and starboard, white superstructure, stacks, spars, etc., buff. *Right*, Relief ships are red with "relief" lettered port and starboard.

1022 Light ships

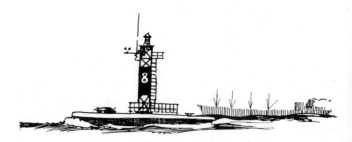

1022A A 40' offshore buoy of the type that has replaced most light-ships

RANGE LIGHTS AND MARKS

1023 Channels are sometimes shown by two marks, often lighted at night, placed some distance apart as on shore, or on shore and a breakwater, or headland, etc. They are so placed that the mariner has but to keep the two marks in line to remain in the channel.

The nearer mark (or target) is always the lower mark and if the farther target is visually kept directly above the lower mark, the ship will be on course. Not much leeway is allowed; often the range will define a narrow dug or dredged channel (as on the Intracoastal Waterway) and allowance must be made for filling in and shoaling at turns or in the path of strong side currents. Run toward the lower mark, even if seemingly "on the shore" or until a buoy or other marker along the range course advises a course change or abandonment of the range. The chart is a must when running ranges, and it should be assumed that tolerances are small and utter accuracy in steering is required.

It is not unusual for a range to cross a range, in which case the ship must run to the junction and most carefully move from one range to the next with not too broad a swing, nor yet too shallow. Running ranges is a fine art, best understood by the Western River pilots whose hourly task when steaming is running the ranges.

In some areas it is not possible to arrange the usual double range targets at each end of the range, so a directional light is used instead. This is a light, usually occulting with equal dark and light periods, that has a special lens showing a narrow band of white along the range, with a red band on one side of it and a green band on the other. The trick is to keep in the channel by keeping the light white, no easy job because the division between white and color is anything but sharp, the two colors tending to blend and produce merely a reduced or tinted white. When the color "turns" to red or green, positively, it is almost too late, because the edge of the channel is at hand. Directional lights may also be multiple, directing from range to range, in which case use extreme caution, for, while dredging engineers usually allow for intersection "swing" where channels meet, currents and wind and prop wash are apt to fill the dredged material right back in.

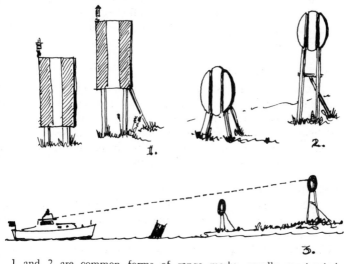

1 and 2 are common forms of range marks, usually constructed of boards or sheet metal and painted a distinctive color. The color means nothing. The farthest mark is always the highest and is kept *above* the nearer mark until shore contour or a navigation aid indicates the continuation of the channel. Any range may be lighted in any combination of white or colored lights, sometimes flashing.

1023 Range marks on the Atlantic Intracoastal Waterway

Both day and night identification can be learned from the chart and *Light List*. Lights may be fixed or flashing and be colored. Their lenses usually direct the most brilliant rays along the correct course, and, therefore, when running a range, a dimming of the light may be taken to mean that the boat is not on the range. Ranges marking straight channels are not difficult to follow.

LIGHTED BEACONS

1024 Beacons on land or over shoals are often lighted and are classified somewhere between lighthouses and lighted buoys. In so far as possible, their painted coloring and light characteristics in dicate their position in relation to the channel.

Characteristics are noted on the chart and in the *Light List*.

If they have reflectors, the letters REF appear adjacent to the symbol on the chart. If lighted, the symbol is a five-pointed open-center star (distinguished from a lighthouse, which has a six-pointed star as a symbol).

AVIATION LIGHTS

1025 Aviation lights likely to be within range of water-borne traffic are listed in the *Light List* and shown on charts. They may be used exactly as lighthouses are, and because of their great power and height, are often seen before navigational lights are raised. Listed characteristics and color identify them, and they are extremely useful in getting a fix far offshore.

FOG SIGNALS

1026 Practically all lighthouses and lightships have fog-sounding equipment, the type being noted on the chart. Devices used include:

The bell is used on inshore stations and for short warning distances.

The gong is used as a distinguishing signal in areas in which there are other and many nearby sound signals in operation. Four tones are sounded.

The whistle is used on lightships or their replacements. It has a steady note, possibly chimed.

The horn is used on any lighthouse or ship. May be of reed or diaphragm type but always has a steady tone. (Also listed as oscillator, tyfon, reed horn, and nautaphone.) Generally is marked HORN on charts.

The diaphone is used on any lightship or lighthouse. It has a two-toned note, ending on the lower pitch.

The siren is used on any lighthouse or lightship. It has a typical siren sound but pitch rises and falls very quickly; not prolonged like a fire siren.

While the chart denotes the type of sound, the period and phase of the sound, which is timed, is listed in the *Light List* only. The station may, of course, be identified by the sound characteristics.

Fog signals are put into operation when visibility falls to about six miles. The vagaries of sound in fog are unpredictable, and the mariner should not place too much reliance on sound signals for determining direction. The signal may skip large areas quite close to the source, or may be misdirected and deflected upwards or sidewards. Half of a two-toned signal may be lost, or distorted. Direction may be reversed; or the signal may be justifiably estimated close aboard when it is quite distant, or quite distant when it is close aboard. The true signal and direction is best heard from the highest point aboard, away from superstructure, as on a mast.

Lead, log, and lookout are by all means more important than fog signals to the navigator. Fog signals are intended as *warnings* only; not directional aids.

RADIO AIDS TO NAVIGATION

1027 On the lightships and many major lighthouses (as well as on coastal points) the United States Coast Guard maintains radio beacons. These are simply radio transmitting sets which project an identifying signal by which the navigator whose boat is equipped with a radio direction finger may orient himself. Signals are sent on the 285–315 *kHz* band periodically as each radio beacon of the same frequency takes its turn.

Stations in a general geographic area are assigned the same frequency, up to six beacons per frequency. Each beacon broadcasts in the same sequence for one minute, giving first its distinguishing Morse identifier than an uninterrupted dash to help in zeroing the direction finder to null. On charts, the beacon's frequency and number in the series (I to VI) is noted. The full six-beacon cycle takes six minutes. Each beacon will thus be on the air for ten minutes in the hour. Local, Class D marker beacons, however, are on the air continuously; they have no special pattern, but send a series of dashes. Aerobeacons are on the air continuously and normally transmit a two- or three-letter Morse identifier that alludes to their location—"JF" for the beacon just south of JFK International Airport, for example.

There are four classes of radio beacons:

Class A	200-mile range
Class B	100-mile range
Class C	20-mile range
Class D	On markers—10 miles or less.

Each station has an identifying signal (Example: Cape Cod sends − − · −). The *Light List* and radio-beacon charts give full information with changes posted in the *Notice to Mariners*.

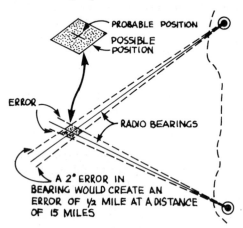

1027 Probable and possible position from two radio bearings

To take a bearing, the navigator merely tunes the direction finder to the listed frequency of the station desired, adjusts the pointer until the faintest (or no) signal is heard, and reads the bearing. Depending upon the type of instrument, this bearing may be a degree bearing from the ship's head or a true bearing on the station. A simple procedure indicates which of the two possible bearings (180° separated) is the correct one.

As the bearing or bearings so ascertained are in no way different from visual bearings, methods of working a fix or line of position are exactly the same. What applies to working visual bearings in the following chapter, applies also to radio-beacon bearings; the methods are interchangeable. It should be noted, however, that radio bearings are assumed to have a plus or minus error of about 2°, and that a fix is liable to a small error. This is shown, for illustrative purposes, in Figure 1027.

This is true only when the fix has been obtained by all radio bearings (as in fog). By crossing a radio bearing or bearings with a visual bearing or bearings, an *approximately* exact position may be determined.

1028   Radio bearings may be taken on standard broadcasting stations of known location, or on any of the directional air-navigation radio beacons, as well as on marine radio-beacon stations. The air-navigation beams operate continuously 24 hours a day and have an identifying signal superimposed upon the constant beam—letters A and N. However, warning is given that such beams are extremely wide and therefore subject to great errors in exact position fixing, and are to be regarded as auxiliary to the regular marine radio beacons. They are useful, generally, only if *happened* upon and serve to check, or roughly estimate, position.

1029   Radio-compass stations are simply direction finders on shore. The ship communicates with one, requests bearings, and, after several shore stations have taken a bearing on the *ship*, the position is transmitted to it. Small boats do not use the radio-compass stations, and they are not to be confused with radio beacons.

1030   Distance-finding stations are radio-beacon stations equipped to transmit a *sound* signal simultaneously with the radio signal. The interval between the reception of the radio signal and the sound signal (read by a stop watch) is converted into distance. The radio and the sound signal are identical, the sound signal being made by the station's foghorn, or siren, or whistle.

Another system makes use of the submarine bell of a lightship and her radio beacon, the submarine bell being heard through an electrical receiving apparatus composed of port and starboard underwater microphones.

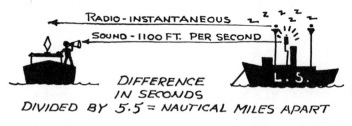

1030

For the small boat the following table shows the distance from the sending station. Direction is taken (one bearing only required) in the usual way.

Interval between radio and sound signal, in seconds	Distance away in nautical miles
1	0.2
2	0.4
3	0.5
4	0.7
5	0.9
6	1.1
7	1.3
8	1.4
9	1.6
10	1.8
20	3.6
30	5.4
40	7.2
50	9.0
60	10.8

To approximate the distance, divide the time between signals in seconds by 5.5 for nautical miles, or 5 for statute miles.

1031   Sound travels as per the following table:

at 40 degrees F. 1,100 ft. per sec. or 1 mile in 4.8 sec.
     50   "   1,110   "   "   4.78 sec.

60	"	1,120	"	"	4.73 sec.
70	"	1,130	"	"	4.68 sec.
80	"	1,140	"	"	4.63 sec.
90	"	1,150	"	"	4.59 sec.

⚓

CHAPTER XI

COASTAL AND INLAND NAVIGATION

1101   Navigation is the art of conducting a vessel from "here" to "there" over any of the earth's watery surfaces, and of determining the vessel's position at any time.

Navigation is subdivided into:

Celestial navigation—which is the art of navigating solely with the aid of celestial bodies.

Coastal navigation—which is the art of navigating with the aid of audible or visible landmarks and aids to navigation.

Coastal navigation is called *piloting,* and is the branch with which small-boat men and coastwise sailors are concerned. Piloting is divided (as is celestial navigation) into two branches, observation and dead reckoning.

Both branches solve the problems of navigation; that is, the problems of position, direction, and distance.

1102   Observation makes use of observed objects and their bearings, from which one or more *lines of position* are plotted; from the lines is obtained a *fix,* or the exact location of the vessel at the time of the observation. (A line of position is a line, straight or circular, somewhere along which the vessel must be. The point at which two lines of position cross is, obviously, the exact location of the observing vessel, and is called a fix.)

A line of position may be established from seen or heard objects, radio beacons, foghorns (with caution), buoys, lighthouses, headlands, prominent objects, etc., of known location (determined, of course, from the chart). A line of position established by visible objects may be crossed with a line of position established by audible objects, a radio bearing with a sighted bearing, a sighted bearing with a sound bearing, a sound bearing with a depth reading, etc., ad infinitum.

Visible bearings are the most reliable and the most desirable, and are the commonest in use for ordinary piloting. Radio bearings are equally reliable, and the *only* reliable bearing in thick weather.

The method of determining the fix is a matter for the navigator alone to decide. The important thing to remember is that it must be as exact as is humanly possible.

1103 When lines of position are unobtainable (as at night, or in thick weather, or offshore), the vessel's approximate position is determined by dead reckoning. Dead reckoning is the navigator's best guess, made in the light of the course, speed, sea condition, current, wind, etc., as to the vessel's exact position. It is not correct—but it is as correct as it can be until a fix by observation can be obtained. The vessel's position between observations at any time or under any conditions of visibility is a dead-reckoning position; each fix by observation is *corrected* dead reckoning. Piloting is therefore a healthy combination, dictated by circumstances, of observation and dead reckoning.

1104 Any voyage starts from a fix, proceeds along the desired direction, at the desired speed, for the desired distance. En route, as the course is changed, as land is dropped or sighted, new fixes are required, either to check or locate the vessel's exact position.

The actual plotting of the course of the vessel is called the *track* and is done, graphically, on the appropriate chart of the waters sailed. Fixes are noted at the intersection of two or more lines of position by a prick of the dividers, or a penciled dot or cross, and is labeled and the time noted. Courses are straight lines drawn from a fix to a future desired or estimated fix, and are drawn in pencil, aided by the parallel rules or course protractor, and are labeled *above the line* as to direction (in degrees or points) and *below the line* as to speed and distance. Lines of position (which form the fix at their intersections) are labeled *above the line* as to bearing and *below the line* as to the time of the observation.

A bearing is always expressed as from the ship, not from the object observed—and it is true unless otherwise labeled.

THE COURSE LINE

1105 The course line is drawn from a fix to some distant point to which it is desired to proceed, the direction being determined by the topography, the water depths, intervening dangers, currents, leeway allowances, etc. It is a graphic straight line from a known "here" to a known "there" and represents an *intended* course.

The direction of the course is obtained as follows:

With a course protractor, measure the direction of the course line against the built-in compass rose on the instrument.

If the course is read from the inner rose it will be a magnetic course and will need to be corrected only for deviation error.

If the course is read from the outer rose it will be a true course and must be corrected for both deviation and variation error.

Either may be used. Magnetic is generally used for coastwise work and short distances. In either case the resultant course will be the steering course.

It will be seen that a sailing vessel may or may not be able to lay a course and make it good. If not (as when close-hauled), she must establish herself on the best course possible toward the objective and then lay down the course line. The course is taken from the compass, corrected to magnetic or true, and then, with the course protractor, the course line is drawn on the chart.

Abbreviations Used in Coastal Chart Work

A—antemeridian before noon*	M—miles
C—course	P—postmeridian, after-noon*
Corr—corrected	R—running (as R fix)
DR—dead reckoning, or dead-reckoning position	S—speed
Dev—deviation	Var—variation
	Yd—yards

* Time is usually indicated by four digits in the 24-hour system. Thus: "1020" equals 10:20 a.m.
"1320" equals 1:20 p.m.

1106 Distance or run is worked on a coastwise chart by the dividers, stepping off the scaled units of distance on the course line, between fixes. The scale is obtained from the scale of nautical miles printed on every coastwise chart. While distance may be obtained from the border (which is marked off in degrees and parts of degrees of latitude and longitude), there is no practical advantage in this on a large-scale chart.

Distance is shown on the chart in nautical miles (6,080' per mile). Distance is measured on the course line in nautical miles and as a convenience the *Coast Pilot* often gives distance in yards. On lake and river charts, and on those of the Atlantic Intracoastal Waterway the distance is indicated in statute miles of 5,280 feet.

1107 The following shows the difference between the nautical mile, 6,080 feet, and the land or statute mile, 5,280 feet:

CONVERTING NAUTICAL MILES TO STATUTE MILES

Nautical Miles.	Statute Miles.	Nautical Miles.	Statute Miles.
1	1.151	22	25.333
2	2.303	23	26.484
3	3.454	24	27.636
4	4.606	25	28.787
5	5.757	26	29.938
6	6.909	27	31.090
7	8.060	28	32.242
8	9.212	29	33.392
10	11.515	30	34.544
11	12.666	35	40.302
12	13.818	40	46.060
14	16.121	45	51.818
15	17.272	50	57.574
16	18.424	60	69.088
17	19.575	70	80.604
18	20.727	80	92.120
19	21.878	90	103.636
20	23.030	100	115.148
21	24.181		

1108 Dead reckoning commences immediately upon leaving a fix. Careful record is kept of speed, log readings (distance), course, and changes in any of these; the record is converted into graphic plottings along the course line. In a sense, the course line is a line of position, but it is a very uncertain one. In thick weather it is of some comfort, but of very little practical use. This is because the errors of steering and the effects of current and leeway have probably made it anything but a straight course, therefore any course must be corrected for current and leeway if subject to their effects. Methods for making these corrections are given in Paragraphs 1122–28.

LINES OF POSITION

1109   The simplest line of position is that taken from a range. Two objects of known location are "lined up," a pencil line extended seaward from them on the chart, and the ship will be somewhere along that line. No compass bearings are required, and there can therefore be no compass errors.

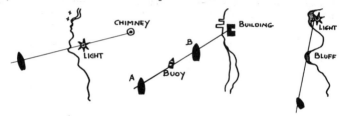

1110   Line of position from ranges

To obtain an exact fix, one or more lines must be crossed with the first. It would be good luck, but highly unlikely, to obtain two ranges for a fix. However, a single bearing and a range are usually possible.

This is obtained by sighting across the compass (aided by a pelorus, though not necessary) to any prominent charted object and noting its compass bearing. If a degree bearing, it must be uncorrected for variation and deviation, if a magnetic bearing, it must be uncorrected for deviation only (*Paragraph 912*). With the parallel rules, step off the corrected direction from the chart rose to the object sighted; then extend the line seaward. The ship will be somewhere along that line.

The exact point of intersection of two lines of position will be the fix. The center of the triangle formed by the intersection of three lines of position will be the fix.

A circular line of position is obtained by determining the distance off from any object. The ship will be somewhere on a circle of which the object is the center. A fix on this circle can be obtained by another line of position crossing it, including a line of position to the object itself.

1110 In Figure 1110, the examples at left and right are true ranges, as is *A* in the center. *B* is not a range but a bearing. Here, the compass bearing from boat to buoy must read exactly the opposite of the bearing from boat to building. Sight alone cannot take such a bearing with accuracy. The right-hand situation is the familiar *open-up* range, expressed as *open up the light on the bluff* (or over the bluff, etc.).

FIX BY BEARINGS

1111 Figure 1111 shows a line of position from a single bearing. Another, crossing bearing is needed for an exact fix. The course is often used as a line of position, but, because of the vagaries of a steered course, it is inexact and using it as a component might result in a fix at any one of many points, only one of which would be correct.

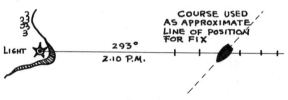

1111 Single bearing

1112 A circular line of position (*Figure 1112*) is established by calculating the distance off. A bearing on the sighted object used as the center of a circle will give a fix on the circumference of that circle. However, the right-hand situation shows how a bearing taken to an object outside the circle might result in two possible fixes. Bearings must be taken on another object, or the center object, to determine in which of the two possible positions the vessel may be.

Distance off is determined by a sextant and certain Bowditch tables, or by bow and beam bearings (*Figures 1118–1119*), or by a running fix (*Figure 1115*), or by a distance-off calculator, which is a simple graphed card from which the fix may be calculated on the one-bearing principle. The card is obtainable from marine supply houses under various names at very slight cost.

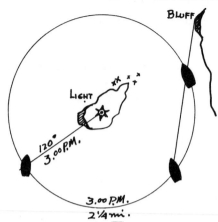

1112 Circular line of position

1113 Two cross bearings provide a reasonably accurate fix (*Figure 1113*). It is to be noted that the less the degree of intersection, the greater the likelihood of error. Ideally, the two bearings should cross nearly at right angles. Less than a 30° angle between bearings is likely to result in error.

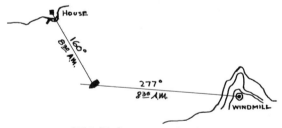

1113 Fix by two cross bearings

1114 A fix by three bearings is desirable whenever possible, as the error is averaged by locating the fix in the center of the triangle resulting because of error (*Figure 1114*). The smaller the triangle, the more accurate the fix. If the triangle is large, its center may be found by the same methods by which triangular sail centers are found. It will often pay, if possible, to take the three bearings again and try for a smaller, tighter triangle.

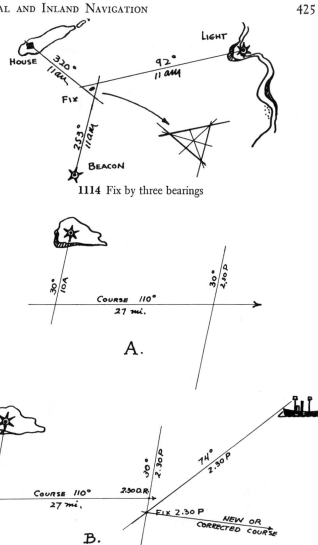

1114 Fix by three bearings

A.

B.

1115 Running fix

1115 Advancing a bearing line to get a running fix is a method of obtaining a fix from two objects observed at different times (*Figure 1115*). A single bearing is taken and the position ticked off on this line of position. The distance off must be a dead-reckoning position, of course (A). Course and distance are dead reckoned when the ship finds herself able to take another bearing, the position ticked off, and through this point a line parallel to the original line of position is drawn. The running fix is then made exactly like any two-bearing fix (B).

It is a thoroughly accurate and reliable method, provided that the course and distance are carefully dead reckoned and are the ship's exact progress and direction *over the bottom*.

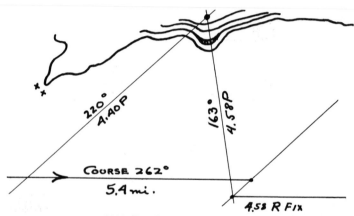

1116 Two bearings on same object

1116 Two bearings on one object to get a running fix and distance off are diagramed in Figure 1116. By noting the log reading between two bearings on a straight course and advancing the original bearing by that course and distance, a cross of this line with the second line of position will provide a running fix.

1117 Course and two bearings are plotted on the chart (*Figure 1117*). With the dividers scaled to the distance run between the bearings, adjust the two legs so that each is on a line of position and both are equidistant along a right angle from the course line. The ship's position will be indicated on the second line of position.

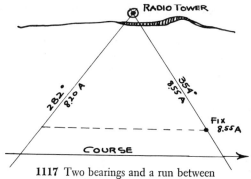

1117 Two bearings and a run between

1118 Bow and beam bearings may be taken from the compass—considering it merely as a protractor—or by relative bearings. When the object bears 45° (or four points) from dead ahead, read

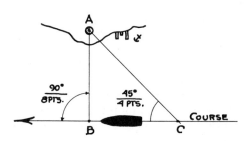

1118 Bow and beam bearings

the log. When the object bears 90° (or eight points), or on the beam, read the log.

The distance off on the line of position A-B is equal to the distance run between B-C.

1119 Another method of finding distance off is called *doubling the angle on the bow*. Bearings are taken as above. The log is read when the object bears 22½° (two points). It is read again when the angle has doubled, or at 45° (four points). The distance run between D and C equals CA or the distance off at this point. Distance off, BA, will equal 7⁄10ths of the distance run between D and C.

This method is valuable in that it *predicts* the distance off when abeam.

The above calculation is merely an example. Any angle observed from D to A may be doubled and logged to obtain CA. For instance, when D is 30°, C will be 60°. (However, the 7/10ths rule holds good only for the 22½°–45° bearings.)

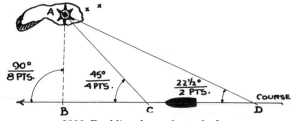

1119 Doubling the angle on the bow

FIX BY SOUNDING

1120   A sounding can be used as one component in obtaining a fix, and is especially useful for finding distance off. A one-point bearing and a sounding taken at the same time as the observation provide a reliable fix. A fix on a circular line of position can often be obtained by a sounding.

A series of soundings (called a *chain*) is the most certain method of obtaining a thick-weather fix for the ship without radio direction-finding equipment. A chain of soundings is taken and applied as follows (*Figure 1120*):

Make and log a series of soundings along the ship's course, noting the time of each cast, depth of water, and distance between.

Example: Course NNE ½ E   9.00 A   68 Ft   14.5 M
                                 9.10   71   14.9
                                 9.20   69   15.3
                                 9.30   64   15.7

Graph this on a small piece of tracing paper, marking the course line oriented to a meridian, or to north. Along the course line, mark the depths encountered, spaced by the dividers set for the distance run between each sounding (or by time-ruler) and by the chart scale. Every 10 minutes, on the nose, take a sounding and keep the dividers set at the distance run in 10 minutes. Then lay the tracing paper on the chart, the course lines matching, and match the first

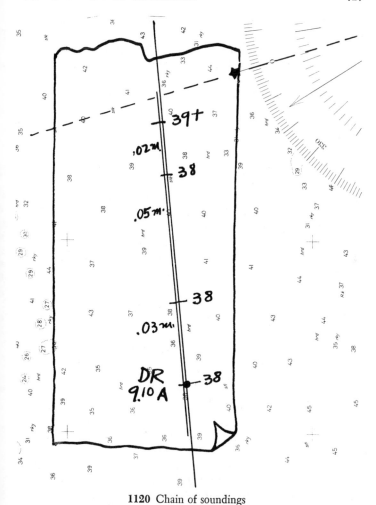

1120 Chain of soundings

sounding taken with the boat's dead-reckoned position at the time the sounding was made. If the chart soundings agree with the graphed soundings, the ship is on that course. If they do not agree, move the series of soundings around on the chart, keeping it properly oriented until a place of agreement is found. Except on a featureless flat bottom, the individual chain of recorded soundings should correspond to one—and only one—such series on the chart.

If the estimated position is in an area of changing bottom, taking samples of the bottom will aid in proving the fix. In passing along a coast bottoms do not change in composition very rapidly. They do change coming on to the coast, or when approaching a river mouth, sound, etc.

DANGER BEARING

1121 A danger bearing is a convenient way in which to keep clear of hidden dangers (shoals, reefs, etc.) without frequent fixes or reliance on dead reckoning.

Draw a line from some prominent landmark well ahead so as to clear all dangers (*as the dotted line, Figure 1121*) and note its direction by compass rose. Take frequent bearings on the object as the ship proceeds. As long as the bearings are to the right of the dotted line's bearings, the ship is to the left and safe side of the danger bearing.

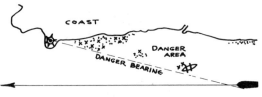

1121

CURRENT AND LEEWAY

1122 All courses, fixes, lines of position—in fact every feature of the chart—are shown in relation, or drawn in relation, to the bottom, a fixed, permanently oriented quantity. The water through which the boat moves (except in some inland lakes, etc.) is not fixed but moves *as a mass* in accord with tidal and current laws. The course, it might be said, is laid out on the *bottom*, not on the surface of the water. Yet the vessel attempts to sail that course through a moving element. Obviously, the course must be corrected by the amount of such movement and its direction.

Correcting for current in coastwise sailing is an extremely difficult procedure, involving a thorough knowledge of the tidal flow, its slacks, reverses, and directions. Tidal set and drift is fully tabulated in the government publications previously listed. The information gleaned from them must be assessed by the navigator and then applied to his particular problem.

It is by all means best done graphically, on the chart, and to the same scale as the chart. In practice it becomes quite foolish to plot courses corrected for current for any but long courses, or courses to be made good in thick weather. On the average coastal run there are so many opportunities for getting fixes that it is far wiser to depend upon even a hasty fix than a course corrected for current. River mouths, depths of water, submerged topography, backeddies around headlands, bays, and islands all contort the tidal currents into waters little short of whirlpools, varying by the minute and the yard in drift, set, and behavior, and by no means decently reversing themselves upon the change of the tide. Obviously, it would be impractical—well-nigh impossible—to anticipate the effect of the current upon a course were its direction and velocity to change six times in an hour; yet there are many coastal locations where it does change this often, and more.

However, in a long run (as eastward or westward through Long Island Sound), it would be folly to disregard the current completely. It should be stated, however, that a 100% current-corrected course can be achieved only with the aid of local tidal knowledge, and that the average coastwise navigator has learned to select the *main* and *important* factors of the problems raised by current and to apply only these in correcting his course.

Tidal and current predictions in government or other publications are for normal weather. The amount by which the predictions will be affected by periods of wind, storm, rivers in flood, ice conditions, etc., can only be estimated. Such estimates are best made by persons having local knowledge: fishermen, boatmen, ferrymen, Coast Guard stations, etc.

CURRENT DEAD AHEAD OR DEAD ASTERN

1123   The effect of currents parallel to the course is on speed over the bottom alone. They have no effect whatsoever on course, and whether the current be with you or against you, no course correction has to be made.

However, since speed is movement through the water at a stated rate per hour for that boat, and since the water itself is moving in relation to the bottom (over which speed or distance is measured for chart purposes), the velocity of the current will directly affect speed over the bottom.

A head current will reduce speed over the bottom by the speed of the current.

Examples:

Vessel, still-water speed	10 k.	4.5 k.
Head current, drift	− 2 k.	− 2.8 k.
Speed over bottom	8 k.	1.7 k.

A stern current will increase speed over the bottom by the speed of the current.

Vessel, still-water speed	9 k.	6.3 k.
Stern current	+ 2 k.	.9 k.
Speed over bottom	11 k.	7.2 k.

CURRENT BROAD ON THE BEAM

1124   To graphically solve the problem of correcting the compass course between two points so as to allow for current and for steering a corrected course between the two points (*Figure 1124A*):

Draw on the chart a straight line between the point of departure and the destination. Mark, to the chart scale, a distance along this line from the start equal to the distance the boat will cover in one hour (determined by the planned speed).

Draw from this point, parallel to the line of current but against the direction of its flow, a straight line. Mark, to the chart scale, a distance along this line, from the intersection, equal to the distance the current will flow in one hour.

By completing the triangle, the resultant hypotenuse enables the navigator to:

1. Find the corrected course by measuring the angle between the hypotenuse and the original course line and by transferring this angle to the compass rose to obtain the correct steering course in degrees or points.

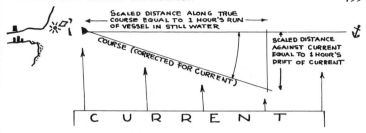

1124A Correcting the course for current

2. Find the time it will take to sail this course—for the distance scaled on the original course—by measuring and scaling the hypotenuse, then converting this distance into time by the usual methods.

Any proportional part of an hour's run scaled on the original course line may be used, providing the hour's draft of the current is scaled in proportion. It is thus possible to correct a very short course of less than an hour's run.

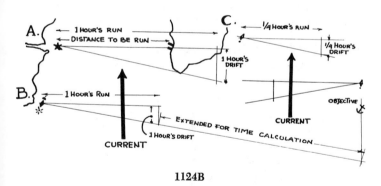

1124B

Examples of this and other methods are shown in Figure 1124B. All are based on the above, however, and are merely worked out in these corollary ways because of possible chart limitations, convenience, or the navigator's preference.

1125 There is a minor and inconsequential error inherent in the formula, which has no effect upon the accuracy of the result unless the speed of the current is 33% or more of the speed of the boat. The error is generally disregarded by coastwise navigators and is, in any case, very slight. Even over a long course the error would not result in the vessel's being so far off course that expected visual aids to navigation, or means of getting a fix, would be denied the navigator.

The usual course corrections for deviation, variation, or both must be applied to the course corrected for current, of course.

It should be unnecessary to state that current drift and set (velocity and direction) are obtained from the *Tidal Current* and the *Tide Tables*. It is highly unlikely that a run will encounter a uniform drift and set for its entire distance. Judgment alone can estimate allowances to be made for such conditions. Current vagaries are mostly near shore, and it is therefore sound navigation to calculate correct courses so as to steer from between offshore marks, such as buoys, between which the current will often be found more uniform than 'longshore.

Long courses may see the current lessen, increase, change direction, etc., and such changes must be considered in laying down the steering course. In some localities it is possible to take advantage of a rotary current, which is more or less constant in direction at least.

CURRENT ON THE BOW OR QUARTER

1126 Any current forward of the beam retards the progress over the bottom.

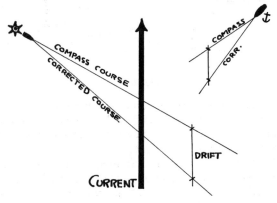

1126A Current on the bow

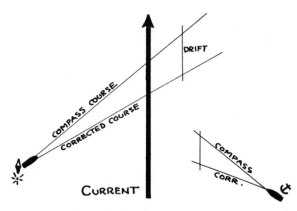

1126B Current on the quarter

To solve the problem graphically and lay a corrected course, the same basic principles apply as in calculating a beam current.

Figure 1126 shows the method. Note that its graphic solution varies only in laying down the current line. This *must* be parallel to the direction of the current, and, of course, against it.

Any current aft of the beam helps the progress over the bottom. The graphic solution is no different from the one above.

LEEWAY

1127 Leeway is the leeward drift of the vessel due to wind or the heave of the sea. The amount of leeway is measured by the angle between the course steered and the course made good. It varies with wind, state of the sea, and the vessel itself. It is a matter to be estimated by the navigator, based upon his experience and judgment.

If leeway can be estimated, it is applied exactly like current to correct the course. If it is disregarded, the error will appear when the next fix is made, and the course and distance then will have to be corrected.

Somewhat the same basic laws as the laws of current apply, but the amount of leeway must always remain an inexact quantity. A vessel with wind on the bow or aft makes no leeway. A beam wind causes maximum leeway. A wind on the quarter causes but slight leeway. Deep vessels make less leeway than shallow ones. Leeway in rough water, or when hove to, greatly exceeds leeway in calm water.

Navigators may be guided somewhat in making their estimates by observing the angle between the vessel's wake and a long line, or the log, towed astern. Such an observation is useless, of course, in broken seas or at slow speeds.

A "ground log" is sometimes used to show approximate drift. This is simply a lead and line of some weight. The vessel is stopped, the lead dropped to bottom, and the rate of drift or leeway noted from a reading of the line. Thus, if a vessel drifts 9' per minute by line reading, she will make 540' of leeway in an hour. This is applied to the course, especially a course of several hours' run, exactly as current corrections are.

OTHER NAVIGATION METHODS

1128 There are many other methods and instruments for solving the problems of coastwise navigation, possibly a total of a hundred or more. No man, especially the nonprofessional, can have all the methods at his fingertips, nor be completely familiar with the sometimes complex instruments (three- and five-arm protractors, maneuvering boards, etc.) required in the solutions. The solutions here given will solve *all* the problems that may be encountered by the pleasure boatman, and it would be wise to understand *these* solutions thoroughly and not become confused by other formulas. Unless one is a mathematician or a practicing engineer, too much theoretical knowledge can only lead to confusion and indecision—and possibly trouble when, at sea, the problem is *real*.

Conceivably, a boatman could use further methods were he navigator on a racing craft, or directing fleet maneuvers, or seeking a particular ocean spot (as for the treasure hunter), but for these jobs he requires not only special knowledge, from special books, but special training as well. So this is a plea to keep this business of navigating simple and sane. It is well within the ability of any man with the brains to make the money to buy a boat; the secret is not to raise boating to an art but hold it down to a craft. The essential reason for safe navigating is safety, and any boatman is going to be a great deal safer knowing a few navigational methods well than a lot of methods halfway.

It is impossible, within the scope of this *Manual,* to discuss celestial navigation in great depth, nor would it be of much use to the boatman, who is 99% of the time a coastwise or inland mariner.

However, it might be stated that a knowledge of the sailings (middle latitude sailing, Great Circle sailing, traverse sailing, etc.) would be of considerable use to the offshore navigator. Additional instruments of navigation are required, including the sextant.

Navigational methods have advanced considerably in the last 50 years, and the modern navigator no longer requires an intricate knowledge of mathematics to solve the problems of celestial navigation. Perhaps the greatest advance in the methods of working has been made by the publication of certain tables necessary to the art. Of these, the latest is known as H.O. (Hydrographic Office) 229, or *Sight Reduction Tables for Marine Navigation* and it is replacing the older types: H.O. 211, and H.O. 214, and others.

Many experienced yachtsmen prefer H.O. 214, however. Its great advantage lies in the fact that only two tables need be referred to and that calculation consists of but simple and very brief arithmetic, thus almost eliminating the chance of error, as well as speeding up the entire working out of position. Yachtsmen who have used H.O. 214 are enthusiastic, and report time savings of 50% or more over older methods, with error practically nil for anyone who can add and subtract. Although H.O. 214 is no longer published, it is still available from some navigation equipment suppliers.

With an esteemed collaborator, Mr. John Montgomery, who taught this method of celestial navigation to Navy airmen, I have written a useful book which, in a direct and quick manner, presents celestial navigation to the layman. Its title is *Navigation the Easy Way* and it is published by the publisher of this *Manual.* It concerns itself with how rather than why and utilizes the quick method based on the *Air Almanac.*

All these "methods" are not shortcuts, in the sense that observations and sights are no longer required. Basically, there has been no change in the science of nautical astronomy, and up to the point of referring to the tables, the navigator today must know everything he had to know 50 years ago, or 100 years ago.

As a conclusion to this section on coastal navigation, let the navigator and the mariner never forget a basic truth, unalterable by human emotion, weather conditions, or anything else, short of an explosion of the universe:

> ### The Compass Never Lies.

Have a good compass, properly adjusted for deviation; take care of it; and from that moment on

> ### Trust Your Compass Over All Else.

NAVIGATING THE INLAND WATERWAYS

1129 The small-boat owner with his home port located on or near the 34,000 miles of improved waterways and countless natural and man-made lakes that abound in the United States has some special problems; indeed handling a small boat in inland waters is as different from coastal navigation as night is from day. Most of our inland waterways have been improved to a 8′ draft and have commercial uses vital to the economy of the entire continent. Yet yachting is also an important factor in these waters and there is no one area in the United States with as many units as the Midwest. The St. Louis district of the Coast Guard has more yachts numbered than any other district in the nation! In this vast system are the Great Lakes, Lake Champlain and many lakes as yet unnamed but rapidly forming behind power dams. An increasingly popular long cruise is from an Ohio port, down the Mississippi, say in October when the current is quiet, through the inland waterways to Carrabelle, Florida; thence down the Gulf to Tarpon Springs, through the waterways or across Lake Okeechobee to the east coast of Florida, north through the inland waterways to the Chesapeake, the Delaware, the Hudson, the Erie Canal, through the Great Lakes to Chicago, down the Illinois River to Cairo on the Mississippi and back up the Ohio. This is some 7,000 miles of cruising and less than 10% of it is in ocean waters! No ocean cruiser on a coasting cruise in the U. S. can equal this distance and remain in new and virgin waters.

Our inland waterways are all free and open to pleasure craft; there are no tolls, few permits necessary and the draft of your boat and its minimum vertical clearance alone fixes your route. For the most part these inland routes, so-called, are on improved rivers or

1129 The "inland waters" of the United States in 1979

bays, are fresh water, and demand some special considerations by
the navigating department of the average cruiser.

Following are presentations of these problems and their solutions.
However, just as the coastal cruiser should use his "bible" both
charts and the various *Coast Pilots*, so should the inland voyager use
his special inland charts and the several helpful booklets distributed
by the various government agencies concerned. Sources for inland
navigation information are listed at the end of this chapter.

LOCAL LORE AND KNOWLEDGE

1130   Unlike the salt-water navigator for whom it has been possible to compile more or less standard aids and procedures, the inland navigator depends very much on local knowledge; i.e., that vast store of information never set down in print but existing only in the minds and experience of local boatmen, pilots, lock tenders, fishermen and the river engineers. Your job, in a new and strange area, even though it is apparently amply charted, is to—somehow—discover the essentials of this information.

For example, an aid to navigation, clearly defining a channel, can become utterly useless and false within six hours after a thunderstorm 100 miles upriver. Bars build and melt, chutes open and shut. Sawyers—large uprooted trees caught on the bottom by their roots, which sweep the channel as the current lashes them—fetch up and lie in wait for you in swept channels, and entire islands move, disappear or are formed between sunup and sundown.

It is therefore of paramount importance to ask questions before you attempt what seems a simple and safe passage. Study the charts. Read all you can. Draw on your own experience. And then ask questions. It is expected and you are respected for asking. Read Mark Twain's *Life on the Mississippi* if you would like to find out what a working river pilot must know before he can appear in his own middle window and pass steering orders to his wheelman.

Inland waters are not subject to direct tidal effects. However, water levels may and do change, at times rather unpredictably, in areas near the confluence of tidal waters or other rivers. While the tidal range may not be great—only 18″ at the mouth of the Mississippi for example—winds and other local conditions may build a high on a high so that the water level change is actually 36″. A sudden rain-swollen current may blank out an incoming tidal current, negate a low tide, or create a high stage 10 times that of a normal tide. Again, your best course is to ask questions of those who know the river.

Wind affects water stages. This is especially true on the shallower lakes where waves build into trochoidal forms, soon become large and powerful, and result in far greater danger to a boat than the smooth cycloidal seas of the coast, which may be five times higher.

Inland waters are navigated with constant reference to the "stage of the water" or, on rivers, to "the pool stage." This simply means how much plus or minus you have from the datum for that lake or pool. It is somewhat akin to allowing for the stage of the tide in coastal waters, except that the stage is not predictable by ordinary observation or by tables. On rivers, pool stages are often noted on bulletin boards located at dams or along the river banks. River charts indicate their location. Usually 9′ is taken as normal pool depth and a pool noted as minus 0.5 would be 5″ below normal or a pool depth of 8′7″.

Lake waters are subject to wind and also to barometric pressures, which sometimes cause a noticeable alteration in water level called a *seiche*. Many artificial lakes feed powerhouse dams and levels will become markedly lower in dry spells. Dams and locks will usually post the stage; a call to the engineers will give you the stage and, sometimes, any contemplated changes in the immediate future.

Inland rivers or improved rivers usually have a constant current downstream, interrupted only by wind or backing-up tide. The current varies greatly, depending much upon drought conditions or upon upriver rain, which, in places, may raise the river stage 50′ in a few days. This occurs often during the spring snow runoff and sometimes results in devastating floods. This ever-present current, even when calm and confined, works constantly to change the river bottom and its course. When speeded up by melting snow or rain, river currents scour the bottom and move vast quantities of sand and mud in a few day.s They not only nibble into banks, create new river channels, and widen rivers, but also cast up sand or mud bars in former channels: when at last the current meets opposition in the form of tide or wind, it meekly slows down and drops its suspended silt and sand—and a new bar is formed!

The Western rivers slowly carry downstream a great mass of mud and muck, not much compressed, called *flocculation*, which at times rolls surfaceward and appears to be a new or forming bar. Commercial vessels plough through it; most pleasure boats glide over it. It is unpleasant stuff indeed to draw into your engine jackets and pumps. A little like chilled consommé, it contains sand and grit which can ruin engines, strut bearings, and propeller shafts in short order.

RIVER CURRENTS

1131   River currents have a pattern familiar to men who know the rivers, and many pilots use this pattern to their advantage. Here are the general rules:

1. Run downstream in midstream, following the deepest channels where the current is swiftest.
2. Run upstream as close as possible to the banks.
3. Running upstream, cut into coves and behind points where counter (upstream) currents lurk to help you.
4. Work river tides. In the Hudson River, for example, if you start at the right time you can carry a favorable, helping tide the entire 153 miles to Troy. This is possible because as you ride north on a rising tide, it neutralizes the river current, and you do not at any time oppose either tidal or river current. The trick is to ride the crest of high tide as nearly as possible since it takes some hours to travel the length of the river, even as you do.

The meanderings of a river such as the Mississippi are almost continuously punctuated by points and capes. At these places, the current usually crosses to the *outside* of the curve and follows close to the bank opposite the cape or point. As it crosses it scours a deep channel and this is usually the recommended and/or marked channel. At times of higher stages, however, the current is driven toward the inside of the curve, but at a slower rate than in its deep, normal channel. Hence, it drops sand and mud and the *inside* of most of such curves should be assumed to be shallow or barred.

Remembering always that the current has probably swept out the natural and best deepwater channel, and that any improvements or dredging have probably been made to and in this natural channel, you should try to traverse these channels in a natural swing rather than in a straight course from buoy to buoy. Watch your wake and if it curls, seemingly "bucking" a counter or side current, you are probably off to one side of the channel, though not necessarily in shallow or dangerous waters. The natural channel will most likely be ideally balanced between *all* the factors that affect its course. You have many of these factors on your local chart—bluffs, heights of land, nature of the bottom, adjacent swamps or lowlands, entering or leaving estuaries or creeks, and the contour of the bottom, which is shown on some but not all inland charts. The stage of the river, the direction of the wind, your own draft, the velocity of the current, all these inform you of what is probably the natural—and therefore the best—channel.

River currents create islands and bars in mid river, which are seen only at low-water stages. Currents will visibly flow over these, often with a distinct ripple or crest on the upriver edge, and such areas are likely to appear lighter than the deeper waters. Roots and bushes are sometimes grounded on them and serve as warnings.

When a river cuts behind a bank it forms a "towhead" and the upriver entrance is apt to be a shoal or barred. When a river cuts across a cape or point, literally forming a new river, the cut is called a "chute." Chute water is apt to be foul with stumps and snags. Avoid both chutes and towheads as channels, however inviting. They should be used as overnight anchorages with caution.

Even in main channels you may encounter a snag, which is a water-logged stump, often of some hard wood such as gum or walnut. Avoid any current aberration as possibly caused by a snag, or by a sawyer, which is an entire tree caught on the bottom by the roots and lying in the current, literally sawing from side to side in a wide and destructive swath. Government sweepers work the Western rivers year round in an attempt to reduce snags and sawyers.

In general, a river should be navigated by pleasure craft only under the best conditions and it is no disgrace to lay over because of an unfavorable current. Vessels that "bull" through find all manner of trouble at times—sand-ruined pumps and bearings, strandings and minor collisions, docks, landings, and fuel pumps submerged, and the riverbanks deserted. October is the best month on the Western rivers, with channels cleared and current at low velocities. April and May are the hard months with high currents, much floating debris and flocculation sluicing downstream and jamming coves. Marine services are often suspended until later in the year when the river is safe.

ANCHORING

1132 The easy way to "anchor" is, of course, to tie up in one of the many marinas on the Western and inland waterways. To actually lie to a hook is sometimes a problem on inland waters.

The bottoms of most rivers are unstable and it is always wise to seek out an anchorage free of current and wind, present or anticipated. It is usual to lie under banks, especially at bends where you can get out of the main channel. Beware of traffic. The big tows do not lay over at dark, and by means of radar and twin searchlights, churn on course in fog and on the darkest of nights.

Favorite river anchorages are: behind a towhead, especially one that has developed a bar on the upriver end and has become a quiet cove; a short way into a creek or tributary that does not have much current; in the "lesser channels" usually found behind river islands, these being on the side of the island opposite the main or marked channel; and behind a wooden or cement pile dike, constructed in the river by engineers to protect the banks. In times of flooding waters, it may become necessary to anchor with a view toward avoiding debris; the dike and towhead are particularly good at such times.

If the stage is stable, river boats freely tie up to any shore, frequently to islands or sand bars. The deepest water is usually on the upriver side or edge. River boatmen run a line from the bow to a tree or buried anchor ashore, cut a 25' sapling to hold out the stern, and then run a preventer line from the stern to shore.

Anchorages on lakes are no problem. The charts will indicate coves; local fleets may be moored in some. Where creeks and rivers enter a lake, a deep spot is often found immediately behind the bar that usually forms off the mouth. Select an anchorage away from traffic swells and from the sudden "northers" that spring up on most fresh-water lakes in summertime. A tie-up to shore or trees or rock ledges is common; indeed many lakes, such as Lake Champlain are so deep that an average cruiser would not carry sufficient cable to anchor in a safe manner in many of its rocky coves.

For river anchoring you will require a "hook" with broad flukes and of some weight. Very light patent anchors or wispy "dory" anchors are not sufficient. In most cases, it is necessary to penetrate considerable bottom muck or flocculation, and the rule that scope equals at least five times the water's depth becomes essential.

River bottoms, particularly in areas of slow or sluggish current, are apt to be foul and studded with water-logged stumpage and vegetation. It behooves the prudent skipper *always* to rig an anchor trip. Chapter VI on ground tackle discusses anchoring and anchor trips and buoys.

Modern lightweight anchors, while having sufficient fluke area to hold, frequently do not have the weight to penetrate to a holding bottom. The old dodge of rigging a fathom or two of chain immediately ahead of the anchor will usually solve the problem, but it raises the obvious question: Why not stick to the old-fashioned heavy anchor in the first place?

Dragging and grounding is a real threat on Western rivers. The considerable wake of passing traffic gives the anchor an uneasy hold. The heave and surge impose heavy strains that can break out an anchor while you snooze. A sudden current—perhaps stemming from an up-country rain—can also break out an anchor. If you drag and ground there is usually no tide to assist in getting off. If, after power has failed to move you, the boat still remains grounded, you must wait for a friendly haul or a wake. As the first swells of a wake hit, gun the boat into deeper water. The *second* swell may be too late since it will tend to wash you further aground. Another trick is to create a wake by running around the grounded boat in circles with the dinghy and an outboard. Each time its small wake hits the grounded boat, gun her off and, little by little, you can gain deeper water.

The normal practices of carrying out a kedge anchor or towing off with the dink and outboard should also be tried. During all of this, guard against sucking sand and silt into your engine cooling system.

AIDS TO INLAND NAVIGATION

1133 These differ somewhat from coastal navigational aids and marks as well as from each other. All inland waters have adequate charts and these should be consulted for chart symbols. River charts are in the form of strip maps, sometimes bound in volumes. They indicate north but do not show a compass rose, for compass courses on most Western rivers are impractical. The Great Lakes are charted in the more familiar National Ocean Survey form and a *Great Lakes Pilot*, sister to the *United States Coast Pilot*, gives all pertinent information. Many inland charts do not indicate water depths because of the great variance in pool and river stages. However, they do show in most cases the favored channels (often buoyed or on a range, or both), and these are maintained at project depth or pool depth, plus or minus the water stage at the moment.

Aids to navigation are numbered from a common point and the

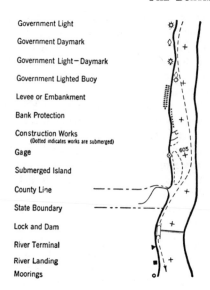

Government Light

Government Daymark

Government Light – Daymark

Government Lighted Buoy

Levee or Embankment

Bank Protection

Construction Works
(Dotted indicates works are submerged)

Gage

Submerged Island

County Line

State Boundary

Lock and Dam

River Terminal

River Landing

Moorings

1133 Symbols on Mississippi River charts between Cairo and Minneapolis, printed in black and white

number of the aid is the number of miles from this point. On the Illinois River, for example, Barry Island Light would be noted in this way:

Otter Island Light	166.1 miles from	On right bank
Fl.W. 2 sec.	Newberry	(descending)

It will also be noted that this mark is visible 360° with a 3° directional beam oriented upstream.

On the lower Mississippi the reference point is A.H.P., which means "above head of passes," some miles south of New Orleans. On the Ohio, mileage is reckoned from Pittsburgh. On the Champlain Canal, mileage is reckoned from Lock #1, which is the federal lock at Troy, N. Y., and must be traversed by all traffic whether bound in or out of the Erie or the Champlain canals.

There is no sounder advice than to obtain all the information and charts pertaining to the waters you plan to cruise well in advance of the cruise. (*See the publications list following*). Study these and become familiar with the basics. There is good reason for the difference in the inland systems from standard or from federal systems; usually it is because of the fluctuation of water levels and the relatively small and narrow waters involved. Most inland waters cannot be related to the heavens, to celestial navigation, to magnetic north, and to predictable tidal ranges. They are therefore related to other fixed values such as mileage, visible marks (towns, bridges, dams etc.), to the character and topography of the surrounding observable country, and to the buoyage system found to be best and safest for that particular water.

One basic and common characteristic of river aids is that most are not floating buoys but are driven piles or distinctive marks on trees, bridge abutments, or posts on the banks. Ranges, properly marked with targets, are quite common. At all times there are vessels at work on the river—dredging, clearing snags and sawyers, building up levees and revetments, and servicing navigational aids— and their signals should be heeded when the workboats are anchored in a fairway or working a main channel. The favored passing channel, if the vessel has made no signal, is the one toward deepest middle water.

At night the aids are lighted sufficiently to indicate the channel and course to *pilots of experience*, men who have run the river by daylight. No novice should attempt night navigation, for the tendency at night is to run from light to light in straight lines, and as previously noted, the channel is apt to follow a natural curve and be anything but a straight line except in dredged areas. It might be safe to navigate at night on a lake, or on deep water such as found in sections of the Tennessee system.

A depth sounder is of considerable practical use in river navigation. So is a knowledge of echo navigation and, of course, that ancient and reliable standby, local knowledge. Larger craft employ radar with success and commercial traffic so equipped drives on through fog, mist, and snow, which should see small craft tied up. A direction finder is of use on the Great Lakes, but not on the rivers.

Throughout the literature of river pilotage, the terms left and right bank are used. Aids are noted as being on the left or right bank. *In all cases*, the left bank is the bank to your left as you face or head *downstream*. Steaming upstream, you must make the conversions, and an aid noted as on the right bank will appear on your left side. Exceptions to this rule are found on the Champlain Canal, where the term "starboard" (right) is used and this means the right-hand or east side of the channel leaving the federal lock at Troy. (Below Troy the coastal buoyage system prevails.) If bound into the Erie Canal, the right-hand side becomes north. *Both hands are reversed when approaching the Troy lock.*

REGULATIONS

1134   While Inland Rules prevail for the regulation of navigation and traffic on inland waters, there are the following exceptions to be remembered:

1. On the Mississippi River system, Inland Rules hold as far as the Huey Long Bridge, 16 miles north of New Orleans. From there to its source, and including its tributaries and also the Red River of the North, the regulations of the Pilot Rules for Western Rivers prevail.
2. On the Great Lakes and its tributaries, as far east as Montreal, the entire system is under the regulations of the Great Lakes Rules. No part of these lakes are under Inland Rules though some are under Canadian law, which differs little from United States regulations. Canadian navigational aids near U. S. waters are often marked with the letter "C."

Many special or local rules have crept into use, some of them not codified into law. Here are some to remember:

1. General lock signals are one long and one short blast as the vessel approaches a lock of the Mississippi system. It will be answered by the lock tender but is not necessarily a signal to enter. Entrance may be controlled by lights, similar to traffic lights, or by hand or sound signals.

   On the New York State Barge Canal system (Erie and Champlain canals), the signal is three "distinct" blasts and the entrance permission is a green signal light.
2. Special lock signals on the Ohio River:
   (*a*) Light signals mean:

   Flashing red .... Do not enter, stay clear
   Flashing amber .. Approach, slowly and under control
   Flashing green .... Enter and prepare to lock

(b) Multiple locks (two or more). Lockmaster makes sound signal on air or other horn:

1 long .... Enter landward lock
2 long .... Enter riverward lock
1 short .... Leave landward lock
2 short .... Leave riverward lock

3. The order of entering locks for locking through are as follows:

First .... U. S. military or naval craft
Second .... Vessels carrying U. S. mail
Third .... Commercial passenger craft
Fourth .... Commercial tows, full or empty
Fifth .... Commercial fishermen
Sixth .... Pleasure craft

The great number of pleasure craft using the locks has made it necessary to revise these rules at some locks, like those controlling pools near populous centers such as St. Louis or Cincinnati. Some have adopted a rule to lock through all accumulated and waiting pleasure craft once every hour. On the Ohio, every fourth locking-through operation is for pleasure craft. Sometimes a single tow, 1,200 or more feet in length, requires five or six lockings for all its barges, which must be broken and then reassembled below the lock—an operation consuming half a day!

4. Any craft but pleasure craft, when giving a sound or whistle signal, must at the same time flash an amber light synchronized with the sound signal.

5. Fog signals for power vessels on Western rivers:
2 short and 1 long blast once every minute, on *whistle*.

6. Fog signals for sailing vessels on Western rivers:
2 short and 1 long blast once every minute on *horn*.

7. Fog signals for tows on Western rivers (signal given by tow or push boat and, if push boat, by leading barge also):
3 blasts of equal length every minute.

8. Power vessels at anchor or lying to, upon the approach of another vessel, in fog, give the following bell signals:
1 tap every minute if lying against the right bank.
2 taps every minute if lying against the left bank.

9. Meeting vessels, by law, assume the following rights and burdens:

Downstream-bound vessel has the right of way and is privileged.

Upstream-bound vessel is burdened and must sound the first passing signal.

However, cross signals here are not illegal and the vessels *pass on the side signalled by the privileged (downstream) vessel*.

10. Vessels bound upstream and approaching a narrow channel occupied by, or *about to be occupied by*, a vessel bound downstream must lay to and allow the descending vessel to pass through.

11. At the junction of two navigable waterways or channels, the vessel having the other to port must give the first signal.

12. A privileged vessel in any situation (as when bound downstream) is obliged to *hold its course* but may reduce or increase its speed. However, if risk of collision exists, *both or all* vessels involved must reduce speed or stop if necessary.

13. On Western rivers, the signal when approaching a bend, or other "blind" feature that reduces visibility ahead to less than 600 yards, is three "distinct" blasts. Any approaching vessel, whether or not seen, must reply by the same signal.

Only when the vessels sight each other do they exchange the usual passing signals in the usual manner.

On inland lakes, the same situation calls for one long blast on the whistle (as do all other pilot rules).

14. Commercial tows (sometimes composed of forty barges laced together and pushed by a modern triple-screw diesel "towboat") are by courtesy given certain rights by pleasure craft in recognition of the difficulty of stopping, steering and controlling such a "vessel." It takes such a tow up to a mile to stop, even with engines rung down to full astern. Loss of way at critical points, such as in a narrow channel or in a bend, can strand and even damage such a tow. They must be given—if only for the safety of the pleasure craft involved—the power of steering, which stems only from their engine power.

The pilots of these tows see you and want to know where you are. Don't "hide" under their barges, or pace them just ahead of the lead barge; don't cut circles around them. If you must pass, do so in a long straight stretch; in a bend, you are likely to be pushed or washed into the bank because of the swing of such a vast tow. When two tows meet, each pilot has his problems; don't complicate them by demanding at this time the rights which by law may be yours. As someone once pointed out, the vast new inland cruising area came to us because commercial interests promoted and needed it, not because your Congressman or anybody else was much concerned about giving a few thousand yachts some new thrills.

LOCKS AND LOCKING

1135 Until a few decades ago, our Western rivers were, by and large, unnavigable. Only special types of vessels, such as the old Mississippi River steamboat and the Missouri stern-wheeler could negotiate the natural Western rivers. To go where commercial vessels do now used to require a flat boat or a raft—or just reasonably high boots! By building a complex system of dams and by controlling the depths of connecting lakes and waterways at all times, we have created a continuous navigable pathway from the heartland of our country to the ports of the world. (*Figure 1135A shows the TVA system.*) And, right along with inland waterways, we have created a source of hydro-electric power.

The connecting link for the inland boatman is the lock, a simple device which, with a vessel afloat on its "locked-in" water, raises or lowers the water and the vessel to the level of a new body of water. The common lock form on our Western rivers is the gate lock, the operation of which is shown in Figure 1135B.

The small craft skipper has some problems—not great—in mastering the art of "locking through."

Lock signals have been given in Paragraph 1134. When waiting for clearance into the lock, keep the boat well under control. If a wait seems indicated, tie up at the lock wings; that's why they are there. Keep far away from the gate and allow space for the vessel locking against you, and probably causing the delay, to clear the lock wings and the dam boom and to enter the regular channel. On the Mississippi, there is a "dead line" clearly marked and noted beyond which no vessel is to proceed without the lockmaster's permission.

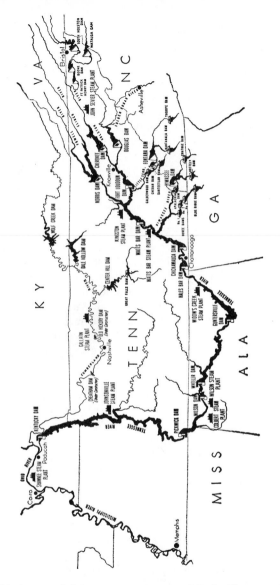

1135A A map of the vast waterways created in the Tennessee Valley (TVA) by a system of dams, impounded waters and connecting rivers. All are navigable to the farthermost dam and carry a minimum depth of 9′

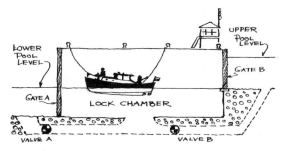

1135B A simplified diagram of the operation of a canal lock Valves A and B are electrically controlled from the lockmaster's station. In this diagram the vessel entered the lock at upper pool level, with Gate B open and Gate A closed and chamber level the same as the upper pool. Gate B and Valve B were then closed and Valve A opened. The chamber water level was allowed to lower until it matched the water level of the lower pool. Valve A was then closed and Gate A opened and the vessel proceeded on her course.

On some locks, at this point, there is a whistle cord to alert the lock tender and for use by very small craft.

The down-current end of a lock is likely to have considerable current near the lock entrance and genuine turbulence when the lock is emptying and before the downstream gates open. Fenders, needed inside the lock, might be useful here as well.

Enter the lock slowly and watch for the lockmaster's signal as to your berth. Proceed there and stay there. In some locks, lines are passed down to you; in others you receive a hauling line ending in a monkey fist to which you make your own lines fast. Send your lines aloft, with the hauling line secured to the eye of your line, and the lock attendant will pass the eye over one of the many bollards studding the lock wall. Use good line, with a large-sized eye splice rove in (say 18″ in diameter), and be *very* sure it is long enough. It must be as long, plus 50%, as the rise of the water in the lock. Obviously, this is important or you are going to lose control of the boat on a lock drop.

Locks are of concrete, usually rough, often dirty or oil-smeared, and probably dripping wet. You will need fender protection. Fancy yacht fenders are not the thing unless you use them inside a fender board, and fender boards are not to be trusted unless tended at all times. They have a tendency to catch or trip on the rough lock wall. Tires, covered with canvas, are excellent fenders but are forbidden in some lock systems. On the New York State canals, it is common to take a gunny sack or two, pack it full of grass or hay and use these as disposable fenders. Two-by-fours covered with carpet scraps are used by many experienced canal cruisers.

Very few locks, even large and deep ones such as the one at Whitehall, N. Y., or the easterly lock on the Lake Okeechobee waterway, throw up a disturbance great enough to endanger small

1135C How to handle locking lines when single-handed

craft. The lockmasters carefully control the inlet valves, and the stories sometimes batted around about maelstroms inside lock gates are fantasies. While there is a beam current tending to move the boat toward or away from the lock wall, it is at no time strong enough to take control of a yacht-sized vessel. (The writer and his wife, in a boat with *no* fenders of any kind, have many, many times locked through with no more than a line to a bollard and a boathook or a sneakered toe to hold her off the wall.)

Ease yourself up by hand or boathook, have a fender ready if you are super-careful, and stand by for orders from the lockmaster. Do *not* ease yourself up by boathook on the rungs of the iron ladders found in vertical channels; some lock keepers positively forbid it, others just think it's a nice way to break your arm and it's your own business if you want to. Be prepared to give the attendant your boat name, port, registration number, last port, and destination. All Western river and TVA locks are free. No permit is required to use them. New York State canals are also free but a permit is required. This may be obtained at no cost from the lock tender of the first lock you encounter.

Do not under any circumstances cleat both ends of your locking lines down to your deck. Boats have been damaged and capsized by this thoughtless practice. Tend your lines, bow and stern, every moment of the time in the lock. Some cruising men carry a double-length locking line, which the lock tender passes over the bollard. When ready to leave the lock, it is necessary only to haul in on the fall and you are free. This plan is not practiced by other boatmen because the line often brings down a bushel of grass clippings and a faceful of pebbles and dust. It becomes dirty and oily by contact with the lock wall and, finally, the end may fall into the water and then the rope must be dried before stowing—or, possibly, unwound from the propeller.

Guard gates may sometimes be found closed in a stretch of canal before a lock. These are lowered while lock gates are under repair, but since repair schedules are known, such information is noted at locks and in appropriate nautical publications.

Watch, when canaling and locking, your overhead clearances. It is generous for yachts in all places except the Champlain Canal—15′6″ being the limiting height here. Sailing boats unstep spars and carry them on deck. Cruisers fold back small spars. It is a good precaution to measure your boat height above water and note it in the log. A gentleman we know on Lake Oneida can enter the lake only with full fuel and water tanks—but he knows it and is never in trouble.

On the Western rivers, it is often possible—indeed can be so ordered—to go over the dam rather than through the lock. At periods of extra high water, when both pools connected by a lock are at the same level, wickets, normally upright to protect vessels from going over the dam, are lowered and the navigating channel is then through the so-called "bear trap." The sill depth in the dam passage will be at least the depth of the controlling pool, and when the signals to use the bear trap are up, it applies to all traffic, including big tows and tugs. Knowing these craft can slide over the dam should ease the minds of the small-craft skipper who can't get used to the idea of sailing over a dam.

LOCKING THROUGH   SEQUENCE ★

A   VESSEL ENTERS FROM POOL TO
LOCK CHAMBER - BOTH AT O LEVEL

B   WATER FROM LEVEL +15 IS VALVED
INTO CHAMBER TO +15 LEVEL

C   CHAMBER LEVEL IS NOW AT +15,
GATE IS OPENED AND COURSE RESUMED.

1135D

On the Ohio, where many such dam wickets are found, lock information is posted on a conspicuous bulletin board well above the lock entrance. The board is scarlet, the lettering is white and the heading of the bulletin is always the word "PASS." At night distinguishing lights give the same information and the bulletin board is brightly spot-lighted.

Even if one lock has its wickets open, there is no assurance that others adjacent to it will also be open. Carefully study each lock as you approach and handle it as a separate and unrelated navigating problem.

In some locks you are requested not to smoke. In others you are required to shut down your engines while locking through. In no locks or lock approaches may you tie up for the night. Near some locks there are terminals for commercial use and, if not in use, there is no objection to lying there. Most canal towns have a town landing or stage and invite the passing yachtsman to leave a few dollars in their community. It is usually difficult to find anchorages near locks, or their canalized approaches, and therefore the day's run should be planned with overnight stops in mind. If you *must* lay over, pick a creek entry, or a bight well away from the wash of passing tows, which operate around the clock. Beware also of proximity to railroad tracks or major truck arteries; there is not much sleep in such places.

Locks become dangerous for small craft when ice begins forming or drifts downstream. In many areas locks are closed to vessels under certain tonnages for periods of up to 10 weeks. High water loaded with debris may also close a lock to small craft. If closed, the information will be noted in appropriate bulletins to mariners.

1136 Chapter IX lists the sources of charts and inland river information. The Mississippi River Commission, Corps of Engineers, U. S. Army, P.O. Box 80, Vicksburg, Miss., 39180 will provide the very latest catalog and listings of charts pertaining to *all* the Western rivers and the Great Lakes. Charts are for sale at the various Corps of Engineers offices in many major river cities; also the periodic issue of the *Notice to Navigational Interests* (correcting charts as changes occur).

Of special interest to inland boatmen are the following publications:

New York State Canals and Waterways Official map, with condensed information on canal system, navigational aids, pleasure boat regulations, data on locks, etc. Superintendent of Operation and Maintenance, State Department of Transportation, Albany, N. Y. 12232

Mississippi River Navigation Division Engineer, Lower Mississippi Valley Division, Corps of Engineers, U. S. Army, P.O. Box 80, Vicksburg, Miss. 39180

Locking Through Things you should know if you use navigation locks. District Engineer, St. Louis, Mo. 63101

Your Key to the Lock U. S. Army Engineer District, Corps of Engineers, Room 322, Federal Building, P.O. Box 991, Albany,

N. Y. 12207 Pamphlet prepared for the guidance of yachtsmen passing through the federal lock at Troy, N. Y.

Ohio River Handbook   Piloting information pertaining to the Ohio and its tributaries. Young & Klein, Inc., 1351 Spring Lawn Ave., Cincinnati, Ohio. 45223

Your Ohio   Pamphlet of general interest. Corps of Engineers, Ohio Division. P.O. Box 1159, Cincinnati, Ohio. 45202

Recreation in TVA Lakes   Tabulates boat docks and related services, with map. Information Office, Tennessee Valley Authority, Knoxville, Tenn. 37902

Boating and fishing guide to the Great Lakes of the South   The Nashville Tennessean, Nashville, Tenn. 37202

Navigation Locks and Dams, Mississippi River   District Engineer, St. Louis, Mo. 63101

Tips on River Safety   District Engineer, St. Louis, Mo. 63101

Mississippi River, Chain of Rocks Canal and Locks   District Engineer, St. Louis, Mo. 63101

⚓

PART IV

BOAT
MAINTENANCE

CHAPTER XII

MARLINESPIKE SEAMANSHIP

THE CARE, handling, knotting, splicing, and use of rope, whether fiber, synthetic, or wire, is called *marlinespike seamanship*. The small-boat man will require some knowledge of marlinespike seamanship, especially the sailboat man. There are some 1,500 knots, hitches, and splices. About a dozen of them will serve the small-boat man all his days afloat and in any situation. All the others are either trick or fancy knots or special-purpose knots, left over from squarerigger days when there was possibly more need for a knowledge of marlinespike seamanship than there is today.

It is far better to understand rope and its care, and to thoroughly understand how to tie a *few* useful knots (in darkness, ice, or snow!) than it is to know several hundred knots only slightly. Old shellbacks, sitting in the lee of the dory shop, love to while away time by recalling or inventing knots, but in their days aloft they found fifteen sufficient to sail the ship and keep them in jobs.

ROPE

1201 The chief natural fiber ropes are made of manila, hemp, cotton, sisal, and flax. Manila, or abaca, comes from a plant resembling the banana tree and is grown chiefly in the Philippines. Almost none are in use to-day and many cannot even be bought. With possible exception of manila, and occasionally sisal, the mariner's choice is restricted to the synthetics, but it is not a disastrous choice by any means. The synthetics overcome a great fault of the vegetable ropes, that of rotting unless stored dry and in a dry place.

461

TABLE OF STRENGTHS (BREAKING)

SIZE (inches) Dia. Circ.		MANILA			NYLON			DACRON		
		Net Wt. 100'	Ft. per lb.	Breaking Strength	Net Wt. 100'	Ft. per lb.	Breaking Strength	Net Wt. 100'	Ft. per lb.	Breaking Strength
¼	¾	1.96	51	600	1.5	66	1,700	2.1	47	1,700
⅜	1⅛	4.02	25	1,350	3	28	3,650	4.7	21.3	3,500
½	1½	7.35	13	2,650	6.6	15	6,650	8.2	12.2	6,100
⅝	2	13.1	7	4,400	10.5	9.5	10,300	13.2	7.6	9,500
¾	2¼	16.3	6	5,400	14.5	6.9	14,600	17.9	5.6	13,200
⅞	2¾	22	5	7,700	20	5	19,600	24.9	4	17,500
	3	26.5	3.77	9,000	26	3.84	25,000	30.4	3.3	22,000
¼	3¾	40.8	2.5	13,500	39	2.56	37,800	46.2	2.16	30,500
1½	4½	58.8	1.7	18,500	55	1.8	55,000	67	1.5	43,000

Synthetics are also far stronger, for the same diameter, than natural-fiber rope. Splicing the synthetics presents some problems, not insurmountable; on the other hand, whipping does not since synthetic ends can be "burned" to prevent unlaying. They are still subject to abrasion and must be handled with care, but a good synthetic line, properly cared for and protected against chafe, should outlast an equal fiber line.

The synthetics currently popular and readily available are:

Nylon—Used for mooring and anchor lines because it has about 20–25% stretch. Will serve as a sheet on small boats. White.

Dacron—Harder than nylon and has much less stretch. Used for halyards, sheets, lifts, and tackles. Both nylon and Dacron come braided, double-braided, twisted, and double-twisted. White, tan, or colored.

The "Polys"—Polypropylene, polyester, polyethylene are used for lashings dinghy towlines, buoy-pickup lines, or more-or-less permanent ropings. Not recommended for tackles since the type has a low abrasion resistance point. Popular with fishermen, crabbers, and lobstermen. The polys float. Yellow, blue and varicolored.

TABLE OF STRENGTHS (BREAKING)

POLYOLEFINS (H.T.) (Polypropylene) and/or Polyethylene			DOUBLE NYLON BRAID			POLYESTER/ POLYOLEFIN DOUBLE BRAID		
Net Wt. 100'	Ft. per lb.	Breaking Strength	Net Wt. 100'	Ft. per lb.	Breaking Strength	Net Wt. 100'	Ft. per lb.	Breaking Strength
1.24	80	1,250	1.66	60.3	2,100	1.7	60.2	1,700
2.9	34	2,600	3.33	30	4,200	3	28	3,500
4.9	20.4	4,150	6.67	15	7,500	6.8	15	6,800
7.8	12.8	5,900	11.1	9	12,000	11	9	11,000
11.1	9	7,900	15.0	6.7	17,000	15	7	15,000
15.4	6.5	11,000	20.8	4.8	23,700	20	5	20,000
18.6	5.4	13,000	25.0	4	28,500	28	3.6	28,000
27.5	3.6	20,000	40.0	2.5	44,000	40	2.5	40,000
39.5	2.5	29,000	60.0	1.6	65,000	60	1.6	60,000

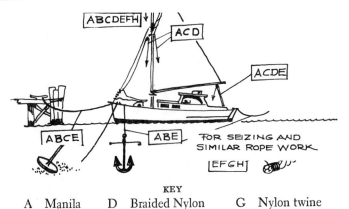

KEY

A	Manila	D	Braided Nylon	G	Nylon twine
B	Nylon	E	Braided Dacron	H	Linen
C	Dacron	F	Cotton		

1201 The right rope for the right service Note that the "poly" ropes are not generally recommended, though they may be acceptable for towing.

The synthetics' enemy, like manila's, is wear and chafing, and they should be protected by serving at points of wear (chocks, etc.). When unreeling, handle a synthetic line like wire rope and do not take the end from the center of the coil as you would manila or coil rope. Special techniques, discussed later, are required to splice synthetic rope.

1202   Rope is made by machinery that twists the fibers into yarns or threads, then twists the threads into strands, and finally the strands into finished rope. As the rope is built, each successive part is twisted in an opposite direction. Right-handed yarns make left-handed strands and right-handed rope, called *plain-laid rope*. Plain-laid rope twisted to form another rope will be left-handed, and is called *cable-laid rope*. Four-stranded rope, made for ease in passing over sheaves and for longer life, is right-handed, and has a small strand or heart laid in the center as a core. (*Figure* 1202)

Right-handed rope, held verticle, runs, //////////
Left-handed rope, held vertical, runs   \\\\\\\\\\

Plain-laid   Cable-laid   Four-strand
right-handed rope   left-handed rope   right-handed rope

1202

1203 A coil is a standard method of coiling a rope for shipment from the ropewalk and is 200 fathoms or 1,200 feet in length
no matter what the size. If a vegetable rope, not nylon, it must be
uncoiled in the following manner in order to avoid kinks: Loosen
the burlap cover and lay the coil, flat down, with the inside end
nearest the deck. Reach down through the center and draw this end
up and out. Coil down in lengths required in a clockwise direction,
i.e., from left to right. Any other method will put additional turns
in the rope, in which case it will have to be thoroughfooted.

1204 To thoroughfoot a rope, it is coiled down *against* the
lay (a right-handed rope is coiled from right to left). Then reach
down into the center (exactly as in uncoiling properly), draw the
end up and out, and coil down *with* the lay. If one end is belayed,
coil opposite the lay from the belaying point, dip the end down
through the coil, capsize the coil, and coil with the lay.

1205 Once out of the original coil, rope is coiled except when
in use.

Straight coil: Lay a circular bight on the deck, following it with
additional bights to the bitter end. Pass kinks and turns aft, coiling
with the lay. Capsize the coil and it will be clear for running.

Flemish down: Make a small tight circle of the free end and continue to lay down circles outside each other. The coil will be flat
and will resemble a wound clock spring.

Fake down: Lay the free end out in a straight line (as along the
waterways), then turn back a loop to form a close flat coil. Continue to lay flat coils with the ends on top of the preceding coil.

1206 Rope diameter is designated by "thread" as follows:

Dia.	³⁄₁₆″	4	thread
	¼″	6	"
	⁵⁄₁₆″	9	"
	⅜″	12	"
	⁷⁄₁₆″	15	"
	¹⁵⁄₃₂″	18	"
	½″	21	"

(Above ½″ diameter, rope is properly designated by circumference. This is approximately three times the diameter, but see Table
of Strengths.)

To determine the thread of a rope: Number of yarns per strand ×
number of strands = thread.

Strength. Manila rope strength may be roughly figured by squar-
ing the circumference and multiplying by 150 pounds. For instance,
a 3″ rope—3 × 3 = 9, 9 × 150 = 1,350 pounds as a safe working
load.

For nylon rope use the same formula but multiply by 250; for
Dacron multiply by 200. Note that the result is a working strength,
not a breaking strength.

1207 A hawser is any rope more than 5″ in circumference.

1208 Rope sizes above ½″ in diameter are correctly given or
called by their *circumference* in inches. (Thus a 3″ rope is 1″ in
diameter.) But line sold for small-craft use is nearly always measured
by diameter.

1209 Rope will last a long time if properly cared for. Such
care includes:

1. Keep rope clean. Avoid grit in fibers to guard against abrasion,
but if the rope does get gritty, wash it down and sun-dry immediately. Do not use water under force as it may drive the grit in further. To remove oil and tar, use a solvent of low power (like a paint
thinner or turpentine) and then, if at all possible, soak the area in
hot water, hose down *several times,* then sun-dry.

Avoid exposing the rope to wet or tacky paint, linseed oils, battery acid, or other chemicals *and* their fumes. Rust is slow to destroy but nevertheless ruthless. Discoloration by water is not dangerous and may be discounted as an enemy.

Look for breakdowns in the fibers, brittleness, and definite small
spots of deterioration. Not much can be done *after the fact* except
to retire the rope or use it for jobs requiring well under the working strength, such as docklines, fender-board lanyards, strops, and
baggywrinkle.

2. Start it right. Uncoil properly (*Paragraph 1203*) and avoid
kinks at all costs. Synthetic ropes are uncoiled by simply placing
the spool, reel, or coil on an axle of some sort (such as a broom-
stick between two chair backs) and taking it off as the spool turns—
the same way you take off wire rope from a spool. If a kink develops, work it out at once or it may be with you for the life of the
rope once strain is applied.

It is a good idea, when taking off only part of a coil, to tag the remaining end, for ease the next time rope is needed. When cutting synthetic line, tape both sides of the cut before slicing, to avoid unraveling.

3. Stow with care. Fiber ropes must be stored *dry*, or soon rot will set in and the rope will be destroyed. Synthetic ropes need not be dry for the health of the rope, but to keep a sweet, healthy ship and to discourage below-decks dry rot in wood boats, it should be dry. A good rule is: sun-dry all rope before stowing, no matter what the type or material.

Both Dacron and nylon suffer from undue exposure to ultraviolet rays and should be covered if long on deck, or stowed below or in deck boxes. They are apt to "go" first at the ends where rust from thimbles, shackles, etc., might have begun the deterioration.

4. Avoid abrasion and chafe. Anything that will cut even one tiny fiber—and successively many tiny fibers—should be avoided like the plague. This means, in their proper places, worming, par-

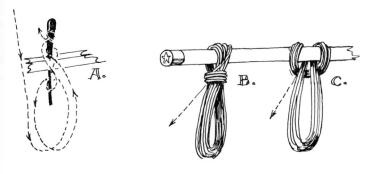

1209 *To coil sheets and halyards properly:* A) A halyard belayed to a pin or the horn of a cleat. Form the line, except the last half-fathom, into a coil, pass the end around the top of the pin, then through the coil and around the lower part of the pin; bring it back and take a clove hitch over the top of the pin. B) and C) *To stow main sheets:* B is merely looped over the boom and secured by a few round turns around the bundle. C is made by coiling the sheet in long bights then passing half over the boom and pulling it through the remaining bight until snug.

celing, and serving, the use of canvas or trade chafing gear (rubber hoses, canvas firehose, etc.) and chocks and hawses that are truly smooth and faired. Watch out for dockside mooring devices—heavy, unfinished castings, concrete mooring posts, rough pilings, or rough wooden cleats. In no case should a line be led over a rough edge, sharp edge, or any edge at all. This refers to decks, buffalo rails, dock-plank edges, cement dock edges, or another crossing line. If such cannot be avoided, pad and apply chafing gear.

5. Avoid knots insofar as possible. Knots weaken rope, sometimes permanently. They reduce working strength by 25 to 40%. A splice reduces strength about 10 to 15% only. A belayed rope (as on a cleat or bollard) loses about 40% of its original strength; the weakness is at the point where the rope leads from the belay to the load.

LOSS OF ROPE STRENGTH DUE TO KNOTTING AND SPLICING

Splices	Loss of Strength
Short splice	15%
Long splice	12.5
Eye (over thimbles)	7.5

Knots	
Bowline	40
Two half hitches	30
Square knot (reef)	50
Anchor bend	25
Clove hitch	40
Belay (as to a cleat)	40

6. Stow running rigging properly. Figure 1209 shows how. The idea is to stow (hang) in such a way that dew, rain, and spray will naturally run off and then the air will dry them rapidly. Reverse the running rigging from time to time to bring wear on newer parts of the rope.

7. Avoid too small sheaves in blocks. Wear here occurs both at the sheave and at the sides (cheeks) of the block. Here is a table of recommended block sizes:

CHART FOR MATCHING
ROPE TO BLOCK

Size of Block (Length of shell in inches)	Size of Rope (Diameter)
3″	⅜″
4″	½″
5″	9⁄16″–⅝″
6″	¾″
7″	13⁄16″–⅞″
8″	⅞″–1″
9″	1″
10″	1⅛″
12″	1¼″

8. Do not lubricate rope. This has been done at the ropewalk on both fiber and synthetic ropes and will prolong life and strength for as long as the rope lasts. You cannot help by adding proprietory compounds, no matter what the claim made.

9. Do not burn rope. Burning occurs when rope being handled by a winch or drum is allowed to slip. Both abrasion and burning can occur with severe damage to the rope. Do not freeze rope but if it freezes, never use it when frozen. The ice crystals cut deeply and destroy strength rapidly. This is less true of synthetics, which absorb far less moisture than fiber ropes.

1210 A worn or weak rope will look bleached and possibly hairy. The true condition may be determined by driving a marlinespike into a strand and opening it up. If it is powdery, the fibers broken or easily broken, or the strands pulled greatly out of a round shape, the rope may be considered weak and not to be trusted. Look for first wear *inside the rope*, especially in the way of blocks and lizards.

A worn or weak spot in a synthetic line will have visible broken strands, usually pin sharp and readily discovered by feeling the area. Look for wear at points of flex, such as at a block. Suspect any synthetic line that has been exposed to acid, its worst enemy. In unclean harbor waters, near large cities and industrial areas, acid may well be present and dangerous, especially to nylon line.

SMALL STUFF

1211   Small stuff (or cordage) are lines of 1¾″ in circumference or less, and are usually designated by "threads," 24-thread or 1¾″ rope being the largest. Halyards, sheets, and other running rigging lines are not considered small stuff, but lines.

Small stuff includes the following cordage:

Marline: For seizings and general service. It is two-stranded and laid left-handed. Untarred, it is used for sennit. Tarred, it is used in rigging.

Spun yarn: Loosely laid, multistranded, tarred, spun yarn is used for seizings and general service of a temporary or emergency nature.

Seizing stuff: Heavy seizing line. A finished rope, usually right-handed and three-stranded. It is tarred.

Ratline stuff: As above but in sizes 6–24 thread.

Houseline: Three-stranded, left-handed, for general uses.

Roundline: Three-stranded, right-handed, for general uses.

Hambroline: Two-stranded, right-handed, of fine-quality yarns.

Whiteline or codline: Small stuff, untarred.

Sail twine: Small, light-cotton stuff, for sewing canvas.

Fishermen's lines, while not truly "small stuff," may be considered so by yachtsmen in need of less than working lines. Here are their characteristics:

Lobster pot warp. Now almost exclusively of poly types, in sizes 6-thread (¼″ diameter) to 15-thread. ³⁄₁₆″ diameter pot warp is called 6-thread fine.

Haul, seine, gill net, and outhauler rope. Available in all sizes and is soft layed, both fiber and synthetic.

Shrimp net rope. In all sizes and especially layed to prevent kinking.

Purse seine rope. A hard lay rope in many sizes.

Crab line. Hard 6 thread fine.

Swordfish warp. Medium lay 6, 9, and 12 thread.

PARTS OF A ROPE

1212   Any rope, when being knotted or bent or hitched divides itself into three parts. It is customary to refer to these parts when giving instructions in knot tying. They are:

The standing part: The long unused or belayed end.

The bight: The loop, or half loop, formed by turning the rope back on itself.

The end: The remaining short end. (If passing through a block it is called the *fall*.)

KNOTS, HITCHES, AND BENDS

1213   The knots, hitches, and bends following are all that the average boatman will require. They should be thoroughly and well learned; then used in the right place. At least the bowline, reef (or square) knot, half hitch, and clove hitch should be used and the user able to tie these in the dark, under water, behind the back, or with one hand and the teeth. A "good" knot is not always the one which serves the situation best, but the one that can be securely tied under the circumstances, that will not jam if it becomes wet or frozen, and that will not chafe the line unduly.

Overhand Knot

Stopper knot to keep the end of a rope from fraying or running through a block.

Reef or square knot

Strong, will not slip, is easily tied and easily cast off, even when wet or frozen, by pushing the standing parts and ends against each other. Should not be used when trying two ropes of different circumference.

Sheet bend

Used for securing a small rope to the bight of a larger rope. May be double for extra holding power.

Double carrick bend

Used for joining large ropes, such as hawsers. As there are no sharp bends, it does not cripple the rope fibers. It passes through chocks and hawseholes easily. The ends must be seized to standing parts for security.

Bowline
Called the king of knots. It will not slip. A double turn is taken around rings, etc., to prevent chafing.

Bowline on a bight
A strong, secure loop, which can be made in a rope, both ends of which are to be belayed.

Two half hitches
A temporary fastening to a spar or Samson post. For extra security, or on a line not under constant strain, seize down the end.

Clove hitch
A secure fastening which can be made over a post or yardarm even with the ends belayed. It will not slip either way. Recommended only for a line on which there is a constant strain.

Figure eight knot
A fine stopper or end knot. Easily made to keep a line from running through a block and does not crimp the rope. Study it; it is just two turns of the standing part around itself and drawn tight.

Fisherman's knot, or overhand
Used for joining two lines, made by securing each end to the opposite standing part by an overhand knot.

Fishermen's bend
Used for making fast to a spar or ring. It is popular, with ends seized to standing part, as an anchor knot.

Timber hitch
Good fastening and will hold when hauled at acute angles to a spar, or when hauling a spar, or sending aloft.

Rolling hitch
A hitch that can be moved along the spar by slacking off, then putting strain on again. Also used to make fast to the standing part of another rope.

Belaying to a cleat
Make the turn around the cleat first; then form a bight in the fall, turn half over, and slip over the cleat ear.

Mousing
A seizing to prevent a hitch or sling from accidentally jumping off the hook.

1213

WHIPPING AND END KNOTS

1214 All rope ends require either burning, whipping, back splicing, or one of the crown knots to prevent the rope from unlaying. Whipping is used if the rope is to be passed through a block. A knot is used to prevent the rope from passing through a block by accident (such as the end of a sheet or halyard) as well as to keep the lay intact.

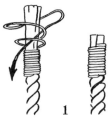

1214A Whipping

Whipping is done by one of the methods shown in Figure 1214A. The whipping is small stuff; for most small boats codline or sail twine will be suitable. A dab of paint or varnish will prevent the whipping from wearing or slipping off.

The synthetics are handled quite differently—by flame. A match, cigarette lighter, hot knife, or soldering iron held briefly to the strands or yarns will effectively fuse the ends together. When handling the synthetics, it is well to remember that they are slippery —especially polypropylene—and will unravel much faster than fiber rope. It is usual to wrap the ends *before cutting* with masking or other tape and then cut. To whip (if you do not care to burn) form the whip below the band of tape, making it extra long and tight and only then cut. An electrically heated "tile cutter" is very useful for cutting synthetic line because it seals as it cuts and prevents immediate unlaying of the slippery strands.

The backsplice
The crown is made as shown, hauled taut, and the ends tucked over and under the strands of the standing part. It will not pass through a block.

The wall knot
Make the crown, haul taut, relay the strands, and whip the end. A wall and crown knot is made by laying a backsplice crown over the wall crown and cutting off the ends.

1214B Other treatments for rope ends

Stopper knots are simple knots that are temporarily tied to prevent rope ends from unlaying. The overhand knot is the one generally used. Better, especially for the slippery synthetics, is the figure eight. Likewise, for joining the synthetics use the sheet bend rather than the square knot or the fisherman's overhand (*Figure 1213*). Remember—always—that synthetic line needs extra turns or tucks to give it friction. Dacron will hold its strand shape and requires only end whipping to keep it in original form. Nylon immediately disintegrates into a brush of unformed strands and yarns; it must be confined before cutting. This is especially noticeable when splicing and it is wise to tape each strand of nylon almost the full length to be tucked.

1215 Splicing is the art of joining any two parts of a rope together permanently. Splicing introduces all the strands involved to each other in such a manner that a continuation of this introduction will result in re-laying the rope with equal tension on all the strands.

The most important step in splicing is the start. Introduce (or marry) the strands correctly and the remaining steps follow almost automatically. (*Figure 1217*)

To prepare the rope for splicing, unlay the end for about 12″ to 18″, tape or whip each end, if the rope is over 21 thread, with a temporary whipping or seizing of small stuff. If the rope is four-stranded, the heart is cut off short where the unlaying commences.

A tapered tool of wood or steel (called a fid or marline spike) is used to aid in opening the lay of the rope at the point where a strand is to be introduced. On small rope mere twisting of the rope *against* the lay will open it sufficiently for hand tucking.

Four tucks will hold any splice providing they are full strands; i.e., not tapered off. Tapering off is made after the fourth tuck, and is done by reducing all strands by one third, tucking, reducing by another one third, and finally tucking and trimming off close. For neatness, or to prevent chafing (as in the eye splice of a mooring line), the splice may be served with small stuff. Serving is started at the "thin" side of the splice and proceeds outward, served against the lay, and ended as in a whipping. A serving board is used for ropes of large circumference; and worming or parceling or both may be done under the serving.

Again, be warned against splicing the synthetics. Their smoothness makes them require added friction in the form of increased tucks of the full strand—six is sufficient—and longer tails for tapering, which means additional final tucks also. After completion of such a splice, pass the splice over a hot, quick flame to burn off the hairy yarns that may remain. It is not necessary to burn the ends of a tapered splice. If not tapered, put in a few extra full-strand tucks and burn the ends—but *do not* seal these ends to the standing part!

THE SHORT SPLICE

1216 For joining two ropes that do not have to pass through a block, or small chocks, or spill pipe, etc. (*Figure 1216*)

"Marry" the ropes first (with a seizing around the standing part if there is an inclination to unlay), then seize down one set of strands and proceed with tucking in the other set, over and under for four tucks. Cast off the strand seizing and tuck the first set, over and under. Do not trim too short if untapered. Shape the splice by rolling underfoot. Very large ropes may require pounding with a wooden mallet as the tucks are made to preserve shape.

1216 The short splice

THE LONG SPLICE

1217   For joining two ropes together without enlarging the diameter (as for a rope that is to pass through a block):

Unlay six to eight times the circumference of each rope and "marry" exactly as for the short splice. Now, unlay one strand carefully and lay in the matching strand from the opposite side. Repeat now with *two strands* but in the opposite direction. Two strands will remain in the center and the splice appear as in A, Figure 1217.

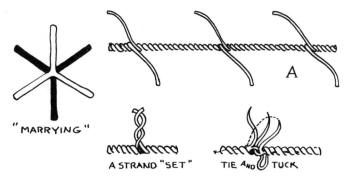

"MARRYING"

A STRAND "SET"   TIE AND TUCK

1217 The long splice

Each set of strands is now cut short, divided and an overhand knot tied with them. Each end is then tucked once *with the lay*, reduced again, tucked and trimmed. The splice must be rolled or pounded into shape and size. Well made, it should appear as a continuous length of rope.

THE EYE SPLICE

1218   The eye splice is used to form a permanent loop in rope, the end being spliced into the standing part. "Marrying" is the important step and is shown in Figure 1218. The first two tucks are shown left and middle; the right-hand cut shows the splice turned over, strand three tucked and the strands all hove taut.

Proceed now over and under, as in short splicing, in rotation. May be tapered and served.

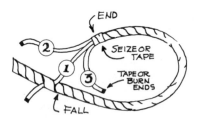

1. Lay out rope on table or lap like this. Seize or tape end. Unlay rope about 20 to 24 times the rope diameter, being careful not to unlay the strands. Tape or burn strand ends. Separate rope at point of joining with fid or marling spike. Select the middle strand (usually the top one) at the seizing and pass in through the opened rope, pulling through about 2 inches of the strand. Call this number 1 so you can follow the diagram.

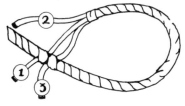

2. Now pass strand number 3, which is the one to the right of the middle or number 1 strand and pass it through the opened rope strand of the fall next to and right of where number 1 enters. Pull through about 2 inches of the strand.

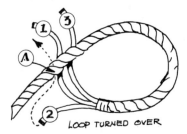

3. Then turn the loop over, with the fall still to your left. It will look like this. Now pass the remaining strand, which is number 3, under the lay of the rope next to and to the left of where number 1 exits from the rope lay. This strand is marked A on the diagram and the remaining loop must pass under it.

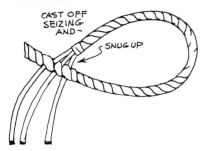

4. Turn the loop over again, as it was when started. Note that now each strand exits from between each of three successive rope strands and looks like this. Pull the tucked strands through until the end, with the seizing cast off, lies snug against the fall. To complete the splice forget about numbers and just tuck over and under each strand under the rope lay to the *left* . . . i.e., follow the lay, over and under. 4 to 6 tucks and the same number of taper tucks are sufficient. Seize the splice for a real yacht job after burning off the thread ends and a mild beating into shape.

Figure 1218 How to eye splice

ADDITIONAL KNOTS, HITCHES, AND BENDS

1219   Granny (or lubber's) knot. A misformed square knot, dangerous because it slips.

Single carrick bend. For joining large ropes and hawsers. The absence of sharp bights makes it easy on the rope.

Reef point (or slippery reed or draw knot). For tying-in reefs in sails. May be quickly cast off by jerking the fall.

Fisherman's knot. For securing leaders or trolling lines together.

Rope-yarn knot (or marline knot). Small and tight knot for tying small stuff together.

Heaving-line bend. For tying a small rope to a large one, and for making fast the heaving line to a hawser.

Reeving-line bend. For connecting two hawsers or cables. The ends must be seized securely.

Running bowline. Slip noose.

French bowline. Useful for sending men aloft or over the side. The man sits on one loop, passing the other under the armpits and leaving both hands free.

Granny

Single carrick bend

Reef point or slippery reef

Fisherman's knot

Rope-yarn
or marline
knot

Heaving-
line bend

Reeving-
line bend

1219A

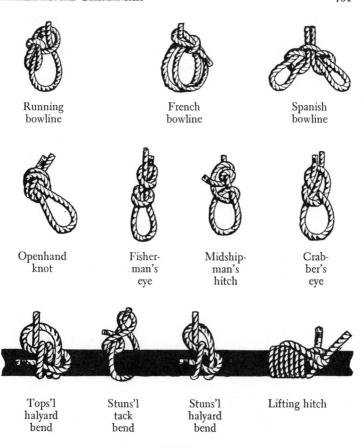

Running bowline   French bowline   Spanish bowline

Openhand knot   Fisherman's eye   Midshipman's hitch   Crabber's eye

Tops'l halyard bend   Stuns'l tack bend   Stuns'l halyard bend   Lifting hitch

1219B

Spanish bowline. Two loops, neither of which will slip.

Openhand knot. A quickly formed loop, but dangerous as it will jam.

Fisherman's eye. Another loop form.

Midshipman's hitch. A useful knot. It will not "set up" until hauled taut over an object within the loop; therefore it will hold.

Crabber's eye. A no-slip noose.

Tomfool knot. Two loops, both of which can be drawn taut and held.

Jury masthead knot. Placed over the masthead, each loop may be used to secure stays or halyards to. Sometimes used on sheerlegs.

Round turn and two half hitches. The double turn relieves the strain on the hitches.

Killick bend. For extra security. The left-hand part of the bend is the timber hitch.

Stopper hitch. Used to fasten a rope to a spar or the standing part of another rope. Can be slid, then hauled taut.

Tops'l sheet bend. For bending a sheet to the clew of a sail.

Tops'l halyard bend. To make a rope fast to anything.

Stuns'l tack bend (buntline hitch). Strong, providing there is constant strain on it.

Stuns'l halyard bend. A simpler and quicker form of the tops'l halyard bend.

Lifting hitch. For lifting, or when the strain is to be exerted parallel to the spar.

SEIZINGS

1220 Seizings are lashigns of small stuff of a more or less permanent character, such as the seizing used for rattling down shrouds. Any small stuff is suitable and should be tarred if it is expected to remain exposed for any length of time, or if it is part of the standing rigging. (*See Figure 1220*)

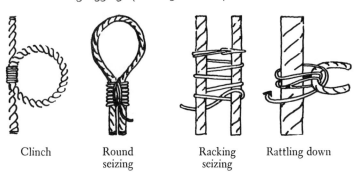

Clinch   Round   Racking   Rattling down
              seizing   seizing

1220

Clinch (or throat seizing). Used to secure a bight on the standing part of a rope, to take another rope, or a block or a tackle.

Round seizing. Used to hold two or more ropes together or one rope in a bright. Ten to twelve round turns are passed around the parts and these secured by two or three frapping turns taken around the round turns.

Racking seizing. Another method of securing several lines together. It is very strong and nonslip. Note the eye at the start. (A round seizing is used when all the strain will be from one end. A racking seizing is indicated when the strain will be from alternating directions.)

Rattling down. Used to secure ratlines to the shrouds. On steel shrouds, a few frapping turns are taken around the seizing for extra power.

END KNOTS

1221 Double wall knot. (*See* Figure 1213) Made exactly as the wall knot, but each strand is followed around again until the end comes out on top.

Diamond knot. Made exactly as the wall knot, but each strand is brought up through the bight of the second strand.

Manrope knot (Double wall and crown). Make a single crown, then *underneath* it make a single crown around the standing part.

Matthew Walker knot. Starts as a single wall knot but each strand is taken under the two other strands and brought up alongside their own parts. *Keep the twist in the strands.* (*Figure 1221A*)

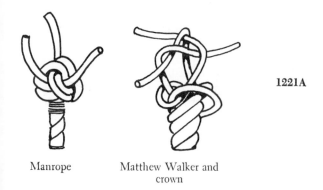

1221A

Manrope   Matthew Walker and
                        crown

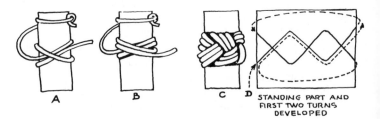

STANDING PART AND
FIRST TWO TURNS
DEVELOPED

1221B Three-strand Turk's-head

The three-strand Turk's-head. A separate knot, not made with the rope's own strands. Used for rope's ends, tiller handles, stanchions, and for other ornamental uses.

As shown in Figure 1221B, tie short end out of the way (A) and make the end into a clove hitch. Follow the clove hitch around, making a two plait; then follow again, making a three plait. This is the principle of making the knot. To make the overlays or convolutions of the knot, several hitches of the bight, over and under, are taken (D) and the lay of it followed for three or four strands round. The ends are tucked under and cut off.

ADDITIONAL SPLICES

1222   Sailmaker's splice. (*Figure 1222A*) Make the first tuck in the same manner as the ordinary eye splice. Follow with the other strands then, but *around* the strands of the standing part and *with the lay* (not over and under). Two full tucks, then taper for four tucks, makes a long neat splice and takes leather serving well.

Flemish eye splice. (*Figure 1222A*) Unlay all strands for about a foot; then unlay one strand further for the full length of the bight to be made. Form the eye by looping the two (paired) strands around to the point where the single strand has been unlaid. Lay up the single strand in its own groove but in the opposite direction. Finish by tucking the three strands as in the common eye splice. It gives additional strength and a short splice, as two tucks are sufficient to hold it.

Cut splice. (*Figure 1222B*) Each end is made as in the common eye splice, the standing part of one end splicing into the standing part of the other. Both sides of the eye should be the same length.

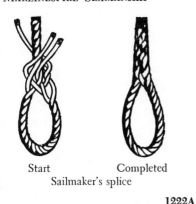

Start   Completed
Sailmaker's splice

Flemish
Eye splice

1222A

Cut splice

Chain splice

1222B

Chain splice. (*Figure 1222B*) Unlay the end and reeve two of the strands through the chain link or shackle. Unlay the third strand back still farther, following it and filling its groove by one of the first two (rove) strands as in the long splice. Tie overhand knot and tuck, exactly as in long splice. The remaining end is tucked and tapered where it is.

ROPE-TO-WIRE SPLICE

1223 This is a handy but very difficult splice, and most professional riggers have a self-developed method for making it. The rope part is unlaid and the strands tapered *at once*. Then the wire part is unlaid *in pairs* and the two parts married as for the short splice. Proceed, over and under, with the wire part only, for *several feet*, halving the wire pair to one at the finish. The splice

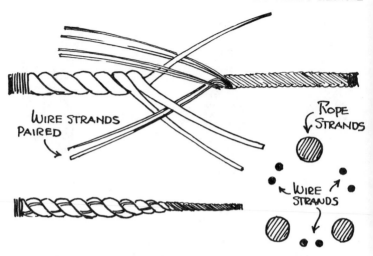

1223 Rope-to-wire splice

must be very tightly served for its entire length. Professionals sometimes (as with 7 x 19 wire) end the splice by sewing in the wire strands individually, using a sail needle.

1224 The splicing of braided line is quite a different art. One of the most popular brands issues instructions for the yachtsman in step-by-step drawings. Note that special tools are required, available from the rope manufacturer at nominal cost. Needed are: a fid, a pusher (an ordinary ice pick), tape, knife, and marking pen. The process is shown using only these aids, which are surely available to the layman.

PROTECTING ROPE FROM WEAR

1225 Rope requires protection from wear when subject to handling on deck, on docks, or where it passes over or through fixed objects, such as bollards or chocks. Serving usually offers ample protection and has the advantage of not stiffening the rope the way complete protection does.

To keep moisture, dampness, and frost out of the rope, mainly that which is used as standing rigging, it is wormed, parceled, *and* served. This makes a very stiff rope, hardly flexible enough for rope which is required to run.

Worming is done with small stuff which fills the lay evenly and presents a fairly uniform surface for the *parceling*, which is done with strips of canvas. Sometimes, as in the case of standing rigging, the parceling may be wrapped so as to shed water, like shingling, the lap being down. Parceling is sometimes painted with red or white lead, or hot tar, and immediately *served* with small stuff, often tarred, wound tightly over the parceling with the aid of a serving mallet.

The turns proceed as in the following jingle:

> Worm and parcel with the lay,
> Turn and serve the other way.

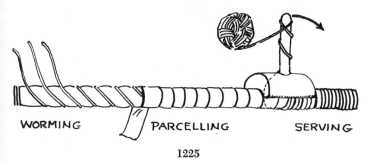

WORMING   PARCELLING   SERVING

1225

WIRE ROPE

1226   Standard wire rope consists of a center around which is laid six strands. Strands consist of 7, 12, or 19 wires each. (*Figure 1226*) Wires are made of galvanized iron, cast steel, plow steel, and sometimes copper, bronze, or phosphor bronze. The coppers are generally much less strong than iron wire of the same diameter. The most enduring wire is made of stainless steel and other alloys, usually nonrusting and very much stronger than ordinary steel wire.

Wire rope is always designated by the *diameter* of the rope, not the circumference as in fiber rope. It is put out in reels or coils. Reels should be placed on a spindle and the wire used directly from it. Coils should first be rolled (like a hoop) and the wire taken from it in this way, not as from fiber rope coils.

If wires and strands are laid in the same direction, it is called *lang-lay* wire rope; if in opposite directions, it is called *regular-lay* wire rope, the lay of most yacht rigging.

Yacht wire today is almost universally of stainless steel. It is preformed as is all wire rope today. Special terminal fittings are required, with various manners of attachment. (*see Paragraph 1227*)

COMMON WIRE SPECIFICATIONS AND USES

7 × 7	For running in blocks, halyards, tiller cables, lifelines, Genoa sheets.
7 × 19	Semi-flexible uses, including backstays and topping lift.
1 × 19 (or 19-wire strand)	Standing rigging.

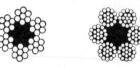

7 x 7   7 x 19   1 x 19 or 19-wire

1226 Common wire-rope forms

1227 To form wire into terminals or join to another wire, several methods are in use. These are splicing; wire-rope sockets, usually requiring highly specialized equipment to attach and causing the entire assemblage to be "custom made"; and wire-rope clamps. The use of clamps is for temporary joining or eyeing only (such as to make up a wire towline) and it is considered lubberly to use clamps in standing-rigging applications.

The near universal use of stainless steel preformed wire today has almost eliminated hand splicing of wire from the rigger's art. Terminal fittings of stainless steel designed to connect wire to chain plates, snaps, shackles, blocks, vangs, and other wire are available but require special equipment to exert the super-high pressures needed to press together the wire and the fitting. In small yacht sizes, the average sailmaker's loft would have the wire, fittings, and special hand tools required to furnish complete rigging assemblies. In larger sizes (⅝″ diameter and upward) power machinery is required. Some full-service yacht yards and most ship chandlers can have this work done on a custom basis. In both cases *exact* lengths are required, measured most carefully with a steel tape and allowances made for the insertion of turnbuckles, lizards, etc. in the assemblage.

There are other methods of terminal-affixing beside the above, (which is a patented process called Nicro-press). One method makes use of a threaded cone that spreads the wire strands and forces them into grooves in a tubular cavity in the terminal fitting. It is difficult to exert sufficient power by hand to make a wire-to-terminal connection as strong as the wire or fitting itself and, in addition, this type of attachment is subject to eventual further weakening from corrosion of the more-or-less mangled strands. Another method, which is well suited to genuinely "heavy" requirements, provides a large terminal with a basket-like depression into which the wire-rope end is inserted and sealed there by pouring in hot metal, usually a lead-zinc alloy. This is sometimes seen on really large cruising yachts, especially in the standing rigging.

1228 By and large, hand splicing of wire is not for the average pleasure boatman. It requires a great deal of specialized equipment, many tools, special benches, vises, and rigging screws, and hands of tanned leather—the hand-splicing of wire is a bloody business! For the rare wire-splice that may have to be done by hand, the novice should understand and use the simple grommet splice. This is easy to understand, can be done by anyone with today's pre-formed wire and is, properly made, quite as strong as other forms. While the figure and instructions relate to the eye-splice, it can be formed over a thimble as well and thus readily joined with other rigging parts by a common shackle; or to the shackle-end fittings of many blocks, turnbuckles, etc. (*Figure 1228*)

WIRE-ROPE CLAMPS (CLIPS)

1229 These are U-shaped units, used to make temporary splices or eyes, with or without a thimble. The correct-sized clip must be ordered for both the size and type of wire.

They are correctly applied only when the U (or staple) grips the end and the shoulder grips the standing part. Any other manner of application will crush the standing part and weaken the entire line. All clips are put on the same way, not staggered. Three clips are sufficient for any splice so made.

Another form of wire-rope clamp is made (especially for tiller cables), both parts of which are scored and which exert equal

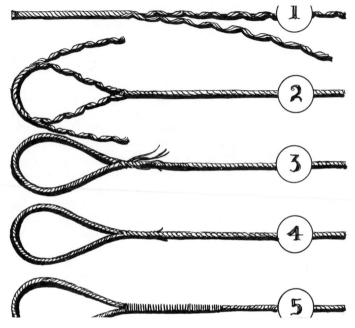

1228 How to grommet splice

1) Cut wire rope off clean. There is no need to whip the ends as preformed rope will not spring apart. Unlay, three strands on either side, carefully retaining natural curves, a length just twice the circumference of the eye to be formed.

2) Draw the two groups toward each other without unnatural bending and tie a simple overhand knot. The knot will form a small-sized section of complete rope at the top of the bight.

3) Now lay each strand into the loop, letting the strands fall in their grooves. The fiber heart should be worked in carefully as the laying up proceeds. Bring the ends snug to the crotch and cut the individual strands off at varying short lengths from 1″ to 2″.

4) Work these ends into the lay of the standing part by tapping with a wooden mallet.

5) Serve the ends down tightly with stainless steel annealed serving wire, drawing it taut with a wire serving tool.

Properly done, this splice is just as strong as a tucked splice and can be finished in one quarter of the time.

TABLE OF BREAKING STRENGTHS—WIRE ROPE

7 x 7 CONSTRUCTION

Diameter, Inches	1/16	3/32	1/8	5/32	3/16	7/32	1/4	9/32	5/16	3/8	7/16	1/2	9/16	5/8	3/4
Bronze	77	172	306	478	688	940	1,225	....	....	....	....	....	....	....	....
Galv. Iron	236	459	711	980	1,220	1,580	1,980	2,400	2,720	3,900	5,280	6,860	8,640	10,600	14,200
Galv. Cast Steel	....	....	....	....	....	....	3,500	4,300	5,600	7,800	10,600	13,600	17,000	20,800	29,600
Galv. Plow Steel	....	....	....	....	....	....	4,200	5,300	6,570	9,270	12,400	16,200	20,300	24,800	35,600
Stainless Steel	355	780	1,150	2,000	2,750	4,000	4,800	6,100	7,500	10,600	14,200	18,500	23,400	28,800	36,900

7 x 19 CONSTRUCTION

Diameter, Inches	1/8	5/32	3/16	7/32	1/4	9/32	5/16	3/8	7/16	1/2	9/16	5/8	3/4
Phosphor Bronze	....	....	....	....	2,140	....	3,310	4,720	6,370	8,300	10,400	12,700	18,000
Galv. Cast Steel	....	....	....	....	3,500	4,300	5,600	7,800	10,600	13,600	17,000	20,800	29,600
Galv. Plow Steel	....	....	....	....	4,390	5,400	6,840	9,650	12,800	16,500	20,500	25,400	36,100
Stainless Steel	1,280	2,000	2,900	3,950	5,090	6,700	7,900	11,100	14,700	19,000	23,800	29,100	41,500

1 x 19 OR 19-WIRE STRAND CONSTRUCTION

Diameter, Inches	1/16	3/32	1/8	5/32	3/16	7/32	1/4	9/32	5/16	3/8	7/16	1/2
Stainless Steel	500	1,100	2,100	3,200	4,600	6,100	8,000	10,000	12,500	17,500	23,500	28,500

pressure on both parts of the wire. They have the advantage of not crushing the wire at any point. One is sufficient for tiller cables. In general, they do not have the strength of a U-clip because the setup is by slotted screw and not by bolt and hex-nut.

GLOSSARY OF ROPE TERMS
1230

Becket   A rope eye for the hook of a block. A rope grommet used as a rowlock; any small rope or strap serving as a handle

Belay   To make fast to a cleat or belaying pin

Bight   A loop formed by bringing the end of a rope around, near to, or across its own part

Bitter end   The last part of a rope as it is paid out; the last link of an anchor chain

Chafe   To wear the surface of a rope by rubbing against a solid object

Coil   To lay down rope in circular turns

Cord   A small rope made by twisting several strands together

Cordage   Ropes or cords; anything made of ropes or cords; used collectively as in speaking of that part of the rigging of a ship composed of ropes, etc.

Fid   A tapered wooden pin used to separate the strands when splicing heavy rope

Frapping turns   Cross turns; turns taken around and perpendicular to the turns of a lashing or seizing

Heart   The inside, center strand of a rope

Heave   To haul or pull on a line; to throw a heaving line

Heave taut   To haul in a line until it has a strain upon it

Irish pennant   The frayed loose end of a line

Jam   To wedge tight

Kink   A twist in a rope

Knot   A twisting, turning, tying, knitting, or entangling of ropes or parts of a rope so as to join two ropes together or make a finished end on a rope, for a certain purpose

Lanyard   A line attached to an article to make it fast, as a knife lanyard

Lashing   A passing and repassing of a rope so as to confine or fasten together two or more objects

Line   A general term for light rope

Marlinespike   An iron or steel pin that tapers to a sharp point, used to splice rope

Marry   Laying two lines together side by side or end to end for the purpose of splicing

Nip   To pinch or close in upon

Part   To break

Pay out   To slack off on a line, to allow it to run out

Rack   To seize two ropes together with crossed turns of lighter stuff

Rigging   A general term applied to ship's ropes, chains, and gear that support and operate masts and spars

Round seizing   To seize two ropes together

Secure   To make fast

Seize   To bind two ropes together

Slack   The part of a rope hanging loose; the opposite of taut

Splice   The weaving of the strands of a rope or ropes by intertwining them to make a strong union

Standing part   That part of a line which is secured

Stopper   A short line, one end of which is secured to a fixed object and used to check or stop a running line, as a boat fall stopper

Strap   A rope ring or sling, made by splicing the two ends of a short piece of rope. Used to handle heavy objects. Small straps used to attach a handy billy to the hauling part of a line

Swage   A special process of mechanically attaching terminal fittings to wire-rope rigging

Take a turn   To pass a line around a cleat or belaying pin to hold on

Taut   Tight; snug; tightly drawn; opposite of slack

Thimble   An iron ring with a groove on the outside for a rope grommet or splice

Toggle   A small piece of wood or bar of iron inserted in a knot to render it more secure, or to make it more readily unfastened or slipped

Trice   To haul up and secure

Unbend   To untie or cast adrift

Veer   To allow rope or chain to run out; to slack off

CHAPTER XIII

BLOCKS AND TACKLES

1301 A block is a mechanical device, like a pulley, to change the direction of the pull of a rope—wire, synthetic, or fiber. It may be needed either to change the direction of pull to "give a better lead" (make it more convenient) or to multiply the power of the pull.

BLOCKS

TABLE OF SHEAVE SIZES FOR VARIOUS ROPE DIAMETERS
(in inches)

Rope Diameter	Sheave Size		
	Diameter	**Score Width**	**Pin Diameter**
⅜	1¾	½	⅜
½	2¼	⅝	⅜
⅝	3	¾	⅜
¾	3½	1	½
⅞	4¼	1	½
1	5	1⅛	⅝

When blocks and rope are combined to multiply power it is called a *tackle.* The following terms are used in connection with a tackle:

Falls—That part of the tackle made of rope

Standing part—That part of the falls made fast to one of the blocks

Hauling part—The end of the falls to which the power is applied

Round in—To bring the blocks together

494

Overhaul—To separate the two blocks

Reeve—To pass the rope through the block, over the sheave

Two-block—To bring the two blocks together (or chock-a-block)

1303 Wire rope should pass over sheaves of very much larger diameter than other rope to reduce fatiguing. Special wire-rope blocks are manufactured, usually with iron or steel shells and sometimes with specially designed sheave grooves, to accommodate the various lays of wire rope. A wire rope ending in a manila or synthetic rope pennant should pass over a sheave grooved for pennant and having a wire-rope groove scored into it.

All types of blocks can be had with ball bearings or other types of frictionless bearings. They are desirable for any block handling regular rope over 2″ and wire rope over ¼″.

Cheek blocks are made to be permanently fastened, sheave against the flat of the object fastened to, and are usually leading blocks (such as those at the foot of a mast used to lead halyards aft). They are generally of all-metal construction.

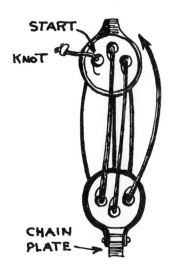

Reeving deadeye lanyards

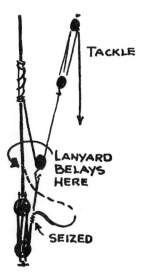

Setting up rigging

Deadeyes (archaic) are a type of sheaveless block, used to set up standing rigging. A tackle is first clapped on the two ends to be set up, then a lanyard rove between the upper and lower deadeyes more or less permanently, it, too, having been set up with the aid of a tackle.

1304 Wooden blocks are generally metal-strapped, though occasionally rope-strapped blocks are still seen, especially aloft. They are called by the number of their sheaves (single, double, triple, fourfold, etc.) or, when part of the rigging of a vessel, by their purpose (sheet block, tops'l halyard block, jib halyard lead block, etc.).

If the block has a latching device, permitting the rope to be rove without the delay of threading it through the swallow, it is called a *snatch block*. These are often used for lead blocks, as when changing direction of the pull between a capstan and a tackle. Single metal-bound blocks are called *gin blocks*. A *secret block* is one having a casing entirely around it, the parts of the falls emerging from two holes in the casing. *Cargo blocks* are of steel, the shell being diamond-shaped.

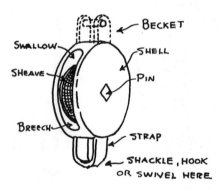

1304A The parts of a block

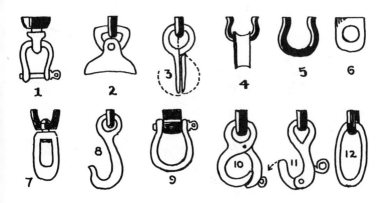

1. Swivel with upset front shackle
2. Flat sheet bridle
3. Front sister hooks
4. Eye and thimble
5. Lashing eye
6. Solid eye
7. Swivel eye
8. Front backstay hook
9. Front shackle
10. Front Coleman hook
11. Anchor trip hook
12. Front ring (or link)

1304B Block fittings

The explosion in sailing fleets has brought forth a vast number of block designs for sailboats, especially racing sailboats. Most of these are designed to save weight (important aloft) and to reduce windage. The shells are of fiberboard, plastic, Tufuol (a proprietary name for a plastic-impregnated fabric), stainless sheet steel, aluminum, and cast aluminum. Sheaves and terminal shackles are usually of

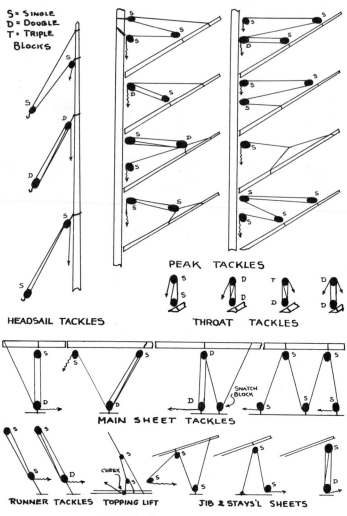

S = SINGLE
D = DOUBLE
T = TRIPLE
  BLOCKS

PEAK TACKLES

HEADSAIL TACKLES

THROAT TACKLES

MAIN SHEET TACKLES

SNATCH BLOCK

RUNNER TACKLES   TOPPING LIFT   JIB & STAYS'L SHEETS

CHEEK

1306 Yacht rigging tackles

stainless steel or a tough plastic and bearings may be ball or roller bearing. Especially sensible designs have come from Sweden and Germany; when such designs are coupled with European craftsmanship, they provide excellent yacht blocks and rigging hardware. Catalogs for this sort of equipment are endless; just check through any yachting periodical. Generally considered, yacht blocks of modern design and construction need to be attached with matching deck and spar straps, eyes, etc.

1305 A general formula for selecting the correct block size follows:

Length of block—three times the circumference of the rope.

Sheave diameter—twice the circumference of the rope.

TACKLES (*Pronounced tayckles*)

1306 Tackles are used to multiply power. Such multiplication can go on almost indefinitely, or until friction becomes so great that there remains no further advantage in multiplying the power. Power is gained at the expense of time; a tackle that increases power by four, for example, must be hauled four times as far (requiring four times as much time) but requires but one fourth the power, friction not considered.

1307 Fixed blocks do not increase power; they merely change the lead. The movable blocks alone provide gain in power.

1308 The block having the greatest number of parts should be placed at the weight to be moved. The number of rope parts leading from the movable block indicates the number of times the power has been theoretically increased.

1309 To determine the power required to raise a given weight with a tackle, divide the weight to be raised by the number of rope parts at the movable block (or blocks). The quotient will be the power required to produce a balance, friction not considered.

Example:	Weight to be moved	1,200 pounds
	Tackle parts	4
	Power required for balance	300 pounds (pull)
	Estimated loss by friction	20%
	Pull required for balance (300 plus friction)	360 pounds

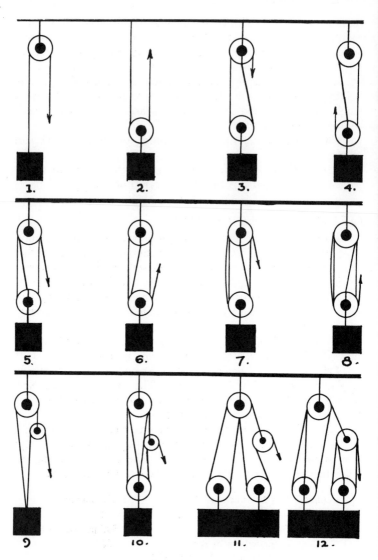

Table of purchases

	Friction Not Considered	Friction Considered	Power Required
No. 1, Single whip	$P = W$	$\dfrac{P}{W} = \dfrac{11}{10}$	1 W
No. 2, Single whip, inverted	$\dfrac{P}{W} = \dfrac{10}{20}$	$\dfrac{P}{W} = \dfrac{12}{20}$	½ W
No. 3, Gun tackle	$\dfrac{P}{W} = \dfrac{10}{20}$	$\dfrac{P}{W} = \dfrac{12}{20}$	½ W
No. 4, Gun tackle, inverted	$\dfrac{P}{W} = \dfrac{10}{30}$	$\dfrac{P}{W} = \dfrac{13}{30}$	⅓ W
No. 5, Luff tackle	$\dfrac{P}{W} = \dfrac{10}{30}$	$\dfrac{P}{W} = \dfrac{13}{30}$	⅓ W
No. 6, Luff tackle, inverted	$\dfrac{P}{W} = \dfrac{10}{40}$	$\dfrac{P}{W} = \dfrac{14}{40}$	¼ W
No. 7, Double purchase	$\dfrac{P}{W} = \dfrac{10}{40}$	$\dfrac{P}{W} = \dfrac{14}{40}$	¼ W
No. 8, Double purchase, inverted	$\dfrac{P}{W} = \dfrac{10}{50}$	$\dfrac{P}{W} = \dfrac{15}{50}$	⅕ W
No. 9, Spanish Burton	$\dfrac{P}{W} = \dfrac{10}{30}$	$\dfrac{P}{W} = \dfrac{13}{30}$	⅓ W
No. 10, Double Spanish Burton	$\dfrac{P}{W} = \dfrac{10}{50}$	$\dfrac{P}{W} = \dfrac{15}{50}$	⅕ W
No. 11, Bell purchase	$\dfrac{P}{W} = \dfrac{10}{70}$	$\dfrac{P}{W} = \dfrac{17}{70}$	⅐ W
No. 12, Luff on luff	$\dfrac{P}{W} = \dfrac{10}{160}$	$\dfrac{P}{W} = \dfrac{26}{160}$	1⁄16 W

1310   A man can pull about 150 pounds maximum, providing he has a firm foothold and is in such a position as to exert his fullest power. This may be down, up, or sideways, and is made up of dead-weight pull and muscular pull, the back muscles being the most powerful.

1311   To determine the amount of purchase (power of tackle) required to raise a given weight with a given power, divide the weight that a single rope will bear multiply by the number of parts at the moving block.

Example:	Weight to be moved	1,200 pounds
	Power available	400 pounds (pull)
	Rope parts needed, therefore	3
	For friction	1
	Total rope parts	4

1312   To determine the weight a given tackle will raise, multiply the weight that a single rope will bear by the number of parts at the moving block.

Example:	Single rope will bear	400 pounds
	Tackle parts	3
	Weight the tackle will raise	1,200

1313   When one tackle is clapped upon another, multiply the two powers together to obtain the total amount of purchase gained.

Example:	Tackle #1	3 powers
	Tackle #2	2 powers
	Total power	6

1314   Angles created by using a rope sling greatly increase the load factor as the sling angle changes from vertical to horizontal. The diagram (*Figure 1314*) shows the load increases rapidly as the angle sharpens. Note that the load at 90° is doubled at 30° and is double-doubled at 15°. Here is the formula used to figure safe loads for slings of known angles:

$$\frac{2 \times \text{tensile strength (of rope)} \times \text{sine of angle}}{5 \text{ (factor of safety)}} = \text{safe load}$$

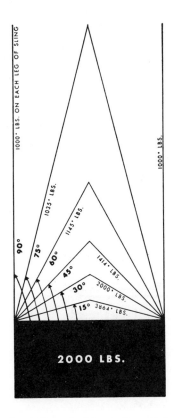

1314 All weights indicate load borne by each leg of the sling.

Thus: For 1″ diameter rope at a 60° angle. Rope strength is 9,000 pounds. The sine of 60 is .866

$$\frac{2 \times 9,000 \times .866}{5} = 3,117 \text{ pounds or safe load.}$$

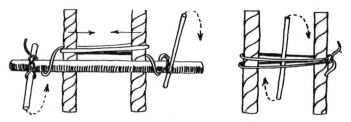

1315 Two forms of the Spanish windlass

1315 The Spanish windlass is a blockless tackle, oftentimes handy. (*Figure 1315*) It is used mainly for rigging jobs.

1316 The parbuckle (*Figure 1316*) is a blockless tackle for taking spars or casks up the side or up an incline (as the gangplank).

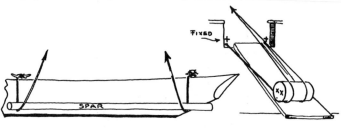

1316 The parbuckle

TO MAKE UP A TACKLE

1317 Place the blocks about three feet apart, hooks pointing up,and coil down *with the sun*, coiling around the blocks. With the end of the fall, clove hitch the tackle about midway between the blocks. Store only if thoroughly dry.

TO FLEET A TACKLE

1318 Place on deck exactly in the position as when made up. Cast off the hitch, lift the coil clear, and capsize. Separate the two blocks.

CHAPTER XIV

DECK SEAMANSHIP

DECK SEAMANSHIP is that branch of seamanship embracing the practical side of boat handling, from the simplest rudiments of marlinespike seamanship up to navigation. It does not include engineering knowledge. The good deck seaman understands and can expertly practice his part of the following maneuvers and operations covered in other chapters of this *Manual*.

In addition, some elemental knowledge of other departments will help to round out the subject. These include, for example, taking soundings by the lead, reading the log, signaling, Rules of the Road, and quartermaster duties (steering and steering orders).

What is presented following is by no means the complete coverage of the subject of deck seamanship. It is, rather, what an average yachtsman would normally be called upon to understand, explain, or himself perform in the course of normal yachting cruise or work sessions. It is certainly what a paid hand would be expected to know well or a family member be expected to know if a regular member of the crew.

Nevertheless, this part of the art must be thoroughly understood by the skipper so that he can instruct others to become his intelligent helpers or, more likely, be able to "do it himself"! In conjunction with what the skipper *must* know, the areas covered by this chapter attempt to instruct others in their roles in the manuevers and procedures which require help. In that sense they become deckhands, and it might be a sensible and prudent notion for all on board to read this chapter and so relieve the hard-pressed skipper of the necessity of personally instructing his deckhands.

HANDLING CARGO AND STORES

1401   Loading the small boat as for an extended ocean cruise is generally not a job calling for complicated cargo-handling gear. What cannot be carried can be handled easily by a jury boom rigged to the masts, or by use of the existing spars fitted with special tackles.

In rigging such jury booms it is essential that the boom-hoisting tackle be secured to the boom at approximately the same point at which the cargo tackle or sling is attached. It would not do, for example, to attach a load to the middle of the main boom and hoist it with the topping lift.

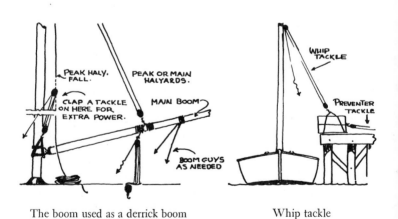

The boom used as a derrick boom   Whip tackle

1401

Whips may be rigged (*Figure 1401*) and are very convenient for taking on a deck load.

1402 For vessels without spars, some form of the sheerlegs make handy derricks. (*Figure 1402*) In guying such hoisting rigs, the sheerlegs must rest on a chafing pad of wood or folded canvas to protect the deck, and the fitting to which every guy is fastened must be carefully examined for strength. Many deck fittings, such as ring bolts and cleats, will stand a tremendous side strain but very little direct pull against the fastenings. Do not trust a fitting that is not fitted with a washer and nut or headed over a washer. Ring bolts, which are often placed on a deck as a convenient place to hook a block to change the direction of a *horizontal* lead, should not be used.

Guys, well padded, secured to a fixed part of the vessel (as a mast, bitts, Samson post) or to a round turn around the vessel's counter itself, are the most secure.

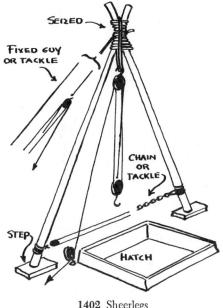

1402 Sheerlegs

1403   By remembering always that the vessel is a movable object or platform, many handling problems become simple. To shift a deck load while the boat is moored to a dock, for example, it is simple to hoist the load by means of a derrick *from the dock* and move the boat under it.

This principle is used in removing heavy engines forward from under a bridge deck, up and then aft, through the hatch, and onto the deck or dock, and saves rigging skids and horizontal purchases.

1404   Slings are usually endless ropes, spliced together to provide a bight for the lifting block hook. The object moved must be raised with a pinch bar to adjust the sling and set down on a block or roller, the sling thrown off, and then the object set fully down. (*Figure 1404*) Engines and machinery should be handled with chain slings or spark-plug hole balancing eyes, screwed into the head of the engine. Many engines are manufactured with lifting rings. The purchase must be made fast above the shaft line in order not to capsize the machine.

In making a rope sling the turns should be taken out of the line before splicing. This is done by coiling the line down *against* the lay and bringing the bottom end up through the coil and short-splicing

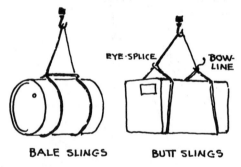

BALE SLINGS   BUTT SLINGS

NON-SLIP SPAR HITCH

1404

the ends. A chain sling should have a ring or long link on one end and a hook on the other. A swivel between load and movable block will permit better handling and placing of the load.

1405   Dunnage is loose wood and wooden blocks laid under and between items of cargo and other items or structural parts of the boat (as mast heels, bulkheads, etc.).

It serves the further purpose of raising the cargo above any bilge water and affords ventilation between items. Dunnage is absolutely necessary for the laden vessel putting to sea. It should serve to prevent the cargo from moving in any *direction*.

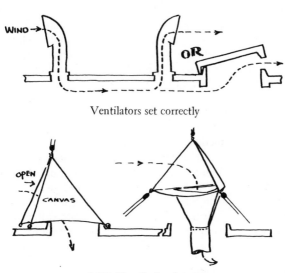

Ventilators set correctly

1406 Ventilation for cargo

1406   Cargo is stowed with liquid always below the dry cargo; barrel bungs *up;* all case markings *up*. Barrels of fuel are stored on deck, ready to be jettisoned in case of fire or other emergency. The small boat should have the heaviest cargo on the bottom, concentrated amidships and near the center line.

In stowing stores to be used during the voyage, great care must be used to make the stores available as might be needed. Careful marking of cases, concentration of like items together (foods grouped, spare parts grouped, tools grouped, etc.), and a full and detailed cargo list and cargo plan are required. Ventilation is of the utmost importance, and a good day at sea should see hatches opened and a wind scoop rigged. The principle of ventilation is to create a draft. A ventilator merely turned to catch the breeze will not ventilate unless there is an outlet.

DECK CARGOES AND STOWAGE

1407   The disposal of cargo on deck is always secondary to the safe operation of the boat. No cargo should ever make it difficult to get at the lifeboats, main bilge pumps, winches, etc., or close up hatches or companionways. In general, and especially if the cargo is heavy, it is best stored amidships, and adequately protected by tarpaulins in such a manner (by lashing) as to positively not shift as the boat rolls and pitches or as it is attacked by boarding seas.

Dunnage should be placed under it always. Cases should be permanently marked with paint, not gummed labels. No baled or inflammable cargo should be placed in the lee of galley stacks or exhaust stacks. Casks and barrels should be stowed forward of cased items to form a protection from spray.

1408   If cargo must be jettisoned (as under storm conditions) heave it to windward and from a point as far aft as possible. Heave floating cargo into the top of a sea, not the trough, or it might "come back." It is dangerous to lighten liquid loads by broaching the casks (except water casks). If it must be done to save time, close all hatches and openings to below decks to prevent fumes, possibly explosive, from collecting in the hull.

MOORING TO A DOCK

1409   When a boat is moored alongside a dock in a more or less permanent manner, mooring lines are put out as follows:

Bow lines. Lines run from the inshore bow to the dock bollard (or cleat or pile head) at an angle of about 30° to the keel.

Stern lines. The same, except that a stern line may lead from an offshore chock.

Breast lines. Lines which lead from the bow and stern chocks, or chocks of their own, at right angles to the keel.

Spring lines. Run from chocks at the bow or stern to the dock at an angle to pull opposite to the bow or stern lines.

The length of line between chock and dock bollard is called the *drift*. After a ship is moored, the drift should be of equal tension on all lines so that the strain is equally divided. If the tide or wind is liable to set the vessel against the dock, fenders may be used, rigged with a fender board as shown in Figure 1409B, but it must be certain that there is no possibility of their "hanging up" on the piles, where there is a rise and fall of tide.

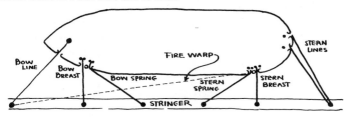

1409A Mooring a vessel

Breasting off   Fending off

1409B

1410 Mooring a large boat is not merely a matter of tying it up. The lines serve at first in conjunction with the rudder and screw to warp the vessel sideways into her berth, and the order of passing lines will come from the helm.

A boat approaching a dock bow first will need the bow line passed, then the bow spring. As her stern swings abreast, the stern line will be required, then the stern spring, and, lastly, the breast lines.

If she is approaching bow first with a strong tide or wind setting her against the dock, other maneuvers may be called for, possibly fenders and breast lines first.

1411 When heaving a dock line, coil about one third of the free end in the heaving hand. Coil the remaining line loosely over the palm of the free hand, arranged so that the outside turns will run out smoothly and without fouling. The heave is made with a sweeping side-arm motion, not directly at but slightly over the person ashore who is to catch it. If the first cast misses, do not try a second until the line is properly re-coiled as above.

1412 If it is necessary to slack off a hawser from the bitts (as when leading it to a winch) a stopper is clapped on to take the strain while the change over is being made. Such a stopper is shown in Figure 1412. The fall must be held onto or belayed.

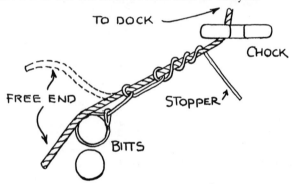

1412 Clapping a stopper on a mooring hawser

DINGHY BOOMS

1413 Only large boats are equipped with boat booms, yet the dinghy on a stern painter constitutes a problem as wind and tide swing it against the boat. (*Figure 1413*)

While the dinghy can often be kept clear by setting a light anchor or some drag off its stern, or hanging a bucket with the bottom punctured from its transom, thus discouraging its "nursing the ship," one of the booming methods in Figure 1413 is more satisfactory.

1413 Jury boat booms

A shows the spinnaker boom or other light spar lashed to the main boom and the dinghy sent to its outboard end on an endless line. B shows the spinnaker pole guyed as a regular boom. The dinghy painter may be rove to an endless line or merely made fast while the boom is alongside, it being controlled by the forward guy.

In a swift tideway, a sea painter may be led over the dinghy's inboard bow and it will ride away from the ship. However, when there is tide enough to accomplish this, the boat will stay astern. It is a useful wrinkle in a crowded anchorage, or if a dinghy light cannot be set at night when the dinghy is moored astern.

TO RIG A BOSUN'S CHAIR

1414 When work aloft or over the side is to be done, the worker may be hauled there in a bosun's chair. (*Figure 1414*) The important part of the chair is the fall and belaying it in a safe manner to make yourself fast aloft.

This is done, once you have reached the point at which the work is to be done, by reaching up above the bend in the bridle eye and seizing both the hauling and standing parts of the fall in the left hand, taking a good grip calculated to hold your weight. The tender on deck now slacks off the hauling part. You reach down and take a generous bight of the slack, pull it through the bridle, slip it over the head, down over the shoulders, and under the chair and the legs. Let the slack overhaul itself until the bight is brought tight and jammed inside the bridle.

To lower away, pay up the hauling part of the fall and let yourself down gently.

If there is no line affording communication to the deck (as on a spar), take a rope aloft, fastened to a leg of the bridle. Paint, tools, etc. can then be hauled aloft as needed.

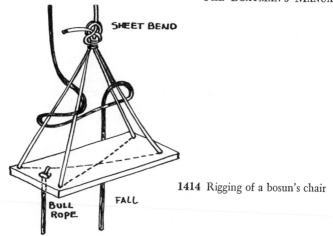

SHEET BEND

1414 Rigging of a bosun's chair

BULL ROPE

FALL

TO RIG A SCAFFOLD

1415   Scaffolds, or hanging stages, are sometimes needed when painting topsides. The plank should be at least 2″ by 12″, with not more than 10′ between bridles nor extending more than 2′ beyond

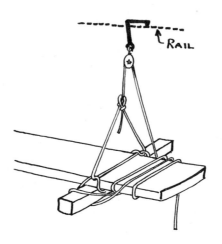

RAIL

1415 Rigging a stage

bridles. Yellow pine or spruce is suitable. Beware of fir, white pine, or soft woods.

Rig the bridle into a bowline with two or more turns around the plank.

A scaffold can be breasted in under the counter by heaving inboard with lines made fast to deck. Breasting into the side may be done with the help of a hook into a port light frame.

TO RIG A GANGPLANK

1416 The small-boat gangplank need seldom be more than a 2″ by 12″ sound plank, rigged between the boat and the dock. If there is a rise and fall in tide, the boat end should be securely lashed permitting the dock end to move. A cleat nailed under the boat end will catch the rail or toe molding to prevent its slipping outboard. Steep gangplanks should be covered with fiber matting or should have light battens nailed across as treads. If possible rig a manrope alongside, as a handrail.

A loading plank must be extra heavy (or double planks) and have no cleats. If material is being taken aboard in hand wheelbarrows, nail two parallel cleats along the center of the plank as wheel tracks.

Special Duties of Deck Seamen

LOOKOUT

1417 Lookouts, wherever stationed, must be on the alert for, and immediately report, vessels, land, rocks, shoals, discolored water, buoys, beacons, lighthouses, floating objects, signals being made, or *anything else which might be of interest to the skipper.*

The lookout is to assume that the skipper has not seen the subject of his report until his report is acknowledged.

1418 Lookouts report anything so sighted in relation to the vessel, not to the compass nor the wind. This system of reporting is called *relative bearings from the ship.* The outboard perimeter of the ship (the rail) is considered a circle divided into 32 sections or points; 16 from ahead to astern on each side.

When an object is sighted, it is reported, for example, "Nun

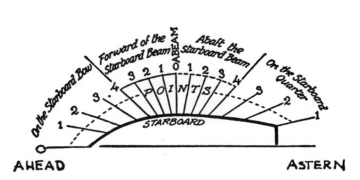

AHEAD   **ASTERN**

1418 Relative bearings The bearings on the port side are designated
the same way

buoy two points on the port bow." Further description may at times
be required as, "Floating object," "Object awash," "Moving object,
possibly a whale," or, "On the horizon," or, "Close aboard."

General Instructions for Lookouts

1. Be alert and attentive.
2. Do not divide your attention.
3. Remain where posted until regularly relieved.
4. Repeat a hail or a report until acknowledged by the skipper.
5. On lookout duty at night, check the lights once a watch.

1419 At night, a dim light can be seen more easily by looking first at the sky *above* the horizon, then dropping the eyes *to* the
horizon. Sweep the horizon, then the sky just above the horizon.

Stand in the dark and be careful that no light shines in your
eyes. Lighting a match, or a flashlight, or tending a coal-stove fire
all cause temporary blindness, lasting for several minutes.

"Look out" with the ears as well as the eyes. In fog or thick
weather, take a post away from engine and other noises and listen
only. Report even the *suspicion* of a fog warning. Fog plays tricks
with sound—it may not be heard again, it may be farther away or
much nearer than it sounds, or in a different direction.

HELMSMAN

1420 When acting as helmsman on a boat under sail, the
steering instructions may be in one of the following forms:

1. *Make the best course*—Steer "by the luff" or the best course possible as to speed with due regard to tide, sea, etc. This order puts the helmsman on his own and requires a knowledge of sailing as well as steering.

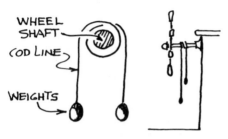

1420 The shrimper's rudder indicator is simply a length of cod line, with a weight (sinker, bolt, nut) on each end that is thrown over the wheel shaft a few turns. The port weight down indicates a port rudder.

2. *Nothing to port (starboard)*—Take extra precautions to prevent the vessel wandering off course in the direction indicated.

   Helm down—Push the tiller to leeward.

   Helm up—Push the tiller to windward.

   Ease the helm—Hold it more amidships.

   Steady—Approval of the boat's course; continue to keep her sailing on it, using the helm without direction from the skipper.

   1421 When being relieved at the helm, always give the relief the exact course and have him repeat it; then report to the skipper or watch captain that you have been relieved. If any peculiarities of steering have developed, such as a tide or wind set, or a change of trim, the new helmsman should be told about it.

   Engine speeds, towed vessels, and other problems related to steering are not normally problems of the helmsman on a large yacht. If he is steering under orders, his duty is to steer only. If he is "in charge" of the boat and steering as well, he may (and on the small boat is quite likely to be expected to) take full command of the ship's movement along the course given.

TO HEAVE A LIFE RING

1422 The life ring or horseshoe buoy is thrown overboard at the cry of "Man overboard," or before the cry, if the man is discovered. If a water light is attached, this is thrown with the ring, *night or day*. If the swimmer is still within range, throw the ring *near* him, not *at* him. A heavy ring or its light can stun a man easily.

It is the duty of the man nearest the life ring (or rings) to get it overboard at once, without orders, then to raise the cry (if not already raised), and keep his eye on the man overboard and his arm pointed at the swimmer. (*See also Paragraph 1615*)

If not underway, a ring buoy with a line may be thrown. This is thrown exactly as a heavy line is thrown. If the line is fitted with a knotted end, it is placed under the left instep. If with a loop, it is slipped over the left wrist. Be very sure that the line will reach the swimmer's position before throwing it. If the buoy fetches up on a short line it will recoil *backwards*, away from the swimmer.

HEAVING THE LEAD

1423 When detailed to "take soundings" by the hand line, the small lead or blue pigeon (7–14 pounds) is used.

A position is taken slightly forward of amidships on the windward side. The line is held about 6′ to 10′ from the lead at the toggle (not always provided) and swung fore and aft; then, when sufficient momentum has been achieved, it is swung twice around with the clock and released on the forward upswing. As the lead enters the sea ahead of the leadsman's position the slack is taken in until the leadsman "feels bottom" or the line is straight up and down; the depth quickly read and reported to the navigator and then the line taken in handsomely.

It must be handed in rapidly and kept clear of the propeller. As the water shallows, soundings are taken more frequently. If directed by the navigator (as in making a soundings track) it is done by time casts, and the time to sound will come from the bridge.

The depth is read from the marks (*Figure 1423*) *at the waterline*. If at night, the line markings are *felt* (or felt with the tongue) at the rail, the distance from rail to water deducted, and the true depth at the waterline reported.

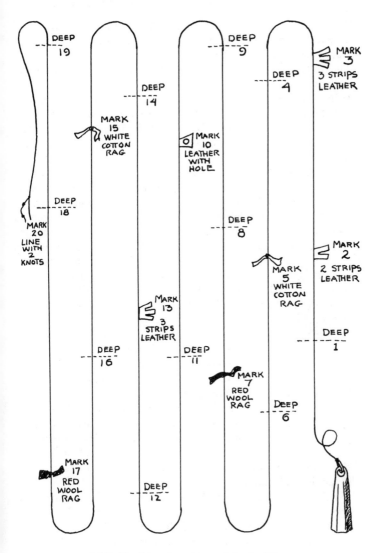

1423 Traditional markings of the lead line

The first two casts are not reported. These are the "soaking casts" and serve to shrink the line to its length when the markings were first attached (always attached to a wet line).

The following is the traditional terminology used in reporting soundings:

When the depth corresponds to any mark on the lead line it is reported as: "By the mark seven," "By the mark nine," etc.

When the depth corresponds to any fathom between the marks on the lead line it is reported as: "By the deep six," "By the deep eight," etc.

When the depth is judged to be a fraction greater or less than that indicated by the marks it is reported as: "And a half seven," "And a quarter five," "Half less seven," "Quarter less nine," etc.

Arming the Lead. This is done by filling the concavely grooved depression in the bottom of the hand lead with tallow, grease, or some similar substance. A sample of the bottom is thus brought up for examination and is reported, following the sounding report, to aid the navigator in determining his position by comparing the bottom reported with his chart. After reporting, the tallow is wiped clean or the lead rearmed if the tallow is below the surface of the depression.

Bottoms are reported, after examination of the sample as follows:

Clay	Shell	No sample
Coral	Stones	Rock (may be "felt" by
Gravel	Weed	bouncing the lead)
Sand (fine or coarse)	Mud (soft, red, black, etc.)	

On a modern yacht, the line is usually ticked off in feet, either with numbered plastic tags or with a piece of small stuff rove in at the marks (long piece for 5', short piece for each foot between) and is about 30' total length. It is good practice to mark off in feet one of the dinghy oars, or a "settin' " pole, to have a convenient depth ruler handy at all times.

1424 The proper use of various types of fire extinguishers likely to be found on small craft is as follows. (*Figure 1424*)

1. Soda-acid (foam) type. This is for use in extinguishing wood, paper or fabric fires and its fumes are detrimental to fabrics and paint. The motion of the vessel tends to mix the chemicals within the extinguisher and it may be found to be "dead."

This kind of fire can be better fought with the newer types of extinguisher—a CO_2-operated cartridge or a pressurized water unit. (Water is very effective against alcohol fires.)

The foam type is also effective against oil or gasoline fires in *static pools*. It will not subdue flames from burning lacquer thinner or some solvents. (For this use the dry chemical type.)

Warning. The foam type is dangerous to use on electrical fires or near electrical apparatus. It leaves a damaging residue.

2. The Carbon-dioxide (CO_2) type. This type is effective on all kinds of fire, including electrical fires, if not too deep-seated. It is the extinguisher to use when fire is first discovered and it readily extinguishes liquid or gasoline fires. It is non-poisonous and will not injure fabrics, paint, clothing or food. Automatic or manually operated systems are available which flood the bilges, tank and engine spaces, and sometimes are piped over the entire ship. Installation of this type, if an approved make, will result in savings in insurance costs.

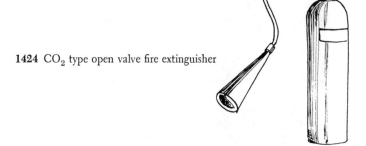

1424 CO_2 type open valve fire extinguisher

3. Dry-chemical type. This extinguisher discharges finely powdered bicarbonate of soda under high pressure and is an extremely efficient fire suppressor for all kinds of fires. It is far less costly than other types; or, at least, the refills are. An objection is that it leaves a residual dust, which must be picked up by vacuum cleaner. This type is probably the kind that is most commonly used on boats today.

Discharge all extinguishers into the base of the fire first; then work upward. Aim to take advantage of wind or draft. Do not let the fire get between you and your escape route. If explosion seems imminent or certain, get off the ship, you can't save her anyway but you may save your life. Before trouble arises, read the directions on your extinguishers and make certain that you and anyone likely to handle them understand how they work. Try a practice run—it doesn't cost much. And, after practice or fire, *refill the extinguisher*.

Helpful Hints for Deck Seamen

TO FOLD THE U. S. FLAG

1425   Fold it lengthwise four folds (*Figure 1425*); then fold in triangular form toward the canton. The flag must never touch the deck and should be gathered in the arms as it falls. Stow it in the flag locker, not between staff and halyards.

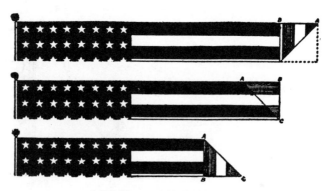

1425 How to fold the U. S. flag

STOWING OTHER FLAGS AND PENNANTS

1426   These are rolled around themselves or around the staff. If stowed in a flag locker, the canvas tabling strip is outside, the bottom of the flag toward the opening, and the name of the signal clearly inked on the tabling strip (or border).

ORDER OF MAKING AND DOUSING COLORS

1427 The U. S. flag is always raised before any other flags (such as club or private signals), and lowered after them. (*See* Chapter XVIII for correct flags to fly, and when.)

COVERING SAILS

1428 Small headsails or yawl mizzens should be taken in. It is simpler than covering them.

Sails to be covered should be carefully furled and stopped down; do not depend upon the cover to hold them secure.

Lay the cover (unroll it) along the boom, fit and lace the throat, making all snug at the gooseneck, halyards outside the cover and the neck drawn tight to shed rain and dew. Then work aft, unrolling, drawing taut against the throat and tying down with slippery reef knots.

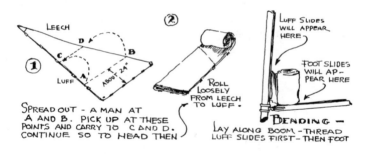

1429 How to fold and bend sails

FOLDING SAILS

1429 After thoroughly dry, sails may be folded as shown in Figure 1429 for rapid bending when used again. Note that two edges will show sail slides—the foot and the luff.

All battens must be removed first and puckering lines slackened. After folding, stow in the sail bag and keep dry.

DO NOTS FOR DECK SEAMEN
1430

Never smoke on deck while taking on fuel, or near open hatches.

Never go up or down ladders with both hands full.

Never work in the hot sun without protecting your head.

Never walk under a hoisting boom or sheerlegs.

Never walk on the weather side in a heavy sea.

Never walk on oily or slippery decks with smooth rubber soles.

Never wear sea boots on deck if it can be avoided.

Never stand in the bight of a line or cable.

Never work aloft or overside without a safety line.

Never trust a line or tackle until tested as safe and secure.

Never go on deck, knowing that you will get wet, without protection.

Never assume anything: investigate, inspect, and test.

BODY AND SOUL LASHINGS

1431   Storm clothing is worn to keep warm by keeping dry, so although warm woolen clothing, not too bulky, should be underneath, every attempt must be made to keep it dry. Deck work under

1431 Storm clothing lashings
(body and soul lashings)

storm conditions may soon see the average suit of foul-weather gear "leaking" due to wind. Lashings may be placed as shown in Figure 1431 to make wind stops.

A small Turkish towel around the neck will help keep water from trickling down inside. "Fisherman" type waterproof canvas gloves are soft, flexible, and waterproof, but not too warm for summer wear. In winter, wear warm gloves under them.

The secret of keeping warm is keeping dry.

TOWING

1432 The deckhand should understand the art of towing; he will be of vital importance to the success of the maneuver because he handles lines, etc. The skipper should detail the maneuver and explain exactly how he means to tow, on a line or alongside, and the hand should immediately break out the correct lines, fenders, etc.

For a genuine tow, prepare a *long* line of manila, Polypropylene, or nylon; nylon being the best because it has the most spring. Lay it out in *capsized* coils on the after deck so that it will pay out readily and without fouling. If you suspect a problem because of the seas running, also prepare a heaving line with a weight, or monkey's fist, on the end. Attach this to the towline so that the towee can haul the towline aboard. If the towline has an eye splice, send it to the towee; you need the free end on the towboat.

Pass the line when the skipper orders it and instruct the towee (what a word!) as to your intentions. Once he has secured the line to his bow post or cleat, he can do little to assist except, if possible, steer, keeping his boat in your wake. Should the boat be on fire, first get the people off; then worry about the boat itself. In such a case, if you cannot get near, try to heave a small grapnel anchor on a short chain into the cockpit or through a sash so that, at least, you can tow the burning boat away from other boats or the dock.

For a sea tow, pay out line, over a stern post or quarter cleat as the skipper applies power, keeping a strain until the towing length has been reached. The skipper will then stop the towing boat (the towee not yet having way on) while you make the line fast.

If available, a towing post or bitts in the towboat's cockpit make the best point of attachment, but these are seldom fitted in the average pleasure boat. A mizzen mast will also serve, if there is one.

However, the average small boat usually has only quarter cleats, and these are usually too flimsy for this kind of work. Since the chances are that sooner or later you may have to take a boat in tow, survey your craft now with an eye to performing that service. Beef up quarter or midships cleats by getting larger fittings, with oversize backup plates on the underside of the deck. If the deck itself is too flimsy, you may have to use the deckhouse itself, taking a padded line completely around it.

To maintain some kind of steering control, the towline's point of attachment to the towboat should be forward of the towboat's propeller. If you use quarter or side-deck cleats, use both of them and

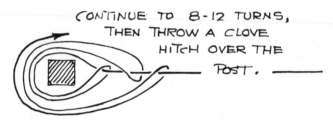

1432 The towboat hitch

rig a bridle over the stern, with the towline attached to its center. Pad the towline where it chafes the hull.

A manila line, under towing strain, will stretch up to 10% of the length—and snap back viciously if a break occurs. Nylon will stretch 25% and snap like a giant rubber band. Both can kill. Stay away from the towline!

Tow so that both vessels are on the same wave plane; i.e., if the towboat is on the forward side of a wave, the towed boat should also be on the forward side of a wave. Use a long, springy line in a seaway. Shorten it in calmer waters and shorten again when about to enter harbor or traffic. If the towee cannot be steered, get the weight (live weight as well) into her stern so she will track more obediently.

1433 If there is no sea or traffic is heavy, it may be wiser to take the tow on the quarter, or "nested." The secret of this is to keep the wheel and rudder of the towboat well astern of the stern of the towee. Properly lashed and fended, the two become a single unit and handle exactly like, and with the ease of, a single unit. Be sure to rig a backing line also. The towed boat should "toe" into the straight-line course of the towboat; not much; 3° to 5° is sufficient to take all the strain from the rudder of the towboat and permit normal rudder angles. (*See also* Chapter III.)

DECK CHORES

1434 In washing down brightwork or paint, use fresh water only, no soap. If dried salt spray is present, rinse the chamois in a second bucket of fresh water; then wring out and rewet in clean fresh water. (Decks should be swept or swept and swabbed first.) Clean topsides at freeing ports or scuppers. Glass is cleaned best using a chamois, well wrung out and with a spot of ammonia in the water.

Brass work should first be rid of dried salt spray, then polished with a good yacht brass polish. Weathered brass or stubborn spots may be brightened by a touch of muriatic acid. Weatherproof waxes applied to the surface will provide a more durable polish.

Extensive paint cleaning is done with a commercial cleaner and plenty of water. High-gloss paint should not be cleaned with an abrasive powder; flat paint can be. Stains or waterline oil streaks can be softened with a paste made of soft water and cleansing powder or an equal amount of powdered soap or detergent.

Rubber matting can be cleaned by rubbing with bronze wool. Paint spots can be removed by applying a hot knife to the spot. Seagull guano should be removed immediately and the spot well washed with water. (It will "eat" into paint, varnish, or canvas in short time.) Rust spots showing through paint (nail sickness) can be cured only by digging out the putty or bung, painting the rusting fastening with thick red lead or white lead; then reputtying or rebunging and touching up the spot with surface paint. Gasoline will remove exhaust smudge on the transom. A fine wire brush will remove scum and growth along the waterline.

⚓

CHAPTER XV

BOAT AND ENGINE MAINTENANCE AND REPAIR

GENERAL REPAIR AND MAINTENANCE WORK

1501 Every boat, however small, should be equipped to make minor repairs at sea. Tools needed in addition to a full complement of engine tools and the usual splicing tools should include the following at least:

Tool Kit for a Small-Boat Cruising Sailor

Ballpeen hammer with 8″ handle but full-weight head
10″ hacksaw frame, spare blades
Small combination wood saw
Several sized screwdrivers, standard and Phillips head
Non-magnetic screwdriver (to fit compass)
Several-sized files
Several-sized chisels
Small wrecking bar
Pliers (electricians, slip-joint, and vise grip)
Metal snips
Hand awl with assortment of bitts
Small hand drill with assortment of drills
Caulking iron and wooden mallet
Measuring tape or pocket ruler
Bolt cutters and socket wrench set (if power boat)
Assorted electrical tape, waterproof sail tape, galvanized wire, screws, bolts, machine screws, washers, waterproof grease, epoxy cement, lubricating and penetrating oils.

A small bench vice is always handy, as well as a T-square and ruler. Tools not regularly used should be oiled to prevent rust and kept in the dryest locker, above the waterline.

The paint locker should include several sealed jars of matching paint so that odd spots can be touched up during the season. White lead, putty, liquid marine glue, and turpentine come in handy. Several small sash brushes, a varnish brush, and an artist's or lettering brush will serve for touching up.

Nothing is useless at sea. A general but small "junk box" should be kept for all manner of small string, nails, wire, bolts, etc. As a foundation for such a store box there should be an assortment of nails, screws, nuts and bolts, leather and metal washers, spare wire, a "snake" for cleaning plugged lines and pipes, a length of rubber tubing for siphoning, a small funnel, spare bulbs and fuses, etc. A few lengths of board, a piece of plywood, piece of inner tube, cork, sail canvas, sheet lead, and strip brass may each have their uses in emergency repairing.

The type and combination of repairs at sea are unpredictable—but "anything might happen." In the following pages some of the more common types of repair work and maintenance are explained.

HOW TO CAULK

1502   (*Figure 1502*) A shows a hollow seam which can never be made tight. B shows a seam that has been caulked too tightly and that will "throw" its putty.

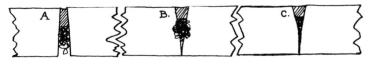

1502

C shows a seam correctly caulked. Note that the cotton has been driven down securely but has not scarred the plank edges. After caulking, the cotton is payed with paint and when set, puttied over. For "hooking out" old caulking there is nothing better than a file tip, heated and bent into a sharp reverse hook.

At considerable nasty and fussy effort, it is sometimes possible to make seam A watertight again. With a sharp, wide chisel, or an electric ripsaw blade, set at about 7°, held against a batten guide tacked to the deck, it may be possible to restore the correct shape to the seam. Finished, it should look like B or C, but much wider. Recaulk about half its depth with oakum, flush with the bottom; then run paint into the seam and let it set. Next caulk lightly with cotton and fill with a silicone-type rubber base seam compound. To get a neat, flush seam, first cover the edges of *both* planks with masking tape; then fill the seam. When dry (or set) trim it flush to the deck with a razor knife or a slightly convex carving tool; then strip off the tape. Hot pitch is no longer used on yacht decks; it is just too messy, even for professionals.

TO KEEP DECKS TIGHT

1503   (*Figure 1503*) In general, souse planked decks down frequently with water. The deck depends upon the swollen condition of the planks for its tightness. Annoying small leaks can sometimes be stopped for a long period by injecting linseed oil into the seams (especially where putty is chipped out) with an ordinary squirt can.

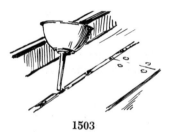

1503

TO RE-COVER A CANVAS DECK

1504   (*Figure 1504*) Start off with a smooth clean deck and tack the canvas along the center line or outboard coaming line so that the canvas is always stretched outward. Use copper tacks only. Make joints between butting pieces of canvas (if necessary) by a double overlap as shown. If laid in oil paint, immediately paint the canvas, thus bonding the canvas between two coats of paint, which will dry together. If laid in a deck glue or mastic, do not paint until glue is thoroughly dry. Use a waterproof marine glue under all mouldings.

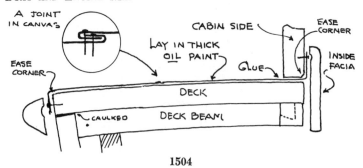

1504

ELECTRICAL CONNECTIONS THROUGH THE DECK

1505 (*Figure 1505*) Either one or the other of the two methods of bringing a wire on deck (to the running lights, horn, etc.) will provide a seatight connection. For protection, keep the loop type in the lee of some fixed deck member, like a cabin trunk or the shroud turnbuckles, and make the loop high enough to get the deck swab under it.

To run a "made-up" electrical line through a deck or bulkhead (such as prewired loops to connect up parts of an autopilot, radio-telephone, radar, etc.), cut a hole the proper size and shape to accept the terminal fitting, then cut a snug hole the *exact* size of the cable itself beside it. Wire up, test it, cover the large hole permanently with a patch of metal, wood, or plywood, and seal off both holes with an epoxy glue. Wherever possible, make entry via a bulkhead (or trunk side). While there are connector plugs available for this service, their sensitivity to saltwater and subsequent corrosion is so great that they promise constant trouble, nor can they solve the problem raised by prewired components.

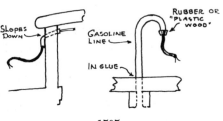

1505

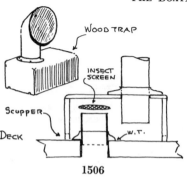

1506

WATERTIGHT VENT

1506 (*Figure 1506*) A simple water-trap arrangement that will give ventilation without soaking the below-deck spaces is shown here. The drawing is self explanatory.

TO SET A MAST COAT

1507 (*Figure 1507*) The proper manner of putting on a mast coat is shown. Make the lashing with several turns of strong tarred marline and set the bottom and the lead gasket in thick paint or marine glue.

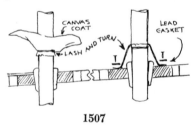

1507

TO MAKE A TEMPORARY PATCH IN PLANKING

1508 (*Figure 1508*) Any heavy, firm bundle of rags or clothing or sails immediately stuffed into a hole in the planking will very much reduce the rate of the leak. With it so under temporary control, prepare a piece of odd wood (floor board, box side, etc.) to fit between the frames at the point of the leak.

Using a woolen cloth, or anything convenient, as a gasket between the temporary patching piece and the inside of the planking, fasten the patch by some means. It can often be braced to some adjacent part of the frame, or a batten and wedge can be rigged as shown in Figure 1508. Such bracing should be nailed in place, because the hull of a boat "works" while underway. The patching piece could be screwed into the planking as well.

The leak will thus be reduced to a seepage, which can only be controlled further by caulking (rope yarns, cotton line, fish line, unraveled woolen garments, etc.).

A split plank can usually be caulked temporarily from the inside. A sprung plank can sometimes be forced back in place by knocking off the butt block and strapping it in by a line passed completely around the boat and given compression with a Spanish windlass. (See Figure 1315)

One of the handiest materials to stop leaks or close up punctures is sheet lead. It can be peened into almost any crevice, and when laid over thick white lead or epoxy glue and tacked around the edges will serve for small leaks.

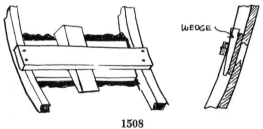

WEDGE

1508

TO MAKE A PERMANENT PATCH IN PLANKING OR PLYWOOD

1509 (*Figure 1509*) Set in a graving piece that is secured to a butt block behind the planking. Use screw fastenings from the inside for a puncture; on the outside for a butt joint (as when fitting in a length of new planking). If in plywood, make a wood-to-wood fit and set in marine glue. If in solid wood, make "caulking joints" (which fit wood to wood only on the inboard edges); then caulk, fill, and putty.

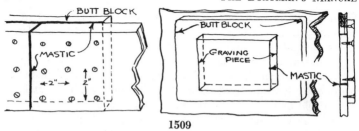

1509

TO SET A BOAT PLUG

1510   (*Figure 1510*) Use soft, clear white pine. Taper to fit the hole exactly when handtight. Drive in snugly from the *outside*, then saw off flush. Do not glue in if it is to be taken out again. If the hole is ragged, rebore it to a larger size. Let the plug (before sawing) extend inside at least the thickness of the planking if possible.

DRIVING FASTENINGS

1511   (*Figure 1511*) While few "dry" fastenings will have to be driven, in either ordinary or emergency repair work, the

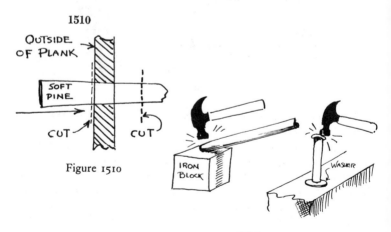

Figure 1510

1511

repair method is shown, in case such a fastening might have to be substituted for a bolt or a nut and bolt. Any metal rod can be so tempered and driven for a temporary fastening (as for a fishing spar). It can be headed on both ends, making a secure fastening. The hole should be 1/16" less diameter than the rod.

When finding this kind of defective fastening in repair work, it is useless to attempt to remove it by pulling. In wet wood, or after it has been set for a long time (especially in oak), it can sometimes be driven through with another and smaller rod—after the head has been hacksawed off. Beware of such a fastening when making a saw cut in wood; it must be hacksawed through with a saw having greater set than the wood saw. Such a hidden fastening, often unsuspected by the non-boatbuilder, is usually found in rudders, centerboards, centerboard cases, watertight bulkheads, deadwood, etc. Look for it in any wide surface. The heads are often covered with a wooden boat bung or putty. It can be located by a magnet or the compass, if iron.

TO KEEP LIMBERS FREE

1512 (*Figure 1512*) Plugged limber holes in inaccessible places may be kept clear by rigging the simple gear shown, which passes through *all* limbers. Use brass fittings only.

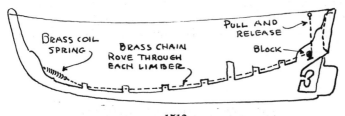

1512

PIPE PLUGS

1513 (*Figure 1513*) Any outboard pipe connection may let go because of corrosion or breaking at any time. If it is made of lead, it is simple to pinch it together and peen it closed with a hammer and block. If a rigid metal, a universal pipe plug of soft

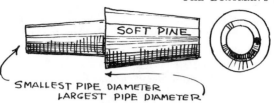

1513 The Coast Guard Auxiliary recommends that such plugs be carried on all boats with through-hull fittings.

pine can be used. Several should be carried aboard, each having tapers from the largest to the smallest diameter pipe on the boat.

CARE OF THE HEAD

1514 Few of the shipboard mechanical parts "get out of order" as often as the hard-used water closet. The repair kit of every boat should have in it a complete replacement kit of gaskets, springs, and washers for the particular head on board. Emergency repairs are impossible save with these patterned parts.

The built-in head is a sturdy affair, but suffers so much because the lubber seldom understands its operation and consequently does considerable damage in his ignorance. The best assurance that it will continue to perform is to post operating rules nearby. One of the best and least offensive, yet good-naturedly effective, is the Long Island Sound classic by Peterkin, which pertain to a common type.

Directions for Landlubbers

It seems this type of bathroom is restricted to a boat,
So follow these directions and don't let them get your goat.
You grasp the handle firmly and work it to and fro,
To make the water in the bowl all disappear below,
Next press the pedal gently, when the tide is almost out,
Pumping in the old Atlantic that the poets rave about.

Release the pedal when it's full, and pump with might and main,
Until you hear the last of it go gurgling down the drain.
A surge of satisfaction will now grace your beating heart,
As you find yourself the master of this oceangoing art.

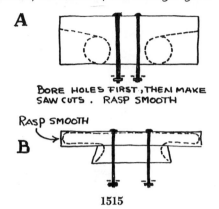

1515

TO MAKE A TEMPORARY WOODEN CLEAT

1515 (*Figure 1515*) Emergency cleats may be easily made to replace one torn out, by following the directions in the sketch. A hard wood will serve best. Through-bolt a cleat if at all possible.

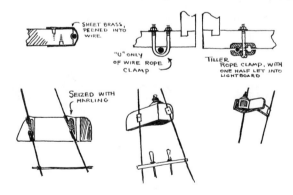

1516 Light boards and methods of securing

TO SECURE LIGHT BOARDS TO SHROUDS

1516 (*Figure 1516*) Several methods are shown for securing these troublesome fixtures. Adjustable fastening methods are to be preferred, making leveling simple in the event shrouds must be adjusted.

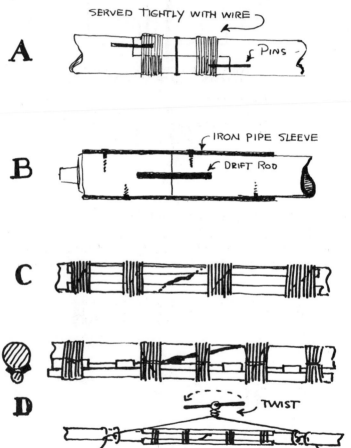

1517

FISHING SPARS

1517 (*Figure 1517*) If a broken spar can be shortened and still be of use, a good and permanent fish can be made, as shown in Sketch A. A mast broken at or below the partners can be fished, as shown in Sketch B.

The broken spar which cannot be shortened (as a main boom or gaff) must be put in "splints," as shown in Sketch C. The splints may be of anything handy, such as floor boards, oars, other lighter spars, etc. The greatest strain on a boom or gaff is at the after end. If possible to do so, reverse the spar so that the fish comes as far forward as possible.

If the fish is made with a single tapered spar, short cleats should be tacked to the broken spar and the sound spar lashed to it securely, taking a few turns around the seizing between the spars. If two tapered spars are used, lash them opposite each other (port and starboard, not top and bottom) and put the heel of one forward and the other aft. (*Sketch D*)

It might be necessary to hold the fractured ends together, in which case a line or several lines are rigged, as shown. Use a stopper hitch or a killick hitch for fastening to the spar, and set the line up by twisting, and then lashing the twisting bar to the spar.

Keep all spar lashings snug by frequent wetting, or possibly wrapping with a wet patch of cloth; remember, wet rope is tight rope.

A fished spar is naturally very much weaker than a sound spar, and a great strain occurs at the point of fracture. If possible change the leads (as of a main sheet or one of the gaff peak halyard leads) so as to bring its tension at or very near the fracture. It is, of course, wise to reef sail when sailing with fished spars.

JURY RUDDER

1518 (*Figure 1518*) For a variety of reasons, the loss of rudder is not an uncommon occurrence. The figure shows several methods of utilizing various boat parts for a jury rudder.

A rolled sail, towed astern, with a line from its outboard end to the boat's quarters, can be used as a rudder by hauling in on one or the other line, thus making a purse or pocket. Deck buckets with

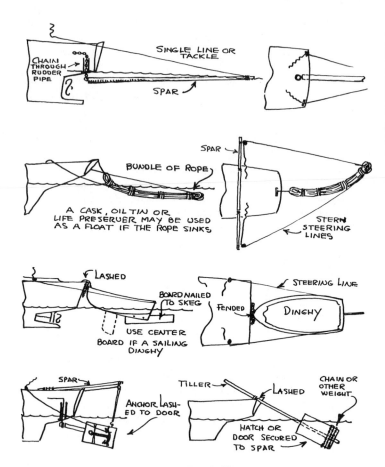

1518 Jury rudders

holes punched in the bottoms and towed from one of the quarters will steer a small boat. Small boats can also be steered by shifting ballast or live weight. A sail raised on a rudderless powerboat will act as a rudder within limits.

CORRECT WAY TO PACK A STUFFING BOX

1519 (*Figure 1519*) Cut the packing into complete circles, ends butted and staggered. Do not make the common mistake of "winding" it in. Put in enough rings to have three complete threads still exposed but not less than three rings of packing. No lubrication other than in the packing is needed.

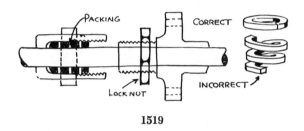

1519

DINGHY FENDER

1520 (*Figure 1520*) Use old, soft line of manila or new cotton line. Tack every second strand *inside* the rope with a pot or copper nail, hauling the rope taut as the nailing proceeds. A tapered short splice at the bow and quarters will give additional protection. Such a rope may be covered with several thicknesses of canvas or old fire hose, in which case the covering is first tacked to the sheer strake; the bed moulding set over the tacks; the rope attached; and the covering drawn tightly over the gunwale and fastened inside, as shown upper left.

"SPLICING IN" BUTTONS

1521 (*Figure 1521*) New buttons are set in mattresses and cushions as shown. A composition button will outlast those covered with fabric or tin caps, and will not rot or discolor the surrounding material.

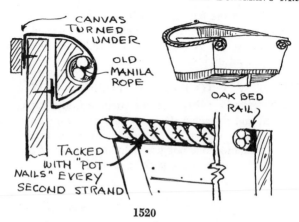

CANVAS
TURNED
UNDER

OLD
MANILA
ROPE

OAK BED
RAIL

TACKED
WITH "POT
NAILS" EVERY
SECOND STRAND

1520

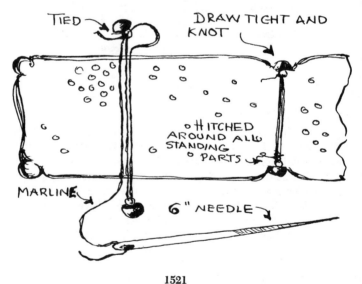

TIED

DRAW TIGHT AND
KNOT

HITCHED
AROUND ALL
STANDING
PARTS

MARLINE

6" NEEDLE

1521

SAILS AND THEIR MAINTENANCE

1522 Look in any general chandlery catalog for *canvas*—and you won't find it. Old-fashioned cotton canvas, the material of sails for generations, has all but disappeared and the synthetics have completely taken over the sailmaker's art. There is nothing wrong with this—save in terms of nostalgia—for modern sailcloth is the answer to the prayers of our forebears who sailed with canvas. Synthetics are fine, long-lived, easily worked materials, no more expensive than canvas. Synthetic cloth has but one fault, and that readily remedied: sunlight tends to slowly destroy it. The remedy, of course, is to keep the sails covered save when in use; if you do this, their lives will be as long as those of canvas.

Nylon and Dacron very nearly have removed the art of sail-making from the novice and amateur. Hand work on these materials (and sail making, as always, is a handcraft) is a highly specialized skill and requires many special techniques, threads, furnishings, and hand machines. For example: synthetics *must* be sewn with synthetic threads compatible with the characteristics of the cloth. Bolt rope can no longer be used, since rope has "movement," while synthetic cloth has little; therefore, tabling—doubling the sail material itself—has replaced it as reinforcement.

Besides sunlight, the only enemy of synthetic sails, really, is mildew, and mildew does not destroy; it merely discolors. It can be controlled by always storing sails dry, by twice-a-season washing in fresh water without *detergent or bleach*, and by use of tight sail covers (or storing sails off the spars). To be sure, synthetic sails will tear if strained or fouled, and they will, as a result of wear and/or strain, "give up" at seams and elsewhere. Because Dacron sailcloth is relatively hard, stitching *stands proud* on it, and does not sink down level with the sail's surface; as a result, the stitching chafes before the sail, and replacing thread is perhaps the most common sail repair today.

Small sailboatmen should be prepared to correct any failures that show up while sailing. The approach should be on a temporary basis—"What to do before the sailmaker comes." One of the simplest repair materials is simply rigging tape and/or spinnaker tape. Plaster it over any rent or hole, however slight, or anything in

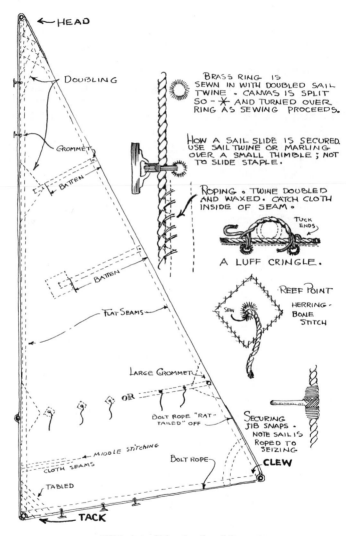

←HEAD

DOUBLING

GROMMET

BATEN

BATTEN

FLAT SEAMS

LARGE GROMMET

OR

BOLT ROPE "RAT-TAILED" OFF

MIDDLE STITCHING

CLOTH SEAMS

BOLT ROPE

TABLED

←TACK

BRASS RING IS SEWN IN WITH DOUBLED SAIL TWINE. CANVAS IS SPLIT SO - ✳ AND TURNED OVER RING AS SEWING PROCEEDS.

HOW A SAIL SLIDE IS SECURED. USE SAIL TWINE OR MARLING OVER A SMALL THIMBLE; NOT TO SLIDE STAPLE.

ROPING. TWINE DOUBLED AND WAXED. CATCH CLOTH INSIDE OF SEAM.

TUCK ENDS

A LUFF CRINGLE.

REEF POINT

SEW

HERRING-BONE STITCH

SECURING JIB SNAPS. NOTE SAIL IS ROPED TO SEIZING

CLEW

1522 A traditional sail and its parts

the way of broken stitching or a fray or chafed spot. It will last the cruise out at least. Later you can go into the shop for a professional job.

Repairs may also be made in the old-fashioned manner and these could be permanent. The following tools should be in the sailmaker's bag:

1. (*a*) *Sail needles.* Long spur needles, triangular in shape, rounded at the eye end for general sewing. Number 15, 2½″ long is a favorite.

   (*b*) *Roping needles.* Short spur needles, stockier than sail needles. Used for sewing to boltropes and other heavy work.

2. *Twine.* Cotton twine of four to eight ply for general work, the heavier ply for heavier cloth. Comes in a ball of one-half pound. Roping is done with nine- to twelve-ply twine.

3. *Palm.* A heavy leather half glove worn over the hand. The palm has a lead casting sewn in, which is used to push the needle through the cloth or rope.

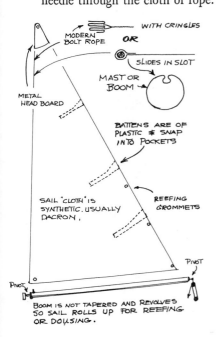

1522A A modern sail, usually self-furling or self-reefing

FLAT STITCH

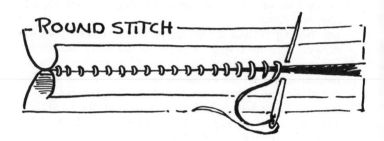

ROUND STITCH

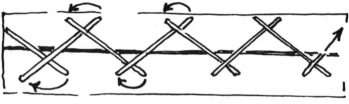

HERRINGBONE STITCH

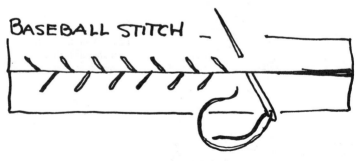

BASEBALL STITCH

1523A

4. *Pricker*. A long, sharp steel-pointed tool, used to puncture a needle hole through several thicknesses of fabric.

5. *Creasing stick*. A tool having a slot at one end, used to crease the seams preparatory to sewing; made of metal, bone, or wood.

6. *Sail hook*. A large barbless hook on a length of line, which is fastened to any handy object and hooked into the fabric to hold it in a convenient working position.

7. Lump of beeswax to lubricate needles and thread.

8. Dacron and nylon sail thread.

SEAMS

1523 The flat seam (*Figure 1523A*) is the commonest seam used for joining two pieces of cloth together. Patches in sail are made with it as follows: Make the patch generously larger than the hole; then sew the patch to the hole edge and the patch edge to the sail, using flat stitches.

The round seam. Used for joining two edges together but leaves a ragged edge on one side. Excellent for sea bags, binnacles and wheel jackets but not often used for sail work.

The herringbone stitch. To sew a rip in canvas.

The baseball stitch. The same as herringbone.

The shoemaker's stitch. Used for leather serving or for fastening oar leathers. Two needles are required, as shown. (*Figure 1523B*)

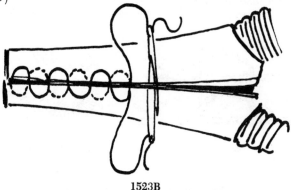

1523B

The bolt rope stitch. Used for sewing to a bolt rope. The stitch picks up each successive rope strand and its length is therefore governed by the strand twist. Doubled twine is often used for bolt rope sewing.

SAIL REPAIR

1524 Cloth seams are sewn with flat stitches, the fabric being doubled under itself. Batten pockets and reef-point doubling are put in with herringbone stitches. The sail is never sewn to the bolt rope without folding under twice.

It should be noted that while the old-fashioned bolt rope—an actual hard-laid rope—is no longer used on synthetic sails, the name "bolt rope" still persists as the proper name for the replacement. The modern synthetic bolt rope is really a "tabling"; that is, a strong edging, a reinforcement made up of several thicknesses of heavy synthetic cloth, machine-sewn together into a veritable "rope." The advantage, of course, is that it has the same stretch factor as the sailcloth and thus, in theory at least, forbids puckering, bagging, or ruinous draft. A modern bolt rope cannot be made or applied by hand.

In addition to functioning as a bolt rope, tabling is used extensively at the head, tack and clew to take the extra strain at these parts. Grommets are generally shaped over a small brass ring but may be made without the ring by folding the cloth back several times and following around the edge with a round stitch. Middle stitching is a row of stitches between two seam stitches for extra strength.

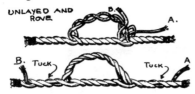

Turning in a reef cringle over a round brass thimble

Turning in a head, tack, or clew cringle. Note that bolt rope goes *outside*

1524 To replace cringles on old-fashioned sails

SAILMAKING

1525   Sails are not flat areas as they seem but have definite shape and draft depending upon their use. The novice should not attempt sailmaking without the aid of some technical advice beyond the scope of this *Manual*. Machine sewing will hasten the work much and make a more satisfactory job in general. A few general hints follow:

Arrange the cloths in main and foresails so that they parallel the boom or make about a 15° angle with the waterline. The cloths in headsails usually follow both the angle of the mainsail cloths and a vertical line, meeting at the bisected angle of the clew. Use genuine "bolt rope" for the bolt rope, not common manila which stretches and shrinks too much for this use. Make batten pockets several inches longer than the batten. On racing sails the reef points are not rove until needed. Sails will stretch considerably and should be made about 8% less than spar limits.

CANVAS PROTECTION

1526   Mildewproofing canvas is simply waterproofing it to resist the moisture which encourages mildew.

UNITED STATES DEPARTMENT OF AGRICULTURE WATERPROOFING FORMULA

Petroleum asphalt	8½ pounds
Vaseline (amber)	1½ pounds
Dry-earth pigment (ochre or umber)	5 pounds
Gasoline	3 gallons
Kerosene	2 gallons

Melt the first two items slowly over a fire while stirring constantly. Remove far away from flame and pour into the mixed gasoline and kerosene. A small amount is withdrawn and made into a paste with the pigment. When smooth it may be further thinned and finally mixed with the main batch. If the waterproofing material settles to the bottom, the batch must be reheated by setting in a tub of hot water—*never over a flame.*

This quantity will be a khaki color and will cover about 450 square feet of canvas, one side. It may be sprayed or painted on and permitted to dry thoroughly. Folding and stowing away before completely dry may cause spontaneous combustion.

If a white treatment is desired use zinc oxide in place of the earth pigment.

Another waterproofing mixture is made as follows:

Boiled linseed oil	2 quarts
Bronzing powder	½ pound
Japan drier	¼ pint

Dissolve the powder first in a small quantity of oil; then add to the mix. No heating is necessary and it may be used at once. The quantity above will cover about 75 square feet, one side, in a light khaki color. It will make a much stiffer surface than the first formula and is best used on standing panels, dodger cloths, etc., rather than on sail covers, jackets, etc.

Another formula is merely a mixture of one gallon of turpentine to one half pound of refined beeswax. The canvas is soaked in it and dried thoroughly for a long period. The color will be quite yellow. This is the dressing used on most oilers and storm clothing with canvas unrubberized fabric. Old oilers may be restored by so treating.

Painting

1527   There probably can be no more important thing said about small-boat painting than to caution the boatman to *use only marine paints*. Any paint other than one labeled a marine paint by a reliable manufacturer is utterly useless and lifeless on shipboard. House paints simply will not stand up on the sea, and to use them is to waste the time and effort put into the work, and, even ultimately to detract from the appearance and value of the boat.

The next most important thing is that the undersurface be properly prepared before painting; that it be dry, oil-free, and firm, and that the paint be applied under fair-weather conditions.

PREPARING THE SURFACE

Remove all scaled or powdery paint, using a paint or varnish remover or a blowtorch. If a paint remover has been used, wash down thoroughly with turpentine or a thinner. Then sand the surface thoroughly until smooth, even, and firm. Check back then for loose putty and re-putty where necessary. If a new raw place is to be puttied, prime first with thin paint or shellac to stop the suction that would soon draw the oil from the putty and permit it to powder. Shellac over knots, give a final light sanding, *dust well*, and only then apply the first paint.

Metal surfaces must be chipped, scraped, and wire-brushed free of scale or rust. Paint applied over rust will not stop the rust nor will the paint long remain bonded to the spot. Once clean, smooth, and dry, a first coat of red lead should be applied; then finish coats. Red lead alone will fully seal iron against the action of oxidization, or rust.

Galvanized surfaces by nature repel paint. A good prime coat, after a wash-down with vinegar, is shellac. Ammonia washes are used before prime coats of paint. Old galvanized surfaces, which have been exposed to the weather for a period of time, will form a far better bonding surface than new galvanizing.

It is not usual to paint bronze or brass work. If it must be, however, all trace of the polishing agent must be removed before the paint will hold. Bronze surfaces can be roughened somewhat if they are brushed with muriatic acid, permitting it to "eat" slightly, then washed off and painted.

Varnished surfaces should be prepared as for painting. A hook-type scraper will come in handy here; it will bite into ancient varnish that sandpaper won't touch. Sand well, then dust and touch up and even the color (if not natural) with an oil stain.

Canvas decks are treated as woodwork. However, if they are badly checked, they are hopeless and a recanvasing is indicated: To remove the paint with a paint remover from such a deck requires immense quantities of remover. Burning off will result in burned-through areas even when done by experts. Either method will destroy the bond of the canvas to the deck beneath it.

WHEN TO PAINT

Paint and varnish only when:
1. The surface is absolutely dust-free.
2. Work above it has been completed.
3. The surface is thoroughly dry.

4. The weather is fair, with no prospect of change, and the temperature at least 50°.
5. The wind, or the possible future winds, will not bring dust, sand, or insects.
6. The coat beneath is thoroughly dry and set.
7. A painting, not a scrubbing, is indicated.

PAINTING TOOLS
Check List for Fitting-out Painting

Brushes	Paint cleaner
Sandpaper	Wiping rags
Bronze wool	Mixing buckets
Turpentine	Wire brush
Reducing oil	Scrapers
Paint & varnish remover	Putty knives
Naphtha, alcohol, etc.	Blowtorch
Tack rags	

Clean paint and varnish brushes in turpentine; then wash with ordinary "brown soap" and dry thoroughly. Clean shellac brushes in alcohol. Never stand a brush on end. Suspend (in a can of clean turps if desired) in such a way that the bristles do not touch the bottom of the can. A hole bored through the handle as illustrated in No. 15, Figure 1527A provides a handy way to suspend brushes in turpentine. If a brush has been softened by a commercial brush reconditioner, wash it *many* times before using again. A very slight trace of softener will destroy a paint job done with the brush later.

APPLYING PAINT AND VARNISH—HINTS
1. To mix prepared paint. Pour off most of the vehicle (liquid). Stir and paddle the pigment thoroughly, adding small quantities of the liquid from time to time, until the liquid and pigment are combined. Then box the paint by pouring back and forth until smooth and without lumps.
2. Do not mix in driers (if any are to be used) until immediately before ready to paint.
3. Thin paint and varnish with turpentine; shellac, with alcohol.
4. Hard-pulling enamels spread more easily if naphtha is poured thinly over the surface of the enamel as used. It will aid in

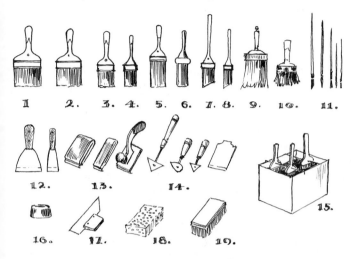

1–4, flat brushes 2″ to 4″. 5–6, long-bristled varnish brushes, oval or round. 7–8, bevel-point sash brushes. 9, dusting brush. 10, old brush for paint and varnish removing. 11, assorted flat and round lettering and artists' brushes. 12, putty knives. 13, hook scrapers. 14, knife scrapers. 15, brush reservoir. 16, rubber antidrip caps for overhead painting. 17, sheet-metal guard for painting sash and corners and around fittings. 18, sponge rubber or cork sanding block. 19, wire scrub brush.

1527A Tool set for a 35-footer, crew of 3 painters

spreading the enamel but will evaporate almost immediately. Watch the ventilation when so doing.

5. Paint should be brushed out thin, not flowed on, with the grain, with brush strokes underneath, and with the "long" way of the surface or panel.

6. Varnish should be flowed on and not brushed out too thin.

7. Sand lightly between coats of both paint and varnish. Dust.

8. Keep paint well mixed during use. Do not mix varnish or enamel during use as it will form bubbles and "foam" at the brush stroke.

PUTTIES AND CEMENTS

Nail holes, seams, etc., are best puttied with white lead putty, not ordinary "sash" putty. A small quantity of litharge will cause putty to set quickly and dry very hard. Blemishes, scrapes, and other hull nicks are best patched with such a mixture.

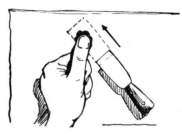

1527B Putting

Professionals handle the putty as shown in Figure 1527B. The palm of the left hand is used as a magazine for a "sausage" of putty, and it is fed between the thumb and the second joint of the forefinger and pressed firmly into the crack with the thumb; then cut off with a quick motion of the knife. A long seam is done in exactly the same way, from right to left, hitching the hand along and following with the putty knife.

Seams that are subject to motion, like deck seams, should be puttied with a commercial elastic seam compound, applied exactly like white lead putty. Liquid and plastic woods are not used in seams but are excellent for patching holes and scars. When dry either type can be sanded, sawn, and screws driven into it. (*See Paragraph 1502*)

PAINT REQUIREMENTS AFTER PRIMING
FOR VARIOUS TYPES OF BOATS

	Din-ghies	Row-boats	Plain Launches	Run-abouts	Cruis-ers	Sail-boats	Auxil-iaries	Yachts
Average length (feet) ...	10	15	25	25	30–32	20	35	60
Topside paint	1 qt.	—	2 qts.	—	2 gals.	2 qts.	2 gals.	9 gals.
Varnish ...	2 qts.	—	—	1½ gal.	1 gal.	1 qt.	2 gals.	5 gals.
Deck paint	—	2 qts.	1 gal.	1 qt.	1 gal.	1 gal.	2 gals.	5 gals.
Interior enamel ..	—	—	—	—	2 qts.	—	3 qts.	3 gals.
Bottom (anti-fouling) ..	—	1 qt.	2 qts.	1 gal.	1½ gal.	3 qts.	3 gals.	6 gals.
Boot topping	—	—	—	½ pt.	½ pt.	½ pt.	½ pt.	1 pt.

BOTTOM PAINTS

1529   Whenever a boat is used in waters that support marine growth or barnacles or teredo worms, a copper or "poisonous" paint is used on the hull below the waterline. There are many grades of such paint on the market. The cheapest kind, which is a brown color, is satisfactory for its prime purpose, discouraging growth and attack. The most expensive kinds, some of which are guaranteed on a money-back basis to keep a hull clean for a normal season, are finely ground and compounded paints, and provide a racing surface as smooth as an enamel.

Each section of the country has its favorite color and brand. As the manner and intensity of growth and attack vary with the water and water temperatures, it is always wise to use the favorite in that section. Commercial boats and fishermen have usually discovered the best type and are using it.

Seasonal repainting of the bottom seldom requires that the old copper paint be removed. It is powdery and usually, when dry, flakes and falls away. However, the under surface should be prepared and made as smooth as any other painting surface, in order to reduce skin friction to a minimum. Wire brushing and sanding are generally required, and possibly re-puttying of some of the seams and fastening holes. A white lead litharge putty may be used on the holes but a white lead putty is best for the seams. When cleaning off flaking copper paint, wear a mask or a wet cloth tied over the nose and mouth as the powder is highly poisonous, especially with those paints having mercury in them.

Depending upon the protection necessary, every part of the underwater surface is copper painted, including rudder, propeller, and outside ballast castings. The only exceptions are the small zinc block sometimes let into the deadwood to discourage electrolysis, the copper plate of a radio ground, and the face of the depth sounder transducer.

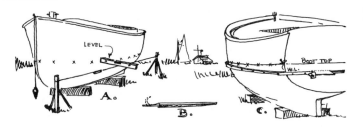

1529 Marking waterlines

The waterline may be "sprung" as shown in Figure 1529. The boat must be plumb but need not be level. The line (*Sketch* A) is level with the bow and stern painted waterlines, and a series of reference points, level with the line, marked off on the hull. A batten is now sprung through these points (*Sketch* C) and the waterline permanently marked with a hook file (*Sketch* B) or a backsaw. A curved waterline or boot topping is swung by letting a line "drape" naturally and marking its curve on the hull. The ends of such a curved waterline sweep upward from the level in about the same proportion as the sheer does, usually more at the bow than the stern. The boot topping on a flat transom stern is always level and never follows the deck crown.

Painting the bottom of a fiberglass boat entails some special requirements. Generally speaking, the cuprous oxide paints are best on this surface, and tributyltin oxide (TBTO) or tributyltin fluoride (TBTF) are better suited to steel and aluminum hulls for which they were formulated. The new vinyl anti-fouling paints are occasionally damaging to fiberglass. Paint a small test patch first, and if the old paint lifts, the new is incompatible with it.

Occasionally a new fiberglass boat's anti-fouling will peel off in huge patches. This generally means that the mold release agent, applied to the new hull to help it part easily from the mold, has not been properly removed. The only thing to do is scrub down the bottom, then remove the slippery release agent—a kind of wax—with any household cleaner designed to remove the wax from floors.

1530

COVERAGE AND DRYING TIME FOR PAINTS, VARNISHES, ETC.

Product	Drying Time Before Re-coat (hrs.)	Coverage per Gallon (in sq. feet)
Primers		
Metal primers	2	400
Zince chromate	18	500
Red lead	24	500
Canvas and vinyl primers	2	250
Undercoaters		
White (topsides)	24	400
Fiberglass	24	400
Sealer, clear	4	600
Stain-filler combinations		
Paste	2	—
Flow or brush	3	350
Paints		
Yacht whites and topsides	24	350
Deck	24	750
Workboat, including white	24	600
Bilge aluminium	24	700
Boot topping	20	800
Plastic paints	24	450
Bottom		
Plastic bottom	96	400
Hard (racing types)	36	800
Average (red, green)	6–18	550
" (blue, white)	12–24	500
Bronze	4–18	450

Handy Formulas

RED LEAD
1531

To make one gallon

Dry red lead	20 pounds
Raw linseed oil	5 pints
Turpentine	½ pint
Liquid driers	½ "

PURE WHITE LEAD PAINT
1532

To make approximately six quarts

White lead paste	25 pounds
Raw linseed oil	6 pints
Turpentine	1 pint
Liquid driers	¼ "

MARINE GLOSS WHITE (OUTSIDE)
1533

To make approximately one gallon

White lead paste	5 pounds
White zinc paste	9 "
Raw linseed oil	3 pints
Turpentine	3 gills
Liquid driers	7 ounces

HULL BLACK
1534

To make approximately one gallon

Red lead paste	4¼ pounds
Carbon black in oil	.33 gallons
Prussian blue in oil	.08 "
Raw linseed oil	.40 "
Turpentine	.06 "
Liquid driers	.06 "

SOLVENT TYPE PAINT REMOVER
1535

To make approximately one gallon

Benzol	2 quarts
Household paraffin (shave and dissolve into benzol)	1½ pounds
Denatured alcohol	1 quart
Acetone	1 "

STARCH TYPE PAINT REMOVER
1536

Caustic soda (98%)	4 pounds
Bolted whiting	4 "
Cornstarch	2 quarts
Water	2 "

(Mix together and use as a thick paste. This mixture should not be used on oak as it will discolor the wood.)

PAINT CLEANER

1537 Mix as above but add three to five times the quantity of water. Use on a scrub brush or a sponge rubber pad with a circular motion and wash off with clean salt or fresh water.

This cleaner will also serve as a so-called liquid sandpaper. Mix as before with at least six times the quantity of water. Brush on paint and varnish work, *after* rough sanding, sponge off and, after one hour, finish paint.

TO KEEP A CLEAN SHIP

1538 Mildew is the great threat on the water, especially in the warm waters and damp zephyrs of the southland. Mildew is a living mold, having a musty odor, its spores borne by the wind and attaching themselves wherever there is a microscopic foothold and some moisture—if only a wet wind, fog, or even just lack of dry air.

It can be prevented on shipboard by drying the air, which means by positive air circulation, by air conditioners, by heat (which takes moisture out of the air), and by placing chemical absorbents in lockers, wardrobes, and the other small spaces usually found on boats. Commercial mildew preventatives—the chemicals—are silica gel, activated alumina, and calcium chloride. These are placed in the threatened area in open containers. The first two chemicals may be dried (after absorption of moisture for a few days) in an oven and used over and over again. Calcium chloride also picks up and retains moisture but most types, once wet, must then be discarded.

Prevention is better than cure; hence be sure that anything that can absorb moisture is *dry and clean* before storage. Leather, especially vulnerable to mildew, should be wrapped in paper and sealed, after a spray treatment with commercial paradi-chlorobenzene. Luggage ditto.

Additives to paint and varnish, calculated to discourage mildew, which in no way affects color or life, may be had for a few cents in marine chandleries. In brown paper bags, at half the price, this additive is known as zinc oxide, chlorinated phenol, phenyl mercurial compound, or, simply, a fungicide. In paint it is effective for about 12 months. Use only in the last coat of paint or varnish.

To remove mildew from paint and varnish, you need small quantities of water, into which a generous splash of chlorine bleach has been poured, and huge quantities of elbow grease, usually yours. Sponge the mixture on the surface, let it "set" briefly, and then go to work. A small nail brush helps in corners, and so does a sponge with one abrasive surface (the kind used in the galley when doing pots and pans; swipe it). A rough cloth-like wad—wrung-out chamois is excellent—helps also. The removal requires some slight abrasion, especially in the corners. When clean, spray or wash down the surface with a commercial mixture of mildew suppressant, and keep your portholes and hatches *open*; for basically all that is needed is the circulation of good, sun-dried air in huge quantities.

The Marine Engine

1539 Marine gasoline engines are either of the two-cycle or four-cycle type. The basic operating principle of each, regardless of make or model, are exactly the same. The variation in engine styles is chiefly a matter of the engine accessories; such as carburetors, starters, electrical equipment, etc. It is impossible to describe and list each of the hundreds of different accessories separately. However, the service pamphlets and booklets of instruction supplied with the engine contain the peculiar instructions, tables of clearances for valves, bearings, points, spark plugs, and lists of replacement parts. These references should be kept on board at all times.

The following information is applicable to all motors:

THE FOUR-CYCLE ENGINE

1540   In a four-cycle engine, four piston strokes are required to complete each power cycle. During the exhaust and intake strokes the piston functions as an air pump and this operation actually consumes power. Each new air charge must be "stretched" into the cylinder. (*Figure 1540A*)

Note: When the engine is operating at 2,500 rpm, the above cycle of operations is repeated 1,250 times per minute in each cylinder. The complete cycle of intake, compression, explosion, and scavenging is therefore completed in 1/1,250 of a minute, or roughly 1/20 of a second. Any single stroke, involving only one fourth of the cycle, thus requires only a small instant of time, about 1/80 of a second. From this, it will be clear why it is necessary to set valve tappet clearances accurate to measurements of a thousandth of an inch.

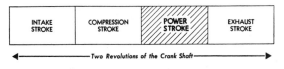

1540A   The cycle of a four-cycle engine

THE TWO-CYCLE ENGINE

1541   In a two-cycle engine, a charge of fuel is burned every time the piston comes to top dead center, and consequently there is one power impulse per cylinder for each revolution of the crankshaft. In other words, a two-cycle engine with six cylinders has twice

Intake stroke: The intake valve starts to open just before top dead center, connecting this particular cyclinder with the intake manifold and carburetor. The piston, in descending, forms a vacuum that pulls fuel through the carburetor and draws into the cylinder a charge of the air and gasoline from the intake manifold.

Compression stroke: On the upstroke of the piston, following intake, both valves are closed and the explosive mixture of air and gasoline is compressed into a small space between the top of piston and the cylinder head.

Power stroke: At the instant the piston reaches its highest point of travel, and compression is greatest, a spark is timed by the distributor to occur across the points of the spark plug, igniting the mixture. The subsequent burning of the inflammable mixture, which is commonly called the "explosion" because it occurs within a very small fraction of a second, causes a very large increase in gas volume; the resulting pressure on the top of the piston forces the piston downward, producing work. Through the connecting rod, this power is transmitted to the crankshaft.

Exhaust stroke: The exhaust valve opens during the latter part of the power stroke, so that the pressure in the cylinder can equalize with atmospheric pressure, then the burned gases are pushed out through the exhaust valve and into the exhaust manifold by the rising piston. At the top of this stroke, the operating cycle is completed, and intake starts again.

1540B Operation of a four-cycle engine

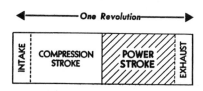

1541A The cycle of a two-cycle engine

as many power impulses as a four-cycle engine with six cylinders operating at the same speed.

In a two-cycle engine, intake and exhaust takes place simultaneously at the bottom of each stroke. The two-cycle engine, therefore, does not function as an air pump during any part of the cycle, so an external means of supplying air must be provided.

In the two-cycle gasoline motor, air and fuel are taken into the crankcase, through a check-valved breather, by the upstroke of the piston, then driven, through a bypass and air port, into the cylinder on the downstroke. In the two-cycle diesel motor, a mechanism, such as a blower or air injector, supplies the air directly to the cylinder and at the proper time. The principle in both is the same, though diesel engines make use of mechanical valves while the two-cycle gasoline motor is valveless as a rule. Outboard motors and lighting-plant motors are generally of the two-cycle type and operate on the same principle. (*Figure 1541B*)

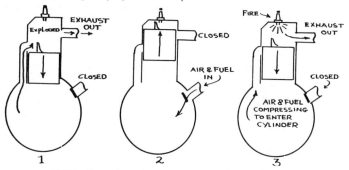

1541B Operation of a two-cycle gasoline engine

THE OPERATION OF A MODERN DIESEL ENGINE

1542 The engine represented in Figure 1542 is the Gray Marine diesel.

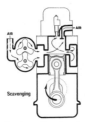

A series of ports cut into the circumference of the cylinder wall above the piston in its lowest position admit the precompressed air from the blower into the cylinder as soon as the top face of the piston uncovers these ports. The one-way flow of air toward the exhaust valves sweeps out the exhaust gases, leaving the cylinder full of clean air when piston covers the ports again.

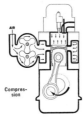

As the piston continues on the upward stroke, the exhaust valves close and the charge of fresh air is compressed to one sixteenth of its initial volume. This happens on every upward stroke of the piston in a two-cycle engine.

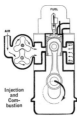

Shortly before the piston reaches its highest position, the required amount of atomized fuel is sprayed into the combustion space by the unit fuel injector. The intense heat generated during the high compression of the air ignites the fine fuel spray immediately, and the combustion continues as long as fuel enters the cylinder. The resulting pressure forces the piston downward until the exhaust valves are opened again.

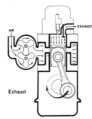

The burnt gases escape into the exhaust manifold and the cylinder volume is swept with clean scavenging air as the downward piston uncovers the inlet ports. This entire combustion is repeated in each cylinder for each revolution of the crankshaft. The quantity of fuel burned each cycle is controlled by the injector, and is varied by the operator or the governor.

1542 Operation of a diesel engine

MAINTENANCE INSTRUCTIONS FOR A TYPICAL
FOUR-CYCLE GASOLINE ENGINE
1543

DAILY

Check lubricating oil level in crankcase, and when necessary refill to high-level mark on depth stick.

Give grease cup on water pump one half turn per day. Use water-proof grease. If the engine is running continuously this should be done every four hours.

Check overflow water every time the engine is started, to make certain that pump is functioning.

EVERY 50 HOURS OF OPERATION

Remove oil from crankcase, using sump pump, and refill to high mark on oil-depth gauge.

Check water level in battery. Proper fluid gravity is 1.275.

Remove cap of oil cooler and clean out any accumulated dirt or debris.

Put three or four drops of engine oil (S.A.E. 30) in oiler on generator, and two drops in oiler on starting motor.

Put three to five drops of engine oil (S.A.E. 30) in the oiler on the outside of distributor body.

Check oil level in housing for driving gears on sea-water pump. Refill as necessary to level of inspection plug. Most gears use A-type oil.

ONCE A MONTH

Inspect flame arrester to make sure the air passages are clean and free from oil or lint. If dirty, remove and wash in kerosene. Blow out with compressed air if available.

Check adjustment of clutch and reverse gear.

Clean sediment bowl on fuel pump.

EVERY 150 HOURS

Replace cartridge in lubricating-oil filter, regardless of apparent condition.

Apply one drop only (no more) of light engine oil (S.A.E. 10) to the breaker-arm hinge pin in distributor.

Remove the distributor rotor and apply three to five drops of light engine oil (S.A.E. 10) to the felt in the top of the breaker cam.

TWICE-A-SEASON "TUNE UP"

Clean and adjust breaker points on distributor. Points should contact evenly.

Remove the distributor head and smear a bit of vaseline or grease the size of a match head on the lobes of the breaker cam.

Check spark plugs and set gap, using feeler gauge. Clean fouled plugs and search for cause of fouling. Replace cracked or doubtful plugs.

Check distributor setting.

Check carburetor adjustment.

Inspect all wiring for loose connections or worn insulation. Clean battery terminals with soda solution and coat lightly with vaseline or grease.

Check engine coupling for misalignment. Tighten lag screws holding engine to bed.

Remove clean-out plate and look for signs of sludge in oil sump. Inspect oil pick-up screen. If you find sludge, the motor is running too cold, or there may be a leak in oil cooler.

Check valve-tappet adjustment.

Clean the engine thoroughly.

EVERY 1,000 HOURS

Give engine a thorough going over.

Grind and adjust valves.

Check valve stems for carbon.

Clean commutator on generator, using No. 00 sandpaper.

If compression is weak, look for imperfectly seated valves or rings stuck in grooves on piston.

EVERY 2,500 HOURS

Time for a major overhaul.

Install new piston rings. Check piston clearance.

Check bearings. When oil pressure drops below 20 pounds, this is an indication of worn bearings.

MAINTENANCE INSTRUCTIONS FOR A TWO-CYCLE ENGINE

1544 The simplicity of the two-cycle gasoline engine makes maintenance a matter of external oiling and cleaning only. As there is no lubricating oil in the crankcase (it is mixed with the gasoline in the fuel tank in the proportions recommended by the manufacturer), maintenance may be reduced to the following daily operations:

Turn down all grease cups.

Refill drop oiler (if so equipped) every 50 hours of operation.

Drain carburetor bowl or strainer for water.

With sump pump, draw off raw gas and oil from crankcase.

Clean points of make-and-break mechanism, or, if equipped with high-tension system, proceed as for four-cycle engines.

EVERY SEASON

Tighten all hold-down bolts.

Check shaft alignment.

Check carburetor adjustment.

Renew batteries (or recharge if storage type).

Remove carbon from cylinder by scraping.

The two-cycle engine will operate for years if properly maintained, without the overhauls necessary to the four-cycle type. Once the correct carburetor and timing adjustments have been reached, the engine requires little more than daily oiling of external moving parts, such as pump plunger, timing mechanism, and thrust bearing.

Outboard motors are lubricated through the carburetor. Ignition parts may be inspected and cleaned by removing the flywheel or rope-starter plate and exposing the magneto and timer built into the flywheel, and serviced as for high-tension systems (*See four-cycle motor instructions*). External greasing is done by removing the screw caps and injecting the grease by means of the tube in which the grease is packaged. Waterproof grease must be used for underwater transmission parts.

The outboard motor that has become soaked or has been submerged should be serviced as described in Paragraph 1546.

DIESEL ENGINES

1545 Diesel engines vary greatly in operating principle, and no general remarks may be made which would serve as a complete guide to maintenance. The manufacturer's recommendations, as they apply to his motor, should be followed.

However, lubricating-oil levels in crankcase and transmission should be checked daily, and all grease cups turned down. Freshwater cooling systems should be checked for content (if so equipped) and, if in winter, the freezing point checked. Every 24 hours of operation, the sediment and water should be drawn off from oil and fuel filters.

Every 50–75 hours of operation, the crankcase oil should be changed, all air screens cleaned. Transmission oil will last for 250–350 hours of operation. Elements in fuel and lubricating-oil filters should be replaced about every 500 hours. Intake ports in some types require cleaning about every 2,500 hours, and possibly new cylinder liners, or piston rings, or both.

Electrical starting and generating equipment on the diesel is serviced exactly like similar equipment on gasoline engines.

OVERHAULING AN ENGINE AFTER SUBMERSION IN SALT WATER

1546 It is important to understand that damage is done primarily by the action of air (oxygen) on the surfaces exposed to salt water. The damage can be minimized by leaving the engine submerged until you are ready to do the entire job. If the engine has been flooded only, not sunk, treat it as soon as possible with Tectyl (*see instructions following*) or if this chemical is not readily available, the best procedure is to leave the water in the engine, or to submerge the engine in fresh water at once, until ready to proceed with the overhauling.

Regardless of what precautions are taken or how long the engine has been under water, it is well to bear in mind that the sooner the overhaul is begun after the engine is exposed to the air, the less likely it is that pitting and serious corrosion of the parts will have taken place.

EMERGENCY TREATMENT WITH TECTYL

Tectyl is the name of a chemical that is of particular value in salvaging engines after exposure to salt water, having the property of displacing water from contact with metal and leaving a tenacious, moisture-resisting film. Tectyl is said to do two things: (1) it separates water from iron or steel, (2) it forms an oily protective coating on the metal. It is electromagnetically attracted to steel, and forms what are known as *polar films*.

Tectyl grade No. 511 is recommended for marine engines.

As soon as possible after the engine has been immersed or flooded it should be drained of oil and water and treated with Tectyl 511 as follows:

1. Fill the base of the engine with Tectyl 511 and circulate it through the engine's oil system by cranking the engine over, either with the starter or by hand. After the Tectyl is removed from the base, the water will separate out from it, and the undiluted Tectyl can be saved and used again.

2. Remove the spark plugs and flush the cylinders with Tectyl 511, cranking the engine over by hand to aid in spreading the compound. *Caution:* Do not replace spark plugs during this operation, because the liquid above the pistons will be compressed and may break something.

3. Remove the cover to the valve chamber and flush the entire chamber thoroughly with Tectyl 511, using a brush or a spray gun.

4. Squirt some Tectyl 511 into the flame arrester on the carburetor.

5. Remove cover on reverse-gear housing, and flush clutch and reverse gear, also inside of housing, thoroughly with Tectyl 511.

6. Spray or paint all accessories and exterior surfaces with Tectyl 511. Wipe off at once from electrical parts, as it has a tendency to cause the insulation to swell.

7. Remove Tectyl from base of engine and refill to high-level mark on depth stick with regular lubricating oil of the correct grade, to which a pint of Tectyl 511 has been added. (Tectyl is soluble in oil or gasoline.)

8. As soon as possible, give the engine a complete dismantling and thorough cleaning.

LAYING-UP SUGGESTIONS FOR WINTER STORAGE
1547

1. First run the engine, under load with clutch engaged, until it is completely warmed up. (Hot oil is thinner and will drain more easily; also it has the accumulated impurities held in suspension.) Then shut it off and remove crankcase oil, using the sump pump. The reason for removing the old oil is that it may have an acid content, because most fuels have a trace of sulphur, and sulphur-dioxide gas (SO_2), which is a product of combustion, plus water (H_2O), plus heat, forms sulphurous (H_2SO_3). Refill slightly over the "full" mark with fresh oil of the correct viscosity.

2. Start up the engine again to distribute clean oil through the engine, and while it is running at good speed, choke it off by pouring a cupful of regular No. 30 engine oil into the air intake on the carburetor. This may have the effect of making the engine a trifle hard to start in the spring (although not if you clean the spark plugs) but it will coat the combustion chamber as well as the carburetor jets with a protective film of oil. Turn off ignition switch.

3. Drain all water jackets and piping, and don't forget the drain cock on the oil cooler, if your engine has one. Prodding the drain cocks with a piece of wire after draining will make sure they are fully open and not clogged with sediment. Then close all drain cocks, and fill all the water passages with kerosene or fuel oil, through the water-outlet tube. This is particularly important if the boat has been operated in salt water, as this treatment will exclude oxygen and thus retard rusting. After filling, open the lowest petcock and drain out about a quart; water, being heavier than oil, will be forced out at the bottom. Close petcock and refill.

4. Drain the fuel tank, gasoline lines, and carburetor dry. This will prevent "sweating" and consequent water in the gasoline next spring. Most yards require this as a precaution against fire. Remember also that gasoline will get "stale," losing its more volatile fractions by evaporation; also ethyl gasoline has a chemical property of depositing a rubberlike gum or gel that will foul up the fuel pump and carburetor. Clean the gas tank now; it will be easier than in the spring.

5. Protect cylinder walls by coating them with a thin film of lubricating oil (S.A.E. 30). Simplest way to do this is to remove spark plugs and pour a half cupful of oil into each cylinder. Then crank the motor over a few times by hand, with the spark plugs out, to distribute this oil evenly over the cylinder walls. *Caution:* If you use the electric starter for cranking the motor at this time, the spark plugs *must be out,* otherwise the oil may be compressed enough to break the pistons.

6. Care of electrical equipment: Remove the coil, the high-tension wires, and the magneto (if any). These parts can best be kept clean and dry in some safe place at home. Starter and generators may also be removed, but if they are left on the motor they should be cleaned and wrapped with rags. Spark plugs should be replaced in the cylinder head and tightened down firmly. These protect the threads and seal out dirt. Do not use corks in spark-plug holes.

7. Care of batteries: Replenish water to bring level ⅜″ above the plates. Fully charge the battery to 1.275 gravity, then store in a clean dry place and keep charged. Battery should be inspected once a month during the winter; your marine dealer will take care of this for you at small cost. Clean the cable terminals by dipping them in a solution of baking soda, then dry them and coat lightly with vaseline or thin grease. Badly corroded terminals should be replaced.

8. External care of the engine:

   a. Cover all surfaces having a tendency to rust by painting or spraying with oil. Use an oily rag, a paint brush, or a spray gun, and pay particular attention to rusty spots. Remove the valve-cover plate, and paint or spray the valve springs, valve stems, and all exposed metal parts that are not painted. (A valve spring which is protected against rust will seldom, if ever, break.)

   b. Examine the paint on the outside of the engine, and repaint any damaged spots before rust appears.

   c. Always disconnect the propeller shaft from the engine at the coupling *before hauling boat from the water.* This is to prevent straining or bending the shaft. Now is a good time to check your propeller for bent blades.

   d. Put a tarpaulin or waterproof canvas cover loosely over the engine to protect it from water drips and snow. Be sure the covering is not too tight, because good ventilation is desirable; this discourages condensation and rust.

9. How about overhauling? If your engine has been in use for several years, its performance will be improved by a general overhaul. Winter is the time to do it. Don't wait until the spring rush season.

10. Order spare parts at this time through your dealer; you will get best service. Be sure to supply identification of model and serial number. These will be found on a brass plate, usually riveted to the cylinder block, manifold, or reverse-gear cover.

YOU'LL WANT TO THINK OF THESE THINGS IN THE SPRING

1548

1. Fill the tanks with a good grade of clean gasoline, of the octane rating recommended for your engine.

2. Double check your gasoline line and fittings for leaks.

3. Check the lubricating oil, and make sure the crankcase is filled to the high-level mark on depth stick, with any good nationally advertised oil of the correct viscosity, as recommended in the instruction book for your engine.

4. Put new grease in all grease cups, and a few drops of oil in the oil cups of generator and starter, also on all control joints. Remove all old grease carefully from grease cups before refilling.

5. Brighten up the terminal posts on the batteries, using steel wool, and attach cables. After tightening down the clamps, smear lightly with vaseline or grease to exclude acid and air. Do not put vaseline on the battery posts *before* attaching the cables, as vaseline is a nonconductor.

6. Clean all contacts inside the distributor with fine sandpaper (No. 00) or a small file. If the points are pitted, dress them down evenly on an oil stone, or better still, replace them with a new set of points; these are inexpensive and easily installed. Wipe inside of distributor clean, and rub a very thin film of cup grease around the cam and the terminals inside the cap.

7. Inspect top of pistons by looking through the spark-plug holes, using a flashlight, and make sure there is no excess oil standing on top of the pistons. Inspect spark plugs and check to make certain they are set for the correct gap, as specified in instruction book. If they look doubtful, replace them with new plugs of the correct heat range, or have them sand-blasted and tested. One faulty plug can cause you no end of trouble.

8. Now is a good time to check over your stock of spares. It is good policy to carry on board an extra condenser, distributor rotor, distributor cap, coil, set of distributor points, and set of spark plugs. These are inexpensive items, and having them may save you a day's cruising sometime. Some owners also carry a spare water pump and spare propeller.

9. Tighten down all bolts, nuts, screws, etc., paying particular attention to the cylinder head studs, the lag screws holding engine to the bed, and electrical connections.

10. Reconnect the coupling *after* the boat is put in the water, and check the alignment. Tighten up on stuffing boxes and water-pump packing glands.

11. *Caution:* Before starting the motor, open the hatches and let the boat "air out." If boat is equipped with an engine-room ventilating fan, let the fan run long enough to insure a complete change of air. Make sure the bilge is dry. Be sure there is no possible cause of fire—rags, gas or oil leaks, open tins of kerosene or gasoline, etc.—anywhere around the boat.

12. Finally, with gas in the tank, oil in the base, propeller tight on the shaft, stuffing boxes tight, and the motor hitting on every cylinder, water coming freely through the overflow, oil gauge and ammeter readings OK, you will be ready for a trial run. It is very important to check your clutch and reverse gear carefully at this time to make sure they are properly adjusted. A loose clutch will wear prematurely.

ENGINE TOOL KIT FOR A BOAT

1549   Engine tools, at times, can be quite as vital to the safety of lives afloat as the life preservers. Not many boats have *all* the tools they might require; but although it is not necessary to sail with a machine shop, certain basic tools are a *must*. Even the outboard boater—or perhaps we should say especially the outboard boater—should have a simple kit. It should contain slip-joint pliers, a screwdriver to fit the screws on his particular motor (straight, crosshead, or both) spark-plug wrench and a test lamp of the same voltage as the electrical system on the boat.

The outboarder will find anything further of little use, for outboard motors today are assembled with special factory tools and processes that cannot be duplicated with average hand tools. Take it to the dealer, as was intended by the manufacturer. A ditty box of "junk" might be of more use than sophisticated tools, because most trouble is simple. Thus a fine wire or two, some tape, a length of fuel hose, a spark plug could very well send you on your way.

The owner of a large cruising boat might well use more sophisticated tools, especially the special tools needed for *his* engine. This would include a spark-plug wrench, with extension handle, a box or spanner capable of handling bolts such as stuffing-box bolts, engine bolts, all the through-hull fittings, etc.

Following is the tool box inventory of my own vessel, the Penbo trawler *Penobscot*, which is included as a start from which to take off and specify *your* tool kit. *Penobscot* has a single Gray diesel, a generator, an outboard motor, and the usual appliances—themselves sometimes needing quite sophisticated tools! This is in *addition* to the carpentry and painting tools carried.

1 medium-size ball peen hammer
1 12″ hacksaw and frame
1 wire cutters
1 electrician's pliers
Assorted small pliers, grips
1 small vise-grip
1 large vise-grip
Assorted files, all shapes
1 small rasp
Straight screwdrivers, square shank, in 3 sizes
Cross-head screwdrivers, square shank, in 4 sizes (Reed & Prince or Phillips)
Combination angle screwdriver (cross-straight)
1 set ratchet socket wrenches ⅜″ to 1″ × 1/16 ths.

Large spanners, 1″ to 2¼″
1 set valve wrenches
3 sizes of Stillson wrench
1 adjustable monkey wrench
1 hand drill and metal drills/countersinks
1 reamer
1 9″ tin snips
1 16″ wrecking bar
3 assorted cold chisels
1 soldering gun, 110 V. A. C.
1 leaf gauge
1 probe
1 heavy magnet (on a brass chain) for retrieving
1 test light
1 polarity tester
1 battery terminal cleaner
Assorted punches, pricks, and sets.

—and I have used every tool!

PROPELLER SIZES

1550 Printing suggested propeller sizes in table form is an unusual procedure. However, the following tables have been prepared by the Gray Marine Motor Company of Detroit, Michigan, after many years of experience in the marine motor field and in the light of many thousands of individual problems that this large manufacturer has solved for the boatowner. The Gray Marine Motor Company points out that to apply these charts intelligently is to remember that the sizes given are *average*; also that for extreme economy and for special cases, larger sizes are often used to advantage. These suggested wheel sizes will not fit all boats, and it should be remembered that diameter and pitch have to be varied according to the characteristics of the hull. Propeller sizes given are for three-blade wheels. For auxiliary two-blade propellers, increase diameter. Wheel sizes given are mostly unsuited for towing service, which requires more diameter and less pitch. The general rule when slip is excessive is to increase diameter and decrease pitch. When highest economy is wanted, use more diameter or pitch. Twin-screw installations usually need a higher ratio of pitch to diameter, because one engine takes the load off the other.

Propeller and engine manufacturers generally maintain a service for their users which recommends proper propeller sizes. In requesting such information, provide the manufacturer with length, beam, and draft; type of boat and uses; speed desired and size of the present wheel (if any). A picture of the boat, out of water, if possible, helps greatly, as well as any general information, such as thickness of deadwood, distance from it to wheel, and type of rudder. Naturally, the make, horsepower, drive, and all information about the motor including the rated rpm and piston displacement is necessary as well.

It may be noted that both four- and five-blade wheels have been tried in recent years, replacing the standard traditional three-blade propellers of the past. The five-blade wheel is an efficient forward propeller but almost completely lacks backing power and has largely been abandoned in small craft. However, the four-blade wheel is a fine performer and is gradually becoming the standard yacht propeller. Up to about a 30″ diameter, the rule for replacement is: same diameter as a three-blade wheel but 1″ less pitch. Thus three-blade tables such as Figure 1550 may be used for four-blade wheels with the above adjustment.

Variable-pitch wheels, which require a complex, manually adjusted mechanism, have some specialized uses (as in a utility craft that may be called upon for high speed as well as towing) and are occasionally found on yachts. Feathering wheels, the feathering sequence usually automatic as soon as shaft power is removed, are popular on sailing craft, especially racers. The drag of an idle propeller can be considerable in light breezes, and it is usual when power is shut down to let the wheel turn with the boat's progress; a practice of dubious advantage at high speeds under sail when gear trains operate for long periods in reverse. A cure is a single-way clutch astern of the engine clutch/reduction gear train.

High-speed wheels are very sensitive to imbalance and when nicked or bent should be immediately sent for a reconditioning. Use of a wheel seriously out of balance, even at moderate speeds, can result in a bent or sprung shaft, excessive wear in the stuffing gland and stern bearing, crystallized struts, and a high, unpleasant vibration and noise level.

LARGE CENTER FIGURES REFER TO AVERAGE DIAMETER AND PITCH. THE LOWER FIGURES COVER SUGGESTED RANGES.

Horse-power	Med. & Hvy. Duty Eng.	Direct Drive	1.5:1 Ratio	2:1 Ratio	2.5:1 Ratio	3:1 Ratio	3.5:1 Ratio
16	69 cu. in.	12 x 8 14 x 8—10 x 10		16 x 12 18 x 10—15 x 13			
22	91 cu. in.	12 x 10 15 x 8—11 x 8		17 x 12 19 x 10—15 x 14			
27	112 cu. in.	13 x 10 15 x 9—12 x 11		18 x 12 20 x 12—15 x 15			
37	140 cu. in.	14 x 10 16 x 9—12 x 12	15 x 13 17 x 11—16 x 12	18 x 14 21 x 14—18 x 16	20 x 16 22 x 16—18 x 18	20 x 18 20 x 20—18 x 20	22 x 20 20 x 22—20 x 20
42	162 cu. in.	15 x 10 17 x 10—13 x 12	16 x 13 18 x 11—15 x 12	22 x 14 20 x 14—18 x 18	22 x 18 22 x 20—22 x 16	22 x 20 24 x 20—24 x 18	24 x 20 26 x 20—22 x 22
55	200 cu. in.	14 x 11 16 x 9—13 x 12	16 x 13 18 x 10—15 x 12	20 x 14 19 x 14—16 x 18	22 x 16 20 x 18—18 x 20	24 x 18 22 x 20—20 x 22	24 x 22 28 x 20—22 x 24
68	218 cu. in.	15 x 11 16 x 10—13 x 12	16 x 14 17 x 12—15 x 14	20 x 15 22 x 16—18 x 16	22 x 18 24 x 16—20 x 20	24 x 20 22 x 22—22 x 20	26 x 22 28 x 20—24 x 24
83	244 cu. in.	15 x 12 17 x 10—14 x 12	17 x 13 18 x 12—15 x 15	20 x 16 24 x 16—18 x 18	24 x 18 26 x 18—22 x 24	26 x 20 28 x 18—24 x 24	28 x 26 30 x 26—28 x 28
87	290 cu. in.	16 x 10 17 x 10—14 x 12	17 x 14 19 x 12—17 x 15	22 x 18 26 x 16—20 x 18	24 x 20 26 x 18—22 x 24	26 x 22 28 x 20—24 x 24	30 x 24 32 x 22—28 x 28
96	330 cu. in.	16 x 11 18 x 10—15 x 11	18 x 14 20 x 12—18 x 18	20 x 20 26 x 18—24 x 20	26 x 20 28 x 18—24 x 24	28 x 22 30 x 20—26 x 26	32 x 24 34 x 22—30 x 26
101	383 cu. in.	18 x 10 18 x 13—16 x 14	20 x 18 22 x 16—20 x 16	26 x 22 28 x 24—24 x 24	30 x 24 28 x 26—28 x 28	34 x 24 30 x 28—32 x 26	36 x 26 32 x 28—34 x 28
122	372 cu. in.	15 x 14 18 x 12—17 x 11	19 x 16 22 x 14—18 x 17	24 x 20 22 x 20—22 x 22	24 x 24 26 x 22—26 x 24	26 x 26 28 x 24—28 x 22	28 x 28 32 x 24—30 x 24

1550 Table of three-bladed propeller sizes

WHEEL SIZE FOR HIGH-SPEED DIRECT-DRIVE ENGINES

Horsepower	Wheel Size
45	10 x 10
	10 x 9
62	11 x 11
	11 x 12
75	11 x 12
	12 x 12
86	12 x 12
	11 x 12
90	12 x 12
	12 x 13
103	12 x 13
	12 x 12
125	13 x 14
	13 x 13
140–160	12 x 14
	13 x 14
	12½ x 16
	13 x 15
180	15 x 14
	15 x 15

SOME PROPULSION FORMULAS

1551   Approximate speed formula: Multiply the power of your engine by 1,000 and divide by the total weight of your boat in pounds. Take the cube root of this figure and multiply it by the square root of the waterline length. Next multiply your last figure by from 1.2 to 1.6, depending upon the type of boat. For a heavy, beamy cruiser use 1.2; a medium cruiser, 1.3; a light cruiser, 1.4; a husky open boat, 1:5, and a light runabout, 1.6. The result will be the estimated speed in statute miles per hour. Speed is usually expressed in knots. To obtain nautical miles divide the result by the factor 1.15.

Another formula for speed: Multiply the length of your boat by the horsepower and take the cube root of the result. Divide this by the beam of the boat and then multiply by a figure ranging between 8 and 10 for the average boat, although you can go as high as 20 for an extremely fast, lightweight boat.

Horsepower formula: Square the bore in inches and multiply by the stroke in inches, in each case changing fractions to decimals.

Then multiply by the number of cylinders, then by the r.p.m. and finally by a factor ranging between .65 for an ordinary machine up to 1.2 for the most efficient possible type of engine. On the average, it is better to use a factor of about .8. Divide the result of all this multiplication by 10,000 and the result should be horsepower.

Shaft diameters: Shaft diameters will vary considerably due to the speed of the boat, the power of the engine and many other factors. However, for a rough estimate, you can assume that a propeller not more than 10″ in diameter will need a ¾″ shaft. 12″ wheels will need a ⅞″ shaft; 14″ wheels a 1″ shaft; 16″, a 1¼″ diameter; 18″ wheels, 1⅜″ shaft, and 20″ wheels, 1½″ shafts. These diameters were figured for hardened bronze shafts; they will be slightly less for a stainless steel or Monel shaft.

RUDDER AREA

1552 For boats between 20′ and 30′ in length, the rudder blade should be about 5% of the figure found by multiplying the waterline length of the boat by the extreme draft. Boats between 40′ and 50′ need rudders of about 4%, while larger ones need an area of about 3%. If the boats are very fast, these areas may be reduced, or if very slow, or sailing boats, they must be increased.

⚓

PART V
SAFETY

CHAPTER XVI

SAFETY AT SEA

1601 Safety at sea is the twin art of *keeping out of trouble* and *getting out of trouble* if you get into it.

The more the boatman is prepared by experience and equipment and common sense to keep out of trouble, the less he will have to get out of trouble. Very few of the troubles that beset the ship at sea are to be dismissed by that all-inclusive phrase "dangers of the sea." A storm at sea is not a deadly hazard if the boat is seaworthy and the ship and crew prepared for the blow. Yet a mild gale at sea can be a disaster to the ship that ought never to venture from smooth water because of design or condition, and whose crew have not suspected the blow until it descended upon the unprepared ship. A fire on shipboard is a disaster; yet most fires anywhere are preventable, not by the use of an extinguisher, but rather by proper design and insulation, and safe and sane equipment, thought of long before the extinguisher is needed.

Keeping out of trouble starts with an intelligent and unemotional survey of the boat, in which every possible contingency is understood, and means taken to prevent that contingency. The means taken include the following:

1. Correction of the basic elements of a hazard or a danger.
   (Examples: Clear, unobstructed decks to make tripping and falling overboard unlikely. Backfire traps on carburetors.)
2. Proper equipment at hand to control mishaps that, uncontrolled, could become tragedies.
   (Examples: Life preservers, accessible and usable. Means of signaling. Fire extinguishers.)

3. Training and experience.
   (Examples: Thorough understanding of the Rules of the Road.
   Knowledge of the use of danger-fighting equipment. Common
   sense and sanity applied to weather, speed, organization, etc.)

The last mentioned is the most important. The boatman of experience and judgment seldom has to worry about getting out of serious
trouble because he doesn't often get into it. He sails only when his
boat is in top-notch condition, and fully equipped; when the
weather—present and predicted—is suitable and safe for *his* boat;
when he is prepared to meet any possible danger—including the
danger of boatmen not of his own experience and common sense.

On board will be the equipment peculiarly suited to his boat and
his problems in meeting danger. The skeleton of such equipment
will be the items of equipment required by the government. To
them he will add whatever is still needed to make his vessel as safe
as possible. Government equipment is required to prevent collision
at night or in fog, to fight fire, to prevent gasoline fire and explosion, and to sustain persons afloat in the water. (*Chapter IV*) Voluntarily, the boatman must provide his own means of anchoring,
signaling, preventing fire or explosion from other sources than the
engine, heaving to, calming waves, stopping leaks, and a great many
other things. The amount, utility, and fitness of all this equipment,
plus the amount of knowledge and experience in the crew, make a
ship safe or not safe.

Two of every known safety device on board and a lubber at the
wheel do not make a safe ship.

No safety devices on board and an experienced seaman and navigator at the wheel do not necessarily make a dangerous ship.

Getting out of trouble starts with a basic knowledge of seamanship and the ability to use, under emergency conditions, safety devices and maneuvers. It means preparation by drill and organization,
and having ready and in usable condition the devices required to
control or remedy the trouble.

When trouble comes at sea, it is usually complex, a combination
of several troubles. There are few situations for which a specific can
be prescribed. Only by understanding the nature of each trouble
can the vessel again be put into a safe condition. Thus, a fire might
disable the engine and burn away the steering control. Putting the

fire out saves the ship for the moment but a jury sail and rudder are still needed, or signals must be made, the vessel anchored, and a tow called to save the life of the boat and its company.

Fire

KEEPING OUT OF TROUBLE

1602 Government regulations for motorboats require a back-fire trap on every gasoline marine engine except an outboard motor. These traps must be of approved make, and those sold with marine plants are of approved make. Lighting plants or gasoline-driven pumps must have the carburetors so fitted.

As an additional precaution, the safe installation will always see a drip pan placed under the carburetor. This is covered with a fine flame-arresting mesh and a sump pump led to the intake manifold to draw off any raw gasoline which collects.

Government regulations also require that a motor that is boxed in (as under a bridge deck, cockpit floor, etc.) must be ventilated outboard. Cowl- or equal-type ventilators are required, and are so arranged as to form a positive draft. General ventilation of the hull is desirable, not only to disperse dangerous gases but to prevent dry rot in the hull parts and to keep the boat "sweet."

1603 Both the backfire trap and ventilator regulations are aimed at preventing gasoline explosion.

Gasoline fumes may come from leaking or ruptured fuel lines or from improperly installed tanks.

Fuel lines should be strapped down with broad metal straps, screwed to woodwork (not nailed) at frequent enough intervals to prevent any movement of the line. A chafing pad should be inserted between strap and pipe. When led through bulkheads or structural members, the pipe should pass through a hole several times its own diameter. Shut-off valves, manufactured for gasoline lines, should be at the tank outlets, fuel pump, or vacuum tank and carburetor.

Fuel tanks should be most securely chocked and strapped in place. The filler pipes should positively be outboard, so that spilled gasoline and gasoline fumes will pass overboard. Vent pipes for tanks should positively be outboard, so that fumes are drawn away from the boat. The same precautions are to be observed in the installation of other fuel tanks (cooking fuels, lighting-plant fuels, etc.). Diesel-oil tanks are not excepted.

1604   Fire may start from an electric spark. Switches and fuses, if at all possible, should be kept out of the small engine compartment and at least 3' above the floor level. Power ventilators should be equipped with a motor shielded against sparking or, if not, located outside the exhaust duct. Inspection of the electrical system should frequently be made to locate any ruptured or weakened wire before it breaks and sparks and becomes a potential danger. Knife switches should be kept out of the bilge area.

1605   Any minute spark may explode gaseous fumes if present in the boat. Such fumes are heavier than air and settle into the lowest and most difficult to ventilate parts of the boat; hence the required backfire traps and ventilation requirements.

Such fumes are generated chiefly while fueling. Unless the wind is blowing outboard from the filler pipe (not forward, aft, or inboard) all hatches and companions should be closed lest such fumes be whirled into the ship's below decks. Watch also boats that are fueling nearby. Fumes may be undetected by ordinary methods yet be present in dangerous quantities or mixtures. It is safest to assume that they are present and to ventilate carefully before any fire is lighted or engine started. It should be needless to point out that, when fueling, all fires should be out, engine stopped, and smoking on board and nearby strictly prohibited.

There are commercial devices for sale which detect the presence of dangerous gaseous fumes, including fumes from cooking gas, alcohol, turpentine, etc.

1606   Overheated engine parts may cause fire on shipboard. The exhaust line should be lagged with asbestos wherever not water-cooled, especially the engine end of it. Sheet asbestos should line the engine compartment and underneath side of hatches, etc. Shaft bearings should be frequently lubricated; an overheated one can cause fire, especially if the inflammable parts surrounding it have been allowed to become oil-soaked.

1607   Heating and cooking stoves can cause fire. Pressure stoves using kerosene or alcohol for fuel must be most carefully handled at all times. Under no circumstances fill a nearby fuel tank while the stove is lighted. The stoves seldom fail if kept clean and in an unleaky condition. Stove fires are almost always the fault of a careless operator. Any wick or open-fount-type oil stove is dangerous on shipboard and should be replaced by a stove approved by the Underwriters' Laboratories.

LP gas is one of the most dangerous fuels if allowed to escape. Being heavier than air, it is apt to settle deep in the bilges.

Coal, briquet, and wood-heating stoves should be of a "marine" variety and design. This will see adequate provision made for lashing and securing them and assure that all doors are equipped with a seagoing latch, not to be easily or accidentally opened by heeling or pitching.

All stoves should have pot rails to hold cooking pots securely. A spilled pot will cause the flame to jump and possibly ignite some nearby object. All sailing vessels should have pot rails and have the stove hung in gimbals, preferably athwartships. If the stove is not equipped with gimbals and pot rails, no cooking should be done on board at all.

Woodwork adjacent to stove spaces should be protected from the danger of fire by asbestos covering, or metal stove shields, or a similar device. Stovepipes should pass through the deck in a water iron,

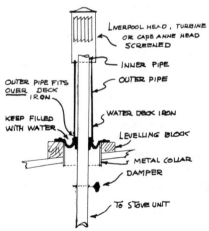

1607 A safe through-deck installation of a smoke pipe from a heating or galley stove. Stainless steel is best for components.

kept filled with water at all times, to prevent scorching the deck and deck beams in their way. The head of the smoke pipe should be fitted with a Charlie Noble or a similar screened device to prevent sparks from flying.

1608 Spontaneous combustion has caused many shipboard fires. Any oil-soaked material may self-ignite under conditions of warmth and absence of ventilation. Suspect paint rags, storm clothing, wiping rags, oil mops, and waxing rags. Usually such fires smolder until given air by opening a locker or bin; then they burst into furious flame. Old oilskins are the gravest offenders. Discard them when the finish becomes tacky. Store new ones in ventilated lockers only, and after thorough drying.

1609 Liquid Petroleum (LP) gas refrigerators in themselves are fairly safe appliances, since they are equipped with automatic shut-offs should the flame be extinguished. However, the lines leading to them, usually hidden outboard in an inaccessible area, are suspect, as are the pipe fittings. Check these regularly, using a soapy water and a soft brush and watch for bubbles. *Do not* test with a match! A proper LP system—and gas is a clean, satisfactory fuel for stoves, refrigeration, and even space heating—should have a master valve on the tank itself *and* another controlling the cooking stove. The latter should be *off* whenever the stove is not in service.

Refrigerators will operate well, even in a moderate seaway, and if the burner and flue are clean. The *average* stance of the flue must be plumb; the occasional roll will not cause trouble. However, if the ship is not plumb in still water, if she is misballasted or has a permanent list, the flue will soot up and the flame become wild. It is best to shut the refrigerator down when in a heavy sea for long periods, especially if there is a chop.

GETTING OUT OF TROUBLE

1610 The types and quantity of required legal fire-fighting apparatus are listed for various classes of boats in Chapter IV. These are *minimum* requirements and may be quite inadequate on all types of boats within the class. Every vessel's fire-fighting equipment should suit that particular vessel.

Any boat with enclosed engine spaces should be equipped with a permanently installed basic fire-suppression system of the carbon-dioxide type. These may be obtained to operate either automatically or manually; the former affording protection 100% of the time, the latter only when an operator is on board.

Fire extinguishers and controls for manually operated CO_2 systems should be located within easy reach. It should not be necessary to reach *through* a fire area for them, or to have to open lockers. Thus, the galley extinguisher should be located between the stove and the exit, not beyond or above the stove nor in a corner opposite to the exit. The main extinguishing system should be within reach of the helmsman on the average small boat.

Some thought of fighting fire should be exerted *before* an emergency. A fire-station bill can be very simply worked out for the organized cruise. Fire drill might be engaged in at the outset of a cruise. A sample fire-station bill is given in Paragraph 726, Chapter VII.

While the actual methods of using the various types of fire extinguishers are given in detail in Paragraph 1424, Chapter XIV, all are dependent upon a smothering action, and, upon the outbreak of a fire, it is good to close hatches, portholes, and ventilators in order to keep the fire-suppressing agent at the fire, not blown away.

If the fire breaks through the deck, head the burning end of the boat to leeward, at slow speed if the fire is forward of the steersman. At all costs keep it from spreading toward the wheel or the life preservers or the lifeboat. A fire can be fought effectively from windward even after extinguishers have become useless (as they usually are in the wind at sea) by water or soaked blankets or chopping away. A burning boat headed to windward will catch completely in a few seconds and drive the crew overboard without a chance of fighting or securing life preservers. If the air is calm, do not hesitate to reverse. Getting to shore is of secondary importance. Maneuvering to control the fire is first.

Auxiliary fire-fighting gear, on a larger yacht, might well include a fire ax, several buckets of sand, water pails (to which a short filling line has been rove), and possibly a pump and hose. A simple system of Y-switches on the electric-bilge pump, or cooling water pump or hand pump can provide a small stream of water of sufficient strength to reach any part of a small boat.

Man Overboard

KEEPING OUT OF TROUBLE

1611 In the ordinary operation of a boat, many situations develop that require taking the risk of falling overboard. There is little to be done about the matter save to remember the old adage of the square-riggers, "One hand for the ship and one for yourself."

Beyond that only a few precautions can be observed to lessen the possibility of such an accident.

Lifelines should be rigged on any vessel, sail or power, that goes to sea, in any place on deck that does not afford a foothold and a *handhold*. Lifelines serve two purposes: one is to provide a handhold (as in going forward along the waterways); the other to serve as a net in the event that one is swept outboard by a boarding sea. The lifeline (or storm rails) should therefore be rigged to exceptionally strong stanchions, should be of wire rope, and should be spaced no more than 12″ apart. A height of 26″ to 30″ from the deck is sufficient. They should positively extend around the stern.

If permanently installed rails or lifelines are absent, every man on deck during rough weather or at night should have an individual lifeline harnessed from himself to some firm part of the ship. It should be in the form of a broad leather or canvas belt around the middle, to which is attached a stout line of about 2″ circumference, of sufficient length not to hinder normal movement about deck, and having the end terminate in a husky snap hook. Many harnesses have double lines, with hooks on each, so a wearer can hook on a new point before unhooking the old line.

When at sea, every boat person should make a habit of reaching up *from* the companionway, before going on deck, to snap the line to a ring. A line fastened to the boat at both ends along the center line, or one along each waterway, should have been rigged before the one along each waterway, should have been rigged before the weather made up. Individuals required to go forward on duty snap their lifelines to this, changing them to shrouds or bowsprit rigging, etc., while working. Naturally, only men who can swim should be detailed to any duty where there is risk of falling overboard.

Untidy decks, or decks cluttered with cleats, halyard leads, uncoiled rope, or ship's gear, cause tripping and should certainly be redesigned with as few tripping hazards as possible.

Proper footgear must be carefully selected for nonslip soles. Rubber boots are slippery and almost impossible to swim in as they fill and weigh down the feet. Any boat liable to an "icing-up" should carry ice creepers for attaching over ordinary footgear. Rubber-soled footgear, even with the popular, fine-treaded soles now so common, is dangerous when worn smooth. They can be kept in a roughened condition by cutting cross slices, or branding in a grid with hot wire or a soldering iron, or by painting with benzol in uneven patches (which will soften and dissolve the rubber).

It should be needless to state that life jackets should be worn by every man having deck duty during rough weather. The soft "racing jacket" is most comfortable and does not retard movement. Look for new, wearable life jackets soon; the Coast Guard is presently developing a new type.

1612 Life preservers are required equipment on motorboats. While the original Motorboat Law did not specify life preservers for sailboats, under the regulations of the Coast Guard (which cover *all* vessels) they are legally required equipment. (*See Paragraph 407*)

The jacket-type life preserver is required on all boats carrying passengers for hire. There must be child's-sized life preservers available if children are in the passenger list. Life preservers should be kept instantly available, either in racks or in plainly marked boxes or lockers.

Supplementary (but not required) lifesaving equipment might include a raft (easily stowed and easily launched and capable of supporting four to eight persons in the water). Federal law now requires at least one throwable preserver—ring, horseshoe or cushion—on all boats over 16', *in addition* to a wearable preserver for each person aboard.

1613 The life preserver jacket is worn exactly like a vest with the lashing in front or zippered and snapped closed.

1614 The ring buoy should be used as shown in Figure 1614. The shoulders may be let through a large ring buoy and the weight rests on the arms. Putting the head through the ring helps somewhat to break the seas and permits easier breathing.

1615 The first duty upon the call "Man overboard" is to get a ring buoy or raft launched. Launch *near*, not *at*, the swimmer. The helmsman should stop the propeller at once and head sharply toward the side from which the person fell, thus swinging the pro-

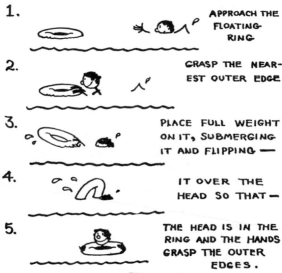

1. APPROACH THE FLOATING RING

2. GRASP THE NEAR-EST OUTER EDGE

3. PLACE FULL WEIGHT ON IT, SUBMERGING IT AND FLIPPING —

4. IT OVER THE HEAD SO THAT —

5. THE HEAD IS IN THE RING AND THE HANDS GRASP THE OUTER EDGES.

1614 How to get into a ring buoy

peller away from the man overboard. A member of the crew should point to the man overboard and keep pointing for the benefit of the helmsman and, if it is launched, the lifeboat. The water light will cast a light by night and thick smoke by day. Man the searchlight at once if at night. See Man Overboard station bill Chapter VII.

It is generally quite useless to launch a small boat of the dinghy type at sea in a storm. Attempt the rescue from the large boat, taking the person aboard on the lee side. If a search must be made mark the course by any handy means, such as leaving a trail of oatmeal, an oil slick, or paper, or by taking shore ranges, so that the same water is not covered twice. If a transmitter is aboard, send a "Pan" urgency call for more searchers.

Shipwreck

KEEPING OUT OF TROUBLE

1616   Shipwreck is usually caused by faulty navigation or poor seamanship or a combination of both. There is no positive way in which to keep out of trouble except to know the boat, its habits and peculiarities and capabilities, and to have the knowledge, judgment, sense, and courage to operate it under safe and sane conditions of weather and sea, and in a safe and sane manner.

It is largely a matter of what has been done and planned long before the moment of danger; the preparation and skill of the skipper and the seaworthiness and condition of the vessel. To elaborate would be to run in circles. Suffice to mention that, in the final analysis, a vessel is no better or safer than the human beings who operate her. She will seldom meet with shipwreck, grounding, stranding, or dismasting unless she has been placed in such danger by ignorance, or stupidity, or carelessness, or drunkenness, by the hand at her controls.

DISMASTING OR BEING SWEPT

1617 The great danger after such a disaster is that spars and loose gear will batter the boat. Cut everything away as soon as possible, saving what can be *safely* saved only. Get hatches on at once (tarpaulin, boards, overturned tables, mattresses) and pump the ship dry. Heaving to, and jury rigs and rudders are discussed elsewhere in this *Manual*.

STRANDING AND GROUNDING

1618 Such accidents on a rising tide are seldom more than annoying, providing the hull has not been punctured. If it has been, judgment must decide whether to abandon ship, or make temporary repairs and remain on board until help comes.

On a falling tide, it may become far more serious than at the moment of striking. The boat can sometimes be placed in a better situation by jettisoning cargo or ballast, or shifting them for balance. Sound the water nearby. A channel may be found ahead or astern and, with weights shifted, the boat might be pried or kedged off, or run out under her own power or sails.

Kedge anchors should be taken out in the proper direction and the warp led to a winch, the capstan or a block and tackle. A lead from an anchor to the masthead, or a parbuckle arrangement, will often heel a stranded boat to the point that she will float off a reef or shoal. Sometimes it is possible to swamp a small boat in such a manner that it will lift the stranded boat as it is pumped dry. Every such accident presents its own peculiar problem, and an effective solution depends upon the skipper's knowledge of seamanship and engineering, as well as his resourcefulness and ingenuity.

Upon stranding, check the bilge at once. Put out all fires. Plug tank vents if the boat has heeled enough to cause spillage. Get a lifeboat or raft over and ready for use. Ventilate or jettison the batteries (salt water and batteries form chlorine gas in lethal quantities). Take steps to prevent the wreck from settling into a still worse position. Pad the hull with life preservers, cushions, etc. if it bears on rocks.

Make distress signals. (Paragraph 801, *Chapter VIII*)

1619 Do not hesitate to ask and take the assistance of the Coast Guard. Such assistance is the primary function of that service and accepting its aid does not create a salvage situation. They should be considered as "in charge" after their appearance; they well understand their duties—the first of which is to save life in danger, then to rescue property.

VESSEL INFORMATION DATA SHEET

When requesting assistance from the Coast Guard, you may be asked to furnish the following details.

1. *Description of Vessel Requiring Assistance:*
   Hull markings
   Home port
   Draft
   Sails: color and markings
   Bowsprit
   Outriggers
   Flying bridge
   Other prominent features

2. *Survival Gear Aboard*
   Personal flotation devices
   Flares
   Flashlight

Raft
Dinghy or tender
Anchor
Spotlight
Auxiliary power
Horn

3. *Electronic Equipment*
   Radiotelephone(s)   VHF   MF   HF
   Channels/frequencies   Ch. 22   2670 kHz
      available (in addition to emergency frequencies)
   Radar
   Depth finder
   Loran
   Direction finder
   EPIRB (Emergency Position-indicating Radio Beacon)

4. *Vessel Owner/Operator*
   Owner name
      Address
      Telephone number
   Operator's name
      Address
      Telephone number
   Is owner/operator an experienced sailor?

5. *Miscellaneous*
   Be prepared to describe local weather conditions.

VESSEL IDENTIFICATION

1. For quick identification at night shine spotlights straight up.
2. If aircraft are involved, once you are identified, turn lights away so as not to blind aircraft crew.

OPERATING CG DROPPABLE PUMPS

1. Make sure suction hose is tight—connect discharge hose.
2. Fill gas tank.

3. Pull stop switch away from spark plug.
4. Close carburetor choke—turn lever in direction of arrow.
5. Open throttle at base of engine.
6. Attach starting cord and spin engine.
7. After engine starts, open choke.
8. Normally, pumps are self-priming. If difficulty arises, prime.
9. When finished, flush out pump with fresh water.

PREPARATIONS FOR TOWING
1. Have forecastle cleared.
2. If line-throwing gun is used, keep all personnel out of way until projectile clears boat.
3. Have material handy for chafing gear.
4. Secure tow line to bitt.
5. Remove heaving line.

IF IT IS A MEDICAL CASE, FOLLOWING ADDITIONAL INFORMATION REQUIRED
1. Is patient stretcher case or can he walk?
2. Temperature and pulse readings.
3. Any vomiting or diarrhea?
4. Any swelling or pain?—give location.
5. Medication you have given.
6. General condition of patient.
7. What you have done for patient and first-aid materials and medicine you have aboard.

HELICOPTER EVACUATION CHECKOFF LIST
As Captain, each member of your crew is your responsibility and although the Coast Guard, the doctors, and other agencies may assist you, he is your man.

Helicopter evacuation is a hazardous operation to the patient AND the plane crew, and should only be attempted in a matter of life or death. Provide the doctor with all the information you can concerning the patient so that an intelligent evaluation can be made concerning the need for evacuation.

Today's helicopters can operate no farther than between 100 and 150 miles offshore for a pickup, and then only if weather conditions permit; so, if an evacuation is necessary, you must be prepared to proceed to a spot within this range.

WHEN REQUESTING HELICOPTER ASSISTANCE

1. Give accurate position, time, speed, course, weather conditions, sea conditions, wind direction, and velocity, type of vessel, and radio frequencies.
2. If not already provided, give *complete* medical information, including whether or not patient is ambulatory.
3. If you are beyond helicopter range, advise your diversion intentions so that a rendezvous point may be selected.
4. If there are any changes in any items, advise immediately. Should the patient die prior to arrival of the helicopter, be sure to advise.

PREPARATIONS PRIOR TO ARRIVAL OF THE HELICOPTER

1. Provide continuous radio guard on Channel 16 (VHF), 2182 kHz or specified VOICE frequency if possible.
2. Select and clear most suitable hoist area. This must include securing of loose gear, awnings, and antenna wires. Trice up running rigging and booms.
3. If hoist is at night, light pickup areas as well as possible. Be sure you *do not shine any lights* on the helicopter and blind the pilot. If there are obstructions in the vicinity, put a light on them so the pilot will be aware of their positions.
4. Advise location of pickup area *before* the helicopter arrives so he may adjust for and make his approach to aft, amidships, or forward, as required.
5. Remember, there will be a high noise level under the helicopter, so voice communication is almost impossible. Arrange a set of hand signals among the crew who will assist.

HOIST OPERATIONS

1. If possible, have patient moved to or close to the hoist area as his condition permits—*time is important*.
2. Normally, if a litter is required, it will be necessary to move the patient to the special litter which will be lowered by the 'copter. Be prepared to do this as quickly as possible. Be sure patient is strapped in, face up, with life jacket, if his condition permits.
3. Be sure patient is tagged to indicate what and when medication, if any, was given.
4. Again, if patient's condition permits, be sure he wears life jacket.
5. Change course to permit the ship to ride as easily as possible with the wind on the bow, preferably on the port bow. Try to choose a course to keep stack gases clear of hoist area.
6. Reduce speed to ease ship's motion but maintain steerageway.
7. If you do not have radio contact with the helicopter, when you are in all respects ready for the hoist, signal it with a "Come On" with hand, or use flashlight at night.
8. *Allow basket or stretcher to touch deck prior to handling to avoid static shock.*
9. If a trail line is dropped by the helicopter, guide basket or stretcher to deck with line; keep line clear at all times. Line will not cause shock.
10. Place patient in basket, sitting with hands clear of sides, or in the litter, as described above. Signal the hoist operator when ready for hoist. Patient nods head if he is able. Deck personnel give thumbs up.
11. If necessary to take litter away from hoist point, unhook hoist cable and keep free for the helicopter to haul in. *Do not secure cable to vessel or attempt to move stretcher without unhooking.*
12. When patient is strapped in stretcher, signal the helicopter to lower cable, hook up, and signal hoist operator when ready to hoist. Steady stretcher against swinging or turning.
13. If trail line is attached to basket or stretcher, use to steady. Keep feet clear of line.

To Handle an Emergency via Marine Telephone to Coast Guard

1620

DISTRESS COMMUNICATIONS FORM

Instructions: Complete this form now (except for items six through nine) and post near your radiotelephone.

Speak   *Slowly — Clearly — Calmly*

1. Make sure your radiotelephone is on.
2. Select either VHF *Channel 16* (156.8 MHz) or *2182* kHz.
3. Press microphone button and say "MAYDAY — MAYDAY — MAYDAY."
4. Say: "This is _____, _____, _____
                 your boat name   your boat name   your boat
   _____, _____."
   name   your call letters
5. Say "MAYDAY 3 _____."
                 your boat name
6. Tell where you are (What navigational aids or landmarks are near?).
7. State the nature of your distress.
8. Give number of adults and children aboard, and conditions of any injured.
9. Estimate present seaworthiness of your boat.
10. Briefly describe your boat: _____; _____
                                State Registration No. Length

    Feet; _____ Feet; _____; _____ Hull; _____ Trim;
          Draft   Type   Color   Color

    _____ Masts; _____ Power; _____
    Number   Type; Horsepower   Construction

    _____.
    Material

    Anything else you think will help rescuers to find you.
11. Say: "I will be listening on *Channel 16   /   2182*."
                        Cross out one which does not apply.

12. End Message by saying: "This is _____

your boat name and call

_____. Over."

letters

13. Release microphone button and listen: Someone should answer. *If they do not, repeat call, beginning at item 3 above.* If there is still no answer, switch to another channel and begin again.

Notify the Coast Guard Promptly As Soon As the Emergency Terminates

SIGNALS FROM AN AIRCRAFT

1621   The international signal for an aircraft that wants to direct a surface craft to a distress is: Circling the surface craft, opening and closing the throttle or changing propeller pitch (*noticeable by change in sound*) while crossing ahead of the surface craft, and proceeding in the direction of the distress. If you receive such a signal, you should follow the aircraft. If you cannot do so, try to inform the aircraft by any available means. If your assistance is no longer needed, the aircraft will cross your wake, opening and closing the throttle or changing propeller pitch. If you are radio equipped, you should attempt to communicate with the aircraft on 2182 kHz when the aircraft makes the above signals or makes any obvious attempt to attract your attention. In the event that you cannot communicate by radio, be alert for a message block dropped from the aircraft.

THE FLOAT PLAN

1622

Prudent cruisers, even if only weekending, often file a form containing the information suggested below. It can be written out and left with a yacht club steward, the marina operator, mailed (on a postcard) to a friend, your wife, your office, the local police, or the nearest Coast Guard station. It can save frustration and anguish and hours of time and danger. And remember, when you return, call in and clear yourself.

Float Plan for:
(Name of boat, owner or skipper) _____
If overdue, contact: local area Coast Guard, Police, etc. Advise them
as follows:

BOAT

Name of vessel _____
Registry number _____
Power _____
                          (inboard, outboard, sail)
Length overall _____
Color of hull _____ Rig _____
                  (white hull, blue top, etc.)   (type, sloop, etc.)
Radio aboard _____ _____
                  transmit frequency   receive frequency
Number of persons aboard _____
                                    adults   children
Departure from _____
Date and time of departure _____
Destination _____
Date and estimated time of return _____
Route or cruising plans _____
Time after which boat is overdue _____

BOARDING A WRECK—HINTS

1623 It is best in most cases to approach and board a vessel,
whether stranded or afloat, from the lee side. The greatest danger
lies in the sea's crashing your boat against the vessel or in being
swamped as the sea breaks away from it. The sea is always more
violent on the weather side of the vessel. A vessel stranded broadside to the sea presents such hazards as wreckage alongside, which
may damage the boat, and the possibility of a falling mast, a stove-in
lifeboat, or other gear that may have become awash. The presence
of these dangers may make it advisable to carry out rescue from
bow or stern.

To carry out rescue from a drifting wreck, come in from leeward
keeping a sharp lookout for floating wreckage. In a strong wind lay
off and heave a line aboard. Instruct a seaman aboard the wreck (if
there is one) to secure the line to one person's body with a French
bowline and have the person jump overboard. Haul him aboard and

repeat the operation. Remember that there is great danger of swamping if you take your boat alongside a wreck that is rapidly drifting to leeward. If you must go alongside, do so with bow or stern to the sea ladder and hold your boat at right angles to the wreck. From this position it will be much safer when pulling away.

A wrecked craft with very low freeboard is best boarded from the weather quarter. This action cuts down the danger from her main booms, chains, etc.

FOG

1624   Fog has no terror for the capable navigator. He knows exactly where he is at all times and proceeds in such a manner as to be in a position to avoid collision, indicating his position and course to other traffic.

Rules of the Road provide that speed in fog or thick weather should be reduced or maintained at "moderate," with due regard to circumstances and conditions. When any fog signal is heard forward of the beam, the law provides that the vessel hearing it must stop and then navigate with extreme caution until danger of collision is past. A boat should always be able to stop within one-half the distance of visibility.

Motorboats 16' to 26' must be equipped with (and use as a fog signal) a whistle capable of being heard one half mile. On larger boats, the whistle must be audible at least one mile, and a fog bell must be carried as well. No motorboat makes fog signals on a foghorn. Boats under 16' need not carry whistle or bell.

SOUND SIGNALS FOR FOG (INLAND RULE)
1625

Motorboats (On Whistle)

1. Under way.—A prolonged blast at least once every minute.
2. Towing.—One prolonged blast and two short blasts, in succession, at least once every minute.
3. Towed.—Same (but no other signal).
4. At anchor.—A rapid ringing of the bell for at least five seconds at least once every minute.

Sailboats (On Foghorn)

1. Starboard tack.—One blast at least every minute.
2. Port tack.—Two blasts at least once every minute.
3. Wind abaft the beam.—Three blasts at least once every minute.
4. At anchor.—Same as motorboat.

Fog distorts, blankets, and magnifies sound in unpredictable ways, and bearings taken from sound signals during thick weather are not to be relied upon. The cautious and experienced navigator relies upon the three L's of navigation in thick weather—log, lead, and lookout. Radio bearings, on the radio-equipped boat, are reliable during fog.

1625 Fog in itself is in no way dangerous. Fog combined with poor navigation or seamanship can be dangerous and may cause shipwreck or collision. Beyond that the worst that can happen is to become lost—and the only way to get out of such trouble is to anchor. Deepwater men of long experience do not fear fog. They navigate to the best of their ability—and the moment they become lost, they humbly and wisely anchor.

There is no alternative within the bounds of prudence or good seamanship.

SAFETY EQUIPMENT FOR SMALL BOATS
IN ADDITION TO REQUIRED EQUIPMENT

1626 Auxiliary fire-suppression apparatus
Life rafts
Water lights
Shoulder gun (for throwing line)
Very pistol (for signaling and lighting dangerous waters at night)
Signaling gear (such as a gun, blinker, flares, etc.)
Sheet and storm anchors (with lines)
First-aid kits
Auxiliary lights (may be oil, or spare standard lights)

⚓

CHAPTER XVII

FIRST AID AND SANITATION

First Aid *

INTRODUCTION

First aid, in any situation, consists of the emergency treatment of the sick and injured before trained medical attention can be obtained. The purposes of first aid are:

1. To save life.
2. To prevent further injury or unfavorable progression.
3. To preserve resistance and vitality.

A real knowledge of first aid and its purposes, when properly applied, may mean the difference between life and death, between rapid recovery and long hospitalization, between temporary disability and permanent injury.

Proper knowledge and skill in first aid are musts for every boatman. Boats frequently operate at a considerable distance from sources of medical care and certain injuries or illnesses may be fatal unless intelligent care is given immediately.

This brochure provides the boatman with information pertinent to life threatening injuries. The first aid advice is based on the American National Red Cross Standard First Aid and Personal Safety Textbook, Cardiopulmonary Resuscitation Manual (CG-139), and Handbook of the Hospital Corps (NAVMED-P-5004).

Before discussing care of the wounded and injured, a word or

---

* U.S. Coast Guard 1978 edition of "First Aid for the Boatman," Aux-206.

two is directed to the boatman who will have the responsibility of providing first aid. You should:

1. Keep calm, never permitting yourself to become excited or confused.
2. Act quickly, with efficiency and confidence, making a decision on priorities as soon as possible.

You should practice the first aid skills described in this brochure before you are involved in an emergency situation. An even better idea is to enroll in the Standard First Aid Course conducted by the American Red Cross. You will gain additional first aid knowledge and skills that could save a life or prevent unnecessary suffering.

THE FOUR PRINCIPLES OF FIRST AID

The following four principles of first aid present a topical outline for learning and retaining the essential knowledge and skills in first aid. Memorizing these principles will also assist you in knowing how to act and in what order to act if you encounter a situation requiring first aid:

1. Check and Clear the Airway.
2. Stop the Bleeding.
3. Protect the Wounds.
4. Treat for Shock.

Check and Clear The Airway

Resuscitation is a general term which covers all of the measures taken to restore life or consciousness to an individual who is apparently dead. These measures include artificial respiration to restore normal respiratory function, and closed chest heart massage to restore normal heart beat. Time is of prime importance. SECONDS COUNT. If a person stops breathing, he can die within 4–6 minutes. Mouth-to-mouth or mouth-to-nose artificial respiration should be started at once in any case where breathing has ceased.

Only after artificial respiration has been initiated and after it has been determined that the heart has stopped, should external heart massage be started and combined with artificial respiration to give cardiopulmonary resuscitation.

The following techniques should govern cardiopulmonary resuscitation (C.P.R.) procedures:

Mouth-To-Mouth Breathing

1. This is ALWAYS started first, and then the necessity for external heart massage is determined.
2. Place victim on his back.
3. Kneel beside the victim's shoulder.
4. Clear the victim's mouth and air passages of foreign objects, i.e., chewing gum, dentures, seaweed (drowning victim), etc.

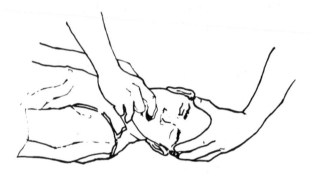

Figure 1

5. Place one hand under victim's neck.
6. Place other hand on victim's forehead so that thumb and forefinger can close the nose.

7. Lift gently with hand under neck while pushing down with hand on forehead. This will extend the neck and open the air passages in the vast majority of cases.

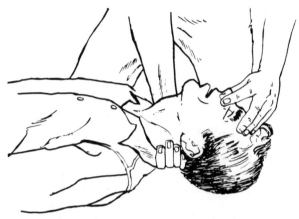

Figure 2

8. Initially, give the victim four (4) quick breaths without interruption, then take a deep breath (about twice the normal), open your mouth wide, place your mouth over the victim's mouth and blow.

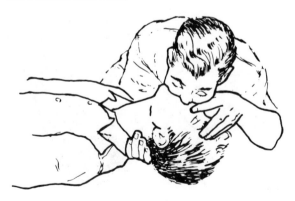

Figure 3

9. Watch for victim's chest to rise. As soon as this happens, remove your mouth from the victim's and allow the air to expire naturally from the victim's chest.
10. Repeat 12–14 times a minute for adults, 18–20 for children and infants.
11. If the chest does not rise, one or more of the following conditions exists and must be corrected:
    a. Airleak.
       (1) Make sure that there is an airtight seal between your mouth and the victim's and that the seal on the victim's nose is secure.
    b. Airway obstruction (more likely).
       (1) Insert your finger in the victim's mouth and remove any foreign objects (false teeth, etc.), vomit and/or blood clots.
       (2) For adults—see section on "Choking Accidents."
       (3) For children—Roll infant over your forearm and give a sharp blow between the shoulder blades.
12. If the chest still fails to rise, remove hand from neck, insert your thumb into the victim's mouth and grab lower jawbone (mandible) between the thumb and finger, lift jawbone upward, holding it in this position while you continue to perform mouth-to-mouth breathing.

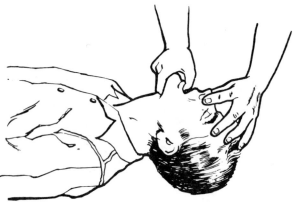

Figure 4

13. In children and infants, a lesser amount of air is necessary. In infants, the amount of air that can be held in your cheeks may be sufficient. The rescuer must cover both the mouth and nose of the infant or child with his mouth. Inflate the lungs once every three seconds (18–20 per minute). Forceful backward tilting of the infant's head may obstruct the breathing passages. Therefore, do not exaggerate the head tilt position.

14. Mouth-to-nose breathing may be carried out using much the same technique as for mouth-to-mouth, except, of course, the victim's mouth is held closed while your mouth is placed over the victim's nose.

15. If you are hesitant to place your mouth over the victim's, satisfactory mouth-to-mouth breathing can be carried out through a handkerchief. Airways and tubes should not be used. Not only are they dangerous when used by untrained personnel, but also are usually not available when such an emergency arises.

External Heart Massage

1. After artificial respiration has been instituted with four quick breaths, and only then, check to see if external heart massage should be started.
   a. It is needed only if the heart has stopped.
   b. In many cases, the initiation of artificial respiration will be sufficient to cause resumption of the heartbeat.

2. Check for pulse.
   a. The best pulse to check is the carotid in the neck. This is a large artery lying close to the surface on either side of the Adam's apple. Practice feeling your own carotid pulse.

3. Check the pupils.
   a. If the pupils are dilated and do not constrict (get smaller) when light hits them, the blood flow to the brain is insufficient.

4. If there is no pulse and/or the pupils are dilated and do not constrict, start external heart massage.

5. For external heart massage to be effective, the victim must be on a firm surface, i.e., ground, spineboard, or floor.

6. Locate notch at top of breastbone.
7. Locate the lower end of the breastbone. Great care must be exercised *not* to place your hand over the tip of the breastbone (xiphoid process).
8. Measure two fingerwidths up from the xiphoid process, and place the heel of one hand over lower one-third of breastbone, and the other hand on top of first.

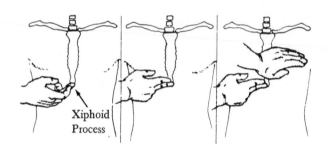

Figure 5

9. Bring shoulders directly over the victim's breastbone. Keep your arms straight and rock back and forth slightly from the

hip joints exerting pressure vertically downward to depress the lower breastbone.

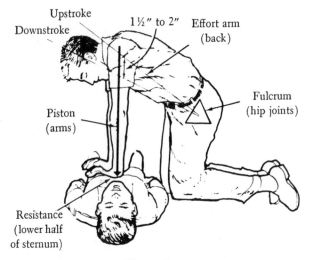

Figure 6

10. Then release pressure immediately. Compression and relaxation must be of equal duration. Do not remove the heel of your hand from the victim's chest when the pressure is released. Be sure that the pressure is completely released so that the breastbone returns to its normal resting position between compressions.

11. The breastbone should be compressed 1½ to 2 inches for adults. For small children only the heel of one hand is used; for infants, only the tips of the middle and index finger are used to compress the sternum. In small children and infants, the heart lies higher in the chest and external compression should be applied over the mid-sternum.

12. This cycle is repeated 60–80 times per minute in adults, 80–100 in children, and *should be in a smooth, rhythmic fashion.*

13. Keep your fingers away from the victim's ribs to avoid fractures. Fingers may be interlocked during this procedure to assist in keeping them off the chest wall.

14. Check pulse frequently to see if the victim's heart has restarted.

Techniques of C.P.R. For One and Two Rescuers.

1. If only one rescuer is present, he must of necessity, administer both artificial respiration and external heart massage. This can be managed by interrupting external heart massage every 15 beats to give 2 deep lung inflations. Because of the interruptions for the lung inflation, the single rescuer must administer each series of 15 chest compressions at a more rapid rate, 80 compressions per minute, in order to achieve an actual compression rate of 60 compressions per minute. The two deep inflations must be administered in quick succession, within a period of 5 seconds. DO NOT allow full, long exhalation between breaths.

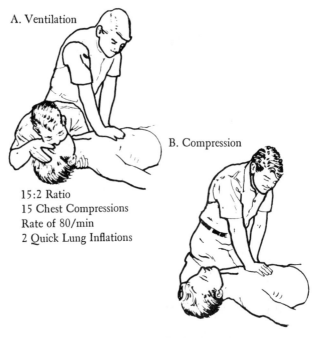

A. Ventilation

B. Compression

15:2 Ratio
15 Chest Compressions
Rate of 80/min
2 Quick Lung Inflations

Figure 7

2. If two rescuers are present, they should work as follows:
   a. One, positioned at the victim's head
      (1) Administers artificial respiration
      (2) Monitors pulse at carotid artery (neck) without interrupting artificial respiration.
   b. One positions himself on the *opposite side* of the victim's body at shoulder level and begins external heart massage.

5:1 Ratio
5 Chest Compressions
Rate of 60/min
1 Full Lung Inflation

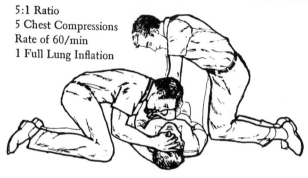

Figure 8

Some Additional Factors in Cardiopulmonary Resuscitation

1. The victim's stomach may become distended with air. This is especially true in children and if the airway is not clear. It is not dangerous, but may interfere with lung inflation. It can be remedied by applying pressure over the stomach with the palm of your hand. This expels the air, but may also lead to regurgitation of the stomach contents, so you must be ready to turn the victim's head to one side and clean out the mouth with your fingers or a cloth.

2. Cardiopulmonary resuscitation, once started, must be continued until spontaneous breathing and heartbeat occur or until the victim is turned over to a physician. In many cases, this will mean that the procedures must be continued while the victim is being transported to a medical facility. Under no circumstances should cardiopulmonary resuscitation be interrupted for more than a five (5) second period.

STOP THE BLEEDING

After checking the victim's airway, or having reestablished his breathing and/or heartbeat, the next most important step is to stop the bleeding.

Bleeding is the escape of blood from arteries, veins, or even capillaries because of a break in their walls. Control of severe bleeding is an urgent matter. Arterial bleeding from a major blood vessel can cause a casualty to bleed to death in a very short time.

Identification of the types of bleeding may be as follows:

1. *Arterial bleeding:* Blood escaping is bright red, gushes forth in jets or spurts which are synchronized with the pulse.
2. *Venous bleeding:* Blood is dark red and escapes in a steady flow.
3. *Capillary bleeding:* Blood is intermediate in color, and oozes from the wound.

To control severe bleeding apply DIRECT PRESSURE with the palm of your hand over the entire area of the wound. Also, raise the affected part to a level higher than the heart, if there are no fractures, or if additional pain or harm will not be inflicted.

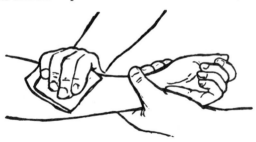

Figure 9

If immediately available, a thick pad of cloth should be held between your hand and the wound, or add the cloth as soon as possible.

Preferably, the cloth should be sterile or clean. However, unclean material can be used. Do not remove this dressing if it becomes blood soaked. Rather, add more layers of cloth and continue direct pressure and elevation.

A pressure bandage can replace direct hand pressure on most parts of the body. Apply the pressure bandage by placing the center of the bandage or strip of cloth directly over the pad; hold the pad in place by circling the bandage ends around the body part and tie off with a knot directly over the pad.

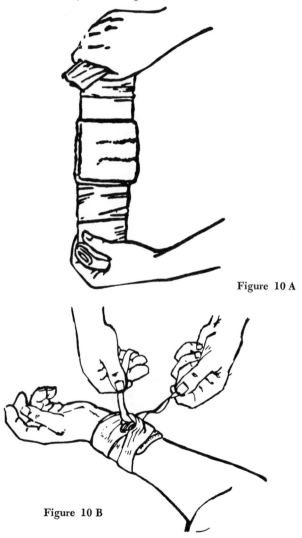

Figure 10 A

Figure 10 B

If direct pressure does not control the bleeding, apply pressure at the appropriate PRESSURE POINT *maintaining pressure over the wound and elevation.* Pressure on the PRESSURE POINT will control arterial bleeding in the region supplied by that artery.

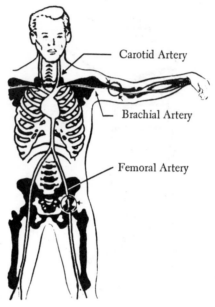

Carotid Artery

Brachial Artery

Femoral Artery

Figure 11

If the bleeding is from a wound in the lower arm, apply pressure to the *brachial artery.* This pressure point is located on the inside

of the arm in the groove between the biceps and triceps, about midway between the armpit and the elbow.

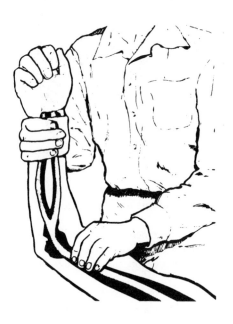

Figure 12

Pressure should be applied by grasping the midde of the victim's
upper arm, with the thumb on the outside of his arm and your
fingers on the inside. Press or pull your fingers toward your thumb,
using the flat inside surface of your finger, not your finger tips.

If the bleeding is from a wound in the leg, apply pressure to the
femoral artery. This pressure point is located on the front center
part of the diagonally slanted "hinge" of the leg, in the crease of
the groin area, and over the pelvic bone.

Apply pressure by placing the heel of your hand directly over the spot described above. Lean forward with the arm straightened to apply pressure.

Figure 13

It is IMPORTANT when using the pressure points (brachial and femoral arteries) that you maintain pressure over the wound as well as elevation.

It is also important to remember, especially in situations involving mass casualties, that a conscious victim may apply pressure to his own wound to restrict or stop the bleeding allowing you to assist others.

If the above methods do not control severe bleeding and the victim is in danger of bleeding to death, a tourniquet may be used as a last resort to save a life.

The TOURNIQUET should be used ONLY for the severe, life-threatening bleeding that cannot be controlled by other means. This method is used only on the arm or leg. To apply a tourniquet:

1. Place the tourniquet just above the wound edges. If the wound is in a joint area or just below, place the tourniquet directly above the joint.
2. Wrap the tourniquet band tightly twice around the limb and tie a half knot.
3. Place a short strong stick, screwdriver or any similar object that you can find on the half knot and tie a full knot.
4. Twist the stick until bleeding stops.
5. Secure the stick in place.

6. Attach a note to the victim giving the location of the tourniquet and the time it was applied.

7. Once the serious decision to apply a tourniquet has been made it should not be loosened (except on the advice of a physician).

8. Treat for shock and get medical attention IMMEDIATELY.

NOTE: A TOURNIQUET SHOULD ONLY BE TIGHT ENOUGH TO STOP THE BLEEDING.

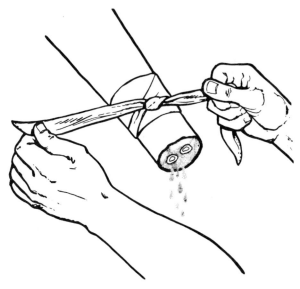

Figure 14 A

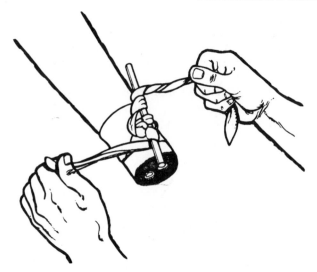

Figure 14 B

Figure 14 C

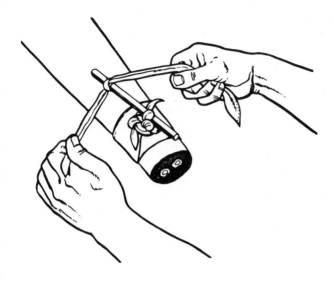

Figure 14 D

PROTECT THE WOUNDS

When the airway has been checked or breathing/heartbeat re-established and the bleeding has been stopped, the next step is to protect the wounds. Wounds may be classed as open flesh wounds, fractured bones and burns. Regardless of the class of wound, all must be protected from further aggravation or injury while transporting the victim to a hospital to help relieve his pain and discomfort. Burn wounds will be considered in detail at this point since they are most crucial and are common in boating accidents.

BURNS

Burns are usually classified by depth and degree of skin damage. Three general classifications are: (1) First degree—redness, mild swelling and pain; (2) Second degree—deeper, with blister formations appearing; and (3) Third degree—very deep burns with complete loss of all layers of skin. The burn may looked charred.

Burns are sometimes described according to the extent of total body surface involved. For example, a severe sunburn (first degree) is considered serious and should receive prompt medical attention.

First aid for burns according to classification: First degree—running water (preferably cold) or cloths soaked in ice water on the burned area until pain is relieved. Dry sterile dressings may be used. Second degree—running water (preferably cold, but not ice water) or clean cloths wrung out in ice water until pain subsides. Blot dry with sterile or clean cloth. Apply sterile gauze, or a clean cloth, as a protective dressing. DO NOT break blisters, remove shreds of tissue, or apply additional home medications. DO treat for shock and obtain medical attention. Third degree (or deep second degree)—Cover the burn to exclude air. This can be done, for example, with sterile dressings, fresh laundered sheets, or other clean linen. It is extremely important to treat for shock and to obtain medical attention. Elevate the affected parts. DO NOT remove charred clothing that sticks to the burn. DO NOT apply ice water to the burn. DO NOT apply home medications.

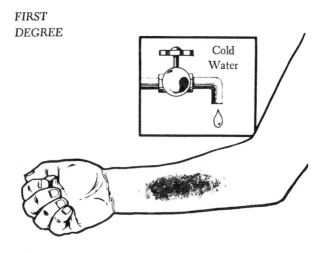

Figure 15 A

SECOND
DEGREE

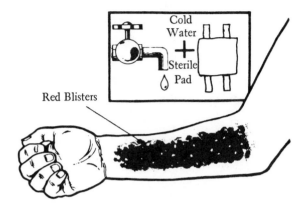

Red Blisters

Figure 15 B

THIRD
DEGREE

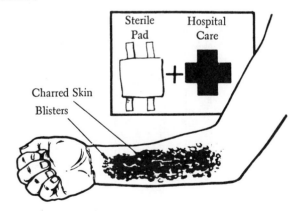

Charred Skin
Blisters

Figure 15 C

The following quick reference chart gives first aid advice for burns according to classification:

FIRST AID

Burn	Do	Don't
First Degree (redness, mild swelling and pain)	Apply cold water and/or dry sterile dressing or additional commercial or home medication.	Apply butter, oleo-margarine, etc.
Second Degree (deeper and blisters develop)	Immerse in cold water, blot dry with sterile cloth, and apply dry, sterile cloth for protection. Treat for shock. Obtain medical attention if severe.	Break blisters. Remove shreds of tissue. Use antiseptic preparation, ointment, spray, or home remedy on severe burn.
Third Degree (deeper destruction, skin layers destroyed)	Cover with sterile cloth to protect. Treat for shock. Watch for breathing difficulty. Obtain medical attention quickly.	Remove charred clothing that is stuck to burn. Apply ice. Use home medication.
Chemical Burn	Remove by flushing with large quantities of water for at least 5 minutes. After flushing eye apply sterile pad for protection. Obtain medical attention.	

Figure 16

CHEMICAL BURNS to the skin or eyes produce the same type of burn as do agents such as flash fires, flame, steam, or hot liquids. First aid for this type of burn is to wash away the chemical completely with large quantities of water as quickly as possible. Continue flushing the burn for at least five minutes.

When the burn involves the eye, flush the burn with water for five minutes, then cover both eyes with a dry, clean protective dressing and seek medical attention as quickly as possible. Give first aid for shock.

TREAT FOR SHOCK

Shock is a state of circulatory deficiency associated with depression of the vital processes of the body. It must be considered and followed for each victim, regardless of the nature or extent of his injuries. Always remember that a victim may go into shock hours after he is rescued and given first aid.

Injury related shock, commonly referred to as traumatic shock, is decidedly different from electric shock, insulin shock, and other special forms of shock. This section relates to traumatic shock which is a condition resulting in a depressed state of many vital body functions that could threaten life, even though the injuries would not otherwise be fatal.

Evaluation of the situation, according to the extent and severity of the injuries, is more important than any particular sign or symptom. The shock syndrome (set of symptoms which occur together) is variable and the symptoms listed below do not appear in every casualty, nor are they equally noticeable. The following findings are, however, representative of the varied picture which may be presented by the casualty in shock:

1. Eyes may be glassy, lackluster, pupils are dilated or suggest fear and apprehension.
2. Breathing may be normal, rapid, or labored.
3. The lips may be pale or cyanotic (bluish-gray).
4. The skin may be very pale or a peculiar ashen-gray (if dark complexion).
5. The skin temperature may be lowered and the body covered with a clammy sweat.
6. The pulse may be nearly normal or it may be rapid, weak, thready, and of poor volume.

7. There may be retching (trying to vomit; heave), nausea, vomiting, hiccups and dryness of the mouth, lips and tongue.
8. Restlessness, apprehension, are usual signs.

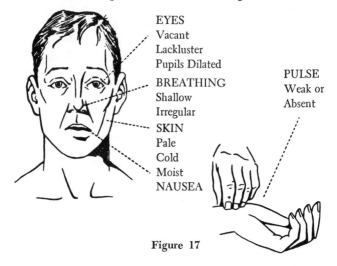

EYES
Vacant
Lackluster
Pupils Dilated

PULSE
Weak or
Absent

BREATHING
Shallow
Irregular

SKIN
Pale
Cold
Moist

NAUSEA

Figure 17

9. Veins in the skin are collapsed. Veins normally visible at the front of the elbow or forearm, and back of hands, may become invisible.
10. Frequent complaints of thirst. Shock victims may complain of thirst rather than pain, even when they are severely wounded. It's easy to recognize the fully developed picture of shock, but it is not so easy to recognize the victim about to go into shock.

First aid for SHOCK should be given to any seriously injured person.

To prevent or give first aid for shock, the following steps should be taken: (1) Keep the victim lying down; (2) Maintain the victim's normal body temperature; and, (3) Get medical care as soon as possible.

Depending on the injury, the victim's body should be positioned to minimize the danger of shock. The most desirable position is lying down with the feet raised 6 to 8 inches. If you are uncertain as to the type of injury, keep the victim flat on his back. The following chart gives variations in this position based on the injuries the victim has sustained:

Injury or Condition	*Position*
1. Back or neck	1. Do not move the victim
2. Wounds of face and jaw	2. Sitting and leaning forward
3. Unconscious	3. On side
4. Head injury	4. Flat or propped up (head never lower than body)
5. Breathing difficulty	5. Head and shoulders raised

1. Keep Victim Lying Down
2. Maintain Normal Body Temperature
3. Get Medical Care as Soon as Possible

Figure 18 A

If he can breathe well, put him like this:

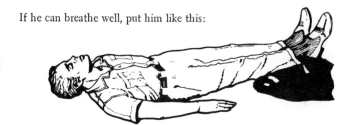

Figure 18 B

If he cannot breathe, put him like this:

Figure 18 C

If he is bleeding from the mouth, put
him on his side with knees bent and
his head on his arm. Watch carefully
to see that he keeps breathing.

Figure 18 D

Maintain normal BODY TEMPERATURE (98.6 degrees F.).
If environmental conditions are cold or damp, protect the victim
by placing blankets or additional clothing over and under the victim. If conditions are hot, provide protection from the heat or sun
(shade) and do not add heat.

Obtain MEDICAL CARE as soon as possible. If this care will
be delayed for an hour or more, water, preferably containing salt
and baking soda (½ level teaspoon of salt and ½ level teaspoon of
baking soda to each quart of water) is recommended. An adult

should be given about 4 ounces every 15 minutes, a child approximately 2 ounces, and an infant about one ounce. DO NOT give fluids if the victim is unconscious, having convulsions, vomiting, becoming nauseated, or if surgery is likely.

MISCELLANEOUS INJURIES AND ILLNESSES

Injuries and sudden illnesses other than those mentioned previously may occur. The following steps are first aid measures only. Medical advice and attention should be obtained as soon as possible.

If a medical emergency occurs on the water and your boat is equipped with a two-way radio, do not hesitate to call the Coast Guard to obtain medical advice and possible evacuation.

1. Choking Accidents or "Cafe Coronaries." Choking accidents are often called "Cafe Coronaries" because they happen so frequently in restaurants. Although choking casualties are often difficult to differentiate from heart attack victims, it is imperative to recognize the difference between them, because the emergency procedures may differ. You can often tell the difference simply by watching the victim.

   a. Heart Attacks. Unless the heart attack is so massive as to cause almost instant death, the victim will likely clutch at his chest. He will perspire, make sounds of excruciating pain, perhaps even cry out. He will be short of breath, but able to breathe.

   b. The Choking Victim. If the windpipe is blocked, and after the initial reflex of coughing, the victim will NOT be able to BREATHE or even GROAN. He may become very agitated. He then becomes cyanotic (blueness or grayness of the skin, fingernails, and mucous membranes) and slides into unconsciousness. It should be noted that some victims suffering from choking accidents leave the area fearful of causing a scene, and may collapse in the restroom, unattended. Some one should always follow the victim to ascertain his condition.

   If the victim is coughing, or otherwise trying to eliminate the foreign matter, initially, it is best NOT to interfere with these efforts and NOT to strike him on the back. He should be encouraged to breathe slowly and deeply. DO NOT question him needlessly. Be calm and try to encourage him to cough. If these efforts of expulsion cease, and the victim becomes anoxic (oxygen deficient), semiconscious, or unconscious he should be rolled onto his side toward you. Deliver a firm blow with the heel of your hand over the victim's spine and between his shoulder blades.

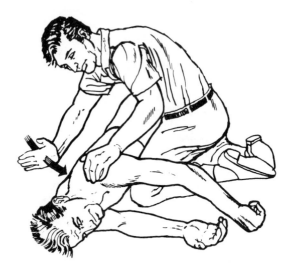

Figure 19

Figure 20

c. *The Heimlich Techniques.* The Heimlich Technique is a
   method of treating choking victims. This technique calls
   for the rescuer to stand behind the victim, put both arms
   around him, just above the beltline, allowing the victim's
   head, arms, and upper torso to hang forward. Grasping
   your own right wrist, quickly thrust upward into the victim's abdomen, forcing the diaphragm up. This compresses
   the lungs and expels the residual air in the lungs upward.
   The foreign object will often pop out of the victim's windpipe like a cork from a wine bottle. If the victim is lying

face down on the floor, sit astride the victim's lower torso or buttocks and perform the hug the same as for a standing victim. If the victim is on his back, sit astride the pelvis, and place one hand on top of the other and forcefully thrust into the upper abdominal region. A second person, if available, should be ready to remove the foreign matter from the mouth. If the victim vomits, his mouth should be immediately cleaned out by turning his head to one side and cleaning out his mouth with your fingers or cloth.

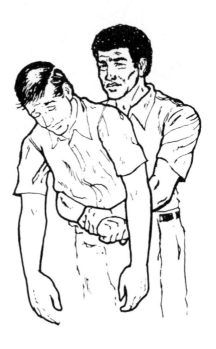

Figure 21

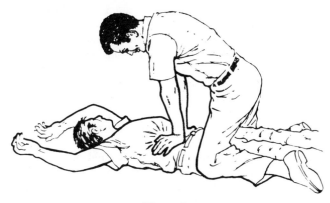

Figure 22

2. Broken Bones (fractures).
   a. Symptoms may include:
      (1) Pain, swelling and discoloration at the site of the injury.
      (2) Misalignment (deformity) of the injured part.
   b. Treatment.
      (1) Treat every suspected fracture as if it were a fracture until it is proven to be otherwise. Protect and immobilize all injured victims until the diagnosis is made. "SPLINT THEM WHERE THEY LIE."
      (2) Always use gentleness and care in handling any broken limb.
      (3) Eliminate unnecessary handling of the injured part. Roughness is inexcusable.
      (4) Disturb the victim as little as possible.
      (5) Do not be deceived by the absence of deformity and disability; in many cases of fracture some ability to use the limb persists.
      (6) Make sure that you are not dealing with more than one fracture.
      (7) Keep the broken bone ends and the joints above and below the injury immobilized.

(8) A splint is intended to maintain immobilization of a fracture.

(9) Splints should be applied before the victim is moved. Any unnecessary manipulation must be avoided.

(10) Rules governing the application of splints:

    (a) Apply splint snugly but do NOT cut off the circulation.

    (b) Never hide a tourniquet with a splint or bandage.

    (c) Splints should be well padded.

    (d) Splints must be long enough to immobilize the joint above and the joint below the point of the injury.

    (e) Apply the splint where the person lies.

    (f) Make use of assistance and use enough splint. Do not be stingy.

    (g) Minimize moving and handling the victim.

    (h) Leave tips of victim's fingers and toes out and check them often for circulation adequacy.

(11) The specific splint selected is of far less importance than the immobilization achieved.

(12) Treat for shock.

3. Heart Attack. Symptoms include shortness of breath, chest pains, bluish color of the lips and about the fingernails, a chronic cough, and swelling of the ankles. These symptoms may occur in combinations, but usually one or the other is outstanding. Treat for shock, maintaining normal body temperature and placing in position of greatest comfort for breathing. Administer cardiopulmonary resuscitation if necessary. Assist in obtaining or administering prescribed medicine. NOTE: You can improve your knowledge of how to recognize the need for and apply appropriate Cardiopulmonary Resuscitation (CPR) measures by taking courses offered by such agencies as the American Red Cross, American Heart Association, etc.

4. Emergencies Due to Heat. When a person exerts himself in a hot environment, a considerable part of his circulation must

be directed into blood vessels of the skin in order to radiate heat from the surface and to support activity of the sweat glands. When the nerves which control expansion and contraction of blood vessels and heart output are inadequate to meet the needs of increased skin circulation, in addition to muscle and brain circulation, the individual collapses.

a. *Heat Exhaustion* is a physiologic disturbance following exposure to heat. It can occur in even the most physically fit man and woman by heavy enough work in a severe enough environment. However, it is usually non-fatal.

  (1) Symptoms. In heat exhaustion, faintness, usually with a sense of pounding of the heart, is the predominant symptom. Nausea, vomiting, fainting, headache, and restlessness are also common. The victim who has collapsed in the heat and is perspiring freely almost surely has heat exhaustion. Even though his temperature may be somewhat elevated, *sweating rules out* the diagnosis of *heat stroke*. Under general supportive treatment the victim of heat exhaustion will usually recover consciousness promptly, even though he may not feel well for some time.

  (2) Treatment:
    (a) Move victim to a cool place.
    (b) Keep victim lying down; treat for shock.
    (c) If the victim is conscious, water to which has been added ½ teaspoon of salt to each glass, or stimulants such as coffee or tea may be given freely.

b. *Heatstroke*—Heatstroke has for its distinguishing characteristic of an extreme elevation of body temperature. This is due to a failure of the sweating mechanism and it may occur whenever heat regulation is dependent upon sweating for a long period of time. Heatstroke calls for heroic measures to reduce body temperature immediately to prevent brain damage and death.

  (1) *Symptoms.* Headache, dizziness, frequent desire to urinate, irritability, disturbed vision, usually objects

have a red or purplish tint. Patient suddenly falls unconscious; skin is hot and dry; pupils are constricted; pulse is full, strong, and bounding; may be convulsions; body temperature is from 105 to 109 degrees F.

(2) *Treatment.*

    (a) Place the victim in the shade or a cool place.

    (b) The aim of the treatment in heatstroke is to reduce the body temperature to a safe range as rapidly as possible. Brain damage is the product of time as well as temperature. Total immersion in an ice-water bath is probably the most efficient method.

    (c) Remove the victim's clothing. Lay victim in a supine position with head and shoulders slightly elevated.

    (d) Try to decrease the victim's body temperature by one of the following methods:

        1. Pour cold water over the body.

        2. Rub body with ice. Place pieces of ice in armpits.

        3. Cover with sheets soaked in ice water.

    (e) Give cool (not iced) drinks after consciousness returns.

    (f) DO NOT give stimulants.

c. Heat Cramps—Heat cramps are painful contractions of various skeletal muscles brought about by the depletion of sodium chloride (salt) from the body fluids, via excessive sweating.

    (1) *Symptoms.* In the typical picture, the victim has his legs drawn up, is thrashing about, grimacing, and crying out from the excruciating pain.

    (2) *Treatment.* The treatment is salt and water. Drinking cool water with ½ teaspoon of salt will afford relief and continued protection.

NOTE: THE USE OF HOT PACKS ON CRAMPED MUSCLES WILL ONLY MAKE IT WORSE.

5. Minor wounds (without severe bleeding). Cleanse the wound thoroughly and apply a sterile or clean dressing. Have the victim obtain medical attention, if signs of infection (swelling and discoloration, pain, fever, pus, nodules, and red streaks) develop.

6. Foreign Bodies On or In the Eye. Symptoms include spasms of the eyelid, a feeling of sand in the eye, or a scratchy sensation.

   a. Treatment:
      (1) Attempt to remove the foreign body first by flushing the victim's eye with water. The water should be warm and the stream directed away from the nose. Use very little force. Position the victim so that the stream will not run into the other eye.
      (2) Carefully remove a loose foreign body with moistened cotton-tip applicator (Q-tip).
      (3) If the foreign body is embedded in the surface of the eyeball, or if it has penetrated the eyeball, the victim should be taken immediately to the care of a specialist.
         (a) Evacuate the victim lying down on a litter with his head fixed to prevent movement.
         (b) Instruct the patient not to squeeze his eyelids together or place any pressure on the eyeball.
         (c) Caution the victim not to strain, lie on stomach, or even to perform such ordinary tasks as removal of clothing.
         (d) Put NOTHING in the victim's eye.
         (e) Patch BOTH of the victim's eyes.

7. Poisoning by Mouth. If this occurs, it is vital that proper first aid be given immediately. If a person takes poison orally, the following first aid steps should be taken:

   a. Dilute the poison by having the victim drink milk or water.
   b. If the victim *is* conscious and the poison *is not* a strong acid, strong alkali, or petroleum product, then induce vomiting. Vomiting may be induced by causing the victim to gag by inserting one or two fingers in his throat or by

giving him warm, soapy water to drink. Specific procedures for combating poisoning are often included on the product container.

c. Seek medical attention IMMEDIATELY. It is important to identify the type of poison involved, therefore, take the container of poison with the victim when seeking medical attention.

8. Stroke. The symptoms of a major stroke are unconsciousness, heavy breathing and paralysis of the limbs on one side of the body. However, if the brain damage is slight, the only symptoms may be dizziness, headache, or muscular difficulty involving some body part. TREAT FOR SHOCK. If the victim has difficulty breathing, help him maintain an open airway and give cardiopulmonary resuscitation if needed.

9. Hypothermia (Exposure to Cold). The victim will be numb, move with difficulty, and may be unconscious. If breathing has stopped, begin artificial respiration. The victim's body temperature must be raised. Ashore, a warm bath can be used. However, on most boats the best way to raise the victim's temperature is by close physical contact with someone who is already warm or by wrapping him in blankets with an external heat source such as a hot water bottle. It is very important to reheat the victim's trunk (core) before reheating the limbs in order to avoid "after drop" (cold blood placing an added strain on the heart). Once the victim is warmed, keep him well insulated with blankets or personal flotation devices. Be sure to give particular protection to the areas of rapid heat loss: the head, neck, sides, and groin.

10. Fish Bites and Stings.

a. *Bites*. Sharks and barracuda bites generally result in the loss of large amounts of tissue. Prompt and vigorous action to control bleeding and shock are necessary to save life. Bleeding should be controlled with pressure dressings if at all possible. If not, tourniquets may be used. Seek medical help immediately.

b. *Stings*.

(1) For *Portuguese Man-of-War* stings, remove tentacles

immediately and wash skin surface with alcohol—
then apply calamine lotion or ammonia water.

(2) For *Jellyfish*, treatment is about the same; apply
meat tenderizer, ammonia water, vinegar, or soothing lotion. Cardiopulmonary resuscitation is sometimes needed.

(3) NOTE: In experimental studies, heat has been
proven to have a deactivating effect on the pain-
producing faction of the venom as well as other
known toxin components. Hot water soaks which
have been used since antiquity in many parts of the
world are recommended for stings of many sea crea-
tures such as scorpionfish, weeverfish, toadfish, cat-
fish, venomous sharks, rays and ratfish.

HANDLING AND TRANSPORTATION OF THE INJURED

One of the major problems in dealing with injured persons aboard
small boats is that of transporting the victim to medical help. In
many situations, it would be difficult, if not impossible, for medical
help to reach the victim; therefore, the boatman must have a basic
knowledge of transportation of injured persons so that the victim
may be safely and quickly delivered to medical help.

The sooner the victim can be moved, the better. It is normally
the responsibility of the boatman giving first aid to see that the
victim is transported safely and without being subjected to further
injury, shock, or unnecessary pain.

Moving an injured person is precise work. It calls for close team-
work and great care. Even the act of placing the victim on a
stretcher demands coordination and practice. The simple movements involved in lifting the stretcher-bound victim and walking
with him call for specific procedures.

There are two important rules to remember when transporting
an injured person. If possible, never move the victim until he has
been examined and his injuries have been protected by properly ap-

plied splints and dressing. Always transport seriously injured victims in a lying down position.*

COMPRESSES AND DRESSINGS

1701 These are packaged sterilized cloth swatches to be placed directly upon the wound after it has been made ready for dressing and bandaging. They are assumed to be sterile if the wrapping has not been broken, and if the first-aider has not fingered or dropped them before applying. Do not open until needed; then place upon the wound immediately.

SPLINTS

1702 Splints are materials of wood, wire, paper, etc., used to prevent broken bones from moving at the point of fracture. They may be improvised from any rigid object or material (rolled magazines and newspapers, sail battens, floor board, oars, etc.).

In applying, the splint should be padded, having first been measured on the sound limb (not the injured one). If the limb is deformed put a pillow or a sweater under it so that it can be fastened above and below the joints on either side of the break. Use a roller bandage or a wide strip of cloth, not rope or small stuff, and immobilize the break by making the sound parts of the limb fast to the splint. Square knots are used, the knot being tied against the splint, not the limb. No binding is placed near the fracture as swelling will occur here very soon.

FRACTURES

1703 A fracture is a broken bone or bones.

A simple fracture is one in which the broken bone does not pierce the skin. There is no danger from infection.

A compound fracture is one in which the broken bone does pierce the skin. It is treated as a wound; there is great danger of both bone and flesh infection.

The first-aider must use care that improper handling of the in-

---

*U. S. Coast Guard 1978 edition of "First Aid for the Boatman," Aux-206.

jured person does not make a compound fracture of a simple one. The first-aider should never attempt to set bones.

SIMPLE FRACTURE

Symptoms

The victim may have heard or felt the bone snap

Pain at the point of fracture

Tenderness at the point of fracture

The limb deformed

Voluntary movement limited or completely lost

Swelling

Shock

Treatment

Apply splints.

Move only as necessary.

Lay the patient down if possible.

Treat for shock.

Transport to doctor (splinted), or call doctor (before splinting).

COMPOUND FRACTURE

Symptoms

The same as for a simple fracture *plus*:

Protruding bone

Bleeding

Severe shock

Treatment

Treat as for a wound.

After bandaging, treat as for a simple fracture.

WARNING: Never apply water to a compound fracture.

FRACTURED RIBS

1704

Symptoms

Pain on breathing following injury

Tenderness at point of fracture

Treatment

Apply cravat bandage (folded, triangular slings), hauled quite tightly, with the victim in full expiration.

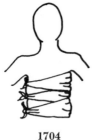

1704   1705

FRACTURE OF THE UPPER ARM
1705
Use two padded splints. Place the arm in a narrow sling, and bind the arm to the body with a wide cravat bandage.

FRACTURE OF THE FOREARM AND WRIST
1706
Use two padded splints, back and front. Place in a sling with the thumb up and the hand arised slightly above the elbow.

1706

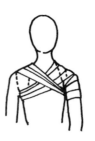

1707

FRACTURE OF THE COLLARBONE
1707
Apply an arm sling, raised high. Bind the arm to the body.

ting may be encourage
in water, or milk of ma
ing requires medical care

(AINE)

omen

ea

quantities of water.
gnosis and treatment.
tic plus tickling the back of the
miting.)

ean out, using a toothpick and a bit
soaked in oil of cloves.
is suspected, apply heat or cold, whic

ver treat for severe abdomen distress with
assured that the complaint is not ap-

spected if the pain is general over all or
tended by nausea and vomiting (possibly
nd accompanied by pain, tenderness, and
t part of the abdomen, and slight rise in

FRACTURE OF THE ELBOW
1708

Splint the upper and lower arms; then place in a sling. But never force the elbow into a right-angle position if it does not do so easily.

1708

FRACTURE OF THE SKULL
1709

Symptoms
Bruise (likely)
Bleeding from the ears, nose, or eyes
Depressed bone
Dizziness
Loss of consciousness
Repeated vomiting
Double vision (likely)
Treatment
Lay the victim down with the head elevated.
Treat for shock, but *do not give any stimulants.*
Do not attempt to stop the bleeding of the ears unless it is excessive.
Check the bleeding of the bruise or wound, being careful not to place too much pressure on the compress, and thus on the brain.
Cold cloths on the head will help.
There is always a question to the first-aider whether such an in-

jury is a concussion or a fracture or both. Great car
immediate medical assistance and hospitalization

FRACTURE OF THE LEG
1710
Use two splints, well padded, top and bottom. Roll
or bed pad.

FRACTURE OF THE KNEECAP
1711
Use one splint on the back of the leg. Place extra paddi
the knee and at the heel.

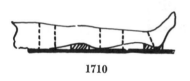

1710

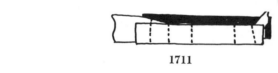

1711

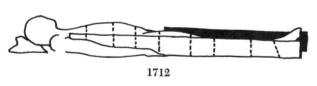

1712

FRACTURE OF THE THIGH
1712
Use two splints—one from the armpit to the heel on the outer
side, and the other from the crotch to the heel. These should be
heavy (¾″ x 5″) and well padded. In emergencies in which long
splints are not to be found, use the short splint only and bind the
injured leg to the sound one.

These methods failing, vom
an emetic followed by soda
Severe or persistent hiccougl

FOOD POISONING (PTO
1717
Symptoms
Discomfort in the upper abd
Pain and cramps
Nausea and vomiting; diarrh
Prostration
Treatment
Dilute by swallowing large
A doctor is required for di
Induce vomiting. (An eme
will cause immediate v
Treat for shock.

TOOTHACHE
1718
Search for cavities and cl
cotton.
Apply and pack in cotto
If infection of the tooth
ever relieves pain bes

CRAMPS
1719 WARNING: Ne
or without diarrhea unti
pendicites.
Appendicitis is to be s
most of the abdomen, at
of only short duration),
rigidity in the lower righ
temperature.

Treatment

If Appendicitis Is Suspected

Put such person to bed at once.
Get immediate medical aid. (*See Chapter on Signaling.*)
Do not give a laxative.
Do not give food.
Do not apply heat to abdomen.
Operation at once is indicated, and the patient must be sent ashore in the *quickest possible manner.*

If Appendicitis Is Not Present

Do not attempt to stop cramps; if diarrhea is present, medication may be given.
Give plenty of water.
Withhold food for 24 hours.

TREATMENT OF THE ORDINARY COLD

1720 Not generally serious, the ordinary cold is common and will seldom send the boatman ashore for medical aid. Prompt measures will often break it up in its early stages.

Avoid unnecessary exposure.

Drink plenty of fluids, eat lightly.

Take a hot bath and a hot drink; then turn in. Do not get chilled.

Gargle (if the throat is sore) with lukewarm water, to which has been added salt. Gargle often. Sea water which has been first boiled is satisfactory.

Rest is the best remedy known.

If the cold persists, or if a serious cough develops and the temperature remains above normal, seek medical aid. Any cold which seems to be traveling toward the chest or lungs and is *more than a head cold* should be regarded as serious.

A person having a cold should always sleep alone. He should guard against coughing or breathing heavily near other persons. Individual towels, utensils, and bedding should be provided, and these sterilized before being used by others. Frequent washing of the hands by the victim and his mates will prevent the spread of the cold.

1721 A severe cold, especially following exposure or injury, may develop into pneumonia.

Symptoms

Severe chill and rapidly rising temperature

Head and body pains, particularly a stabbing pain in the chest

Bloody or "rusty" sputum (sticky in nature)

Delirium

Treatment (Get a physician *immediately*)

Plenty of fresh air.

A fluid or semifluid diet

Bowels must be kept open (by enemas, if necessary).

If the pulse is weak, give strong tea or coffee.

Under no circumstances attempt to nurse through a pneumonia case. Special drugs and care are needed.

REMOVING FISHHOOKS IN THE FLESH

1722 Paint the exposed part of the hook with iodine; push it entirely through the flesh; cut off the eye with a nippers and draw it free. If it is necessary to draw it out toward the eye, nip off the hook beyond the curved part, paint it with iodine and draw it out backwards.

Make the wound bleed and treat as an open wound.

SUNBURN

1723 Sunburn is treated as a first-degree burn, occasionally as a second-degree burn. Calomine lotion or emollient creams are soothing. If blistering develops, as in second-degree burns, treat as a wound, liable to infection. If fever occurs as a result of an extensive sunburn, medical aid is required; cold compresses will reduce fever temporarily.

TRANSPORTATION OF THE INJURED

1724 Unless it is absolutely necessary, it is wisest not to move the injured person. Provide comfort as best as possible (pillows, cover, heat, or shade), and wait for the doctor.

If removal is essential, the victim, in every case of injury except one to the arms or hands, should be transported lying down. Lacking a stretcher, the following improvised carrying devices may be used.

1. A blanket. Carried by four or six persons under the command of a leader, who directs the movements and synchronizes them.
2. Shirts, overcoats, or a mattress cover might be rove over two oars or short spars, thus making a "stretcher."
3. A pipe berth, a hatch cover, or a floor rack of a small boat, may also serve as a firmer stretcher.

In transporting an injured person from ship to ship in a rough sea, lash him to a firm rigid base (hatch cover, battened planks, etc.). He may be placed in a small, light dinghy and the dinghy regarded as the stretcher. Coast Guard rescue planes and ships have special basket stretchers that will be brought or lowered to the ship by the rescuers.

FIRST-AID KITS

1725 A good first-aid kit contains such articles as the following:

1-inch compress on adhesive in individual packages
*Sterile gauze squares—about 3″ x 3″—in individual packages
*Assorted sterile bandage in individual packages
*Triangular bandages
Sterile gauze in individual packages of about one square yard
Roll of ½″ adhesive tape
*Burn ointment
Inelastic tourniquet
*Aromatic spirits of ammonia
Scissors
3″ splinter forceps
1″ and 2″ roller bandages
Wire or thin board splints
Castor oil or mineral oil, for use in eyes (This should be sterile; may be obtained in small tubes.)

---

* These items provide a simple first-aid kit for canoes and open boats.

Thermometer

Aspirin tablets, laxative tablets

The boat kit may well include the following items also:

Oil of cloves	Boric acid
Bicarbonate of soda	Cough medicine
Epsom salts	Antihistamines
Olive oil	Hot-water bottle
Tannic acid powder	Elastic bandages
Eye cup	*Analgesic ointment for sunburn*

A first-aid kit is useless unless kept in order and stocked up. Ship inspection should include the checking of the kit and the immediate replacing of items used.

MEDICINE CHEST

1726 Few small boats require a true medicine chest unless they do extended offshore cruising or sail waters where prompt professional medical attention is difficult to obtain. However, if for these reasons, or others, one should be required, the following representative list will suffice, in addition to the first-aid kit, for most needs. The use of these drugs and medicines is not recommended except under unusual emergency circumstances, or as directed by radio or signaling by medical authorities.

CAUTION: Preparations containing opium, such as paregoric, laudanum, camphor and opium pills, etc., should be given only when absolutely necessary as they are habit-forming.

Antiseptics and Disinfectants

Bichloride of mercury
  (7½-grain tablets and bulk)
Chloride of lime
Tincture of iodine
Solution of cresol (compound)
Formalin
Argyrol solution (20%)
Mercurochrome solution (1%)
Picric acid (½% solution)
Cocaine solution (1%)

Ointments

Vaseline
Mercury ointment (External
  use only)
Ichthyol ointment (20%)
Sulphur ointment
Glycerine base burn ointment

Liniments

Turpentine
Camphorated oil

Permanganate of potash
(1-grain tablets or crystal
form)

Soap liniment

Powders

Calomel (½ grain)
Boric acid
Bismuth subnitrate

Cathartics

Compound cathartic pills
Castor oil
Epsom salts

Internal Medicines

Aromatic spirits of ammonia
Bicarbonate of soda (baking
soda)
Bromide of potash
Copaiba and Santal oil (5-grain
tablets)
Sweet spirits of niter
Ipecac (alcresta) (5-grain
tablets)
Aspirin (5-grain tablets)
Quinine sulphate (5-grain cap-
sules)
Paregoric

SHIPBOARD SANITATION

1727   Any boat, especially a cruising boat having living quarters in the usual cabin, forecastle, etc., may become infested. The
presence of any object carrying in, or on it, cockroaches, fleas, lice,
bedbugs, etc., plus rats and mice presents the potential of infestation.

Most small boats have no serious pest problem. However, the
boat that berths near large foreign vessels, or at waterside docks,
shipyards, or bulkheads known to harbor rats may very easily become the home of one of these pests, which are not uncommon in
the large vessels of the merchant marine.

No government regulations for the control of small-boat sanitation exist, save when that boat has entered from a foreign port.
Such a vessel must present a consular bill of health certifying the
state of any quarantinable disease at the port of clearance. Quarantine may be required upon recommendation of the health officer
making the inspection of the boat's crew.

1728   The disinfection of an infested boat can be accomplished by boiling or steaming (as 20 pounds pressure for 15
minutes) all objects, clothing, etc., from the boat or the part of
the boat that is suspect. With cabins stripped bare, bulkheads,
ceilings, decks, and all furniture are washed with a disinfectant.

Bichloride of mercury (1:500) is recommended. Mix one part bichloride of mercury with 500 parts of sea water. A 5% carbolic-acid solution (50 parts of carbolic acid to 50 parts of alcohol, mixed and added to 900 parts of sea water) is also effective.

1729 Fumigation is not practical for the small boat. Fumigation is used for disinfestation, not disinfection. The average small boat can be freed of infestation by simpler methods such as use of the common aerosal bombs.

1730 Rats and mice can be trapped on small boats with ordinary baited traps set in the galley or near food lockers. Flooding the boat by opening sea cocks, letting the water reach the level of the floor boards, will drive these pests into places where they can be caught. In laying to any dock or wharf infested by rodents, always put out booms and have rat guards on them and all hawsers; also draw in the gangplank whenever possible, especially at night. Suggest you do *not* shoot these pests. Sounds unlikely, but it has been done!

1731 Fleas normally live on rats and mice as well as on the ship's pet. Fleas can be gotten rid of by pouring boiling water in crevices and cracks in sleeping quarters. Kerosene so applied will also kill them. A very effective method is to place a small animal on board for several days (cat or dog) and then de-flea the animal. The fleas will have taken the animal as host. Bedding should be boiled or steamed.

1732 Cockroaches are more of a nuisance than a menace. Boric acid will rid the boat of them. In southern states, various powders and poisons are available in any chain store.

1733 Lice are found on human beings and may transmit disease from diseased to other persons. The person having head lice, body lice, or pubic lice (crabs) should be deloused, his clothing and bedding disinfested, and his surroundings disinfected.

1734 Bedbugs are gotten rid of as fleas are by pouring boiling water or kerosene in cracks and disinfesting clothing and bedding.

1735 Flies and mosquitoes both carry disease. Sanitation and comfort are both achieved by complete screening of every opening in the boat. The unscreened boat may control these pests by liberal use of antifly sprays or an insect repellent placed at all openings.

DRINKING WATER

1736   Clean and sterile drinking water is absolutely necessary on shipboard, especially on long offshore cruises. The secret is clean tanks and clean piping, and a sterilizing agent in the water, no matter how pure when first tanked.

Tanks should be mechanically cleaned often (through the handholes) and then filled with a one-ounce solution of hypochlorate of lime (Clorox) to each 300 gallons of water. Pipes are filled as well. Let it stand for 24 hours; then discharge, flush and fill with pure water.

1737   Drinking water should be treated in one of the following ways to assure disinfection and sterilization:

Add one-quarter teaspoonful of dry hypochlorate of lime (bleaching powder or liquid bleach, such as Clorox), to 50 gallons of water. It will not affect taste.

One tablespoonful of tincture of iodine to 50 gallons of water. Stir and do not use for 30 minutes thereafter.

Small boats having tanks that are difficult to clean should use tank water exclusively for cooking and washing and carry drinking water in sanitary containers, kept clean. Water should never be carried in copper tanks unless the tank has been tinned inside.

⚓

PART VI

CUSTOM AND ETIQUETTE

CHAPTER XVIII

NAUTICAL ETIQUETTE AND FLAGS

Flag Etiquette

THE UNITED STATES FLAG

1801 This (the regular United States flag) is properly flown by all except documented yachts, which fly the yacht ensign. It is properly flown only at anchor, and shown underway when passing or saluting other vessels, lighthouses, or signal stations, or upon entering a harbor, or fortification.

It is flown from a stern staff on all boats at anchor. A sailing vessel having a boom which interferes with such a staff carries the staff slightly to starboard of the boom. Underway, a powerboat may carry the flag from a gaff of the aftermost mast. Under sail, the flag is flown from the peak of the aftermost sail. Marconi-rigged boats carry the flag about two-thirds of the length of the leech from the clew, or about where the flag would be were the rig gaff headed. A recent ruling of the U. S. Yacht Racing Union sanctioned (assuming they have this right) the wearing of the flag at the stern staff by sailing craft under sail. This decision, already widely adopted, merely brings American practice in line with that of other nations'. Old-timers consider it lubberly.

Traditionally, it is always hoisted by halyards and is two-blocked. It may be dipped for saluting when required. If it is flown at half-mast (as on Memorial Day from 8 a.m. until noon), it is first hoisted fully aloft, then lowered to the half-mast position. The flag is always broken out flying, never bundled into a ball, and broken from stops or halyard hitches arranged to release it after hoisting aloft.

The flag is flown from 8 a.m. until sunset; never at night.

It is never used as a signal of any kind, save with one exception. It is universally recognized as a distress signal if flown from any part of a vessel upside down (canton to the bottom).

The flag should be flown when entering a foreign port or foreign territorial waters, or when meeting any vessel on the high seas. Showing the flag, however, does not exempt or protect any vessel from further revealing her identity. Before law, the papers and documents alone reveal identity, and the flag in itself is not sufficient proof of nationality to any challenging vessel or station.

THE YACHT ENSIGN

1802   This is the familiar ensign, exactly like the United States flag, except that the canton contains a circle of 13 stars and a fouled anchor, in white against a blue field. It is authorized by law as a yacht signal for documented yachts of 16 tons or over, and indicates that such a yacht is exempted by law from certain port clearing and entering regulations.

However, its use has become general for all yachts, and custom has sanctioned it as an ensign replacing the United States flag on vessels of the pleasure class. When used in place of the standard United States flag it must be accorded the same respect.

Its use in territorial or inland waters is in no way frowned upon by law or by custom. However, any vessel sailing foreign, or sailing upon the high seas should meticulously observe the law, flying the United States flag only and the yacht ensign, *in addition*, as a signal, if documented as a yacht.

THE JACK

1803   This flag is similar to the 50-starred canton of the United States flag and is, strictly speaking, a naval flag and not a yachting or small-boat flag. It is flown only from a jack staff—a staff on the cap of the bowsprit—never from the bow staff of any powerboat. It may be properly flown from the bow staff of a two-masted sailing vessel or auxiliary (assuming the presence of a bow-sprit), or from the jack staff of a clipper-bowed steam vessel.

It is hoisted only on festive occasions, or Sundays and holidays, and *never* underway; nor is it shown at any time unless the boat is ready for visitors and all deck and other work done, wash taken in, and owner and crew "off duty."

The jack has fallen into disuse among small-boat men.

THE PRIVATE SIGNAL OR OWNER'S FLAG

1804 This is generally a rectangle or a swallowtail upon which are worked certain devices and colors, in patterns selected by the owner, and which serves as an identification signal.

Any signal should be designed so as not to duplicate any other private signal, and, before adopting it, the design is submitted to the publishers of *North American Yacht Register** who rule upon the appropriateness of the design. When accepted, it may be registered with this publisher, who then publishes it, for a fee, together with other American owners' flags. The publication is therefore the key for identifying owners' flags.

Owner's signals are located in the *Register* by simply noting the color combinations of the observed signal. All color combinations are shown together (such as all the white and blue flags, or all the red and black flags). The correct color-combination lists show the identifying designs, devices or initials, give the owner's name and will refer you to other information concerning the owner of the signal.

It is flown from the points shown in Figure 1813.

THE BURGEE

1805 The burgee, or club flag, is generally a triangular pennant upon which have been worked the colors and devices selected by yacht clubs (or other clubs having a yachting division) as their own identifying signal. Its design and selection and registry follow the *North American Yacht Register* procedure of the private signal, and club burgees are shown in that publication.

It is flown from the points shown in Figure 1813.

---

* Formerly *Lloyd's Register of American Yachts*. Now published annually by F. F. Livingston, 17 Battery Place, New York, N. Y. 10004 under the name of *North American Yacht Register*.

OFFICER'S FLAG

1806 This is a flag of varying design and color flown by a yacht club officer on his own boat. It is flown only upon a boat belonging to the same club as the officer flying it; never, for example, when he is on a cruise with another club. It flies night and day as long as the yacht is in commission, and is hoisted to the points diagramed hereinafter. Some clubs show this flag from the yardarm of the shore signal mast when the officer whose flag it is is on the grounds.

The officer's flag becomes his private signal and is flown as the private signal while the owner holds club office.

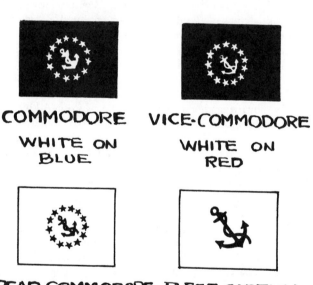

COMMODORE   VICE·COMMODORE

WHITE ON   WHITE ON
   BLUE   RED

REAR COMMODORE   FLEET CAPTAIN
RED ON WHITE   BLUE ON WHITE

1806   Common forms of yacht club officers' flags

OWNER ABSENT FLAG

1807 A blue rectangular flag is shown from the starboard yardarm or spreader to indicate that the owner is not on board. It is never flown underway, whether the owner is on board or not. At night, the signal is made by a blue electric light or lantern, hung in the same place.

GUEST FLAG

1808 A blue rectangular flag, diagonally crossed by a white stripe, is used to show that the boat is being used by guests of the owner. It is flown from the starboard yardarm or spreader during their stay but is lowered at night, whether or not the guests are on board. It is flown *underway* and at anchor.

OWNER'S MEAL FLAG

1809 Flown from the starboard yardarm or spreader during daylight hours, this white rectangular flag indicates the fact that the owner is at table and not to be disturbed. Flown only when at anchor.

CREW'S MEAL PENNANT

1810 A red pennant, flown from the foremost mast, at the port yardarm or spreader, indicating that the crew is at table and cannot, for the moment, be expected to render usual services. Flown only when at anchor and during daylight hours.

OTHER FLAGS

1811 A night or wind pennant is sometimes hoisted to the truck of the aftermost mast as a hawk (or telltale). This pennant may also be used during daylight hours as a hawk, while underway.

A rectangular yellow flag is used as the quarantine flag.

On large vessels, a rectangular flag is hoisted when fuel is being taken aboard as a warning. All nearby fires are put out and smoking on or in the vicinity of the boat that is fueling is prohibited.

A square red flag, with a white stripe cutting diagonally from upper left to lower right, indicates that there is a diver nearby. If he has come off a large boat that is at anchor, the flag is flown from its yardarm. If he is diving at some distance from his boat, the flag is flown from a float with a short flagpole. If he has used a dinghy or pram to get to the diving area, the flag flies from it. In any case, it means keep away; keep well clear.

Dressing ship is done with the International Code flags, bent alternatingly [two flags and one pennant] on national holidays and for special occasions, such as a regatta or a launching. (*Figure 1813*) The ensign, the private signal, or the burgee are never part of such a hoist.

Ship is dressed while at anchor only; never while under way. It is highly improper to dress ship at any time with college banners, or any flags having letters or words, and especially advertising pennants such as those sometimes supplied with stock boats.

1812   The United States flag may be half-masted on any day of national mourning and always on Memorial Day. The burgee may be half-masted upon the death of a club officer or member. The private signal may be half-masted upon the death of the owner or a member of his immediate family.

When half-masting any flag or signal, it is always first hoisted and then secured at half-mast. Upon lowering, it is first run up; then lowered and taken in.

1813   Flags are displayed from 8 a.m. until sunset. It is considered courteous to take the hour for making and lowering from the yacht club in whose harbor the boat is lying or from the boat of the senior officer present. The usual signal is a gun salute.

Flags are raised in the following order: ensign or United States flag, burgee, and private signal; and lowered in the reverse order. If sufficient hands are present, all flags should be handled simultaneously, immediately upon the signal. Upon lowering, the night pennant is sent up at once and anchor lights lighted and set. Power vessels generally show their range light as an anchor light. Sail vessels hang a lantern from the forestay.

If a passage is started before 8 a.m. or finished after sunset, it is proper to have flags set until coming to anchor, but under no circumstances are they to be flown during darkness (officer's flags and wind pennant excepted).

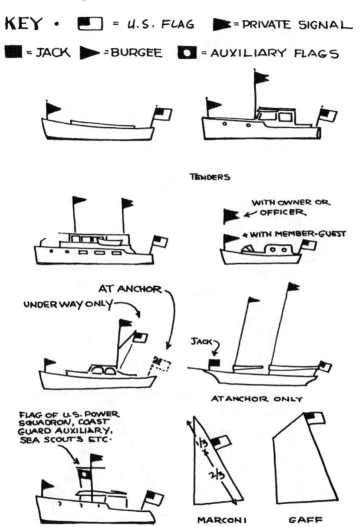

KEY · ▭ = U.S. FLAG   ▶ = PRIVATE SIGNAL
■ = JACK ▶ = BURGEE   ◖◗ = AUXILIARY FLAGS

TENDERS

WITH OWNER OR
OFFICER

WITH MEMBER-GUEST

AT ANCHOR
UNDER WAY ONLY

JACK

AT ANCHOR ONLY

FLAG OF U.S. POWER
SQUADRON, COAST
GUARD AUXILIARY,
SEA SCOUTS ETC.

MARCONI   GAFF

1813 Flag etiquette

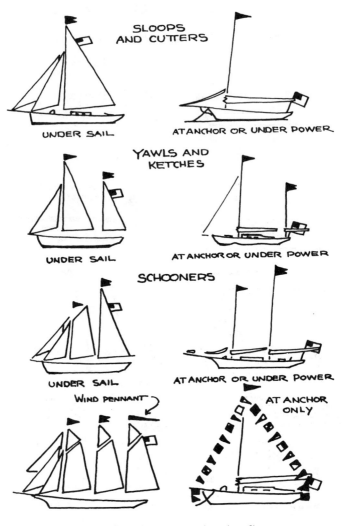

SLOOPS
AND CUTTERS

UNDER SAIL

AT ANCHOR OR UNDER POWER

YAWLS AND
KETCHES

UNDER SAIL

AT ANCHOR OR UNDER POWER

SCHOONERS

UNDER SAIL

AT ANCHOR OR UNDER POWER

WIND PENNANT

AT ANCHOR
ONLY

1813 Flag etiquette (*continued*)

SALUTES

1814   Formal salutes are made with a gun or the ensign. In any case the junior always salutes first and is answered promptly by the senior, and in the same manner in which it is made.

A gun salute is one gun.

A flag salute is one dip of the flag.

It is a nice courtesy to salute American and foreign naval vessels.

It is courtesy to salute senior officers upon meeting afloat or upon their arrival at an anchorage, and to salute upon arriving at the home anchorage of another yacht club.

(The standard three blasts, calling a shore boat or club tender, is not a salute.)

It is a nice courtesy to hand-salute the quarterdeck upon boarding any boat.

Boat salutes are made to seniors by breaking the stroke for a moment and resting upon the oars, or by tossing the oars, or, in a sailboat, by letting the sheet fly for a moment. Boats (as power tenders) salute with the flag. (NOTE: No rowing boat rowing less than four oars flies the ensign, and therefore salutes as provided above.)—All a bit archaic, but then perhaps someday you will be in Boston.

DISPLAY OF FLAGS BY NAUTICAL CLUBS

1815   While there is no general or legal rule, custom seems to have decreed the following pattern for the display of flags on a pole often used to indicate a yacht or nautical club or establishment. Remember, the starboard yardarm is the one to the right when you look out to sea.

	Staff with Yard	Staff with Gaff	Staff with Yard and Gaff
U. S. Flag	Masthead	Gaff	Gaff
Club Burgee	Starb'd yardarm	Masthead	Masthead
Officer's Flag(s)	Port yardarm	—	Starb'd yardarm
Jack	—	—	Port yardarm

The jack is flown only on Sundays and holidays. Flags are made at 8 a.m. and lowered (to a single gun) at sundown. The distinguishing colored light signals of the club are immediately raised after lowering the flags. The U. S. flag is made first and lowered last. See Chapter XIV, for folding the ensign.

RACECOURSES

1816   While a boat racing has no legal rights over a boat not racing, it is courteous not only to give racing boats every right but also to try to forecast the rights she may desire and *keep well out of her way*. Do not enter the limits, present or future, or any racing boats. Follow racing sailboats on the leeward side and well astern of the *last* boat. Keep turning points clear. Large vessels under sail should keep well clear of smaller racing sailboats, so as not to create eddies or disturb the free flow of the wind to the racing boats.

YACHTING UNIFORM

1817   The coat is a double-breasted navy-blue jacket. The trousers are of the same material and without cuffs. For summer or tropical wear, an all-white suit may be worn, cut the same. Either the blue or white cap may be worn with the blue uniform, but the white uniform calls for only the white cap. On shore, black shoes are worn with the blue uniform, and white shoes (not sneakers) worn with any uniform combination having white trousers. The blue-uniform jacket is often worn with white trousers.

The style of uniform, or "dress of the day," is indicated by the senior officer, and other officers and members dress as he does. White and blue cap-tops are alternated upon orders from the senior officer, or by date, generally the white top indicated between June first and October first.

The formal yachting dress may be worn at regattas, when visiting a yacht club, and at all social occasions connected with cruising or yachtclub activities. Guests, as well as visiting officers of any yacht club, are received on board in the uniform. It is entirely appropriate for wear when visiting customs or port officials on boat business.

A simple work uniform, usually of khaki, is prescribed by the code of many clubs for general service, especially for the owner-skipper, who may dispense with the formal dress except for the special social and other occasions noted above. The cap may be worn with the work uniform, and footgear is of the utility type.

YACHT INSIGNIA FOR CAP AND UNIFORM

1818   Members of yacht and similar nautical clubs (but not the United States Power Squadron, Coast Guard Auxiliary, or Sea Scouts) follow the general insignia rules given below.

Paid hands wear only the cap devices, in gold bullion, shown in Figure 1818. While these are actually officers' insignia, the paid hand on small boats, whose status is somewhere between crew and officer and who at times acts as each or both, is generally permitted by custom to wear them.

Paid hands who serve as officers only (as on a large yacht) may wear the cap device shown in Figure 1818, also of gold bullion. Inside the wreath may be the owner's flag only, or the crossed owner's and club flag, both in enamel.

Deck Dept.

Engineer Dept.

Radio Dept.

Paid hands cap insignia

1818 Paid officers' cap insignia

Cap insignia of club member but not boat owner

1819

Cap insignia of club member who is a boat owner (not an officer)

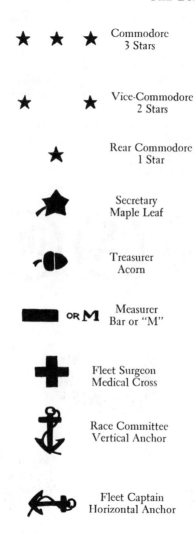

Commodore
3 Stars

Vice-Commodore
2 Stars

Rear Commodore
1 Star

Secretary
Maple Leaf

Treasurer
Acorn

Measurer
Bar or "M"

Fleet Surgeon
Medical Cross

Race Committee
Vertical Anchor

Fleet Captain
Horizontal Anchor

1820 Insignia worn in addition to crossed anchors to show rank

1819 The device for a club member who is not a boat owner is the simplified insignia with the club disk, shown in Figure 1819, left. The right-hand device, same figure, is worn by the member who is a boatowner but not a club officer. Both are in gold bullion, with the club disk in enamel.

1820 Club officers wear the same basic device, to which is added the gold-bullion devices showing rank, as in Figure 1820. The insignia of rank is worn only during incumbency. Occasionally rules permit past flag officers to wear the insignia devices of rank, but in silver.

1821 Sleeve insignia of a commodore

1821 Sleeve insignia (Figure 1821) is worn on the uniform jacket, both sleeves, as follows:

Commodore	four plain stripes, one stripe with trefoil, three stars
Vice-commodore	three	"	"	"	"	"	"	two stars
Rear-commodore	two	"	"	"	"	"	"	one star
All other flag officers	two	"	stripes	"	"	"	"	no stars
Nonofficer member	one	"	stripe	"	"	"	"	" "

(Past flag officers wear the stripe of their former office but not the stars.)

The sleeve braid is usually ⅜" wide, and local regulations establish the distance between, the distance from the cuff and the size of the stars. Black stripes are worn on the blue-uniform jacket, and white stripes on the white uniform jacket. The stars are gold in any case. Sleeve insignia are not worn on work-uniform jackets of any kind; nor on topcoats or storm clothing.

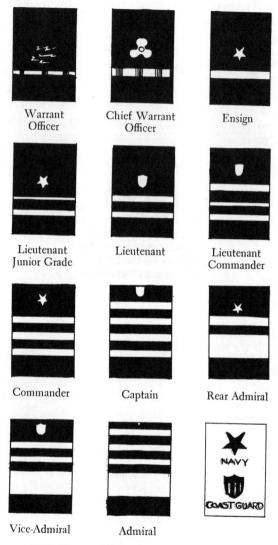

Warrant Officer	Chief Warrant Officer	Ensign
Lieutenant Junior Grade	Lieutenant	Lieutenant Commander
Commander	Captain	Rear Admiral
Vice-Admiral	Admiral	

1822 Navy and Coast Guard sleeve insignia

MILITARY INSIGNIA

1822 Boatmen often come in contact with Coast Guard or U. S. Navy officers and their insignia of rank are therefore given in Figure 1822.

Warrant officers and commissioned officers are addressed by rank or as "Mister" until the rank of captain, after which they are addressed by rank (as Commander Jones, Admiral Smith, etc.).

Insignia of Navy and Coast Guard are alike.

Rank	Sleeve Insignia	Shoulder-Strap Insignia
Warrant Officer	¼" gold	On black background same width and type of stripes
Chief Warrant Officer	½" gold	Same as sleeve
(Note—Warrant officer stripes are broken at 2" intervals by ½" dark-blue silk thread.)		
Ensign	½" gold	Same as sleeve
Lieutenant (Junior Grade)	One ½" gold with one ¼" gold above	Same as sleeve
Lieutenant	Two ½" gold	Same as sleeve
Lieutenant Commander	Two ½" gold with one ¼" between	Same as sleeve
Commander	Three ½" gold	Same as sleeve
Captain	Four ½" gold	Same as sleeve
Rear Admiral	One 2" gold with one ½" gold above	Anchor with 2 stars on gold lace background
Vice-Admiral	One 2" gold with two ½" gold above	Anchor with 3 stars, etc.
Admiral	One 2" gold with three ½" gold above	Anchor with 4 stars, etc.

⚓

APPENDICES

APPENDICES

APPENDIX I

DEPARTMENT OF TRANSPORTATION U. S. COAST GUARD CG-2901 (Rev. 2-75)	U. S. COAST GUARD AUXILIARY COURTESY MOTORBOAT EXAMINATION	DATE

REGISTRATION NUMBER (or name and document number)	LENGTH FT IN	OWNER(S)

NOTE TO BOAT OWNER: This is one of the services rendered by the Coast Guard through the Coast Guard Auxiliary. This examination is unofficial, is made as a courtesy, and is made only with your consent. This check list is furnished for your information. No violation report is made to the Coast Guard or to any law enforcement agency. There is no assumption of liability of any kind for either services given or any opinions expressed in connection with this examination. Please remove decal if vessel is sold.

FEDERAL REQUIREMENTS

YES	NO	ITEM DESCRIPTION	YES	NO	ITEM DESCRIPTION
		1. IDENTIFICATION AND NUMBERING - Papers are in order. Numbers block type, proper size, properly spaced, distinctly visible. Name and Hailing Port displayed and Official Number marked on main beam (documented yacht only).			3. DISPLAY OF CAPACITY INFORMATION - Proper location, proper display (if required) (boats for which construction began after 10-31-72). See AUX-204(1 - 75)
					4. CERTIFICATION OF COMPLIANCE - Proper location proper display (if required)(boats for which construction began after 10-31-72). See AUX-204(1 - 75)
		2. HULL IDENTIFICATION NUMBER - Proper location, proper display (boats for which construction began after 10-31-72).			5. BELL - .26 ft. or over only.

FEDERAL REQUIREMENTS / AUXILIARY REQUIREMENTS

YES	NO	ITEM DESCRIPTION	YES	NO	ITEM DESCRIPTION
		6. PERSONAL FLOTATION DEVICES - Approved type - Required number, satisfactory condition, readily accessible.			6. One approved personal flotation device for each person on board but not less than one for each bunk or less than two.
		7. VENTILATION - Adequate; each engine & fuel tank compartment. Boats built after 4-25-40.			7. Conforms with Auxiliary standards regardless of date of construction.
		8. BACKFIRE FLAME CONTROL - Properly attached to each carburetor of each gasoline engine, except outboard engines, installed after 4-25-40			8. Satisfactory installation required; except outboard engines, regardless of date of construction.
		9. FIRE EXTINGUISHERS - Approved type. Adequate in size & number. Satisfactory condition; readily accessible. Except boats less than 26 ft. outboard open construction.			9. One portable unit in boats less than 26 ft. regardless of construction or fixed F.E. system.
		10. WHISTLE OR OTHER SOUND PRODUCING DEVICE - Adequate; meets Federal requirement for length of boat on which installed or carried. 16 ft. or greater only.			10. Required for all boats.
		11. NAVIGATIONAL LIGHTS - Display required underway between sunset and sunrise, white, red, green. White when anchored.			11. Running and anchor lights installed and operating satisfactorily. (Boats 16 ft. or greater in length)

ADDITIONAL AUXILIARY REQUIREMENTS

YES	NO	ITEM DESCRIPTION	YES	NO	ITEM DESCRIPTION
		12. PORTABLE FUEL TANKS AND CONTAINERS - Condition satisfactory, free of leaks, properly stowed.			16. DISTRESS FLARE - Preferably hand-held red flares, fuse type or burning torch. Check state law for required permit on other types such as very pistols, signal guns, flare guns, etc.
		13. PERMANENTLY INSTALLED FUEL TANKS - Condition and installation satisfactory. Fill pipe tight to deck plate, located outside coaming or within self bailing cockpit. Fuel tank vents leading clear.			17 GALLEY STOVE - Marine type, properly installed.
					18. PADDLE OR OAR - Required for under 16 ft. only.
					19. MANUAL PUMP OR BAILER - Required for under 16 ft. only.
		14. CARBURETOR DRIP COLLECTOR - Installed satisfactorily to prevent spill into bilge.			20. ANCHOR AND ANCHOR LINE - Suitable size and length for vessel and operating area.
		15. ELECTRICAL INSTALLATION - Wiring in good condition, circuits fused, no knife switches in bilge, batteries properly installed.			21. GENERAL CONDITION - Vessel in good overall condition, bilges clean, free from fire hazards. Bilge pumps operable.

STATE SAFETY-RELATED EQUIPMENT REQUIREMENTS

These items of state safety-related equipment (not covered above) are required by the state listed below and are either not presently aboard or are not in good condition. This list must be corrected before award of the CME Decal can be made.

CME conducted in _____ (state)	I CERTIFY that I have personally examined this vessel and find its condition as stated above.
DECAL ISSUED (Number) DISTRICT	SIGNATURE OF EXAMINER
DIVISION FLOTILLA	
REMARKS	

Reverse of CG-2901 (Rev. 2-75)

OWNERS CHECK LIST FOR RECOMMENDED CONDITION AND EQUIPMENT STANDARDS

While not cause for withholding the decal, the Auxiliary recommends the following standards of condition and equipment. Your boating pleasure depends upon the condition of your craft and how you outfit and maintain her:

☐ Through hull fittings should have shut-off valves or wooden plugs accessible for use.

☐ Fuel lines must lead from the top of the tank and be equipped with shut-off valves at the tank and engine.

☐ Auxiliary generators should have separate permanently installed fuel tanks.

☐ Switches should not be located in bilges.

☐ Distress signaling equipment should be carried on every boat.

☐ A manual bilge pump should be carried on every boat irrespective of any mechanical pumping devices.

☐ Handrails should be secured with through bolts.

☐ Spare cannisters should be carried for horns or whistles which operate from compressed gas.

☐ Spare batteries and spare bulbs should be carried for battery operated lights.

☐ A fully equipped first aid kit should be carried in every boat.

☐ Have tools and spare parts on board in usable condition.

The following items of equipment are advisable to have aboard, depending on size, location, and use of boat.

ANCHORS (1 light, 1 heavy)
ANCHOR CHAIN OF LINE (long)
BAROMETER
BILGE PUMPS
BINOCULARS
BOAT HOOK
CHAMOIS
COAST PILOT
COMPASS
COURSE PROTRACTOR, OR PARALLEL RULES
DECK SWAB
DEVIATION TABLE
DIRECTION FINDER, RADIO
DISTRESS SIGNALS
   FLASHLIGHT
   SIGNALING MIRROR
   SMOKE SIGNALS
   WATER DYE MARKERS
DIVIDERS
EMERGENCY RATIONS AND WATER
FENDERS
FIRST AID KIT AND MANUAL
HEAVING LINE
INSECT REPELLENT
LANTERN
LEADLINE (for soundings)
LOCAL CHARTS
LIGHT LIST
MEGAPHONE
MOORING LINES
MOTOR CRANK HANDLE
MOTOR OIL AND GREASE (extra)
NAILS, SCREWS, BOLTS, PINS, WASHERS, WIRE, TAPE
PATENT LOG
PELORUS
RADIO TELEPHONE
RING BUOYS
R.P.M. TABLE
SEARCHLIGHT
SPARE BATTERIES
SPARE PROPELLOR
SUN GLASSES
SUNBURN LOTION
SUNBURN PREVENTIVE
SPARE PARTS
   COIL
   CONDENSER
   DISTRIBUTOR HEAD
   DISTRIBUTOR POINTS
   DISTRIBUTOR ROTOR
   FUEL PUMP REPAIR KIT
   FUSES
   LIGHT BULBS
   SPARK PLUGS
TOOLS
WATER PUMP

The Coast Guard Auxiliary's Courtesy Motorboat Examination program is a public service effort designed to provide the boating public with a convenient method of learning the equipment requirements for boating safety. In addition to checking these equipment requirements, each Auxiliary Courtesy Examiner will gladly pass on any boating tips that may make your recreation more pleasurable. Please feel free to discuss any questions that you may have concerning your boat and/or sport. Your Courtesy Examiner is not a marine surveyor and will not advise you on the soundness of your boat's construction, but does have reference material available or can direct you to others with the required information.

Listed below are some of the more important safety points to be kept in mind. If you have questions about any of these points, contact your Courtesy Examiner.

1. Rules of the Road place certain responsibilities on you with regard to signals and navigation lights. You should be aware of the ones that apply to you.
2. Small boats should keep out of the way of large vessels, even if the boat has the "right of way."
3. Your speed should be kept down when proceeding through anchorage, moorings, or near berths. You are responsible for your wake.
4. It is illegal to moor to buoys, daybeacons, or other aids to navigation maintained by the government.
5. In the event that your boat overturns or floods, put on personal flotation devices and STAY WITH THE BOAT.
6. By accepting this CME Decal you are pledging to maintain your boat and equipment to the standards of safety of the examination.

FOR FURTHER INFORMATION CONTACT YOUR NEAREST COAST GUARD UNIT, STATE BOATING AUTHORITY, OR THE COAST GUARD AUXILIARY FLOTILLA NEAR YOU.

YOUR AUXILIARY CONTACT IS:

APPENDIX II

State agencies which register, number, and in some cases administer the boating laws of that state. Addresses of the central administration offices are also listed. Each state listed has a system which meets the minimum requirements of the Federal Boat Safety Act of 1971. Its laws may or may not match exactly the federal law or the laws of other states. Most listed states offer, free, a descriptive booklet and registry application forms.

ALABAMA Department of Conservation, State Administrative Building, Montgomery, Alabama 36104.

ALASKA The State of Alaska does not have a boat registration and numbering law, but general information on boating can be obtained from Department of Natural Resources, Division of Lands, 344 6th Ave., Anchorage, Alaska 99501.

ARIZONA Game and Fish Department, 2211 W. Greenway Rd., Phoenix, Ariz. 85023.

ARKANSAS Revenue Department, State Revenue Building, Little Rock, Ark. 72201

CALIFORNIA Department of Harbors and Watercraft, 1416 9th Street, Room 1336, Sacramento, California 95814.

COLORADO Game, Fish & Parks Department, 6060 Broadway, Denver, Colorado 80216.

CONNECTICUT Boating Commission, Department of Agriculture & Natural Resources, State Office Building, Hartford, Connecticut 06115.

DELAWARE Small Boat Safety Division, Commission of Shell Fisheries, P. O. Box 512, Lewes, Delaware 19958.

DIST. OF COLUMBIA The District of Columbia does not have a boat registration and numbering system; this is done by the Coast Guard.

FLORIDA State Board of Conservation, 107 West Gaines Street, Tallahassee, Florida 32304.

GEORGIA State Game and Fish Commission, Room 715, Trinity-Washington Bldg., Atlanta, Ga. 30334.

HAWAII Harbors Division, Department of Transportation, Box 397, Honolulu, Hawaii 96809.

IDAHO Motor Vehicle Division, Department of Law Enforcement, P. O. Box 34, Boise, Idaho 83707.

ILLINOIS Conservation Department, 400 South Spring Street, Springfield, Illinois 62706.

INDIANA Department of Natural Resources, 605 State Office Building, Indianapolis, Indiana 46209.

IOWA State Conservation Commission, State Office Building, 300 4th Street, Des Moines, Iowa 50319.

KANSAS Forestry, Fish & Game Commission, P. O. Box 1028, Pratt, Kan. 67124.

KENTUCKY Division of Boating, Department of Public Safety, New State Office Bldg., Frankfort, Ky. 40601.

LOUISIANA Wild Life & Fisheries Commission, Wild Life & Fisheries Building, 400 Royal Street, New Orleans, Louisiana 70130.

MAINE Bureau of Watercraft Registration and Safety, State Office Building, Augusta, Maine 04330.

MARYLAND Department of Chesapeake Bay Affairs, State Office Building, Annapolis, Maryland 21404.

MASSACHUSETTS Division of Motorboats, 100 Nashua Street, Boston, Massachusetts 02114.

MICHIGAN Department of State, 2100 N. Larch Street, Lansing, Mich. 48906.

MINNESOTA Department of Conservation, 625 North Robert Street, St. Paul, Minnesota 55101.

MISSISSIPPI Boat and Water Safety Commission, 605 West Capitol Street, Jackson, Mississippi 39203.

MISSOURI Boat Commission, P.O. Box 603, Jefferson City, Missouri 65101.

MONTANA State Board of Equalization, Capitol Building, Helena, Montana 59601.

NEBRASKA State Game, Forestation & Parks Commission, Lincoln, Nebraska 68509.

NEVADA Fish and Game Commission, Box 10678, Reno, Nev. 89501.

NEW HAMPSHIRE Division of Motor Vehicles, Department of Safety, 85 Loudon Road, Concord, New Hampshire 03301. The State of New Hampshire registers powerboats operated on inland or nontidal waters. As this registration system does not comply with the Federal Boating Act of 1958, the Coast Guard has retained the responsibility for registering and numbering undocumented vessels chiefly used on navigable waters of the United States within the territorial limits of New Hampshire.

NEW JERSEY Bureau of Navigation, Department of Conservation & Economic Development, Box 1889, Trenton, New Jersey 08625.

NEW MEXICO State Park and Recreation Commission, P. O. Box 1147, Santa Fe, New Mexico 87501.

NEW YORK Division of Motor-boats, State Conservation Department, New York State Campus, 1220 Washington Avenue, Albany, New York 12226.

NORTH CAROLINA Wildlife Resources Commission, Box 2919, Raleigh, North Carolina 27602.

NORTH DAKOTA State Game & Fish Department, Bismark, North Dakota 58501.

OHIO Watercraft Division, Department of Natural Resources, 802 Ohio Departments Building, Columbus, Ohio 43215.

OKLAHOMA State Tax Commission, 2101 N. Lincoln Blvd., Oklahoma City, Okla. 73105.

OREGON State Marine Board, State Agriculture Building, 635 Capitol Street, N. E., Salem, Oregon 97310.

PENNSYLVANIA Miscellaneous License Division, Pennsylvania Dept. of Revenue, Harrisburg, Pennsylvania 17127.

RHODE ISLAND Registry of Motor Vehicles, Executive Department, State Capitol Building, Providence, Rhode Island 02903.

SOUTH CAROLINA Wildlife Resources Department, P. O. Box 167, Columbia, South Carolina 29202.

SOUTH DAKOTA Department of Game, Fish & Parks, State Office Building, Pierre, South Dakota 57501.

TENNESSEE Game & Fish Commission, 706 Church Street, Doctors Building, Nashville, Tennessee 37203.

TEXAS Highway Department, Motor Vehicle Division, 40th & Jackson, Austin, Texas 78703.

UTAH Boating Division, Utah State Park & Recreation Commission, 132 South Second West, Salt Lake City, Utah 84101.

VERMONT Marine Division, Department of Public Safety, Montpelier, Vermont 05602.

VIRGINIA Game & Inland Fisheries Commission, P. O. Box 1642, Richmond, Virginia 23213.

WASHINGTON The State of Washington does not have a boat registration and numbering law.

WEST VIRGINIA Department of Natural Resources, State Office Building, Charleston, West Virginia 25305.

WISCONSIN Conservation Department, P. O. Box 450, Madison, Wisconsin 53701.

WYOMING Game & Fish Commission, P. O. Box 1589, Cheyenne, Wyoming 82001.

PUERTO RICO Marine Operations Department, Ports Authority, San Juan, P. R.

VIRGIN ISLANDS Department of Commerce, Marine & Aviation Services, Charlotte Amalie, St. Thomas Island, Virgin Islands.

APPENDIX III

Additional state requirements over federal requirements:

The following equipment is required, on power- and sailboats, by the state law of the state listed *in addition* to Federal law. The last item (marine toilets) is a restriction; not a piece of equipment.

EQUIPMENT	*STATE*
Distress flag	New York, Ohio
Flares	Delaware (3), New York (3 red) if over 18'
Battery covers	Illinois, Indiana (if over 10 hp), Wisconsin, Wyoming
Flashlight/lantern	Massachusetts, Nebraska
Length of "stout rope"	New Mexico
Marine toilet restrictions	On *all* waters of the state: Illinois, Indiana, Michigan, Minnesota, New York, Ohio, Virginia
	On *some* waters of the state: California, Maine, Massachusetts, Missouri, Nebraska, Nevada, New Hampshire, Texas, Vermont

APPENDIX IV

OFFSHORE RACING COUNCIL

JANUARY, 1978

SPECIAL REGULATIONS GOVERNING MINIMUM

EQUIPMENT AND ACCOMMODATIONS STANDARDS

1.0   PURPOSE AND USE

1.1   It is the purpose of these special regulations to establish uniform minimum equipment and accommodation standards for yachts racing under the International Offshore Rule and thereby to aid in promoting uniform offshore racing throughout the world.

1.2   These regulations do not replace, but rather supplement, the requirements of governmental authority, the Racing Rules and the International Offshore Rule. The attention of owners is called to restrictions in the rules on the location and movement of equipment.

1.3   The Offshore Racing Council strongly recommends the use of these special regulations by all organizations sponsoring races under the International Offshore Rule. Race Committees may select the category deemed most suitable for the type of race to be sailed. They are urged to depart from the regulations or modify or make exceptions thereto only when the most compelling circumstances so dictate.

2.0   OWNER'S RESPONSIBILITY

2.1   The safety of a yacht and her crew is the sole and inescapable responsibility of the owner, who must do his best to ensure that the yacht is fully found, thoroughly seaworthy and manned by an experienced crew who are physically fit to face bad weather. He must be satisfied as to the soundness of hull, spars, rigging, sails and all gear. He must ensure that all safety equipment is properly maintained and stowed and that the crew know where it is kept and how it is to be used.

2.2   Neither the establishment of these special regulations, their use by sponsoring organizations, nor the inspection of a yacht under these regulations in any way limits or reduces the complete and unlimited responsibility of the owner.

681

2.3   It is the sole and exclusive responsibility of each yacht to decide whether or not to start or continue to race.

3.0   BASIC STANDARDS

3.1   Yachts shall be self-righting. They shall be strongly built, watertight and, particularly with regard to hulls, decks and cabin trunks, capable of withstanding solid water and knock-downs. They must be properly rigged and ballasted, be fully seaworthy and must meet the standards set forth herein (see I.O.R. Part XII).

"Properly rigged" means (*inter alia*) that shrouds shall never be disconnected.

3.2   All equipment shall function properly, be readily accessible and be of a type, size and capacity suitable and adequate for the intended use and the size of the yacht, and shall meet standards accepted in the country of registry.

3.3   Inboard engine installation shall meet standards accepted in the country of registry and shall be such that the engine, when running, can be securely covered, and that the exhaust and fuel supply systems are securely installed and adequately protected from the effects of heavy weather.

4.0   INSPECTION

4.1   A yacht may be inspected at any time. If she does not comply with these special regulations her entry may be rejected, or she will be liable to disqualification or such other penalty as may be prescribed by national authority or the sponsoring organization.

5.0   CATEGORIES OF OFFSHORE EVENTS

5.1   The International Offshore Rating rule is used to rate a wide variety of types and sizes of yachts in many types of races, ranging from long-distance ocean races sailed under adverse conditions to short-course day races sailed in protected waters. To provide for the differences in the standards of safety and accommodation required for such varying circumstances, four categories of races are established, as follows:

5.2   *Category 1 race.* Races of long distance and well offshore, where yachts must be completely self-sufficient for extended periods of time, capable of withstanding heavy storms and prepared to meet serious emergencies without the expectation of outside assistance.

5.3   *Category 2 race.* Races of extended duration along or not far removed from shorelines or in large unprotected bays or lakes, where a high degree of self-sufficiency is required of the yachts but with the reasonable probability that outside assistance could be called upon for aid in the event of serious emergencies.

5.4   *Category 3 race.* Races across open water, most of which is relatively protected or close to shorelines, including races for small yachts.

5.5   *Category 4 race.* Short races, close to shore in relatively warm or protected waters.

In the following lists, the star indicates the item applies to the category in that column.

6.0   STRUCTURAL FEATURES

6.1   "Hatches, companionways, ports, vents, spinnaker launchers, and other fittings which breach the hull or deck shall be essentially watertight, that is, capable of being strongly and rigidly secured. Cockpit companionways, if extended below main deck level, must be capable of being blocked off to the level of the main deck at the sheer line abreast the opening. When such blocking arrangements are in place this companionway (or hatch) shall continue to give access to the interior of the hull.

Cockpits opening aft to the sea. The lower edge of the companionway shall not be below main deck level as measured above. The opening shall not be less than 50 per cent of max. cockpit depth X max. cockpit width. The requirement in 6.31 and 6.32 that cockpits must drain at all angles of heel, applies.

6.2   *Cockpits* must be structurally strong, self-draining and permanently incorporated as an integral part of the hull. They must be essentially watertight, that is, all openings to the hull below the main deck level must be capable of being strongly and rigidly secured. Any bow, lateral, central or stern well will be considered as a cockpit for the purpose of 6.21, 6.22, 6.31 and 6.32.

6.21   The maximum volume of *all cockpits* below lowest coamings shall not exceed 6% L times B times FA. The cockpit sole must be at least 2% L above LWL.

6.22   The maximum volume of *all cockpits* below lowest coamings shall not exceed 9% L times B times FA. The cockpit sole must be at least 2% L above LWL.

6.31   *For yachts 21 feet rating and over.* Cockpit drains adequate to drain cockpits quickly but with a combined area (after allowance for screens, if attached) of not less than the equivalent of four ¾ ins. (2.0cm) diameter drains. Yachts built before 1-1-72 must have drains with a combined area (after allowance for screens, if attached) of not less than the equivalent of two 1 ins. (2.5cm) drains. Cockpits shall drain at all angles of heel.

Yachts built before 1-1-77 may conform to 6.32 for races in Categories 3 and 4.

6.32   *For yachts under 21 feet rating.* Cockpit drains adequate to drain cockpits quickly but not less in combined area (after allowance for screens, if attached) than the equivalent of two 1 ins. (2.5cm) diameter drains. Cockpits shall drain at all angles of heel.

6.4   *Storm coverings* for all windows more than two square feet in area.

6.51   *Sea cocks or valves* on all through-hull openings below LWL, except integral deck scuppers, shaft log, speed indicators, depth finders and the like, however a means of closing such openings, when necessary to do so, shall be provided.

Does not apply in Category 4 races to yachts built before 1-1-76.

RACE CATEGORY

	1	2	3	4
6.1	★	★	★	★
6.2	★	★	★	★
6.21	★			
6.22		★	★	★
6.31	★	★	★	★
6.32	★	★	★	★
6.4	★	★	★	
6.51	★	★	★	★

RACE
CATEGORY
1 2 3 4

6.52 Soft wood plugs, tapered and of various sizes.   ★ ★ ★ ★

6.6 *Life lines and pulpits:*

6.61 *For Yachts 21 Feet rating and over*

6.61.1   *Taut double life-lines,* with upper life-line of wire at a height of
not less than 2 feet (60cm) above the working deck, to be permanently
supported at intervals of not more than 7 feet (2.15m). When the   ★ ★ ★
cockpit opens aft to the sea, additional life-lines shall be fitted
so that no opening is greater in height than 22 ins. (56cms.).

6.61.2   *Life-line terminals.* A taut lanyard of synthetic rope may be used
to secure life-lines, provided that when in position its length does not   ★ ★ ★
exceed 4 ins. (10cm).

6.61.3   *Stanchions* shall not be angled from the point of their attachment
to the hull at more than ten degrees from vertical throughout their length.   ★ ★ ★

6.61.4   *Pulpits.* Fixed bow pulpit (forward of headstay) and stern pulpit
(unless life-lines are arranged as to adequately substitute for a stern pulpit).
Lower life-lines need not extend through the bow pulpit. Upper rails of
pulpits shall be at no less height above the working deck than upper life-   ★ ★ ★
lines. Upper rails in bow pulpits shall be securely closed while racing.
Any lifeline attachment point will be considered as a stanchion in
so far as its base shall not be situated outboard of the working deck.

6.61.5   *Overlapping pulpits.* Life-lines need not be affixed to the bow
pulpit if they terminate at, or pass through, adequately braced stanchions   ★ ★ ★
2 feet (60cm) above the working deck, set inside of and overlapping the
bow pulpit, provided that the gap between the upper life-line and the bow
pulpit shall not exceed 6 ins. (15cm).

6.61.6   *Pulpit and stanchion fixing.* Pulpits and stanchions shall be
through-bolted or welded, and the bases thereof shall not be further inboard from the edge of the working deck than 5% of B max. or 6 ins. (15cm), ★ ★ ★
whichever is greater. Stanchion bases shall not be situated outboard of the
working deck.

6.62 *For Yachts under 21 feet rating*

6.62.1   *Taut single wire life-line,* at a height of not less than 18 ins. (45cm)
above the working deck, to be permanently supported at intervals of not
more than 7 feet (2.15m). If the life-line is at any point more than 22 ins.
(56cm) above the rail cap, a second intermediate life-line must be fitted.   ★ ★ ★
If the cockpit opens aft to the sea additional life-lines must be fitted so
that no opening is greater in height than 22 ins. (56cm).

6.62.2   *Life-line terminals,* as in 6.61.2.   ★ ★ ★

6.62.3   *Stanchions,* as in 6.61.3.   ★ ★ ★

6.62.4   *Pulpits.* Fixed bow pulpit and stern pulpit (unless life-lines are
arranged as to adequately substitute for a stern pulpit). Lower life-lines   ★ ★ ★
need not extend through the bow pulpit. Upper rails of pulpits must be

RACE CATEGORY

at no less height above the working deck than upper life-lines. Upper rails in bow pulpits shall be securely closed while racing. The bow pulpit may be fitted abaft the forestay with its bases secured at any points on deck, but a point on its upper rail must be within 16 ins. (40cm) of the forestay on which the foremost headsail is hanked. Any lifeline attachment point will be considered as a stanchion in so far as its base shall not be situated outboard of the working deck.

	1	2	3	4
6.62.5 *Overlapping pulpits,* as in 6.61.5, but for 2 feet read 18 inches (45cm).	★	★	★	
6.62.6 *Pulpit and stanchion fixing,* as in 6.61.6	★	★	★	
6.63 As in 6.61 and 6.62, except that a stern pulpit is not required, provided the required height of life-line must be carried aft at least to the midpoint of the cockpit.				★
6.7 *Ballast and Heavy Equipment.* Inside ballast in a yacht shall be securely fastened in position. All other heavy internal fittings such as batteries, stoves, gas bottles, tanks, outboard motors, etc., shall be securely fastened.	★	★	★	★
6.8 *Sheet winches* shall be mounted in such a way that no operator is required to be substantially below deck.	★	★	★	★
7.0 ACCOMMODATIONS				
7.11 *Toilet,* securely installed.	★	★		
7.12 *Toilet,* securely installed, or fitted bucket.			★	★
7.2 *Bunks,* securely installed.	★	★	★	★
7.31 *Cooking stove,* securely installed with safe accessible fuel shutoff control capable of being safely operated in a seaway.	★	★		
7.32 Cooking stove, capable of being safely operated in a seaway.			★	
7.41 *Galley facilities,* including sink.	★	★		
7.42 Galley facilities.			★	★
7.51 *Water tanks,* securely installed and capable of dividing the water supply into at least two separate containers.	★			
7.52 At least one securely installed water tank, plus at least one additional container capable of holding 2 gallons.		★		
7.53 Water in suitable containers.			★	★
8.0 GENERAL EQUIPMENT				
8.1 *Fire extinguishers,* readily accessible and of the type and number required by the country of registry, provided there be at least one in yachts fitted with an engine or stove.	★	★	★	★

RACE
CATEGORY

	1	2	3	4
8.21 *Bilge pumps,* at least two, manually operated, one of which must be operable with all cockpit seats and all hatches and companionways closed.	★	★		
8.22 One manual bilge pump operable with all cockpit seats, hatches and companionways closed.			★	
8.23 One manual bilge pump.				★
8.31 *Anchors.* Two with cables except yachts rating under 21 feet, which shall carry at least one anchor and cable.	★	★	★	
8.32 One anchor and cable.				★
8.41 *Flashlights,* one of which is suitable for signaling, water resistant, with spare batteries and bulbs.	★	★	★	
8.42 At least one flashlight, water resistant, with spare batteries and bulb.				★
8.5 *First.aid kit* and manual.	★	★	★	★
8.6 *Foghorn.*	★	★	★	★
8.7 *Radar reflector.*	★	★	★	★
8.8 *Set of international code flags* and international code book.	★			
8.9 *Shutoff valves* on all fuel tanks.	★	★	★	★
9.0 NAVIGATION EQUIPMENT				
9.1 *Compass,* marine type, properly installed and adjusted.	★	★	★	★
9.2 *Spare compass.*	★	★	★	
9.3 *Charts, light list and piloting equipment.*	★	★	★	
9.4 *Sextant, tables and accurate time piece.*	★			
9.5 *Radio direction finder.*	★	★		
9.6 *Lead line or echo sounder.*	★	★	★	★
9.7 *Speedometer or distance measuring instrument.*	★	★	★	
9.8 *Navigation lights,* to be shown as required by the International Regulations for Preventing Collision at Sea, mounted so that they will not be masked by sails or the heeling of the yacht.	★	★	★	★
10.0 EMERGENCY EQUIPMENT				
10.1 *Emergency navigation lights* and power source.	★	★		

RACE CATEGORY

	1	2	3	4
10.21 *Special storm sail(s)* capable of **taking the yacht to windward in** heavy weather.	★	★		
10.22 Heavy weather jib (or heavy weather sail in **boat with no forestay**) and reefing equipment for mainsail.			★	★
10.23 Any storm or heavy-weather jib if designed for a seastay or luff-groove device shall have an alternative method of attachment to the stay or a wire luff.	★	★	★	★
10.24 No mast shall have less than two halyards each capable of hoisting a sail.	★	★	★	★
10.3 *Emergency steering equipment.*	★	★	★	
10.4 *Tools and spare parts,* including adequate means to disconnect or sever the standing rigging from the hull in case of need.	★	★	★	★
10.5 *Yacht's name* on miscellaneous buoyant equipment, such as life jackets, oars, cushions, etc. Portable sail number.	★	★	★	
10.61 *Marine radio transmitter and receiver* with minimum transmitter power of 25 watts. If the regular antenna depends upon the mast, an emergency antenna must be provided.	★			
10.62 *Radio receiver* capable of receiving weather bulletins.		★	★	★

11.0 SAFETY EQUIPMENT

	1	2	3	4
11.1 *Life jackets,* one for each crew member.	★	★	★	★
11.2 *Whistles* attached to life jackets.	★	★	★	
11.3 *Safety belt* (harness type) one for each crew member.	★	★	★	
11.41 *Life raft(s)* capable of carrying the entire crew and meeting the following requirements:	★	★	★	

Must be carried on deck (not under a dinghy) or in a special stowage opening immediately to the deck containing life raft(s) only:
Must be designed and used solely for saving life at sea:
Must have at least two separate buoyancy compartments, each of which must be automatically inflatable; each raft must be capable of carrying its rated capacity with one compartment deflated:
Must have a canopy to cover the occupants:
Must have been inspected, tested and approved within two years by the manufacturer or other competent authority: and
Must have the following equipment appropriately secured to each raft.

    1 Sea anchor or drogue

RACE
CATEGORY
1   2   3   4

1 Bellows, pump or other means for maintaining inflation of air
  chambers
1 Signaling light
3 Hand flares
1 Baler
1 Repair Kit
2 Paddles
1 Knife

11.42   Provision for emergency water and rations to accompany raft.

11.51   *Life ring(s),* at least one horseshoe type life ring equipped with a
waterproof light and drogue within reach of the helmsman and ready for
instant use.

11.52   At least one horseshoe-type life-ring equipped with a drogue and
a self-igniting light having a duration of at least 45 minutes within reach of
the helmsman and ready for instant use.

11.53   At least one more horseshoe-type life-ring equipped with a whistle,
dye marker, drogue, a self-igniting high-intensity water light, and a pole and
flag. The pole is to be attached to the ring with 25 feet (8m) of floating line
and is to be of a length and so ballasted that the flag will fly at least 8 feet
(2.45m) off the water.

11.61   *Distress signals* to be stowed in a waterproof container, and
meeting the following requirements for each category, as indicated:

11.62   Twelve red parachute flares.

11.63   Four red parachute flares.

11.64   Four red hand flares.

11.65   Four white hand flares.

11.66   Two orange smoke day signals.

11.7 *Heaving line* (50 foot (16m) minimum length, floating type line)
readily accessible to cockpit.

INDEX

694

U.S. Ensign and Merchant Flag

Yacht Ensign

Union Jack

Club Burgee

Owner
Absent
Flag

Guest
Flag

Private Signal

Owner's
Meal
Flag

Officers' Flag

Crew Meal
Pennant

Yacht Flags